Lecture Notes in Artificial Intelligence 12576

Subseries of Lecture Notes in Computer Science

More information about this subseries at http://www.springer.com/series/1244

Marcus Gallagher · Nour Moustafa ·
Erandi Lakshika (Eds.)

AI 2020: Advances in Artificial Intelligence

33rd Australasian Joint Conference, AI 2020
Canberra, ACT, Australia, November 29–30, 2020
Proceedings

Springer

Editors
Marcus Gallagher ⓘ
School of Information Technology
and Electrical Engineering
University of Queensland
Brisbane, QLD, Australia

Nour Moustafa ⓘ
School of Engineering
and Information Technology
University of New South Wales
Canberra, ACT, Australia

Erandi Lakshika ⓘ
School of Engineering
and Information Technology
University of New South Wales
Canberra, ACT, Australia

ISSN 0302-9743   ISSN 1611-3349   (electronic)
Lecture Notes in Artificial Intelligence
ISBN 978-3-030-64983-8   ISBN 978-3-030-64984-5   (eBook)
https://doi.org/10.1007/978-3-030-64984-5

LNCS Sublibrary: SL7 – Artificial Intelligence

This Springer imprint is published by the registered company Springer Nature Switzerland AG
The registered company address is: Gewerbestrasse 11, 6330 Cham, Switzerland

Preface

This volume contains the papers presented at the 33rd Australasian Joint Conference on Artificial Intelligence (AI 2020). Due to the COVID-19 global pandemic, the conference was virtually held during November 29–30, 2020, and was hosted by the University of New South Wales, Canberra, Australia. This annual conference is one of the longest running conferences in artificial intelligence, with the first conference held in Sydney in 1987. The conference remains the premier event for artificial intelligence in Australasia, offering a forum for researchers and practitioners across all subfields of artificial intelligence to meet and discuss recent advances. AI 2020 received 57 submissions with 174 authors from 16 countries and 63 different institutions. Each submission was reviewed by at least three Program Committee (PC) members or external reviewers. After a thorough discussion and rigorous scrutiny by the reviewers and the dedicated members of the Senior PC, 36 submissions were accepted for publication as full papers.

AI 2020 had two keynote talks by the following distinguished scientists:

- Prof. Alice E. Smith, Auburn University, USA, on November 29, 2020.
- Prof. Chengqi Zhang, University of Technology Sydney, Australia, on November 30, 2020.

We thank the authors for submitting their research papers to the conference, preparing videos, and presenting their work online to cope with the consequences of the COVID-19 pandemic. We are grateful to authors whose papers are published in this volume for their cooperation during the preparation of the final camera-ready versions of the manuscripts. We especially appreciate the work of the members of the PC and the external reviewers for their expertise and tireless effort in assessing the papers within a strict timeline. We are very grateful to the members of the Organizing Committee for their efforts in the preparation, promotion, and organization of the conference, especially the general chairs for coordinating the whole event. We acknowledge the assistance provided by EasyChair for conference management.

To celebrate the diversity of talent working with, developing, and educating for emerging technology, the Women in Artificial Intelligence (WAI) committee worked in conjunction with IEEE Women in Computational Intelligence (WCI) and Women in Big Data (WiBD) to present three events. The panel event, Perspectives on Trust and Intelligence, brought together experts to discuss the diversity required to realize ethical and capable technology. The WAI/WCI keynote event focused on career experiences, and development tips for all emerging AI/CI professionals. Finally, the WAI/WiBD event provided an opportunity for anyone within AI, CI, or data to pitch their achievements and goals, whether working in research, industry, or academia.

Lastly, we thank Springer, the National Committee for Artificial Intelligence of the Australian Computer Society, and the University of New South Wales, Canberra, Australia, for their sponsorship, and the professional service provided by the Springer LNCS editorial and publishing teams.

October 2020

Marcus Gallagher
Nour Moustafa
Erandi Lakshika

Organization

General Chairs

Hussein Abbass   University of New South Wales, Australia
Chin-Teng Lin   University of Technology Sydney, Australia

Program Chairs

Michael Barlow   University of New South Wales, Australia
Jie Lu   University of Technology Sydney, Australia

Conflict of Interest Chairs

Xiaodong Li   RMIT University, Australia
Pablo Moscato   The University of Newcastle, Australia

Proceedings Chairs

Marcus Gallagher   The University of Queensland, Australia
Nour Moustafa   University of New South Wales, Australia

Organizing Committee

Local Arrangements Chairs

Erandi Lakshika   University of New South Wales, Australia
Jiangjun Tang   University of New South Wales, Australia

Finance Chair

Kathryn Kasmarik   University of New South Wales, Australia

Sponsorship Chair

Andy Song   RMIT University, Australia

Tutorial Chair

Sreenatha Anavatti   University of New South Wales, Australia

Publicity Chairs

Essam Debie   University of New South Wales, Australia
Raul Fernandez Rojas   University of New South Wales, Australia

Women in AI Chairs

Heba El-Fiqi   University of New South Wales, Australia
Kate Yaxley   University of New South Wales, Australia

Workshop Chair

Matthew Garratt   University of New South Wales, Australia

Senior Program Committee

James Bailey   The University of Melbourne, Australia
Junbin Gao   The University of Sydney, Australia
Yuefeng Li   Queensland University of Technology, Australia
Jinyan Li   University of Technology Sydney, Australia
Jixue Liu   University of South Australia, Australia
Kathryn Merrick   University of New South Wales, Australia
Frank Neumann   The University of Adelaide, Australia
Bernhard Pfahringer   University of Waikato, New Zealand
Abdul Sattar   Griffith University, Australia
Markus Stumptner   University of South Australia, Australia
Kay Chen Tan   City University of Hong Kong, Hong Kong
Xingquan Zhu   Florida Atlantic University, USA

Program Committee

Brad Alexander   The University of Adelaide, Australia
Harith Al-Sahaf   Victoria University of Wellington, New Zealand
Zhuoyun Ao   Defence Science and Technology Group, Australia
Peter Baumgartner   CSIRO, Australia
Regina Berretta   The University of Newcastle, Australia
Will Browne   Victoria University of Wellington, New Zealand
Weidong Cai   The University of Sydney, Australia
Stephan Chalup   The University of Newcastle, Australia
Jeffrey Chan   RMIT University, Australia
Archie Chapman   The University of Queensland, Australia
Qi Chen   Victoria University of Wellington, New Zealand
Gang Chen   Victoria University of Wellington, New Zealand
Songcan Chen   Nanjing University of Aeronautics and Astronautics,
                          China
Stephen Chen   York University, Canada
Sung-Bae Cho   Yonsei University, South Korea
Michael Cree   University of Waikato, New Zealand
Andreas Ernst   Monash University, Australia
Daryl Essam   University of New South Wales, Australia
Tim French   The University of Western Australia, Australia
Xiaoying Gao   Victoria University of Wellington, New Zealand
Tom Gedeon   The Australian National University, Australia

Manolis Gergatsoulis	Ionian University, Greece
Ning Gu	University of South Australia, Australia
C. Maria Keet	University of Cape Town, South Africa
Asanka Nuwanpriya Kekirigoda Mudiyanselage	Defence Science and Technology Group, Australia
Alistair Knott	University of Otago, New Zealand
Jérôme Lang	Université Paris-Dauphine, France
Ickjai Lee	James Cook University, Australia
Andrew Lewis	Griffith University, Australia
Hong-Cheu Liu	University of South Australia, Australia
Jing Liu	Chinese Academy of Sciences, China
Wan Quan Liu	Curtin University of Technology, Australia
Hui Ma	Victoria University of Wellington, New Zealand
Frederic Maire	Queensland University of Technology, Australia
Brendan Mccane	University of Otago, New Zealand
Yi Mei	Victoria University of Wellington, New Zealand
Nina Narodytska	VMware Research, USA
Chrystopher L. Nehaniv	University of Hertfordshire, UK
Aneta Neumann	The University of Adelaide, Australia
M. A. Hakim Newton	Griffith University, Australia
Bach Nguyen	Victoria University of Wellington, New Zealand
Oliver Obst	Western Sydney University, Australia
Laurent Perrussel	Université de Toulouse, France
Marcus Randall	Bond University, Australia
Inaki Rano	University of Southern Denmark, Denmark
Ji Ruan	Auckland University of Technology, New Zealand
Rafal Rzepka	Hokkaido University, Japan
Rolf Schwitter	Macquarie University, Australia
Andrea Soltoggio	Loughborough University, UK
Yanan Sun	Sichuan University, China
Maolin Tang	Queensland University of Technology, Australia
Binh Tran	Victoria University of Wellington, New Zealand

Additional Reviewers

Shadi Abpeikar	Kevin Huang
Shohel Ahmed	Jae Hyuk
Fayeem Aziz	Gongjin Lan
Ali Bakhshi	Minyi Li
Andrew Ciezak	Dongnan Liu
James Dannatt	Jing Liu
Suranjith De Silva	Yuqiao Liu
Chuanxing Geng	Luke Mathieson
Behrooz Ghasemishabankareh	Alexandre Mendes

Munyque Mittelmann
Mohammad Mobasher
Mohammad Nazmul
Tung Nguyen
Hung Nguyen
Nasimul Noman
Nima Salimi
Dilini Samarasinghe
Tao Shi
Ye Shi
Avinash Singh
Aaron Snoswell
Han Sun

Yuan Sun
Russell Tsuchida
Rudy Veerbeck
Bing Wang
Min Wang
Chen Wang
Dulakshi Wannigamage
Mingfu Xue
Shuo Yang
Qing Ye
Yamin Yin
Tony Ynot
Bo Zhang

Contents

Evolutionary Computation

Fairness and Ethics

Games and Swarms

Machine Learning

Applications

Multi-diseases Classification from Chest-X-ray: A Federated Deep Learning Approach

Sourasekhar Banerjee[1]($\boxtimes$) , Rajiv Misra[2]($\boxtimes$), Mukesh Prasad[3]($\boxtimes$),
Erik Elmroth[1]($\boxtimes$), and Monowar H. Bhuyan[1]($\boxtimes$)

[1] Department of Computing Science, Umeå University, 901 87 Umeå, Sweden
{sourasb,elmroth,monowar}@cs.umu.se
[2] Department of Computer Science and Engineering, Indian Institute of Technology
Patna, Patna, India
rajivm@iitp.ac.in
[3] School of Computer Science, FEIT, University of Technology Sydney, Ultimo,
Australia
mukesh.prasad@uts.edu.au

Abstract. Data plays a vital role in deep learning model training. In large-scale medical image analysis, data privacy and ownership make data gathering challenging in a centralized location. Hence, federated learning has been shown as successful in alleviating both problems for the last few years. In this work, we have proposed multi-diseases classification from chest-X-ray using Federated Deep Learning (FDL). The FDL approach detects pneumonia from chest-X-ray and also identify viral and bacterial pneumonia. Without submitting the chest-X-ray images to a central server, clients train the local models with limited private data at the edge server and send them to the central server for global aggregation. We have used four pre-trained models such as ResNet18, ResNet50, DenseNet121, and MobileNetV2 and applied transfer learning on them at each edge server. The learned models in the federated setting have compared with centrally trained deep learning models. It has been observed that the models trained using the ResNet18 in federated environment produce accuracy up to 98.3% for pneumonia detection and up to 87.3% accuracy for viral and bacterial pneumonia detection. We have compared the performance of adaptive learning rate based optimizers such as Adam and Adamax with Momentum based Stochastic Gradient Descent (SGD) and found out that Momentum SGD yields better results than others. Lastly, for visualization, we have used Class Activation Mapping (CAM) approaches such as Grad-CAM, Grad-CAM++, and Score-CAM to identify pneumonia affected regions in a chest-X-ray.

Keywords: Federated learning · Optimization · Transfer learning · Medical imagery analysis · Class activation mapping

M. Gallagher et al. (Eds.): AI 2020, LNAI 12576, pp. 3–15, 2020.
https://doi.org/10.1007/978-3-030-64984-5_1

1   Introduction

Deep learning creates a massive impact on the data-intensive applications in diverse domains from healthcare [10] to autonomous systems [4] to disaster management [11]. The availability of biomedical and healthcare-related data brings opportunities and challenges to the health care research [10]. In this domain, the application of Deep Neural Network (DNN) is required for the analysis of the Clinical Imaging [14] and Electronic Health Records [7].

In medical imagery analysis, applying deep learning methods can produce significant results but requires a considerable amount of quality data. An individual client may not have sufficient data to train and build a quality model, so, collaborating with different clients may solve the data insufficiency problems in deep learning but introduce privacy-constraints. Federated learning plays an essential role in solving such issues. Instead of storing highly sensitive patients personal and medical data to a centralized server, keep it at the individual client. Each client separately trains models based on locally available data and shares local models with a centralized server for global aggregation [17].

This paper proposes a federated deep learning approach for multi-diseases classification from chest-X-ray, specifically pneumonia. We have taken the following assumptions to alleviate this problem such as (a) The Client use their private data for training (b) Imbalanced distribution of data across edge servers, (c) The communication between clients/hospitals with the central server is stable, (d) The learning follows a cross-silo federated learning architecture where each edge server actively participates in training for every round. The main contributions are as follows.

- The training of the Convolutional Neural Network (CNN) on chest-X-ray images using transfer learning to classify different kind of pneumonia at the client-side in federated setting. The training includes the client-side local update and central server-side global aggregation.
- The impact analysis of different adaptive learning rate-based optimization methods, including Adam, Adamax, and momentum-based SGD, to train deep neural network model training in a federated environment.
- Visualization using CAM based methods (Grad-CAM, Grad-CAM++, and Score-CAM) to show the impact of the proposed model for detecting viral and bacterial pneumonia from chest-X-ray images.

The rest of the paper is organized as follows. In Sect. 2, a brief literature review is reported. The problem formulation is given in Sect. 3, whereas in Sect. 4, we describes the proposed model. Experimental results provided in Sect. 5, and finally, Sect. 6 concludes the work.

2   Related Work

Deep learning has been played a significant role in medical imagery analysis. It was used in various areas such as brain-tumors detection [17], electronic health records analysis [3], pneumonia detection from chest-X-ray images [2,14]. For these tasks, the goal was to develop a medical decision support system by employing data-driven machine learning-based modeling on patient data. A recent work [19] on Covid19 detection from chest-X-ray images using the deep convolutional neural network reported promising results. In [14], the model can detect pneumonia from chest-X-ray and produce the radiologist level outcome.

Training of deep neural networks requires a massive amount of data. Different clients work collaboratively to address this problem. However, putting sensitive information of patients in a centralized location may violate privacy constraints. Federated learning, introduced by google [9] as a replacement of traditional centralized learning solutions can alleviate this problem. In the traditional learning method, different clients store data in a centralized server for training. However, in the federated learning, each client trains its model locally. Instead of sharing data, they only send the parameter updates or models to the centralized server. The server aggregates the parameter updates and sends the recent updates to the clients for further training [9]. By preserving privacy, federated learning is showing a great impact on the healthcare analysis domain [20]. In [17], the performance of federated semantic segmentation models on multimodal brain scans are similar to models trained by data sharing. Authors in [8] has prepared a model using federated learning based on Covid19 and other pneumonia chest-X-ray images. In [12], authors applied split learning for the collaborative neural network in health care.

In federated deep learning, optimization plays an important role. Federated averaging (FedAvg), a stochastic gradient descent (SGD) based optimization method [9], is massively used in federated learning. Now, momentum [13] accelerates SGD in the proper direction and dampens oscillations. Adaptive Moment Estimation (Adam) [6] computes adaptive learning rate for each training parameter. Adamax [6] is a variant of Adam optimizer. In adaptive federated optimization [15], the federated version of the adaptive optimizers such as Adagrad, Adam, and Yogi have been proposed.

Visual interpretation of the result is one of the important part of medical imagery analysis. Class Activation Mapping (CAM) based methods are useful here. Three types of visual explanation methods are very popular such as Grad-CAM [16], Grad-CAM++ [1], and Score-CAM [18]. One application of Grad-Cam has been found in versatile domains including healthcare [14] and disaster management [11].

3   Problem Formulation

This paper's main objective is to build an optimal federated deep learning model to detect multiple pneumonia diseases from normal and infected chest-X-ray images. So, the problem turns into an optimization problem with two parts, such as optimize loss function and optimal weights generation.

a. **Optimize loss function:** The training images are consist of two parts, such as batch of input images $X = [X_1, X_2, \ldots, X_N]$ and the label of the images

$Y = [Y_1, Y_2, \ldots, Y_N]$ as desired output of the model. The loss function produces the error of the model. The objective here is to minimize the error on a set of data divided into batches. We have assumed that each hospital (H_i) has one edge server (E_{ser_i}) and, its local dataset $(D_{E_{ser\_i}})$ to train local models. Edge servers individually train their model for E epochs. The local loss function $F_{E_{ser\_i}}(w_i, X, Y)$ at E_{ser_i} is estimated using Eq. (1).

$$F_{E_{ser\_i}}(w_i, X, Y) = \frac{\sum_{j=1}^{|D_{E_{ser\_i}}|} f_j(w_j, X_j, Y_j)}{|D_{E_{ser\_i}}|} \tag{1}$$

where loss per data point at E_{ser_i} is $f_j(w_j, X_j, Y_j)$ and updated weight is w_i. Here w_j refers to the parameter update per iteration at E_{ser_i}.

The global loss function on distributed datasets is computed based on the Eq. (2).

$$F(w^*) = \min_{t=1,2,\ldots,T} (\underset{i=1,\ldots,N}{avg} F_{E_{ser\_i}}(w_i^t)) \tag{2}$$

where T is the total number of rounds for federated training and N is the total number of participating edge server.

In this paper, we attempt to solve this problem not only by binary classification (i.e., normal and pneumonia) but also with multi-class classification (i.e., normal, bacterial pneumonia, and viral pneumonia). For these two problems, we have used categorical cross-entropy [21] as loss function.

b. **Learning problem:** The learning problem is to minimize the loss function and converge towards a pre-defined threshold. Each edge server optimizes the loss function locally; then, the loss function will be globally optimized in the global update step. Each edge device eventually gets the best-optimized model (w^*) from the central server after T rounds of iteration.

$$w^* = \underset{where\ t=1,2,\ldots,T}{\arg\min} F(w^t) \tag{3}$$

Here, w^t indicates model weights at t^{th} round.

4   System Model

A typical Cross-silo federated learning involves the participation of all clients/hospitals and a central server to learn a model. Clients train models locally using their private data and upload the model to the central server. The central server orchestrates the training and generates global models.

Training of deep neural network models in federated learning needs a large amount of data and computational power at the client level. So, clients (e.g., edge servers, micro data-center) with high computing and storage power may involve in training. The trained model can be deployed at devices (e.g., smartphone, laptop, tablet) registered with the central server. This paper assumes that each client contains one edge server, and each client participates in model training. Figure 1 describes the architecture of the proposed system.

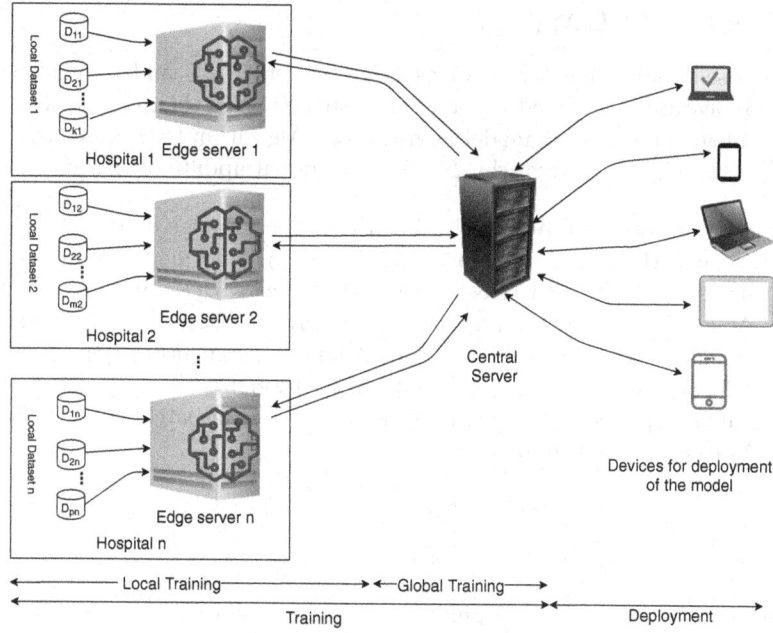

Fig. 1. System architecture

1. **Training:**
   (a) Each client/hospital is an autonomous entity, and they are registered with the central server. Each hospital has its own set of chest-X-ray images and uses them for local training at the edge server.
   (b) At the initial phase of federated deep learning, each registered edge server downloads the pre-trained model and weights from the central server.
   (c) Each edge server then re-train the model using transfer learning according to their private chest-X-ray images and uploads the model updates to the central server.
   (d) The central server performs the global update using the federated averaging method.
   (e) The edge server of each hospital download the globally updated model and initiate the next round of training.
   (f) The above procedure will continue until the convergence of the model.
   (g) CAM based methods (Grad-CAM, Grad-CAM++, and Score-CAM) would be applied to the optimal global model to detect pneumonia infected regions.
2. **Inference:**
   (a) The optimal trained model would be inferred by the devices registered with the central server for real-time pneumonia prediction.

4.1   Proposed FDL Approach

The proposed FDL approach involves Edge Server (E_{ser}) and Central Server (C_{ser}) for learning. Each edge server is responsible for learning locally, and the central server performs model aggregation. Algorithm 1 describes the local update at the E_{ser} and Algorithm 2 refers the global update of the model.

1. **Client Side Local Update:** In Algorithm 1, each edge server (E_{ser}) parallelly trains their model on local data ($D_{E_{ser}}$). The model computes loss for each epoch (E_i) and selects the best model with minimum validation loss. At local training, the algorithm uses any of the three optimizers such as Momentum with SGD, Adam and, Adamax. Momentum (β) accelerates the performance of SGD and calculates model weights using Eq. (8) and (9). Adam uses exponentially moving averages on a mini-batch B using Eq. (4) and (5) to calculate the moments.

$$m^b = \beta_1 m^{b-1} + (1 - b_1)\nabla^b \tag{4}$$

$$v^b = \beta_2 m^{b-1} + (1 - b_2)[\nabla^2]^b \tag{5}$$

Then it calculates the bias regulated estimators using Eq. (6) and (7).

$$\bar{m}^b = \frac{m^b}{(1 - b_1{}^b)} \tag{6}$$

$$\bar{v}^b = \frac{v^b}{(1 - b_2{}^b)} \tag{7}$$

Apply value of $\bar{m}^b$ and $\bar{v}^b$ in Eq. (10) to generate the parameter weights of the model. Adamax also use same approach but use the value v as the $L2$ norm of the gradient (∇). Using Eqs. (11) and (12), it calculates model weights. After all epochs, the best model will be selected using Eqs. (13) and (14) and send the local model to the C_{ser} for generating global model.

2. **Global Update at Central Server:** Algorithm 2 contains two parts: (a) Central Server-side Global Update, and (b) Optimal Global Model generation.
   (a) **Central Server side Global Update:** Each E_{ser} train model parallelly and returns the local models to the C_{ser} for global aggregation. C_{ser} applies a federated averaging(FedAvg) method to update the global model. Each E_{ser} downloads the global model for the next round of training.
   (b) **Finding Optimal Global Model:** For each round, C_{ser} stores the global model, so after T rounds, it will contain T global models. The global model with minimum loss will be the optimal global model.

The CAM based techniques to be applied to the optimal model to visualize the pneumonia infected areas using heat maps. The optimal global model will be deployed at the edge for real-time processing and detection of diseases.

5   Evaluation

We divide the experiments into three parts. In the first part, we detect pneumonia from chest-X-ray using federated and centralized learning. In the second part, we have extended the experiments towards a different type of pneumonia detection (Bacterial and Viral) from chest-X-ray images using federated deep learning. In the final part, we will use CAM based techniques (e.g., Grad-CAM, Grad-CAM++, and Score-CAM) to detect pneumonia infected regions from chest-X-ray.

In Sect. 5.1, we have given a detailed description of the dataset. The simulation setup and the performance metrics have given in Sect. 5.2. In Sect. 5.3, we have shown corresponding results.

Algorithm 1. Client Side Local Update

Input : D_{Local}, B = mini batch Size, E = Total Epochs
Output : Optimal model parameters w_e , Optimal local loss function $F(w_e)$

1: **procedure** CLIENTSIDE_LOCAL_UPDATE(D_{local}, B, E)
2:     **Initialize :** $w_e^0 = w_e^1$, λ, β, $\beta 1$, $\beta 2$
3:     **for** $e = 1; e \leq E; e+ = 1$ **do**
4:         **for** $b = 1; b \leq |\frac{D_{Local}}{B}|; b+ = 1$ **do**
5:             compute local update at each E_{ser} using any of the following optimizers
6:             **Momentum + SGD :**

$$V^b = \beta V^{b-1} + (1 - \beta)\nabla_{w_e^b} F_{E_{ser}}(w_e, X, Y) \tag{8}$$

$$w_e^b = w_e^{b-1} - \lambda V^b \tag{9}$$

7:             **Adam :** calculating bias regulated first and second moment using Equation 4, 5, 6, and 7 and then calculate

$$w_e^b = w_e^{b-1} - \lambda \frac{\bar{m}^b}{\sqrt{\bar{v}^b} + \epsilon} \tag{10}$$

8:             **Adamax :**

$$v^b = \max(\beta_2 v^{b-1}, |\nabla^b|) \tag{11}$$

$$w_e^b = w_e^{b-1} - \lambda \frac{\bar{m}^b}{v^b} \tag{12}$$

9:             compute loss using Equation 1
10:         select the local model using

$$F_{E_{ser}}(w_e) = \min_{e=1...E}(F_{E_{ser}}(w_e)) \tag{13}$$

$$w_e = \underset{e=1...E}{\arg \min}(F_{E_{ser}}(w_e)) \tag{14}$$

11:     **return** $w_e, F(w_e)$ ▷ The best local model to be returned

---

Algorithm 2. Central Server Side Global Update

Input : $E_{ser} = [E_{ser_1}, E_{ser_2} \ldots E_{ser_N}]$, total rounds $= T$
Output : final model parameters w^* , Global optimal loss function $F(w^*)$

1: **procedure** CENTRALSERVER_SIDE_GLOBAL_UPDATE(E_{ser})
2:    **for** $t = 1, 2, \ldots T$ **do**
3:        **for** each $E_{ser_i} \in E_{ser}$ in parallel Compute: **do**
4:            ClientSide_Local_Update()
5:            $w^t = $ FedAvg(all clients local updates)   ▷ Calculate weights and loss using federated averaging
6:        Send w^t to the E_{ser}s
7:        **Optimal Global Model**

$$w^* = \underset{where \ t=1,2,\ldots T}{\arg\min} \ F(w^t) \tag{15}$$

8:    apply CAM based methods on optimal global model for visualization
9:    infer optimal global model for real-time processing

5.1   Datasets

We consider a public dataset of chest-X-ray [5] to perform experiments. The dataset contains 5,232 labeled images of chest-X-ray from children. It includes 3,883 pneumonia (including 2,530 Viral pneumonia and 1,353 bacterial pneumonia) and 1,349 normal chest-X-ray images. In the beginning, we only use this dataset to classify pneumonia and normal chest-X-ray images using federated deep learning. The dataset is divided into three hospitals/clients, so that each Hospital can train its model locally. In this experiment, the whole data is

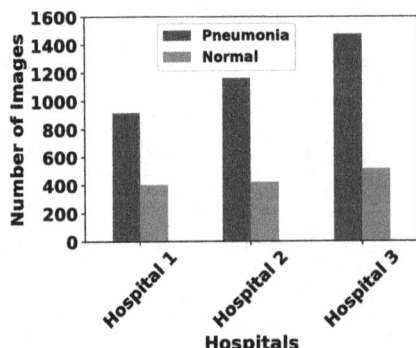
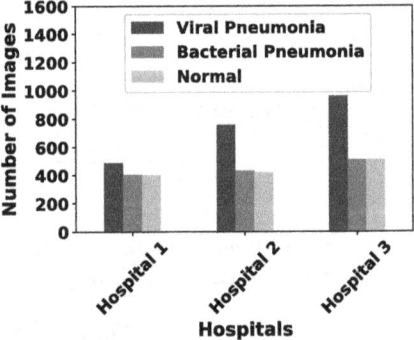

(a) Distribution of Pneumonia and Normal chest-X-ray images among hospitals

(b) Distribution of Viral Pneumonia, Bacterial Pneumonia and Normal chest-X-ray images among hospitals

Fig. 2. Characteristics of data

distributed into 30%, 32%, and 38% between Hospital 1, Hospital 2, and Hospital 3, respectively. Figure 2a describes the distribution of pneumonia and normal chest-X-ray, and Fig. 2b depicts the distribution of viral pneumonia, bacterial pneumonia, and normal chest-X-rays among three hospitals.

The dataset in each edge server further is divided into training, validation and test set with a ratio of 6:3:1.

5.2 Simulation Setup

We have taken four pre-trained models for the experiments including ResNet18, ResNet50, DenseNet121, and MobileNetV2. Each edge server first downloads the pre-trained model with pre-defined imagenet weights from the central server. The edge server in each hospital applies transfer learning here and trains the model with their local data. The edge server sends the updated model to the central server for model aggregation. This process will continue until the optimal model is produced. The description of the federated setting is described in Table 1.

Table 1. Parameters description in federated setting

Parameter(s)	Value	Description
Clients	3	Edge servers for model training
Client participation	100%	Full participation of each client
Total epochs	10	Train model locally
Batch size	16	Batch size per round
Rounds	5	Number of interaction between hospitals (clients) and central server
Optimizer	3	Adam, Adamax, and SGD+Momentum
λ	0.001	Learning rate for optimizer
β	0.9	Momentum term
β_1	0.9	The exponential decay rate for the first moment estimates
β_2	0.999	The exponential decay rate for the second moment estimates
ϵ	$10E-8$	A small number to prevent the division by zero
Momentum	0.9	
Learning rate decay	0.1	After 7 epochs learning rate will be decayed
Performance metrics	5	Loss, Accuracy, F1-score, Precision, Recall

5.3 Results and Analysis

We have performed 5 consecutive rounds of model training of ResNet18, ResNet50, MobileNetV2, and DenseNet121 using transfer learning in federated domain using datasets of Fig. 2a and Fig. 2b, respectively and compared the loss convergence among them. Figure 3a describes the performance of every model on dataset Fig. 2a, the ResNet18 model produces the loss 0.052 which is minimum compared to other methods. In Fig. 3b, loss convergence of ResNet18 and ResNet50 model have carried out on dataset 2b. ResNet18 model gives better convergence than ResNet50 model. It produces the minimum loss 0.365 whereas ResNet50 model provide minimum loss 0.381.

Next, in Fig. 3c, we have compared FedAvg method with centralized method. We have trained the ResNet18 model in both centralized and federated setting on the chest-X-ray dataset given in Fig. 2a. The performance of the model in both environments is equivalent.

In Table 2, we made a comparative study between the performance of different optimizers in this problem. We compared adaptive learning rate based optimization techniques such as Adam and Adamax with momentum-based SGD technique in the federated setting. We test it for both datasets in Fig. 2a and Fig. 2b, respectively. In both cases, ResNet18 based model gives the best performance, and Momentum + SGD outperforms adaptive learning rate based methods.

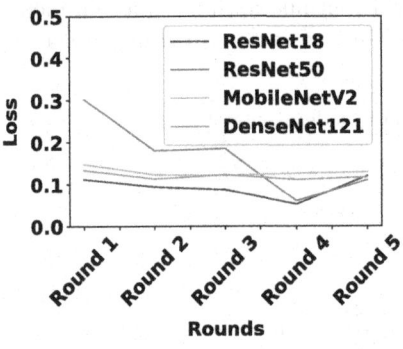

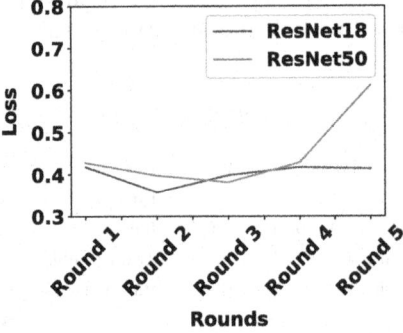

(a) Loss convergence of different models in federated setting on dataset in Figure 2a

(b) Loss convergence of different models in federated setting on dataset in Figure 2b

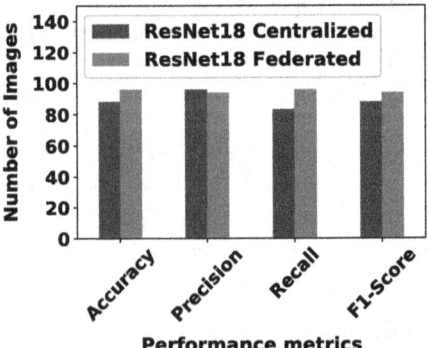

(c) Performance evaluation between centralized and federated deep learning models

Fig. 3. Performance evaluation between centralized and federated deep learning models

Table 2. Comparison among optimizers

Classification of pneumonia and normal chest-X-ray						
Methods	Adam		Adamax		Momentum + SGD	
	Loss	Accuracy	Loss	Accuracy	Loss	Accuracy
ResNet18	0.13	95.8%	0.146	95.8%	0.052	98.3%
ResNet50	0.12	95.6%	0.126	95.6%	0.06	97.6%
Classification of viral pneumonia, bacterial pneumonia, and normal chest-X-ray						
ResNet18	0.486	81%	0.517	79.4%	0.365	87.3%
ResNet50	0.533	78.6%	0.529	79.2%	0.381	84.9%

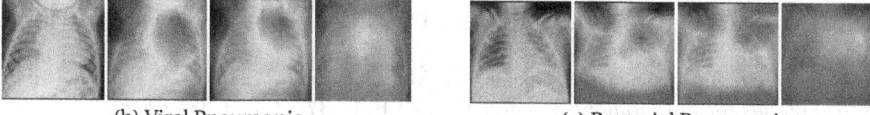

(a) Normal

(b) Viral Pneumonia   (c) Bacterial Pneumonia

Fig. 4. Visualization of pneumonia and normal chest-X-ray

To visualize pneumonia from chest-X-ray images, we have applied three different CAM based methods such as Grad-CAM, Grad-CAM++, and Score-CAM on the ResNet18 model. It produces the heatmap for the chest-X-ray images. Figure 4a shows the normal chest-X-ray. Figure 4b shows the viral pneumonia affected regions and Fig. 4c depicts the bacterial pneumonia infected regions.

6   Conclusion and Future Work

This paper has shown a CNN-based deep learning model for efficiently detecting pneumonia from chest-X-ray images in a federated setting. The proposed approach is validated by employing four pre-trained models such as ResNet18, ResNet50, Dense- Net121, and, MobileNetV2 and re-trained using transfer learning on the chest-X-ray dataset in the federated as well as centralized environments. In both settings, the performance of ResNet18 based model with Momentum + SGD optimizer performs better than other models. ResNet18 achieves 98.3% accuracy for a pneumonia detection problem and 87.3% accuracy for classifying viral, bacterial pneumonia, and normal chest-X-ray images in federated settings. To visualization of pneumonia infected regions in a chest-X-ray, we used CAM based methods including Grad-CAM, Grad-CAM++, and Score-CAM on trained ResNet18 model.

In the future, we will extend this problem to classify different types of chest diseases efficiently from chest-X-ray images in a hybrid federated setting.

Acknowledgement. This work was partially supported by the Wallenberg AI, Autonomous Systems and Software Program (WASP) funded by Knut and Alice Wallenberg Foundation.

References

1. Chattopadhay, A., Sarkar, A., Howlader, P., Balasubramanian, V.N.: Grad-cam++: generalized gradient-based visual explanations for deep convolutional networks. In: 2018 IEEE Winter Conference on Applications of Computer Vision (WACV), pp. 839–847. IEEE (2018)
2. Chouhan, V.: A novel transfer learning based approach for pneumonia detection in chest x-ray images. Appl. Sci. **10**(2), 559 (2020)
3. Farahani, B., Barzegari, M., Aliee, F.S.: Towards collaborative machine learning driven healthcare internet of things. In: Proceedings of the International Conference on Omni-Layer Intelligent Systems, COINS 2019 pp. 134–140. Association for Computing Machinery, New York (2019)
4. Grigorescu, S., Trasnea, B., Cocias, T., Macesanu, G.: A survey of deep learning techniques for autonomous driving. J. Field Rob. **37**(3), 362–386 (2020)
5. Kermany, D., Zhang, K., Goldbaum, M.: Labeled optical coherence tomography (oct) and chest x-ray images for classification. Mendeley Data **2**, (2018)
6. Kingma, D.P., Ba, J.: Adam: A method for stochastic optimization. arXiv preprint arXiv:1412.6980 (2014)
7. Lauritsen, S.M., et al.: Early detection of sepsis utilizing deep learning on electronic health record event sequences. Artif. Intell. Med. **104**, 101820 (2020)
8. Liu, B., Yan, B., Zhou, Y., Yang, Y., Zhang, Y.: Experiments of federated learning for covid-19 chest x-ray images. arXiv preprint arXiv:2007.05592 (2020)
9. McMahan, B., Moore, E., Ramage, D., Hampson, S., Arcas, B.A.: Communication-efficient learning of deep networks from decentralized data. In: Artificial Intelligence and Statistics, pp. 1273–1282 (2017)
10. Miotto, R., Wang, F., Wang, S., Jiang, X., Dudley, J.T.: Deep learning for healthcare: review, opportunities and challenges. Brief. Bioinf. **19**(6), 1236–1246 (2018)
11. Patel, Y.S., Banerjee, S., Misra, R., Das, S.K.: Low-latency energy-efficient cyber-physical disaster system using edge deep learning. In: Proceedings of the 21st International Conference on Distributed Computing and Networking, pp. 1–6 (2020)
12. Poirot, M.G., Vepakomma, P., Chang, K., Kalpathy-Cramer, J., Gupta, R., Raskar, R.: Split learning for collaborative deep learning in healthcare. arXiv preprint arXiv:1912.12115 (2019)
13. Qian, N.: On the momentum term in gradient descent learning algorithms. Neural Netw. **12**(1), 145–151 (1999)
14. Rajpurkar, P., et al.: Chexnet: radiologist-level pneumonia detection on chest x-rays with deep learning. arXiv preprint arXiv:1711.05225 (2017)
15. Reddi, S., et al.: Adaptive federated optimization. arXiv preprint arXiv:2003.00295 (2020)
16. Selvaraju, R.R., Cogswell, M., Das, A., Vedantam, R., Parikh, D., Batra, D.: Grad-cam: visual explanations from deep networks via gradient-based localization. Int. J. Comput. Vis. **128**(2), 336–359 (2019)

17. Sheller, M.J., Reina, G.A., Edwards, B., Martin, J., Bakas, S.: Multi-institutional deep learning modeling without sharing patient data: a feasibility study on brain tumor segmentation. In: Crimi, A., Bakas, S., Kuijf, H., Keyvan, F., Reyes, M., van Walsum, T. (eds.) BrainLes 2018. LNCS, vol. 11383, pp. 92–104. Springer, Cham (2019). https://doi.org/10.1007/978-3-030-11723-8_9

18. Wang, H., et al.: Score-cam: score-weighted visual explanations for convolutional neural networks. In: Proceedings of the IEEE/CVF Conference on Computer Vision and Pattern Recognition Workshops, pp. 24–25 (2020)

19. Wang, L., Wong, A.: Covid-net: a tailored deep convolutional neural network design for detection of covid-19 cases from chest x-ray images. arXiv preprint arXiv:2003.09871 (2020)

20. Xu, J., Wang, F.: Federated learning for healthcare informatics. arXiv preprint arXiv:1911.06270 (2019)

21. Zhang, Z., Sabuncu, M.: Generalized cross entropy loss for training deep neural networks with noisy labels. In: Advances in Neural Information Processing Systems, pp. 8778–8788 (2018)

Comparing Three Data Representations for Music with a Sequence-to-Sequence Model

Sichao Li[(✉)] and Charles Patrick Martin

Research School of Computer Science, Australian National University, Canberra, Australia
{sichao.li,charles.martin}@anu.edu.au

Abstract. The choices of neural network model and data representation, a mapping between musical notation and input signals for a neural network, have emerged as a major challenge in creating convincing models for melody generation. Music generation can inspire creativity in artists and the general public, but choosing a proper data representation is complicated because the same musical piece can be presented in a range of expressive ways. In this paper, we compare three different data representations on the task of generating melodies with a sequence-to-sequence model, which generates melodies with flexible length, to explore how they affect the performance of generated music. These three representations are: a monophonic representation, playing one note each time, a polyphonic representation, indicating simultaneous notes and a complex polyphonic representation, expanding the polyphonic representation with dynamics. The influences of three data representations on the generated performance are compared and evaluated by mathematical analysis and human-cantered evaluation. The results show that different data representations fed into the same model endow the generated music with various features, the monophonic representation makes the music sound more melodious to humans' ears, the polyphonic representation provides expressiveness and the complex-polyphonic representation guarantees the complexity of the generated music.

Keywords: Machine learning · Music generation · Data representation · Sequence-to-sequence model

1 Introduction

Musical melodies can be described as a sequence of notes that form a convincing pattern [3]. To generate such sequences via neural networks, previous works have explored Deep Neural Networks (DNN) and Recurrent Neural Networks (RNN) and demonstrated the potential of sequence models to generate musical scores [2,15]. The musical performance has been improved further by using the long short-term memory (LSTM) model [6]. However, most of these systems generate a sequence of equal length of the given melody from the musical

© Springer Nature Switzerland AG 2020
M. Gallagher et al. (Eds.): AI 2020, LNAI 12576, pp. 16–28, 2020.
https://doi.org/10.1007/978-3-030-64984-5_2

rules, which is not desirable in practice. We aim to design a system that is able to automatically learn and generate sequences of different length of the given sequence. This process can be modelled as a translation problem, from a set of notes to an accompanying sequence, leading to the Sequence-to-Sequence model and researchers have made excellent progress using the system in terms of translation between two different fields, such as text and video [20].

Data representation is critical for machine learning models. The representations of numbers and letters are clear and well-explored, while the representation of a melody is complex and diverse, as a convincing melody takes pitch, duration, dynamics and other expressive factors into account. One melody can be represented in different ways as long as the representation can be transformed back into the same melody. Most recent works only consider one data representation [5,11]; however in this research, three representation methods are explored and systematically compared.

The first data representation is a monophonic representation. Monophonic music is the simplest musical form, one note at a time, without accompanying chords or harmony. Typke and his team claimed that this type of music can be expressed by one-dimensional sequence, consisting of three events: note-played, note-on and note-off [19]. This is the easiest way to think of the melody but it lacks expressive timing or dynamics. To produce chords or polyphonic music, the data representation needs to allow notes that play simultaneously and this format is defined as polyphonic representation. To deal with the chords, taking advantage of a time-by-notes matrix is helpful, which enables the model to generate polyphonic music. Our last representation, complex polyphonic, also accounts for dynamics, or MIDI velocity, another expressive factor when playing music. The idea behind the representation is similar to the monophonic-sequence, whereas the events consist of time, velocity, note-on, note-off instead of note-on and note-off, leading the model to predict dynamically [17].

This work introduces a simple sequence-to-sequence model for generating harmonic and convincing music with flexible length, which can be applied in future creativity support tools and which supports each of the three representations. Our system allows us to compare melodies generated by models trained with each representation directly. We analyse these melodies using both a mathematical approach and through a human-centred study on perceived quality. We show that the representation used for a music generation model provides different features in the resultant music, including complexity, musicality and expressiveness.

1.1 Symbolic Music Generation

Music can be recorded in a variety of digital formats ranging from the Waveform Audio File Format (WAV), or raw digital audio, to a more understandable and manipulable format, such as Musical Instrument Digital Interface (MIDI). MIDI files contain high-level symbolic information and can be transformed into an appropriate numerical representations for machine learning purposes.

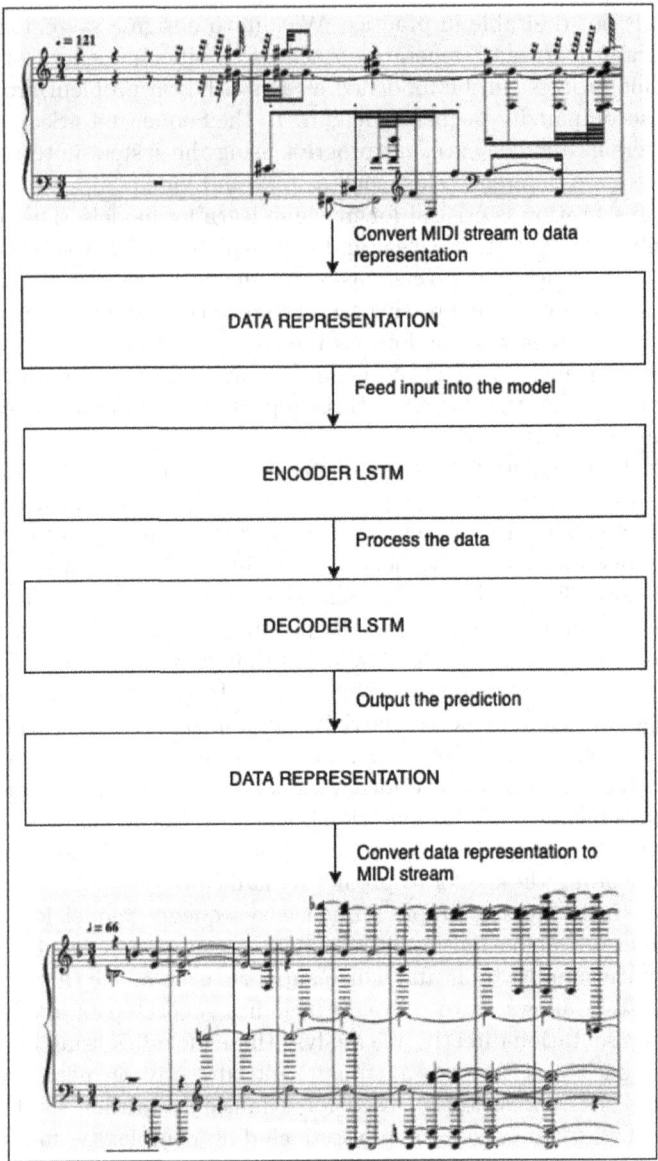

Fig. 1. Our musical sequence-to-sequence architecture for melody generation. Our system is compatible with three data representations used in this study.

To predict a musical sequence, Markov models [1] can be used to predict a sequence of possible events based on the Markov assumption. This approach is widely used in natural language processing. However, Markov chains take extremely long time to converge in the number of samples of the dataset [13] so that Markov model might not be perfect for music generation. Recurrent Neural Networks (RNN) with ability to "memorise" the previous information and learn to predict next notes based on its knowledge are also explored and demonstrated its feasibility in time series data. RNNs also have limitations when it comes to long-term dependency and it may lead to vanishing gradient and exploding gradient. The Long Short-Term Memory (LSTM) RNN cell [6] tackles this issue by implementing gated cells than can learn to selectively remember or forget information in order to capture the long-term dependencies. Based on LSTM, the sequence-to-sequence architecture [18] was proposed to provide more flexibility where the length of the input and output may differ. The architecture consists of two separate parts, an decoder and an encoder. Typically, the basic idea is that both decoder and encoder are LSTM layers and the encoder is responsible for mapping the input sequence into a vector of fixed dimensionality, while another LSTM cell decodes the vector to the target sequence.

2   Model and Data Representations

In this research, we use a sequence-to-sequence LSTM-RNN model illustrated in Fig. 1. The encoder and decoder are both LSTM layers with 512 hidden units. An LSTM cell outputs the cell state and hidden state according to the initial state and input, in which the cell state is the memory information of the network accumulated upon that point. The hidden state is the output of the cell. We defined the training model and inferring model separately.

Our training model consists of an encoder and a decoder. The decoder takes 3 inputs, 2 states from the encoder and a set of encoded notes offset by one timestep from the encoder input, which algorithm, named "teacher forcing", is proposed by Williams's team [21]. We trained the network with a categorical cross-entropy loss function and Adam optimizer following the conventions [9], and set the batch size to 64. The model was trained for 200 epochs on all different data representations.

Our training and inference models both have the same encoder, while the decoder of the inferring model is a starting symbol instead of the expected note. Given the signal and the states from the encoder, the model starts predicting up to the expected length. Normally, we set the start point as 0, while end point depends on how long the user wants the melody to be. Figures 2a and 2b show the structure of training model and inference model.

2.1   Monophonic Representation

The first data representation is the monophonic representation. We followed existing procedures [3] to convert the MIDI stream into a sequence of integers. Standard MIDI files allow 128 pitches, from 0–127, e.g. the number 60 represents "middle C" so that each line of music score can be represented by a sequence of integers. Also, we configure 128 to stand for "note-off" and 129 for "no-event". In short, all events in this representation can be mapped to 0–129 and the explanation are interpreted as follows:

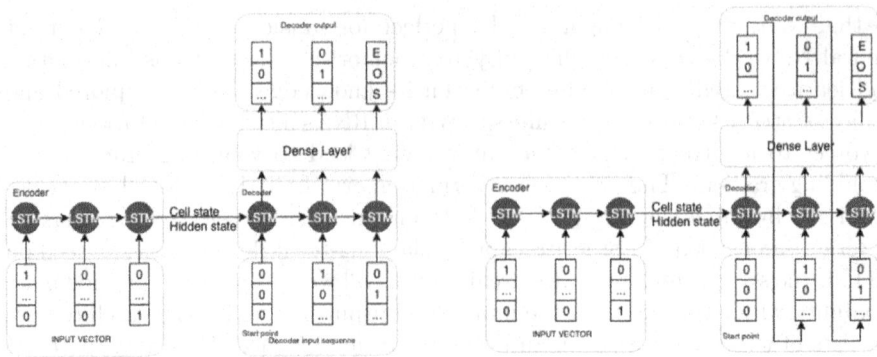

(a) Training model with feedback   (b) Inference model with prediction

Fig. 2. The training and inference models. The difference between the training and inference model is that the expected notes are provided to the decoder of the training model, while the decoder of the inference model predicts from the starting point.

- 0–127 Note-on: plays a MIDI note at that number.
- 128 Note-off: stop the note played.
- 129 No-action: do nothing.

Another crucial factor in representing melody is timing. In this representation, we assume a minimum time duration of sixteenth note (or semi-quaver), so that each integer in the sequence represents an event lasting for one 16th of the time of a bar. Where several notes sound together, we only pick the highest pitch at each semiquaver. An example is shown in Fig. 3.

71 129 129 129 65 129 129 129 74 129 76 129 77 129 129 129

Fig. 3. Integer representation of a monophonic melody. The first chord is represented by the highest pitch (71) followed by three 129 s, indicating that there is no change for the next three semiquavers.

2.2   Polyphonic Representation

The polyphonic representation introduces chords and more dynamic timing. To achieve that, we treat the piano roll as a 2D matrix of notes and time [14]. We construct a $128 \times n$ matrix corresponding to all 128 MIDI-pitches and a time length of n. The overall duration can be easily extracted from MIDI files with Python libraries and we slice the time into small pieces so that we can quantise the events. 0.02 s was chosen as the minimal time.

2.3   Complex Polyphonic Representation

The last data representation consists of polyphonic piano performances with velocity (the force that a note is pressed on the piano keyboard, corresponding to volume), which sounds more human instead of mechanical. The performance is converted into a sequence of events as proposed by [7], which is like the first representation but with more events. The velocity event is quantised into 32 bins from 128 possible MIDI velocities [16]. We also need to quantise the time shift event, the duration from one event to another. According to the study by [4], the just noticeable difference (JND) when temporally displacing a single tone in a sequence is about 10 ms so 100 time shifts are available from 10 ms to 1 s. The total vocabulary has 388 symbols, as follows, and an example can be seen in Fig. 4.

- 0–127 Note-on event
- 128–256 Note-off event
- 256–288 Velocity event
- 288–388 Time-shift event

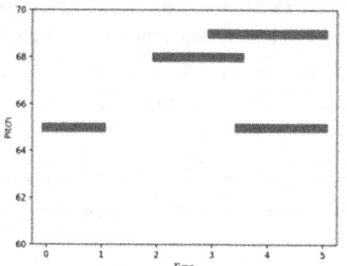

SET_VELOCITY<80>, NOTE_ON<65>
TIME_SHIFT<1000>, NOTE_OFF<65>
TIME_SHIFT<1000>
SET_VELOCITY<100>, NOTE_ON<68>
TIME_SHIFT<1000>
SET_VELOCITY<100>, NOTE_ON<69>
TIME_SHIFT<500>, NOTE_OFF<68>
SET_VELOCITY<80>, NOTE_ON<65>
TIME_SHIFT<1000>, TIME_SHIFT<500>
NOTE_OFF<65>, NOTE_OFF<69>

Fig. 4. A visualised excerpt of a piano roll and its complex polyphonic representation.

3   Experiments

To train sequence-to-sequence models for each representation we used the International Piano e-Competition dataset [8]. This contains piano performances by experts in MIDI and WAV format recorded by internal sensors on the piano. From the International Piano e-Competition dataset, we picked MIDI files for 4 years' of competitions, which contains 502 performances. The performances then were split into validation and training partitions (10:90). To be fair, we can train the model on either the same time length or sequence length, e.g., 30s segments, a sequence of 150 events [12]. We obtained more than 100k training sequences for each data representations from this dataset. In the experiment, we trained the model on the segments of 120 events length. This was because the monophonic representation contains 8 events per second, while the polyphonic and complex-polyphonic representations use 50 events per second. The same length could add burden to the model, making calculation harder and it makes more sense for a neural network to treat the same lengths of input as identical instead of the same time shifts since it does not even have the definition of "time". We trained the model with monophonic representation, polyphonic representation and complex-polyphonic representation separately with 50 epochs. After around 72 hours of training, melodies were generated from each model separately.

4   Model Evaluation

4.1   Mathematical Evaluation

It is difficult to evaluate the quality of music directly, such as musicality and expressiveness, and mostly, those generated melodies are evaluated by human ears [10]. Sometimes it is hard to compare the quality of music even by experts because there is not a standard benchmark for testing music and lack of comparability with similar systems. [22] proposed a set of objective matrix by extracting the meaningful features in a melody to evaluate and compare the outputs of music generative systems. The approach contains two measurements, absolute matrix, giving insights to the characteristics of dataset and relative matrix, comparing two datasets and it defined a set of features. Here, we focused on the absolute matrix and chose 5 representative features listed below:

Table 1. Experimental result of monophonic, polyphonic, complex polyphonic and test data set evaluation. The highest values are bold and the lowest are Italic within four samples

	Monophonic				Polyphonic				Complex Polyphonic				Test-samples			
	Absolute measure		Intra-set		Absolute measure		Intra-set		Absolute measure		Intra-set		Absolute measure		Intra-set	
	Mean	STD	Mean	STD	Mean	STD	Mean	STD	Mean	STD	Mean	STD	Mean	STD	Mean	STD
PC	37.300	6.420	8.111	5.078	37.500	7.645	9.444	6.379	**40.3**	9.209	11.311	7.780	32.400	7.605	9.511	6.170
NC	155.200	33.555	40.133	29.857	**447.0**	260.346	325.911	210.724	153.200	67.427	78.756	62.455	224.800	85.533	106.533	70.060
PR	50.500	10.122	12.200	8.878	59.700	13.499	16.156	11.996	**61.7**	12.248	15.089	10.280	50.700	8.450	9.622	8.130
PI	9.523	2.197	2.660	1.910	11.845	3.559	4.493	2.821	*9.006*	1.034	1.276	0.864	10.983	3.845	4.831	3.086
IOI	0.204	0.039	0.049	0.031	*0.085*	0.059	0.070	0.054	0.203	0.101	0.124	0.086	0.151	0.057	0.071	0.048

- PC (pitch count): the number of different pitches within a sample
- PR (pitch range): the difference between the highest pitch and lowest pitch

– PI (average pitch interval): average value of the interval between two pitches
– NC (note count): the number of used notes
– IOI (average inter-onset-interval): the time between two consecutive notes

The intra-set results represent the distance histograms per feature and the value is computed by applying pairwise exhaustive cross-validation to the distance of each sample in the same dataset.

To extract those features and compare them fairly, we generated 10 30 s-long melodies for all three performances given the same the initial state and test data set, 10 30 s segments, and saved the generated songs in MIDI format. After we applied the feature extraction measurements, we calculated the mean and standard deviation of each feature of the data set for analysis and the results are shown in Table 1.

We make the following observations on these results: First, the PC and PR extracted from complex polyphonic representation are the highest among those representations and it indicates that the melodies generated with complex polyphonic representation is more complex than others since the wider pitch range means higher diversity. Also, PI of the result of the complex polyphonic representation is the lowest, which gives us an insight into the performance as well. The smaller value of PI reveals that the difference between two consecutive pitches are smaller, resulting in a more flowing melody. The note relevant matrix, NC and IOI, shows that the polyphonic performance is able to produce more notes within the same time, which amounts to 3 times more than the monophonic and complex polyphonic and 2 times more than the test sample.

Figure 5 provides a visualisation of the features between different samples. Those figures give us straightforward feeling of how similar our generated melodies are to the ground-truth test samples. The amount of overlap in the distributions reveals which performances have similar characteristics. In terms of PC, polyphonic and complex polyphonic performances' distributions are almost identical and complex polyphonic performance overlaps most in the NC distribution. All perform similar in PR. The polyphonic representation's average pitch interval and the time between two consecutive notes are most like the test sample. Based on the analysis above, in general, the polyphonic representation is the most similar to the test sample.

4.2 Human-Centered Evaluation

The goal of this evaluation was to compare the performances generated with different data representations by asking for feedback from human listeners. We conducted a survey where we played 3 samples generated using the three different data representations and 1 test sample to 20 participants (who were not made aware of how each example had been generated). The participants included music experts and non-experts. Each participant was asked to indicate agreement with the following 5 questions on a 9-point scale for each example:

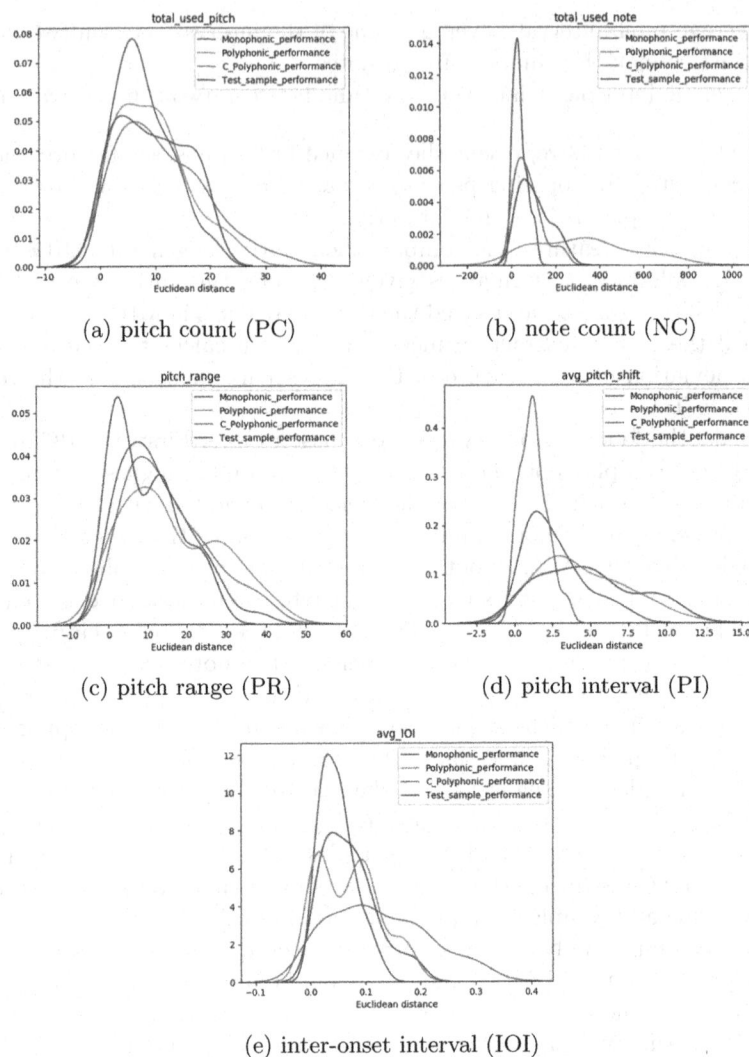

(a) pitch count (PC)

(b) note count (NC)

(c) pitch range (PR)

(d) pitch interval (PI)

(e) inter-onset interval (IOI)

Fig. 5. Distributions of features for generated samples from Monophonic, Polyphonic, Complex Polyphonic and test samples.

1. How much do you like the melody? (*preference*)
2. The performance contained complex melodies. (*complexity*)
3. The performance contained expressive melodies. (*expressiveness*)
4. The performance was musical. (*musicality*)
5. The performance was human-made. (*human-made*)

The distributions of all ratings are displayed in Fig. 6. The findings for each example melody are as follows:

textbfComplex Polyphonic: The ratings on performance complexity is the highest among 5 samples, corresponding to the result of objective assessment, and it sounds even more complex than the test sample to listeners, while the expressiveness is the lowest.

Monophonic: The sample contains a relatively simple melody but it sounds musical, only lower than the test sample, and the overall performance is better than expected.

Polyphonic: The overall performance of the sample is the worst. The melody is comparatively complex and expressive, which expressiveness is only lower than test sample. This mirrors the findings of the systematic analysis above.

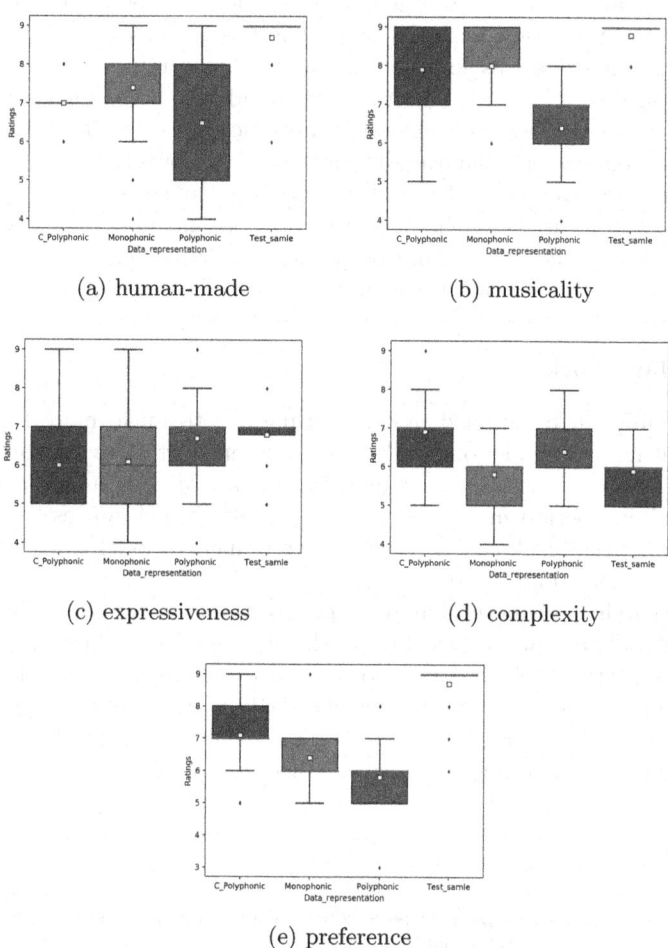

(a) human-made   (b) musicality

(c) expressiveness   (d) complexity

(e) preference

Fig. 6. The distributions of survey responses for samples generated from our complex-polyphonic, polyphonic, monophonic data representations, and a human-generated test melody.

5 Conclusion

In this research we tested a sequence-to-sequence music generation LSTM-RNN with three different data representations: a monophonic, polyphonic, and complex polyphonic representation. Generated music from all three models were compared with held-out melodies from the dataset using a mathematical evaluation and a human-centred survey. The results from our study indicate that the music generated from sequence-to-sequence model sounds broadly human-made as the human ratings for each model generally exceeded the neutral point of the rating scale. Our comparison of the influence of three data representations on the generated performance revealed that different data representations offer different musical features to the generated music. We observed that complex polyphonic representation achieved the highest score in terms of complexity, whereas expressiveness was limited. The monophonic representation performs moderately against all criteria and it almost sounds like human-generated. With polyphonic representation, the generated music sounds most like machine-made among those samples and the overall scores were the lowest.

To summarise, the order of overall performance by score is a complex polyphonic representation, monophonic representation and polyphonic representation. These results, however, could be influenced by participants, and a larger survey size could be used in future studies.

5.1 Further Work

This technique can be applied in other situations to make more flexible and pleasant music. Our model only consists of one encoder layer and one decoder layer and the model is trained for only 50 epochs. More complex models and a longer training period may achieve better results, which makes us optimistic about the potential results for the sequence-to-sequence model, particularly with complex-polyphonic data representation.

This research has shown that data representations can equip final performances with different properties. This work could be extended to other symbolic music representations. Music generation systems could make use of different data representations to achieve specific musical goals; using another representation provides surprising and creative results. This flexibility could allow generated music to be more varied and expressive, and inspire creativity in society.

References

1. Ames, C.: The Markov process as a compositional model: a survey and tutorial. Leonardo **22**(2), 175–187 (1989)
2. Eck, D., Schmidhuber, J.: Finding temporal structure in music: blues improvisation with LSTM recurrent networks. In: Proceedings of the 12th IEEE Workshop on Neural Networks for Signal Processing, pp. 747–756. IEEE (2002)

3. Faitas, A., Baumann, S.E., Næss, T.R., Torresen, J., Martin, C.P.: Generating convincing harmony parts with simple long short-term memory networks. In: Queiroz, M., Sedó, A.X. (eds.) Proceedings of the International Conference on New Interfaces for Musical Expression, pp. 325–330. UFRGS, Porto Alegre (2019)

4. Friberg, A., Sundberg, J.: Perception of just-noticeable time displacement of a tone presented in a metrical sequence at different tempos. J. Acoust. Soc. Am. **94**(3), 1859–1859 (1993)

5. Goel, K., Vohra, R., Sahoo, J.K.: Polyphonic music generation by modeling temporal dependencies using a RNN-DBN. In: Wermter, S., et al. (eds.) ICANN 2014. LNCS, vol. 8681, pp. 217–224. Springer, Cham (2014). https://doi.org/10.1007/978-3-319-11179-7_28

6. Hochreiter, S., Schmidhuber, J.: Long short-term memory. Neural Comput. **9**(8), 1735–1780 (1997)

7. Huang, C.Z.A., et al.: Music transformer: generating music with long-term structure. In: Proceedings of ICLR 2019 (2019)

8. Piano junior competition 2002–2018 (2018). https://www.piano-e-competition.com. Accessed 20 Aug 2019

9. Ketkar, N., et al.: Deep Learning with Python. Springer, Heidelberg (2017). https://doi.org/10.1007/978-1-4842-2766-4

10. Malik, I., Ek, C.H.: Neural translation of musical style. arXiv preprint arXiv:1708.03535 (2017)

11. Mao, H.H., Shin, T., Cottrell, G.: Deepj: style-specific music generation. In: 2018 IEEE 12th International Conference on Semantic Computing (ICSC), pp. 377–382. IEEE (2018)

12. Meade, N., Barreyre, N., Lowe, S.C., Oore, S.: Exploring conditioning for generative music systems with human-interpretable controls. arXiv preprint arXiv:1907.04352 (2019)

13. Mossel, E., Vigoda, E., et al.: Limitations of Markov chain monte Carlo algorithms for Bayesian inference of phylogeny. Ann. Appl. Prob. **16**(4), 2215–2234 (2006)

14. Machine learning blog (2017). https://blogs.technet.microsoft.com/machinelearning/2017/12/06/music-generation-with-azure-machine-learning/

15. Olof: C-rnn-gan: Continuous recurrent neural networks with adversarial training. arXiv preprint arXiv:1611.09904 (2016)

16. Oore, S., Simon, I., Dieleman, S., Eck, D., Simonyan, K.: This time with feeling: learning expressive musical performance. Neural Comput. Appl. **32**(4), 955–967 (2018)

17. Sordoni, A., Bengio, Y., Vahabi, H., Lioma, C., Grue Simonsen, J., Nie, J.Y.: A hierarchical recurrent encoder-decoder for generative context-aware query suggestion. In: Proceedings of the 24th ACM International on Conference on Information and Knowledge Management, pp. 553–562. ACM (2015)

18. Sutskever, I., Vinyals, O., Le, Q.V.: Sequence to sequence learning with neural networks. In: Advances in Neural Information Processing Systems, pp. 3104–3112 (2014)

19. Typke, R., Wiering, F., Veltkamp, R.C.: A survey of music information retrieval systems. In: Proceedings of 6th International Conference on Music Information Retrieval, pp. 153–160. University of London, Queen Mary (2005)

20. Venugopalan, S., Rohrbach, M., Donahue, J., Mooney, R., Darrell, T., Saenko, K.: Sequence to sequence-video to text. In: Proceedings of the IEEE International Conference on Computer Vision, pp. 4534–4542 (2015)

21. Williams, R.J., Zipser, D.: A learning algorithm for continually running fully recurrent neural networks. Neural Comput. **1**(2), 270–280 (1989)
22. Yang, L.C., Lerch, A.: On the evaluation of generative models in music. Neural Comput. Appl. **32**(9), 4773–4784 (2018). https://doi.org/10.1007/s00521-018-3849-7

Real-Time Decision Making for Train Carriage Load Prediction via Multi-stream Learning

Hang Yu[1], Anjin Liu[1], Bin Wang[1], Ruimin Li[2], Guangquan Zhang[1], and Jie Lu[1(✉)] (iD)

[1] Australian Artificial Intelligence Institute, University of Technology Sydney, Sydney, Australia
{HangYu,BinWang-7}@student.uts.edu.au,
{AnjinLiu,GuangquanZhang,JieLu}@uts.edu.au
[2] Sydney Trains, Transport for NSW, Sydney, Australia
ruimin.li2@transport.nsw.gov.au

Abstract. Real-time traffic planning and scheduling optimization are critical for developing low-cost, reliable, resilient, and efficient transport systems. In this paper, we present a real-time application that uses machine learning techniques to forecast the train carriage load when a train departure from a platform. With the predicted carriage load, crew can efficiently manage passenger flow, improving the efficiency of boarding and alighting, and thereby reducing the time trains spend at stations. We developed the application in collaboration with Sydney Trains. Most data are publicly available on Open Data Hub, which is supported by the Transport for NSW. We investigated the performance of different models, features, and measured their contributions to prediction accuracy. From this we propose a novel learning strategy, called Multi-Stream Learning, which merges streams having similar concept drift patterns to boost the training data size with the aim of achieving lower generalization errors. We have summarized our solutions and hope researchers and industrial users who might be facing similar problems will benefit from our findings.

Keywords: Real-time application · Multi-stream learning · Concept drift · Sydney trains

1 Introduction

Overcrowding in public transportation places a major strain on the quality of service and causes delays during peak hours [1]. Passenger load prediction for public transportation can benefit society from two perspectives. From the service provider perspective, an accurate load estimation can help traffic planning and scheduling, reducing the cost and increasing the reliability of transport systems. From the travelers' perspective, knowing the level of crowding and enjoying the

© Springer Nature Switzerland AG 2020
M. Gallagher et al. (Eds.): AI 2020, LNAI 12576, pp. 29–41, 2020.
https://doi.org/10.1007/978-3-030-64984-5_3

trip could be more important than having the shortest travel time, or the least number of interchanges [2].

Being able to include reliable information on crowdedness, requires knowledge about current and future levels of passenger loads. The availability of an increasing amount and complexity of data describing public transport services allows us to explore the detection methods and analysis of different phenomena of public transport operations now better than ever [3,4]. Transport NSW provides the possibility to use open data for occupancy information [5]. However, such information is only available for a trip at a current stop but cannot provide predictions for the next service, making it hard to incorporate it into real-time recommendation models. More importantly, if a disruption or a special event occurs, the occupancy information will become misleading. This is a typical data stream learning problem [20] under a dynamic learning environment [6,21].

Train carriage load prediction aims to estimate the number of passengers in a carriage when the train departs the platform. This information can be used by station crew to manage the flow of passengers while they are waiting at the platform, thereby improving boarding and alighting efficiency. Carriage load prediction also has the potential to provide the trip planner with a forecasting capability to advise passengers to avoid overcrowding.

Since there are eight carriages for a train, the prediction task can be considered as a multi-output problem [19]. However, some of the carriages share the same concept drift [7] patterns, which makes the problem more interesting. From the perspective of generalization error, that is, the more training data a model fits in, the lower the generalization error the model will have, we consider that vertically merging the streams having similar concept drift patterns would improve the overall performance. We label the task as Multi-stream Learning.

In summary, the main contribution of this paper are as follows:

- A real-time train load prediction model to handle Waratah, Non-Waratah trains and be capable of handling disruption situations.
- A discussion of the findings in the model selection, and feature engineering during the development of this application.
- A discussion of the findings in the multi-stream learning strategy.

The rest of this paper is organized as follows. Section 2 details the background and objectives of the study. Section 3 describes the methodology proposed to solve the learning task. Section 4 summarizes the obtained results. Section 5 concludes the paper.

2   Backgrounds and Objectives

2.1   Sydney Trains

As the operator of the suburban passenger rail network, Sydney Trains serve the city of Sydney, New South Wales, Australia. The network is a city-suburban hybrid railway system with a central underground core, 813 km of track covering eight lines and 175 stations [8]. It has subway-comparable train frequencies of every three minutes or shorter at the underground core, 5–10 min off-peak at most major and inner-city stations, and 15 min off-peak at most minor stops. The network is managed by the Department of Transportation, NSW, and is part of its Opal ticketing system. In 2018–2019, the network carried out roughly 377.1 million passenger journeys.

As Sydney Train acknowledged, this study is the first to employ machine learning techniques to implement real-time passenger load forecasting. It will provide the public transport planning and management with a better tool, and play an important role for the development of Intelligent Transport Systems in Sydney in the near future.

2.2   Waratah Train Set

Reliance Rail designed and built the Waratah carriages. The initial order for series 1 Waratahs was the largest rolling stock order in Australia's history. Waratah trains have many advanced features, including a portable boarding ramp, wheelchair-accessible entrances, symbols on accessible entrances, real-time carriage loading sensor, and much more [9]. The specifications of Waratah trains are shown in Table 1.

Table 1. The specifications of Waratah train set [9]. The seating capacity is critical for noise and outlier identification. For example, if we assume the average weight of a passenger is 75 kg, the maximum load of a carriage would be 75 kg × 118 = 8850 kg. If a carriage load exceeded this threshold, it might be due to a faulty sensor.

Specifications	Measurment
Seating capacity	101–118 passengers
Weight	48–51 tons (approx.)
Length	19393-20,000 mm
Width	3,035 mm
Height	4,410 mm

At current stage, Sydney Trains has over 60% trains operated by Waratah Trains. This means there is around 40% trains cannot provide real-time carriage loading information for prediction. The coverage of Waratah trains is important to the prediction accuracy and the actual departure loading information is the only available true label for evaluations [10].

2.3   Data Source

Transport for NSW is opening up its data to provide Open Data Hub, a platform for developers, entrepreneurs, and data analysts to form a united community to create innovative solutions for smart transportation [5]. As one of the leaders in the open data space, the NSW Government has seen its related apps downloaded millions of times. With Open Data Hub, researchers and developers can create the next generation of real-time transportation management systems. They have now serviced an open data community of more than 30,000 users [5].

The data is well documented and access is via an application programming interface (API). Open Data Hub has an application management system for users to organize their API keys, which they can use to access real-time data an via HTTP GET request. An open source data such as this helps researchers to contextualize our solutions and will be beneficial to further improvement of related learning tasks.

2.4 Application Objectives

The transport network can be divided into nine lines serving different areas. There are two types of trains, Waratah and non-Waratah, running on the network. One of the important differences between the two is whether or not a carriage is equipped with an occupancy weighting system. This means only the data collected from Waratah trains have carriages' loading weight when arriving or departing at a platform.

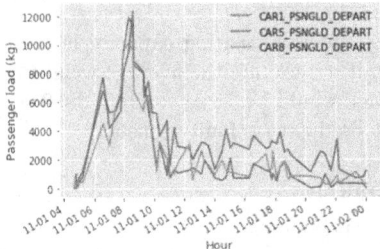 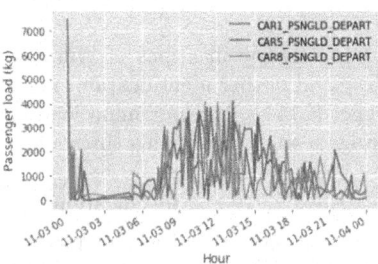

(a) Origin station: Central; Destination station: Schofields; Current station: Redfern; Platform: RD05; Date: 2019-11-01 and 2019-11-03.

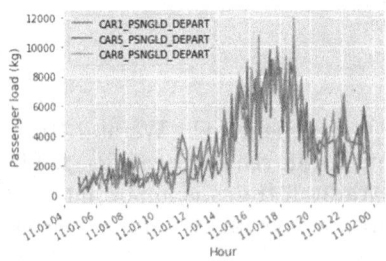 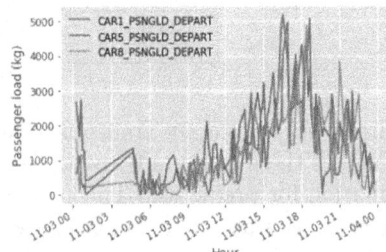

(b) Origin station: Central; Destination station: Schofields; Current station: Central (the origin station); Platform: CE18; Date: 2019-11-01 and 2019-11-03.

Fig. 1. A demonstration of the passenger load patterns during different time periods with different locations.

Figure 1a shows loading examples at platform RD05 of Redfern station on 2019-11-01 (Friday) and 2019-11-03 (Sunday). Note that each train has eight carriages, numbered 1–8 from head to end, and the weights of arrival and departure are recorded. We select the departure weights of Carriages 1, 5, and 8 as examples. In the left figure, there is a distinct peak phenomenon. During peak hours, around 8:00 am, the weight difference among three carriages is minimal, while for off-peak hours, Carriage 5 is much heavier. This may be attributed to the passengers' riding habits, preferring to choose the middle carriage to ride. In the right figure, there is no clear peak time on Sunday, but there is still a large passenger flow at midnight. Figure 1b shows the cases in Central station. As the point of origin, its peak times move from morning to afternoon. The difference in flow trend between Friday and Sunday is not very prominent, except that the passenger flow on Friday register as significantly higher.

In summary, several factors have a significant impact on passenger load, including calendar factors (hour, day of the week), position of the train carriage, and location of the platform, to mention only a few. This can generate a high variability in prediction.

3   Carriage Load Forecasting Methodology

3.1   Models Selection

We evaluate five models for train carriage load forecasting on all stations in Sydney regions. These range from the classical baseline model to advanced machine learning models. Since it is difficult to find in the literature what is the most suitable model for our task, we choose the most commonly used models for solving forecasting problems [18]:

1. Last Value (Baseline): The simplest forecasting is to forward the last observed load on the train to the next one at the same station. More specifically, this model will predict the departure load of a train carriage as the same as its arrival load.
2. Linear Regression: This is the most intuitive regressor solution, able to optimize the weight of each features to link the feature to a target variable function. In our case, the features are the train status, and the target variable is the carriage load.
3. Gradient Boosting (LightGBM): LightGBM is an open source non-linear regressor model that produces prediction models in the form of an ensemble of weak decision trees and weighting average prediction by boosting. It can handle both numerical values and category features.
4. Random Forest: This regressor model produces a prediction model in the form of an ensemble of weak decision trees where the prediction is given by bagging. This model is like gradient boosting, but it does not iteratively update the cost for each base learner.
5. Neural Network: Our final model is a universal approximator, one that can capture any form of relationship in data [11,12]. In this study, both a recurrent

neural network and convolutional neural network are inapplicable. Therefore, we deploy a simple feed forward neural network to model the relationship between the input and output.

3.2   Feature Engineering

The forecasting of train passenger load when a train departs a station is an essential and challenging task, largely due to the influence of several factors [5] which are related to transport demand and supply and can be summarized as follows:

- Calendar factors, including the day of the week, time of the day, peak hours or non-peak hours, and the month of year. It is worth mentioning that public and school holidays are also influential. This information is included in the peak hour and non-peak hour features.
- Spatial factors such as the local information about the area where the station is located. For example, residential, employment, commercial, and leisure. Since this information will not change dramatically in the days of our life, we consider it is dependent with the station name, that is, for a given station, its residential information can be automatically considered by the model.
- Transport network factors, such as the train timetable which may vary slightly if there is an increase in local population or the development of a new public transport interchange hub. Track work and emergent service disruption might also contribute to the carriage load.
- External factors, such as the climatic conditions, special events like music concerts, Rugby League, or New Year's Eve events. Collecting this information is very demanding and could be just a minority record in the data. Therefore, we have not taken them into account.
- Sensors that collect the flow of passengers boarding or alighting the trains and which could provide data subject to different interpretations depending on the context. For example, null value has different meanings, such as no passengers, missing value, or sensor malfunction.

In addition to these factors, generated when a train stopped at a station, we also manually create two features to reflect the trend of the carriage load in the context of a trip.

- Contextual moving average consists of using the average load of trains committed on the same day type and time slice in the history. The moving average shows the passenger flow's historical pattern, and is an important indicator in reflecting the increasing or decreasing of the carriage load.
- Last stopped Waratah train information is adopted to provide information regarding to the most recent traffic condition.

The records of these factors are the features of the data. The actual carriage loads measured during operation is the target variable. The purpose of the features is to understand the context of the forecasting problem more readily and then to model it.

3.3 Multi-stream Learning

This section introduces a novel concept that classifies the forecasting task as a multi-stream learning problem. The fundamental idea of multi-stream learning is to merge streams having similar concept drift to increase the training set size, thereby reducing the model's generalization error.

Some researchers translate the multi-stream learning into multiple-output learning [13,22]. However, in our opinion, two learning have many differences in essential. The point of departure in multi-output learning is the idea that the multiple outputs might have a structure representing the relationship between outputs [14]. Traditionally, based on the structure of outputs, multi-output regression can be divided into global and local methods [15]. However, in multi-stream learning, the structure of outputs might be neither local nor global. For example, assuming there are three data streams and each stream with one output attribute $\{Y_1(t), Y_2(t), Y_3(t)\}$, where the attribute Y_1 has a relationship with Y_2 attribute, but the attribute Y_3 is independent of Y_1 and Y_2, the structure of these three output attributes should be presented as $\{(Y_1, Y_2), (Y_3)\}$. More important, data streams have concept drift problems, i.e., the underlying relationship between input and output attributes can change. Different data streams have different patterns of concept drift. In multi-output learning, the problem of concept drift have not been considered.

Hence, we use the modularity property of data streams to distinguish them from the multiple-output methods. In our proposed method, we explore the similarity between each carriage load in terms of load distribution and concept drift happening, then carriage loads with high similarity are built as a modularity. For example, if we observed the passenger load of carriage 1 is similar to carriage 8, and the rest of the carriage loads are similar, there would be two modularities {Car1, Car8} and {Car2, Car3, Car4, Car5, Car6, Car7}. Then, for each modularity, we learn a prediction model to boost the overall performance.

4 Experiment Evaluations

To evaluate the learning performance of different models, and to analyze the importance of different features, we use the Waratah train operation records of Nov 2019 and Dec 2019. Most of the data is available from Open Data Hub. Only the occupancy feature is different. The carriage loading data provided by Sydney Trains is in kilograms but not in levels as provided in Open Data Hub. Therefore, we use mean absolute error (MAE) as the evaluation metric.

4.1 Experiment 1. Model Selection

The first thing we need to confirm is the base model. As mentioned in Sect. 3.1, in this experiment, we search out the models on the basic features with the lowest MAE. Then we finetune the model's parameters and evaluate it with different cost functions.

Experiment Settings The implementation of the models is as follows.

- Last Value (Baseline): The last value regressor has no specific settings. For a non-Waratah train, we use the mean of the training set as the prediction.
- Linear Regression: Linear regressor is implemented by scikit-learn Linear-Regression module with intercept fitting and normalization.
- LightGBM: The parameters for LightGBM are Objective←Poisson; num_{leaves} ← 20, $learning_{rate}$ ← 0.05; $num_{estimators}$ ← 1000. The resets are set as default values.
- RandomForest: Random forest regressor is implemented by scikit-learn Random Forest module with $num_{estimators}$ ← 20; max_$depth$ ← 10.
- NeuralNetwork: Neural network regressor is implemented by scikit-learn MLPRegressor module with $hidden\_layer\_sizes$ ← 32; $relu$ activation function; $adam$ optimizer; $adaptive$ learning rate.

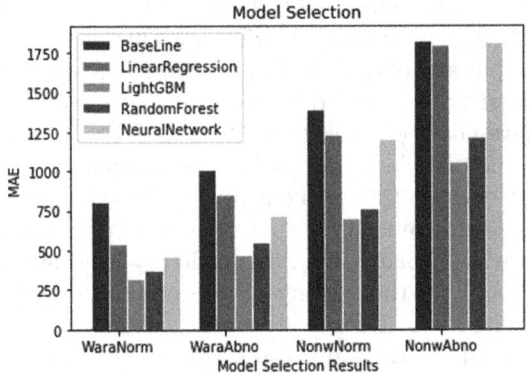

Fig. 2. Model selection result on the four tasks. WaraNorm: Waratah trains operate normally without disuptions; WaraAbno: Waratah trains operate abnormally with disruptions; NonwNorm: Non-Waratah trains operate without disruptions; NonwAbno: Non-Waratah train operate with disruptions.

Findings and Discussions. From Fig. 2, we can glean that LightGBM had the best performance on all four tasks, followed by RandomForest, NeuralNetwork, LinearRegression and Baseline. Since we only used a very shallow neural network structure, future study on this regressor should be undertaken. But for the Baseline, LinearRegression, LightGBM and RandomForest, we are confident to conclude that LightGMB is the best one for our learning tasks, and it follows that we focus on evaluating it for the rest of our experiments. Besides, we also compare the run time of each algorithm, LightGBM has better performance than other machine learning algorithms except for linear regression.

4.2 Experiment 2. Feature Engineering

In this experiment, we evaluate the contribution of the base features and our new proposed features (Historical Mean and Last Available Waratah Information). Sensitivity analysis of the variables/features could complement the insights about the importance of the selected features presented in terms of total gain (in Fig. 3). The experiment settings and evaluation metric are the same as we used in Experiment 1.

Table 2. The results (MAE) of LightGBM model with different features. The historical mean is calculated based on the average departure loads in the previous week. The last available Waratah train information is searched based on the timestamp closest to current trains. There were 116,112 sampled instances for WaraNorm, 11,864 for WaraAbno, 174,440 for NonwNorm, 17552 for NonwAbno.

	WaraNorm	WaraAbno	NonwNorm	NonwAbno	Average
BasicFeatures	321.29	469.86	701.64	1057.39	574.54
HistoricalMean	317.12	498.57	601.88	964.48	514.62
LastAvailableWaratah	305.75	**468.51**	624.23	981.62	522.48
Mixture	**299.68**	489.49	**550.33**	**882.1**	**475.37**

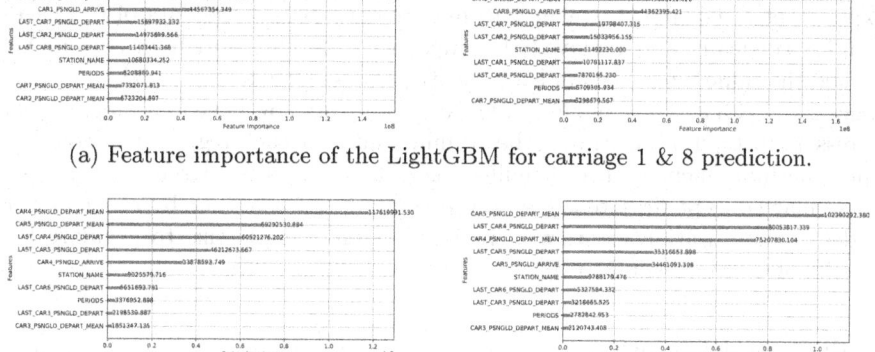

(a) Feature importance of the LightGBM for carriage 1 & 8 prediction.

(b) Feature importance of the LightGBM for carriage 4 & 5 prediction.

Fig. 3. The feature importance of the learning models on each carriage. The historical values of carriage 8 is beneficial to the load prediction on carriage 1. Similar phenomena happened on carriage 8.

Findings and Discussions. Table 2 summarizes the average results of Light-GBM with different features. Figure 3. shows the importance of the top 10 features in terms of total gain for Carriages 1, 8, 4, and 5. The feature importance of Carriages 2, 7, 3, and 6 have similar patterns. In summary, both the historical mean and last available Waratah train contribute to the final predictions. An interesting finding of the feature importance is that for Carriages 1 and 8, the historical means are the top two most important features. We found a similar phenomenon in car 2 and 7, 3 and 6, 4 and 5 as well. Our interpretation of this is that it's due to the head and tail of the trains having similar passenger loading patterns along with the middle carriages. These findings inspired us to think about the multi-stream learning issue. That is, the possibility that merging Carriages 1 and 8 might achieve a better performance than considering them individually.

4.3 Experiment 3. Multi-stream Learning VS. Multi-output Regression

In this experiment, we evaluate the concept of multi-stream learning compared with multi-output learning. Since LightGBM does not support multi-output regression, we adopt the multi-output strategy in sklearn - fitting one regressor per target. The experiment settings were slightly changed, but the evaluation metric is the same as in the previous experiments.

Experiment Settings. For multi-output regression, we built an independent regressor for each carriage with the same model configuration as introduced in Experiment 1. For multi-stream learning, we concatenate the data of Carriages 1 and 8 vertically and removed the duplicated carriage load information. We applied the same multi-stream learning strategy to concatenate the data of Carriages 2 and 7, 3 and 6, 4 and 5 as well. As a result, we now have four independent regressors instead of eight, and the training data for each regressor is doubled. Since the fundamental idea of multi-stream learning is to merge streams having similar concept drift to increase the training set size, thereby reducing the model's generalization error, we chose a different sample size to evaluate the benefits of multi-stream learning.

Findings and Discussions. Table 3 shows the results of multi-stream learning and multi-output. Multi-stream learning always outperforms multi-output, and the average improvement increases as the size of available training data decreases. For sample size 25000, the improvement is 8.87 kg; for 20000, the improvement is 11.03 kg; for 15000, the improvement is 12.18 kg, and for 10000, the improvement is 13.55 kg. This finding strongly supports our assumption that multi-stream learning can boost the number of training data, thereby reducing the generalization error.

Table 3. The results (MAE) of multi-stream learning with different sample size. The average improvement shows how the multi-stream learning enhanced the result compared to multi-output regressor. In this experiment, the multi-output regressor fits one regressor per target. This is a simple strategy for extending LightGMB to support multi-target regression.

Sample size	25000		20000		15000		10000	
Learning method	MulOutput	MulStream	MulOutput	MulStream	MulOutput	MulStream	MulOutput	MulStream
Car 1–8	386.90	**382.14**	392.52	**386.15**	395.32	**386.98**	397.46	**391.44**
Car 2–7	492.63	**486.58**	498.25	**489.57**	501.72	**493.28**	510.84	**502.23**
Car 3–6	513.15	**505.01**	518.86	**510.44**	520.38	**512.51**	531.32	**518.40**
Car 4–5	487.22	**470.69**	492.00	**471.34**	496.92	**472.85**	507.69	**481.03**
Average	469.98	**461.10**	475.41	**464.37**	478.58	**466.40**	486.83	**473.28**
Improvement	8.87		11.03		12.18		13.55	

5   Conclusion and Further Study

In this paper, we investigated train load forecasting with advanced machine learning models and the importance of the features that are part of the construction of these models. The obtained results have shown that machine learning models, and more particularly ensemble learning approaches such as LightGBM or RandomForest can address train load forecasting by using a combination between short- and long-term features that translate influencing factors. Furthermore, the multi-stream learning strategy of merging similar streams has proven its ability to deal with the issue of training sample augmentation. Future work will focus on experiments to enhance multi-stream learning performances through redesigning the merging indicator in terms of the training sample size.

Acknowledgement. This study was undertaken as part of the carriage load prediction project coordinated by Sydney Trains (PRO20-9756), and supported by the Australian Research Council (ARC) under Discovery Grant DP190101733 and Laureate project FL190100149.

References

1. Li, Z., Hensher, D.A.: Crowding in public transport: a review of objective and subjective measures. J. Public Transp. **16**, 107–134 (2013). https://doi.org/10.5038/2375-0901.16.2.6
2. Campigotto, P., Rudloff, C., Leodolter, M., Bauer, D.: Personalized and situation-aware multimodal route recommendations: the FAVOUR algorithm. IEEE Trans. Intell. Transp. Syst. **1**(18), 92–102 (2017). https://doi.org/10.1109/TITS.2016.2565643
3. Vandewiele, G., Van Herwegen F.O.J., Colpaert, P., De Turck, R.V.F., Janssens, O., Mannens, E.: Predicting train occupancies based on query logs and external data sources. In: 26th International World Wide Web Conference, pp. 1469–1474. ACM, Australia (2019). https://doi.org/10.1145/3041021.3051699
4. Lu, J., Liu, A., Song, Y., Zhang, G.: Data-driven decision support under concept drift in streamed big data. Complex Intell. Syst. **6**(1), 157–163 (2019). https://doi.org/10.1007/s40747-019-00124-4

5. TfNSW, Tfnsw Open Data Hub And Developer Portal (2020). https://opendata.transport.nsw.gov.au/user-guide

6. Yu, H., Lu, J., Zhang, G.: Continuous support vector regression for nonstationary streaming data. IEEE Trans. Cybern., 1–14 (2020). https://doi.org/10.1109/TCYB.2020.3015266

7. Liu, A., Lu, J., Zhang, G.: Concept drift detection via equal intensity k-means space partitioning. IEEE Trans. Cybern., 1–14 (2020). https://doi.org/10.1109/tcyb.2020.2983962

8. TrainWiki, Sydney Trains (2020). https://nswtrains.fandom.com/wiki/Sydney_Trains

9. TfNSW, Waratah Trains (2020). https://transportnsw.info/travel-info/ways-to-get-around/train/fleet-facilities/waratah-trains

10. Abadi, A., Rajabioun, T., Ioannou, P.A.: Traffic flow prediction for road transportation networks with limited traffic data. Ieee Trans. Intell. Transp. Syst. $2(16)$, 653–662 (2015)

11. Yu, H., Lu, J., Zhang, G.: Online topology learning by a gaussian membership-based self-organizing incremental neural network. IEEE Trans. Neural Networks Learn. Syst., 1–15 (2020). https://doi.org/10.1109/TNNLS.2019.2947658

12. Toqúe, F., Côme, E., Mahrsi, M.K. El, Oukhellou, L.: Forecasting dynamic public transport origin-destination matrices with long-short term memory recurrent neural networks. In: 19th International Conference on Intelligent Transportation Systems, Proceedings, pp. 1071–1076. IEEE, Brazil (2016). https://doi.org/10.1109/ITSC.2016.7795689

13. Chow, D., Liu, A., Zhang, G., Lu, J.: Knowledge graph-based entity importance learning for multi-stream regression on Australian fuel price forecasting. In: Proceedings of International Joint Conference Neural Networks, pp. 1–8. IEEE, Hungary (2019). https://doi.org/10.1109/IJCNN.2019.8851790

14. Chung, W., Kim, J., Lee, H., Kim, E.: General dimensional multiple-output support vector regressions and their multiple kernel learning. IEEE Trans. Cybern. $11(45)$, 2572–2584 (2015). https://doi.org/10.1109/TCYB.2014.2377016

15. Kocev, D., Vens, C., Struyf, J., Džeroski, S.: Tree ensembles for predicting structured outputs. Pattern Recogn. $3(46)$, 817–833 (2013). https://doi.org/10.1016/j.patcog.2012.09.023

16. Borchani, H., Varando, G., Bielza, C., Larrañaga, P.: A survey on multi-output regression. Wiley Interdiscip. Rev. Data Min. Knowl. Discov. $5(5)$, 216–233 (2015). https://doi.org/10.1002/widm.1157

17. Ke, G., et al.: LightGBM: a highly efficient gradient boosting decision tree. In: 31st Conference on Neural Information Processing Systems, pp. 3147–3155. ACM, USA (2017)

18. Pedregosa, F., et al.: Scikit-learn: machine learning in python. J. Mach. Learn. Res. 12, 2825–2830 (2012). https://doi.org/10.1007/s13398-014-0173-7.2

19. Lu, N., Lu, J., Zhang, G., Lopez De Mantaras, R.: A concept drift-tolerant case-base editing technique. Artif. Intell. 230, 108–133 (2016). https://doi.org/10.1016/j.artint.2015.09.009

20. Lu, N., Zhang, G., Lu, J.: Concept drift detection via competence models. Artif. Intell. 209, 11–28 (2014). https://doi.org/10.1016/j.artint.2014.01.001

21. Wang, B., et al.: Deep uncertainty quantification: a machine learning approach for weather forecasting. In: Proceedings of ACM SIGKDD International Conference Knowledge Discovery Data Mining, pp. 2087–2095 (2019). https://doi.org/10.1145/3292500.3330704
22. Lu, J., Zuo, H., Zhang, G.: Fuzzy multiple-source transfer learning. IEEE Trans. Fuzzy Syst. **6706**, 1–14 (2019). https://doi.org/10.1109/tfuzz.2019.2952792

Novel *Block* Diagonalization for Reducing Features and Computations in Medical Diagnosis

Tahira Ghani and B. John Oommen[✉]

School of Computer Science, Carleton University, Ottawa K1S 5B6, Canada
tahira.ghani@carleton.ca, oommen@scs.carleton.ca

Abstract. Diagonalization is an "age old" technique from Linear Algebra, and it has had significant applications in Pattern Recognition (PR) and data pre-processing. By using the eigenvectors of the covariance matrix of a single class as the basis vectors describing the feature space, the transformed data can be rendered to have a diagonal covariance matrix. If the covariance matrices of two classes are utilized, the covariance matrix of transformed data of the first class can be the made the Identity, while that of the second can be diagonal, implying independence in the case of Normally distributed data (Similar diagonalizing schemes form the basis of the Principal Component Analysis (PCA) and some feature selection/reduction etc. schemes.). In all of the cases reported in the literature, the entire covariance matrix is diagonalized, which is, computationally, a very tedious and cumbersome process. In this paper, we propose a radically different paradigm where we opt to render the transformed data to be *block* diagonalized. In other words, the covariance of the transformed data is made up of a predetermined number of block matrices, implying that *these* corresponding features are assumed to be correlated, while the others are assumed independent. Regression is now done by getting the best value based on each of these sub-blocks and averaging between them. This is essentially an ensemble machine, where the sub-blocks lead to their own respective regression values, which are then averaged to obtain the overall solution. This technique has been used to analyze the survival rate of cancer patients depends on the type of cancer, the treatments that the patient has undergone, and the severity of the cancer when the treatment was initiated. In our *prima facie* study, we consider adenocarcinoma, a type of lung cancer detected in chest Computed Tomography (CT) scans on the entire lung, and images that are "sliced" versions of the scans as one progresses along the thoracic region. The results that we have obtained using such a *block* diagonalization are quite amazing. Indeed, they surpass the results obtained from some of the well-established feature selection/reduction strategies.

Keywords: Diagonalization · Block diagonalization · Medical image processing · Lung cancer treatment · Prediction of survival rates

B. John Oommen—*Chancellor's Professor; Life Fellow: IEEE* and *Fellow: IAPR*. This author is also an *Adjunct Professor* with the University of Agder in Grimstad, Norway.

© Springer Nature Switzerland AG 2020
M. Gallagher et al. (Eds.): AI 2020, LNAI 12576, pp. 42–54, 2020.
https://doi.org/10.1007/978-3-030-64984-5_4

1   Introduction

There numerous ways by which one can reduce the dimensionality of a problem when it concerns Pattern Recognition (PR) and classification. The question of determining which features contain the most discriminating power is not easy to resolve. The strategy that has been used for a few decades is to examine the data by considering the eigenvalues and eigenvectors of the feature space, and by projecting the data onto its most "prominent" eigenvectors. Similar principles are, typically, used in designing feature selection and feature reduction methods. Indeed, almost all of the acclaimed methods deal with the eigenvectors of the covariance matrices of the classes. Since this matrix is symmetric and positive-definite, the problem is less tedious, because the eigenvectors are orthogonal.

The problem, although easily stated, is rather complex because one has to compute the eigenvectors of the covariance matrix of the entire feature space. This is, usually, a very difficult problem, especially if the dimension of this space is large. In this paper we resolve the problem in a completely different manner. The paradigm that we advocate is the following: Rather than work with the entire set of features, we split them into small blocks, which are then *individually* diagonalized. The tacit assumption of invoking such a partitioning is that within each of these small blocks, the intra-block features are correlated, but also that the inter-block features are uncorrelated. Resolving the problem in this manner leads to a block diagonal matrix. Observe that with such a modelling philosophy, the PR-related processing is much easier because the inversion of these block diagonal matrices involves block diagonal operations, and to achieve this, we only have to work with matrices of much smallers sizes.

The specifics of the partitioning, the block diagonalization and the subsequent regression, are detailed in the body of the paper. As far as we know, such a block diagonalization paradigm has not been proposed or applied in the PR or regression literature. In particular, we have used these techniques in a regression analysis, by which we can predict the survival times of lung cancer patients based on various features of the tumor. The results that we have obtained surpass the results obtain by invoking the best-known feature selection and reduction techniques.

1.1   Contributions of This Paper

The contributions of this paper can be summarized as follows:

- The fundamental contribution of this paper is to demonstrate the advantages of utilizing a "block diagonalization" paradigm, instead of invoking a diagonalization process of the entire feature space;
- Rather than achieve a regression analysis based on the entire set of features, we have shown that we can perform such an analysis on the various subsets of the data (each obtained from the block diagonalized submatrices);
- The overall regression will then be obtained by combining the results of the regression analysis of the blocks. Observe that this is equivalent to merging the concept of "ensemble" machines with the latter "block diagonalization" phase;

- Although a lot of work has been done when it concerns the diagnosis of lung cancer, the work related to the survival times and their correlation to the size/shape of the tumor is relatively unexplored. In an earlier paper [10], we had shown that by a regression analysis, we can predict the survival times based on various features of the tumor. This paper builds on those results to use ensemble machines and block-diagonal phenomena.
- While these results have been proven to be relevant for our lung cancer scenario, we believe that these phenomena are also valid for other tumor-based cancers, and hope that other researchers can investigate the relevance of the same hypothesis for *their* application domains.

2   Diagonalization and Block Diagonalization

2.1   Diagonalization

To initiate discussions, we submit a few brief paragraphs about the phenomenon of diagonalization. A square matrix A is referred to as being "diagonalizable" if it is similar to a diagonal matrix. In other words, there exists an invertible matrix P and a diagonal matrix D, such that $P^{-1}AP = D$, which equivalently implies that $A = PDP^{-1}$. Diagonalization is the process of finding the above P and D.

Diagonalizable matrices are especially easy for computations. One can raise a diagonal matrix D to a power by simply raising the diagonal entries to that power, and the determinant of a diagonal matrix is simply the product of all its diagonal entries. Such computations generalize easily due to $A = PDP^{-1}$.

The process of diagonalization is implicitly related to the set of A's eigenvectors $\{\underline{e}_1, \underline{e}_2, \dots \underline{e}_d\}$, and its respective eigenvalues, $\{\lambda_1, \lambda_2, \dots \lambda_d\}$. Indeed, if A can be diagonalized, the diagonalizing matrix P contains the eigenvectors of A as columns, where the ith column is the ith eigenvector, $\underline{e}_i$, and the corresponding diagonal entry is the respective eigenvalue, λ_i. The invertibility of P also suggests that the eigenvectors of A are linearly independent and form a basis of A, which is the necessary and sufficient condition for diagonalizability. Thus,

$$P^{-1}AP = \Lambda, \quad \text{or} \quad AP = P\Lambda, \tag{1}$$

where, $P = [\underline{e}_1, \underline{e}_2, \dots, \underline{e}_d]$, and Λ is the $d \times d$ diagonal matrix, $\text{Diag}[\lambda_1, \lambda_2, \dots, \lambda_d]$.

Diagonalization is a fundamental phenomenon in PR and classification, where A is the covariance matrix of the underlying distribution, and since this is always positive-definite and symmetric, the eigenvectors are orthogonal, implying that:

$$P^T AP = \Lambda. \tag{2}$$

Similar diagonalizing schemes form the basis of the Principal Component Analysis (PCA) and some feature selection/reduction etc. schemes.

If the covariance matrices of two classes are utilized, the covariance matrix of transformed data of the first class can be made Identity, while that of the second can be diagonal, implying independence in the case of Normally distributed data. Geometrically, a diagonalizable matrix is an inhomogeneous dilation (or anisotropic scaling) - it scales the space, as does a homogeneous dilation, but by a different factor along each eigenvector axis, the factor given by the corresponding eigenvalue. For most applications, the matrices are diagonalized numerically using computer software, and numerous packages exist to accomplish this.

2.2 Invoking Block Diagonalization and Ensemble Regression

We shall now show how we can use a non-traditional eigenvector matrix to further enhance the accuracy of the scheme, and also simultaneously minimize the computations.

The monumental task associated with a covariance matrix of large dimensions is to obtain its eigenvalues and eigenvectors. While this is surely advantageous, the task is daunting especially when we deal with a feature space whose dimensionality is greater than 100. It would have been meaningful if we were working with simultaneous diagonalization where we tried to diagonalize or whiten data from *two* classes. In our case, however, since the problem we tackle is regression (rather than classification), we are dealing with only a single class which makes the problem less cumbersome.

In our application domain [9,10], the dimensionality of the feature vector is 110. Computing the eigenvalues and eigenvectors of such a large matrix is, certainly, time consuming. The novel contribution in this section is that we advocate dividing the feature vector into multiple sub-vectors, for example, 5 sub-vectors. We are now faced with a problem of getting 5 sets of eigenvectors, each of dimension 22, which is a significantly smaller problem. Of course, this leads us to an approximated world in which the features within these subspaces are correlated, but it leads to a model in which the features outside of these blocks are assumed to be uncorrelated. This, in turn, leads to the concept of a block diagonal matrix, as displayed in Fig. 1, where the blocks, B_n where $n = 1...5$, represents the subset of features chosen (i.e., 5 sets of 22-dimensional vectors), and all other elements outside of the blocks are set to zero.

$$\begin{bmatrix} B_1 & 0 & 0 & 0 & 0 \\ 0 & B_2 & 0 & 0 & 0 \\ 0 & 0 & B_3 & 0 & 0 \\ 0 & 0 & 0 & B_4 & 0 \\ 0 & 0 & 0 & 0 & B_5 \end{bmatrix}$$

Fig. 1. Block diagonal matrix.

Our task now, is to diagonalize each of these blocks within the block diagonal approximation, and to choose a subset of their prominent eigen-directions, determined by the corresponding largest eigenvalues. For example, if we extracted the 5 principal eigen-directions in each of these blocks, the 110-vector space would reduce to 5 blocks of 5 features each, i.e., a feature vector of dimension 25.

Regression is now done by getting the best "regressed" value based on each of these sub-blocks and averaging between them. The reader will observe that this is essentially an ensemble machine, where the 5 blocks lead to their own respective regression values, which are then averaged to obtain the overall solution. Although this involves computations that are significantly less than working with the 110-dimensional space, the results that we have obtained are actually marginally superior. This seems to be paradoxical but the reason for this is probably because the higher dimensional world tries to impose a dependence on the various variables when, in fact, there may not be such an explicit dependence.

3   Predicting Survival Times for Lung Cancer

Problem Domain: Research in computer vision in medicine has advanced to focus on automatic segmentations, feature extraction and classification for the presence of specific diseases or pathologies. CAD systems are divided into two sub-categories, computer-aided detection (CADe) and computer-aided diagnosis (CADx). Both branches are being actively researched, with CADe being more focused on computationally-efficient early detection with a higher sensitivity and low false-positive rate, and CADx being more focused on the lesions' characterization and classification. The most famous use-case for such an application is the detection (or classification) of a nodule being cancerous. However, if we can push this envelope one step further and are able to judge the *severity* of a nodule, the prognosis and determination of treatment plans can be adjusted to yield a greater chance of success. The results we have obtained [10] deal with the cancer treatments done on 60 patients[1] at varying levels of severity and with a spectrum of survival rates. For patients who survived up to 24 months, the average relative error is as low as 9%, which we believe is very significant.

This research is the continuation of previous work of the authors as part of a Masters program thesis study, whereby the foundation is the evaluation of a cancer nodule through computation of 2D features in the Chest Computed Tomography (CT) scan. In this work, we aim to evaluate the cancer nodule as a single entity in its 3D form rather than "slices" as 2D images. Furthermore, we evaluate the feature sets of the 3D cancer nodules through the lens of various feature reduction and feature elimination techniques, with the most extensive analysis on the process of diagonalization.

Aspects of Lung Cancer: Apart from folklore, the statistics about cancer are disheartening. The American Cancer Society (ACS) estimated their annual

---

[1] Understandably, it is extremely difficult to obtain training and testing data for this problem domain! Thus, both authors gratefully acknowledge the help given by Drs. Thornhill and Inacio, from the University of Ottawa, in providing us with the dataset.

statistics for 2018, based on collected historical data [17]. Lung cancer is now the second leading type of cancer for newly diagnosed patients, behind breast cancer, and it has the highest mortality rate out of all cancer sites. The ACS projected 234,030 new cases of lung cancer. They also forecasted that 154,050 deaths would be caused by lung cancer. However, cancers diagnosed at an early phase, such as Stage 1, can be treated with surgery and radiation therapy with an 80% success rate. The low survival rate of lung cancer patients is primarily because of the late diagnosis, which results in ineffective treatment due to the growth and stage of the cancer.

The most common tests to detect lung cancer include (but are not limited to) sputum cytology, chest X-rays, computed tomography (CT) scans, and biopsies. The emerging domain of radiomics is the field of study that extracts quantitative measures of tumor phenotypes from medical images using data-characterization algorithms. These features are explored to uncover disease characteristics that are not visible to the naked eye, but which can then be used for further prognosis and treatment plans. Many researchers have begun focusing on the engineering of feature sets through implementation of radiomic analysis [8, 16]. Our goal, however, is that of predicting the survival rate of lung cancer patients *once they have been diagnosed*, and the result of this study is to demonstrate that a lot of this information resides in the *3D shape* of the tumor. Our hope is that our study can provide insight into the severity of the cancer, and can additionally, aid in formulating the treatment plans so as to increase the chances of survival.

3.1 *Brief* Literature Review

Apart from the mathematical foundations of diagonalization highlighted above, the main objective of the application domain of this research is to explore and investigate the existence of relations between statistical measures with regards to the texture and shape of a nodule classified as adenocarcinoma (a type of cancer) to the *survival time* of the patient post-diagnosis. The task at hand is a regression problem, instead of the more traditional classification problem.

When considering the applications of ML in healthcare, classification problems have been the dominant area of focus such that the presence, or lack thereof, of a specified anatomical structure can be stated. However, transforming the context of the application to a regression domain can enable a critical advancement in CAD systems. By suggesting a survival time for a given patient, the trajectory of the illness and treatment plan can be evaluated at a deeper level. Through a more extensive literature review, discussed in more detail in Chap. 2 of the thesis[2] [9], we have identified a significant gap in such regression analyses.

We aim to engineer a prognostic feature set based on quantitative measurements that are not visible with a simple glance or reading of the scan, and aspire to reduce the inherent subjectivity and variability when evaluating medical reports with such measures. It is important to note that our focus is heavily

---

[2] Unfortunately, due to space limitations, a comprehensive review is not possible. It is found in [9] and can be provided to interested readers if requested.

on the construction of the feature set, rather than the customization of regression models that have been used as testing thresholds. With this in mind, we also adjust the focus to form a valuable feature set through applying various block-diagonalization-based feature elimination and reduction techniques.

3.2 Data Source

We have used the publicly available data from The Cancer Imaging Archive[3] (TCIA), a service which hosts an archive of data for de-identified medical images of cancer. The dataset used for this work is the "LungCT-Diagnosis" data [11] on TCIA, uploaded in 2014. The set consists of CT scans for 61 patients that have been diagnosed with adenocarcinoma, a type of lung cancer, with the number of images totalling up to about 4,600 over all the scans. However, considering only images that have the presence of a cancer nodule, the count reduces to approximately 450 images. With healthcare, we are constrained to work with what we can obtain and what we are "provided" with, subject to privacy considerations. As we will see, it suffices for the purpose of regression analyses. Throughout the experiments and results explained in this paper, the condensed dataset of 450 images, or 61 scans, has been consistently split into training and testing data with a 70% and 30% split respectively. The dataset also includes the clinical metadata, where the survival time of the patient associated with each scan, is listed.

4   Fundamental Operations and Feature Sets

Computed Tomography (CT) Scans: The most common radiological imaging technique incorporates CT scans where X-ray beams are used to take measurements or images (i.e., "slices") from different angles, as shown in Fig. 2, as the patient's body moves through the scanner. Depending on the section thickness and the associated reconstruction parameters, a scan can range anywhere from 100 to over 500 sections or images [1]. The scan records different levels of density and tissues which can be reconstructed to, non-invasively, create a 3-dimensional image of the human body.

High-resolution Computed Tomography (HRCT) is specifically used in detecting and diagnosing diffuse lung diseases [7] and cancerous nodules, due to its sensitivity and specificity. It enables the detection and analysis of feature aspects such as morphological lesion characterization, nodule size measurement and growth, as well as attenuation characteristics.

Nodule Segmentation: Rather than segmenting the entire lung region as our Region of Interest (ROI), in this research, we segment only the cancerous nodule in the "slices" where the presence of the tumor is observed. Similar to the topic of lung segmentation, there is an abundance of published work discussing the automation of so-called nodule segmentation and extraction [2,15] and [19]. Since

---

[3] More information can be found at https://www.cancerimagingarchive.net/.

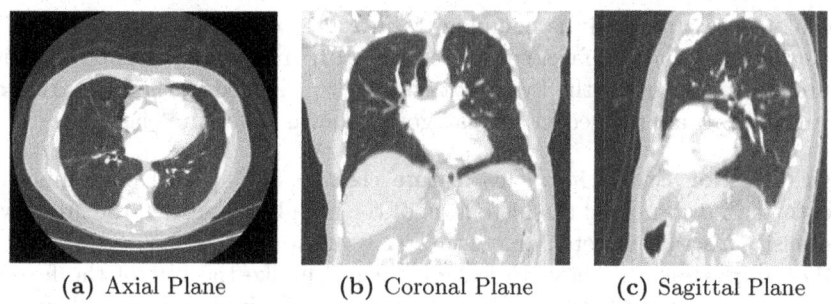

(a) Axial Plane   (b) Coronal Plane   (c) Sagittal Plane

Fig. 2. Planes captured in a Computed Tomography (CT) scan.

this is not the primary goal of our research, in our work, we opt to segment the scans manually to obtain the nodules, as our focus is on the creation of an informative feature set.

We made masks of the tumors using the ImageJ software[4]. This was done by manually tracing a contour around the nodule on the images where it was present, filling the shape as "white", and clearing the background to "black". The images that did not contain the nodule were cleared to a "black" background. The CT scans were reviewed, and the segmentation of cancer tumors were validated by a clinical doctor from the Ottawa Heart Institute.

We achieved this by creating a mask for each scan in the dataset. This enabled us to obtain a simpler implementation of the algorithm to achieve the ROI extraction. For each scan, the respective segmentation mask was loaded and all images were iterated. If a connected component was found (signifying the presence of a nodule) in a mask image, the original image was multiplied against the mask to precisely extract only the nodule. In this manner, we were able to attain the 3D matrix of the nodule in a scan, which could be further used for visualization and feature extraction.

3D Feature Set Compilation: Proceeding now with the work that we did, the next stage included the exploration, compilation and modification of a 3D feature set, which essentially implies that we considered the entire lung as a single entity (or observation) as opposed to the images considered for the 2D feature sets alluded to in the previous sections. We used the `Pyradiomics` library[5], an open source Python package, for extracting radiomics[6].

The main emphasis for this feature set was to compute measures in a 3D consideration. Compared to the benchmark feature set, which contained quantification measures of texture analysis in the 2D domain, this feature set included

---

[4] The ImageJ Software is a Java-based program developed at the National Institutes of Health and the Laboratory for Optical and Computational Instrumentation.

[5] Documentation is available at https://pyradiomics.readthedocs.io/en/latest/.

[6] Radiomics is the field of study that extracts quantitative measures of tumor phenotypes from medical images using data-characterization algorithms. These features are explored to uncover disease characteristics that are not visible to the naked eye.

recalculated texture analysis components in a 26-connectivity capacity, i.e., if the centre pixel shares a face, edge or corner with another pixel. The radiomics features extracted using the `Pyradiomics` library (defined in the `Pyradiomics` documentation) are defined in sub-categories known as feature classes as:

- **First Order Statistics:** This feature class [9,10], focused on computing features that described the histogram of the nodule image, i.e., the grey-level intensity distribution etc., amounting to a total of 19 features.
- **3D Shape-based:** These 16 features [9,10], unlike the rest of the feature classes, computed the values from the mask of the given nodule as they were independent of the grey level intensities. The `Pyradiomics` library built a triangle mesh from the provided mask using the marching cubes algorithm.
- **Grey Level Cooccurrence Matrix (GLCM):** This matrix was computed based on the probability function where the $(i,j)^{th}$ element represents the number of times grey levels i and j appeared next to each other in the image, and led to a total of 24 features [9,10].
- **Grey Level Run Length Matrix (GLRLM):** This matrix captured grey level runs, in which, a *run* refers to the number of consecutive pixels that had the same grey level value. The GLRLM was quantified by individual measures such as short run and long run emphasis, non-uniformity values, run variance, etc., amounting to a total of 16 features [9,10].
- **Grey Level Size Zone Matrix (GLSZM):** This matrix was similar to the GLRLM, however, voxels of the same grey level intensity were taken into consideration rather than just pixels. It was quantified by individual metrics such as area and zone emphasis etc., amounting to 16 features [9,10].
- **Neighbouring Grey Tone Difference Matrix (NGTDM):** This matrix evaluated the difference between a pixel or voxel's grey value and the values of its neighbours. From it, we extracted to a total of 5 features [9,10].
- **Grey Level Dependence Matrix (GLDM):** This matrix measured the grey level dependencies in the image. From it, we extracted a total of 14 features, as explained in [9,10].

5   Implementation and Results

Model Evaluation: To evaluate the performance of the tested regression models, we utilized two measures, namely the Mean Absolute Error (MAE), measured in months, and the Mean Relative Error (MRE), both of which are defined in Eq. (3) and (4) respectively:

$$MAE = \frac{1}{n}\sum_{i=1}^{n}|y_i - z_i|, \qquad \text{and} \tag{3}$$

$$MRE = \frac{1}{n}\sum_{i=1}^{n}\frac{|y_i - z_i|}{z_i}, \qquad \text{where:} \tag{4}$$

- n is the number of test-set data points,
- y_i is the predicted value (i.e., the expected survival time in months), and
- z_i is the true value (i.e., the survival time in months).

The MAE is the average difference between the true values and the predicted values. It provides an overall measure of the distance between the two values, but it does not indicate the direction of the data (i.e., whether the result is an under or over-prediction). Furthermore, this is also seen to be a scale-dependent measure, as the computed values are heavily dependent on the scale of the data, and can be influenced by outliers present in the data [5]. In order to circumvent the scale-dependency, we also computed the MRE which introduces a relativity factor by normalizing the absolute error by the magnitude of the true value. This means that the MRE should, generally, consist of values in the range $[0, 1]$.

As mentioned earlier, all regression tests were done on the data with a 70% to 30% split of the data for training and testing, respectively.

Regression Results: The diagonalization technique applied to the dataset, defined in Eq. (5), is a linear transformation that transforms a set of vectors, $\{X\}$, with a given covariance matrix to a new set of vectors, $\{Y\}$, with a covariance that is the Identity matrix. This indicates uncorrelated features with a variance of 1 satisfying:

$$Y = W^T X. \tag{5}$$

The transformative factor here is defined by W, which is a $d \times d$ matrix such that:

$$W^T \Sigma_X W = \Lambda, \text{ and} \tag{6}$$

$$\Lambda = \begin{bmatrix} \lambda_1 \dots 0 \\ \ddots \\ 0 \dots \lambda_d \end{bmatrix}, \tag{7}$$

where $\lambda_1 \dots \lambda_n$ are the eigenvalues of the covariance matrix. It is important to note that W also satisfies the following condition:

$$W^{-1} = W^T. \tag{8}$$

As mentioned, the context at hand is a regression problem and hence, we are dealing with data from only a *single* class. Therefore, we implemented a simple diagonalization rather than a simultaneous diagonalization of multiple classes.

We computed the covariance matrix of the scaled dataset, resulting in a 110×110 matrix. However, computing the eigenvalues and eigenvectors of the covariance matrix was computationally complex and inefficient, resulting in negligibly-small negative and complex eigenvalues[7]. To combat the inaccuracy of these results, we broke down the 110-dimensional covariance matrix into five 22-dimensional covariance matrices from which we could compute the eigenvalues. This led to the resemblance of an ensemble-based model, as we transformed the

---

[7] This was, of course, due to the computations involving very small quantities.

data five times with only the kth group of features extracted from the covariance matrix. Running the regression models with selecting the corresponding transformed features of the first d significant eigenvalues (where d is the number of eigenvalues that have values above a threshold of 1.0), we took the average of the five predictions and attained our final regressed prediction.

Table 1. Performance of regression models with complete baseline and PCA-reduced feature set.

Model	Baseline		PCA	
	MAE	MRE	MAE	MRE
Linear regression	34.41	1.95	14.83	0.78
kNN regression	16.73	0.97	17.15	0.90
Gradient boosting	14.76	0.85	18.36	1.00

Table 2. Performance of regression models with block diagonalized reduced feature set.

Model	MAE	MRE
Linear regression	14.28	0.76
kNN regression	15.41	0.83
Gradient boosting	15.13	0.80

Table 2 shows the regression results on the diagonalized data. Compared to results from PCA (Table 1), there seems to be an overall improvement across all models with gradient boosting improving the most, with a 20% decrease in the MRE. Table 3 displays the regression results on the subset data where the survival time was less than or equal to 24 months. As expected, all the regression models improved greatly with an average decrease in the MAE of over 50%, and the MRE reaching as low as 41% with gradient boosting.

Table 3. Performance of regression models with block diagonalized reduced feature set on subset data.

Model	MAE	MRE
Linear regression	6.98	0.53
kNN regression	6.10	0.42
Gradient boosting	5.89	0.41

6   Conclusions and Future Work

In this paper, we discussed the domain of healthcare imaging for diagnostics and the implementation of radiomics on CT scans, in particular, to predict the survival rates of lung cancer patients. We explored the engineering of a feature set based on 3D analyses and the related computations associated with the tumor.

We used `Pyradiomics` for the computation of the relevant features to both shape and texture, in the 3D aspect. This resulted in a 110-dimensional feature vector, which was subjected to feature selection and dimensionality reduction using a novel block diagonalization scheme. We achieved an overall improvement in performance from the baseline of the 3D feature set, with the greatest difference in Linear Regression from an MRE of 1.95 to 0.76. Notably, all models achieved better in a short term prediction with the 3D feature sets, enforcing the results found in [10].

With regard to future work, the use of block diagonal strategies for other PR and regressions methods is a fertile field. Besides, the further extension of our research by computing actual 3D features which can be used to augment the feature vector to the previously-computed 3D features through aggregation of successive 2D slices, can surely be applied to other types of cancers.

References

1. Al Mohammad, B., Brennan, P.C., Mello-Thoms, C.: A review of lung cancer screening and the role of computer-aided detection. Clin. Radiol. **72**, 433–442 (2017)
2. Armato III, S.G., Giger, M.L., MacMahon, H.: Automated detection of lung nodules in CT scans: preliminary results. Med. Phys. **28**, 1552–1561 (2001)
3. Armato III, S.G., Sensakovic, W.F.: Automated lung segmentation for thoracic CT: impact on computer-aided diagnosis. Acad. Radiol. **11**, 1011–1021 (2004)
4. Chabat, F., Yang, G.Z., Hansell, D.M.: Obstructive lung diseases: texture classification for differentiation at CT. Radiology **228**(3), 871–877 (2003)
5. Chen, C., Twycross, J., Garibaldi, J.M.: A new accuracy measure based on bounded relative error for time series forecasting. PLoS ONE **12**, e0174202 (2017)
6. Demir, O., Camurcu, A.Y.: Computer-aided detection of lung nodules using outer surface features. Bio-Med. Mater. Eng. **26**, S1213–S1222 (2015)
7. Elicker, B.M., Webb, W.R.: Fundamentals of High-Resolution Lung CT. Wolters Kluwer, Alphen aan den Rijn (2013)
8. Fan, L., et al.: Radiomics signature: a biomarker for the preoperative discrimination of lung invasive adenocarcinoma manifesting as a ground-glass nodule. Eur. Radiol. **29**(2), 889–897 (2018). https://doi.org/10.1007/s00330-018-5530-z
9. Ghani, T.: On *forecasting* lung cancer patients' survival rates using 3D feature engineering. MCS thesis, Carleton University (2019)
10. Ghani, T., Oommen, B.J.: Enhancing the prediction of lung cancer survival rates using 2D features from 3D scans. In: Campilho, A., Karray, F., Wang, Z. (eds.) ICIAR 2020. LNCS, vol. 12132, pp. 202–215. Springer, Cham (2020). https://doi.org/10.1007/978-3-030-50516-5_18

11. Grove, O., et al.: Quantitative computed tomographic descriptors associate tumour shape complexity and intratumor heterogeneity with prognosis in lung adenocarcinoma. PLoS ONE **10**, e0118261 (2015)

12. Hall, E.L., Kruger, R.P., Dwyer, S.J., Hall, D.L., McLaren, R.W., Lodwick, G.S.: A survey of preprocessing and feature extraction techniques for radiographic images. IEEE Trans. Comput. **100**, 1032–1044 (1971)

13. Haralick, R.M., Shanmugam, K., Dinstein, H.: Textural features for image classification. IEEE Trans. Syst. Man Cybern. **6**, 610–621 (1973)

14. Kim, N., Seo, J.B., Lee, Y., Lee, J.G., Kim, S.S., Kang, S.-H.: Development of an automatic classification system for differentiation of obstructive lung disease using HRCT. J. Digit. Imaging **22**, 136–148 (2009). https://doi.org/10.1007/s10278-008-9147-7

15. Messay, T., Hardie, R.C., Tuinstra, T.R.: Segmentation of pulmonary nodules in computed tomography using a regression neural network approach and its application to the lung image database consortium and image database resource initiative dataset. Med. Image Anal. **22**, 48–62 (2015)

16. Paul, R., Hawkins, S.H., Schabath, M.B., Gillies, R.J., Hall, L.O., Goldgof, D.B.: Predicting malignant nodules by fusing deep features with classical radiomics features. J. Med. Imaging **5**, 011021 (2018)

17. Siegel, R.L., Miller, K.D., Jemal, A.: Cancer statistics. CA Cancer J. Clin. **68**, 7–30 (2018)

18. Singadkar, G., Mahajan, A., Thakur, M., Talbar, S.: Automatic lung segmentation for the inclusion of juxtapleural nodules and pulmonary vessels using curvature based border correction. J. King Saud Univ. Comput. Inf. Sci. (2018)

19. Zhao, B., Gamsu, G., Ginsberg, M.S., Jiang, L., Schwartz, L.H.: Automatic detection of small lung nodules on CT utilizing a local density maximum algorithm. J. Appl. Clin. Med. Phys. **4**, 248–260 (2003)

20. Zhou, S., Cheng, Y., Tamura, S.: Automated lung segmentation and smoothing techniques for inclusion of juxtapleural nodules and pulmonary vessels on chest CT images. Biomed. Signal Process. Control **13**, 62–70 (2014)

A Novel Face Detector Based on YOLOv3

Sabrina Hoque Tuli[(✉)], Anning Mao, and Wanquan Liu

Department of Computing, Curtin University, Perth, WA, Australia
{s.tuli,anning.mao}@postgrad.curtin.edu.au, w.liu@curtin.edu.au

Abstract. Face detection has broad applications. Recently, there has been lots of advancement in face detection based on deep learning methods. However, small face detection in a real-world environment is still a challenging task due to its low resolution, variability in size, different poses and occlusions. YOLOv3 is one of the main approaches for object detection, which has achieved comparatively better performance for small target detection in real-time. However, it still struggles to detect a group of small size faces with inaccurate localization as well as an increasing number of false positives. In this paper, we propose an efficient multi-scale deep learning network based on YOLOv3 to detect a group of small faces. First, we select the optimum number of anchors, and this will help us understand the small face targets better; secondly, we change the bounding box regression loss in the YOLOv3 to a new CIoU loss to improve the false positives; thirdly, we extend the detection scale from 3 to 4 in YOLOv3 especially for detecting small faces; fourthly, we simplify the four convolutional layers to two residual blocks from six convolutional layers in each detection scale to avoid the derivative vanishing. The proposed model can achieve the state-of-the-art performance on the WIDER FACE face detection benchmark, especially in the hard subset that has a high number of small faces with the variability of scale, poses and occlusions. Our model has achieved 86.5%AP in the WIDER FACE hard validation subset compared to 72.9%AP by the YOLOv3. The run-time is also satisfactory for real application for VGA resolution image with 64.3 FPS using the Nvidia Titan RTX.

Keywords: Small face detection · YOLOv3 · Deep learning · Computer vision

1 Introduction

Face detection is an essential preliminary step for many successive face-associated applications, such as face verification [15], face alignment [13, 14] and face recognition [16, 17]. Before 2000, despite extensive research conducted in face detection, the outcome was far away from the optimal until the remarkable detector developed by Viola and Jones [18, 19]. However, such detector had several critical drawbacks such relatively required large feature size and was not adequate for the detection of real-world small faces.

In recent years, deep learning, especially the deep convolutional neural networks (CNN), has achieved tremendous successes in various computer vision applications, ranging from image classification to object detection and semantic segmentation, etc. In

© Springer Nature Switzerland AG 2020
M. Gallagher et al. (Eds.): AI 2020, LNAI 12576, pp. 55–68, 2020.
https://doi.org/10.1007/978-3-030-64984-5_5

contrast to traditional vision-based approaches, deep learning methods avoid the hand-crafted design modules and have dominated many well-known benchmark evaluations. Along with the increasing usage of deep learning in computer vision, a surge of research attention is appearing to explore the deep learning for resolving face detection tasks.

In current literature, researchers then focused on resolving face detection by applying deep learning methods [8, 10, 28] used for usual object detection and segmentation problems. The frameworks for generic object detection can mainly be categorized into two types. One follows the traditional object detection pipeline, generating region proposals at first and then classifying each proposal into different object categories such as R-CNN [21], SPP-net [20], Faster R-CNN [22]. However, they are not end-to-end target detection algorithms. The other group regards object detection as a regression or classification problem, adopting a unified framework to achieve final results (categories and locations) directly, such as YOLO [1], YOLOv2 [23], YOLOv3 [2], SSD [3], DSSD [24]. These algorithms can predict the target location and category information directly through the network without generating region proposal. They are end-to-end algorithms, and the speed of these direct target detection algorithms is also faster. Among them, the anchor-based detection [1–3, 23] has become popular as they can drastically reduce the computational cost in comparison to the sliding window based approach [25] and this would make the real-time detection possible. Among the single-stage anchor-based algorithms, YOLO is one of the state-of-art object detection methods, and YOLOv3 has an excellent performance improvement in detecting small objects. We would utilize this advantage of YOLOv3 to revise the network for small face detection. It becomes more challenging for better accuracy in detecting small faces in the wild when the face becomes smaller with low resolution, different pose and illumination changes.

In this paper, a multiscale face detection approach based on YOLOv3 is proposed. The proposed network model based on YOLOv3 can detect more small faces with better localization and accuracy. Our aim is to improve the detection accuracy for small faces based on the YOLOv3.

The structure of this paper is as follows. We briefly explained the framework of YOLOv3 in Sect. 2. In Sect. 3, we elucidate the details of our improved proposed model based on YOLOv3 and the mathematical derivation method to select the appropriate candidate anchor boxes for each scale. In Sect. 4, the comparative experimental analysis and results on the WIDER FACE dataset. Finally, the conclusion of this paper is drawn in Sect. 5.

2 YOLOv3

As our paper is based on YOLOv3, we will briefly introduce the YOLOv3 in this section. YOLO (You Only Look Once) is a one stage target detection algorithm, wherein this series the third version is called YOLOv3. YOLOv3 is an end-to-end object detection algorithm that can predict the class and the location of the objects simultaneously, and the performance of object detection in real-time is quite impressive. The structure of YOLOv3 is shown in Fig. 1, which can perform feature extraction from the backbone Darknet-53. YOLOv3 uses successive 3×3 and 1×1 convolutional layers with a shortcut or residual connections. There are five residual blocks composed of multiple residual units. As the depth of the network becomes deep, the residual unit would make use of feature more times and help to avoid gradient fading. The network of YOLOv3 is shown as below.

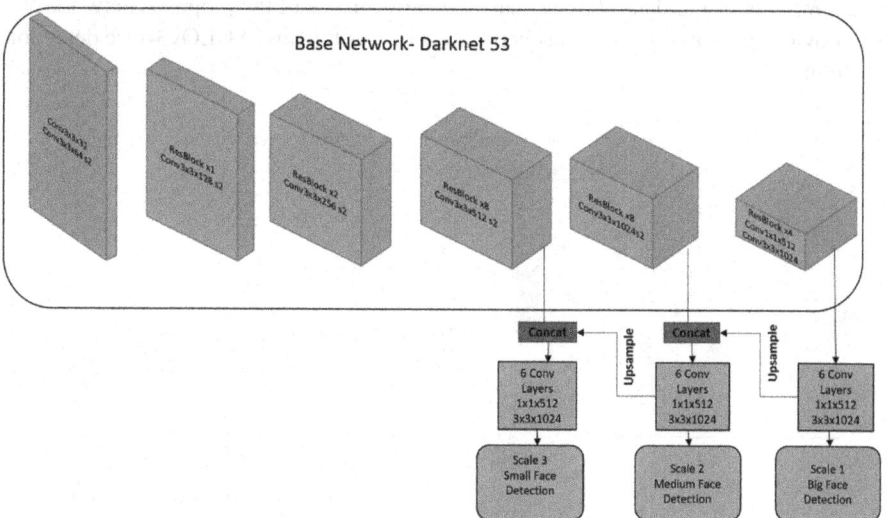

Fig. 1. The network architecture YOLOv3

The input image is downsampled five times, where YOLOv3 prediction is conducted from the last 3 downsampled layers. There are 3 prediction scales with downsampled features from x32, which mainly predicts the big objects, then downsampled features x16 is responsible for the medium objects and downsampled features x8 is for small object detection. The concept of feature fusion is utilized to detect targets, where local feature maps from the earlier layer can provide deep semantic information as large feature maps would provide more fine-grained information of the targets. To perform feature fusion, YOLOv3 would upsample and resize the global feature map and merge them with the local feature map by concatenation. This feature fusion can help YOLOv3 to detect small objects better.

The above YOLOv3 is comparatively better for small target detection, but it still struggles to detect a group of small faces with low resolution, different poses and poor contextual information. To tackle these problems, we will revise the YOLOv3 algorithm for detecting smaller faces aiming to achieve better localization accuracy and reduce false positive. Figure 2, shows our improved YOLOv3 model architecture.

The main contributions of our work can be concluded as follows: (1) We have figured out the optimum number of anchor boxes with the aspect ratio dimensions of the candidate anchors for each scale especially keeping the small anchor size in mind; (2) To further detect more small faces with this revised network, the detection scales of YOLOv3 have been extended from 3 to 4 where we can concatenate more local features after downsampling 4 times with the fine-grained global features; (3) For better regression and accurate localization of small faces, we change the regression loss function to the

CIoU loss; (4) To avoid gradient fading and enhance the reuse of the features, the four out of six convolutional layers in the detection layer of each scale are transformed into two residual units and the global features are collected from last residual unit of each detection layer; (5) We compare our approach with the state-of-the-art face detection algorithms on the WIDER FACE dataset to evaluate the performance of the proposed network. We also provide qualitative evaluations between our algorithm and YOLOv3-face detection algorithm.

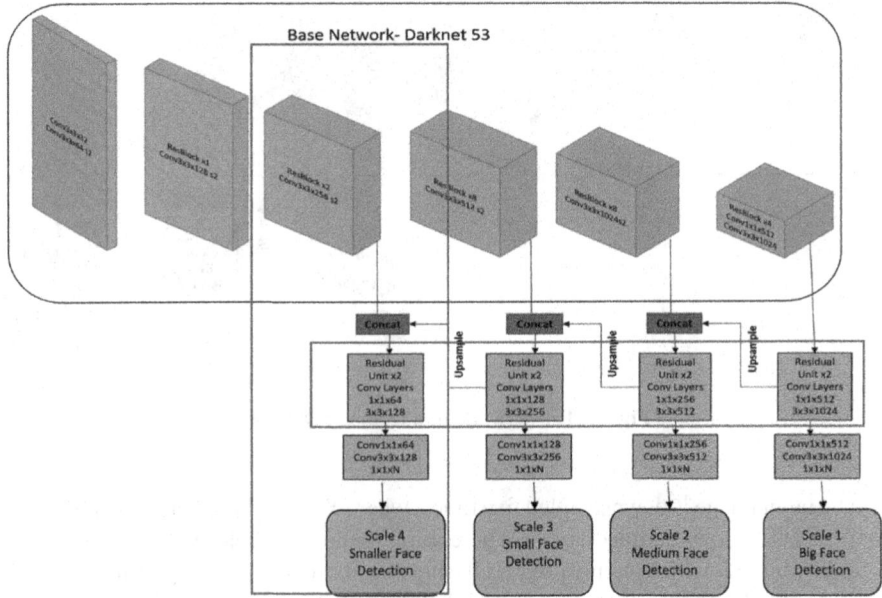

Fig. 2. The network architecture of our proposed YOLOv3 model

3   The Proposed Approach

As anchor boxes are prefixed in YOLOv3, but object target size is continuous, so we need to select anchors in a manner that can fit our purpose to match small faces better. Technically, we ran the K-means clustering algorithm with the different number of anchors and aspect ratios on mostly the small faces in the training set to understand our dataset better. Finally, we choose those anchors that have the highest IOU in the overall training dataset.

3.1   Selecting Appropriate Anchor Size and Number

Anchor boxes or priors are pre-selected candidates with adjusted width and height. The selection of the initial anchors has a significant impact on detection accuracy and speed. Instead of hand-picked priors, YOLOv3 runs the K-means clustering on the dataset to get a better detection indication on the chosen dataset. The original YOLOv3 uses the COCO dataset [26] for object detection. Based on the COCO dataset, they obtained 9 clusters and 3 scales to distribute the anchors across scales evenly.

For face detection, we used the WIDER FACE [11] dataset with a high degree of variability in scale, pose, and occlusion, so that our network can be better trained for face detection. We found that using the pre-selected anchors for the original YOLOv3 is not appropriate in our case to achieve better detection, especially for small faces as the width and height of those anchor boxes are quite different from face images. So, we generated 9 anchors from the WIDER FACE dataset and evenly distributed these anchors in 3 detection layers for 3 different scales. Though it helps the network to get a better understanding of faces in different scales for our chosen dataset during training, we still got an increasing number of false-positive when detecting small faces.

In the process of K-means clustering, choosing an optimum number of clusters is essential for better clustering. With few clusters, some disconnected groups of data are forced to fit into one larger cluster. So whenever we train our model with the fewer number of anchor boxes, which are not adequate to understand the shape of small faces, it may lead to more false-positive detection in small faces. Again, too many clusters would make artificial boundaries within actual data clusters that lead to an increasing number of false positives as it becomes too specific and ignores the actual small faces. To solve this problem, we need to obtain an optimum number of anchor boxes which can minimize the false positive and also does not occur false negative. After extensive experimental searching, we found 12 anchors are good for the dataset, and we distributed these anchors across 4 scales. On the WIDER FACE dataset the 12 clusters are: (4×6), (7×12), (11×19), (16×30), (25×42), (34×65), (59×56), (52×101), (107×105), (82×169), (159×231), (268×353).

3.2 Detecting Small Faces with Extra Layer and Better Regression

To improve the detection performance of the faces, especially small faces, we extend the detection scale of YOLOv3 from 3 to 4. In original YOLOv3 the input image is downsampled 32 times, that means if the input image is 608×608, the final feature map size 19×19. For the original YOLOv3 the last detection layer takes the feature map from 76×76 for small object detection. We found this resolution is not good enough for detecting small faces. So, we have added another detection layer to grab the features from earlier layers with size 152×152. We found adding one more detection layer is significantly beneficial for detecting more small faces.

Detecting more small faces as well as predicting the bounding box properly is a challenging task. Though the YOLOv3 has achieved remarkable performance in detecting small targets, it still struggles to localize small faces properly. YOLOv3 uses the IoU loss for bounding box regression. The IoU loss is only effective when the prior box overlaps with the target box. As previous boxes consist of fixed sizes, but the target box sizes are changing continuously, It is likely not to overlap with the target box, especially for small face target boxes. As a result, the IoU loss would converge to a bad result which could cause an inaccurate localization as well as an increasing number of false positives for small face detection. To solve this problem, we have applied the DIoU loss reported in [12] with complete form CIoU, which is more effective for non-overlapping cases and can give us better detection accuracy and faster convergence. The CIoU loss consists of two parts, 1) DIoU (Distance IoU) loss, which is responsible for normalizing the distance between the predicted box and target box with an aim of achieving faster convergence, 2) The consistency of aspect ratios for bounding boxes is also an important geometric factor for more accurate regression, and hence CIoU (Complete IoU) loss is adopted in this paper. For the DIoU, the penalty term can be defined as:

$$R_{DIoU} = \frac{\rho^2\left(b, b^{gt}\right)}{c^2}$$

where b and b^{gt} denote the central points of B and B^{gt}, $\rho(.)$ is the Euclidean distance, and c is the diagonal length of the smallest enclosing box covering the two boxes. And then the DIoU loss function can be defined as

$$L_{DIoU} = 1 - IoU + \frac{\rho^2\left(b, b^{gt}\right)}{c^2}$$

In Fig. 3, we can see DIoU loss aims at considering the overlap area and central point distance of bounding boxes simultaneously. However, the consistency of aspect ratios for bounding boxes is another important geometric factor. Therefore, based on DIoU loss, we considered the CIoU loss by imposing the consistency of aspect ratio

$$R_{CIoU} = \frac{\rho^2\left(b, b^{gt}\right)}{c^2}$$

where α is a positive trade-off parameter, and v measures the consistency of aspect ratio,

$$v = \frac{4}{\pi^2}\left(\arctan\frac{w^{gt}}{h^{gt}} - \arctan\frac{w}{h}\right)^2$$

Then the loss function can be defined as

$$L_{CIoU} = 1 - IoU + \frac{\rho^2\left(b, b^{gt}\right)}{c^2} + \alpha v$$

And the trade-off parameter α is defined as

$$\alpha = \frac{v}{(1 - IoU) + v}$$

by which the overlap area factor is given a higher priority for regression, especially for non-overlapping cases.

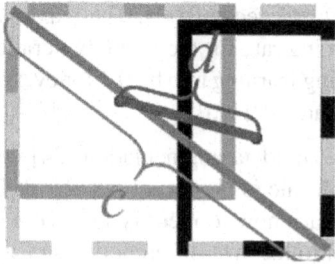

Fig. 3. DIoU loss for bounding box regression, where the normalized distance between central points can be directly minimized. c is the diagonal length of the smallest enclosing box covering two boxes, and $d = \rho(b, b^{gt})$ is the distance of central points of two boxes.

3.3 Better Performance with More Residual Connection

The original YOLOv3 has a backbone (Darknet-53) of 53 convolutional layers. As the YOlOv3 network is significantly large and there are multiple downsampled layers in Darknet-53, so the feature maps become coarse. Also, in each detection layer, there are 6 convolutional layers stacked one after another. These can lead to gradient fading problem that makes sub-successive detection layers less effective, so the loss doesn't improve as expected for small faces. The gradient is back-propagated to earlier layers, so the repeated multiplication may make the gradient infinitely small. As a result, as the network goes deeper, its performance gets saturated or even starts degrading rapidly.

To solve this problem and reuse the features from earlier layers, we use 2 residual connections in 6 Conv layers of each detection layer. The Resnet [27] has several compelling advantages: it can remove the vanishing-gradient problem, strengthen feature propagation, encourage feature reuse, and considerably reduce the number of parameters. After adding 2 residual connections before each detection layer, it can significantly improve the AP to 4%, 0.5%, 0.2% in the hard, medium and easy subset of the WIDER FACE dataset respectively.

4   Experiments and Results

To evaluate the performance of the proposed network on small face detection, we conduct some comparative experiments with other target detection algorithms on the WIDER FACE dataset. The experimental setup is as follows. The operating system is Ubuntu 18.04. The deep learning framework is the Darknet. The machine is with CPU: Intel(R) Xeon(R) Gold. Memory: 1 TB, GPU: NVIDIA GeForce TITAN RTX.

4.1   Training Dataset and Data Augmentation

Our model is trained based on 12880 images from the WIDER FACE training set. We have also trained the original YOLOv3 for faces on the same dataset with similar training configuration. The input image size is set to be 608 × 608, and the batch size we used is 64 with a subdivision of 16 to reduce the GPU memory usage. We use the optimizer of SGD with momentum 0.9 and decay 0.005. The maximum number of iterations is 160k, and we use 0.001 learning rate for the first 64k iterations, then continue training for 96k iterations with reducing learning rate by 0.1 for every 8000 steps. The following data augmentation strategies are adopted.

Mosaic Augmentation: Mosaic data augmentation [34] combines 4 training images into one in specific ratios. Mosaic is the recent popular data augmentation technique, which allows the model to learn how to identify faces at a smaller scale than normal. It also encourages the model to localize different types of images in different portions of the frame. It also helps to detect faces out of their usual context. Besides, we have also used the existing data augmentation technique in YOLOv3 like changing the hue, saturation and exposure of training images.

4.2   Model Analysis

We analyze our model on the WIDER FACE validation set by extensive experiments. The WIDER FACE validation set has easy, medium and hard subsets, which roughly correspond to large, medium and small faces, respectively. Hence it is suitable to evaluate our model. Our model has achieved overall mAP of 93.8%, 92.4% and 86.5% respectively in Easy, Medium and Hard validation sets of WIDER FACE.

Ablative Setting: To understand the effect of different techniques in our model, we conduct ablation experiments to examine how each proposed component would affect the final performance. We evaluated the performance of our method with three different settings. (i) Our model (C): it only changes the loss function to CioU; (ii) Our model (C + 4L): it has the addition of 4 scale detection layers including CIoU loss implementation; (iii) Our model (C + 4L + R): it is our complete model, consisting of 4 detection layer including two residual layers in each detection module and implementation of CIoU loss function. The results are summarized in Table 1, and one can see that our proposed model can achieve much better results than YOLOv3.

Better Accuracy and Localization of Bounding Box with CIoU Loss. We found more accurate bounding box and less false positives overall large, medium and small face detection. Especially, for small faces the anchors take more time to converge with target boxes and the localization error rate is high in predicted boxes. In comparison with IoU and GIoU loss, we found CIoU loss is better for detecting small face with less false detection and better regression. After applying the CIoU loss to our model, we have achieved 1% AP increase on the easy and medium subsets and 1.6% AP increase on the hard subset of the WIDER FACE dataset.

More Detection with an Extra YOLO Layer. As for YOLOv3 the input image is downsampled 32 times, so the earlier layers with big feature map contains more contextual information on small faces and downsampling make the feature map coarse. For getting more small faces we have added an additional YOLO detection layer, where the final feature map is derived from by concatenating more earlier feature map with fine-grained information for small faces. After adding 4 YOLO detection layer with the CIoU loss to our model, we have achieved 1.1% AP increase on the easy, 0.9% AP in medium and 1.6% AP increase on the hard subset of the WIDER FACE dataset.

More Residual Connection for Re-Using Feature Map. As network becomes bigger and each of the detection layer has multiple convolutional layers stacked over one another, so the performance degrades rapidly in later detection layers which are responsible for detecting small faces and loss doesn't improve as expected. To avoid gradient fading and enhance performance for big network residual connection has no alternative, so we added 2 residual block in each detection layer to reuse the features maps. It boosts the network performance by 4.2%, 0.5%, 0.2% in the hard, medium and easy subset of the WIDER FACE dataset respectively.

Table 1. The comparative analysis with YOLOv3 and ablative results of our model with different methods on WIDER FACE validation subset.

Methods	Easy (mAP%)	Medium (mAP%)	Hard (mAP%)
YOLOv3	87.6	85.8	72.9
Our model (C)	92.5	91.0	80.1
Our model (C + 4L)	93.6	91.9	82.3
Our model (C + 4L + R)	**93.8**	**92.4**	**86.5**

4.3 Comparative Evaluation

In this section, we evaluate our model on the WIDER FACE face detection in comparison with other existing approaches. It has 32203 images and labels 393703 faces with a high degree of variability in scale, poses and occlusion. The database is divided into training (40%), validation (10%) and testing (50%) set. Moreover, the images are categorized into three levels (Easy, Medium and Hard subset) according to the difficulties of detection. Our model is trained on the training set and tested on validation and test set against recent face detection methods including YOLOv3 [2], and [5–7, 30]. SFD [5] is a single shot CNN based well-known face detector that detects faces with scale-equitable framework with anchor matching strategy. SSH [6] is an effective face detector with single stage scale-invariant and scale-wise anchor matching approach. Face R-CNN [7] is an improved Faster R-CNN based approach with multi-scale training and bounding box regression with pre-defined anchors. MS-CNN [30] is an another recent multi-scale object detection with scale-dependent anchor generation. We choose these state-of-art algorithms because these are multiscale, bounding-box based CNN methods using regression, which is similar to the network architecture of our proposed model. Besides, training has performed in different scales, and the final detection is performed by combining the multiscale detections as did similarly in this paper. The precision-recall curves and mAP values are shown in Fig. 4 and Table 2. It achieves the better average precision in all level faces, i.e. 0.938 (Easy), 0.924 (Medium) and 0.865 (Hard) for validation set and 0.931 (Easy), 0.920 (Medium) and 0.859 (Hard) for the test set. These results show the effectiveness of the proposed method with competency in detecting small and hard faces.

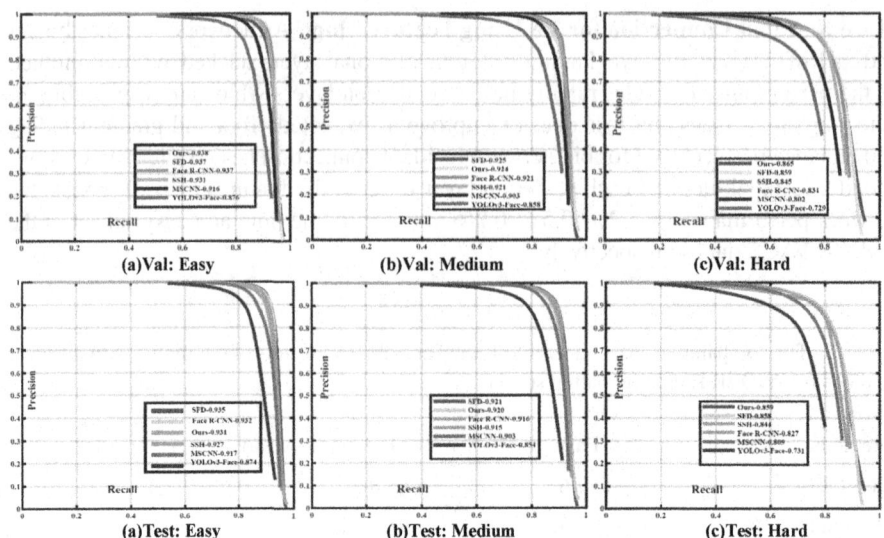

Fig. 4. Precision-recall curves on WIDER FACE 1) validation set 2) test set.

Table 2. Detection mAP of Ours, YOLOv3 and other face detectors on the WIDER FACE validation and test dataset.

Method name	WIDER FACE validation set			WIDER FACE test set		
	Easy (mAP%)	Medium (mAP%)	Hard (mAP%)	Easy (mAP%)	Medium (mAP%)	Hard (mAP%)
YOLOv3 face	87.6	85.8	72.9	87.4	85.4	73.1
MS-CNN	91.6	90.3	80.2	91.7	90.3	80.9
SSH	93.1	92.1	84.5	92.7	91.5	82.7
Face R-CNN	93.7	92.1	83.1	93.2	91.6	84.4
SFD	93.7	92.5	85.9	93.5	92.1	85.8
Ours	**93.8**	**92.4**	**86.5**	**93.1**	**92.0**	**85.9**

4.4 Experimental Demonstration

Here are some qualitative results emphasized on small faces with low resolution in wild environment with a high degree of variability in scale, pose and occlusion. We selected four photos with many small faces, and the detected results by YOLOv3 and the proposed model are shown below.

(a.1) Ours

(b.1) YOLO3

(a.2) Ours

(b.2) YOLO3

Fig. 5. Comparison of qualitative performance on small faces **(a) Ours (b) YOLOv3.**

In Fig. 5, the green bounding boxes represent the ground truth and blue boxes are predictions detected by our model and original YOLOv3. One can see that our proposed model is able to detect more small faces with better accuracy and a lower number of false positives in comparison to the original YOLOv3.

4.5 Running Time for Detection

As to the effectiveness of our proposed approach, we measured the running time in comparison to the original YOLOv3. We measured testing speed using NVIDIA GeForce TITAN RTX and cuDNN v7.6 with Intel(R) Xeon(R) Gold@2.30 GHz. For VGA resolution image with batch size 1 using a single GPU YOLOv3 can run at average 68.2 FPS including NMS (Non-max Suppression) and drawing bounding boxes. Our face detector can run in the same condition at average 64.3 FPS. Our model performs in a total of 151 BFLOPS (Billion Floating Point Operations) during testing and for YOLOv3 141 BFLOPS. As it is well known that the original YOLOv3 can be used in many real applications and our approach is comparable to the original YOLOv3, so the proposed approach can be used in practical applications in the future.

5 Conclusions

In this paper, a small face detection approach based on YOLOv3 is proposed. The main contributions of the proposed network are as follows: First, we have figured out the optimum number of anchor boxes with the aspect ratio dimensions for the revised YOLOv3. Second, to enhance the localization accuracy and to reduce false positives for small faces, we changed the regression loss to CIoU loss function. Third, to further improve the detection performance of the network, the detection scales of YOLOv3 have been extended from 3 to 4 to detect the smaller faces. Fourth, to avoid gradient fading and enhance the reuse of the features in lower layers of our network, the four out of six convolutional layers in front of each output detection layer were transformed into two residual units, that boost performance mostly in the smaller face detection layer. Finally, we did a comparative analysis with the state-of-the-art face detection algorithms on the WIDER FACE dataset with their evaluation tools.

In future, we will work on contextual information for small faces for better understanding the faces in large groups or crowds with deep network architecture. Also, we intend to train different detection models separately based on different face solutions to improve detection accuracy.

References

1. Redmon, J., Divvala, S., Girshick, R., Farhadi, A.: You only look once: unified, real-time object detection. In: Proceedings of the IEEE Conference on Computer Vision and Pattern Recognition, Las Vegas, NV, USA, 27–30 June 2016, pp. 779–788 (2016)
2. Redmon, J., Farhadi, A.: YOLOv3: An Incremental Improvement. https://arxiv.org/abs/1804.02767. Accessed 8 Aug 2019

3. Liu, W., et al.: SSD: single shot multibox detector. In: Leibe, B., Matas, J., Sebe, N., Welling, M. (eds.) ECCV 2016. LNCS, vol. 9905, pp. 21–37. Springer, Cham (2016). https://doi.org/10.1007/978-3-319-46448-0_2

4. Da, J., Li, Y., He, K., Sun, J.: R-FCN: object detection via region-based fully convolutional networks. In: Advances in Neural Information Processing Systems 29 (NIPS 2016) (2016)

5. Zhang, S., Zhu, X., Lei, Z., Shi, H.: S^3FD: single shot scale-invariant face detector. https://doi.org/10.1109/iccv.2017.30

6. Najibi, M., Samangouei, P., Chellappa, R., Davis, L.: SSH: single-stage headless face detector. In: ICCV, pp. 4885–4894 (2017)

7. Wang, H., Li, Z., Ji, X., Wang, Y.: Face R-CNN. arXiv:1706.01061 (2017)

8. Zhu, C., Zheng, Y., Luu, K., Savvides, M.: CMS-RCNN: contextual multi-scale region-based CNN for unconstrained face detection. In: Bhanu, B., Kumar, A. (eds.) Deep Learning for Biometrics. ACVPR, pp. 57–79. Springer, Cham (2017). https://doi.org/10.1007/978-3-319-61657-5_3

9. Zhang, K., Zhang, Z., Li, Z., Qiao, Y.: Joint face detection and alignment using multitask cascaded convolutional networks. IEEE Signal Process. Lett. 23(10), 1499–1503 (2016)

10. Yang, S., Luo, P., Loy, C.-C., Tang, X.: From facial parts responses to face detection: a deep learning approach. In: ICCV (2015)

11. Yang, S., Luo, P., Loy, C.C., Tang, X.: Wider face: a face detection benchmark. In: CVPR, pp. 5525– 5533 (2016)

12. Zheng, Z., Wang, P., Liu, W., Li, J., Ye, R., Ren, D.: Distance-IoU loss: faster and better learning for bounding box regression. In: AAAI Conference on Artificial Intelligence (AAAI) (2020)

13. Xiong, X., De la Torre, F.: Supervised descent method and its applications to face alignment. In: CVPR, pp. 532–539 (2013)

14. Zhu, X., Lei, Z., Liu, X., Shi, H., Li, S.Z.: Face alignment across large poses: a 3D solution. In: CVPR, pp. 146–155 (2016)

15. Sun, Y., Wang, X., Tang, X.: Deep learning face representation from predicting 10,000 classes. In: CVPR, pp. 1891–1898 (2014)

16. Parkhi, O.M., Vedaldi, A., Zisserman, A.: Deep face recognition. In: Proceedings of the British Machine Vision Conference, vol. 1, p. 6 (2015)

17. Schroff, F., Kalenichenko, D., Philbin, J.: FaceNet: a unified embedding for face recognition and clustering. In: CVPR, pp. 815–823 (2015)

18. Viola, P., Jones, M.: Rapid object detection using a boosted cascade of simple features. In: CVPR, vol. 1, p. I–511. IEEE (2001)

19. Viola, P., Jones, M.J.: Robust real-time face detection. Int. J. Comput. Vis. 57(2), 137–154 (2004). https://doi.org/10.1023/B:VISI.0000013087.49260.fb

20. He, K., Zhang, X., Ren, S., Sun, J.: Spatial pyramid pooling in deep convolutional networks for visual recognition. TPAMI 37(9), 1904–1916 (2015)

21. Girshick, R., Donahue, J., Darrell, T., Malik, J.: Rich feature hierarchies for accurate object detection and semantic segmentation. In: CVPR, pp. 580–587 (2014)

22. Ren, S., He, K., Girshick, R., Sun, J.: Faster R-CNN: towards real-time object detection with region proposal networks. In: Advances in Neural Information Processing Systems (NIPS), pp. 91–99 (2015)

23. Redmon, J., Farhadi, A.: YOLO9000: better, faster, stronger. In: CVPR, pp. 7263–7271 (2017)

24. Fu, C., Liu, W., Ranga, A., Tyagi, A., Berg, A.C.: DSSD: deconvolutional single shot detector. https://arxiv.org/abs/1701.06659. Accessed 8 Aug 2019

25. Navneet, D., Triggs, B.: Histograms of oriented gradients for human detection. In: Computer Vision and Pattern Recognition (CVPR) (2005)

26. Lin, T.-Y., et al.: Microsoft COCO: common objects in context. In: Fleet, D., Pajdla, T., Schiele, B., Tuytelaars, T. (eds.) ECCV 2014. LNCS, vol. 8693, pp. 740–755. Springer, Cham (2014). https://doi.org/10.1007/978-3-319-10602-1_48

27. He, K., Zhang, X., Ren, S., Sun, J.: Deep residual learning for image recognition. In: CVPR, pp. 770–778 (2016)

28. Li, H., Lin, Z., Shen, X., Brandt, J., Hua, G.: A convolutional neural network cascade for face detection. In: CVPR (2015)

29. Jiang, H., Learned-Miller, E.: Face detection with the faster R-CNN. arXiv:1606.03473 (2016)

30. Cai, Z., Fan, Q., Feris, R.S., Vasconcelos, N.: A unified multi-scale deep convolutional neural network for fast object detection. In: Leibe, B., Matas, J., Sebe, N., Welling, M. (eds.) ECCV 2016. LNCS, vol. 9908, pp. 354–370. Springer, Cham (2016). https://doi.org/10.1007/978-3-319-46493-0_22

31. Tang, X., Du, D.K., He, Z., Liu, J.: PyramidBox: a context-assisted single shot face detector. In: Ferrari, V., Hebert, M., Sminchisescu, C., Weiss, Y. (eds.) ECCV 2018. LNCS, vol. 11213, pp. 812–828. Springer, Cham (2018). https://doi.org/10.1007/978-3-030-01240-3_49

32. Yang, S., Luo, P., Loy, C.C., Tang, X.: Faceness-Net: face detection through deep facial part responses. IEEE Trans. Pattern Anal. Mach. Intell. 40(8), 1845–1859 (2018)

33. Ju, M., Luo, H., Wang, Z., Hui, B., Chang, Z.: The application of improved YOLO V3 in multiscale target detection. Appl. Sci. 9, 3775 (2019). https://doi.org/10.3390/app9183775

34. Jocher, G.: Ultralytics LLC YOLOv3. https://github.com/ultralytics/yolov3

Reducing Traffic Congestion in Urban Areas via Real-Time Re-Routing: A Simulation Study

Mauro Vallati[1]([⊠])[iD] and Lukáš Chrpa[2][iD]

[1] University of Huddersfield, Huddersfield, UK
M.vallati@hud.ac.uk
[2] Faculty of Electrical Engineering, Czech Technical University in Prague,
Prague, Czech Republic

Abstract. Traffic congestion problems of urban road networks are having a strong impact on economy, due to losses from accidents and delays,
and to public health. The recent progress in connected vehicles is expanding the approaches that can be exploited to tackle traffic congestion,
particularly in urban regions. Connected vehicles pave the way to centralised real-time re-routing, where a urban traffic controller can suggest
alternative routes to be followed in order to reduce delays and mitigate
congestion issues in the network. In this work, we introduce a centralised
architecture and we compare in simulation a number of approaches that
can be exploited for re-routing vehicles.

Keywords: Urban traffic control · Real-time re-routing · Traffic
optimisation

1 Introduction

Nowadays, the traffic in urban areas becomes one of the major economical problems due to losses from traffic accidents and travel delays. In rush hours, the
problem with traffic jams, road congestion and travel delays is far more apparent. With continuing growth of global urbanisation, the problem with traffic
congestion is expected to exacerbate. Hence there is a need for intelligent traffic
control techniques that can, at least to some extent, mitigate the problem. With
the recent progress in the area of *connected vehicles* we have more options for
designing intelligent traffic control techniques [10].

One of the well studied options is to control traffic lights in order to optimise
traffic flow in intersections. Such techniques include SCOOT [1], MOVA [13] or
SCATS [6] that adapt green phase lengths according to current traffic conditions. Apart of reactive techniques, there are techniques leveraging Automated
Planning that take into account longer time period in which traffic in the urban
road network evolves [8,11].

Intelligent traffic light control, however, is only able to tackle one aspect
of urban traffic congestion as it can only affect bandwidth of intersections. A

© Springer Nature Switzerland AG 2020
M. Gallagher et al. (Eds.): AI 2020, LNAI 12576, pp. 69–81, 2020.
https://doi.org/10.1007/978-3-030-64984-5_6

complementary approach that can be leveraged to mitigate road congestion is intelligent vehicle routing [2]. That is, in a nutshell, routing vehicles from their locations of origin to their destination location throughout the road network in a smart way –maximising some aspects specified by the traffic controller. In consequence, two different vehicles might take different routes even though they have identical locations of origin and destination. Leveraging Automated Planning to tackle the problem of intelligent vehicle routing throughout the road network achieved promising results [3,4]. Those techniques approach the problem from centralised perspective, i.e., there is a central urban traffic controller that suggests routes to all the navigating vehicles [14].

One of the known drawbacks of centralised approaches is the scalability issue: since a controller is in charge of a whole region, it may struggle in the presence of a large number of vehicles. Overcoming the scalability issue can be done, for example, by considering computationally inexpensive metrics for re-routing vehicles – so that the central controller can more easily deal with large volumes of traffic. Another opportunity is to consider decentralised approaches, where vehicles do not rely on a centralised system to decide the route to follow (see, for instance [9,12]). A version of this approach is commonly exploited in satellite navigators, but some drawbacks include the fact that it may lack reliable information about the evolution of the network conditions, or require strong vehicle to vehicle communication. For the interested reader, a comparison between centralised and decentralised approaches for traffic light controlling has been recently performed by Manolis *et al.* [7].

In this paper, we introduce an architecture that supports the real-time re-routing of vehicles approaching a controlled urban region, and we exploit such architecture to compare a number of criteria that can be used to re-route vehicles with the aim of reducing the congestion of the network links. We specified six different criteria that determine whether a vehicle should re-route. Three of the criteria consider the current situation in the road network, and can therefore be exploited also in a decentralised fashion where each vehicle is considering the condition in isolation, while the other three criteria consider estimates of the near future traffic situation, and are typical of a centralised approach where a traffic controller can predict the evolution of the network conditions. Effectiveness of the criteria is evaluated on the Milton Keynes road network while considering historical data. The results indicate that criteria based on the current or (near) future road occupancy are promising for effective and efficient vehicle re-routing, when a large number of vehicles follow the provided suggestions.

2 Investigated Architecture and Approaches

This section is devoted to describe the investigated architecture, and the metrics considered to be used for performing the real-time re-routing of vehicles, in order to spread vehicles in the urban network with the aim of reducing congestion.

Figure 1 provides an overview of the architecture that is designed and considered for this investigation. The main aim of the framework is to support

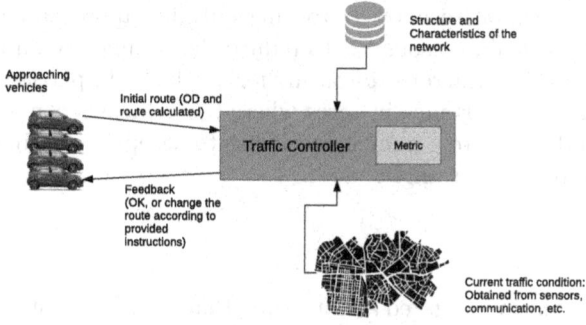

Fig. 1. An overview of the considered architecture.

the exploitation of techniques for maximising the use of the controlled urban network via real-time re-routing, each vehicle approaching the controlled area will receive re-routing instructions based on its current destination, and on the current traffic conditions.

The main element of the framework is the *traffic controller*; by taking into account the vast amount of available information and data, the controller is in charge of deciding what are the best routes to be followed by the connected vehicles that are approaching the network, according to the considered optimisation metric. The traffic controller relies on three types of input:

– Structure and characteristics of the network; This includes a description of the topology of the network in terms of links, junctions, traffic lights, etc.
– Current traffic condition; Available sensors distributed in the controlled region can provide additional information about the status, for instance in terms of air quality, congestion, accidents, etc. Further, connected vehicles can directly communicate with the traffic controller, providing information about their current location, speed, etc.
– Approaching vehicles; Connected vehicles that are approaching the controlled urban area can communicated with the controller in order to share their current path, and their destination.

On the basis of the available information, and taking into account the metric to optimise, the traffic controller is in the best position for deciding the route to be assigned to the approaching vehicles. They can of course maintain their current route, or they can be assigned a different one. For the sake of this analysis, and following the common practice, here we consider a path (or a route) to be an ordered sequence of links that a vehicle has to navigate for reaching its destination.

We designed the traffic controller to provide re-routing instructions to vehicles entering the controlled region. For every approaching vehicle, or every x seconds, the controller assess the condition of the network and, considering the metric to be optimised, takes a decision. In other words, the controller does not built a single overall simulation of the area to control, but keeps re-assessing conditions. The decision to allow re-routing only for approaching vehicles has been taken for two main reasons: (i) to reduce the complexity on the controller side, and (ii) to avoid numerous re-routing for a vehicle. In particular, the latter point is of primary importance in cases where the vehicle is connected, but not autonomous, and therefore a human driver has to accept re-routing instructions and modify the path accordingly.

2.1 Metrics

A key element of the investigated architecture, that is a blue print for a connected urban traffic controller, is of course the metric to be used to re-route approaching vehicles, with the aim of optimising the traffic conditions of the network.

Our analysis is focused on metrics that can be computed in real-time, and are therefore computationally cheap, and that can allow to compare two or more paths. The aim is to be able to decide the path that is expected to be less congested, in order to distribute vehicles.

We identify two main classes of metrics that can be designed: metrics that gives an overview of the current network conditions, and metrics that aim at predicting the evolution of traffic conditions. For the sake of operationality, i.e. making sure that the re-routing can be done in real-time, the prediction of the evolution of the traffic conditions has to leverage on features and elements that can be easily computed, also in large urban areas. For the first class of approaches, we designed the following metrics:

- **Occupancy**. the current occupancy of a path P is calculated as the total number of vehicles across all the links that are part of the path P. Formally:

$$occ(P) = \sum_{n \in P} vehicles(n) \tag{1}$$

  Where $vehicles(n)$ represents the number of vehicles that are currently on link n, either moving or queuing.
- **Density**. The proposed measure of occupancy does not take into account the maximum capacity of a link, in terms of the maximum number of vehicles that can physically fit it. This may potentially lead to cases where paths composed by short extremely congested links are preferred over paths that include longer links. To address this potential issue, the notion of Density takes also into account the maximum capacity of each link, in order to provide a more accurate overall evaluation of the congestion:

$$density(P) = \sum_{n \in P} \frac{vehicles(n)}{maxCapacity(n)} \tag{2}$$

For the sake of readability, we assume that the *density* function can also accept a single link as an input parameter. In that case, the density of the single provided link is returned.

- **Journey time**. The current estimation of the journey time for a path P is calculated as a sum of travel times for each link (note that waiting time at intersections is incorporated in the link travel time):

$$travelT(P) = \sum_{n \in P} travelT(n) \tag{3}$$

Where $travelT(n)$ represents the most recent travel time measurement for link n. If no measure is available, then the minimum "physical" travel time is considered, as the ratio between the length of the link and the allowed maximum speed. Notably, this is the metric traditionally leveraged by connected Satellite Navigators such as Waze[1] and Navfree[2], as is therefore deemed to be extremely informative.

The second class of approaches focuses on providing an estimation of the evolution of the traffic conditions on the considered paths. We will later refer to this class as "cumulative", and it includes the following metrics:

- **Cumulative occupancy**. The cumulative occupancy of a path P is calculated as a sum of the number of vehicles that are currently passing the links or are routed through them in future:

$$cumulativeOcc(P) = \sum_{n \in P} \sum_{v \in V} expected(v, n) \tag{4}$$

Where $expected(v, n)$ represents the expected number of vehicles to navigate through link n, and is calculated as follows.

$$expected(v, n) = \begin{cases} 1 : n \in path(v) \\ 0 : \quad otherwise \end{cases} \tag{5}$$

$path(v)$ represents the remaining path that vehicle v has yet to navigate in order to reach its destination. In other words, the cumulative occupancy value of a path gives a very pessimistic overview of traffic conditions, by assuming that all the vehicles in the network, that are expected to navigate through some links of the path, are occupying all the links at the same time. It is as if a vehicle is actually "booking" all the links that it is planned to navigate in the future. This gives an unrealistic view of the traffic conditions to the traffic controller, but forces the controller to pre-actively take action in order to distribute traffic as much as possible from early stages.
- **Cumulative density**. This is an extension of the notion of density, where the cumulative occupancy of each link is considered, instead of the current occupancy.

$$cumulDensity(P) = \sum_{n \in P} \frac{\sum_{v \in V} expected(v, n)}{maxCapacity(n)} \tag{6}$$

---

[1] https://www.waze.com/.
[2] http://navfree.android.informer.com/.

As for the cumulative occupancy, also the cumulative density gives a pessimistic overview of the traffic conditions, but it is aiming at providing an estimation of how much links may become congested, rather than providing the raw number of expected vehicles.

– **Cumulative journey time**. This measure is a combination of the previously described cumulative occupancy and journey time metrics. The idea is to acknowledge the fact that an increased occupancy is likely to have a detrimental impact on the travel time of a path. Therefore, the estimate of the travel time of a path is increased according to the calculated cumulative occupancy, as follows:

$$cumulTravelT(P) = \sum_{n \in P} \frac{travelT(n) \times \sum_{v \in V} expected(v, n)}{vehicles(n)} \tag{7}$$

In cases where $vehicles(n) = 0$, only $travelT(n) \times density(n)$ is considered for a link n. The above equation has been designed so that future travel time is directly affected by the cumulative occupancy. Since the cumulative occupancy is generally expected to be higher than the maximum link capacity, due to the way in which it is calculated, this measure is ignoring that travel time is not a linear function of the number of vehicles. This has also been done to reduce the complexity of calculating the metric, and to ensure that it can cope also with unexpected travel conditions.

It is worth noting that the *cumulative* dimension of the metrics can be optimised according to the characteristics of the network, and of the traffic. In the above definitions we considered that a vehicle is occupying at the same time, all the links of its current path. However, this can be modified in order to consider only the next few links, or the links corresponding to the next 1 km of the path.

3 Simulation Investigations

3.1 Setup

To study and compare the performance of the six introduced metrics for real-time re-routing of connected vehicles in urban areas under realistic traffic conditions, the network of Milton Keynes centre has been used. In particular, here we consider a SUMO microsimulation model [5], and the network is shown in Fig. 2. Milton Keynes is a town of the United Kingdom, located about 80 km north-west of London. Milton Keynes has a population of approximately 230,000. The model covers an area of approximately 2.9 km^2, and includes more than 25 junctions and more than 50 links.

The model simulates the morning rush hour, and has been built by considering historical traffic data collected between 8am and 9am on non-holiday weekdays. Data has been provided by the Milton Keynes Council, and gathered

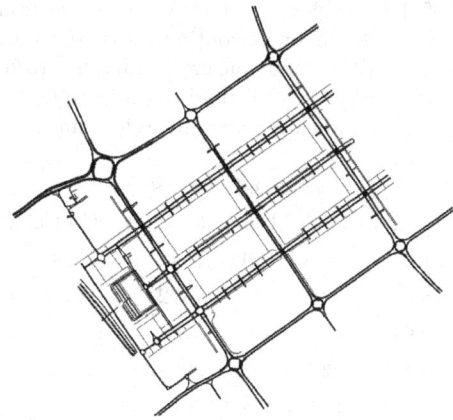

Fig. 2. The modelled central Milton Keynes urban area. Large influx of traffic, for the considered morning peak time, comes from the West roundabout, and from the North East roundabout.

Table 1. Performance of the cumulative metrics when run in simulation with *normal* traffic conditions, and *all vehicles* follow re-routing instructions. Occ, Den, and JourneyT stand for, respectively, Occupancy, Density, and Journey Time. A-* (n5-*) indicates that all the remaining path (next 5 links) is considered as occupied by a vehicle. Bold indicates the best performance.

	Considered metrics					
	A-Occ	A-Den	A-JourneyT	n5-Occ	n5-Den	n5-JourneyT
Departed vehicles [#]	**1882**	1731	1842	1860	1823	1848
Arrived vehicles [#]	1533	1045	1605	**1668**	1443	1634
Avg, speed [m/s]	2.8	0.9	3.9	**4.8**	2.5	4.0
Avg, trip length [m]	**1937.0**	1942.7	2079.7	2049.5	2055.4	2120.9
Avg, trip duration [s]	476.7	696.1	404.7	**356.5**	532.1	383.3
Avg, time loss [s]	335.7	555.0	253.1	**207.2**	382.6	228.8

by sensors distributed in the region between December 2015 and December 2016. Traffic signal control information has been provided again by the Council. The model has been calibrated and validated.

The presented architecture has been implemented in Python, and uses the TRaCI interface to interact with the SUMO simulation environment, in order to get the current network status, communicate with approaching vehicles, and inform vehicles of re-routing. For every couple of origin-destination, described by the traffic flows of the model, between 2 and 3 alternative routes are considered for distributing traffic. Such routes have been provided by a human expert, that has a good understanding of the dynamics of the modelled region. Alternatives can, in principle, be automatically calculated (by using approaches based on the

Table 2. Performance of the considered metrics when run in simulation with *normal* traffic conditions, and *all vehicles* follow re-routing instructions. Default indicates that no traffic control is in use. Occ, Den, and JourneyT stand for, respectively, Occupancy, Density, and Journey Time metrics. C-* is used to indicate the cumulative version of the corresponding metric. Bold indicates the best performance.

| | Default | Considered metrics | | | | | |
		Occ	Den	JourneyT	C-Occ	C-Den	C-JourneyT
Departed vehicles [#]	1669	1818	1808	1842	**1860**	1823	1848
Arrived vehicles [#]	801	1628	1611	1572	**1668**	1443	1634
Avg, speed [m/s]	0.6	4.6	**5.2**	3.7	4.8	2.5	3.9
Avg, trip length [m]	2297.4	2098.5	2136.6	2059.9	**2049.5**	2055.4	2121.0
Avg, trip duration [s]	788.9	**354.3**	378.2	407.7	356.5	532.1	383.3
Avg, time loss [s]	622.1	**201.6**	222.7	257.5	207.2	382.6	228.8

Dijkstra algorithm, for instance), relying on human expertise can allow to exploit some insights that are based on knowledge that is not captured by the symbolic model of the network. The simulation is run for 1 h and then stopped. For each set of experiments, the simulation is run five times and results are averaged, to account for non-determinism.

The simulation results are summarised in terms of the following SUMO-calculated performance indices:

– number of departed (arrived) vehicles. Indicates the number of vehicles that entered the region (reached destination) during the simulation. A vehicle can enter the region if the entry point link has enough space to accommodate it, otherwise it is assumed to be queuing outside the region.
– average speed (m/s) of the vehicles.
– average trip length (m) and duration (s). Length and duration reports the average measurement of the trips of the vehicles to reach their destination from the entry point.
– Average time loss (s). This value indicates the time that has been lost due to vehicles queuing, or travelling at a speed that was lower than the maximum allowed.

3.2   Results and Discussions

A first pivotal aspect to investigate, for metrics of the cumulative class, is to identify the most promising number of links to be considered as occupied by a vehicle that is following an assigned path. After a number of preliminary experiments, we found that a lookahead of 5 links allows the traffic controller exploiting the metrics to deliver consistently good performance. Table 1 shows the performance of the cumulative metrics when a vehicle is occupying (A)ll the remaining links of the path, or only the next 5 (n5). In most of the cases, the

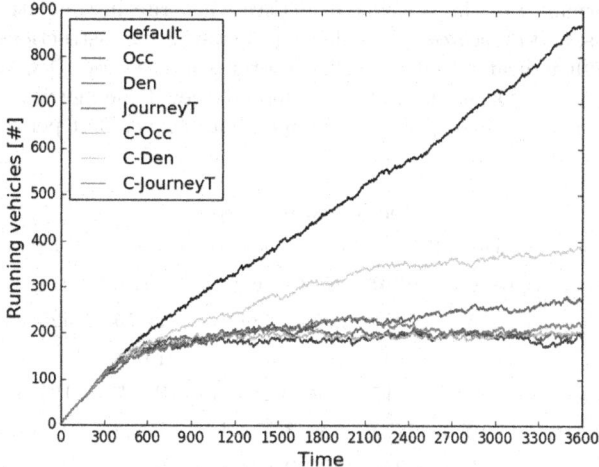

Fig. 3. The number of vehicles running, i.e. navigating the controlled region, at any point in time during the simulations. Occ, Den, and JourneyT stand for, respectively, Occupancy, Density, and Journey Time metrics. C-* is used to indicate the cumulative version of the corresponding metric.

n5- cumulative version allows the corresponding metric to deliver better performance than the All one. Given the presented results, in the remainder of this analysis we will use the n5- version for the cumulative class of metrics.

Having identified the most promising value to be used by the cumulative metrics, we can now turn our attention to an extensive comparison of the considered techniques. In the first scenario, we consider ideal conditions: traffic is normal –as for the historical data collected in the area– and all the vehicles are connected and are following the re-routing instructions provided by the traffic controller. This scenario should provide an idea of how different metrics can help to distribute traffic in the urban region when used under the best possible conditions; it is a sort of upper bound of the achievable performance. The results are presented in Table 2, and includes the default performance of the network, achieved when no traffic control is in operation. In the Default settings, vehicles enter the network and follow their pre-calculated path to the destination, that does not take into account the network conditions. As expected, all the techniques are significantly outperforming the default; this is an indication that the proposed architecture can effectively reduce traffic congestion via re-routing. Notably, there is no metric that allows to deliver the best performance according to all the indicators. In general, Occupancy and Cumulative Occupancy seem capable of delivering the best performance, and show very similar results. Metrics based on the notion of Density do not perform well when the cumulative version is used, as a limited number of vehicles can reach its destination during the simulation time. Remarkably, the use of Density allows to achieve the highest average speed of vehicles in the network, even though at the cost of longer

Table 3. Performance of the considered metrics when run in simulation with *heavy* traffic conditions, and *all vehicles* are following the re-routing instructions of the traffic controller. Default indicates that no traffic control is in use. Occ, Den, and JourneyT stand for, respectively, Occupancy, Density, and Journey Time metrics. C-* is used to indicate the cumulative version of the corresponding metric. Best performance are in bold.

		Considered metrics					
	Default	Occ	Den	JourneyT	C-Occ	C-Den	C-JourneyT
Departed vehicles [#]	1869	**2945**	2778	2678	2919	2215	2858
Arrived vehicles [#]	495	2071	2054	1844	**2075**	1425	2008
Avg, speed [m/s]	0.2	**1.9**	1.7	1.2	1.6	1.1	1.6
Avg, trip length [m]	2295.0	2117.4	2164.5	2108.7	**2097.4**	2191.5	2159.0
Avg, trip duration [s]	1107.5	777.6	**659.3**	714.4	722.4	891.5	704.7
Avg, time loss [s]	935.0	623.5	**502.0**	561.1	569.6	732.0	547.6

journeys on average. With regards to the Journey time metrics, the use of the cumulative version allows to deliver consistently good performance.

In order to shed some light on the performance of the compared techniques, Fig. 3 shows the evolution over time of the number of vehicles running in the controlled region. In other words, the number of vehicles that entered the area but has not yet reached the destination. This indicator can help relating and understanding the departed and arrived vehicles measurements provided in Table 2. On the one hand, the number of arrived vehicles are an important factor that shows the ability of the technique in letting traffic move, while the departed vehicles indicator focuses on the ability of the traffic controller in maintaining the entry points of the network free. The number of running vehicles shows to us what happens between these 2 extremes. From this perspective, it is easy to notice that the Cumulative Density metrics is having issues in keeping the traffic moving in the region, with approx. 400 vehicles in the region at the end of the simulation time. The Journey time metric is facing some issues as well, but those are less pronounced. The remaining techniques are all showing similar performance with regards to this indicator, having approx. 200 vehicles in the region at the end of the simulation time.

We then considered a second scenario, with heavy traffic conditions. To simulate heavy traffic, we assumed that twice the normal amount of vehicles (3, 800) are accessing the network over the same 1 h simulation time. We are again assuming that all the vehicles are connected and are following the re-routing instructions. Table 3 shows the results of the performed analysis. Under such circumstances, the improvement that can be obtained by using the investigated framework, compared to the default network behaviour, is even more significant. Under default conditions, 495 vehicles would reach their destination within the simulation time: the worst metric is allowing 1, 425 vehicles to reach their destination, with an improvement of approx 290%. The Density metric seems to

Table 4. Performance of the considered metrics when run in simulation with *normal* traffic conditions, and 50% *of the vehicles* are following the re-routing instructions of the traffic controller. Default indicates that no traffic control is in use. Occ, Den, and JourneyT stand for, respectively, Occupancy, Density, and Journey Time metrics. C-* is used to indicate the cumulative version of the corresponding metric. Best performance are in bold.

		Considered metrics					
	Default	Occ	Den	JourneyT	C-Occ	C-Den	C-JourneyT
Departed vehicles [#]	1669	1801	1787	1784	**1807**	1789	1797
Arrived vehicles [#]	801	**1540**	1484	1464	1539	1454	1465
Avg, speed [m/s]	0.6	**3.9**	2.8	3.0	3.7	3.1	2.8
Avg, trip length [m]	2297.4	2303.5	2330.1	2288.0	2280.0	**2264.3**	2310.1
Avg, trip duration [s]	788.9	**434.0**	466.8	493.3	439.1	499.8	491.1
Avg, time loss [s]	622.1	**266.6**	297.4	327.0	273.3	335.4	323.24

exploit well the available network, by minimising time loss and the average trip duration. In terms of trips length and number of vehicles arrived/departed, the Occupancy-based metrics are still delivering the best performance. As before, the Journey time metrics do not seem to be capable of effectively re-route the traffic in the network.

Finally, our third scenario investigates the importance of penetration rate for the proposed metrics. Table 4 shows the performance achieved when the traffic condition is normal, but only 50% of the vehicles are following the provided re-routing instructions. By considering the results presented in Table 2, it is apparent that the Density and Journey time metrics are the most sensitive to the penetration rate, as its performance are the most affected by the reduction of vehicles following instructions. On the contrary, Occupancy-based metrics are robust with regards to this aspect, and are still capable of delivering generally good performance according to the indicators.

4   Conclusion

In this paper, we performed an extensive simulation study aimed at comparing six criteria for real-time re-routing of connected vehicles in an urban region. Vehicles are re-routed in order to minimise congestion in some part of the network, by spreading the traffic. The criteria are divided into two main classes, one that considers only the current condition of the network for re-routing vehicles, and the other that is also taking into account some prediction of the traffic evolution. To ensure the exploitability of the criteria in a real-world scenario, we focused on aspects that are computationally cheap to assess, in order to support a centralised urban traffic control architecture.

The simulation study considered the central Milton Keynes urban area in the morning rush hour. Data has been provided by the Milton Keynes council, and the considered model has been calibrated and validated. The experimental results indicated that: (i) Journey time, that is the criteria most used by satellite navigators, does not provide outstanding performance; (ii) Occupancy-based criteria tend to be robust and to consistently support a good redistribution of vehicles; and (iii) criteria based on predictions can improve network conditions, particularly when all the vehicles follow an expected behaviour.

For future work, we are interested in evaluating the criteria in different urban regions. We plan also to consider more computationally expensive re-routing criteria, with the aim of identifying the best ratio between computability and accuracy. Finally, we are interested in assessing also the performance of re-routing techniques that are based on vehicle-to-vehicle communication.

Acknowledgement. Mauro Vallati was partially funded by the EPSRC grant EP/R51343X/1 (AI4ME). Lukáš Chrpa was partially funded by the Czech Science Foundation (project no. 18-07252S).

References

1. Bretherton, R.: Scoot urban traffic control system: philosophy and evaluation. In: Proceedings of the 6th IFAC/IFIP/IFORS Symposium on Control, Computers, and Communications in Transportation (1989)
2. Cao, Z., Jiang, S., Zhang, J., Guo, H.: A unified framework for vehicle rerouting and traffic light control to reduce traffic congestion. IEEE Trans. Intell. Transp. Syst. **18**(7), 1958–1973 (2017)
3. Chrpa, L., Magazzeni, D., McCabe, K., McCluskey, T.L., Vallati, M.: Automated planning for urban traffic control: strategic vehicle routing to respect air quality limitations. Intelligenza Artificiale **10**, 113–128 (2016)
4. Chrpa, L., Vallati, M., Parkinson, S.: Exploiting automated planning for efficient centralized vehicle routing and mitigating congestion in urban road networks. In: Proceedings of SAC (2019)
5. Lopez, P.A., et al.: Microscopic traffic simulation using sumo. In: Proceedings of ITSC (2018)
6. Lowrie, P.: The Sydney coordinated adaptive traffic system-principles, methodology, algorithms. In: Proceedings of the International Conference on Road Traffic Signalling, no. 207 (1982)
7. Manolis, D., Pappa, T., Diakaki, C., Papamichail, I., Papageorgiou, M.: Centralised versus decentralised signal control of large-scale urban road networks in real time: a simulation study. IET Intel. Transport Syst. **12**(8), 891–900 (2018)
8. McCluskey, T.L., Vallati, M.: Embedding automated planning within urban traffic management operations. In: Proceedings of ICAPS, pp. 391–399 (2017)
9. Pan, J., Popa, I.S., Zeitouni, K., Borcea, C.: Proactive vehicular traffic rerouting for lower travel time. IEEE Trans. Veh. Technol. **62**(8), 3551–3568 (2013)
10. Vallati, M., Chrpa, L.: A principled analysis of the interrelation between vehicular communication and reasoning capabilities of autonomous vehicles. In: Proceedings of ITSC, pp. 3761–3766 (2018)
11. Vallati, M., Magazzeni, D., De Schutter, B., Chrpa, L., McCluskey, T.L.: Efficient macroscopic urban traffic models for reducing congestion: a PDDL+ planning approach. In: Proceedings of AAAI (2016)

12. Vasirani, M., Ossowski, S.: A market-inspired approach to reservation-based urban road traffic management. In: Proceedings of AAMAS, pp. 617–624 (2009)
13. Vincent, R., Pierce, J.: Self-optimising signal control for isolated intersections. Crowthorne: Transport and Road Research Laboratory Research Report, no. 170 (1988)
14. Zambrano-Martinez, J.L., et al.: A centralized route-management solution for autonomous vehicles in urban areas. Electronics 8(7), 722 (2019)

A Mixed-Integer Programming Approach for Scheduling Roadworks in Urban Regions

Mauro Vallati[1](✉) and Lukáš Chrpa[2]

[1] University of Huddersfield, Huddersfield, UK
M.vallati@hud.ac.uk
[2] Faculty of Electrical Engineering, Czech Technical University,
Prague, Czech Republic

Abstract. In order to keep roads in acceptable condition, and to perform maintenance of essential infrastructure, roadworks are required. Due to the increasing traffic volumes and the increasing urbanisation, road agencies are currently facing the problem of effective planning frequent –and usually concurrent– roadworks in the controlled region. However, there is a lack of techniques that can support traffic authorities in this task. In fact, traffic authorities have usually to rely on human experts (and their intuition) to decide how to schedule and perform roadworks. In this paper, we introduce a Mixed-Integer Programming approach that can be used by traffic authorities to plan a set of required roadworks, over a period of time, in a large urban region, by specifying constraints to be satisfied and suitable quality metrics.

Keywords: Mixed-Integer Programming · Roadworks · Urban traffic management

1 Introduction

It is expected that, during the 21st century, there will be a huge growth in urbanisation as the global population living in urban areas is projected to rise to 66% by 2050 from 54% in 2014[1]. Together with the expected socio-economic motivation for increasing mobility, a significant increase of pressure on the urban traffic network seems to be inevitable. Given the increasingly demanding use of the urban traffic network, road maintenance works are becoming more frequent, extremely time-constrained, and of primary importance [3]. Furthermore, the continuous growth of the size of urban areas is requiring additional road works to be performed, in order to maintain in operation (or to improve) all the infrastructure needed by the growing urban population, e.g., electricity, gas, network cables, etc. As a result, on top of the other urban traffic management tasks, transport controllers are currently facing the problem of coping with the large

---

[1] United Nations - https://rb.gy/nsqvcw.

© Springer Nature Switzerland AG 2020
M. Gallagher et al. (Eds.): AI 2020, LNAI 12576, pp. 82–93, 2020.
https://doi.org/10.1007/978-3-030-64984-5_7

amount of roadworks to be planned and performed at a regional level. Planning ahead is crucial, because the impact of roadworks can be dramatic on the traffic of the area. A notable example is represented by the roadworks required in the Manchester (UK) area in 2018, which resulted in an almost daily traffic jams and, consequently, in dramatic disruptions to the local economy[2].

Despite the pressing need for efficiency, and the large body of works for optimising problems and situations daily faced by traffic controllers, there is a lack of approaches designed for supporting agencies in the decision process of creating a plan of roadworks for a controlled urban area. Beside a very recent preliminary exploration of the use of AI planning for planning roadworks [15], the body of existing works in the area is focused on providing formal frameworks for the analysis of the impact of works [6], or on the evaluation of the process exploited by local authorities [7]. For this reason, roadwork plans are usually generated manually, without any explicit notion of "quality", and with a very limited control on constraints and assessment of the impact of works on the managed network traffic, as highlighted by the above-mentioned Manchester example.

In this paper we propose a principled approach that leverages Mixed-Integer Programming (MIP) [2] to provide an effective Decision Support tool for planning roadworks in urban areas. Mixed-Integer Programming provides a powerful framework for maximising an objective function subject to one or more constraints, where variables can have Boolean or Integer values. Examples of use of MIP in real-world applications include the generation of optimal scheduling for constellation observation [14], optimising the loading of boxes into air cargo containers [10], the generation of fiducial marker dictionaries [5], and the design of reliable chemical plants [16].

Here we provide a formalisation of the roadworks scheduling problem, and using the well-known MiniZinc tool [1], we specify and develop a MIP model that allows to represent the constraints related to roadworks planning within large urban regions, and to include notions of quality in order to shape the generated solutions. Notably, MiniZinc is able to translate MIP models, encoded in a human-readable language, in the FlatZinc language [9], that is supported by a wide range of solvers: solvers can therefore be used as "black-boxes" that can be easily embedded (and are easy to change and update) into a larger system. We empirically validate our approach by considering the Kirklees urban region of Yorkshire (UK), and by modelling scenarios based on roadworks performed in the region.

2 Problem Definition and Modelling

Roadworks are needed for three main purposes: (i) maintenance of the existing road network; (ii) extension or improvement of the network, and (iii) works not strictly related with the traffic network. The third case includes works such as water or gas supply pipes maintenance. For the sake of this investigation,

---

[2] https://bbc.in/2C6l1mu.

we focus on cases (i) and (iii), as they are the most common in large urban areas, and only temporarily affect the performance and the characteristics of the network. Case (ii) works are rarely put in place in well-established urban networks, and may require a specific planning and scheduling.

2.1 Assumption

We assume that a number of roadworks need to be performed in a controlled urban region. Each roadwork is characterised by:

- *Duration*: The length of time required to complete the work. This is fixed and known before optimising the roadworks schedule.
- *Deadline*: The latest available time in which the work can be completed.
- *Start*: The earliest available time in which the work can be started.
- *Location*: The location of the roadwork. Here the location can be specified in terms of a urban *area*, or in terms of the specific affected road(s). The number of works in a given area, or in adjacent areas has to be limited to mitigate traffic congestion issues.
- *Company*: The company that is in charge of performing the roadwork. We assume that each company has a maximum number of works that can carry out concurrently.

We focus on works that have already been identified and accepted, and that are ready to start in the near future. We assume that at schedule time the set of works and their information as specified above are known and fixed. Managing works then involves determining which roadwork can be performed, considering constraints on the number of works a company can perform at the same time and the number of works that can be done concurrently in a given urban area. The optimisation requires that works are scheduled as early as possible. We assume that time is suitably discretised.

2.2 Model

Let us introduce the different variables and sets used in our optimisation model. Let $W = \{w_1, ..., w_n\}$ denotes the set of works that are being scheduled, and let $B = \{b_1, ..., b_n\}$, $D = \{d_1, ..., d_n\}$, and $E = \{e_1, ..., e_n\}$ denote, respectively, the lists of Begin, Duration, and Deadline times for each work. The begin value provides the earliest time step in which the corresponding work can be started, duration refers to how many time steps the work requires, and deadline refers to the latest time step in which the work has to be finished. Intuitively, given a work w_i, the corresponding values are identified by b_i, d_i, and e_i. The following constraints illustrate the relationships between the values that has to meet (otherwise a work violating those constraints cannot be scheduled).

$$\forall w_i : (1 \leq b_i \leq e_i) \tag{1}$$

$$\forall w_i : (d_i \leq (e_i - b_i)) \tag{2}$$

In particular, constraints 1 and 2 are used to encode aspects related to the timings of works to be scheduled, and to make sure that the problem at hand is feasible –at least from this perspective. In particular, Constraint 1 defines the relationship between begin and deadline time of each work, and at the same time it makes sure that the earliest begin time is a positive number. Constraint 2 is used to enforce the fact that the time window which is allowed for a work is sufficient, according to the duration.

To represent an actual starting time of each of the works, we introduce the list $S = \{s_1, ..., s_n\}$, which is also the objective of the optimisation.

In this paper we consider that each time unit t_i corresponds to one week, but that can be easily adjusted without changes to the model. The week time discretisation has been selected because it allows some flexibility, with regards to works that are requiring a slightly longer amount of time than the initially budgeted.

We do not explicitly model roads, but focus instead on the notion of areas, which represent a group of connected roads. The notion of area allows to effectively and efficiently encode the proximity of roadworks, as discussed later in this section. Let $A = \{a_1, ..., a_m\}$ be the set of considered areas for the given urban region. Areas that are adjacent are identified by a predicate $nextTo(a_i, a_j)$. Each area has a maximum number of roadworks that can be concurrently performed, denoted by $maxWorks(a_i)$. For the sake of assessing the number of works performed at the same time, we introduce a counter $active(a_i, t_j)$, that is used to count how many works are planned to performed at time t_j in the area a_i.

Similarly, we would like to constrain the number of concurrent works performed by a single company. The maximum number of works that a company c_i can perform at the same time is defined via $maxWCompany(c_i)$. Works are assigned to a company using a predicate $assignedTo(w_i, c_j)$, while the number of active works of a given company is specified by the counter $activeWCom(c_i, t_j)$.

Combining the assumptions and constraints described above, we can then define the model used for scheduling a set of roadworks in a urban region:

$$\forall w_i : (s_i + d_i \leq e_i) \tag{3}$$

$$\forall w_i : (s_i \geq b_i) \tag{4}$$

$$\forall a_i, \forall t_j : (active(a_i, t_j) \leq maxWorks(a_i)) \tag{5}$$

$$\forall c_i, \forall t_j : (activeWcom(c_i, t_j) \leq maxWCompany(c_i)) \tag{6}$$

$$\forall t_j, \forall a_i, a_x : nextTo(a_i, a_x) \wedge$$
$$(active(a_i, t_j) < maxWorks(a_i)) \wedge \tag{7}$$
$$(active(a_x, t_j) < maxWorks(a_x))$$

```
set of int: WEEKS = 1..period;

constraint forall (w in WORKS)
    (schedule[w] => begin[w]);

constraint forall (a in AREA,
    b in AREA where nextTo[a,b] == true ) (
        forall (t in WEEKS)
            (active[b,t] < maxWorkArea[b] /\
            active[a,t] < maxWorkArea[a]));
```

Fig. 1. MiniZinc encoding of constraints 4 (top) and 7 (bottom). The first line shows how the time period can be manually defined.

Constraints 3 and 4 are used to enforce the correct scheduling of a work, with regards to the deadline (3) and the earliest begin time (4).

Constraints 5 and 6 allow to encode limits related to the maximum works that can be active at the same time step t_i. Constraint 5 focuses on limits due to works being performed in the same area, while Constraint 6 is used to limit the number of works that a company has to perform concurrently. Finally, Constraint 7 is used to specify that it is not allowed to perform concurrently too many roadworks on adjacent areas. This has been encoded by constraining the fact at the same time, the maximum number of allowed works can not be performed in two neighbouring areas.

The mixed-integer problem is solved when all the required roadworks have been scheduled, via the dedicated list S, while respecting all the constraints of the model. The quality of a solution is calculated by considering the scheduled starting time of the works, the idea is to schedule all the works as early as possible, and the function to optimise can be modelled as follows.

$$min \sum_{i=1}^{n} s_i \tag{8}$$

2.3   Implementation

We decided to implement the described Mixed-Integer Problem using the well-known MiniZinc [1] constraint modelling language. This is because MiniZinc provides a valuable middle ground for encoding problems. On one hand, it is high-level enough to express most constraint problems easily. On the other hand, it can be mapped onto existing solvers easily and consistently via the translator that allows to generate FlatZinc models.

The overall encoding of the above described constraints required a few tens of lines of code in MiniZinc. Figure 1 provides an example of the implementation of two constraints, namely 4 (top) and 7 (bottom). While the vast majority of the code should be self-explanatory, there are a couple of caveats that should be

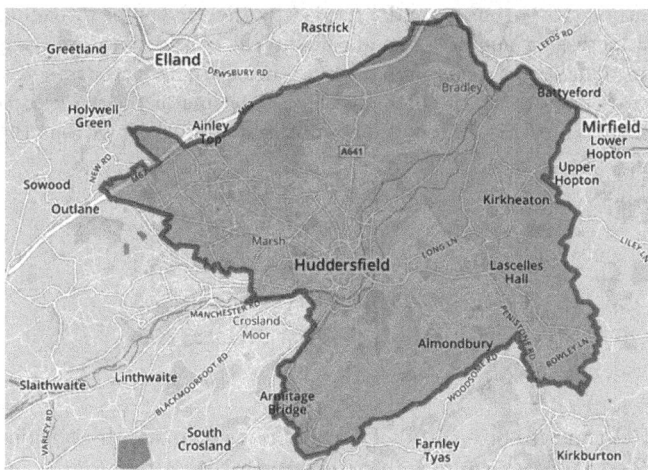

Fig. 2. The urban region considered in the experimental analysis, part of the Yorkshire county of the United Kingdom. (Color figure online)

described in order to support the readability. The first line is used to define the time period that is considered for the scheduling. The `period` value is provided as input, and represents the number of weeks to consider. This approach greatly simplifies the encoding of constraints that need to be enforced for each time step. Finally, the symbol indicates a *logic or* operator in the MiniZinc language.

3   Evaluation of the Approach

The MIP model has been encoded using MiniZinc version 2.2.3. Generated problems have been solved using three general solvers: Chuffed 0.10.3[3], Gecode 6.1.0 [12], and CBC 2.9 [4]. The first solver is based on lazy clause generation, which is a hybrid approach that combines features of finite domain propagation and Boolean satisfiability. Gecode is the winner of all categories at the MiniZinc Challenges between 2008 and 2012 [13], and is extremely optimised for the FlatZinc language. Finally, CBC is a branch-and-cut solver that requires MIP models to the provided via the COIN-OR open solver interface.

In this context, quality is measured in terms of starting time of works, as indicated in Eq. 8. In other words, works have to be scheduled as soon as possible. Better quality corresponds to works which, on average, are started as early as possible. This is the key indicator of quality, in the light of the fact that, in a typical urban context, all the roadworks which need to be planned are usually essential, and should be completed as soon as possible.

Experiments have been performed on a system equipped with 2.0 Ghz Intel i7-3667U Processors, 8 GB of RAM and Linux operating system. We set a cutoff

---

[3] https://github.com/chuffed/chuffed.

Table 1. Runtime (CPU-time seconds) needed by the solvers for providing a plan for performing an increasing number of roadworks in the considered area, over a 6-month period of time. Quality of generated plans is measured as the average delay (time units–weeks) with regards to the first possible start time of the work. Bold indicates best results, * indicates that the solution is different from those of the other solvers.

	Runtime			Quality		
# works	5	10	20	5	10	20
Chuffed	0.3	0.4	**18.3**	2.2	2.8	**5.1**
Gecode	**0.2**	**0.3**	60.0	2.2	2.8	7.6
CBC	0.5	3.8	60.0	2.2	2.8*	5.7

time of 1 CPU-time minute (60 s). Due to the way in which considered solvers work, generated plans are guaranteed to be valid with regards to the provided MIP model.

Our analysis has been focused on the northern part of the Kirklees urban region. Kirklees is a council of the West Yorkshire county, located in the north-east part of United Kingdom. Here, 11 different areas has been identified, following the local classification and organisation: Ashrbow, Almondbury, Marsh, Lindley, Edgerton, Crosland Moor, Netherton, Dalton, Huddersfield centre, Lindley, and Newsome. For the sake of this analysis, here we considered only areas as a whole. It should be noted that roads can be easily added according to the network that needs to be modelled and to the level of granularity required. Figure 2 (coloured) shows an overview of the considered region.

3.1 Empirical Results

In order to collect informative and realistic data, we analysed the number of roadworks being executed in the considered region during 2017. According to the observed data, we synthetically generated a set of instances, with the following main characteristics: number of roadworks to be planned ranging from 5 to 20; plan horizon of 6 months, roadworks duration ranging between 1 and 10 weeks; at most 2 roadworks can happen concurrently in the same area, but two nearby areas can not have, at the same time, the maximum amount of works scheduled. This is to avoid too much pressure on the network due to traffic navigating in those adjacent areas. Start time and deadline values have been randomly generated. For each considered number of roadworks to be planned, we randomly generated three instances with different durations and start times. As a general common deadline, we required all the works to be completed by the end of the modelled 6-months period. We considered the roadworks to be assigned evenly to 5 companies, and that each company can perform a single work at a time.

Presented results are averaged on the three instances, in order to take into account noise and variability due to the randomised aspects.

The results of this first set of experiments, designed for testing the fact that the proposed approach is effectively able to plan the roadworks required in the controlled region, are presented in Table 1. As a first remark, it is worth noting that all the considered solvers are able to generate solutions in a very reasonable amount of time. In fact, the process of planning roadworks is not required to be performed in real time, and longer amount of CPU time can be devoted to the task. Nevertheless, less than 1 CPU-time minute has been enough to generate solutions to all the considered cases. It should be noted that the considered solvers run in an "anytime" fashion: they keep running until they are not able to find a better quality solution to the considered problem. Furthermore, they also provide intermediate solutions found in the meanwhile; an interested user can therefore let the system run for a higher amount of time, and at the same time can have insights about the current best solution. Among the considered solvers, Chuffed is the one that is generally the fastest. CBC is possibly negatively affected by the fact that an additional translation step has to be performed in order to provide the solver with the required input format.

With regards to the quality of generated plans, the easiest tasks are solved optimally by all the considered solvers. As multiple plans can share the same overall quality value, due to the fact that the measured quality corresponds to an average delay among works to be started, it is interesting to notice that Chuffed and Gecode tend to return the same plans, while CBC seems to "prefer" plans where shortest works are scheduled as soon as possible, while longest works are delayed. On the contrary, the other considered solvers tend to schedule longest works earlier.

Figure 3 shows (top) how the output can be shaped using the MiniZinc language, and (bottom) part of an example output provided by the proposed approach. In the shown case, four roadworks are planned to start in different weeks –which correspond to the time unit of our model. The company that has to perform the work is also listed. The shape of the output can be modified according to needs, as the MiniZinc interface provide significant flexibility on this regards.

To check the validity of generated plans, they have been visually inspected by transport experts, which confirmed their overall quality and that they look similar to plans one would expect from an expert-generated solution.

3.2   Time Horizons

To study the impact on performance of the number of roadworks to be planned, in the previous section we focused our analysis on scenarios with increasing numbers of roadworks, where time windows are randomly generated: the end time of all the works was fixed at the end of the 6-months period, but the different starting time lead to different time windows for each of the works. Intuitively, the size of the time window is an extremely important aspect: loose time windows give a significant degree of freedom to the solver to schedule works, while very strict time windows instead steadily drive the search process. Here we therefore aim to assess the impact of time windows on the performance of the proposed MIP-based approach. Focusing on the 10 roadworks scenario, we generated four problems by varying (i) the duration of roadworks, either 1 or 10 for all the considered works, and (ii) the size of the time window of each

```
output [ "\(assignedTo[w]) starts \(w) in \(schedule[w]);\n" | w in
WORKS ];
```

```
Company1 starts workA in week 5
Company2 starts workB in week 5
Company4 starts workC in week 11
Company1 starts workX in week 9
```

Fig. 3. Top: the command used in MiniZinc to format the provided output. Bottom: Excerpt of plan provided by the MiniZinc framework for planning four roadworks (namely, workA, workB, workC, and workX) in the controlled region. The provided week indicates the planned start time, and company to which the work has been assigned.

work, that can be exactly the same size of the duration, or can cover the whole modelled period.

As a first remark, we note that the duration of the considered works has no significant impact on the performance of the considered solvers: neither CPU-time nor the quality of the generated schedule plans is affected. On the other hand, the size of the time window has a remarkable impact on performance. The more constrained the time windows are, the easier it seems to be for the solvers to generate a solution. In the more constrained cases, all the 3 approaches can find a plan in approximately 0.3 CPU-time seconds. Conversely, larger time windows lead to a higher computational complexity (up to 15 CPU-time seconds for CBC), and a remarkable variability in terms of shape of the generated solution plans.

3.3   Assess the Feasibility of Roadworks

Noteworthy, the proposed approach can also be a valuable tool for assessing the feasibility of performing the required roadworks in the considered period of time, with the constraints in terms of companies and maximum works per area.

As a case study, we manually designed scenarios where no feasible plan exists. This has been done by providing time windows for roadworks which are smaller than the actual duration of the works, or by forcing too many works to be done in parallel in the same area/by the same company. In the mentioned case studies, all the solvers very quickly (less than 0.2 CPU-time seconds) identified that no plan could satisfy all the constraints.

Given the ability of the proposed approach that quickly identified infeasible scenarios, it can be used for evaluating the usefulness of additional resources, or for relaxing some of the constraints. Different solutions can be tested and compared. In many of the generated cases, the best solution was to re-negotiate initial time or deadlines for roadworks; in some cases our analysis indicated that the only viable solution was to relax some of the constraints.

Unfortunately, the considered solvers are not designed to indicate which of the constraints is the most stringent, or which resources are the most limiting. In that, the evaluation and exploration process has to be performed manually, by investigating how relaxing some constraints or increasing some resources affect the solvability of the problem at hand.

3.4 Discussion

The experiments demonstrate the extent to which the proposed approach is able to efficiently and effectively generate roadwork plans according to specified constraints and available resources. Given the notion of quality, that in our case corresponds to starting works as early as possible, MIP solvers can generate optimised solutions for the problem at hand. Remarkably, the quality metric can be easily modified using the MiniZinc language, and can therefore be specified by the local authorities on the basis of their requirements. Different quality metrics can also be specified and mixed together, for instance using a weighted sum of the relevant aspects to be considered. In cases where a quality metric can not be easily specified, a very intuitive notion of quality can be included in the MIP model, and the generated best solutions –all the solutions of the best quality found can be returned by the solvers– can then be manually compared.

The proposed model includes a number of constraints, focusing on the area of the region and on the company performing the works. It should be noted that the set of constraints can be easily extended. For instance, the number of roadworks performed per time unit in the whole controlled region can be limited, or restrictions can be specified in terms of works performed on the same road of the urban network, or on directly connected roads. It is also possible to provide constraints that vary over time: for instance the maximum number of works that a company can perform in parallel may be affected by other commitments of the company in the modelled period, that should be taken into account. Constraints can also be specified in terms of minimum required traffic throughputs for roads or areas. From this perspective, the model can encode a notion of usual throughput of roads and expected reduction due to a given roadwork: the planning engine can take these elements into account in order to generate plans where a minimum throughput is guaranteed.

In the performed experiments, we focused on cases where no works were already planned for the controlled region during the modelled time period. However, roadworks that are already planned, or are already being performed can be included in the problem model. This can be done in two main ways: by introducing works which have a time window of the same size of the duration, and that corresponds to the period of time were works are being executed; or by implicitly modelling the work by increasing the number of works performed in the relevant area, by the relevant company, in the affected weeks. In the former case, the solver will have to take into account the work explicitly, as if it has yet to be planned. In the latter case, the work is modelled only in terms of its impact on the constraints and resources, so the solver does not need to take it into account when solving the problem.

When comparing the approach introduced in this paper with the preliminary work on using AI Planning for dealing with roadworks scheduling [8,11,15], it was possible to make a number of observations. In terms of quality of the generated schedules, measured as the average delay of planned roadworks with regards to the earliest possible start date, MIP-based approaches tend to provide consistently good solutions; Planning-based techniques instead show a very high variability, making virtually impossible to estimate whether using the approach will be beneficial or not. On the other hand, planning engines are generally able to provide solutions very quickly, while MIP-based solvers can be much slower. Given that, it is easy to highlight the high complementarity of the approaches. Planner can be used to quickly provide potentially low-quality scheduling of roadworks, that can be then refined using MIP approaches. Furthermore, schedules generated via Planning can be used as initial solutions for MIPs, that are then tasked to improve them.

Finally, it is worth noting that the proposed approach does not take into account uncertainty of the duration of roadworks. Here we assume that provided expected durations are reasonably accurate, with regards to the considered time unit. In our experimental analysis, given the selected time unit, any discrepancy of less than a week can be ignored. On the other hand, uncertainty can also be taken into account by providing an overestimated duration of the critical roadworks, or by generating problems where works at-risk have in turn different durations: comparing the generated solutions would then shed some light into the most robust scheduling.

4   Conclusion

In order to assist road agencies and authorities in the critical duty of planning essential roadworks, here we investigated the use of Mixed-Integer Programming techniques to provide an effective decision support tool for roadworks planning. Main contributions of this work are: (i) A formalisation of the roadworks planning problem; (ii) A MiniZinc model encoding the problem; and (iii) A thorough experimental analysis, that considers realistic scenarios and compared plans generated using three different MIP solvers, supported by the MiniZinc framework.

The performed experimental analysis demonstrates the extent to which the proposed approach is able to efficiently and effectively create a roadworks plan that satisfies the identified constraints, and follows the provided notion of quality. Remarkably, plans are generated very quickly –in a few seconds–, and this demonstrates the potential of the approach for being routinely used, also as a feasibility tool, and for assessing different constraints or resources. Furthermore, on the MIP side, we provided class of problems that can be used to benchmark the performance of MIP solvers.

Future work will focus on further validating the proposed approach in different urban regions, and in exploring approaches to explicitly represent uncertainty.

Acknowledgement. L. Chrpa was partially funded by the Czech Science Foundation (project no. 18-07252S). M. Vallati was partially supported by the EPSRC grant EP/R51343X/1 (AI4ME).

References

1. CSPLib language minizinc. http://www.csplib.org/Languages/MiniZinc
2. Bixby, E.R., Fenelon, M., Gu, Z., Rothberg, E., Wunderling, R.: MIP: theory and practice — closing the gap. In: Powell, M.J.D., Scholtes, S. (eds.) CSMO 1999. ITIFIP, vol. 46, pp. 19–49. Springer, Boston (2000). https://doi.org/10.1007/978-0-387-35514-6_2
3. Burningham, S., Stankevich, N.: Why road maintenance is important and how to get it done (2005)
4. Forrest, J., Lougee-Heimer, R.: CBC user guide. In: Emerging Theory, Methods, and Applications, pp. 257–277. INFORMS (2005)
5. Garrido-Jurado, S., Muñoz-Salinas, R., Madrid-Cuevas, F., Medina-Carnicer, R.: Generation of fiducial marker dictionaries using mixed integer linear programming. Pattern Recogn. **51**, 481–491 (2016)
6. Huerne, H.t., Berkum, E.v., Hermelink, W.: A multi objective framework to optimise planning of road works. In: 5th Eurasphalt and Eurobitume Congress (2012)
7. Hussain, R.S., Ruikar, K., Enoch, M.P., Brien, N., Gartside, D.: Process mapping for road works planning and coordination. Built Environ. Proj. Asset Manag. **7**(2), 157–172 (2017)
8. Ghallab, M., Nau, D., Traverso, P.: Automated Planning Theory and Practice. Elsevier, San Francisco (2004)
9. Nethercote, N., Stuckey, P.J., Becket, R., Brand, S., Duck, G.J., Tack, G.: MiniZinc: towards a standard CP modelling language. In: Bessière, C. (ed.) CP 2007. LNCS, vol. 4741, pp. 529–543. Springer, Heidelberg (2007). https://doi.org/10.1007/978-3-540-74970-7_38
10. Paquay, C., Schyns, M., Limbourg, S.: A mixed integer programming formulation for the three-dimensional bin packing problem deriving from an air cargo application. Int. Trans. Oper. Res. **23**(1–2), 187–213 (2016)
11. Scala, E., Haslum, P., Thiébaux, S., Ramírez, M.: Interval-based relaxation for general numeric planning. In: Proceedings of ECAI, pp. 655–663 (2016)
12. Schulte, C., Stuckey, P.J.: Efficient constraint propagation engines. ACM Trans. Program. Lang. Syst. (TOPLAS) **31**(1), 2 (2008)
13. Stuckey, P.J., Feydy, T., Schutt, A., Tack, G., Fischer, J.: The MiniZinc challenge 2008–2013. AI Mag. **35**(2), 55–60 (2014)
14. Valicka, C.G., et al.: Mixed-integer programming models for optimal constellation scheduling given cloud cover uncertainty. Eur. J. Oper. Res. **275**(2), 431–445 (2018)
15. Vallati, M., Chrpa, L., Kitchin, D.: How to plan roadworks in urban regions? A principled approach based on AI planning. In: Rodrigues, J.M.F., et al. (eds.) ICCS 2019. LNCS, vol. 11540, pp. 453–460. Springer, Cham (2019). https://doi.org/10.1007/978-3-030-22750-0_37
16. Ye, Y., Grossmann, I.E., Pinto, J.M.: Mixed-integer nonlinear programming models for optimal design of reliable chemical plants. Comput. Chem. Eng. **116**, 3–16 (2018)

A Tri-level Programming Framework for Modelling Attacks and Defences in Cyber-Physical Systems

Waleed Yamany$^{(\boxtimes)}$, Nour Moustafa, and Benjamin Turnbull

School of Engineering and Information Technology,
University of New South Wales at ADFA, Canberra 2600, Australia
w.yamany@student.adfa.edu.au,
{nour.moustafa,benjamin.turnbull}@unsw.edu.au

Abstract. Smart power grids suffer from coordinated attacks that exploit both their physical and cyber layers. It is an inevitable requirement to study power systems under such complex hacking scenarios to discover the system vulnerabilities and protect against those vulnerabilities and their attack vectors with appropriate defensive actions. This paper proposes an efficient tri-level programming framework that dynamically determines attacking scenarios, along with the best defensive actions in cyber-physical systems. A tri-level optimisation framework is proposed to fit the optimal decisions of defence strategies, malicious vectors and their operators for optimising the unmet demand while launching hacking behaviours. Defending resource allocation is designed using an evolutionary algorithm to examine coordinated attacks that exploit power systems. The proposed framework includes a Genetic Algorithm (GA) to solve each of the model levels in power systems. This proposed framework can flexibly model malicious vectors and their defences. IEEE 14-bus benchmark is employed to evaluate the proposed framework.

Keywords: Tri-level programming · Evolutionary algorithm · Power system · Coordinated attacks

1 Introduction

Cyber-Physical Systems (CPSs) are the underlying technologies of global critical infrastructure, that have different functions, such as managing the power supply and distribution, water management, and manufacturing. CPSs are uniquely susceptible to cyber-attacks, such as false-data injection, to breach vulnerable elements. The impact of such attacks would disrupt power supply and its services [1]. For example, in 2005, a distribution substation explosion in Moscow disrupted electricity distribution for an estimated 2 million customers [2,3]. Another incident, in 2015, an organised cyber-attack targeting the Ukraine power grid

The original version of this chapter was revised: numerous corrections were implemented. The correction to this chapter is available at https://doi.org/10.1007/978-3-030-64984-5_37

led to an estimated 225,000 customers losing power, with further analysis indicating that there was potential for this attack to be even more serious [4]. Due to these malicious attacks and increase in network connectivity between CPSs and corporate networks, there has been a significant work to understand the cyber risks and develop countermeasures.

Advanced cyber-attacks can exploit power systems that lead to a kinetic impact with unpredictable consequences. Cyber-attacks against CPSs would damage control systems [5]. There exist two types of attacks against control systems: cyber and physical. Cyber-attacks utilise malware for obtaining access to network components, such as routers and switches, while physical-attacks directly manipulate physical elements, such as sensors and actuators, to disrupt CPS operations [6]. Cyber-attacks have various and complex scenarios that could hack CPS's components, but existing security systems cannot identify those scenarios [7]. One of the main issues is that the coordinated attacks, including cyber and physical malicious techniques, would have a significant impact on electricity suppliers, as the power systems are prone to these attacks [8]. A typical trend adopted by attackers is the concealing of physical damage to the components of the power grid systems by injecting incorrect data in the control system or the communication network to cause cascading failures [9].

This study aims to design an optimal defence framework that can understand the interaction between coordinated attacks in power systems, and find the optimal defence strategies. Optimisation-based cybersecurity applications are an emerging field, aiming to develop new algorithms that could understand attack and defence interactions. By implementing information protection models, the overall security protection of power systems can lead to patching vulnerable nodes [10]. The development of optimisation-based cybersecurity techniques is complex, as multiple security controls should be chosen and each of them should defend against the manipulation of any potentially conflicting vulnerabilities [11]. The development of optimisation-based security applications can be applied to CPSs to optimise the control system's efficiency [12]. Optimisation models, especially bilevel [13] and min-max [14], can assist in formulating the relationship between attack and defence scenarios. Therefore, in this paper, we propose a tri-level optimisation model to investigate the best optimal defence strategy to reduce the unmet demand and hedging against coordinated attacks in power systems.

This paper is structured as follows. Section 2 outlines both the issues in CPS security for power grids, and outlines the current state of utilising optimisation in cybersecurity. Section 3 presents the model assumptions and structure, along with the mathematical formulation. Section 4 outlines the proposed approach. Numerical results and comparisons are presented in Sect. 5. Finally, Sect. 6 concludes the work and outlines future work in this work.

2   Existing Literature

There is significant academic work that investigates the impact of coordinated attacks on power systems. For example, Akl et al. [9] handled the formulation of an attack strategy based on incorrect data injection inside an AC-model causing voltage drop. The security of power systems against potential adversarial cyber-attacks was analysed by Hughes [15]. Zhang et al. [16] found that cyber-attacks posed a potential risk to the robustness of photovoltaic power systems. Extensive mitigation approaches have been conducted to prevent malicious attacks [17,18]. These schemes involved decentralised strategies for energy management [19], where the development of a decentralised electricity market was designed using the blockchain technology [20]. Deng et al. [18] explored the impact of coordinated attacks on power systems that inject incorrect information on measurements by phasor units, in order to neutralize the effects of physical-attacks. The unmet demand for electricity triggered by load redistribution of attacks combined with physical-attacks on the power systems generators was calculated by Xiang [21].

Various studies have been conducted on the use of tri-level optimisation algorithms to mitigate the damage triggered by attacks. These algorithms are known as the Defender-Attacker-Defender (DAD) paradigm. This paradigm aims to reduce the unmet demand caused by attacks and obtain the optimal defence technique that involves the hardening of the component, configuration of the topology, expansion of the transmission, and generation. Wu et al. [1] employed a DAD paradigm to determine the optimal defence strategy to reduce the unmet demand under the worst-case scenario of physical-attacks. Costa et al. [22] incorporated microgrid islanding with a topology configuration in the DAD paradigm to improve the flexibility of distribution against potential attacks.

In [23], the DAD paradigm was extended to respond to physical-attacks based on the resource expansion of renewable energy. Fang et al. [24] integrated switch installation and capacity expansion in power systems to improve the flexibility against malicious attacks. Ding et al. [25] studied the relation between the best optimal DAD paradigm defence strategy and the load types. Further, in [26], the uncertainty was incorporated into the DAD paradigm to choose the optimal defence strategy, where the authors utilised the probability distribution function to handle the uncertainty.

The majority of the existing approaches based on the DAD paradigm was focused on either cyber-attack or physical-attack, with considering a coordinated or synchronized attack in small-scale systems. The current research assumed that power failures because of malicious attacks would continue for many days [27]. In this paper, the optimisation model is employed for minimising the unmet demand caused by coordinating attacks operating within 24 h. Depending on the attack strategy, the attacker can choose the attack duration and which components would be attacked. The coordinated attack contains physical-attack scenarios which target the transmission lines and cyber-attack which target the protective relays. The cascading failures happen when the corresponding protective relays to the transmission line affected by the attack.

Table 1. Nomenclature

Sets and indices	
T	Time index, where t=1,2,..T
R	Protective relays (devices) index
L	Transmission lines index
N	Buses index
G	Generators index
RU_l	Upstream of protective relays
RD_l	Downstream protective relays
LU_n	Upstream voltage of bus n
LD_n	Downstream voltage of bus n
BG_g	Buses connected to generator g
GN_n	Generators connected to bus n
BU_l	Upstream connection of lines l
BD_l	Downstream connection of line l
Decision variables	
spd_l	Status of physical defend on line l
scd_r	Status of cyber defend on protective relays r, (0 or 1), 1 means the relay is cyber defended, 0 otherwise
spa_l	Status of physical-attack on line l,(0 or 1), 1 means the line is physically attacked, 0 otherwise
sca_r	Status of cyber-attack on the protective relays
at_t	Start time of attack/restoration
$LSH_{n,t}$	Unmet demand/Load shedding on bus n at time t
$po_{g,t}$	Generator power output at time t
$pof_{l,t}$	Line power flow at time t
$\theta_{n,t}$	Bus phase angle at time t
System variables	
et_t	Attack/restoration end at time t
SLU_l	The upstream status side of line l
SLD_l	The downstream status side of line l
SN_n	The status of bus n, (0 or 1), 1 means the bus is shutdown, 0 otherwise
Constants	
A_{max}	Maximum attacker budget
D_{max}	Maximum defender budget
AD	Attack duration/ restoration time
$RampU_g^{max}$	Raming up limit of the generator g
$RampD_g^{max}$	Raming down limit of the generator g
$opf_{g,t}$	Power output of generator g during normal operation at time t
B_l	Susceptance of transmission line l
pf_l^{max}	Maximum power flow on the line l
$load_{n,t,d}$	Demand/ load on bus n at time t

3   Problem Definition

Given an electrical bus system under possible coordinated attack strategies, on cyber (protective relays) layers and physical (transmission lines). The strategies might cause a bus shutdown if its lines and corresponding relays were targeted at the same time, also called cascading failure [3]. It worth to mention that during the normal operation, the power system is operated by a multi-period Direct Current Optimal Power Flow (DC-OPF) model. For mitigating the attack effects during the attack time, the proposed model is developed to obtain the system operation. It assumed that the attacker can hack multiple lines and corresponding protective relays simultaneously, within a limited budget and a certain attack duration. Also, the components (transmission lines or protective relays) which already defended, cannot be attacked. The system will back to normal operation when there is no unmet demand which caused by the attacker.

Based on a tri-level hierarchical structure, the interactions between the upper level (defender), the middle level (attacker), and the lower level (operator) are mathematically formulated. The main objective of the upper level is to minimise the unmet-demand/load-shedding resulting from the coordinated attack with considering the operator conditions. The defender chooses which relays and lines would be defended according to limited defended budget (the allowed defended components). According to the upper level decision variables (the defend strategy), the attacker in the middle level tries to maximise the unmet demand by choosing a specific time for starting the coordinate attacks with a certain attacker budget. At the lower level, the operator attempts to alleviate the damage caused by the attacker in the middle level, considering the prior information from the previous two levels.

3.1   Mathematical Formulation

Sets and indices, decision variables, system variables, along with constants are highlighted in Table 1, which is followed by a mathematical model.

$$
Min_{[spd_l,scd_r]}\left\{Max_{[spa_l,car,at_t]}Min_{[po_{g,t},pof_{l,t},LSH_{n,t},\theta_{n,t}]}\sum_{t\in AD}\sum_{n}LSH_{n,t}\right\}
$$

$$(1)$$

Subject to:

$$
\sum_{l} spd_l + \sum_{r} scd_r <= D_{max}
$$

$$(2)$$

$$
\sum_{l} spa_l + \sum_{r} sca_r <= A_{max}
$$

$$(3)$$

$$\sum_{t=1}^{T} at_t = 1 \tag{4}$$

$$\sum_{t=1}^{T} et_t = 1 \tag{5}$$

$$\sum_{t=1}^{T} at_t * et_{t+AD-1} = 1 \tag{6}$$

$$SLD_l = (1- \sum_{r \in RD_l} scd_r) \times \sum_{r \in RD_l} sca_r \times min\{(1-spd_l) \times spa_l + (\sum_{n \in BU_l} SN_n + \sum_{n \in BD_l} SN_n), 1\}, \forall l \tag{7}$$

$$SLU_l = (1- \sum_{r \in RU_l} scd_r) \times \sum_{r \in Ru_l} sca_r \times min\{(1-spd_l) \times spa_l + (\sum_{n \in BU_l} SN_n + \sum_{n \in BD_l} SN_n), 1\}, \forall l \tag{8}$$

$$SN_n = min\{(\sum_{l \in LU_n} SLU_l + \sum SLD_l), 1\} \forall n \tag{9}$$

Operator Constraints:

$$0 \leq Po_{g,t} \leq P_g^{max} \times (1 - \sum_{n \in NG(g)} SN_n), \forall g, t \in AD \tag{10}$$

$$- RampD_g^{max} \leq (p_{g,t+1} - po_{g,t}) \leq RampU_g^{max}, \forall g, t \in AD \tag{11}$$

$$- RampD_g^{max} * at_t \leq (p_{g,t} - opf_{g,t-1}) \leq RampU_g^{max} * at_t, \forall g, t \in AD \tag{12}$$

$$pof_{l,t} = B_l \times (\sum_{n \in BU_l} \theta_{n,t} - \sum_{n \in BD_l} \theta_{n,t}) \times (1 - \sum_{n \in BU_l} SN_n) \times (1 - \sum_{n \in BD_l} SN_n)\{1 - spa_l \times (1 - spd_l)\}, \forall l, t \in AD \tag{13}$$

$$- pf_l^{max} \leq pof_{l,t} \leq pf_l^{max}, \forall l, t \in AD \tag{14}$$

$$- \pi \leq \theta_{n,t} \leq \pi, \forall n, t \in AD \tag{15}$$

$$0 \leq LSH_{n,t} \leq load_{n,t}, \forall n, t \in AD \tag{16}$$

Equations (1)–(16) formulate the tri-level optimisation model, which describes the defender behavior (i.e., the upper level), the attacker action (i.e., the middle level), and the operator reaction (i.e., the lower level). In more detail,

Eq. (1) represents the single objective function for the three levels, which is the unmet demand during the coordinating attacks under the operation constrains. Equation (2) is the upper level constraint, which identifies the defender budget. Equations (3)–(6) determine the constraints of the middle level (attacker), which denote the optimal time of the attacks and the optimal components (the transmission lines or the protective relays) that should be attacked. The attacker budget (the number of attacked components) is calculated by Eq. (3). The start, end and duration of attacks was estimated by Eqs. (4)–(6).

The logical schema for describing the bus status (shutdown or not) is formulated by Eqs. (7)–(9). Equation (7) determines the downstream status of the line (SLD_l), Eq. (8) describes the upstream status of the line (SLU_l), and Eq. (9) defines the bus status (SN_n) corresponding to the previous line. The lower level (operator) constraints are represented by Eqs. (10)–(16). The output power of the generator is limited by Eq. (10). Depending on the generator power output during the normal operation, Eqs. (11) and (12) handle the ramping up and down limits of the generator, respectively. During the attacks, Eq. (13) handles the transmission line power flow. The limits of the capacity of power flow and bus phase angle are represented by the constraints (14) and (15), respectively.

4   Proposed Methodology

Based on the mathematical formulation illustrated above, the problem is defined as Mixed Integer Non-linear Programming (MINLP), where the production of continuous and binary variables occurs. Given the powerful of the Genetic Algorithm (GA), as one of the most popular population-based evolutionary algorithms, to handle such constrained optimisation problems [28]. Additionally, the ability of column and constrained generation ($C\&CG$) method for solving and linking multi-level linear and nonlinear problems [29, 30].

In this paper, a GA embedded with $C\&CG$ was proposed for solving the tri-level min-max optimisation framework to select the optimal defence strategy against the coordinated attacks. This framework consists of a master problem and a bilevel sub-problem. The master problem contains the upper (defender) level which represents the minimisation component. The sub-problem contains the hierarchical attacker-operator problem which represents the maximisation component, as shown in Fig. 1.

A single level GA, on the one hand, is utilised for solving the master problem to minimise the unmet demand/load shedding, Eq. (1), which returns the

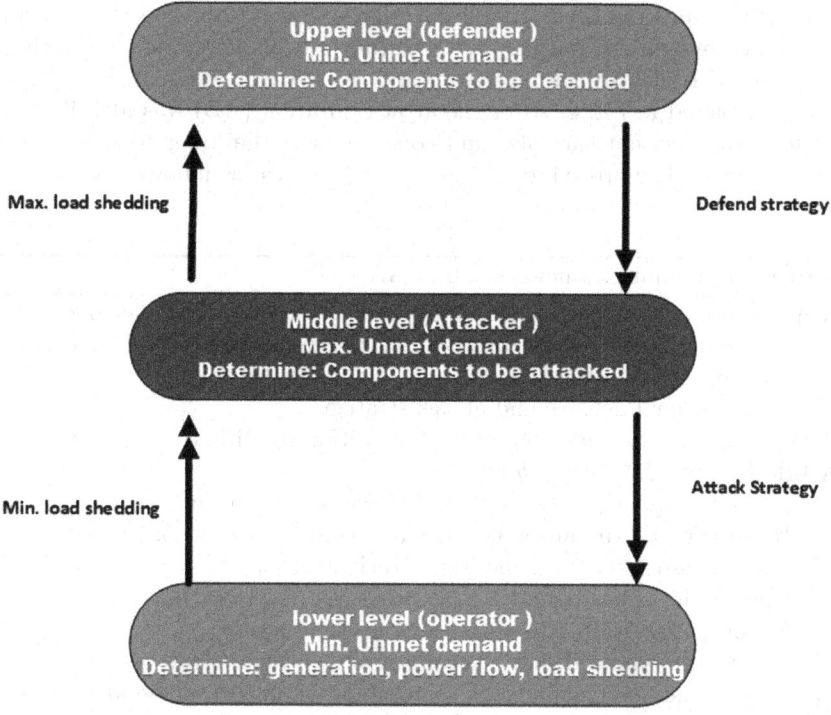

Fig. 1. Structure of tri-level framework

lower bound (LB) of the $C\&CG$, subject to the defender and operator variables and constraints using Eqs. (2) and (10)–(16), respectively. On the other side, a bilevel GA is used to handle the hierarchical interaction between the middle level (attacker) and the lower level (operator), Eqs. (3)–(16), which preserve the primal structure of the original formulation. Unlike the previously proposed methods in [1,3], where the bilevel problem merged into one level by using the duality method which leads to increase the problem dimension and computational efforts. The bilevel sub-problem returns the best attack strategy to feedback the master problem and the maximum unmet demand/load shedding which considers the upper bound (UB) of the $C\&CG$.

4.1   Main Framework

The $C\&CG$ heuristic method is used to connect the multiple GA optimisation to create a Defender-Attacker-Operator (DAO) tri-level model as illustrated in Algorithm 1 [9]. The master and sub-problem are solved through the iterative process until convergence tolerance is reached. DAO based on GA starts with a random initialisation to investigate the best attack strategy, where the initial defence strategy is set to zero and the lower and upper bound are set to negative and positive infinity, respectively. To obtain the load flow during the normal operation (input data), the DC-OPF model is solved by utilising Matpower 7.0b1 which installed in MATLAB R2018b [31]. These data determined the constant value of the generators' output and the direction of power flow through the power system to identify the upstream and downstream sides of the lines and buses, as depicted in Fig. 2. After the attack duration (AD) was identified, the number of the decision variables and constraints of the lower (operator) level was determined. The procedure of the iterative process as follows:

Algorithm 1: Main framework (DAO-GA)

Input: population size of the upper level, defender budget, defended components, attack duration, set the upper bound (UB) and lower bound (LB), threshold,

Output: optimal defence and attack strategies

Data: power flow under the normal operation conditions (DC-OPF)

1 **while** $(UB - LB) < threshold$ **do**
2   Perform Algorithm 2 to solve the bilevel sub-problem
3   Return the maximum unmet demand caused by the coordinated attacks associated with the best attack strategy
4   Update the upper bound $UB_t = min(UB_{t-1}, unmet\ demand)$
5   Perform Algorithm 4 to optimise the defend strategy
6   Return the unmet demand according best defence strategy
7   Update the lower bound $LB_t = max(LB_{t-1}, unmet\ demand)$

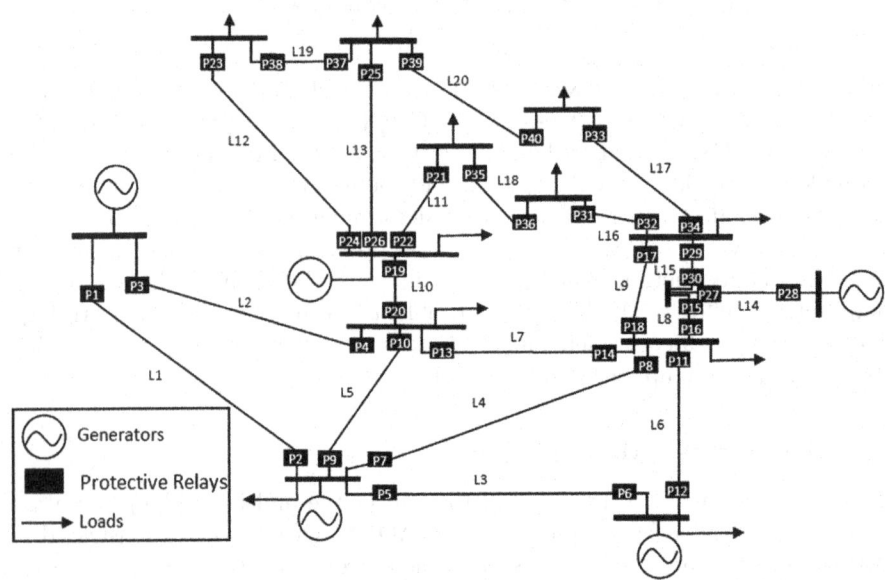

Fig. 2. IEEE14 bus system [3].

Firstly, the bilevel sub-problem solved by calling Algorithm 2 which takes the initial defence strategy as an input and returns the maximum unmet demand/Load shedding associated with the best attack strategy as an output. Then, the UB of the $C\&CG$ will be updated by choosing the minimum between the current unmet demand and the previous value of the UB. Secondly, the best attack strategy will forward to the master problem as an input. By calling Algorithm 4, the defender single level problem will be solved to minimise the unmet demand and obtain the best defence strategy. Then the LB will be updated by choosing the maximum between the current unmet demand and the previous value of the LB.

4.2   Bilevel Sub-problem

For solving the bilevel attacker-operator maximisation subproblem Algorithms 2 and 3 are proposed. The steps for handling the middle (attacker) level using GA is illustrated in Algorithm 2. The MATLAB inbuilt GA has been utilised with its default settings. Algorithm 2 starts with the random initialisation of the attacker population while considering the binary limitation. For each individual in the attacker population, the objective function is evaluated by calling the lower (operator) level, Algorithm 3, which returns minimum unmet demand. Afterward, the constraint violation is calculated and the number of function evaluations (NFE) will be updated. The evolutionary process will continue until the total number of function evaluation reach the maximum. For every iteration, a new population is created by applying the evolutionary process of GA over the old (parents) population. Again, by calling the operator level Algorithm 3, the objective function and constraint for every individual in the new population is evaluated. This algorithm returns the maximum unmet demand associated with the optimal attack strategy in terms of which lines and protective relays would be attacked.

Algorithm 2: Bilevel sub-problem

    Input: population size of the middle level (Pm), defend strategy, number of function evaluations NFE

    Output: optimal attack strategy for maximising the unmet demand

1   Generate initial population pop_m

2   perform Algorithm 3 to evaluate pop_m

3   **while** $NFE < TFE$ **do**

4   Evolve the current (parents) population to create a new child population pop_c

5   Perform Algorithm 3 to evaluate pop_c by calculate the objective function and constraints violation

6   Combine the the parents and child population $\{pop_t = pop_m + pop_c\}$

7   Sort pop_t

8   Reduce pop_t

9   select the best

10   Update NFE

Algorithm 3: Lower (operator) level

Input: population size of the lower level (Pl), defend strategy, attack strategy, maximum number of function evaluations TFE, and set $NFE = 0$

Output: minimising unmet demand during the coordinated attack

1 Generate initial population $poppop_l$
2 Evaluate pop_m by calculate the function evaluation and constraint violation of the lower level problem
3 Update the number of function evaluation NFE
4 **while** $NFE < TFE$ **do**
5 | create new child population
6 | Evaluate the child population by calculate the objective function and constraints violation
7 | Combine the the parents and child population $\{pop_t = pop_m + pop_c\}$
8 | Sort pop_t
9 | Reduce pop_t
10 | Select the best
11 | Update NFE

Algorithm 4: Upper(defender) level

Input: population size of the upper level (Pu), attack strategy, maximum number of function evaluations TFE

Output: Optimal defence strategy

1 Generate initial defender-operator population pop_u
2 Evaluate pop_u the objective function equation (1) and constraint violation equations (2) and (10)-(16)
3 **while** $NFE < TFE$ **do**
4 | create new child population pop_c
5 | Evaluate the child population by calculate the objective function and constraints violation
6 | Combine the the parents and child population $\{pop_t = pop_u + pop_c\}$
7 | Sort pop_t
8 | Reduce pop_t
9 | Select the best
10 | Update NFE

4.3   Master Problem

The master problem contains the decision variables from the upper (defender) level and lower (operator) level, while the middle (attacker) level variables are constants returned from sub-problem output. Based on the best attack strategy and with considering the operator condition, Algorithm 4 explains the steps to optimise the defence strategy and minimise the unmet demand. The algorithm begins with random initialisation and follows the same GA process considering the defender constraint Eq. (2). The algorithm returns the optimal defence strategy associated with the minimum unmet demand.

5   Experimental Results

The proposed framework has been tested on the IEEE 14-bus system [32]. This system contains 5 generators, 20 lines, 14 buses, and 11 loads. For each line, 2 protective relays were installed, giving a total number of 40. To illustrate the interactions between the defender and the attacker, several experiments were carried out with different criteria. These criteria include attacker budgets, attack duration, and defender budgets, were developed to judge the effects of different parameters on unmet demand. The proposed framework is coded using MAT-LAB R2018b in a Windows 10 64-bit system with an i7 core processor. The parameters for GA is setting as default value exist in MATALB R2018b except the population size which set as 100, 100 and 100 for attacker, operator and defender, respectively. The results reported after function evaluations reached 10000, 100000 and 100000 for attacker, operator and defender-operator, respectively.

Table 2. Results of different various attacker budgets (a_{max}) and attack duration (AD) with 3 defended components $(d_{max} = 3)$ for IEEE14-bus system

Attack duration	Attacker budget	Attacked components		Defended components
AD=2 h	$a_{max} = 2$	l_{11}, p_{21}	$at(15)$	l_3, l_{14}, p_{27}
	$a_{max} = 3$	l_1, l_{16}, p_{32}	$at(16)$	L_{13}, p_2, p_{36}
	$a_{max} = 4$	l_8, l_9, p_7, p_{17}	$at(18)$	l_5, l_{13}, l_{16}
	$a_{max} = 5$	$l_{17}, l_{20}, p_3, p_{25}, p_{40}$	$at(18)$	l_{12}, l_{17}, p_{19}
AD=3 h	$a_{max} = 2$	l_8, p_{15}, p_{16}	$at(8)$	l_1, l_{16}, p_7
	$a_{max} = 3$	l_1, l_{16}, p_{36}	$at(14)$	l_{13}, p_2, p_{36}
	$a_{max} = 4$	$l_{20}, p_{10}, p_{25}, p_{40}$	$at(17)$	l_7, p_8, p_{21}
	$a_{max} = 5$	$l_9, p_{17}, p_{20}, p_{27}, p_{28}$	$at(20)$	$l_3, l_{20}, p1$
AD=4 h	$a_{max} = 2$	l_7, p_{14}	$at(6)$	l_{12}, p_2, p_{19}
	$a_{max} = 3$	l_3, l_{19}, p_{38}	$at(17)$	l_{15}, p_8, p_{37}
	$a_{max} = 4$	$l_{13}, p_{25}, p_{31}, p_{39}$	$at(16)$	l_9, p_3, p_{38}
	$a_{max} = 5$	$l_5, l_{10}, l_{13}, p_{10}, p_{20}$	$at(19)$	l_2, p_{23}, p_{35}

The numerical results are depicted in Tables 2, 3, and Fig. 3, respectively. Tables 2 and 3 present the optimal defence and attack strategies with various attacker budgets, defender budgets, and attack times. It can be observed from theses tables, that optimal attacking and defending strategies change with attacker budgets, defender budgets, and attack duration. The results demonstrate the rationality of the attackers, as they prefer to select an attack strategy that causes cascading failures, which leads to an increase in the unmet demand.

Table 3. Results of different various defender budgets (d_{max}) and attack duration (AD) with 3 attacked components ($a_{max} = 3$) for IEEE14-bus system

Attack duration	Defender budget	Attacked components		Defended components
AD=2 h	$d_{max} = 1$	l_{18}, p_{26}, p_{36}	$at(3)$	l_{14}
	$d_{max} = 2$	l_5, l_8, p_{15}	$at(13)$	l_{16}, p_{28}
	$d_{max} = 3$	l_2, p_3, p_4	$at(13)$	l_3, l_9, l_{16}
	$d_{max} = 4$	l_6, p_{12}, p_{37}	$at(21)$	$l_{18}, p_{21}, p_{28}, p_{33}$
	$d_{max} = 5$	l_6, p_{12}, p_{37}	$at(21)$	$l_2, l_{13}, p_4, p_{11}, p_{30}$
AD=3 h	$d_{max} = 1$	l_3, l_{19}, p_5	$at(4)$	l_1
	$d_{max} = 2$	l_3, l_{19}, p_5	$at(14)$	l_{17}, p_{33}
	$d_{max} = 3$	l_1, l_{16}, p_{32}	$at(14)$	l_{13}, p_2, p_{36}
	$d_{max} = 4$	l_3, l_{19}, p_6	$at(16)$	$l_{15}, p_{10}, p_{30}, p_{32}$
	$d_{max} = 5$	l_{18}, p_{22}, p_{35}	$at(7)$	$l_5, l_9, p_8, p_{24}, p_{33}$
AD=4 h	$d_{max} = 1$	l_3, l_{19}, p_{38}	$at(17)$	l_8
	$d_{max} = 2$	l_3, l_{19}, p_{38}	$at(17)$	l_2, p_9
	$d_{max} = 3$	l_3, l_{19}, p_{38}	$at(17)$	l_{15}, p_8, p_{37}
	$d_{max} = 4$	l_3, l_{19}, p_{39}	$at(17)$	$l_{15}, p_3, p_{30}, p_{35}$
	$d_{max} = 5$	l_3, l_{19}, p_{38}	$at(14)$	$l_{10}, l_{16}, p_1, p_{23}, p_{40}$

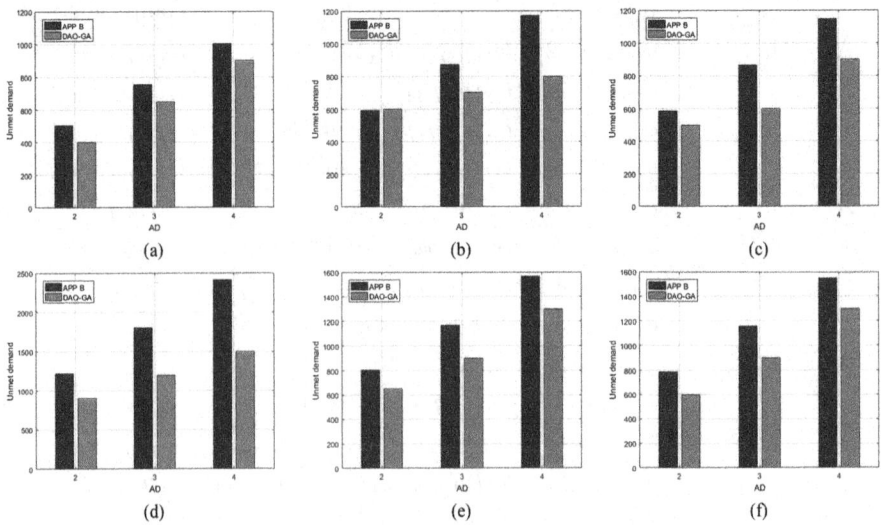

Fig. 3. Comparison of the proposed algorithm and App B based on the unmet demand for the IEEE 14-bus system with 3 defended components (a) $A_{max} = 2$; (b) $A_{max} = 3$; (c) $A_{max} = 4$; and with 3 attacked components (d) $D_{max} = 2$; (e) $D_{max} = 3$; (f) $D_{max} = 4$

Furthermore, the attack duration has an impact on choosing the optimal attack time. From the defender's perspective, the outcome shown in Tables 2 and 3 presents a successful distribution as well as the allocation of defending resources to avert the worst attack strategy. For example, most of the defence strategies focused on protecting the essential lines and relays connected directly to the generators for preventing the malicious attack. In addition, none of the defence strategies selects the transmission line and its corresponding relays to be defended simultaneously, which proves the optimal use of the defend resources. In order to test the efficiency of the proposed framework, a comparison is performed in terms of the unmet demand as a result of the coordinated attacks against (*App B*) [3] which is the most recent algorithm in the literature for the adopted model. This comparison is illustrated in Fig. 3, which reflects the improvement in the unmet demand for all cases compared with the rival algorithm. Also, it is observed that the proposed algorithm was able to achieve a stable value of unmet demand with an increase in the attacker budget. In summary, the proposed framework has shown its efficiency in comparison to the *App B* algorithm for determining the optimal defend strategy against coordinated attacks.

6   Conclusion and Future Work

This paper has presented a tri-level optimisation framework to optimise the attack-defence strategy in CPSs, specifically power systems. The interactions between the defenders, attackers and operators over a 24-hour period were formulated as a tri-level min-max optimisation problem to optimise the unmet demand. The framework is divided into a master and sub-problem, where the master problem was handled by a single level GA algorithm and the sub-problem was handled by a bilevel GA algorithm. The proposed framework was tested on the IEEE 14-bus system. The framework started with investigating the worst-case attack scenario then by the iterative process, the defence actions are optimised with the minimum unmet demand. According to the numerical results, the defending and attacking strategies vary with defender budgets, attacker budgets, and attack duration. Attacker preferred to initiate attacks which produce cascading failures, while the best optimal defence strategy was to prevent cascading failures. The unmet demand decreases with increasing the defender budget, while it increases with increasing the attacker budget and the attack duration. A future direction of this work will consider computing the boundaries of attack and defence strategies in complex power networks.

Acknowledgment. We would like to strongly thank Dr Amany Mohamed Mamdouh AKL, Research Associate at UNSW Canberra, for great support in producing this work.

References

1. Wu, X., Conejo, A.J.: An efficient tri-level optimization model for electric grid defense planning. IEEE Trans. Power Syst. **32**(4), 2984–2994 (2016)
2. Lu, W., Besanger, Y., Zamaï, É., Radu, D.: Blackouts: description, analysis and classification. Network **2**, 14 (2006)
3. Lai, K., Illindala, M., Subramaniam, K.: A tri-level optimization model to mitigate coordinated attacks on electric power systems in a cyber-physical environment. Appl. Energy **235**, 204–218 (2019)
4. Defense Use Case.: Analysis of the cyber attack on the Ukrainian power grid. Electricity Information Sharing and Analysis Center (E-ISAC), 388 (2016)
5. Keshk, M., Sitnikova, E., Moustafa, N., Hu, J., Khalil, I.: An integrated framework for privacy-preserving based anomaly detection for cyber-physical systems. IEEE Trans. Sustain. Comput. (2019)
6. Li, Z., Shahidehpour, M., Alabdulwahab, A., Abusorrah, A.: Analyzing locally coordinated cyber-physical attacks for undetectable line outages. IEEE Trans. Smart Grid **9**(1), 35–47 (2016)
7. Koroniotis, N., Moustafa, N., Sitnikova, E.: A new network forensic framework based on deep learning for internet of things networks: a particle deep framework. Future Gener. Comput. Syst. **110**, 91–106 (2020)
8. Machowski, J., Lubosny, Z., Bialek, J.W., Bumby, J.R.: Power System Dynamics: Stability and Control. Wiley, Hoboken (2020)
9. Akl, A., Sallam, K., Chakrabortty, R., Moustafa, N., Ryan, M., Choo, K.K.R.: A Novel Multi-level Optimization Framework for Enhancing Cyber-Physical Defenses in Smart Power Systems (2020). https://cloudstor.aarnet.edu.au/plus/s/D8JB2G6KGQtPSAT
10. Smith, J.C., Song, Y.: A survey of network interdiction models and algorithms. Eur. J. Oper. Res. **283**(3), 797–811 (2020)
11. Kamarudin, N.D., Rahayu, S.B., Zainol, Z., Rusli, M.S., Ghani, K.A.: Performance comparison of machine learning classifiers on aircraft databases. Def S & T Tech Bull (1985–6571) **11**(2), 154–169 (2018)
12. Liang, G., Weller, S.R., Luo, F., Zhao, J., Dong, Z.Y.: Distributed blockchain-based data protection framework for modern power systems against cyber attacks. IEEE Trans. Smart Grid **10**(3), 3162–3173 (2018)
13. Sinha, A., Malo, P., Deb, K.: A review on bilevel optimization: from classical to evolutionary approaches and applications. IEEE Trans. Evol. Comput. **22**(2), 276–295 (2017)
14. Cortés, J., Dullerud, G.E., Han, S., Le Ny, J., Mitra, S., Pappas, G.J.: Differential privacy in control and network systems. In: 2016 IEEE 55th Conference on Decision and Control (CDC), pp. 4252–4272 (2016)
15. Hughes, L., de Jong, M., Wang, X.Q.: A generic method for analyzing the risks to energy systems. Appl. Energy **180**, 895–908 (2016)
16. Zhang, P., Li, W., Li, S., Wang, Y., Xiao, W.: Reliability assessment of photovoltaic power systems: review of current status and future perspectives. Appl. Energy **104**, 822–833 (2013)
17. Lai, K., Illindala, M.S.: A distributed energy management strategy for resilient shipboard power system. Appl. Energy **228**, 821–832 (2018)
18. Deng, R., Zhuang, P., Liang, H.: CCPA: coordinated cyber-physical attacks and countermeasures in smart grid. IEEE Trans. Smart Grid **8**(5), 2420–2430 (2017)

19. Zhang, Y., Wei, W.: Decentralised coordination control strategy of the PV generator, storage battery and hydrogen production unit in islanded AC microgrid. IET Renew. Power Gener. **14**(6), 1053–1062 (2020)
20. Sikorski, J.J., Haughton, J., Kraft, M.: Blockchain technology in the chemical industry: machine-to-machine electricity market. Appl. Energy **195**, 234–246 (2017)
21. Xiang, Y., Wang, L., Liu, N.: Coordinated attacks on electric power systems in a cyber-physical environment. Electr. Power Syst. Res. **149**, 156–168 (2017)
22. Costa, A., Georgiadis, D., Ng, T.S., Sim, M.: An optimization model for power grid fortification to maximize attack immunity. Int. J. Electr. Power Energy Syst. **99**, 594–602 (2018)
23. Lin, Y., Bie, Z.: Tri-level optimal hardening plan for a resilient distribution system considering reconfiguration and DG islanding. Appl. Energy **210**, 1266–1279 (2018)
24. Nemati, H., Latify, M.A., Yousefi, G.R.: Coordinated generation and transmission expansion planning for a power system under physical deliberate attacks. Int. J. Electr. Power Energy Syst. **96**, 208–221 (2018)
25. Moreira, A., Strbac, G., Moreno, R., Street, A., Konstantelos, I.: A five-level MILP model for flexible transmission network planning under uncertainty: a min-max regret approach. IEEE Trans. Power Syst. **33**(1), 486–501 (2017)
26. Fang, Y., Sansavini, G.: Optimizing power system investments and resilience against attacks. Reliab. Eng. Syst. Saf. **159**, 161–173 (2017)
27. Davarikia, H., Barati, M.: A tri-level programming model for attack-resilient control of power grids. J. Mod. Power Syst. Clean Energy **6**(5), 918–929 (2018)
28. Deb, K., Agrawal, R.B., et al.: Simulated binary crossover for continuous search space. Complex Syst. **9**(2), 115–148 (1995)
29. Zeng, B., Zhao, L.: Solving two-stage robust optimization problems using a column-and-constraint generation method. Oper. Res. Lett. **41**(5), 457–461 (2013)
30. García, R., Marín, A., Patriksson, M.: Column generation algorithms for nonlinear optimization, i: convergence analysis. Optimization **52**(2), 171–200 (2003)
31. Zimmerman, R.D., Murillo-Sánchez, C.E., Thomas, R.J.: MATPOWER: steady-state operations, planning, and analysis tools for power systems research and education. IEEE Trans. Power Syst. **26**(1), 12–19 (2010)
32. Iyambo, P.K., Tzoneva, R.: Transient stability analysis of the IEEE 14-bus electric power system. In: AFRICON 2007, pp. 1–9 (2007)

Three-Way Framework Using Fuzzy Concepts and Semantic Rules in Opinion Classification

L. D. C. S. Subhashini[1,2,3], Yuefeng Li[1(✉)], Jinglan Zhang[1], and Ajantha S. Atukorale[2]

[1] Queensland University of Technology, Brisbane, Australia
shashikala.charles@hdr.qut.edu.au, {y2.li,jinglan.zhang}@qut.edu.au
[2] University of Colombo, Colombo, Sri Lanka
aja@ucsc.cmb.ac.lk
[3] University of Sri Jayewardenepura, Nugegoda, Sri Lanka
subhashini@sjp.ac.lk

Abstract. Binary classification is a critical process for opinion mining, which classifies opinions or user reviews into positive or negative classes. So far many popular binary classifiers have been used in opinion mining. The problematic issue is that there is a significant uncertain boundary between positive and negative classes as user reviews (or opinions) include many uncertainties. Many researchers have developed models to solve this uncertainty problem. However, the problem of broad uncertain boundaries still remains with these models. This paper proposes a three-way decision framework using semantic rules and fuzzy concepts together to solve the problem of uncertainty in opinion mining. This framework uses semantic rules in fuzzy concepts to enhance the existing three-way decision framework proposed by authors. The experimental results show that the proposed three-way framework effectively deals with uncertainties in opinions using relevant semantic rules.

Keywords: Opinion mining · Fuzzy logic · Semantic rules · Three-way decision

1 Introduction

Online reviews are one of the vital opinion sources on the Web. These reviews are analysed using machine learning algorithms. This has become a challenging issue with the uncertainty of reviews. Today, people write a large number of opinions and make them available via the Internet [1]. Most review collections are very long, and the reviews range widely between positive and negative views. Therefore, online customers find it challenging to make decisions based on such reviews. The growth of online customers has led to a reliance on reading previous customer opinions before new customers decide. A three-way framework has been proposed for opinion mining using fuzzy concept [5]. However, with the semantic

© Springer Nature Switzerland AG 2020
M. Gallagher et al. (Eds.): AI 2020, LNAI 12576, pp. 110–121, 2020.
https://doi.org/10.1007/978-3-030-64984-5_9

structure of the text data, these models can create unexpected results in some cases. In opinion classification models, the mechanism for managing uncertainties is a challenging task [10] as much user generated opinions contain uncertainties.

The critical challenge is to automatically deal with opinion uncertainties to enhance the performance of machine learning algorithms. Also, uncertainties are a problematic issue in opinion mining since many frequently used words may be non-relevant to a class. Therefore, a three-way decision framework is proposed using fuzzy concepts and deep learning [5]. The authors argue that using patterns or concepts to link several features to make the meaning clear is a possible solution for dealing with uncertainties in opinions. They put uncertain reviews into an uncertain boundary provisionally, and then design a more specific method to make the right decision [5].

The semantics of opinion is linguistic and philosophical meaning of opinions. It considers the relationship between words, phrases, signs, and symbols [19]. Most of the models ignore the semantics of opinion data, which is an important feature in opinion classification. People write text data in reviews and may use different semantic structures. In opinion mining models, it is a challenging task to consider the semantic rules within text data [16]. Some are developed considering the semantic aspects of opinions [15–17]. These models are less accurate than fuzzy models [5,7,17]. In binary opinion classification, it is hard to understand the difference between positive and negative categories. We used semantic rules in feature selection, which may result in a significant improvement in opinion classification using the three-way framework proposed by Subhashini et al. [5]. We propose to extend the three-way decision framework to select relevant reviews according to semantic rules [17], then identify the uncertain boundary and use a deep learning. The proposed three-way decision framework provides an elegant way to integrate fuzzy logic and semantic rules in a single umbrella to enhance the binary opinion classification.

We have conducted many experiments on two well-known datasets, the movie review and ebook review datasets. The proposed model achieved impressive performance in terms of F-measure. The significance tests show that the proposed framework is better than the baseline models. This paper is organized as follows: Sect. 2 presents the related work, Sect. 3 describes the proposed framework, and Sect. 4 gives evaluation results. Finally, conclusions are presented in Sect. 5.

2   Related Work

2.1   Opinion Mining

Liu [11] defined the opinion mining task that consists of a target of the opinion (entity), attributes of the target at which opinion mining is directed, and the sentiment (polarity), which are labeled as the positive, negative or neutral. The opinion mining includes feature selection, knowledge discovery and classification.

2.2　Feature Selection

Statistical feature selection methods are used to extract term-based features from a collection of reviews [5, 7]. Term based features are TF-IDF, BM25, Uniformity (Uni), and Inverted Conformity Frequency (ICF). The BM25 is a ranking function used to rank matching documents according to their relevance to a given query. When the Uni value is larger, it means that the term is more distinctive in a specific category. Li and Tsai [7] used Uni > 0.2 as a threshold value for feature selection. The ICF indicates term should frequently appear in a specific category. The smaller ICF value indicates, the term frequently appears in specific category. Li and Tsai [7] used $ICF < log(2)$ as a threshold value for feature selection.

Semantic features are used to extract the structure of the opinions [17, 18]. People write different semantic structures in their opinions. According to Samha et al. [17], there are frequent tags relevant for opinion mining. First, they did Part-of-Speech (POS) tagging for all the review collections. After that, they have identified frequent tags that appear first as aspect or opinion.

2.3　Knowledge Discovery

Fuzzy logic and pattern mining are the latest successful knowledge discovery methods in the area of opinion mining. Fuzzy Formal Concept Analysis (FFCA) [7] is a theory that combines fuzzy logic and Formal Concept Analysis (FCA) to represent the uncertainty of data. With the enhancement of fuzzy logic, researchers attempt to evaluate the fuzzy logic classifiers in opinion mining research [7, 12]. A fuzzy composition is a new approach to procuring classification. Pattern-based methods are also used as a higher-level method of discovering knowledge from text data [8, 9]. Pattern mining can discover sequencing terms that frequently co-occur in a customer review, and such set of terms can represent the knowledge of reviews effectively. Frequent patterns and closed patterns are frequently employed to represent knowledge and trends in a dataset [8]. These trends can be used to make decisions in business as well as for customers.

It is vital to select a reliable pattern, which enhances the efficiency of generating frequent itemsets without losing any item. The closed pattern [13] was proposed for handling a large number of frequent patterns.

2.4　Classification

In the classification process, the reviews can be classified into the relevant category. There are supervised, unsupervised and semi-supervised algorithms available for the classification process. Recently, deep learning is employed for the classification using a set of hidden layers. Convolutional Neural Networks (CNNs) is the most popular neural network model used in recent years for opinion mining with a significant performance [3, 4]. The advantage is that parameter sharing saves memory when compared to traditional models. The fuzzy composition is a recently used method for classification [7].

3 Proposed Model

In our model, we first select the reviews according to frequent tags defined in Samha et al. [17]. We select the reviews based on the defined frequent tags. As there are many uncertainties in user reviews, there is an uncertain boundary, a margin that includes both positive and negative samples, between positive and negative reviews [10]. A three-way based classification framework was used to address the problem of uncertain boundary for binary classification [5]. It includes two transformations: 'two-way to three-way' (obtaining three regions: the positive region, negative region and uncertain boundary), and then 'three-way to two-way' (classifying the uncertain boundary into positive and negative regions) [10]. It also used a vector space model to find the uncertain boundary and then classify the uncertain boundary. The problem with using this existing framework for opinion mining is that the uncertain boundary is huge since people are writing different format of semantic structures when they expressed their opinions. Unexpected results could occur due to different semantic structure used in opinions. In this paper, we extend the three-way decision framework for opinion mining using semantic rules [5].

3.1 Select Relevant Reviews and Features for Generating Formal Concepts

In our model, we first select the reviews according to Samha et al. [17] defined frequent tags as in Algorithm 1. According to the algorithm, a collection of reviews are POS tags using Stanford POS tagger. Our post tags algorithms are implemented using Samha et al. [17] frequent tags as follows.

- [NN] [VBZ] [RB][JJ] e.g. "software is absolutely terrible"
- [NNS][VBP] [JJ] e.g. "pictures are razor-sharp"
- [NN][VBZ][RB][JJ] e.g. "earpiece is very comfortable"
- [NN] [VBZ] [JJ] e.g. "sound is wonderful"
- [NNS] [VBP] [RB] e.g. "transfers are fast"
- [VBZ][JJ] e.g. "looks nice"
- [JJ][NN] [IN] [NN] e.g. "superior piece of equipment"
- [JJ] [NN] [CC] [NN] e.g. "decent size and weight"
- [RB][JJ][TO][VB] [DT] [NN] e.g. "very confusing to start the program"
- [VBD] [NN] e.g. "improved interface"
- [JJ] [VBG] e.g. "great looking"

Relevant reviews are selected 93.7% and 95.6% from movie and ebook review datasets respectively. After that, features are selected using three feature selection indexes [5].

We found that term-based feature selection approaches suffered from polysemy and synonymy [9] when using them for dealing with uncertainties within user reviews. Currently, a popular way of solving this problem in text mining is to extend low-level term spaces to higher-level patterns or concepts [5,8].

Algorithm 1. Select relevant semantic tags

Require: collection of reviews R and Frequent tag list F_t
Ensure: $R_{POS} \in F_t$
1: **for** each r **do**
2:     POS tagging $= R_{ipos}$
3: **end for**
4: **for** $R_{ipos} \in R_{POS}$ **do**
5:     **if** $(R_{ipos} \in F_t$) **then**
6:         $L_i = R_{ipos}$
7:         L_i append L_{ipos}
8:     **end if**
9: **end for**

Formal concepts [14] have elegant properties; however, closed patterns only discuss terms' binary appearances and long-closed patterns have very low frequency [21]. To solve these issues, fuzzy concepts were proposed by researchers [5]. They select some relevant term features firstly to reduce the time complexity for finding concepts; then using fuzzy composition to find the associations between concepts and categories.

In this research, selected frequent tags [17] are pre-processed and applied BM25, Uni and ICF (three feature selection techniques) to find the relevant terms [5]. The output will be a set of terms as shown in Table 1. In the table r1,r2,r3,...r7 are refers to reviews.

Table 1. Reviews after feature selection

Review	Funny	Good	Pretty	Great	Comedy	Awful
r1	x		x			
r2	x	x		x		
r3	x		x			
r4		x		x		x
r5	x		x		x	
r6	x	x		x		
r7	x	x				x

In this model multiple indexes of $BM25 > 30$, Uni > 0.2 and $ICF < \log(2)$ are used [5]. The three conditions were checked simultaneously and if one condition did not satisfy, the term is eliminated. Table 1 shows an example of feature selection, where we assume that term set $T = \{funny, good, ..., comedy, awful\}$ and review set $R = \{r_1, r_2, ..., r_7\}$.

The frequency of terms might vary according to user reviews' size. The normalization values of BM25 weights are calculated [5]. A threshold is used to reduce the number of noisy terms. Table 2 shows a simple example of the normalized BM25 weights, where the threshold is 0.5 and we simply assume that all selected terms' normalized weights $nBM25 > 0.5$.

Table 2. Reviews after normalization

Review	Funny	Good	Pretty	Great	Comedy	Awful
r1	0.82		0.70			
r2	0.82	0.69		0.61		
r3	0.82		0.70			
r4		0.69		0.61		0.63
r5	0.82		0.70		0.68	
r6	0.82	0.69		0.61		
r7	0.82	0.69				0.63

All closed patterns and their cover sets which are generated from Table 2 is shown in Table 3. We found that identified patterns are larger than the terms. The minimum support is used to control the size of discovered patterns. The discovered closed patterns are further processed to determine the formal concepts using a suitable minimum support as the threshold [5]. Table 4 shows the selected formal concepts from closed patterns $CP = \{p_1, p_2, p_3, p_4, p_5\}$.

Table 3. Closed patterns

Patterns	Terms	Coverset
p1	Funny, Pretty	r1, r3, r5
p2	Funny, Good, Great	r2, r6
p3	Good, Great, Awful	r4
p4	Funny, Pretty, Comedy	r5
p5	Funny, Good	r2, r6, r7

Table 4. Selected formal concepts

Concept	Intent	Extent	Original pattern
c1	Funny, Pretty	r1, r3, r5	p1
c2	Funny, Good	r2, r6, r7	p5

3.2   Fuzzy-Based Three-Way Decisions

According to the three-way decision framework proposed by Subhashini et al. [5] the relationship between concept and category is generated using fuzzy composition. Algorithm 2 illustrates the idea for classifying user reviews into three regions: the positive region (POS), negative region (NEG), and the uncertain boundary (BND). It firstly describes the training process (the first for loop) to calculate the relation I_{C-Catg} (a concept-category matrix) by using the fuzzy composition. It then calculates a fuzzy value for each new review r to a category j (see the second for-loop). At last, it determines the three regions (POS, NEG, and BND) based on these fuzzy values for a given unlabeled review set U.

Algorithm 2. Three-way Classification

Require: C, I_{C-T}, I_{T-Catg}, U, two categories: $j = 1$ and $j = 0$ and an experimental coefficient δ
Ensure: I_{C-Catg} and three regions: POS, NEG, BND
1: **for** each j **do**
2:     **for** $c_i \in C$ **do**
3:         $I_{C-Catg}(i,j) =$
4:         $max_{k \in T} min[I_{C-T}(i,k), I_{T-Catg}(k,j)]$
5:     **end for**
6: **end for**
7: **for** $r \in U$ **do**
8:     $C_r = \{c \in C | intent(c) \subseteq r\}$
9:     **for** j **do**
10:         $f_j(r) = max_{c_i \in C_r}[I_{C-Catg}(i,j)]$
11:     **end for**
12: **end for**
13: **for** $r \in U$ **do**
14:     $POS = \{r \in R, f_{j=1}(r) - f_{j=0}(r) > \delta\}$
15:     $NEG = \{r \in R, f_{j=0}(r) - f_{j=1}(r) > \delta\}$
16:     $BND = \{r \in R, |f_{j=0}(r) - f_{j=1}(r)| \leq \delta\}$
17: **end for**

3.3 Boundary Classification

Algorithm 3. Deciding parameter δ

Require: R, I_{C-T} two categories: $j = 1$ and $j = 0$
Ensure: δ
1: **for** $r \in R$ **do**
2:     **for** each j **do**
3:         $f_j(r) = \sum_{t_k \in r, intent(c_i) \subseteq r} I_{C-T}(i,k)$
4:     **end for**
5:     $f(r) = \frac{f_0(r) + f_1(r)}{2}$
6: **end for**
7: **for** $r \in R$ **do**
8:     let $\mu = \frac{1}{|R|} \sum_{r \in R} f(r)$
9: **end for**
10: let $\delta = \sqrt{\frac{\sum_{r \in R}(f(r) - \mu)^2}{|R| - 1}}$

Algorithm 3 [5] uses a parameter δ (a very small value) to classify reviews into three regions. It is tough to decide the class of a review when its fuzzy values to the two classes are very close.

Error rates of the three regions when we use fuzzy values to determine the positive and negative regions for two datasets, where we let δ = very small value.

It is evident that the uncertain boundary (BND) includes a lot of uncertain reviews. Table 5 and Table 6 show the size and the percentage of the uncertain boundary in both movie review and ebook review datasets, respectively [5].

Table 5. Boundary reviews-movie review dataset

Category	Boundary reviews	Percentage
Positive	115	11.5%
Negative	102	10.2%
Total	217	21.7%

Table 6. Boundary reviews-ebook review dataset

Category	Boundary reviews	Percentage
Positive	104	10.4%
Negative	101	10.1%
Total	205	20.5%

In this sub-section, we also develop a method to further classify the uncertain boundary (BND) as the data in BND are not linearly separable. In this paper we use word embedding to do the mapping [5]. It can find a higher dimensional space easily. Word embedding models map each word from the vocabulary to a vector of real numbers. We use word2vec model [2] in our experiments and each word was encoded by an 8-dimension vector, that is,

$$\overrightarrow{w} = (x_1, x_2, ..., x_8)$$

for all words $w \in \Omega$, where x_i are real numbers. Algorithm 4 describes the new idea for integrating word embedding vectors and the terms (with assigned fuzzy values) in the formal concepts. The first for loop firstly get the related concepts of each word $w \in \Omega$ for the positive class j. It then uses the average fuzzy value to update the word vector, where $\overrightarrow{e_i}$ are unit vectors. In the second for loop it uses Z-core normalization to normalize the word vectors by using the average vector (μ) and the standard deviation s. The time complexity is $O(|\Omega| * |C|)$ that is decided by the first for loop.

CNN classifier for the uncertain boundary, which consists of an input layer, two convolution layers, two max-pooling layers, and a fully connected layer with softmax as the activation function. The outputs of algorithm 4 are fed to the CNN for the input layer [5].

For using deep learning, people usually transfer textual features into numerical vectors (e.g., using word2vec [2], a word embedding technique to generate a vector for each word). This process requires a huge collection of documents that are related to the given topic; however, normally, the extensive collection is not designed specially for this opinion classification task. Therefore, the input vectors to a deep leaning algorithm describe more general knowledge for the opinion classification. Also, deep learning does not have the capacity for dealing with uncertainties in features; therefore, it is tough to produce satisfactory results for using deep learning directly.

Algorithm 4. New Word Embedding Vector

Require: Ω is a set of words, each word $w \in \Omega$ is a word2vector $\overrightarrow{w}$; and C is the concept set

Ensure: new word vectors $\hat{w}$ for all words $w \in \Omega$.

1: **for** $w \in \Omega$ **do**
2:     let $C_w = \{c \in C | w \in intent(c)\}$ and $j = 1$
3:     $\overrightarrow{w} = \overrightarrow{w} + \sum_{i=1}^{8} \left(\frac{\sum_{c_j \in C_w} I_{C-Catg}(i,j)}{|C_w|} \overrightarrow{e_i} \right)$
4: **end for**
5: **for** $w \in \Omega$ **do**
6:     let $\overrightarrow{\mu} = \frac{\sum_{w \in \Omega} \overrightarrow{w}}{|\Omega|}$
7:     let $s = \sqrt{\frac{1}{|\Omega|} \| \overrightarrow{w} - \overrightarrow{\mu} \|}$
8:     $\hat{w} = \frac{1}{s}(\overrightarrow{w} - \overrightarrow{\mu})$
9: **end for**

---

4   Evaluation

To evaluate the performance of the proposed technique, we adopted three measurements namely, precision, recall, F-measure, and pair wise t-test. Then we compared these measures to the baseline models.

4.1   Dataset

The movie review and ebook review datasets [7] are used in this research. Both collections contain 2000 reviews, and 1000 reviews for each category. However, for evaluation, both positive and negative reviews in the testing sets are used.

4.2   Baseline Models

In this research, we provide a comprehensive evaluation of the proposed model, we have selected six baseline models.

- Three-way decision framework of Subhashini et al. [5].
- Li and Tsai's [7] fuzzy model.
- Support Vector Machine(SVM) which is outperformed model in opinion mining [7].
- CNN model of Kim [4] which is a deep learning model for opinion mining.
- Graph Convolutional Networks (GCN) [20] which is a recent model developed using GCN.
- Attention Network [6] used Multi-sentiment resource Enhanced Attention Network (MEAN) to alleviate the problem by integrating three kinds of sentiment linguistic knowledge.

4.3 Results

In order to evaluate the effectiveness of the proposed model, we compare the results with existing classification models as in Table 7 and Table 8. It is evident that the proposed model has the best performance in the two datasets comparing with baseline models. In Table 8 we have not included CNN [4], GCN [20] and Attention Network [6] because those models were not evaluated with the ebook review dataset.

We also conducted statistical significance testing (a two-tailed t-test). The results for the above models are shown in Table 9 and Table 10. It is obvious that all p-values <0.05 in the two tables, where 0.05 is a recommended threshold for the significance testing. The t-test results show that the proposed model is better than the five baseline models.

In our model we removed reviews which are not followed in Samha's [17] frequent tag list. Thereafter, feature selection is done based on three feature selection indexes. Experiment results are showed that selecting relevant reviews based on frequent tags can improve the F-measure of the model.

The main advantage of the proposed model is that it can ascertain uncertain reviews in the boundary, then conduct a deep learning algorithm. The model can identify the relevant semantic structures from a collection of reviews. Despite, there are different semantic structures that can be available for a extensive collection of reviews, therefore, important reviews may be omitted from the classification process of reviews. The main challenge is to identify all semantic structures from a collection of reviews.

Table 7. F-measure of state-of-the-art models: movie review

Model	Precision	Recall	F-measure
Proposed model	**0.9502**	**0.9512**	**0.9506**
Three-way decision framework	**0.9404**	**0.9509**	**0.9467**
FFCM	0.8870	0.8840	0.8800
CNN	Not available	Not available	0.8150
SVM	0.8770	0.8690	0.8730
GCN	Not available	Not available	0.7674
Attention	Not available	Not available	0.8450

Table 8. F-measure of state-of-the-art models: eBook review

Model	Precision	Recall	F-measure
Proposed model	**0.9811**	**0.9821**	**0.9815**
Three-way decision framework	**0.9710**	**0.9777**	**0.9744**
FFCM	0.9509	0.9508	0.9509
SVM	0.9382	0.9381	0.9382

Table 9. P-values-two tailed-movie review

Model	Precision	Recall	F-measure
Proposed model	**0.9811**	**0.9821**	**0.9815**
Three-way decision framework	**0.9710**	**0.9777**	**0.9744**
FFCM	0.9509	0.9508	0.9509
SVM	0.9382	0.9381	0.9382

Table 10. P-values-two-tailed-eBook review

Model	P values
Proposed model	**0.0010**
Three-way decision framework	**0.0013**
FFCM	0.0219
SVM	0.0101

5 Conclusion

This paper presents an extended three-way based framework for binary opinion classification. The framework extends semantic rules to select relevant reviews. This framework implies that incorporating relevant semantic rules can be enhanced the model F-measure and provide a promising way to construct an opinion classifier using fuzzy concepts. The experimental results show that our model achieved significant performance compared to all other baseline models. The contribution made by the proposed framework is an innovative feature selection method. The performance of the proposed framework relies on selected semantic frequent tags. It is tough to incorporate all semantic structures into the model. It remains as future work to find efficient implementation on this.

Acknowledgment. This work was supported in part by the Queensland University of Technology, Australia, University Grant Commission, Sri Lanka, and University of Colombo School of Computing, Sri Lanka.

References

1. Ciullo, F., Zucco, C., Calabrese, B., Agapito, G., Guzzi, P.H., Cannataro, M.: Computational challenges for sentiment analysis in life sciences. In: 2016 International Conference on High Performance Computing and Simulation (HPCS), pp. 419–426. IEEE (2016)
2. Goldberg, Y., Levy, O.: word2vec explained: deriving Mikolov et al'.s negative-sampling word-embedding method. arXiv preprint arXiv:1402.3722 (2014)

3. Hughes, M., Li, I., Kotoulas, S., Suzumura, T.: Medical text classification using convolutional neural networks. Stud. Health Technol. Inform. **235**, 246–50 (2017)
4. Kim, Y.: Convolutional neural networks for sentence classification. arXiv preprint arXiv:1408.5882 (2014)
5. Subhashini, L.D.C.S., Li, Y., Zhang, J., Atukorale, A.: Integration of fuzzy and deep learning in three-way decisions. In: Proceedings of the 2020 IEEE International Conference on Data Mining Workshop. ICDMW 2020. IEEE (2020)
6. Lei, Z., Yang, Y., Yang, M., Liu, Y.: A multi-sentiment-resource enhanced attention network for sentiment classification. arXiv preprint arXiv:1807.04990 (2018)
7. Li, S.T., Tsai, F.C.: A fuzzy conceptualization model for text mining with application in opinion polarity classification. Knowl.-Based Syst. **39**, 23–33 (2013)
8. Li, Y., Algarni, A., Albathan, M., Shen, Y., Bijaksana, M.A.: Relevance feature discovery for text mining. IEEE Trans. Knowl. Data Eng. **27**(6), 1656–1669 (2015)
9. Li, Y., Algarni, A., Zhong, N.: Mining positive and negative patterns for relevance feature discovery. In: Proceedings of the 16th ACM SIGKDD International Conference on Knowledge Discovery and Data Mining, pp. 753–762. ACM (2010)
10. Li, Y., Zhang, L., Xu, Y., Yao, Y., Lau, R.Y.K., Wu, Y.: Enhancing binary classification by modeling uncertain boundary in three-way decisions. IEEE Trans. Knowl. Data Eng. **29**(7), 1438–1451 (2017)
11. Liu, B.: Sentiment analysis and subjectivity. Handb. Nat. Lang. Process. **2**, 627–667 (2010)
12. Nadali, S., Murad, M.A.: Fuzzy semantic classifier to determine the strength levels of customer product reviews. In: Proceedings of the International Conference on Advances in Computer Science and Application (2012)
13. Pasquier, N., Bastide, Y., Taouil, R., Lakhal, L.: Discovering frequent closed itemsets for association rules. In: Beeri, C., Buneman, P. (eds.) ICDT 1999. LNCS, vol. 1540, pp. 398–416. Springer, Heidelberg (1999). https://doi.org/10.1007/3-540-49257-7_25
14. Poelmans, J., Kuznetsov, S.O., Ignatov, D.I., Dedene, G.: Formal concept analysis in knowledge processing: a survey on models and techniques. Expert Syst. Appl. **40**(16), 6601–6623 (2013)
15. Poria, S., Cambria, E., Gelbukh, A., Bisio, F., Hussain, A.: Sentiment data flow analysis by means of dynamic linguistic patterns. IEEE Comput. Intell. Mag. **10**(4), 26–36 (2015)
16. Samb, S.M.K., Kandé, D., Camara, F., Ndiaye, S.: Improved bilingual sentiment analysis lexicon using word-level trigram. In: 2019 IEEE 5th International Conference on Computer and Communications (ICCC), pp. 112–119. IEEE (2019)
17. Samha, A.K., Li, Y., Zhang, J.: Aspect-based opinion extraction from customer reviews. arXiv preprint arXiv:1404.1982 (2014)
18. Turney, P.D.: Thumbs up or thumbs down?: Semantic orientation applied to unsupervised classification of reviews. In: Proceedings of the 40th Annual Meeting on Association for Computational Linguistics, pp. 417–424. Association for Computational Linguistics (2002)
19. Van Dijk, T.A.: Semantic discourse analysis. Handb. Discourse Anal. **2**, 103–136 (1985)
20. Yao, L., Mao, C., Luo, Y.: Graph convolutional networks for text classification. arXiv preprint arXiv:1809.05679 (2018)
21. Zhong, N., Li, Y., Wu, S.T.: Effective pattern discovery for text mining. IEEE Trans. Knowl. Data Eng. **24**(1), 30–44 (2012)

Evolutionary Computation

Minimising Cycle Time in Assembly Lines: A Novel Ant Colony Optimisation Approach

Dhananjay Thiruvady⬛, Atabak Elmi⬛, Asef Nazari$^{(\boxtimes)}$⬛,
and Jean-Guy Schneider⬛

School of IT, Deakin University, Geelong, Australia
{dhananjay.thiruvady,atabak.elmi,asef.nazari,
jeanguy.schneider}@deakin.edu.au

Abstract. We investigate the problem of mixed model assembly line balancing with sequence dependent setup times. The problem requires that a set of operations be executed at workstations, in a cyclic fashion, and operations may have precedences between them. The aim is to minimise the maximum cycle time incurred across all workstations. The simple assembly line balancing problem (with precedence constraints) is proven to be NP-hard and is consequently computationally challenging. In addition, we consider setup times and mixed model product types, thereby further complicating the problem. In this study, we propose a novel ant colony optimisation (ACO) based heuristic, which unlike previous approaches for the problem, focuses on learning permutations of operations. These permutations are then mapped to workstations using an efficient assignment heuristic, thereby creating feasible allocations. Moreover, we develop a mixed integer programming formulation, which provides a basis for comparing the quality of solutions found by ACO. Our numerical results demonstrate the efficacy of ACO across a number of problems. We find that ACO often finds optimal solutions for small problems, and high quality solutions for medium-large problem instances where mixed integer programming is unable to find any solutions.

Keywords: Assembly line balancing · Sequence dependent setup times · Minimise cycle times · Ant colony optimisation · Mixed integer programming.

1 Introduction

Assembly line balancing deals with subdividing a manufacturing process into simple operations and to assign those operations to workstations to produce goods in an optimal fashion. Assembly lines generally consist of a set of workstations connected by material handling systems including moving belts or robots [12]. Finding an optimal assignment of operations to workstations considering precedences between operations, operation durations and the availability

© Springer Nature Switzerland AG 2020
M. Gallagher et al. (Eds.): AI 2020, LNAI 12576, pp. 125–137, 2020.
https://doi.org/10.1007/978-3-030-64984-5_10

of workstations is called an assembly line balancing problem (ALBP) [11]. The problem has several categories depending on line layouts, variability of durations, objective functions, and so forth. For example, a type I ALBP (ALBP-I) tries to minimise the number of workstations for given cycle time. In contrast, a type II ALBP (ALBP-II) minimises the cycle time or maximises the throughput for a given number of workstations. Moreover, there are other types, namely E and F, where type F focuses on maximising an effectiveness measure and type E is used when there is no specific objective [3].

Assembly line problems are also categorised based on the number of models processed on a line. A single model problem (SALBP), an early variant, aimed to address a high volume of demand for a particular product. To respond to diversified customer requirements for products and to avoid constructing multiple assembly lines, the multi-model and mixed model variants (MMALBP) variants emerged. Here, several models of a product are considered simultaneously but still only a single assembly line [11]. Production systems differ substantially, thus leading to new problem variants. The various ALBP type problems include general (GALBP), resource constrained (RCALBP), robotic (RALBP), worker assignment (ALWABP), robotic (RMMALBP), etc. Of particular interest in this study are the type II SALBP and MMALBP problems with setup times, which are abbreviated as SALBPS and MMALBPS, respectively [1,3,17].

ALBP, in its simplest form, is known to be computationally intractable or NP-hard [7]. A large body of research is devoted to solve the problem in a time efficient manner. Several exact algorithms have been proposed for the problem, but to deal with its complexity, incomplete approaches including dynamic programming, heuristics and meta-heuristics have been attempted [12,15]. Simaria and Vilarinho [14] maximise the production rate of a line (equivalent to minimising cycle time of a line) in a MMALBP with parallel workstations for a pre-determined number of operators using a genetic algorithm. The studies by Kilincci [9] and Hossain [8] investigate SALBP-II, where the first study proposes bounded exact methods while the second study proposes a progressive modelling approach. Seyed-Alagheband et al. [13] propose a simulated annealing algorithm to solve a general assembly line balancing problem with setups (GALBPS-II) by using the Taguchi method. In this work, the author represented the problem as an object-oriented graph. Zheng et al. [20] proposed a version of ant colony optimisation (ACO) method in solving a type II ALBP which essentially searches for different combinations of tasks for each workstation. Despite several approaches (exact and incomplete) being proposed for variants of the ALBP, there is still substantial room for improvement.

In this study, we propose a novel ACO based heuristic and adapt a mixed integer programming approach for tackling the MMALBPS.[1] Previous studies with the MMALBPS have focused on either modifying solutions based on a neighbourhood structure [19] or the assignment of operations to workstations [1,10]. In contrast to these approaches (including also ACO), our ACO approach splits the solution creation into two components. The motivation for this is that ACO

---

[1] Note, SALBPS is a special case of MMALBPS.

is very effective at 'sequence learning' but not as effective in dealing with complex constraints. Hence, the first component learns sequences (or equivalently permutations) of operations (which ACO is very effective at) and the second component takes a sequence and maps it into a feasible assignment of operations to workstations. We show that this approach is indeed very effective for MMALBPS, and our results demonstrate that ACO can find high quality (often optimal) solutions in short time-frames. Moreover, ACO scales very efficiently with problem size.

The paper is organized as follows: Sect. 2 defines the MMALBPS problem and provides its mixed integer programming (MIP) formulation. Section 3 discusses the ACO-based heuristic specifically designed for this problem. Section 4 details the experimental setting followed by a presentation of the results. Section 5 concludes the paper and provides some insights into future work.

2   Problem Definition and Mathematical Model

The MMALBPS can be formally described as follows. We are given N operations which must complete M models of a product in a manufacturing system. The operations are allowed to use W workstations.[2] The assignment of operations to workstations (sequencing) must satisfy precedence relations P_{ij} (an indicator variable), where $P_{ij} = 1$ if operation i must precede operation j. An operation $i \in N$ in model $m \in M$ occupies a workstation $s \in W$ that it is allocated to for a duration T_{im} (process time of operation i in model m). Moreover, when two operations i and j are allocated sequentially to the same workstation, they incur a forward setup[3] time F_{ij}^m (setup time between operations i and j in model m). In this paper we aim to solve an MMALBPS with parameters (N, M, W, P_{ij}, T_{im}, F_{ij}^m), which seeks an optimal assignment of N operations pertaining to M models to workstations so that the maximum cycle time (sum of durations and setup times) of any workstation is minimised. When $M = 1$, we are dealing with the SALBP.

Given the problem definition above, we define the following MIP. Note, we have adapted the MIP from the study of Akpinar [2] where we relax the constraints on cycle time but rather impose constraints on the number of machines. In the following discussion we provide the list of decision variables and detail the objective function and the constraints of the MIP model. In addition to the parameters specified above, we make use of an indicator variable Q_{im}, which is 1 if $T_{im} > 0$.

The model makes use of binary variables y, w and x. y_{is} is 1 if operation i is assigned to workstation s, w_{ijs} is 1 if operation i precedes operation j at machine s and x_{ijms} is 1 if operation j directly follows operation i of model m at workstation s. Additionally, the variable c represents the cycle time.

---

[2] We use workstations and stations synonymously in the remainder of this paper.
[3] Backward setups are assumed to be done within the initial setups for all workstations, at the beginning of a cycle.

$$\textbf{\textit{Minimize}} \; c = \max_{s \in W, m \in M} \left\{ \sum_{i=1}^{N} \left(y_{is} T_{im} + \sum_{j=1}^{N} (x_{ijms} F_{ijm}) \right) \right\} \tag{1}$$

$$\textbf{\textit{subject to}} \; \sum_{s=1}^{W} y_{is} = 1 \quad \forall i \in N \tag{2}$$

$$\left(\sum_{s=1}^{W} s y_{is} - \sum_{s=1}^{W} s y_{js} \right) P_{ij} \leq 0 \quad \forall i, j \in N, \; i \neq j \tag{3}$$

$$w_{ijs} + w_{jis} + x_{ijms} + x_{jims} \leq 2(1 - y_{is} + y_{js}) \quad \forall i, j \in N, m \in M, s \in W \tag{4}$$

$$w_{ijs} + w_{jis} + x_{ijms} + x_{jims} \leq 2(1 + y_{is} - y_{js}) \quad \forall i, j \in N, m \in M, s \in W \tag{5}$$

$$w_{ijs} + w_{jis} + x_{ijms} + x_{jims} \leq 2(y_{is} + y_{js}) \quad \forall i, j \in N, m \in M, s \in W \tag{6}$$

$$P_{ij}(y_{is} + y_{js}) \leq w_{ijs} \quad \forall i, j \in N, i \neq j, s \in W \tag{7}$$

$$w_{iis} = 0 \quad \forall i \in N, s \in W \tag{8}$$

$$w_{iks} + w_{kjs} - 1 \leq w_{ijs} \quad \forall i, j, k \in N, i \neq j \neq k, s \in W \tag{9}$$

$$\left| \sum_{k=1}^{N} \sum_{l=1}^{N} w_{kls} - \sum_{v|v<u}^{N} v \right| \leq N \left| u - \sum_{p=1}^{N} y_{ps} \right| \quad \forall u \in N, s \in W \tag{10}$$

$$\sum_{j=1}^{N} \sum_{s=1}^{W} x_{ijms} \leq 1 \quad \forall i \in N, m \in M \tag{11}$$

$$x_{ijms} + x_{jims} \leq 1 \quad \forall i, j \in N, i \neq j, m \in M, s \in W \tag{12}$$

$$\sum_{s=1}^{W} x_{iims} = 0 \quad \forall i \in N, m \in M \tag{13}$$

$$(y_{is} Q_{im} + y_{js} Q_{jm} - 1) - \left| \sum_{k=1}^{N} w_{iks} Q_{km} - \sum_{l=1}^{N} w_{jls} Q_{lm} - 1 \right| \leq x_{ijms} \tag{14}$$
$$\forall i, j \in N, m \in M, s \in W$$

The objective function minimises the cycle time of the assembly line as given in (1), which is the maximum cycle time across all workstations. Constraints sets (2–3) assign tasks to workstations ensuring that the precedence relations are satisfied. Constraints sets (4–9) order the assigned tasks to each workstation ensuring that the precedence relations within a workstation are satisfied. The constraint set (10) determines the number of orderings between all pairs of tasks at each workstation. Constraints sets (11–13) guarantee that each task can have a single immediate successor in a workstation. Finally, the constraint set (14) determines the immediate successor of each task and relevant setup operation that should be performed between them.

Algorithm 1. ACS for MMALBPS

1: **Input:** An MMALBPS instance, t_{max}, n_s, q_0
2: Initialise($\mathcal{T}$)
3: **while** time elapsed $< t_{max}$ **do**
4:     **for** $j = 1$ to n_s **do**
5:         $\pi^j :=$ ConstructPermutation($\mathcal{T}$, q_0)
6:         $\hat{\pi}^j :=$ AssignOperations(π^j)
7:     $\pi^{ib} := \min_{j=1,\ldots,n_s} f(\pi^j)$
8:     $\pi^{bs} :=$ Update(π^{ib})
9:     $\mathcal{T} :=$ PheromoneUpdate(π^{bs})
10: return π^{bs}

---

3 Ant Colony Optimisation

The ACO variant used in this study is ant colony system (ACS) [5]. ACS is proven as one of the most practically effective ACO methods. In particular, its convergence characteristics are a lot more effective on a range of problems compared to that of the original Ant System [5].

We use π – a permutation that represents a solution to the problem. The permutation has an associated assignment $\hat{\pi}$, which takes the operations in the permutation and assigns them one-by-one in the order they appear into workstations. This assignment heuristic (Sect. 3) ensures that precedence feasible solutions are constructed, and hence the permutation does not need to be precedence feasible.

An ACS implementation for the MMALBPS is shown in Algorithm 1. The algorithm has the following inputs: (a) an MMALBPS problem instance, (b) a terminating criteria, we use a time limit (t_{max}) for this study, (c) the number of permutations n_s to be constructed at each iteration of the algorithm and (d) a pre-defined parameter q_0 that specifies the level of deterministic selection. In the first step of the algorithm, the pheromone trails are initialised (Initialise($\mathcal{T}$)). Here, we set $\tau_{ij} = \frac{1}{|N|}$ $\forall i, j \in N$, where τ_{ij} is the desirability of picking $\pi_i = j$.

The algorithm executes Lines 4–9 until a terminating criteria, or in this study, until a time limit expires. Within this time limit, a number of iterations are executed. In an iteration, the first step is to construct n_s solutions from scratch. Each solution is built by starting out with an empty permutation, and adding operations in successive positions of the permutation using the pheromone trails (ConstructSequence($\mathcal{T}$, q_0)). In the usual ACS way, operations are selected either deterministically or stochastically. For this purpose, a random number q is generated from the interval $(0, 1]$ and is compared to the pre-defined parameter q_0. If $q < q_0$, operation k is chosen in position i of the permutation as:

$$k = \underset{j \in N}{\operatorname{argmax}} \{\tau_{ij} \cdot \eta_{ij}\} \tag{15}$$

If $q \geq q_0$, the operation is selected stochastically according to:

$$P(\pi_i = k) = \frac{\tau_{ik} \cdot \eta_{ik}}{\sum_{j \in N} \tau_{ij} \cdot \eta_{ij}} \tag{16}$$

where a heuristic η_{ik} is used to bias the selection of operation i in position k. In preliminary testing, we investigated several heuristics, for example setup times μ, but the most effective choice was found to be $\eta_{ij} = \frac{1}{T_{im}}$.

In ACS, a local pheromone update is used at every selection step as a mean to reduce the chance of making a repeated selection. That is, when an operation j is selected at position i the pheromones are updated according to:

$$\tau_{ij} = \max\{\tau_{ij} \cdot (1.0 - \rho), \tau_{min}\} \tag{17}$$

where, to ensure that no selection of an operation to a position becomes too low, we set $\tau_{min} = 0.0001$. This ensures that operation j at least has a small chance of being selected in position i.

A complete permutation can be mapped in a greedy way to a feasible assignment of operations to workstations in AssignOperation(π_j) (Sect. 3). In Line 7, an iteration best solution is selected as one that minimises the cycle time across all workstations. In Line 8, π^{bs} is updated to π^{ib} if π^{ib} is an improvement. The final step is to update the pheromone trails ($\mathcal{T} :=$ PheromoneUpdate(π^{bs})) for those solution components seen in π^{bs}:

$$\tau_{ij} = \tau_{ij} \cdot (1.0 - \rho) + \delta \tag{18}$$

where the reward factor $\delta = Q/f(\pi^{bs})$ applies to all solution components and Q is a normalising factor that is chosen to ensure that the reward, relative to the pheromone values, is always between $0.01 \leq \delta \leq 0.1$. For the evaporation rate, it was found that a value of 0.1 is very effective. This is not unusual as for ACO implementations with relatively short run-times (as is the case in this study), a high reward is favourable.

Assigning Operations to Workstations

Previous studies in scheduling have demonstrated the efficacy of learning permutations and mapping these to a schedule [4,18]. Using this idea as a guide, we develop an assignment heuristic, which maps operations in a permutation to workstations.

The high-level algorithm is shown in Algorithm 2. Starting with a permutation π (input), the heuristic assigns operations to workstations ensuring that a minimum cycle time is always maintained. The first step is to initialise the following data structures: (a) $\hat{\pi}$ - the assignment of operations to workstations, (b) W - a waiting list and (c) g - the workstation cycle times. The main loop starts in Line 3 where, for each operation, a feasible assignment to a workstation is found. The operation is tested to see if its preceding operations have been

Algorithm 2. Assigning Operations to Workstations

1: INPUT: π
2: $\hat{\pi} \leftarrow \emptyset \; \forall s \in S, \; W \leftarrow \emptyset, \; g_i \leftarrow 0 \; \forall i \in S$
3: **for** $t \in \pi$ **do**
4:     $\hat{t} \leftarrow t$
5:     **if** Prec(t) not done **then**
6:        $W \leftarrow W \cup \hat{t}$
7:     **else**
8:        **while** $\hat{t} \neq \emptyset$ **do**
9:           $s := $ BestWorkStation($\hat{t}$)
10:          $(\hat{\pi}, g_s) \leftarrow$ Update($\hat{t}$)
11:          $\hat{t} \leftarrow \emptyset$
12:          **for** $j \in W$ **do**
13:             **if** Prec(j) done **then**
14:                $\hat{t} \leftarrow j, \; W \leftarrow W \setminus j$
15:                break
16: OUTPUT: $\hat{\pi}$

completed (Lines 5–7), and if not, it is put on a waiting list W. If the precedences are satisfied, then the operation is assigned to the workstation with the minimum overall cycle time divided by the number of jobs on the workstation - that is, workstation j is chosen for operation i under mode m:

$$j = \operatorname*{argmin}_{s \in S} \left\{ \frac{\hat{C}_s + T_{im} + F_{i-1,i,m}}{|N_s|} \right\} \tag{19}$$

where $\hat{C}_s$ is the current cycle time of workstation s and $|N_s|$ is the number of operations already allocated to station s. In Line 10, the final assignment $\hat{\pi}$ and cycle time of workstation s are updated. An assignment of an operation leads to examining W, to determine if any other operations can now be assigned (Lines 12–15). The procedure completes by returning the final precedence-feasible assignment.

Figure 1 illustrates how the heuristic works. The figure on the left shows a permutation of operations and 5 workstations. The operations are assigned in order to workstations while workstations still do not have operations in them (Fig. 1 – middle). In the figure on the right we see that a new operation is added to a workstation when an operation is already assigned to it. In this case, the operation is assigned to the workstation with the lowest overall cycle time.

4 Experimental Setting and Results

ACS for MMALBPS was implemented in C++ and compiled in GCC-5.4.0. The MIP was implemented in Gurobi 9.0.1 (http://www.gurobi.com/). The experiments were conducted on MonARCH - a Linux cluster at Monash University.[4]

---

[4] https://confluence.apps.monash.edu/display/monarch/MonARCH+Home.

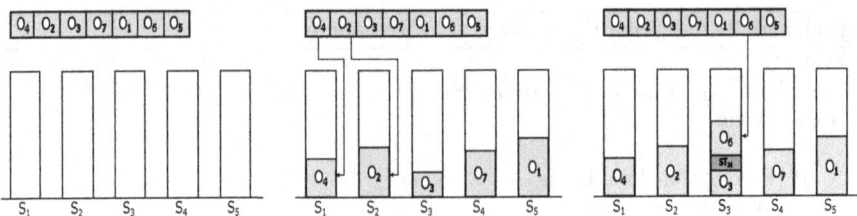

Fig. 1. An example of an assignment of operations to workstations. The figure on the left shows a permutation of 7 operations and 5 workstations. The figure in the middle shows that the first 5 operations are placed in each available workstation (height of a job is its duration). The figure on the right shows that Operation 6 (O_6) is assigned to the workstation with the shortest cycle time (Station 3 here). A setup time ST_{31} is required between the two operations on the workstation.

Table 1. The details of the problem instances; n is the number of operations and **W** the number of workstations; The workstation levels are also provided.

		Instance number																		
		1	2	3	4	5	6	**7**	8	**9**	10	11	12	13	14	15	16	17	18	19	20
n		8	11	12	14	15	16	17	19	21	25	28	29	30	32	35	45	53	58	70	75
W	WL:1	5	6	7	8	8	9	9	10	11	13	15	15	16	17	18	23	27	30	36	38
	WL:2	6	8	9	10	11	11	12	13	15	17	19	20	21	22	24	31	36	39	47	51
	WL:3	7	9	10	11	12	13	13	15	16	19	22	22	23	25	27	34	40	44	53	57

To investigate the performance of the algorithms, we consider the problem instances from [2]. We made two changes: (a) remove the constraint on cycle time and (b) specify the number of workstations as a function of the number of operations n: $\{\frac{n}{2}, \frac{2 \cdot n}{2}, \frac{3 \cdot n}{4}\}$.[5] The details of these problem instances are shown in Table 1. The table shows, for each problem, the number of operations (n), the number of workstations (**W**) split by levels (**WL**). Overall, we have a total of 120 problem instances, with 60 per model type. For ACS, we allow a run-time of 2 min and conduct 30 runs per instance. The MIP executes only once per instance (as it is deterministic) and will allow a time limit of 10 min.[6] ACS is memory efficient requiring only up to 1 GB memory, while the MIP often used up to 10 GB for the large instances.

We used a subset of the problem instances to tune the parameters of ACS. For ρ, we tested values in the range $\{0.2, 0.1, 0.0.5, 0.01\}$ and found that 0.01 was most effective. For q_0 we tested $\{0.5, 0.2, 0.1, 0.01\}$ and found that 0.1 was best. $\tau_{min} = 0.0001$ was used to ensure that an operation at a workstation will always have some small chance of being selected.

---

[5] In the industry, workstations are limited in the number of operations they can handle.
[6] The MIP is given larger run-time as it struggles to find solutions for large problems.

In the following, we use *workstation level (WL)* to denote the varying level of workstations: $1 = \frac{n}{2}$, $2 = \frac{2 \cdot n}{2}$ and $3 = \frac{3 \cdot n}{4}$. Here, WL = 1 can be thought of as the hardest problem consisting of the fewest machines. The instances are numbered such that the number of workstations increases with increasing numbers.

Table 2 shows a comparison of ACS and the MIP solver. The results are split by model M (single = 1, two = 2), workstation level *WL* and solver type. The table shows the cycle time obtained by the MIP, and for ACS, the best, mean and standard deviations of 30 runs are reported. The best solutions found are marked in boldface. When a method fails to find a feasible solution (only in the case of the MIP) it is marked by a "-".

For small problem instances, the MIP can often find optimal solutions (up to problem 8 for single model problems). On instances with many workstations, i.e., WL = 2,3, ACS often finds the optimal solution (on average). In fact for a few small problem instances with two models (e.g., Problem 5), ACS outperforms the MIP. However, for these instances the ACS solutions are not provably optimal. When the problem size increases (≥ 9), ACS easily proves to be the best method, where the MIP is unable to even find a feasible solution on most occasions. Even when solutions are found (e.g.. Problem 10 - Model 1 - WL 2), they have very large cycle times. Interestingly, splitting by models, we see that ACS performs better when there are two models compared to one despite the instances with two models being more complex. These results overall demonstrate that despite running ACS for short run-times, we see very good results.

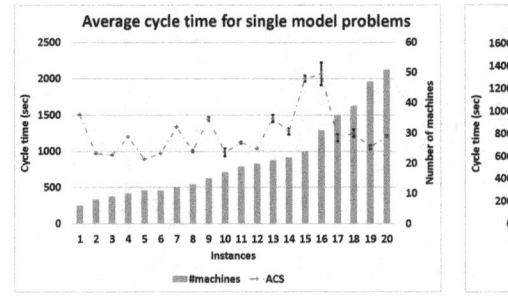 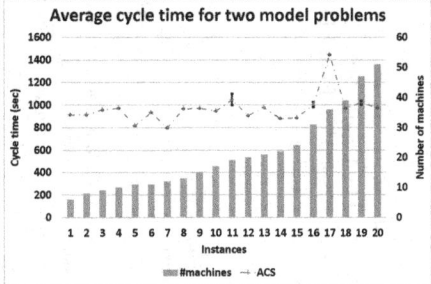

Fig. 2. The performance of ACS on single model and two model instances.

We now delve into the results by focusing on ACS in Fig. 2. The left axis represents the cycle time, the right axis shows the number of workstations and the horizontal axis represents the instances. The bars in these plots show the number of machines. The figure on the left shows the results for single models while the figure on the right shows the same for two models. The ACS run is indicated by the green line. An obvious pattern we see is that the variation in single model problems is much larger than two model problems, demonstrating the usefulness of ACS in dealing with increased complexity.

Table 2. The results the cycle times obtained by the MIP and ACS. Since ACS is run 30 times on each problem instance, the best, average and standard deviations are shown. The results are split by model type (single or two model) - M - and three workstation levels (WL); the values in boldface indicate the best solution found for a problem instance; "-" indicates that no feasible solution was found; b is the best solution, μ is the average solution and sd is the standard deviation considering 30 runs.

M	WL	Solver	1	2	3	4	5	6	7	8	9	10	11	12	13	14	15	16	17	18	19	20
1	1	MIP	**1223.0**	**1017.0**	**997.0**	**1045.0**	**889.0**	**968.0**	**1134.0**	**1183.0**	-	-	-	-	-	-	-	-	-	-	-	-
		ACSb	1796.0	1206.0	1341.0	1728.0	1040.0	1470.0	1611.0	1313.0	**2589.0**	**1424.0**	**1232.0**	**1950.0**	**1845.0**	**3529.0**	**2583.0**	**2812.0**	**4766.0**	**5638.0**	**1500.0**	**1519.0**
		μ	1796.0	1208.3	1341.0	1728.0	1088.9	1481.4	1613.0	1409.8	2640.7	1469.4	1289.2	2600.1	2096.7	3529.0	2583.0	2884.2	4766	6009.7	1646.4	1598.0
		sd	0.0	11.17	0.0	0.0	94.5	38.5	5.5	26.4	54.1	137.7	51.5	340.9	107.2	0.0	0.0	196.0	0.0	295.9	92.6	50.8
	2	MIP	**1067.0**	**969.0**	**945.0**	**969.0**	**889.0**	**968.0**	**1000.0**	**962.0**	1994.0	5007.0	-	-	-	-	-	-	-	-	-	-
		ACSb	1501.0	969.0	945.0	1181.0	889.0	968.0	1333.0	962.0	**1439.0**	**883.0**	**1084.0**	**1011.0**	**1235.0**	**1184.0**	**1880.0**	**1770.0**	**1096.0**	**1174.0**	**966.0**	**1171.0**
		μ	1501.0	969.0	945.0	1192.9	889.0	968.0	1333.0	1003.3	1444.7	985.0	1116.2	1035.0	1451.2	1274.2	1999.0	2063.8	1183.7	1246.7	1054.9	1204.4
		sd	0.0	0.0	0.0	58.2	0.0	0.0	0.0	33.5	26.8	70.0	45.6	5.0	63.8	93.9	81.6	309.4	93.5	118.8	65.7	15.2
	3	MIP	**915.0**	**969.0**	**945.0**	**969.0**	**889.0**	**968.0**	**828.0**	**962.0**	2112.0	1694.0	-	-	-	-	-	-	-	-	-	-
		ACSb	1404.0	969.0	945.0	969.0	889.0	968.0	1333.0	962.0	**1195.0**	**883.0**	**947.0**	**783.0**	**1235.0**	**955.0**	**1448.0**	**946.0**	**971.0**	**949.0**	**956.0**	**992.0**
		μ	1404.0	969.0	945.0	969.0	889.0	968.0	1333.0	962.0	1197.7	883.0	947.0	803.0	1272.6	955.0	1523.0	1065.5	971.0	949.0	956.0	1027.8
		sd	0.0	0.0	0.0	0.0	0.0	0.0	0.0	0.0	9.5	0.0	0.0	67.8	86.2	0.0	78.5	63.9	0.0	0.0	0.0	21.5
2	1	MIP	**1066.0**	**1196.0**	**956.0**	**972.0**	932.0	**933.0**	**1008.0**	1232.0	-	-	-	-	-	-	-	-	-	-	-	-
		ACSb	1134.0	1300.0	1059.0	972.0	**899.0**	933.0	1187.0	**1138.0**	**970.0**	**1363.0**	**1003.0**	**905.0**	**1585.0**	**2191.0**	**898.0**	**1837.0**	**2500.0**	**1013.0**	**1464.0**	**1250.0**
		μ	1134.0	1300.0	1059.0	972.0	899.0	933.0	1246.2	1162.2	976.8	1363.0	1171.4	905.0	1895.2	2191.0	1109.0	2432.1	2500.0	1061.9	1608.1	1275.6
		sd	0.0	0.0	0.0	0.0	0.0	0.0	78.1	44.1	23.6	0.0	146.9	0	279.8	0.0	73.0	272.4	0.0	33.9	77.9	24.1
	2	MIP	996.0	912.0	956.0	972.0	932.0	933.0	809.0	966.0	3186.0	-	-	-	-	-	-	-	-	-	-	-
		ACSb	**913.0**	**912.0**	**956.0**	**972.0**	**817.0**	**933.0**	**797.0**	**965.0**	**970.0**	**946.0**	**962.0**	**905.0**	**975.0**	**877.0**	**885.0**	**967.0**	**1444.0**	**969.0**	**965.0**	**975.0**
		μ	913.0	912.0	956.0	972.0	817.0	933.0	797.0	965.0	970.0	946.0	1047.4	905.0	975.0	877.0	885.0	1002.6	1444.6	969.0	1019.7	975.0
		sd	0.0	0.0	0.0	0.0	0.0	0.0	0.0	0.0	0.0	0.0	173.9	0.0	0.0	0.0	0.0	54.2	2.2	0.0	51.2	0.0
	3	MIP	**731.0**	912.0	956.0	972.0	932.0	933.0	809.0	966.0	5116.0	-	-	-	-	-	-	-	-	-	-	-
		ACSb	731.0	**912.0**	**956.0**	**972.0**	**817.0**	**933.0**	**797.0**	**965.0**	**970.0**	**946.0**	**962.0**	**905.0**	**975.0**	**877.0**	**885.0**	**967.0**	**1444.0**	**969.0**	**965.0**	**975.0**
		μ	731.0	912.0	956.0	972.0	817.0	933.0	797.0	965.0	970.0	946.0	1047.4	905.0	975.0	877.0	885.0	967.0	1445.0	969.0	965.0	975.0
		sd	0.0	0.0	0.0	0.0	0.0	0.0	0.0	0.0	0.0	0.0	173.9	0.0	0.0	0.0	0.0	0.0	2.6	0.0	0.0	0.0

For single model instances, the cycle times tend to increase when the problem consist of 20–30 stations (problem instances 11–16 where the number of tasks are between 28–45). However, for problems with more than 30 stations, the cycle times return to previous levels (900–1500 time units). A similar effect is seen for two model problems at around 35 stations. While this aspect warrants further investigation (e.g.. examining the proportion of operations to workstations or precedence graphs), we leave this to further work due to space limitations.

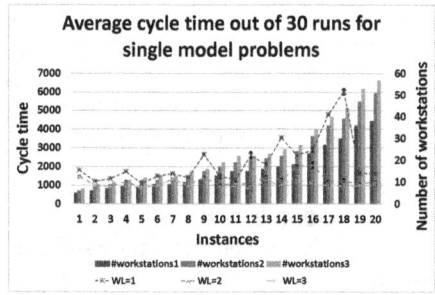 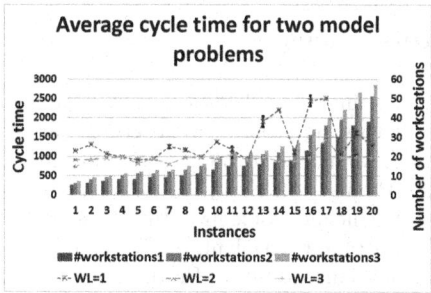

Fig. 3. The performance of ACS with 120 s execution time cap with different workstation levels.

In Fig. 3 we focus on ACS with respect to the level of workstations WL. Like with Fig. 2, the cycle time is presented on the left, the number of workstations on the right and the instances on the horizontal axis. The plots show a split of the performance of ACS depending on the number of workstations. We see that, for single and two models with WL = 1, the cycle times are large and also have high variability. This is not surprising since the instances with a small number of workstations are the hardest ones in the sense of minimising cycle times. In fact, when the instances are "easy", ACS find very low cycle times consistently (a number of which are provably optimal, see Table 2). The large spikes in cycle times seen in Fig. 2 are attributable to those problem instances with relatively few workstations (where workstations were selected as $n \div 2$) for both models.

5 Conclusion and Future Work

We investigate the multi-model assembly line balancing problem with setup times, and propose a novel ant colony system based heuristic for solving it. In comparison to previous ACS methods on similar problems, we focus on learning permutations of operations, which are then mapped to workstations via an efficient assignment heuristic. We compare ACS to a mixed integer programming model and find that ACS performs well overall. In particular, ACS demonstrates clear advantages in three aspects: (a) high quality solutions are found in short time-frames when the number of work stations increase compared to the MIP,

(b) improved performance on two model problems compared to single model problems (c) outperforms the MIP for all medium to large problem instances.

While the proposed ACS approach is effective, there are areas where its performance can certainly be improved. This is especially in the case where there are a small number of workstations leading to large cycle times. For example, the assignment heuristic could be enhanced with probabilistic selection for operations to stations. Furthermore, time-based MIP models could prove very effective, leading to decompositions [6] and hybrid approaches [16].

References

1. Akpinar, S., Baykasoğlu, A.: Modeling and solving mixed-model assembly line balancing problem with setups. part I: a mixed integer linear programming model. J. Manuf. Syst. **33**(1), 177–187 (2014)
2. Akpinar, S., Elmi, A., Bektaş, T.: Combinatorial benders cuts for assembly line balancing problems with setups. Eur. J. Oper. Res. **259**(2), 527–537 (2017)
3. Battaïa, O., Dolgui, A.: A taxonomy of line balancing problems and their solution approaches. Int. J. Prod. Econ. **142**(2), 259–277 (2013)
4. Blum, C., Thiruvady, D., Ernst, A.T., Horn, M., Raidl, G.R.: A biased random key genetic algorithm with Rollout evaluations for the resource constraint job scheduling problem. In: Liu, J., Bailey, J. (eds.) AI 2019. LNCS (LNAI), vol. 11919, pp. 549–560. Springer, Cham (2019). https://doi.org/10.1007/978-3-030-35288-2_44
5. Dorigo, M., Stützle, T.: Ant Colony Optimization. MIT Press, Cambridge (2004)
6. Fisher, M.L.: The Lagrangian relaxation method for solving integer programming problems. Manage. Sci. **50**(12_supplement), 1861–1871 (2004)
7. Gutjahr, A., Nemhauser, G.: An algorithm for the line balancing problem. Manage. Sci. **11**(2), 308–315 (1964)
8. Hossain, S.K.M.: Solving assembly line balancing type II problem using progressive modeling. In Proceedings of the International Annual Conference of the American Society for Engineering Management, pp. 1–10 (2017)
9. Kilincci, O.: A petri net-based heuristic for simple assembly line balancing problem of type 2. Int. J. Adv. Manuf. Technol. **46**(1–4), 329–338 (2010)
10. Kucukkoc, I., Zhang, D.Z.: Mixed-model parallel two-sided assembly line balancing problem: a flexible agent-based ant colony optimization approach. Comput. Ind. Eng. **97**, 58–72 (2016)
11. Scholl, A.: Balancing and sequencing of assembly lines. Physica-Verlag HD, Contributions to Management Science (1999)
12. Scholl, A., Becker, C.: State-of-the-art exact and heuristic solution procedures for simple assembly line balancing. Eur. J. Oper. Res. **168**(3), 666–693 (2006)
13. Seyed-Alagheband, S.A., Ghomi, S.M.T.F., Zandieh, M.: A simulated annealing algorithm for balancing the assembly line type II problem with sequence-dependent setup times between tasks. Int. J. Prod. Res. **49**(3), 805–825 (2011)
14. Simaria, A.S., Vilarinho, P.M.: A genetic algorithm based approach to the mixed-model assembly line balancing problem of type II. Comput. Ind. Eng. **47**(4), 391–407 (2004)
15. Sivasankaran, P., Shahabudeen, P.: Literature review of assembly line balancing problems. Int. J. Adv. Manuf. Technol. 1665–1694 (2014). https://doi.org/10.1007/s00170-014-5944-y

16. Thiruvady, D., Morgan, K., Amir, A., Ernst, A.T.: Large neighbourhood search based on mixed integer programming and ant colony optimisation for car sequencing. Int. J. Prod. Res. **58**(9), 1–16 (2019)
17. Thiruvady, D., Nazari, A., Elmi, A.: An ant colony optimisation based heuristic for mixed-model assembly line balancing with setups. In: 2020 IEEE Congress on Evolutionary Computation (CEC), pp. 1–8 (2020)
18. Thiruvady, D., Wallace, M., Gu, H., Schutt, A.: A Lagrangian relaxation and ACO hybrid for resource constrained project scheduling with discounted cash flows. J. Heuristics **20**(6), 643–676 (2014)
19. Vilarinho, P.M., Simaria, A.S.: ANTBAL: an ant colony optimization algorithm for balancing mixed-model assembly lines with parallel workstations. Int. J. Prod. Res. **44**(2), 291–303 (2006)
20. Zheng, Q., Li, M., Li, Y., Tang, Q.: Station ant colony optimization for the type 2 assembly line balancing problem. Int. J. Adv. Manuf. Technol. **66**(9–12), 1859–1870 (2013)

An Implementation and Experimental Evaluation of a Modularity Explicit Encoding Method for Neuroevolution on Complex Learning Tasks

Yukai Qiao[⊠] and Marcus Gallagher

University of Queensland, Brisbane, Australia
kai.barnes@uqconnect.edu.au

Abstract. Modularity provides advantages in neuroevolution by improving evolvability or efficiency of connections. Many techniques that leverage modularity, either by utilizing human knowledge or adding additional evolutionary objectives, have been studied. In this work, we reimplemented and explored an existing encoding based method, MENNAG, that appears promising but has received little attention. The algorithm is tested on four tasks that are expected to receive different levels of benefits from modularity. The results show that this method is able to produce modular neural networks without directly optimizing modularity, as long as the problem has some degree of modular nature.

Keywords: Neuroevolution · Modularity

1 Introduction

Modularity is a property widely observed in many complex systems: from naturally evolved organisms [15] to artificially defined organizations [14]. A system is modular if it can be divided into sub-parts where interactions within the same part are much more often than between parts.

While the intrinsic merit of such a property is unclear, it has shown that techniques that promote modularity in neuroevolution improve overall performance. Many hypothesized that modularity increases functional stability during mutation. A small mutation within a module barely affects other modules, resulting in increased evolvability. Ellefsen et al. [4]. has also shown that by leveraging modularity, the population gains the ability to remember old skills while learning new ones during evolution.

Most of the techniques proposed to produce modularity in neuroevolution can be classified as one of the following: 1. Manually splitting tasks or neural networks into modules utilizing human knowledge [12,13] 2. Assigning additional evolutionary objectives to apply a biased selective pressure towards modular structure [2,3] 3. To apply a modularity explicit encoding so that the genotype space maps favorably to modular phenotypes [6,10].

© Springer Nature Switzerland AG 2020
M. Gallagher et al. (Eds.): AI 2020, LNAI 12576, pp. 138–149, 2020.
https://doi.org/10.1007/978-3-030-64984-5_11

In this study, we focus on an encoding based method: Modular encoding for neural networks based on attribute grammars (MENNAG) [10]. It is a genetic programming-like algorithm with neural networks as the phenotype. Each genotype is an attribute grammar parse tree that encodes a developmental process of a neural network. The authors claimed that this method produces neural networks with structural properties including hierarchy, regularity, and modularity. However, to the best of our knowledge, no further research has carried out for these claims.

On the basis of the original work [10], we reimplemented MENNAG and extended the experiment on two reasonably complex control problems and a problem that has been widely used in researches on neural network modularity. We analyzed the outcome using a well-known Q metric [11] as a measurement of modularity. The results indicate that the algorithm does indeed exploit the modular nature of some problems and produces modular solutions without directly optimizing modularity, proving the claims of the original work [10].

Our implementation is in Python, the code repository is available at: https://github.com/qyk130/MENNAG.

2 Related Work

Hypotheses of how modularity occurs in biological organisms has been raised [15]. In the most trivial case, fitness directly benefits from modularity. Modularity is proposed to be a direct consequence of selective pressure alone. Another theory proposed that modularity provides advantages in adapting to changeable environments. The environment changes continuously, but not dramatically enough to require changes in all aspects of the organism. The ability to have an adaptation that results in a small functional change but maintaining other functions is essential in evolution [8].

Apart from natural selection, modularity in organisms could just be a side effect from the developmental process. Force showed that new subfunctions and genetic modularity in a population of eukaryote genes can accrue during non-selective processes [5]. This suggests that the genotype-phenotype mapping of eukaryote might be biased towards modularity.

Some studies in neuroevolution have explored the above hypotheses. Clune et al. [2] evolved neural networks on the retina problem [8]. The problem contains two subtasks, each requires recognizing several 4-bit patterns and the solution is only correct when both tasks are solved simultaneously. The authors showed that by penalizing connections, the population discovers a more modular structure than optimizing performance alone and even outperforms it. They concluded that high-performing networks are rare when complexity is high, but many low complexity modular networks perform well. Greedily increasing complexity may increase performance, but also push the search area away from the efficient area. With a selective pressure on lowering complexity the search is limited to a more efficient area where high performing modular networks are found.

3   MENNAG Algorithm

In MENNAG, a genotype is a parse tree generated by an attribute grammar. Evolutionary operators are similar to operators used in genetic programming. The details are stated in the original paper [10], a summary is given here.

3.1   Symbols

A grammar rule consists of symbols and production rules. MENNAG is a context-free grammar, each production rule describes how a single symbol can be reinterpreted regardless of its surrounding symbols. The full abstract grammar rule for MENNAG are shown in Fig. 1. The description of each symbol can be found in Table 1. The exact functionality of each instance of symbols are controlled by its attributes.

```
START ⇒ DIV CONNS            CONN ⇒ ICONN
DIV ⇒ DIV CLONES CONNS       CONN ⇒ ICONN
DIV ⇒ CLONES DIV CONNS       ICONN ⇒ weight node target
CLONES ⇒ CLONE CLONES        IN ⇒ end
CLONES ⇒ CLONE               IN ⇒ IO in1
DIV ⇒ DIV DIV CONNS          IN ⇒ IO in2
DIV ⇒ CELL CELL CONNS        OUT ⇒ end
CELL ⇒ IN OUT                OUT ⇒ IO out1
CLONE ⇒ end                  OUT ⇒ IO out2
CONNS ⇒ CONN CONNS           IO ⇒ weight target
CONNS ⇒ end
```

Fig. 1. Full abstract grammar rules when there are two inputs and two outputs. Rearranged from [10]

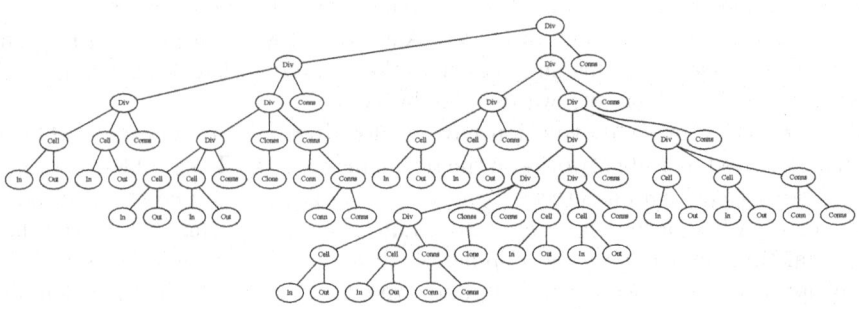

Fig. 2. An example genotype of MENNAG.

Table 1. Description of MENNAG symbols.

CELL	Defines a neuron in the phenotype. It is always reinterpreted as IN OUT where each may define a connection between the neuron and a certain input/output. This also means each neuron can be connected to one input and one output at most
IN/OUT	Defines a connection between its parent CELL and an input/output. The source/destination and the weight of connections can be mutated
DIV	Stands for division. This symbol forms the skeleton of a parse tree genotype. It can be reinterpreted as two CELL, forming a basic division/module of a neural network. It also can consist of two DIV, or, a DIV and its CLONES
CLONE	Allows the reuse of its sibling DIV. It would replicate the sibling DIV as if there is a copy at the CLONE's position in the parse tree. However, a CLONE would shuffle the IO connections using an evolvable array of float numbers. For example, an array of $[0.5, 0.1, 0.7]$ has an order of $[2, 1, 3]$ if sorted ascending. Neurons that should have connected to input 1 in the original DIV would connect to input 2 in the clone
CLONES	Defines a list of CLONE where each one replicates the same DIV, but with different IO shuffling
CONN	Defines a connection between two neurons under the same subtree represented by the symbol's parent
CONNS	Defines a list of CONNs

3.2 Evolutionary Operators

Population Initialization. The population is initialized by the GROW algorithm used in genetic programming [9]. A probability is assigned to every production rule. Each individual starts with a DIV, which is then reinterpreted by a randomly chosen production rule. The production will then be reinterpreted again. This procedure keeps going recursively until every leaf symbol is terminal.

Mutation. There are non-structural mutations and structural mutations. The non-structural mutations changes attributes like connection weights and IO shuffling arrays. Structural mutations, include adding and removing a node in the genotype, must follow a specific procedure so that the resulting parse tree still follows the grammar. For insertion, the procedure follows:

1. Assign each rule a likelihood to be extended during a mutation, p_1. Assign each recursive rule a likelihood to be used to extend the tree, p_2.
2. Select the first rule r_1 randomly according to the likelihood p_1.
3. Select the second rule r_2 randomly according to the likelihood p_2 from valid choices; the LHS symbol of r_2 must belong to the RHS symbols of r_1.

4. Among the existing nodes generated by r_1, randomly select a node n_1 with the same symbol as the LHS of r_2. The symbol of n_1 also needs to belong to the RHS of r_2, which means r_2 must be recursive.
5. Create a new node n_2 with the same symbol as n_1
6. Generate the offsprings of n_2 using r_2
7. Replace n_1 by n_2 in the list of offsprings of the parent of n_1
8. Replace one the the offsprings of n_2 by n_1 where the symbol matches.

Deletion is implemented symmetrically. The conventional random tree mutation is also used at a low probability (0.01) [10].

Crossover. Crossover is implemented the same as one-point crossover in conventional Genetic Programming. An offspring copies from parent A, then replace a sub-tree by a sub-tree from parent B.

3.3   Discussion

There are several potential benefits about having a tree-structured genotype. A tree is hierarchical and modular. It can easily be decomposed into isolated sub-trees. Depending on the actual genotype phenotype mapping, a tree-structured genotype may allow less disruptive evolutionary operators. This certainly does not hold for context-sensitive grammar-based mapping where the interpretation of a sub-tree would depend on the surrounding context. An example is Cellular Encoding [6]. MENNAG, on the other hand, is context-free.

Comparing with neural architecture search algorithms which rely on predefined CNN blocks [16]. This algorithm applies minimum inductive bias about the actual architecture. Instead, it provides a direction of general network properties like modularity to the search. While losing efficiency and the utilization of GPU it has the potential to explore delicate structures without human design.

4   Experimentation

The goal of our experiments is to investigate whether the MENNAG algorithm indeed produces modular solutions while not directly optimizing modularity, and, if so, does it provide modularity regardless of the nature of the problem? We tested MENNAG on a pattern recognition problem and two continuous control task that are expected to receive different levels of benefit from modularity. Firstly, the retina problem has an explicit modular structure. The second problem, inverted pendulum swing up, is non-modular. The third problem, bipedal walker, can be decomposed into sub-problems, but it would require a lot more coordination between possible modules than the retina problem. We used an implementation provided in OpenAI gym environment [1] for the last two problems.

4.1   Modularity Measurement

We measure modularity using a close approximation of Q-score [11]. The metric is defined as [7]:

$$Q = \sum_{s=1}^{K} \left[\frac{l_s}{L} - \left(\frac{d_s}{2L} \right)^2 \right] \tag{1}$$

where K is the amount of modules, L is the amount of edges in the graph, l_s is the amount of edges within a module, d_s is the sum of degrees of nodes in module s. The score is between 0 and 1. It is intuitively higher when edges within modules are more frequent than edges between modules. The approximating algorithm also gives the modular decomposition of a network.

4.2   Experimental Settings

Neural network in all tasks are feed-forward with a logistic sigmoidal activation function. A rank-based EA where the probability of an individual being selected into the next generation is proportional to the rank of the individual's performance, is used. Experiments on all three problems were run 20 times, with a population of 1000. Experiments on the retina problem were run for 2500 generations, the other two were run 1000 generations. These numbers were observed to be sufficient for algorithm to appear to be heading to convergence. All other algorithm parameters are the same as the original MENNAG paper [10].

4.3   The Retina Problem

The retina problem has been covered in numerous studies on modularity in neuroevolution [2,3,8]. The task can be separated into two sub-tasks, each requires recognizing 8 random 4-bit patterns. The input is 8-bit in total. The correct answer is 1 if one of the left patterns is given to the left half and one of the right patterns is given to the right half, the answer would be 0 otherwise. In each evaluation, all 256 possible inputs were tested and the fitness would be the proportion of correct response. A random guessing agent can achieve 75% accuracy since it is a binary classification problem and 75% of the possible inputs are negative.

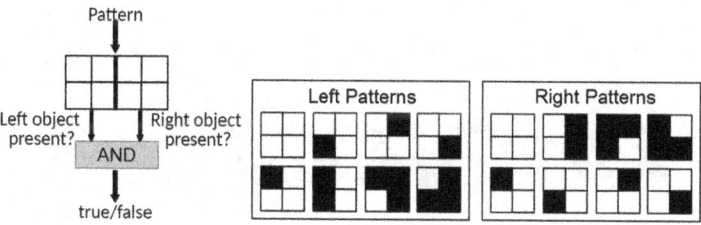

Fig. 3. The retina problem can be decomposed into two sub-tasks connected by a logical AND. Picture based on [3].

A non-modular version is also tested, with 64 8-bit patterns, which has the same difficulty for a random guess agent.

4.4   Inverted Pendulum Swing up

Inverted pendulum swing up is a classic control problem that has been used as a benchmark in reinforcement learning. In this task, the agent must swing an inverted pendulum up and keep it upright. There are three inputs where the first two are the sin and cos of the angle of the pendulum, and, the third input is the angular speed. The output is the torque applied. Each individual is evaluated 8 times from different starting angles. At each time step, a penalty on a linear combination of torque and difference between the current angle and the upward angle, is applied. This encourages the solution to be as efficient as possible. The final fitness would be the sum of all penalties across time steps.

The problem is fully markovian and there is no trivial sub-task decomposition. We do not expect a solution to receive any advantage from having a modular structure for this problem.

4.5   Bipedal Walker

The task requires a robot with two legs to move forward on a randomly generated terrain. Rewards are given by the distance traveled. Applying motor torque receive some penalty to encourage efficient movement. There are in total 24 inputs including angles and velocities of hull and joints, and 10 LIDAR sensors. 4 outputs for the motor torque on four joints—2 for each le.g. The fitness is the distance traveled. The ground environment is shared for all runs.

This task can be intuitively decomposed into several subtasks and potentially benefits from doing so. The control of two legs, while coordination should be required, should also be quite independent. Inputs from the LIDAR sensors should be processed regardless of how legs are being moved.

Fig. 4. A bipedal walker

5   Result and Discussion

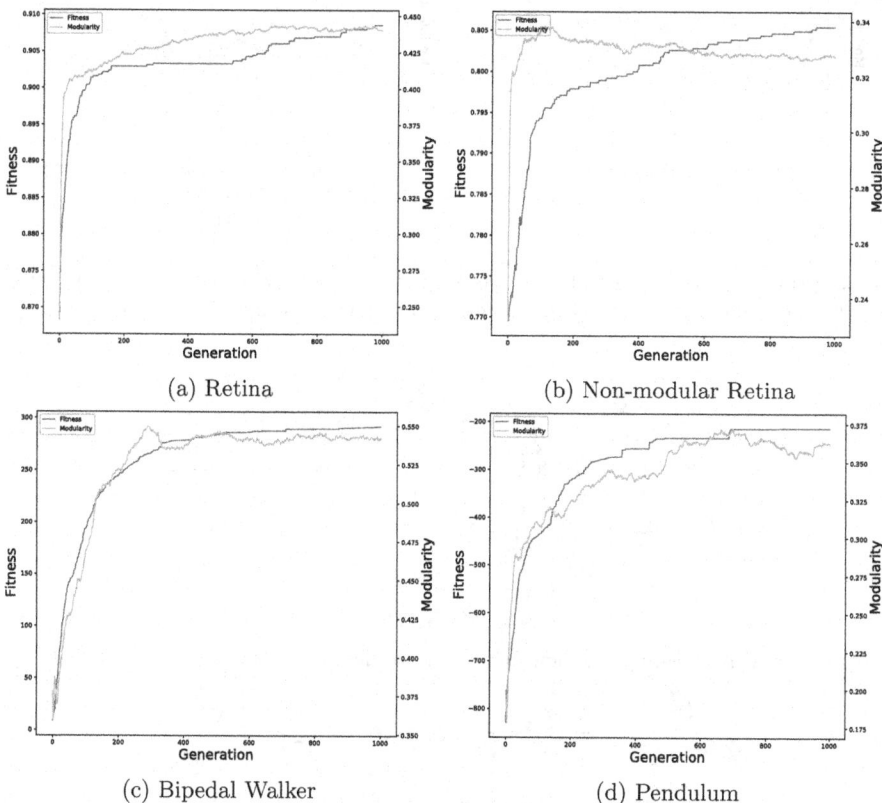

(a) Retina   (b) Non-modular Retina

(c) Bipedal Walker   (d) Pendulum

Fig. 5. Best fit individual performance and population average modularity over generations of different problems.

The results are summarized in Fig. 5. In terms of performance, MENNAG performed well on both control problems. For bipedal walker, 6 out of 20 runs solved the problem (with a score over 300). For pendulum, all solutions were able to keep the pendulum upright from all initial directions. In the original work [10] the authors mentioned that the algorithm would not perform well with a large amount of IO since CLONE operators need to shuffle IO to find a good symmetrical position. Nonetheless, our results showed that it worked well on bipedal walker which has 24 inputs.

For retina problem, however, none of the runs produced a perfect solution. Comparing previous studies where direct encoding methods with limited search space were used, MENNAG performed worse with the same amount of generations. The retina problem requires the neural network to memorize specific

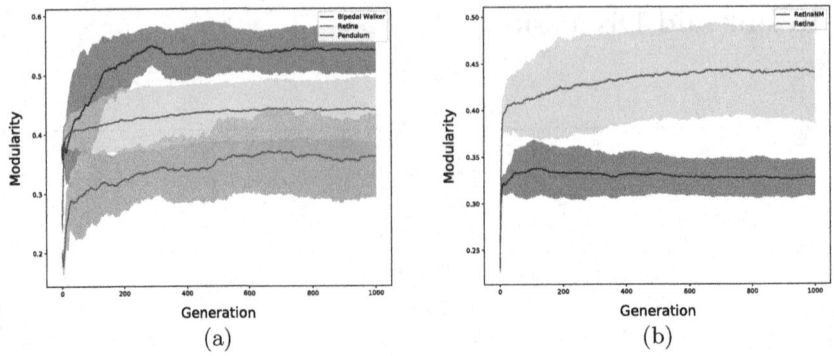

Generation   Generation
(a)   (b)

Fig. 6. (a) Comparison of population average modularity between three problems, with one standard deviation interval (b) Comparison between retina and the non-modular version

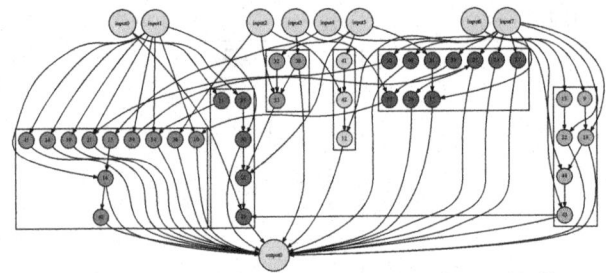

(a) A good performing solution for retina problem $Q = 0.40$ $Fitness = 0.9766$

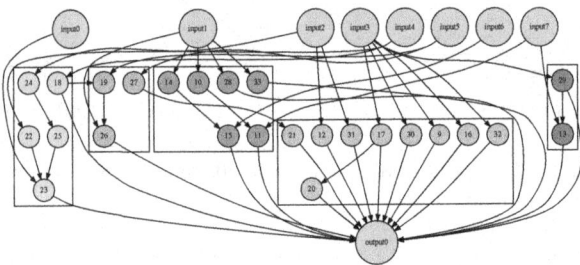

(b) A bad performing solution for retina problem $Q = 0.40$ $Fitness = 0.9023$

Fig. 7. Although having the same modularity score, solution (a) has found better modular decomposition than solution(b). In (a), the two halves of input are relatively separated. In (b) the two halves connect to the same modules more frequently.

patterns precisely. A possible reason for the bad performance is that a genotype that encodes a developmental process, may not be able to fine tune the resulting phenotype to fit discrete, low-level patterns. Apart from fine tuning issue, the algorithm does not always find good modular decomposition. Figure 7a shows a solution that has found a good modular decomposition. The first four inputs and

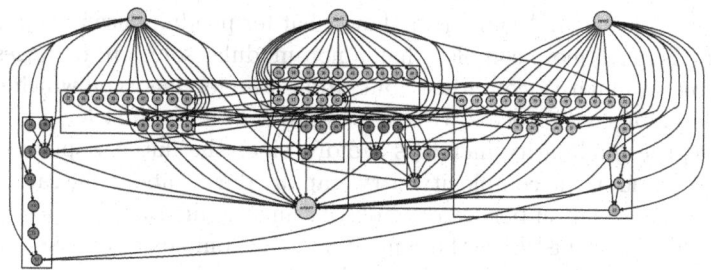

(a) A modular solution for pendulum swing up $Q = 0.42$ *Fitness* $= -117$

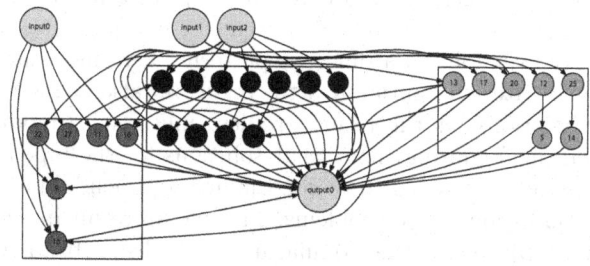

(b) A less modular solution for pendulum swing up $Q = 0.24$ *Fitness* $= -133$

Fig. 8. MENNAG is able to find a modular solution even for a problem with no trivial sub-task decomposition, however, it is significantly more complex than a less modular solution.

the last four inputs are well separated by connecting to different modules. The solution in Fig. 7(b), although having the same modularity score, has a worse decomposition, and consequently performs worse. It is expected as the algorithm does not require any prior information of the modular structure of the problem and simply search according to the performance. Ellefsen et al. suggested to optimize the diversity of the modular decomposition in population to solve this issue in a direct encoding approach [3] which should be explored in future work.

The algorithm performed even poorer on the non-modular retina problem, obtaining about 80 percent accuracy which is 10 percent lower than the outcome of the modular version. This however indicates that MENNAG indeed benefits from the intrinsic modular nature of the problem. The result is also contrary to the previous study where a direct encoding method performed better on the non-modular version but worse on the modular version [2]. It seems that with limited fine-tuning capability, it is easier for the algorithm to find a solution to memorize two of 4-bit patterns then combine them, rather than memorizing an 8-bit pattern.

From Fig. 5(a)(c)(d), population modularity seems to correlate with fitness, even for pendulum swing up. Figure 5(b) follows a different pattern where modularity decreases as fitness increases. It appears that the algorithm has found a non-trivial modular decomposition for pendulum swing up and it failed to do so for non-modular retina. As for Fig. 7 shows that for pendulum swing up a modular solution is much more complex than a non-modular solution. It suggests that the observed modularity could just come from a larger genotype which encodes a larger developmental process. We can observe that in the first few hundreds of generations the modularity increases rapidly, since the initial population complexity is minimum, the complexity grows rapidly during about the same period, which gives a correlation between complexity and modularity. It is possible that some modules might just have the same functional complexity comparing with a single neuron in a non-modular solution. In other words, the modularity growth may not be driven by selective pressure but rather just formality from the biased encoding.

Figure 5(b) however follows a different pattern where modularity decreases as fitness increases after the initial growth. Figure 6b also suggests that MEN-NAG produces solutions for the retina problem much more modular than its non-modular version. Figure 6a shows that solutions for the bipedal walker are significantly more modular than those for the inverted pendulum, which corresponds with our intuition of the problems. The overall result indicates that the selective pressure projected by the modular nature of the problem does affect the modularity of solutions. For an absolutely non-modular task, the non-modular retina problem, the modularity even decreases over generation since there is only disadvantage.

6   Conclusion

We discussed the importance and motivation of modularity in neuroevolution. We reimplemented and extended the experimentation of an encoding based neuroevolution method MENNAG [10]. We showed that the algorithm is capable of solving more complex problems than what had been tested in the original work.

We discussed the origin of modularity in natural and artificial evolution. We analyzed the algorithm's ability to produce modular neural networks on four tasks that intuitively receive different levels of benefit from modularity. The result indicates that the algorithm is able to produce modular solutions without directly optimizing modularity when the problem has some degree of modular nature.

References

1. Brockman, G.: OpenAI gym. arXiv preprint arXiv:1606.01540 (2016)
2. Clune, J., Mouret, J.-B., Lipson, H.: The evolutionary origins of modularity. Proc. Royal Soc. B: Biol. Sci. **280**(1755), 20122863 (2013)
3. Ellefsen, K.O., Huizinga, J., Torresen, J.: Guiding neuroevolution with structural objectives. Evol. Comput. **28**(1), 115–140 (2020)
4. Ellefsen, K.O., Mouret, J.-B., Clune, J.: Neural modularity helps organisms evolve to learn new skills without forgetting old skills. PLoS Comput. Biol. **11**(4), e1004128 (2015)

5. Force, A., Cresko, W.A., Pickett, F.B., Proulx, S.R., Amemiya, C., Lynch, M.: The origin of subfunctions and modular gene regulation. Genetics **170**(1), 433–446 (2005)
6. Gruau, F., et al.: Neural network synthesis using cellular encoding and the genetic algorithm (1994)
7. Guimera, R., Amaral, L.A.N.: Functional cartography of complex metabolic networks. Nature **433**(7028), 895–900 (2005)
8. Kashtan, N., Alon, U.: Spontaneous evolution of modularity and network motifs. Proc. Natl. Acad. Sci. **102**(39), 13773–13778 (2005)
9. Koza, J.R., Koza, J.R.: Genetic Programming: on the Programming of Computers by Means of Natural Selection, vol. 1. MIT Press, Cambridge (1992)
10. Mouret, J.-B., Doncieux, S.: MENNAG: a modular, regular and hierarchical encoding for neural-networks based on attribute grammars. Evol. Intel. **1**(3), 187–207 (2008)
11. Newman, M.E.J.: Modularity and community structure in networks. Proc. Natl. Acad. Sci. **103**(23), 8577–8582 (2006)
12. Reisinger, J., Stanley, K.O., Miikkulainen, R.: Evolving reusable neural modules. In: Deb, K. (ed.) GECCO 2004. LNCS, vol. 3103, pp. 69–81. Springer, Heidelberg (2004). https://doi.org/10.1007/978-3-540-24855-2_7
13. Schrum, J., Miikkulainen, R.: Solving multiple isolated, interleaved, and blended tasks through modular neuroevolution. Evol. Comput. **24**(3), 459–490 (2016)
14. Simon, H.A.: The architecture of complexity. In: Facets of Systems Science, pp. 457–476. Springer (1991). https://doi.org/10.1007/978-1-4899-0718-9_31
15. Wagner, G.P., Pavlicev, M., Cheverud, J.M.: The road to modularity. Nat. Rev. Genet. **8**(12), 921–931 (2007)
16. Zoph, B., Le, Q.V.: Neural architecture search with reinforcement learning. arXiv preprint arXiv:1611.01578 (2016)

A Parametric Framework for Genetic Programming with Transfer Learning for Uncertain Capacitated Arc Routing Problem

Mazhar Ansari Ardeh[(✉)], Yi Mei, and Mengjie Zhang

School of Engineering and Computer Science, Victoria University of Wellington, Wellington, New Zealand
mazhar.ansariardeh@ecs.vum.ac.nz

Abstract. The Uncertain Capacited Arc Routing Problem (UCARP) is an important variant of arc routing problems that is capable of modelling uncertainties of real-world scenarios. Genetic Programming is utilised to evolve routing policies for vehicles to enable them to make real-time decisions and handle environment uncertainties. However, when the properties of a solved problem change, the trained routing policy becomes ineffective and a new routing policy is needed to be trained. The training process is time-consuming. Nevertheless, by extraction and transfer of some knowledge learned from the previous similar problem, the retraining process can be improved. Transfer learning is a challenging task that entails many aspects to decide about, which can influence the degree by which knowledge transfer can be effective. Consequently, in this paper we propose a parametric framework to formalise these details so that it can facilitate studying different aspects of using transfer learning for handling scenario changes of UCARP. Conducting a large number of experiments, we utilise this framework to analyse different transfer learning mechanisms and demonstrate how it can help with understanding dynamics of knowledge transfer for UCARP.

Keywords: Transfer learning · Genetic programming · Uncertain Capacitated Arc Routing Problem

1 Introduction

The Uncertain Capacitated Arc Routing Problem (UCARP), first proposed by Mei et al. [13], is an important optimisation problem which simulates a set of vehicles that serve a set of tasks in an uncertain environment. The goal of solving a UCARP is to find a collection of routes that serve all tasks with minimal total cost while respecting some predefined constraints [13]. The approach of using routing policies is a flexible method that can handle the uncertainties of this problem effectively [1,13]. A routing policy is a real-valued function that assigns a priority value to unserved tasks based on state of environment. Vehicles consider the priority and choose the task to serve next. Liu et al. [13] utilised

© Springer Nature Switzerland AG 2020
M. Gallagher et al. (Eds.): AI 2020, LNAI 12576, pp. 150–162, 2020.
https://doi.org/10.1007/978-3-030-64984-5_12

Genetic Programming as a Hyper Heuristic (GPHH) for evolving UCARP routing policies and showed its superiority to existing methods.

The GPHH method is effective for solving UCARP but it is a time-consuming process. Additionally, if a change occurs the trained routing policies will not perform optimally for the new problem [13] and, it is required to train new routing policies. However, when the change in problem is not drastic, it is reasonable to believe that transfer learning methods can extract reusable knowledge from the old solution(s) of the old problem to help the training process for the new problem. Previous studies have shown that applying transfer learning methods for handling scenario changes of UCARP is a challenging task [1,3]. As a result, a formal framework is needed that facilitates the analysis of the knowledge transfer process for UCARP.

Accordingly, in this paper, we propose a parametric knowledge transfer framework to formalise the steps involved in performing knowledge transfer for handling scenario changes of UCARP. In our framework, different parameters formulate the influence of different aspects of a knowledge transfer scenario. Consequently, we seek to fulfil the following research goals: 1) Propose a parametric transfer learning framework for handling scenario changes of UCARP; 2) analyse the effect of each component of the framework, governed by different parameters, on the success of knowledge transfer; 3) speculate on considerations for effective extraction and update of the knowledge. We study this framework for handling scenario changes of UCARP (Section 2.1). Our preliminary work showed that the Probabilistic Prototype Tree (PPT) structure has a good potential for representing transferable knowledge [4]. Therefore, we select this structure as an explicit representation for knowledge. Knowledge representation is an abstract term in our generic framework and we intend to use this structure to help analyse our framework experimentally and illuminate the potentials and shortcomings of a transfer learning scenario. Our results shows that the framework provides a capable tool for this purpose.

2 Background

2.1 UCARP

UCARP is an uncertain combinatorial problem defined on a connected undirected graph $G(V, E)$ with V as its set of nodes and E as its set of edges [13]. Each node $v \in V$ represents a location and each edge $e \in E$ is a route between two locations and has a stochastic non-negative demand $d(e)$. Edges with positive demand values are called tasks. In UCARP, a set of vehicles, with limited capacity Q, are considered to serve the tasks that are spread over the edges. In the beginning, all vehicles are stationed at a depot node $v_0 \in V$. Serving a task $e \in E$ incurs two costs: 1) the stochastic deadheading cost, which represents the cost of traversing e with or without serving it and, 2) the positive deterministic cost of serving the task. In UCARP, the goal is to find a set of routes for all vehicles that serves all the tasks while minimising the sum of all costs. There are three constraints that should be considered: 1) a vehicle cannot serve more than its capacity without going back to the depot; 2) all vehicles are required to start and end their routes with the depot; 3) each task can be served only once [13].

The best approach for solving UCARP is to search for routing policies that generate solutions in real-time [13]. A routing policy is a real-valued function that assigns a real number as a priority value to unserved tasks, based on the state of environment. Vehicles consider the priority and choose the task with the best priority to serve next. Uncertainty is an important aspect of real-world scenarios [13] and routing policies help vehicles to assess available tasks in real-time and select their next task based on the up-to-date state of their environment. Routing policies can be trained with GP.

GPHH for UCARP. Genetic Programming is an Evolutionary Computational (EC) algorithm that evolves a population of computer programs [5]. Like GA, GP applies the genetic operators to its population iteratively to search for an optimal program. When the search space of GP is the space of heuristics, the algorithm is usually referred to as Genetic Programming Hyper-Heuristic (GPHH). Since routing policies are heuristics in essence, GPHH can be utilised to evolve routing policies for UCARP. GPHH initialises a population of routing policies randomly, evaluates the fitness of each population member on a set of training instances, creates a new population by applying the genetic operators (crossover, mutation, reproduction) to the current population, and repeats these steps until a stopping condition is met. Routing policies are represented with GP trees [20,21].

Routing policies generate the final set of vehicle routes that serve all the tasks. Generating the routes starts with all the vehicles stationed at the depot. Whenever idle, vehicles consider all accessible tasks and utilise the routing policy to assign a priority to each task, select the task with the best priority and, start serving it. This process of selecting and serving tasks is repeated until all tasks are served. The fitness of a routing policy is the mean total cost of the solutions it generates over training instances [13]. Training routing policies is a time-consuming process and this fact is exacerbated by the finding that if a change such as the number of vehicles occurs then training of new routing policies will be required [3]. However, when the change in problem is not drastic, transfer learning methods can help the retraining process.

2.2 Transfer Learning for Genetic Programming

Torrey et al. define transfer learning (TL) as "the improvement of learning in a new task through the transfer of knowledge from a related task that has already been learned" [19]. Therefore, instead of learning a new task from scratch, transfer learning allows salvaging the knowledge learned from similar solved tasks to improve the efficiency and effectiveness of the learning process. However, a *negative transfer* may happen when extracted knowledge decreases the performance. When the learning technique is Genetic Programming (GP), the same criteria can be considered and one can expect a GP-based TL to 1) create a good initial population; and 2) speed up the evolutionary process; 3) achieve a better

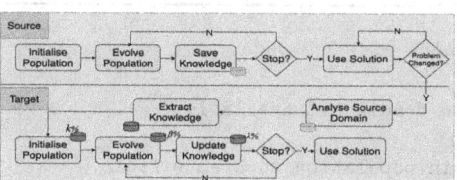

Fig. 1. A general transfer learning framework

Table 1. Framework Parameters

Par	Description
k	Initialisation rate
β	Search contribution rate
x	Crossover rate
m	Mutation rate
r	Reproduction rate
λ	Learning rate

final performance. This section reviews some of TL methods for evolutionary algorithms and interested readers are referred to [9,19] for more comprehensive reviews.

Taylor et al. [18] proposed knowledge transfer for evolutionary algorithms by transferring the whole final population from a solved source domain to initialise a Genetic Algorithm (GA) population on a target domain.

Dinh et al. [6] proposed three methods for initialising GP population. In the *FullTree-k* algorithm, k percent of the best individuals in the final population of a source domain are selected as initial GP individuals on a target domain. Their *SubTree-k* method focused again on the final GP population of the source domain but extracted a randomly-selected subtree from each individual and used them as new individuals in the first GP population of the target domain. Their final method, called *BestGen-k* selected k percent of the best individuals of each generation to initialise a new GP.

Ardeh et al. [3] believed that the subtrees that appear frequently in a source domain must be important because GP created them repeatedly. Their algorithm, *FreqSub*, considered them as new individuals to initialise GP of a target domain. Later [2], they measured the importance of subtrees based on their contribution to fitness and transferred the most contributing ones as new individuals.

Ardeh et al. also performed transfer learning as transfer of feature/function importance [1,4]. In a more recent work, Ardeh et al. [4] learned the probability distribution of creating good individuals from a source domain. They utilised PPTs for representing the learned probabilities and used the transferred PPTs for initialising GP in target domains.

3   The Proposed Parametric Framework for Transfer Learning

Transfer learning is needed when a change in a solved problem creates a new but related problem. In this context, there are a few key decisions: 1) how to represent the transferable knowledge? 2) how to extract the knowledge? 3) how to use the knowledge? 4) how to update the knowledge?

Algorithm 1: Pseudocode for PKGPHH

Input : Training dataset $\wp$
Output: The best learned heuristic ind^*

1: $ind^* \leftarrow null,\ gen \leftarrow 0,\ k \leftarrow 0$
   // Load final population of source domain, if available.
2: $\Im \leftarrow$ loadFinalPopulationSource ()
   // Specify portion of target domain population to create from
      extracted knowledge
3: $k \leftarrow$ getInitPercent ()
4: $\Im' \leftarrow$ Select top members of $\Im$ to learn from
5: **if** $\Im' = \varnothing$ **then**
6: $\quad\vert\quad \mathcal{M} \leftarrow \varnothing$
7: **end**
8: **else**
9: $\quad\vert\quad \mathcal{M} \leftarrow$ Extract knowledge from the selected individuals (e.g extract a
      PPT).
10: **end**
11: **Initialisation:** Create $k \times Popsize$ individuals from the $\mathcal{M}$ by selecting
      functions/terminals for each node based on the probability distribution.
12: Randomly initialise the remaining $(1-k) \times Popsize$ individuals
13: **while** $gen < maxGen$ **do**
14: $\quad\vert\quad$ Evaluate each individual on $\wp$ and update ind^*
15: $\quad\vert\quad$ Apply clearing
16: $\quad\vert\quad$ **if** $\mathcal{M} \neq \varnothing$ **then**
17: $\quad\vert\quad\vert\quad$ Update $\mathcal{M}$ with a learning rate of λ
18: $\quad\vert\quad\vert\quad$ Breed $\beta \times Popsize$ of the population from $\mathcal{M}$
19: $\quad\vert\quad$ **end**
20: $\quad\vert\quad$ Apply crossover, mutation and reproduction
21: $\quad\vert\quad gen \leftarrow gen + 1$
22: **end**
23: **return** ind^*

Knowledge representation can be either *explicit* or *implicit*. In explicit representations, the transferable knowledge is extracted into a reusable model $\mathcal{M}$ that expresses some form of understanding about the source domain. The works of Feng et al. [8] and Ardeh et al. [4] are in this category that respectively, use memes of statistical dependency and probability prototype trees as the explicit representations. In the implicit approach, the model $\mathcal{M}$ is not extracted but some manifestation of the hidden knowledge are considered from the source domain. The work of Dinh et al. [6] is in this category. Knowledge extraction is heavily dependent on the selected representation. It is important to consider that when the two domains are related, the knowledge contributes to the *exploitation* phase of EC methods and relying too much on it may run the risk of early convergence. In the context of EC-based algorithms, the transferred knowledge can be used to 1) initialise $k \in [0, 1]$ portion of the initial population; 2) guide the evolution by contributing to β percent of the search effort. The value of β should be selected in coordination with crossover rate x and mutation rates m.

The knowledge from a source domain may be good enough for giving EC algorithm a better-than-random state but as search becomes more focused on the characteristics of the target domain, its usefulness degrades. Hence, it is needed to update the knowledge with new information. The important decision here is the learning rate $\lambda \in [0, 1]$ that specifies what portion of the old knowledge should be preserved with $\lambda = 0$ meaning no update at all. The details of the update mechanism depends on the knowledge representation.

Figure 1 presents a flowchart of this general framework and a more pseudo code of the framework is given in Algorithm 1. Table 1 gives a summary of the parameters introduced here. In the remainder of this paper, we investigate the proposed general framework with the help of *FullTree*, *SubTree* [6] and *FreqSub* [3] methods. Since all these methods have an implicit knowledge representation and only focus on initialisation, we also extend the model-based method in [4] with the capability of updating the model during the GP run so that it demonstrates different aspects of the framework. This method will be referred to as Probabilistic Knowledge-enabled GPHH (*PKGPHH*). The goal here is to help the better understanding of the framework and illustrate how it can help with gaining a better insight of a transfer learning pipeline rather than proposing a new and more efficient algorithm.

3.1 Probabilistic Knowledge-Enabled GPHH

Knowledge Representation and Extraction. We consider the probability distributions of good individuals of a source domain as an explicit transferable knowledge and utilise PPTs to store the probability distributions. A PPT is a complete binary tree in which each node holds the probabilities that each GP function/terminal may appear in a tree at the corresponding node. It can be proven with maximum likelihood estimation [7] that the probability of a GP function/terminal g appearing in a particular position in the tree is $p_g = M_g/N$ in which N is the total number of individuals considered for learning; M_g is the number of GP trees in the population that contain g at the given node. Figure 2 demonstrates an example PPT for a simple GP configuration for which the terminal set is $T = \{a, b\}$, the function set is $F = \{+, *\}$ and the maximum tree depth is two.

Presence of code bloat and duplicates can have a negative effect on the quality of transfer learning techniques [3]. To fight off this issue, we utilise the clearing method [15]. The clearing method relies on the phenotypic characterisation of GP trees for measuring similarity and is based on the work in [12].

Knowledge Usage. To create new GP individuals in target domains, first a GP function/terminal g is selected for the root node with the probability specified in the PPT root node for g. Then, for each child of the root (if it can have a child), a GP terminal/function is selected based on its PPT probability and this

Table 2. UCARP Terminal Settings

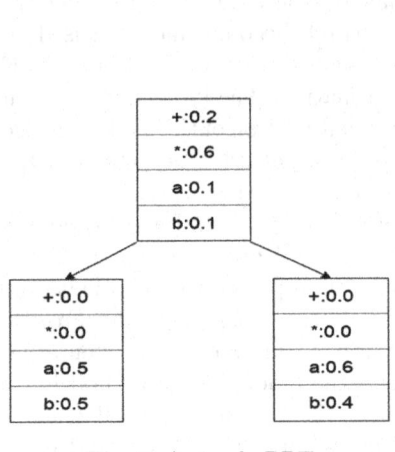

Fig. 2. A simple PPT

Terminal	Description
CFH	Cost From Here
FULL	FULLness (vehicle load capacity)
CR	Cost to Refill
CTT1	Cost To the closest Task
DEM1	DEMand of the closest unserved task
RQ	Remaining Capacity
FUT	Fraction of Unassigned Tasks
SC	Serving Cost
RQ1	Remaining Capacity of closest alternative route
FRT	Fraction of Remaining Tasks
DEM	DEMand
ERC	Ephemeral Random Constant
CFR1	Cost From the closest alternative Route
CTD	Cost To Depot

process is repeated until maximum tree depth is reached. The transferred PPT is used to create k portion of the initial GP population and, β portion of new populations in each generation alongside crossover and mutation operators.

Knowledge Update. To keep transferred PPT updated to the specifications of the target domain, we update each probability value incrementally with $P_g^{t+1} = \lambda P_g^t + (1 - \lambda)\bar{P}_g$. Here, P_g^t is the probability value of GP function/terminal g at generation t and $\bar{P}_g = M_g^t/N$ is the estimated probability value for g from the best individuals of the current population (M_g^t is the number of individuals that contain g at a corresponding node).

4   Experimental Studies

In order to investigate the proposed framework, we consider the scenario in which the difference between source and target UCARP domains is based on the number of vehicles (Table 3). We consider *SubTree*, *FullTree* [6] and *FreqSub* [3] from the body of existing works alongside the *PKGPHH* method (research question in Section 1). The GP terminal set is presented in Table 2. GP function set is $\{+, -, \times, /, min, max\}$ [3]. A population of 1024 individuals is evolved for

Table 3. Number of vehicles on source and target problems

Dataset	Gdb1	Gdb1	Gdb2	Gdb2	Gdb3	Gdb3	Gdb4	Gdb4	Gdb5	Gdb5	Gdb6
Source	5	5	6	6	5	5	4	4	6	6	5
Target	4	6	5	7	4	6	3	5	5	7	4

Dataset	Gdb6	Gdb7	Gdb7	Gdb12	Gdb12	Gdb14	Gdb14	Gdb15	Gdb15	Gdb16	Gdb16
Source	5	5	5	7	7	5	5	4	4	5	5
Target	6	4	6	6	8	4	6	3	5	4	6

Dataset	gdb17		Gdb17	Gdb13	Gdb13	Gdb19	Gdb19	Gdb20	Gdb20	Gdb21	Gdb21
Source	5		5	6	6	3	3	4	4	6	6
Target	4		6	5	7	2	4	3	5	5	7

50 generations with a reproduction rate of 0.05. Max tree depth is 8, and 10 elites of a generation are moved to the next generation. For training, 5 samples are considered which are rotated each generation to improve generalisation while 500 samples are used for testing. We obtained the best results with the $\epsilon = 0, c = 1$ for niching radius and capacity settings [15]. All comparisons are performed with the Wilcoxon rank sum test of 30 independent runs with 0.05 significance level. *SubTree*, *FullTree* and *FreqSub* initialise 10% of GP population in the target domain and are referred to as *SubTree-0.1*, *FullTree-0.1* and *FreqSub-0.1* respectively. For PKGPHH, we extracted the transferable PPT from top 10% individuals of the source domain and considered different initialisation rates k, breeding rate β, learning rate λ and crossover x rate and, is referred to as *PKGPHH(β, x, λ, k)*. For these experiments, we rely on domain expertise for the relatedness of the source and target domains.

4.1 Experimental Results

A major goal of transfer learning is to reduce the time for retraining the routing policies. Accordingly, we considered the earliest generation in which test performance of a transfer learning method is statistically similar to the final population of vanilla GP without knowledge transfer for at least three consecutive generations. Figure 4 depicts the percentage of generations on target domain that could be saved by applying each transfer algorithm, averaged over all experiments. According to Table 4, PKGPHH achieved the final performance of vanilla GP at least 57.2% earlier which indicates its potential for reducing the training time. Interestingly, based on Table 4, the best improvement is achieved by the *Full-Tree* method.

Table 4 presents a summary of how the final performance of each algorithm compares to that of vanilla GP without transfer in the form of ('wins', 'draws', 'losses') triples in which the number of 'wins', 'draws' and 'losses' of an algorithm indicate the number of times its final performance was statistically better than, similar to or worst than the baseline algorithm. According to Table 4, for the majority of the experiments, *PKGPHH* is on par with the existing methods and Table 4 indicate that *PKGPHH* has the potential for transfer learning that is similar to existing methods. In the following subsections, we will consider our research questions and use the results to give an extensive analysis of the framework and gain a better understanding about its dynamics.

4.2   Exploration vs Exploitation

The effect of transferred knowledge on the GP evolution is governed by different parameters. Large values of β place a high focus on the exploitation of old knowledge and can deter GP's search mechanism. We observed that when β is large, GP converges to local optima and even more exploration through large values of mutation rate could not overcome it. For example, for the case of PKG-PHH(0.325, 0.325, 0.3, 0.5), the improvement was 47.13%. We noticed that GP's performance for UCARP is sensitive to the initial state (controlled with k) and GP will converge to local optima if large portion of the initial population is created from the transferred knowledge. This effect was observed in all algorithms. For instance, in Table 4, increasing k from 0.1 to 0.5 reduced improvement from 57.2% to 51.0% and added 4 more negative transfer cases. However, more cases of significantly better final performance were observed with larger initialisation rates too. This usually happens when important regions of the target domain's search space are seen in the source domain and the initialisation can bias GP towards these regions.

Table 4. Performance of algorithms in terms of number of "wins", "draws" and "losses" of algorithms against vanilla GP and, average improvements in training effort achieved

Algorithm	SubTree-0.1	FullTree-0.1	PKGPHH(0.1, 0.7, 0.2, 0.1)
Performance	(1, 30, 1)	(1, 28, 3)	(0, 32, 0)
Improvement	63%	63.3%	57.2%

Algorithm	FreqSub-0.1	PKGPHH(0.1, 0.7, 0.2, 0.5)
Performance	(4, 20, 8)	(3, 25, 4)
Improvement	43.6%	51%

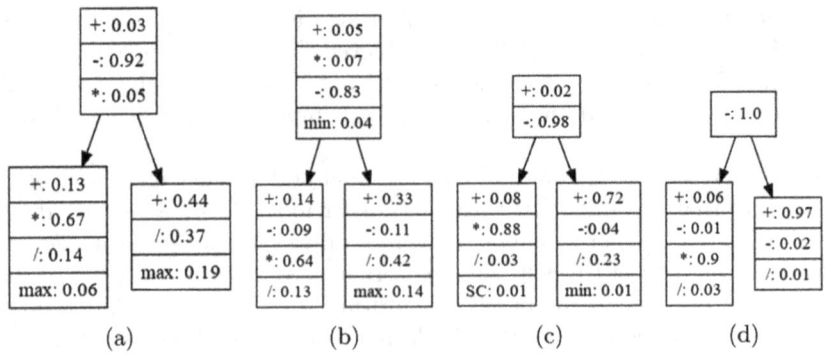

(a)   (b)   (c)   (d)

Fig. 3. Evolution of an extracted PPT (a) after generation 2 (b), 25 (c) and 50 (d) in target domain.

4.3   Quality of Learned Knowledge

Figure 3 shows evolution of a PPT (Figure 3a) extracted from a source domain (only top two levels are shown to save space) and tracks its structure after generation 2 (Figure 3b), generation 25 (Figure 3c) and generation 50 (Figure 3d). The first thing to notice is that one GP function at each shown node has a probability that is very higher than others. We observed the same property in lower levels of the PPT. This indicates a lack of diversity in the source domain. Considering that niching is performed in the source domain, this figure shows that even if the niching algorithm increases phenotypic diversity, the population still can lose its genotypic diversity in the subset of top-performing individuals. Increasing the number of individuals to learn the PPT does not help since either their fitness is not good or they have low probabilities and will not be selected.

4.4   Sensitivity to Learning Rate

Another issue that is evident from Figures 3 is that the probability values do not change over time, even when the learning rate λ is zero. To understand the effect of learning rates, we recorded the fitness of all individuals that were created from the PPT breeding and crossover operators at each generation and Figure 4a plots them for different learning rates for one of the experiments with $\beta = 0.1, k = 0.1$. According to this figure, the fitness of individuals created from PPT (labelled as *PPT* in the plot) are usually worse than the fitness of the individuals created from crossover (labelled as *XOVER* in the plot). Also, it is noticeable that different learning rates do not have any effect and, for all learning rates, standard deviations of PPT-bred individuals is more than crossover-bred individuals. Consequently, we can conclude that the learning mechanism is not very efficient and the population suffers from some sort of convergence to local optima from which GP cannot escape.

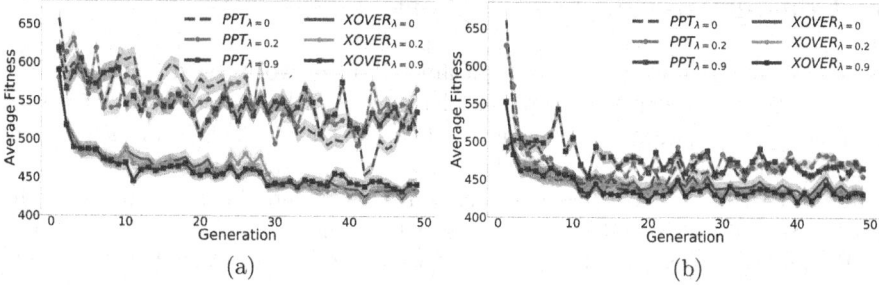

Fig. 4. Average fitness of individuals bred from PPT (PPT) and crossover (XOVER) for different learning rates λ (gdb2, 6 to 7 vehicles) (a) clearing is enabled versus (b) clearing is disabled.

4.5 Effectiveness of Clearing

Previous studies showed that diversity in source domains affects quality of knowledge transfer [3]. To verify this, we disabled the clearing method in both source and target domains and we identified a few more cases of significant final improvements and less cases of negative transfer than the results reported in Table 4. Figure 4b shows that again, different values of λ do not have important effect but disabling the clearing method has an observable effect and it actually improves the quality of the individuals that are created from the PPT. Looking at the structure of the PPT for this experiment showed that the lack of diversity has lead to a PPT that has single probability values in many nodes. This leads to creation of trees that are very similar to the best individuals the PPT was learned from. Conversely, the PPTs that represent more diversity due to the clearing procedure create trees that are more diverse but do not have good qualities because the current structure of PPT does not consider inter-dependence of probability distributions (more investigations in Subsection 4.6). Overall, we suspect that genotypic [17] niching may alleviate this problem.

4.6 Effectiveness of Knowledge Representation

It is possible that the selection of the PPT structure for knowledge representation, $\mathcal{M}$, is limited. A basic assumption of our model is the independence of probability distributions governing each PPT node. While this assumption was effective in the area of probabilistic optimisation [16], other works have also noticed its flaws and have proposed multivariate modelling of the search space with Bayesian networks [10,11,14]. In our investigations, we noticed that good individuals that, for example, have / as the root's right child node, usually have ∗ as the root's left child node. However, the PPT structure does not represent this relationship.

5 Conclusions and Future Work

In this paper, first we proposed a parametric framework for transfer learning and investigated it with a simple implementation that offers straightforward mechanisms for updating and using the transferred knowledge during GP run. Utilising this method, we probed the framework's features with a case study of tackling the UCARP scenario changes. Our experiments demonstrated that the framework can model delicacies of transfer learning.

Formulating a transfer learning task based on our framework, helped us note that although transfer learning can have strong potential, devising a powerful structure for knowledge representation and updating it effectively are key factors for producing an effective and efficient performance in target domains. Striking a balance between exploitation and exploration is another important challenge. In our framework, the transferred knowledge can be used during both GP initialisation and evolution and our experiments showed that both of them should be considered carefully to reach the balance. The transferred knowledge can add to the exploitation phase of GP and relying on it excessively can lead to convergence to local optima. Relatedness of a source domain to a corresponding target domains is also an important considerations that can affect the performance. To the best of our knowledge, there exists no methods for measuring the similarity between UCARP domains. In our experiments, we relied on domain expertise for defining related source and target domains. However, this assumed relatedness is not guaranteed. We leave the investigation of this issue and its integration into the framework for future works.

Although we utilised an experimental transfer learning algorithm implementing the framework, we believe the potentials of the framework are general in nature and our experiments with GP and UCARP are examples that demonstrate how different aspects of the framework can impact the success of knowledge transfer which we aim to demonstrate in our future works.

References

1. Ardeh, M.A., Mei, Y., Zhang, M.: Genetic programming hyper-heuristic with knowledge transfer for uncertain capacitated arc routing problem. In: Proceedings of the Genetic and Evolutionary Computation Conference Companion, pp. 334–335. ACM (2019)
2. Ansari Ardeh, M., Mei, Y., Zhang, M.: A novel genetic programming algorithm with knowledge transfer for uncertain capacitated arc routing problem. In: Nayak, A.C., Sharma, A. (eds.) PRICAI 2019. LNCS (LNAI), vol. 11670, pp. 196–200. Springer, Cham (2019). https://doi.org/10.1007/978-3-030-29908-8_16
3. Ardeh, M.A., Mei, Y., Zhang, M.: Transfer learning in genetic programming hyper-heuristic for solving uncertain capacitated arc routing problem. In: Proceedings of the IEEE Congress on Evolutionary Computation, pp. 49–56 (2019)
4. Ardeh, M.A., Mei, Y., Zhang, M.: Genetic programming hyper-heuristics with probabilistic prototype tree knowledge transfer for uncertain capacitated arc routing problems (accepted to appear). In: Proceedings of the IEEE Congress on Evolutionary Computation (2020)
5. De Lorenzo, A., Bartoli, A., Castelli, M., Medvet, E., Xue, B.: Genetic programming in the twenty-first century: a bibliometric and content-based analysis from both sides of the fence. Genet. Program. Evolvable Mach. 21(1), 181–204 (2019). https://doi.org/10.1007/s10710-019-09363-3
6. Dinh, T.T.H., Chu, T.H., Nguyen, Q.U.: Transfer learning in genetic programming. In: Proceedings of the IEEE Congress on Evolutionary Computation, pp. 1145–1151 (2015)
7. Eliason, S.R.: Maximum Likelihood Estimation : Logic and Practice. Sage, Thousand Oaks (1993)
8. Feng, L., Ong, Y.S., Lim, M.H., Tsang, I.W.: Memetic search with interdomain learning: a realization between CVRP and CARP. IEEE Trans. Evol. Comput. 19(5), 644–658 (2015)
9. Gupta, A., Ong, Y., Feng, L.: Insights on transfer optimization: because experience is the best teacher. IEEE Trans. Emerg. Top. Comput. Intell. 2(1), 51–64 (2018)
10. Hasegawa, Y., Iba, H.: Optimizing programs with estimation of bayesian network. In: Proceedings of the IEEE Congress on Evolutionary Computation, pp. 1378–1385 (2006)

11. Hasegawa, Y., Iba, H.: A bayesian network approach to program generation. IEEE Trans. Evol. Comput. **12**(6), 750–764 (2008)
12. Hildebrandt, T., Branke, J.: On using surrogates with genetic programming. Evol. Comput. **23**(3), 343–367 (2015)
13. Liu, Y., Mei, Y.: Automated heuristic design using genetic programming hyper-heuristic for uncertain capacitated arc routing problem. In: Proceedings of the Genetic and Evolutionary Computation Conference, pp. 290–297 (2017)
14. Pelikan, M., Goldberg, D.E., Cantú-Paz, E.: BOA: the bayesian optimization algorithm. In: IlliGAL Report, GECCO'99, pp. 525–532. Morgan Kaufmann Publishers Inc. San Francisco, CA, USA (1999)
15. Petrowski, A.: A clearing procedure as a niching method for genetic algorithms. In: Proceedings of IEEE Conference on Evolutionary Computation (1996)
16. Sałustowicz, R., Schmidhuber, J.: Probabilistic incremental program evolution: stochastic search through program space. In: van Someren, M., Widmer, G. (eds.) ECML 1997. LNCS, vol. 1224, pp. 213–220. Springer, Heidelberg (1997). https://doi.org/10.1007/3-540-62858-4_86
17. Shir, O.M.: Niching in evolutionary algorithms, pp. 1035–1069. Springer, Berlin (2012)
18. Taylor, M., Whiteson, S., Stone, P.: Transfer learning for policy search methods. In: Proceedings of the International Conference on Machine Learning (2006)
19. Torrey, L., Shavlik, J.: Transfer learning. Handbook of Research on Machine Learning Applications and Trends: Algorithms, Methods, and Techniques, pp. 242–264. IGI Global, Hershey (2010)
20. Zhang, F., Mei, Y., Nguyen, S., Zhang, M.: Evolving scheduling heuristics via genetic programming with feature selection in dynamic flexible job shop scheduling. IEEE Trans. Cybern. (2020). https://doi.org/10.1109/TCYB.2020.3024849
21. Zhang, F., Mei, Y., Zhang, M.: A two-stage genetic programming hyper-heuristic approach with feature selection for dynamic flexible job shop scheduling. In: Proceedings of the Genetic and Evolutionary Computation Conference, pp. 347–355 (2019)

Genetic Programming-Based Selection of Imputation Methods in Symbolic Regression with Missing Values

Baligh Al-Helali[✉], Qi Chen[✉], Bing Xue[✉], and Mengjie Zhang[✉]

School of Engineering and Computer Science, Victoria University of Wellington,
PO Box 600, Wellington 6400, New Zealand
{baligh.al-helali,Qi.Chen,Bing.Xue,Mengjie.Zhang}@ecs.vuw.ac.nz

Abstract. Data incompleteness represents a serious issue in real-world applications of machine learning. Imputation methods are algorithms for restoring missing values in the data based on other available entries. Imputation methods have an influence on the learning performance on incomplete data. Therefore, the choice of a right imputation method has an important role when constructing prediction models. It is common to use one imputation method to impute all the incomplete features. However, the imputation method that works well for some features might not be suitable for others, hence, it would be more useful to select the right imputation method for each feature. In fact, selecting an imputation method for the whole data set is still a challenging issue, let al one selecting different imputation methods for all incomplete features. Therefore, this work proposes the use of genetic programming to search for the right combination of imputation methods for symbolic regression. The role of GP is to select imputation methods for incomplete features and evolve symbolic regression. It incorporates a heterogeneous set of imputation methods as part of the symbolic regression process. The results show that the proposed method can automatically find the most effective combination of imputation methods for a variety of incomplete regression data sets.

Keywords: Symbolic regression · Genetic programming · Incomplete data · Imputation

1 Introduction

Genetic programming (GP) is a popular evolutionary algorithm that automatically generates computer programs for performing a user-defined task [9]. It starts from a high-level definition of the problem and creates a population of random programs and then refines them progressively using genetic operations until getting a satisfactory solution [19]. One typical application of GP is symbolic regression (SR), which is a task with the goal of constructing a mathematical model that best fits a given data set. Unlike traditional regression methods, no

© Springer Nature Switzerland AG 2020
M. Gallagher et al. (Eds.): AI 2020, LNAI 12576, pp. 163–175, 2020.
https://doi.org/10.1007/978-3-030-64984-5_13

priori assumption is required in symbolic regression. This means many benefits for using symbolic regression for real-world applications [8].

Missing values can cause considerable losses in data quality, which in turn, have a potential influence on the whole learning process [16]. There are different reasons for data incompleteness such as unfilled survey fields and sensor failures. Imputation is one of the widely used strategies to address the missing data problem. In imputation, statistical and machine learning methods are used to estimate the original values of missing entries based on the data available in both complete and incomplete instances [16]. Due to the importance of choosing the right imputation method in machine learning, several studies have investigated extensive comparisons between different imputation techniques [7,11,17].

It is common to use a single imputation method to address the incompleteness in a whole given data set. However, it is hard to find an imputation method that suits all features in a given data set, especially when there are various features with different natures. The imputation method that provides highly accurate estimates for the missing values in some incomplete features might not work well for other features. Features can have different data types, distributions, and ranges. This means that it would be more useful to find an effective combination of feature-wise imputation methods in order to improve the learning task. However, finding such a combination is an exhaustive process, even with a small number of features, as there is a need to train the model and evaluate it for each possible choice. This work proposes a method to find such a combination.

GP has been successfully used to select different components of several learning pipelines, but it is rarely adopted for selecting and evolving imputation methods. An attempt to use GP to evolve imputation methods is presented in [15,16]. They incorporate imputation methods as data preprocessors to a recent AutoML approach; the Tree-based Pipeline Optimization Tool (TPOT) [20]. However, these methods work by finding the imputation method for the whole data set, rather than finding suitable imputation methods for individual features. Moreover, their applicability has only been validated on classification tasks.

The main objective of this study is to use GP to automatically find a combination of imputation methods for incomplete features when constructing symbolic regression models. It utilizes GP to incorporate the feature-wise imputations in the evolutionary process of symbolic regression with missing data. This approach has a considerable potential to improve the symbolic regression performance effectively. The use of GP to solve similar tasks has been widely adopted in many studies.

GP has been successfully used to find optimal solutions that involve many possible combinations in several problems. For instance, GP has been successfully utilised for evolving solutions in various learning tasks such as deep learning [24] and job shop scheduling [28]. However, we are not aware of any other study that uses GP for selecting useful combination of imputation methods to improve the symbolic regression performance. Another motivation to select GP over other search methods is the ability of GP to search for the imputation methods while carrying out symbolic regression simultaneously. That is, in this work, GP is used to select imputation methods for incomplete features and evolve symbolic regression.

2   Related Work

Machine learning algorithms use given data sets to build a proper model. In reality, unfortunately, the given data might not be suitable to be used directly due to some issues such as incompleteness. Many real-world data sets have instances with missing values. For instance, in the UCI machine learning repository [12], about one-forth the available regression data sets are annotated as having missing values. There are usually missing values that have to be handled during the learning process. However, doing so without careful investigation might impact the overall pipeline.

There are different categorizations of missing values [13]. Missing values can be classified into missing completely at random (MCAR), missing not at random (MNAR), and missing at random (MAR). In MCAR missingness, the missing values are a random subset of the given data set with a completely random reason. In this kind of missingness, the missingness probability of a value is not related to any other value. For MNAR missingness, the probability that a value is missing is related to non-observed information such as the missing value itself. In the case of missing at random (MAR), the probability for a value to be missing is commonly related to existing data, i.e., missingness depends on other values.

Missing values cause serious problems for regression. Most regression methods could not work directly on incomplete data sets. On the other hand, if the instances with missing values are simply deleted, the amount of available data might be reduced dramatically. There will be insufficient data to represent the true pattern. Moreover, hidden patterns in the missing values might be useful for providing additional insight in the data generating system [6]. Data imputation is one approach to handling the incompleteness in which the missing values are estimated then the learning can be performed using the imputed complete data.

The focus in this work will be on the imputation approach. There are two main types of imputation: single imputation and multiple imputation. Single imputation directly replaces missing values with the estimated ones based on observed characteristics. Single imputation usually ignores uncertainty and underestimates the variance [22]. Multiple imputation addresses this problem by considering both within-imputation uncertainty and between-imputation uncertainty [25]. In multiple imputation, multiple complete copies of the data are produced each for independent estimates for the missing values. Conditional on observed data, a posterior distribution of missing data is modeled to draw a random sample and create several imputed data sets reflecting the uncertainty about imputation [23]. Then, statistical analysis is conducted on the imputed data sets separately and the results are combined to get a value estimate [25].

For symbolic regression with missing values, a few studies have considered imputation to handle the incompleteness. In [10], GP for symbolic regression method is performed on incomplete data. The missing values are handled through prediction models for the variables. In [27], the missingness is treated as having imbalanced data in certain regions of mathematical functions. A hybrid method which combines GP and KNN to impute missing values for symbolic regression is proposed in [1]. In [4], GP is used for selecting and ranking imputation predictors in high-dimensional symbolic regression with incomplete data. In [3], a wrapper imputation method is developed using GP and applied for symbolic regression with incomplete data. In [2], a GP-based method is proposed for selecting imputation predictors while imputing missing values for symbolic regression. In [5], regularized GP models are constructed for imputation predictor selection in symbolic regression with missing values.

There are only a few studies that attempt to evolve imputation methods. In [16], a method for evolving imputation strategies for missing data in classification problems with TPOT is presented. They proposed a GP method to search for the best combination of imputation and classification algorithms on the Python-based TPOT library by incorporating a heterogeneous set of imputation algorithms as part of the machine learning pipeline search. However, this approach produces a high number of unfeasible pipelines. To address this limitation, a strongly-typed-GP based approach that enforces constraint satisfaction is presented in [15]. These studies use GP to find a good imputation method for the whole data set as a preprocessing step within a classification pipeline. They do not aim to find suitable combination of imputation methods (can be different) for different features, which is the goal of our work.

3   The Proposed Method

Selecting and applying a right imputation method is important and usually requires a substantial amount of human intervention. Currently, there are many techniques used to impute missing values, which makes trying all possible methods almost infeasible. Therefore the automatic selection of these methods is desired. Instead of exhaustively evaluating combinations of imputation methods over the incomplete features, GP can be utilized to search for the most effective combination. This is done by designing GP solutions that involve different imputation methods in symbolic regression with missing data.

Usually, for a given data set with missing values, only one imputation method is used to fill in the missing values in different incomplete features. Unfortunately, the selected method might not be the best choice for all incomplete features. For this purpose we present a method called GPEvoIM that uses GP for the selection of imputation methods to estimate the incomplete features while evolving symbolic regression solutions. That is, the role of GP is to select imputation methods per features and evolve symbolic regression.

There are many possible combinations of imputation methods based on the number of incomplete features. For a given data set, trying all possible combinations to identify the one that minimizes the regression error is often unfeasible. Search-based methods are a feasible alternative in this scenario. Therefore, we focus on automatically generating such a combination while constructing symbolic expressions that fit the given data. Assume we have p incomplete features and q imputation methods, the size of the search space is $p \times q$ if the imputations are done independently (or in case of parallel imputation) whereas it can be $\prod_{i=1}^{p} q$ combinations when performing sequential imputations.

To implement the imputation methods on incomplete features, we consider a search space that contains features associated with imputation methods, such that there are $p \times q$ possible combinations for q imputation methods and p features ($\{(Imp_i, F_j), i = 1, ..., q, j = 1, ..., p\}$), where Imp_i refers to the ith imputation method and F_j stands for j^{th} feature. These possible pairs are included in the terminal set as well as random floating-point constants. When evaluating a GP model that contains (Imp_i, F_j), the imputation method Imp_i is applied on the feature F_j providing an imputed one. In addition, basic arithmetic functions, viz. $+, -, *, \div$, are used. The division function is protected, i.e. it returns one if the second input (the denominator) is zero.

For measuring the quality of the produced solutions, a fitness function that evaluates the regression error of the evolved trees is needed. In this work, the relative squared error (RSE) shown in the following equation (Eq. (1)), is used.

$$RSE = \frac{\sum_{i=1}^{n}(y_i - t_i)^2}{\sum_{i=1}^{n}(t_i - \bar{t})^2} \tag{1}$$

where n is number of instances, y_i is the ith predicted value, t_i is the ith desired value, and $\bar{t}$ is the average of the desired values t_i, $i = 1, 2, 3..., n$.

The result of the GP evolutionary process with the above components is a symbolic regression solution, which, in addition to traditional GP elements, involves the selection of a "good" combination of imputation methods that minimizes the fitness function value. An example of a GPEvoIM solution that includes applying imputation to incomplete features is shown in Fig. 1. This example can be read as, $Regression\_Target = (Impute(IM_1, IF_1) * CF_1) * ((Impute(IM_2, IF_3) * Impute(IM_3, IF_4)) + (CF_2 + (C_1 - Impute(IM_1, IF_2))))$, where IM_1, IM_2, and IM_3 are imputation methods, IF_1, IF_2, IF_3, and IF_4 are incomplete features, CF_1, and CF_2 are complete features, and C_1 is a constant. It implies applying the imputation method IM_1 to impute the incomplete feature IF_1 before multiplying the imputed one by the complete feature CF_1. Similarly the imputation methods IM_2, IM_3, and IM_1 are applied to impute the incomplete features IF_3, IF_4, and IF_2, respectively. The overall result of the evaluation of this model represents a prediction value for the regression target variable.

4   Experiment Setup

To evaluate the proposed method, two types of data sets are used, synthetic incomplete data sets and real-world incomplete data sets. The synthetic data sets are generated from real-world complete regression data sets. Table 1 shows the statistics of the original data sets and more details can be found in the associated reference. Each data set is divided randomly into two sub data sets where 70% of the data is used for training and the other 30% is for testing. For

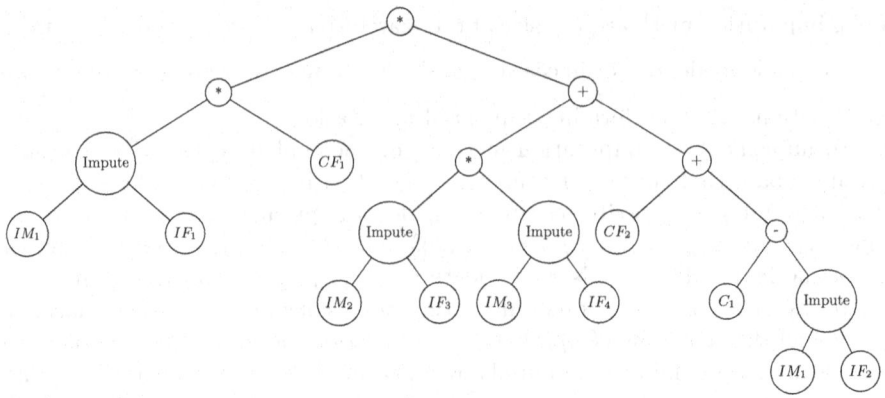

Fig. 1. An example of symbolic tree that includes applying imputation methods to incomplete features.

Table 1. Statistics of the used data sets

Data set	#Features	#Instances	#Incomplete	Ref
SkillCraft1	19	3395	57	[12]
Imports-85	25	205	54	[12]
Auto-mpg	7	398	6	[12]
CCN	122	1994	1676	[12]
fri_c0_100_25 (Fri)	25	100	0	[26]
CPMP	24	2108	0	[26]
Bank32nh (Bank)	33	8192	0	[26]
Selwood	54	31	0	[26]

the data sets with no missing values, each pair of train-test data set, 30% missing at random (MAR) probability missingness is imposed on 50% of the features, which results in 30 synthetic incomplete pairs for each complete data set. The missingness is generated using the R package SIMSEM [21].

In this work, ten imputation methods are considered. These methods represent different imputation approaches implemented in Autoimpute, which is a Python package for handling missing data [18]. The used methods include four simple algorithms: mean, mode, norm, and random, which are self explaining, and other six more advanced methods: linear regression (LR), predictive mean matching (PMM), multinomial logistic regression (MLR), local residual draws (LRD), bayesian least squares (BLS), and last obs carried forward (LOCF).

Table 2 shows the parameter settings for GP runs. These values are selected empirically. GP implementation is done by using the GP framework provided by distributed evolutionary algorithms in python (DEAP) [14]. The comparisons of the methods are based on their effect on the symbolic regression performance.

Table 2. GP settings

Parameter	Value	Parameter	Value
Generations	100	Population size	512
Crossover rate	0.9	Mutation rate	0.1
Elitism	Top-5 individual	Selection method	Tournament
Tournament size	7	Maximum depth	11
Initialization	Ramped-half and half	Function set	$+, -, *, \%$
Terminal set	imputations, features, constants	Fitness	Eq. (1)

The proposed method carries out symbolic regression simultaneously, however, to compare it with the other imputation methods, a separate step is needed. For each data set, the imputation methods are used to produce complete training and test sets. The training data are used to construct symbolic regression models. These models are then applied on the test data and the obtained regression error is considered as the comparison criterion.

5   Results and Discussions

5.1   Evaluation on Synthetic Incomplete Data

To measure the symbolic regression performance, 30 GP runs are performed on each imputed data obtained by applying each imputation method. Note that we have 30 synthetically generated incomplete variations for each complete data

Method	Fri	CPMP	Bank	Selwood
LR	0.2324	83.9530	0.0440	0.1936
PMM	0.2284	74.9300	0.0393	0.1870
BLS	0.2372	72.8660	0.0408	0.1970
ML	0.2138	76.9267	0.0338	0.2008
norm	0.2522	91.5087	0.0452	0.2056
mean	0.2545	93.3087	0.0484	0.2128
mode	0.2561	107.3467	0.0490	0.2311
LRD	0.2333	81.5667	0.0367	0.1902
LOCF	0.2333	86.4433	0.0460	0.2037
random	0.2633	109.2667	0.0497	0.2094
GPEvoIM	0.2013	58.2165	0.0323	0.1768

Fig. 2. The average regression errors of using different imputation methods on the used synthetic incomplete data sets.

set, which means 120 data set in total. The results of the symbolic regression with different methods are shown in Figure 2, which are the average of symbolic regression errors over the 30 runs. To make it easy to observe the pattern of the performance with respect to both the data and the method, we show the results in a heat-map manner. For each data set, the error of each method has a background of a green-scale color, where the darker scale the better the method.

From the shown results, the proposed method, GPEvoIM, has the smallest symbolic regression error compared to any other method on all the data sets. These results are expected as GPEvoIM combines different imputation methods in a feature-wise way while improving the symbolic regression performance during the evolutionary process. However, the other methods are applied on the data sets in an unsupervised manner, i.e. Without considering the regression performance. Moreover, the method is used to impute all missing values in the data set al.though it might not suitable for some features.

It is clear that there is no universal imputation method that can always achieve the best performance on every data set. However, from our results, the methods PMM, ML, and BLS have a consistent good impact on the performance of symbolic regression. Although they do not provide the best performance on all data sets, none of them cause the worst accuracy. On the other hand, the methods mode and random are associated with highest symbolic regression errors over all data sets. This indicates that univariate imputation methods may not be suitable for these data sets under the current circumstances.

The factors that contribute to such results can be the ratio of missingness (both feature-wise and instance-wise), the number of available features and instances, and the approach of the imputation method. In our experiments, having at least 50% complete features in each data set can be appropriate for multivariate methods to utilize these features to impute the incomplete ones. On the other hand, univariate methods use the data in the same feature to impute its missing values and this might not be effective when around 30% of the data are missing in the feature.

To show the significant superiority of the proposed method, comparisons of the symbolic regression performance for using each imputation method against the proposed method are performed. The comparisons are based on the statistical significance pairwise Wilcoxon test with a significance level of 0.05. As we have 30 incomplete variations for each data set, 30 comparison cases are considered for each data set. Table 3 summarizes the amount of cases in which the proposed method wins/losses against each benchmark imputation method on the used data sets. The row "+" ("−") refers to the number of cases in which the proposed method significantly outperforms (is outperformed by) the corresponding method in the table.

In total, there are 1200 comparisons among 10 methods on 30 variations for each of the four data sets. The proposed method, GPEvoIM won in 872 cases ($\approx 73\%$) and it is outperformed only in less than 9% of the comparisons. No significant difference is found in the other cases. The most frequent loosing method was random and it has zero total win on the Fri data set. For the data

Table 3. The count of worse/better $(-/+)$ cases of the proposed method against different imputation methods based on the symbolic regression performance

		LR	PMM	BLS	MLR	norm	mean	mode	LRD	LOCF	random	GPEvoIM
Fri	+	20	19	21	15	25	26	26	20	20	28	220
	−	3	3	4	3	4	1	1	4	4	0	27
CPMP	+	22	20	20	21	24	24	27	22	23	27	230
	−	2	3	3	3	2	2	1	3	2	1	22
Bank	+	25	22	23	19	25	27	28	21	26	28	244
	−	2	2	2	3	2	1	1	2	1	1	17
Selwood	+	15	13	16	17	18	21	26	14	18	20	178
	−	4	5	4	4	3	3	1	5	4	3	36

Table 4. Frequency of imputation methods in the best evolved GPEvoIM models

Method	LR	PMM	BLS	MLR	norm	mean	mode	LRD	LOCF	random
Fri	8	9	7	13	4	3	3	8	8	1
CPMP	6	8	8	7	5	5	2	6	5	2
Bank	4	8	7	11	4	2	1	9	3	0
Selwood	13	14	12	11	10	7	3	14	10	8
Total	31	39	34	42	23	17	9	37	26	11

sets, the best performance of the proposed method is on the Bank data set with 244 wins and the least number of wins is on the Selwood data set. This might be due to the high-dimensionality nature of Selwood data as the number of features is more than the number of instances in this data set.

5.2 Further Analysis

One of the interesting features of GP is its white-box (at least grey-box) nature, which increases the interpret-ability of the developed methods. GP provides explicit expression trees representing the final best models. These models include the arithmetic functions and the features that contribute to the learned model. Moreover, in our method, the contribution of the involved imputation methods can be analysed. Another benefit of the proposed method is the ability of analysing the feature selectability. Interestingly, some incomplete features can be more useful to build the regression model than some other complete features. Moreover, some incomplete features can appear in the constructed model more than once, but imputed with different methods. This can indicate an involvement of an implicit feature construction process.

An additional benefit of the proposed method is that it provides a means to compare the imputation methods indirectly. That is, instead of comparing each pair of the imputation methods based on their results directly, their contribution in the best evolved methods can be considered. The imputation methods that are used in the best trees can be considered as better methods than the other methods. Table 4 shows the frequency of using imputation methods in the best evolved GPEvoIM solutions.

In total of 120 solutions, the MLR method is involved 42 times. It indicates that this method is suitable to impute incomplete features more than the others. However, even the methods that have bad performance when they are used to impute the whole data set can appear in the best GPEvoIM solutions. For example, the mode and random methods appear 9 and 11 times out of the 120 possible occurrences. This is because the involvement is based on the applicability of the methods for individual features rather than the whole data set. Subsequently, methods that might not be suitable for imputing a data set can still be suitable for some features in the same data set.

5.3   The Applicability on Real-World Incomplete Data Sets

To validate the applicability of the proposed method, real-world incomplete data sets are considered. After applying each imputation method, the symbolic regression errors on the imputed test data sets are shown in Table 5. The table shows the mean and the significance test sign when compared to the proposed method.

Table 5. The test results of symbolic regression error on real incomplete data sets using different imputation methods

Method		Auto-mpg	Imports-85	SkillCraft1	CCN
LR	Avg	0.2427	0.3321	0.6141	0.5353
	T	=	+	+	+
PMM	Avg	0.2483	0.3235	0.6256	0.5243
	T	=	+	+	+
BLS	Avg	0.2472	0.3149	0.6371	0.5133
	T	=	+	+	+
MLR	Avg	0.2424	0.3063	0.6286	0.5123
	T	=	+	+	+
norm	Avg	0.2417	0.3127	0.6601	0.5173
	T	=	+	+	+
mean	Avg	0.2418	0.3289	0.6416	0.5303
	T	=	+	+	+
mode	Avg	0.2511	0.3305	0.6431	0.5442
	T	=	+	+	+
LRD	Avg	0.2475	0.3193	0.6246	0.5128
	T	=	+	+	+
LOCF	Avg	0.2476	0.3123	0.6226	0.5073
	T	=	+	+	+
random	Avg	0.2485	0.3294	0.6476	0.5356
	T	=	+	+	+
GPEvoIM	Avg	**0.2413**	**0.2981**	**0.6102**	**0.5013**

For each data set, "T" refers to the result of the Wilcoxon significance test where "+" ("−") indicates that the proposed method is significantly better (worse) than the corresponding method whereas "=" means no significant difference.

As can be seen from the results, the proposed method achieves the best performance on all the used data sets. The difference is significant except for the Auto-mpg data set where the ratio of missing values is too small (only 6 instances in one feature). Even the simple imputation methods can achieve better or at least similar results compared to sophisticated methods on some data sets. For example, norm and mean methods lead to better than PMM, NLS, LR, and ML on the Auto-mpg data set. This might be due to the low missingness ratio in this data sets, which implies that there is no need to use complicated imputation methods when there is a small percentage of missining values.

6   Conclusions and Future Work

In this work, a method for incorporating imputation techniques when using GP for symbolic regression with missing values is presented. Instead of using one imputation method to handle the missing values in a data set, the proposed method works by automatically searching for a good combination of heterogeneous imputation methods for different incomplete features. The method is based on a selective approach to combining different imputation algorithms in a way that improves the symbolic regression performance. The method is compared to several imputation methods on both synthetic and real-world incomplete data sets. The obtained experimental results show that, mostly, the proposed method is better or at least equal to any underlying method.

Although, theoretically, the presented framework can include more imputation techniques and can be applicable for different machine learning tasks, there is a need for more effort in this aspect. This includes more experiments considering more settings. More sophisticated imputation methods can be considered in more complex missingness situations such as having higher missingness ratios. Furthermore, rather than symbolic regression, the proposed approach can be applied on other machine learning tasks such as classification and clustering. These issues can be further investigated when the given incomplete data are high-dimensional.

References

1. Al-Helali, B., Chen, Q., Xue, B., Zhang, M.: A hybrid GP-KNN imputation for symbolic regression with missing values. In: Mitrovic, T., Xue, B., Li, X. (eds.) AI 2018. LNCS (LNAI), vol. 11320, pp. 345–357. Springer, Cham (2018). https://doi.org/10.1007/978-3-030-03991-2_33
2. Al-Helali, B., Chen, Q., Xue, B., Zhang, M.: Genetic programming-based simultaneous feature selection and imputation for symbolic regression with incomplete data. In: Palaiahnakote, S., Sanniti di Baja, G., Wang, L., Yan, W.Q. (eds.) ACPR 2019. LNCS, vol. 12047, pp. 566–579. Springer, Cham (2020). https://doi.org/10.1007/978-3-030-41299-9_44

3. Al-Helali, B., Chen, Q., Xue, B., Zhang, M.: A genetic programming-based wrapper imputation method for symbolic regression with incomplete data. In: 2019 IEEE Symposium Series on Computational Intelligence (SSCI), pp. 2395–2402. IEEE (2019)

4. Al-Helali, B., Chen, Q., Xue, B., Zhang, M.: Genetic programming for imputation predictor selection and ranking in symbolic regression with high-dimensional Incomplete Data. In: Liu, J., Bailey, J. (eds.) AI 2019. LNCS (LNAI), vol. 11919, pp. 523–535. Springer, Cham (2019). https://doi.org/10.1007/978-3-030-35288-2_42

5. Al-Helali, B., Chen, Q., Xue, B., Zhang, M.: Hessian complexity measure for genetic programming-based imputation predictor selection in symbolic regression with incomplete data. In: Hu, T., Lourenço, N., Medvet, E., Divina, F. (eds.) EuroGP 2020. LNCS, vol. 12101, pp. 1–17. Springer, Cham (2020). https://doi.org/10.1007/978-3-030-44094-7_1

6. Angelov, B.: Towards data science: working with missing data in machine learning (2017). https://towardsdatascience.com/working-with-missing-data-in-machine-learning-9c0a430df4ce

7. Arslan, A.K., Tunç, Z., Güldoğan, E., Çolak, C.: Performance comparison of some imputation methods used in missing value (s)analysis: a simulation study. Turk. Klinikleri J. Biostatistics**11**(1) (2019)

8. Austel, V., et al.: Globally optimal symbolic regression. arXiv preprint arXiv:1710.10720 (2017)

9. Banzhaf, W., Nordin, P., Keller, R.E., Francone, F.D.: Genetic programming: an introduction, vol. 1. Morgan Kaufmann San Francisco (1998)

10. Brandejsky, T.: Model identification from incomplete data set describing state variable subset only-the problem of optimizing and predicting heuristic incorporation into evolutionary system. In: Nostradamus 2013: Prediction, Modeling and Analysis of Complex Systems, pp. 181–189. Springer (2013)

11. Çüm, S., Demir, E.K., Gelbal, S., Kışla, T.: A comparison of advanced methods used for missing data imputation under different conditions (2019)

12. Dheeru, D., Karra Taniskidou, E.: UCI machine learning repository (2017). http://archive.ics.uci.edu/ml

13. Donders, A.R.T., Van Der Heijden, G.J., Stijnen, T., Moons, K.G.: A gentle introduction to imputation of missing values. J. Clin. Epidemiol. **59**(10), 1087–1091 (2006)

14. Fortin, F.A., Rainville, F.M.D., Gardner, M.A., Parizeau, M., Gagné, C.: Deap: evolutionary algorithms made easy. J. Mach. Learn. Res. **13**, 2171–2175 (2012)

15. Garciarena, U., Mendiburu, A., Santana, R.: Towards a more efficient representation of imputation operators in tpot. arXiv preprint arXiv:1801.04407 (2018)

16. Garciarena, U., Santana, R., Mendiburu, A.: Evolving imputation strategies for missing data in classification problems with tpot. arXiv preprint arXiv:1706.01120 (2017)

17. Heidt, K.: Comparison of imputation methods for mixed data missing at random (2019)

18. Kearney, J., Barkat, S.: Autoimpute, a python package for handling missing data. https://pypi.org/project/autoimpute/

19. McPhee, N.F., Poli, R., Langdon, W.B.: Field Guide to Genetic Programming. Lulu. com, Morrisville (2008)

20. Olson, R.S., Moore, J.H.: TPOT: a tree-based pipeline optimization tool for automating machine learning. In: Hutter, F., Kotthoff, L., Vanschoren, J. (eds.) Automated Machine Learning. TSSCML, pp. 151–160. Springer, Cham (2019). https://doi.org/10.1007/978-3-030-05318-5_8

21. Pornprasertmanit, S., Miller, P., Schoemann, A., Quick, C., Jorgensen, T., Pornprasertmanit, M.S.: Package 'simsem' (2016)

22. Rubin, D.B.: Multiple Imputation for Nonresponse in Surveys, vol. 81. JohnWiley & Sons, New Jersey (2004)

23. Schafer, J.L.: Multiple imputation: a primer. Stat. Methods Med. Res. 8(1), 3–15 (1999)

24. Suganuma, M., Shirakawa, S., Nagao, T.: A genetic programming approach to designing convolutional neural network architectures. In: Proceedings of the Genetic and Evolutionary Computation Conference, pp. 497–504 (2017)

25. Takahashi, M., Ito, T.: Multiple imputation of turnover in edinet data: toward the improvement of imputation for the economic census, pp. 24–26. Work Session on Statistical Data Editing, UNECE (2012)

26. Vanschoren, J., Van Rijn, J.N., Bischl, B., Torgo, L.: Openml: networked science in machine learning. ACM SIGKDD Explor. Newsl. 15(2), 49–60 (2014)

27. Vladislavleva, E., Smits, G., Den Hertog, D.: On the importance of data balancing for symbolic regression. IEEE Trans. Evol. Comput. 14(2), 252–277 (2010)

28. Zhang, F., Mei, Y., Nguyen, S., Zhang, M.: Evolving scheduling heuristics viagenetic programming with feature selection in dynamic flexible job shopscheduling. IEEE Trans. Cybern. (2020)

A Novel Mutation Operator for Variable Length Algorithms

Saskia Van Ryt[1(✉)], Marcus Gallagher[1], and Ian Wood[2]

[1] School of Information Technology and Electrical Engineering,
University of Queensland, Brisbane 4702, Australia
{s.vanryt,marcusg}@uq.edu.au
[2] School of Mathematics and Physics, University of Queensland,
Brisbane 4702, Australia
i.wood1@uq.edu.au

Abstract. The focus of this paper is variable length optimisation, which is a type of optimisation where the number of variables in the optimal solution is not known a priori. Due to the difference in solution space, traditional algorithms for fixed length problems either require significant adjustment, or cannot be applied at all. Furthermore, there is evidence that variable length algorithms - algorithms that consider solutions with different lengths throughout the optimisation process - may outperform fixed length algorithms on these problems. To investigate this, we have designed an abstract variable length problem that allows for straightforward and clear analysis. The performance of a number of evolutionary algorithms on this problem are analysed, including a fixed length algorithm and a state-of-the-art variable length algorithm. We propose a new mutation operator for variable length algorithms, and suggest potential directions for further research. Overall, the variable length algorithm with our mutation operator outperformed the state-of-the-art variable length algorithm, and the fixed length algorithm.

Keywords: Variable length optimisation · Evolutionary algorithms

1 Introduction

Variable length optimisation is an area of research focused on solving problems where the number of variables in the optimal solution is not known a priori. While a variety of approaches and real world problems have been proposed in the literature, such as wind farm layout problems [1,7], wireless network design [10], laminate stacking [4,7], and more [6], there is little communication outside of specific problem domains [7], and a theoretical understanding of these problems is lacking [8]. Compared to fixed length optimisation - where the number of variables remains fixed throughout the course of optimisation - research into variable length optimisation is in its infancy. Furthermore, it is unclear whether or not variable length algorithms can outperform the obvious alternative - running a fixed length algorithm for each different solution length.

© Springer Nature Switzerland AG 2020
M. Gallagher et al. (Eds.): AI 2020, LNAI 12576, pp. 176–188, 2020.
https://doi.org/10.1007/978-3-030-64984-5_14

The aim of this paper is to investigate the performance of a fixed length evolutionary algorithm compared to a number of variable length algorithms. To aid in analysis, we have designed an abstract shape matching problem, which can be solved by both fixed and variable length algorithms, and is easy to visualise regardless of the solution length. Additionally, we propose a novel variable length mutation operator specifically targeted to address the shortcomings of the existing variable length algorithms.

The first section of this paper contains an overview of variable length optimisation, from basic methods to the state-of-the-art. In the second section we present our abstract variable length problem - referred to as the shape matching problem. The third section gives details about our novel variable length mutation operator, including motivation and hyperparameter tuning. Finally, the performance of a number of algorithms is compared and analysed using the shape matching problem, with suggestions for further research.

2   Variable Length Optimisation

For a given optimisation problem, a candidate solution contains a particular number of variables, known as the solution length. For the vast majority of optimisation problems in the literature, the solution space consists only of solutions with the same length - known as fixed length problems. In contrast, there exist problems where the solution space consists of solutions with multiple different lengths. These are known as variable length problems, or 'trans-dimensional' problems.

Variable length problems pose a challenge for traditional optimisation algorithms. For example, gradient based methods rely on the existence of a clearly defined derivative or method for calculating the gradient [8]. However, the concept of gradients breaks down when the number of variables for a solution can vary. Similarly, methods with strict requirements for the problem representation, such as Linear Programming [8], are unsuitable for handling sets of solutions with multiple different structures.

In response to these difficulties, researchers have proposed techniques to solve variable length problems while still using fixed length algorithms. For example, if only a few possible solution lengths exist, then using a fixed length algorithm for each solution length is a straightforward approach. Another approach is to use a solution representation that allows some variables to be 'turned off', so they are not considered by the objective function [3]. Alternatively, a different problem representation can be used, so that it is fixed length. However, this can lead to representations that do not adequately match the real life scenario they are based on.

Another technique has also emerged - variable length algorithms. These algorithms are typically a variation on evolutionary algorithms, and allow the length of solutions to change throughout the optimisation process. Variable length algorithms have been applied to a diverse range of problems in the literature. However, as identified by Ryerkerk [7], discussion of variable length algorithms rarely

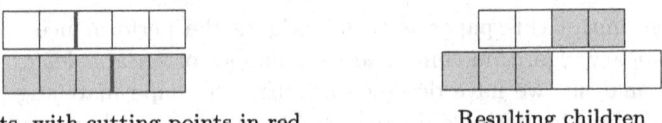

Two parents, with cutting points in red   Resulting children

Fig. 1. One-point crossover, with different cutting points for each parent (Color figure online)

extends beyond a problem's specific context. Consequently, concepts and methods are often proposed repeatedly across different problems, leading to little progress beyond basic variable length methods. The only significant work that has been done to compare different techniques is by Ryerkerk [7], who presented interesting hypotheses about the disruptive behaviour of crossover techniques and the value of length diversity.

While a variety of problem structures can be used for variable length algorithms, Ryerkerk [7] identified that most of these problems have solutions that are made up of a collection of identically structured groups of variables, which we refer to as components. For example, if one was to imagine an optimisation problem where an unknown number of wireless network devices were to be placed in a building, then each device would need its own set of coordinates. A pair of variables would represent the coordinates for a single wireless network device, making a single component. Solutions to this problem would consist of sets of these components - one component for each wireless network device.

Evolutionary algorithms are commonly employed to solve these problems, with authors proposing a range of alterations to existing fixed-length mutation and crossover operators, in order to handle the variable length nature of these problems.

A commonly proposed operator for variable length problems is an operator similar to one-point crossover, demonstrated in Fig. 1. In one-point crossover for fixed length problems, two parents will swap all variables to the right of a randomly chosen cutting point. This is altered for variable length problems by randomly generating different cutting points for the two parents, so the number of variables that are exchanged may be different for each parent. Numerous variations of this concept have been proposed, focused on choosing the cutting points for the two parents [1,9].

A particularly interesting crossover operator, which is used in this paper, is named 'spatial crossover' by Ryerkerk et al. [6], and has appeared in a number of publications [7,10]. If some part of each component represents coordinates in a physical space (such as a problem that places objects on an area of land), then parent solutions can be combined by splitting the area along a line (in the 2D case) and swapping components on one side of that line to produce two new child solutions. For mutation operators, common techniques used in the literature allow mutation to add or delete random components, or add a component based on the location of existing components [6].

Some authors have also proposed new selection operators for variable length algorithms. These selection operators are designed to increase the length diversity for the population - that is, increase the number of different lengths appearing in the parent population. Chang and Sim [2] propose a slight variation on tournament selection with elitism, where instead of just the best solution being placed into the next generation if it is not already there, the best solution of a different length is also included, thus ensuring at least some length diversity. A more complex selection operator, proposed by Ryerkerk, divides the population into niches based on their length, and performs selection as normal within each niche. This selection operator guarantees that some amount of length diversity is maintained between generations, and that solutions only compete with other solutions of similar lengths. Ryerkerk found that this 'length niching' selection operator outperformed existing selection operators on a range of problems, producing higher quality results in less function evaluations.

3   An Example Variable Length Problem: Shape Matching

3.1   Problem Description

To aid in the analysis of variable length optimisation algorithms, we present the shape matching problem, inspired by a similar problem presented by Lee [5]. Informally, the shape matching problem consists of a hidden target shape (a polygon) on a continuous 2D plane, where the goal is to create a shape as close to the target shape as possible. The only information given about the hidden target shape is through the objective function - which returns a real number representing how similar the candidate solution is to the target shape. Observe an example problem in Fig. 2, which contains a target shape and a solution.

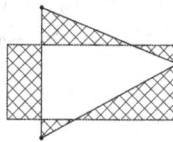

Fig. 2. A target shape (rectangle), and a candidate solution (triangle). The symmetrical difference is marked by the shaded area.

Solutions are represented as an ordered list of vertices. Each vertex is connected by edges to the vertices directly before and after it in the list of vertices, where the first and last vertices are connected by an edge in order to close the shape. Lee's version of the problem, published in the year 2000, included a simple objective function that results in a problem that is now easy to solve. Furthermore, Lee's chosen objective function indirectly penalised candidate solutions with lengths different to the target shape. We believe this gives algorithms too much information about the optimal solution, as the length of the optimal solution is not usually known for typical variable length problems. Additionally, there may even be multiple optimal solutions with different lengths for some problems, so Lee's objective function would not adequately represent real world variable length problems.

Our shape matching problem has a different objective function and solution representation compared to Lee's problem, in order to address these issues. We use Cartesian coordinates to represent vertices, instead of Polar coordinates, for ease of implementation, and our objective function is based on the total area not shared by the candidate shape and the target shape, along with a penalty term for the length of the solution. This penalty term does not take into account the length of the target shape - so that aspect of the optimal solution is not revealed to the algorithm. Without the penalty term in the objective function, algorithms would often produce shapes with many more vertices than is needed to match the target shape. These bloated solutions are not only qualitatively worse than equivalent shapes with less vertices, but are much more computationally expensive. Furthermore, many real world variable length problems, such as the wind farm problem, implicitly penalise larger solutions.

Formally, the shape matching problem, with a target shape t, is defined as follows:

$$\arg \min_{s \in S} f(s) = d(s,t) + \alpha L(s) \tag{1}$$

The set S is the set of all candidate solutions, which is the set of all ordered finite lists of components, where each component is an ordered pair of real numbers. The function $d(s,t)$ is the symmetric difference (defined below) between the candidate solution, s, and the target solution, t. The function $L(s)$ returns the number of components in solution s, and α is a constant weight parameter. For a given component, c, in a solution s, where c is a pair of real numbers, c_1 represents the x-coordinate of a particular vertex, and c_2 represents the y-coordinate. The resulting polygon from solution s is formed by creating an edge between each consecutive pair of vertices in s, including the final edge between the first and last vertices.

Note that the symmetric difference between two 2D polygons, s and t, is the total area in s that is not in t plus the total area in t that is not in s. Mathematically, if the area of shapes s and t are represented as s_a and t_a, respectively, then the symmetric difference is defined as: $d(s,t) = s_a \Delta t_a = (s_a \setminus t_a) \cup (t_a \setminus s_a)$.

4   Algorithm

In this section we present a novel mutation operator designed specifically for variable length algorithms. We provide the motivation and reasoning behind the design of this operator, followed by a detailed description.

4.1   Motivation

As observed by Ryerkerk, selection methods that aim for some amount of length diversity in the set of parent solutions outperform selection methods that focus solely on objective value. Furthermore, it was observed that some operators were quite prone to producing an undesirable number of poorly performing solutions, due to the disruptive effects of changing solution lengths.

We propose that there is another subtle effect produced by these disruptive crossover operators. A new solution may have a comparatively poor objective value, but its structure could have the potential to lead to solutions with better objective values than the parent solutions. However, using rudimentary selection operators, these solutions are unlikely to be chosen for the next generation.

The selection operators aimed at maintaining a level of length diversity in the parent population address part of this problem - they make it more likely for these poorly performing, well structured solutions to be chosen for the next generation. However, these solutions may require more than a few generations of improvements to be competitive, reducing the likelihood that they will reach their potential before being removed from the population.

4.2 Description

The mutation operator we propose in this paper - the 'Nudge' operator - aims to address this issue. Conceptually, this operator collects a few solutions with different lengths over a number of generations, and then improves them individually using a basic fixed length evolutionary algorithm, before placing them into the parent population. This allows these few differently-structured solutions to reach their potential, leading to an algorithm that uses less function evaluations to find good solutions, with a higher likelihood of overcoming local minima.

In the design of this method, one concern was that the number of function evaluations used to 'nudge' the chosen solutions would outweigh any benefits produced by this operator. However, this was found not to be the case.

During each generation, a list of all children larger than the parent and a list of all children smaller than the parent, are collected. After a number of generations, the best child from each of the two lists is collected, along with the best solution found so far. A mutation only, fixed-length, $(1 + 1)$ evolutionary algorithm is then used to improve each of the three solutions individually. After a predetermined number of generations for the fixed length algorithms, the three improved solutions are placed back into the population, and the algorithm continues.

The two hyperparameters for this operator are the nudge frequency, which is the number of generations between each nudge, and the nudge distance, which is the number of generations for the fixed length evolutionary algorithm used in the nudge operator. While the full results of hyperparameter tuning are not included in this paper, it was found that a nudge frequency of 2 and a nudge distance of 50 produced the best results on the shape matching problem.

The algorithm for the Nudge operator can be found in Algorithm 1, along with a demonstration of its placement within an evolutionary algorithm in Algorithm 2. Code is available at https://github.com/saskiavanryt/nudgealgorithm.

5 Methodology

The aim of this experiment is to compare the performance of five selected algorithms on the shape matching problem. Four target shapes were chosen, as seen

Algorithm 1. Nudge Operator

1: **procedure** NUDGE(p, N_r)   ▷ Improves solution p over N_r generations
2:     $r \leftarrow 0$
3:     **while** $r \leq N_r$ **do**
4:         $C \leftarrow \{p\}$
5:         $C \leftarrow C \cup \{mutate(p), mutate(p)\}$
6:         $p \leftarrow$ best solution in C
7:         $r \leftarrow r + 1$
8:     **end while**
9:     **return** p
10: **end procedure**

Algorithm 2. Variable Length Algorithm with Nudge Operator

1: **procedure** EVOLVENUDGE(P_n, t, N_f, N_r)
2:     $P \leftarrow \{$generate P_n random solutions$\}$
3:     $A_U \leftarrow \{\}$
4:     $A_H \leftarrow \{\}$
5:     $g \leftarrow 0$
6:     **while** stop condition not met **do**
7:         **if** $g \mod N_r = 0$ and $g \neq 0$ **then**
8:             $A \leftarrow \{$best solution in $A_H\}$
9:             $A \leftarrow A \cup \{$best solution in $A_U\} \cup\{$best solution in $P\}$
10:            $N \leftarrow \{Nudge(a)$ for each a in $A\}$
11:            $P \leftarrow P \cup N$
12:            $A_U \leftarrow \{\}$
13:            $A_U \leftarrow \{\}$
14:        **end if**
15:        $C \leftarrow$ Generate children from P
16:        $L \leftarrow$ Length of best solution in C
17:        $A_U \leftarrow A_U \cup$ best solution in C with length $> L$
18:        $A_H \leftarrow A_H \cup$ best solution in C with length $< L$
19:        $P \leftarrow Select(C)$
20:        $g \leftarrow g + 1$
21:    **end while**
22:    **return** Best solution in P
23: **end procedure**

Algorithm 3. Evolutionary Algorithm

1: **procedure** EVOLVE(P_n, t)
2:     $P \leftarrow \{$generate P_n random solutions$\}$
3:     $g \leftarrow 0$
4:     **while** stop condition not met **do**
5:         $C \leftarrow$ Generate children from P
6:         $P \leftarrow Select(C)$
7:         $g \leftarrow g + 1$
8:     **end while**
9:     **return** Best solution in P
10: **end procedure**

in Figs. 3, 4, 5, and 6, resulting in four different problems of varying difficulty. These four shapes lie within the bounds of $x = [0, 10]$ and $y = [0, 10]$, approximately centred around the point $(5, 5)$.

There were 30 runs for each algorithm on each problem, with approximately 250,000 objective function evaluations for each run. The same objective function was used for each algorithm, with the α hyperparameter (as in Eq. 1) set to 0.1. Each algorithm was provided an initial set of 5 randomly generated parents, with each parent containing a predetermined number of components. These components all lie within the bounds of $x = [0, 10]$ and $y = [0, 10]$. An angle is calculated for each component, based on its position compared to the point $(5, 5)$, and all components in the solution are ordered based on these angles, to produce shapes with minimal intersecting edges. Note that this ordering of component angle is not maintained during the optimisation process, and is only used when the parents are generated for the initial generation.

The algorithms are listed below, along with the relevant design and the hyperparameter choices that were made after tuning. Note that details about the full hyperparameter tuning process has not been included in this paper.

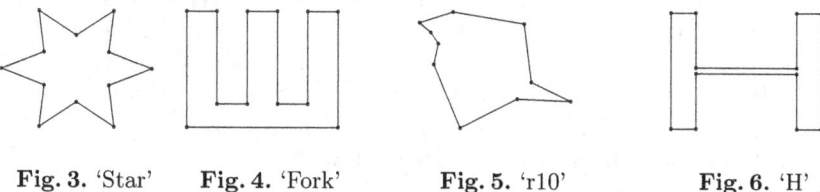

Fig. 3. 'Star'   **Fig. 4.** 'Fork'   **Fig. 5.** 'r10'   **Fig. 6.** 'H'

5.1 Algorithms

Fixed Length Evolutionary Algorithm (FEA). The basic structure of this algorithm follows the pseudocode in Algorithm 3. To generate children, crossover is applied to each pair of different parents twice, and mutation is applied to each parent. For N parents, this gives $N(N - 1) + N$ children. One point crossover was used, along with Gaussian mutation with a standard deviation of 0.1. Each component in a solution had a 20% chance of mutating. For initialisation, 5 parents were randomly generated, with the optimal number of components for that specific target shape. There were 5 parents for each generation, and the parents were chosen using tournament selection on the population of children and parents combined. The best solution in the population was automatically selected as one of the 5 parents.

Basic Variable Length Algorithm (V-Base). The algorithm follows the same structure as the FEA. It has the same selection operator, but uses different mutation, crossover, and initialisation methods. The spatial crossover method was used for this algorithm, with the cutting line being a randomly generated line that passes through the point $(5, 5)$. For initialisation, 5 parents were randomly generated, each with exactly 10 components. For mutation, several different mutation operators were used with different probabilities. For 50% of mutations, the same mutation operator as in the FEA was used. For 10%, a random component is added to the solution, within the bounds $x = [0, 10]$ and $y = [0, 10]$. For 10%, a random component in the solution is deleted. For 30%, a new component is added halfway between two randomly chosen consecutive components. This new component is then mutated using a uniform distribution, with upper and lower bounds -0.25 and 0.25, respectively.

Variable Length Algorithm with Nudge Operator (V-Nudge). This algorithm is identical to the V-Base algorithm, except that it uses the Nudge operator proposed in this paper. For the hyperparameters, the nudge frequency (the number of generations between nudges) is 2, and the nudge distance (number of generations for the fixed-length algorithm used inside the nudge operator) is 50.

Variable Length Algorithm with Length Niching (V-Niche). This algorithm is identical to the V-Base algorithm, except that it uses the Niche selection method as proposed by Ryerkerk et al. Ryerkerk [7] proposed several variations of the Length Niching selection method. The one chosen for this algorithm uses the 'moving window function', with the window width set to 3. Within the Niche selection method, tournament selection was used, with the same implementation as in the other algorithms.

Variable Length Algorithm with Nudge Operator and Length Niching (V-NN). This algorithm is a combination of the V-Nudge and V-Niche algorithms. The implementation and hyperparameters for this algorithm are identical to those in V-Nudge, except that the selection operator used is the same as in V-Niche, instead of tournament selection.

6   Results

Tables 1, 2, 3 and 4 contain the results for each algorithm on each target shape, along with the optimal value for each shape. Figures 7, 8, 9 and 10 show the mean objective value for each algorithm.

On all shapes, the fixed length algorithm produced lower quality shapes, despite knowing the optimal number of vertices a priori. This is in line with the results published by Ryerkerk [7]. It appears as though the poor performance of the fixed length algorithm is caused by local minima - it is unable to escape as effectively as the variable length algorithms. We hypothesise that this is due to the variable length algorithms escaping local minima via changing dimensions, although this would require further research to confirm.

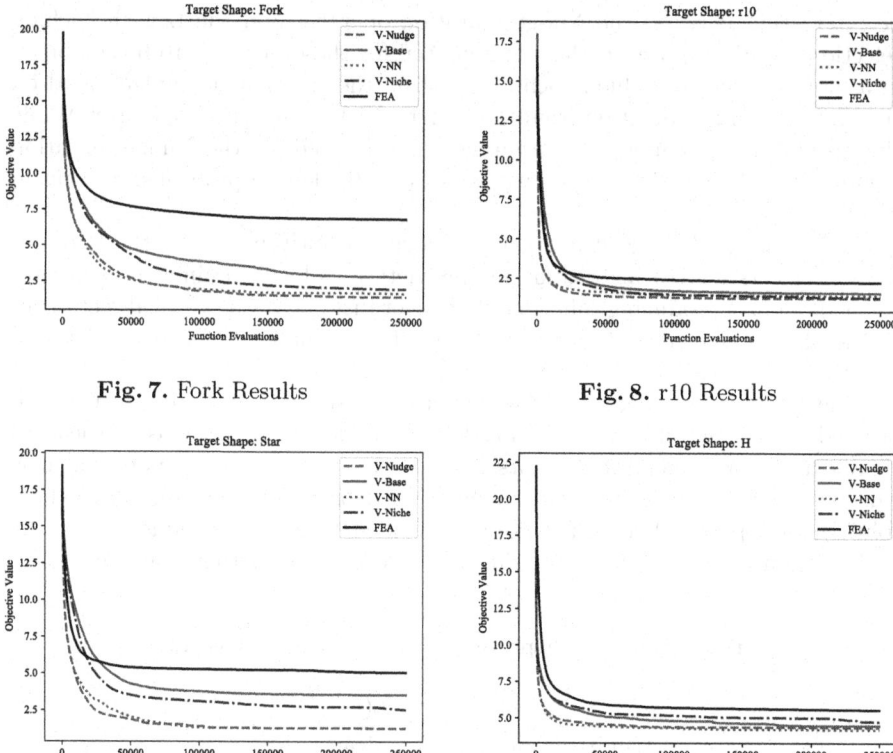

Fig. 7. Fork Results   **Fig. 8.** r10 Results

Fig. 9. Star Results   **Fig. 10.** H Results

Ultimately, the Nudge method proposed in this paper allows algorithms to significantly outperform others, as the V-Nudge and V-NN algorithms were the clear leaders for each target shape. However, the combination of the Length Niching and Nudge methods in the V-NN algorithm did not translate to a significant improvement in results, contrary to the predictions of the authors. While the V-NN algorithm does produce the best solutions on average for the H and Star target shapes, the difference between results for the V-NN and V-Nudge algorithms is fairly minor, and could be attributed to random variation. This is likely due to the V-Nudge and V-Niche methods targeting similar shortcomings of the V-Base algorithm - perhaps a combination of methods with different aims would produce better results.

Furthermore, the combination of the Nudge and Length Niching operators was fairly rudimentary. The implementation of the V-NN algorithm included no interacting between the Nudge mutation operator and the Length Niching selection method. However, there is potential for these methods to be combined in a more intelligent fashion such as choosing the solutions to nudge based on the moving window function from the Length Niching selection operator. While the results in this paper are intriguing, there is need for the Nudge mutation operator to be applied to a wide variety of variable length problems, to confirm its effectiveness.

Interestingly, the algorithms performed significantly poorly on the H target shape. This is due to algorithms falling victim to local minima with greater frequency, often producing solutions that cover just one of the vertical rectangles in the shape. Evidently, there is still need for methods that can consistently recover from harsh local minima.

One of the key conclusions this experiment suggests is that the inclusion of fixed length algorithms nested inside variable length algorithms can lead to significant improvements on results. There are a wide range of potential new variable length algorithms that can be created based on this concept - where solutions are passed between variable and fixed length algorithms during the optimisation process. We suggest this as a direction for further research.

Table 1. Target shape: Star. Optimal value for f(x): 1.2

	f(x)		L(x)	
Algorithm	Mean	Std	Mean	Std
V-Nudge	1.261	0.011	12.0	0.0
V-Base	3.531	2.525	10.033	2.401
V-NN	**1.258**	0.007	12.0	0.0
V-Niche	2.509	1.723	11.167	1.529
FEA	5.064	1.456	12.0	0.0

Table 2. Target shape: Fork. Optimal value for f(x): 1.2

	f(x)		L(x)	
Algorithm	Mean	Std	Mean	Std
V-Nudge	**1.413**	0.363	12.333	1.011
V-Base	2.818	1.712	11.267	1.948
V-NN	1.651	0.791	12.1	1.165
V-Niche	1.944	0.793	12.5	1.147
FEA	6.851	1.55	12.0	0.0

Table 3. Target shape: r10. Optimal value for f(x): 1.0

	f(x)		L(x)	
Algorithm	Mean	Std	Mean	Std
V-Nudge	**1.242**	0.494	8.667	0.745
V-Base	1.57	0.592	8.267	1.062
V-NN	1.418	0.63	8.333	0.943
V-Niche	1.279	0.456	8.7	0.781
FEA	2.25	0.646	10.0	0.0

Table 4. Target shape: H. Optimal value for f(x): 1.2

	f(x)		L(x)	
Algorithm	Mean	Std	Mean	Std
V-Nudge	4.365	1.723	5.867	3.253
V-Base	4.482	1.616	5.8	2.96
V-NN	**4.08**	2.306	6.567	3.422
V-Niche	4.75	1.728	5.367	3.082
FEA	5.555	1.825	12.0	0.0

7   Conclusions

In this paper we investigated the effectiveness of variable length algorithms compared to fixed length algorithms. To aid in this process, we developed an abstract variable length problem known as the 'shape matching' problem, designed for easy analysis of results. In addition to comparing state-of-the-art variable length methods to fixed length methods, we proposed a novel mutation operator for variable length algorithms, named the Nudge mutation operator. We provided evidence that variable length algorithms can outperform fixed length algorithms, and should be seriously considered for appropriate problem types.

The 'Nudge' operator we proposed outperformed the current state-of-the-art for variable length algorithms on the shape matching problem, resulting in higher quality solutions in a smaller number of generations. Our results suggest that further research is needed to investigate methods that combine fixed and variable length algorithms.

References

1. Castro Mora, J., Calero Barón, J.M., Riquelme Santos, J.M., Burgos Payán, M.: An evolutive algorithm for wind farm optimal design. Neurocomputing **70**(16–18), 2651–2658 (2007)

2. Chang, C., Sim, S.: Optimising train movements through coast control using genetic algorithms. IEE Proc. Electr. Power Appl. **144**(1), 65–73 (1997). http://search.proquest.com/docview/27302944/

3. Gad, A., Abdelkhalik, O.: Hidden genes genetic algorithm for multi-gravity-assist trajectories optimization. J. Spacecraft Rockets **48**(4), 629–641 (2011)

4. Giger, M.: Representation concepts in evolutionary algorithm-based structural optimization. Ph.D. thesis, ETH Zurich (2007)

5. Lee, C.Y.: Variable length genomes for evolutionary algorithms. In: In Proceedings of the Genetic and Evolutionary Computation Conference, 806. Las Vegas, p. 806. Morgan Kaufmann (2000)

6. Ryerkerk, M., Averill, R., Deb, K., Goodman, E.: A survey of evolutionary algorithms using metameric representations. Genet. Program. Evolvable Mach. **20**(4), 441–478 (2019). https://doi.org/10.1007/s10710-019-09356-2

7. Ryerkerk, M.: Metameric representations in evolutionary algorithms (2018). http://search.proquest.com/docview/2156231464/

8. Schneider, J., Kirkpatrick, S.: Stochastic Optimization. Springer-Verlag, Berlin Heidelberg (2006)

9. Ting, C.K., Lee, C.N., Chang, H.C., Wu, J.S.: Wireless heterogeneous transmitter placement using multiobjective variable-length genetic algorithm. IEEE Trans. Syst. Man Cybern. Part B (Cybernet.) **39**(4), 945–958 (2009)

10. Weicker, N., Szabo, G., Weicker, K., Widmayer, P.: Evolutionary multiobjective optimization for base station transmitter placement with frequency assignment. IEEE Trans. Evol. Comput. **7**(2), 189–203 (2003)

Improving Distribution-Based Discrete Particle Swarm Optimization Using Lévy Flight

Koya Ihara[1,2] and Shohei Kato[1,2(⊠)]

[1] Department of Computer Science and Engineering,
Graduate School of Engineering, Nagoya Institute of Technology, Gokiso-cho,
Showa-ku, Nagoya 466-8555, Japan
[2] Frontier Research Institute for Information Science,
Nagoya Institute of Technology, Gokiso-cho, Showa-ku, Nagoya 466-8555, Japan
{ihara,shohey}@katolab.nitech.ac.jp
https://www.katolab.nitech.ac.jp

Abstract. Some metaheuristic algorithms such as particle swarm optimization (PSO) are extended and have been shown to perform very well in a wide range of optimization domains though they are originally designed for continuous optimization. In discrete optimization, some extended algorithms handle continuous parameters of a probability distribution, which assumes variable values of a candidate solution instead of directly handling discrete variables. These distribution-based discrete PSOs (DDPSO) sample a variable value from a distribution for every variable to generate a candidate solution. This procedure can be considered as a kind of local search centered on an *intended solution*, which has the highest probability to be generated. Step length from the intended solution increases proportionally and the probability of producing an intended solution decreases exponentially in high-dimensional problems. We propose a novel sampling method to control the step size for DDPSO. In this paper, we describe our new sampling method to control the step size with Lévy distribution in a similar way to Lévy flight. The proposed method is applied to three representative methods of DDPSOs and performance is compared with original algorithms. In our discrete optimization experiments, we demonstrate that our algorithm increases DDPSO's search performance and robustness to dimensionality.

Keywords: Particle swarm optimization · Discrete optimization · Lévy flight

1 Introduction

Discrete optimization problems are problems of finding discrete values for the variables which will give optimum functional values of the objective functions. In

© Springer Nature Switzerland AG 2020
M. Gallagher et al. (Eds.): AI 2020, LNAI 12576, pp. 189–200, 2020.
https://doi.org/10.1007/978-3-030-64984-5_15

these problems, each variable can take only a finite number of states. Based on the decision variables, discrete optimization problems can be classified into two types. One is integer problems, where variables are generally restricted to a set of integer variables and there is an implicit ordering in integer values: integers with a larger difference between them are considered to be further apart. The other is categorical problems, where there is no ordered relationship between values [13]. Recent discrete optimization problems, especially those motivated by real-world problems, have continued to grow in scale. It is important to develop algorithms to provide a sufficiently good solution to such problems in a short time.

Particle swarm optimization (PSO) is a powerful method to find the minimum of a numerical function on a continuous definition domain. It is very simple and highly customizable. A number of improved variants has been proposed and shown to perform very well on a wide range of optimization problems [3,15] Extending PSOs for discrete optimization is also under intense investigation. Some of the extended algorithms outperform comparative methods that are originally designed for discrete optimization in various discrete problems such as multi-cast routing problems in communication networks [12], and high-dimensional feature selection, classification and validation [1]. One of the simplest methods for adapting to discrete problems is real value conversion to the nearest integer by rounding or truncating. Such rounding changes the objective function landscape inefficiently from PSO's point of view by introducing flat areas to the fitness landscape. To avoid this problem, several Discrete PSO variants search probability space instead of solution space [8,13,14] (See Sect. 3). In other words, these methods handle continuous parameters of probability distribution assuming variable values, and candidate solutions are sampled from the distribution similar to estimation of distribution algorithms [9]. We refer to such algorithms as distribution-based discrete PSO (DDPSO).

When generating a candidate solution vector from a distribution vector, DDPSOs generally sample a variable value from each distribution of the vector. We regard this sampling procedure as a kind of local search and focus on its step size. The step size tends to be too large due to many times of probabilistic operations especially on high-dimensional problems.

Our aim is to control directly step size and to set to appropriate step size. We propose a new sampling method for controlling step size of DDPSOs. When producing a candidate solution, our method updates probability distributions such that the step size of any solution sampled from the updated distribution must be a predetermined number. This paper determines step size based on random numbers according to Lévy distribution, inspired by Lévy flight, which is an effective random walk.

2   Proposed Method

This section introduces original continuous PSO and DDPSO. Then we describe DDPSOs' drawbacks and our proposed sampling method to improve it.

2.1 Standard PSO

In standard PSO [5], particle p's position in the search space, $X_p = \{X_{p,1}, X_{p,2}, \ldots, X_{p,n}\}$ directly represents a candidate solution. The particle flies in the search space according to its velocity vector $V_p = \{V_{p,1}, V_{p,2}, \ldots, V_{p,n}\}$, updated at each iteration. The velocity and position are updated as follows:

$$\mathbf{V}_p = \omega\mathbf{V}_p + U(0, \phi_1) \otimes (\mathbf{pBest} - \mathbf{X}_p)$$
$$+ U(0, \phi_2) \otimes (\mathbf{gBest} - \mathbf{X}_p), \tag{1}$$
$$\mathbf{X}_p = \mathbf{X}_p + \mathbf{V}_p,$$

where each operator is performed in a component-wise manner over each variable in the vector, and $U(0, \phi_1)$ and $U(0, \phi_2)$ are uniformly distributed random numbers between 0 and ϕ_1 and 0 and ϕ_2. Vector **pBest** is the best position in the search space that this particle has reached, and **gBest** is the best position in the search space any particle in the swarm has ever reached. The particle moves in the search space by adding the updated velocity to the particle's position vector in the current iteration. The particle's behavior is controlled by adjusting parameters ω, ϕ_1, and ϕ_2.

2.2 Distribution-Based Discrete PSO

In DDPSO, particle p's position or velocity vector directly or indirectly represents probability distribution vector $D_p = [D_{p,1}, D_{p,2}, \ldots, D_{p,n}]$, and candidate solution $x = [x_1, x_2, \ldots, x_n]$ is generated by sampling x_i from distribution $D_{p,i}$ as shown in Fig. 1. Converting a position or velocity vector to distribution differs depending on algorithms.

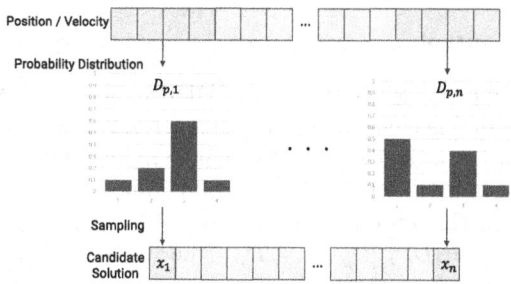

Fig. 1. Generating a candidate solution in DDPSO

In general PSO, search points are updated according to (1). In DDPSO, search points are probabilistically selected by sampling from probability distributions updated by (1). The sampling procedure is considered as a kind of local search centered on a solution having the highest probability of being generated from the distribution. We refer to such solution and each of its variable value as *intended solution* and *intended value*. Then step size ξ is defined as the number of variables taking states other than intended values. This is because the distance between solutions can be defined by the number of different variables in discrete problems, including categorical problems, where the distance between variable states cannot be defined.

In the simplest case, where the probability that the intended value has generated is p in all n variables, step size ξ follows binomial distribution $B(n, 1 - p)$ since each of the n variables takes a value other than the intended value with a probability of $1 - p$. Figure 2 shows probability distributions of the step size on simple DDPSOs ($n = 1000$, $p = 0.5, 0.7, 0.9$). The step size is concentrated around mean $n(1 - p)$ in these distributions. In particular, the probability that the step size will be near 0 is almost 0. Owing to this, DDPSOs' sampling seldom generates candidate solutions close to the intended solution even though the PSO's update equation is intended to search there.

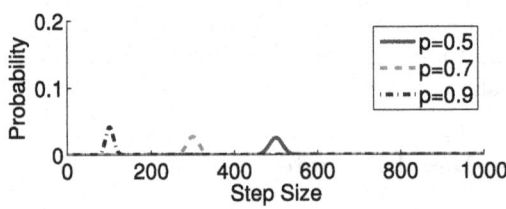

Fig. 2. Probability distribution of step size on simple DDPSOs ($n = 1000$, $p = 0.5$, 0.7, 0.9), where n is the number of decision variables and p is the probability that intended value is generated on each variable.

2.3 Step Size Control

Our method directly controls the step size of DDPSO. For the given step size ξ, a probability distribution is changed so that the step size of any solutions that are sampled from the distribution is ξ. By the change in distribution, ξ variables can take on any value other than the intended value, and the other $n - \xi$ variables are bound to take on the intended values.

Formally, let $\boldsymbol{D_p} = [D_{p,1}, D_{p,2}, \ldots, D_{p,n}]$ be a distribution vector for original DDPSO. Here, each element $D_{p,i} = [d_{p,i}^a, d_{p,i}^b, \ldots, d_{p,i}^k]$ is the probability distribution for variable X_i, and $d_{p,i}^j$ corresponds to the probability by which variable X_i will take on value j for particle p. A set of ξ variables $\boldsymbol{X}_{\text{step}}$ is chosen randomly, and then the distribution is changed as follows:

$$d_{p,i}^j = \begin{cases} 0 & (X_i \in \boldsymbol{X}_{\text{step}} \wedge j = x_{p,i}^*) \\ \frac{d_{p,i}^j}{1-d_{p,i}^{x_{p,j}^*}} & (X_i \in \boldsymbol{X}_{\text{step}} \wedge j \neq x_{p,i}^*) \\ 1 & (X_i \notin \boldsymbol{X}_{\text{step}} \wedge j = x_{p,i}^*) \\ 0 & (X_i \notin \boldsymbol{X}_{\text{step}} \wedge j \neq x_{p,i}^*) \end{cases}$$

where, $\boldsymbol{x}_p^* = x_{p,1}^*, x_{p,2}^*, \ldots, x_{p,n}^*$ is the intended solution of the original distributions. This update changes the distributions such that the ξ variables in $\boldsymbol{X}_{\text{step}}$ must not be the intended value and the $n - \xi$ variables that are not included in $\boldsymbol{X}_{\text{step}}$ must be the intended value while maintaining valid probability distributions.

In the proposed method, the step size is determined in advance for each update of the probability distribution. In this paper, the step size is determined in a similar way to Lévy flight. It is a kind of random walk in which the step sizes follow a Lévy distribution, and various studies [2,11] have shown that the flight behavior of many animals and insects has its typical characteristics. Lévy distribution is a heavy-tailed probability distribution. By frequent small step walk and rare long jump, Lévy flight is efficient to global search, and many researches [7,16] utilize it for continuous optimization. Our proposed method reduces most step sizes in order to more frequently search near intended solutions than original DDPSOs, and ensure effectual use of the search space by long jump via Lévy distribution.

Using Lévy distribution, step size ξ is determined by the following equation.

$$\xi = \text{round}(|s_l l|)$$

where, $s_l > 0$ is a scale parameter and l 1 is a random number following a Lévy distribution. The continuous random value is rounded to an integer and mapped into $[0, n]$. This paper utilized Mantegna's algorithm [10] for a Lévy stable distribution to generate random number l as follows:

$$l = \frac{u}{|v|^{1/\beta}},$$

where, u and v follow normal distributions as follows:

$$u \sim N(0, \sigma_u^2), \quad v \sim N(0, \sigma_v^2)$$

$$\sigma_u = \{\frac{\Gamma(1+\beta)\sin(\pi\beta/2)}{\Gamma[(1+\beta)/2]\beta 2^{(\beta-1)/2}}\}^{1/\beta}, \quad \sigma_v = 1$$

where, Γ is gamma function.

3   DDPSO Implementations

This section describes three representative DDPSO algorithms.

3.1 BPSO

Binary PSO [8] (BPSO) uses bit strings for position vectors. Velocity update is performed using the general PSO's update Eq. (1). After the velocity update, each element of the velocity vector is mapped to $[0, 1]$ using the following standard sigmoid function.

$$S_{p,i} = \frac{1}{1 + \exp(-V_{p,i})}$$

where, $V_{p,i}$ is the i-th value in the velocity vector of particle p. Then using random number $r_{p,i}$ sampled from uniform distribution $[0, 1]$, the position is updated as follows:

$$X_{p,i} = \begin{cases} 1 & (r_{p,i} < S_{p,i}) \\ 0 & \text{otherwise} \end{cases}$$

3.2 VPSO

Veeramachaneni et $al.$ extended BPSO and proposed discrete multi-valued PSO [14] (VPSO), where variables can take M discrete values. Velocity update is performed by the general update Eq. (1) similar to BPSO. After the velocity is updated, each element of the velocity vector is mapped to $[0, M - 1]$ using the following extended sigmoid function.

$$S_{p,i} = \frac{M - 1}{1 + \exp(-V_{p,i})}$$

Then, using random number $r_{p,i}$ sampled from normal distribution $N(S_{p,i}, \sigma(M - 1))$, the position is updated as follows:

$$X_{p,i} = \begin{cases} M - 1 & (r_{p,i} > M - 1) \\ 0 & (r_{p,i} < 0) \\ r_{p,i} & \text{otherwise} \end{cases}$$

3.3 ICPSO

ICPSO is a novel PSO algorithm that has been shown to surpass other discrete PSO algorithms such as BPSO and VPSO [13]. In ICPSO, the representation of the particle's position is changed so that each attribute in a particle is a distribution over its possible values rather than a single value.

In ICPSO, particle p's position $\mathbf{X}_p$ is represented as, $\mathbf{X}_p = [\mathcal{D}_{p,1}, \mathcal{D}_{p,2}, \ldots, \mathcal{D}_{p,n}]$, where each $\mathcal{D}_{p,i}$ is a probability distribution for variable X_i. In other words, each component of the position vector is a set of probabilities expressed as $\mathcal{D}_{p,i} = [d^a_{p,i}, d^b_{p,i}, \ldots, d^k_{p,i}]$, where $d^j_{p,i}$ denotes the probability by which variable X_i takes on value j for particle p. Particle p's velocity, $\mathbf{V}_p$, is a vector of n vector φ, which controls the particle's probability distributions: $\mathbf{V}_p = [\varphi_{p,1}, \varphi_{p,2}, \ldots, \varphi_{p,n}], \varphi_{p,1} = [\psi^a_{p,i}, \psi^a_{p,i}, \ldots, \psi^a_{p,n}]$, where $\psi^j_{p,i}$ corresponds to particle p's velocity for variable i in state j. The velocity and position update equations are directly applied to the values in the distribution following (1).

When a sample produced by a particle exceeds the global or local best values, the best values are updated using both the distribution from the particle position $\mathbf{P}_p$ and sample $\mathbf{S}_p$. For all states $j \in Vals(X_i)$, the global best's probability is updated as follows:

$$
d^j_{gB,i} = \begin{cases}
\epsilon_s \times d^j_{p,i} & (j \neq s_{p,i}) \\
d^j_{p,i} + \displaystyle\sum_{\substack{k \in Vals(X_i) \\ \wedge k \neq j}} (1 - \epsilon_s) \times d^k_{p,i} & (j = s_{p,i})
\end{cases}
$$

where ϵ_s (the *scaling factor*) is a user-controlled parameter that determines the magnitude of the shift in the distribution restricted to $[0, 1)$, and $d^j_{gB,i}$ is the global best position's probability signifying that variable X_i takes value j. This update increases the probability of the distribution producing samples that are similar to the best sample while maintaining a valid probability distribution. The local best is updated in exactly the same way.

4 Experiments

In order to evaluate the performance of the proposed method, we adapted the method to BPSO, VPSO, and ICPSO, and compared the extended algorithm and each original algorithm. We performed minimization experiments using five benchmark functions and compared the fitness of the best solution. We performed 50 trials for each problem setting and performed a statistical comparison.

4.1 Problem Settings

We compared the algorithms on five benchmark functions (Ackley, Griewank, Rastrigin, Rosenbrock, and Sphere) using the same function ranges presented in the literature [4]. In order to evaluate the performance of integer problems and categorical problems, shuffled problems (Shuffled Ackley, Shuffled Griewank, Shuffled Rastrigin, Shuffled Rosenbrock, Shuffled Sphere), in which the order of the values of the variables randomly shuffled is used in a way similar to [13].

For integer problems, integer variables $x \in X$ are mapped to continuous variables $x' \in X'$. In this paper, mapping function $g : X \to X'$ is defined as $g(x) = a_f x$, where a_f is a continuous parameter for a benchmark function f, and it is adjusted so that the nature of f's landscape is not lost as much as possible. Table 1 shows the values of the parameter used in this experiment. Figure 3 illustrates the landscape of f in the domain X'_f. Here, integer variables take on 11 states ($x_i \in X = \{-5, -4 \ldots, 5\}$). The dimensions of the functions n is set to 10, 100, and 1000.

4.2 Algorithm Settings

We adapted our proposed method to BPSO, VPSO, and ICPSO, and we will refer the extended algorithms BLPSO, VLPSO, and ICLPSO respectively.

All PSO algorithms use the same parameters for consistent comparison. Each algorithm uses a swarm of size 10 and is terminated after $1,000$ $(10,000)$ iterations in problems of $n = 10, 100$ (1000). Parameters ϕ_1 and ϕ_2 were set to 1.49618, $\omega = 0.729$. These values are recommended in the work of [4,6]. BPSO and VPSO variants use a parameter, maximum velocity, $V_{\max} = 10.0$ recommended in [8]. VPSO variants use parameter $\sigma = 0.2$ recommended in the original paper [14]. ICPSO variants use parameter $\epsilon = 0.75$ in the same way as [13]. In our proposed method, Lévy distribution's parameter β is set to 1.5 following [17], and scale parameter $s_l = 1.0$.

Table 1. Benchmark functions and mapping parameters used for experiments.

	Function	Domain (mapping parameter)	Optimum solution
Ackley	$f_1(x) = -20\exp(-0.2\sqrt{\frac{1}{n}\sum_{i=1}^{n}x_i^2}) - \exp\frac{1}{n}\sum_{i=1}^{n}\cos(2\pi x_i)$	$\{-2.5,\ldots,2.5\}$ $(a_{f_1} = 0.5)$	$f_1(0,\ldots,0) = 0$
Griewank	$f_2(x) = 1 + \frac{1}{4000}\sum_{i=1}^{n}x_i^2 - \prod_{i=1}^{n}\cos(\frac{x_i}{\sqrt{i}})$	$\{-5.0,\ldots,5.0\}$ $(a_{f_2} = 1.0)$	$f_2(0,\ldots,0) = 0$
Rastrigin	$f_3(x) = 10n + \sum_{i=1}^{n}(x_i^2 - 10\cos(2\pi x_i))$	$\{-1.0,\ldots,1.0\}$ $(a_{f_3} = 0.2)$	$f_3(0,\ldots,0) = 0$
Rosenbrock	$f_4(x) = \sum_{i=1}^{n}(100(x_{i+1} - x_i^2)^2 + (x_i - 1)^2)$	$\{-5.0,\ldots,5.0\}$ $(a_{f_4} = 1.0)$	$f_4(1,\ldots,1) = 0$
Sphere	$f_5(x) = \sum_{i=1}^{n}x_i^2$	$\{-5.0,\ldots,5.0\}$ $(a_{f_5} = 1.0)$	$f_5(0,\ldots,0) = 0$

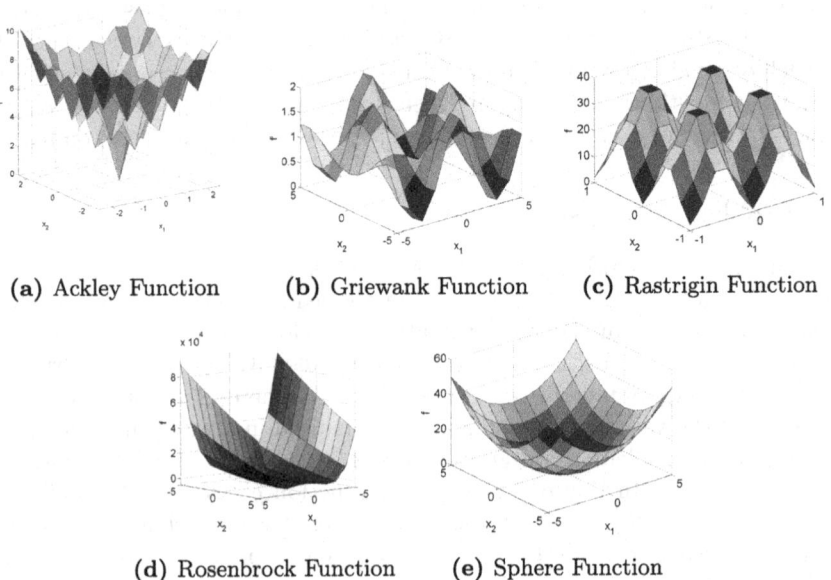

(a) Ackley Function   (b) Griewank Function   (c) Rastrigin Function

(d) Rosenbrock Function   (e) Sphere Function

Fig. 3. Fitness landscape of benchmark functions on one's discrete domain X'_f $(n = 2)$.

Table 2. Average fitness results of DDPSO variants for 20 runs

Dimensions	Problem	BPSO	BLPSO	VPSO	VLPSO	ICPSO	ICLPSO
$n = 10$	Ackley	2.37E+00(6.31E-02)	2.07E+00(4.17E-01)	4.53E+00(1.59E-01)	**2.91E+00(1.36E+00)**	1.12E+00(6.75E-01)	**0.00E+00(0.00E+00)**
	Griewank	4.09E-01(1.23E-02)	4.31E-01(1.51E-02)	8.34E-01(4.56E-03)	**5.81E-01(8.27E-02)**	4.29E-02(1.01E-03)	**5.05E-03(2.55E-04)**
	Rastrigin	1.19E+01(1.40E+01)	**5.11E+00(5.92E+00)**	8.14E+00(3.68E-01)	8.74E+00(1.99E+00)	1.20E+00(4.00E-01)	**0.00E+00(0.00E+00)**
	Rosenbrock	1.05E+03(1.92E+05)	3.93E+03(1.41E+06)	1.37E+04(3.14E+07)	**2.53E+03(1.35E+07)**	1.34E+02(6.83E+03)	**2.02E+01(1.81E+03)**
	Sphere	6.30E+00(9.00E-01)	6.80E+00(3.51E+00)	3.02E+01(6.10E+01)	**8.88E+00(3.72E+01)**	1.20E+00(8.44E-01)	**0.00E+00(0.00E+00)**
	Shuffled Ackley	2.43E+00(2.32E-01)	**1.53E+00(1.35E+00)**	3.16E+00(1.30E-01)	3.14E+00(1.79E-01)	3.46E-01(3.11E-01)	1.12E-01(1.24E-01)
	Shuffled Griewank	3.81E-01(1.07E-02)	**2.59E-01(1.26E-02)**	5.47E-01(1.78E-02)	4.97E-01(2.60E-02)	6.56E-02(1.89E-03)	5.49E-02(5.18E-04)
	Shuffled Rastrigin	8.34E+00(9.17E+00)	**3.30E+00(1.34E+00)**	1.24E+01(2.95E+01)	1.19E+01(2.86E+01)	1.10E+00(1.43E+00)	**0.00E+00(0.00E+00)**
	Shuffled Rosenbrock	1.44E+03(1.29E+05)	3.33E+03(1.08E+07)	2.48E+03(2.00E+06)	2.58E+03(1.85E+06)	1.33E+03(9.29E+03)	7.09E+01(9.15E+03)
	Shuffled Sphere	8.10E+00(5.88E+00)	**4.40E+00(5.16E+00)**	1.02E+01(1.58E+01)	1.01E-01(1.30E+01)	1.20E+00(6.22E-01)	**0.00E+00(0.00E+00)**
$n = 100$	Ackley	5.92E+00(6.89E-03)	3.67E+00(1.99E-02)	5.34E+00(5.51E-02)	**5.27E-01(8.78E-01)**	4.54E+00(5.20E-02)	3.04E+00(5.24E-02)
	Griewank	1.15E+00(2.70E-05)	9.79E-01(4.98E-04)	1.10E+00(2.10E-04)	**3.59E-01(1.66E-01)**	1.06E+00(1.92E-04)	7.70E-01(4.00E-03)
	Rastrigin	6.84E+02(2.72E+02)	2.41E+02(1.91E+03)	4.33E+02(4.33E+02)	**3.63E+02(2.39E+04)**	3.03E+02(1.23E+03)	8.95E-01(1.41E+02)
	Rosenbrock	9.33E+05(8.10E+08)	1.11E+05(6.31E+08)	5.02E+05(1.30E+10)	**1.31E+04(1.74E+08)**	2.82E+05(1.06E+10)	5.37E+04(1.71E+08)
	Sphere	5.74E+02(1.02E+03)	1.17E+02(2.24E+02)	4.03E+02(3.31E+03)	**2.45E+01(9.34E+02)**	2.86E+02(2.12E+03)	1.06E+02(1.55E+02)
	Shuffled Ackley	6.04E+00(7.59E-03)	**3.70E+00(4.22E-02)**	6.02E+00(1.43E-02)	6.12E+00(1.16E-02)	4.60E+00(1.84E-02)	3.11E+00(3.08E-02)
	Shuffled Griewank	1.15E+00(3.50E-05)	1.02E+00(7.11E-04)	1.15E+00(7.89E-05)	1.16E+00(5.24E-05)	1.07E+00(2.33E-05)	8.13E-01(9.47E-03)
	Shuffled Rastrigin	6.24E+02(3.46E+02)	1.82E+02(8.54E+02)	6.26E+02(1.15E+03)	6.46E+02(9.28E+02)	3.07E+02(1.76E+03)	9.36E+01(2.14E+02)
	Shuffled Rosenbrock	8.66E+05(3.52E+09)	1.77E+05(2.55E+09)	8.80E+05(4.41E+09)	9.22E+05(8.50E+09)	2.46E+05(4.85E+09)	4.95E+04(1.03E+08)
	Shuffled Sphere	6.13E+02(9.94E+02)	**1.85E+02(3.60E+02)**	6.21E+02(1.25E+03)	6.34E+02(1.52E+03)	2.80E+02(1.26E+01)	9.29E+01(1.33E+02)
$n = 1000$	Ackley	6.86E+00(3.48E-04)	4.14E+00(6.09E-03)	5.40E+00(7.87E-03)	**1.71E-02(9.28E-04)**	6.14E+00(1.89E-03)	3.22E+00(5.09E-03)
	Griewank	3.14E+00(9.03E-04)	1.48E+00(2.36E-04)	2.02E+00(4.66E-03)	**6.42E-03(2.19E-04)**	2.60E+00(4.21E-03)	1.18E+00(2.63E-03)
	Rastrigin	8.65E+03(3.07E+03)	3.76E+03(1.50E+05)	6.01E+03(8.77E+03)	**1.08E+03(4.94E+06)**	2.58E+03(3.12E-03)	1.22E+03(6.91E+03)
	Rosenbrock	1.65E+07(9.74E+10)	1.16E+06(4.17E+09)	4.93E+06(2.16E+11)	**2.47E+04(1.86E+09)**	9.43E+06(4.09E+11)	3.79E+05(8.87E+08)
	Sphere	8.61E+03(2.44E+03)	1.97E+03(2.50E+03)	4.03E+03(4.09E+04)	**2.65E+00(3.72E+01)**	6.40E+03(5.64E+04)	1.08E+03(2.72E+03)
	Shuffled Ackley	6.80E+00(7.28E-04)	4.12E+00(1.96E-02)	6.80E+00(4.64E-04)	6.85E+00(3.08E-03)	6.11E+00(3.25E-03)	3.24E+00(4.88E-03)
	Shuffled Griewank	3.12E+00(4.95E-04)	1.64E+00(8.77E-04)	3.13E+00(1.51E-03)	3.16E+00(1.26E-03)	2.60E+00(4.21E-03)	1.18E+00(3.80E-03)
	Shuffled Rastrigin	8.27E+03(6.62E+03)	2.24E+03(2.19E+04)	8.25E+03(1.06E+04)	8.32E+03(1.05E+04)	6.42E+03(2.39E+04)	1.20E+03(7.09E+03)
	Shuffled Rosenbrock	1.48E+07(3.77E+10)	3.01E+06(6.74E+10)	1.47E+07(1.82E+11)	1.50E+07(7.86E+10)	9.18E+06(7.68E+11)	3.75E+05(1.69E+09)
	Shuffled Sphere	8.49E+03(5.65E+03)	2.51E+03(2.16E+04)	8.46E+03(1.59E+04)	8.66E+03(1.36E+04)	6.39E+03(5.68E+04)	1.09E+03(5.49E+03)

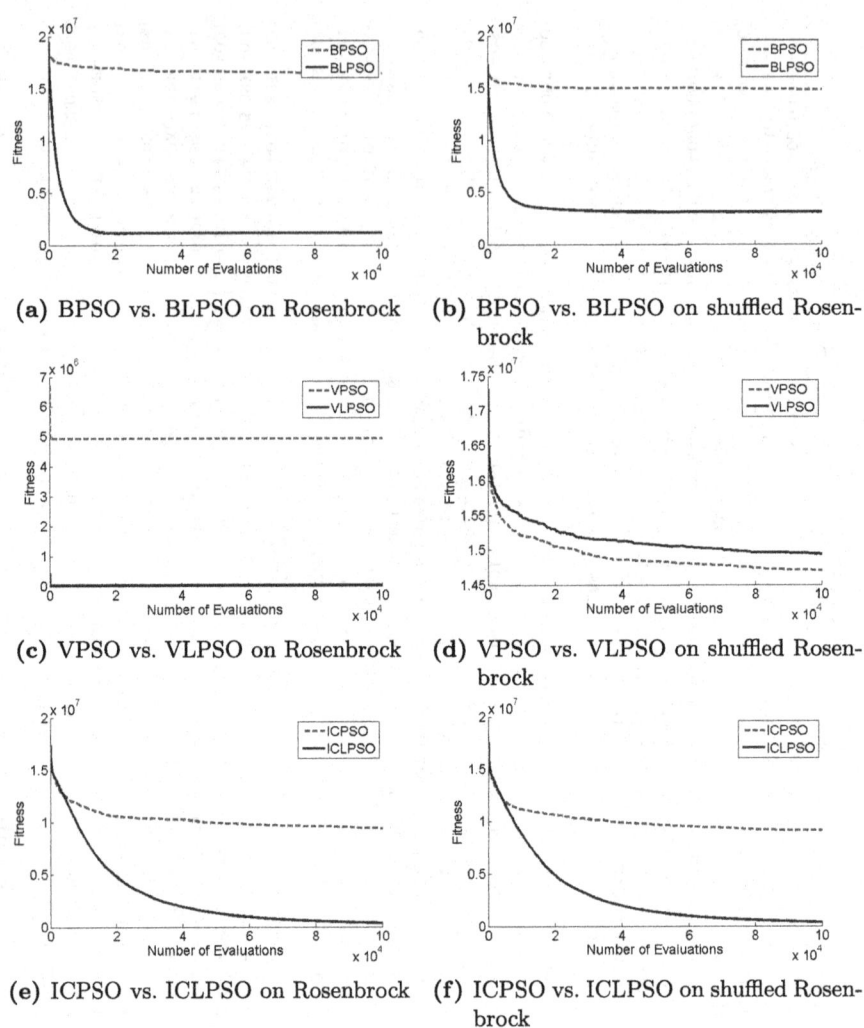

(a) BPSO vs. BLPSO on Rosenbrock

(b) BPSO vs. BLPSO on shuffled Rosenbrock

(c) VPSO vs. VLPSO on Rosenbrock

(d) VPSO vs. VLPSO on shuffled Rosenbrock

(e) ICPSO vs. ICLPSO on Rosenbrock

(f) ICPSO vs. ICLPSO on shuffled Rosenbrock

Fig. 4. Fitness curve of the DDPSOs.

4.3   Experimental Result

Table 2 shows the experimental results. Each value corresponds to the average fitness of the best solution in all trials, and values in parentheses are the standard deviations. Bold values indicate extended algorithms that statistically outperformed the original algorithm (one-tailed Welch's t-test in integer problems, and one-tailed paired t-test in shuffled problem with $\alpha = 0.05$). BLPSO and ICLPSO outperformed original DDPSOs on 25 and 27 of 30 problems. In particular, they performed better in all of the high-dimensional problems ($n = 100, 1000$).

VLPSO outperformed VPSO on only a half of the problems. However, in shuffled problems, VLPSO outperformed VPSO on almost all the problems.

Note that VPSO is designed for integer problems. In integer DDPSOs such as VPSO, the probability distributions are updated with assuming the order relation between variable states and intended solutions can be located on a good point. Since the proposed method with a small step size generates a solution near the intended solution, the search performance of integer DDPSOs is further enhanced in integer problems, whereas in categorical problems it is not.

Figure 4 shows the fitness curves for all the algorithms on the Rosenbrock and shuffled Rosenbrock problems. The X-axis is the number of fitness evaluations, while the Y-axis is the best solution fitness averaged over 20 runs. For BPSO and ICPSO, our proposed method has steep curves than the original algorithms. VPSO variants converged very soon on integer problems and VLPSO has a greater initial fitness gain. The proposed method can return a better solution than the original algorithms even if fitness evaluations are limited to a few times.

5   Conclusion

Our proposed method improved the search performance of all DDPSOs. The proposed method was especially effective in high-dimensional problems. We evaluated the performance on integer and categorical problems. DDPSO implementations designed for both problems are improved on both problems. An algorithm originally designed for integer optimization was improved only on integer problems. This is no problem since it is not necessary to use integer DDPSOs for categorical problems.

The proposed method can be applied to not only DDPSOs but any other discrete optimization algorithms that use probability distributions to generate candidate solutions. In the future, we will apply the proposed method to other algorithms and verify the versatility and effectiveness. In addition, we will investigate a suitable method for selecting a step size according to the original algorithm and target problem.

Acknowledgment. This work was supported in part by the Ministry of Education, Culture, Sports, Science and Technology-Japan, Grant–in–Aid for Scientific Research under grant #JP19H01137, #JP19H04025, and #JP20H04018.

References

1. Ardizzon, G., Cavazzini, G., Pavesi, G.: Adaptive acceleration coefficients for a new search diversification strategy in particle swarm optimization algorithms. Inf. Sci. **299**, 337–378 (2015)
2. Brown, C.T., Liebovitch, L.S., Glendon, R.: Lévy flights in Dobe Ju/'hoansi foraging patterns. Hum. Ecol. **35**(1), 129–138 (2007)
3. Chatterjee, S., Sarkar, S., Hore, S., Dey, N., Ashour, A.S., Balas, V.E.: Particle swarm optimization trained neural network for structural failure prediction of multistoried RC buildings. Neural Comput. Appl. **28**(8), 2005–2016 (2016). https://doi.org/10.1007/s00521-016-2190-2

4. Eberhart, R.C., Shi, Y.: Comparing inertia weights and constriction factors in particle swarm optimization. In: Proceedings of the 2000 Congress on Evolutionary Computation (CEC), vol. 1, pp. 84–88. IEEE (2000)
5. Eberhart, R., Kennedy, J.: Particle swarm optimization. In: Proceedings of the IEEE International Conference on Neural Networks, vol. 4, pp. 1942–1948. Citeseer (1995)
6. Engelbrecht, A.P.: Fitness function evaluations: a fair stopping condition? In: Proceedings of 2014 IEEE Symposium on Swarm Intelligence (SIS), pp. 1–8. IEEE (2014)
7. Jensi, R., Jiji, G.W.: An enhanced particle swarm optimization with levy flight for global optimization. Appl. Soft Comput. **43**, 248–261 (2016)
8. Kennedy, J., Eberhart, R.C.: A discrete binary version of the particle swarm algorithm. In: Proceedings of the IEEE International Conference on Systems, Man, and Cybernetics. Computational Cybernetics and Simulation, vol. 5, pp. 4104–4108. IEEE (1997)
9. Bengoetxea, E., Larrañaga, P., Bloch, I., Perchant, A.: Estimation of distribution algorithms: a new evolutionary computation approach for graph matching problems. In: Figueiredo, M., Zerubia, J., Jain, A.K. (eds.) EMMCVPR 2001. LNCS, vol. 2134, pp. 454–469. Springer, Heidelberg (2001). https://doi.org/10.1007/3-540-44745-8_30
10. Mantegna, R.N.: Fast, accurate algorithm for numerical simulation of levy stable stochastic processes. Phys. Rev. E **49**(5), 4677 (1994)
11. Reynolds, A.M., Frye, M.A.: Free-flight odor tracking in drosophila is consistent with an optimal intermittent scale-free search. PLoS ONE **2**(4), e354 (2007)
12. Shen, M., Zhan, Z.H., Chen, W.N., Gong, Y.J., Zhang, J., Li, Y.: Bi-velocity discrete particle swarm optimization and its application to multicast routing problem in communication networks. IEEE Trans. Industr. Electron. **61**(12), 7141–7151 (2014)
13. Strasser, S., Goodman, R., Sheppard, J., Butcher, S.: A new discrete particle swarm optimization algorithm. In: Proceedings of the Genetic and Evolutionary Computation Conference (GECCO), pp. 53–60. ACM (2016)
14. Veeramachaneni, K., Osadciw, L., Kamath, G.: Probabilistically driven particle swarms for optimization of multi valued discrete problems: design and analysis. In: IEEE Swarm Intelligence Symposium, pp. 141–149. IEEE (2007)
15. Wang, Z.J., et al.: Dynamic group learning distributed particle swarm optimization for large-scale optimization and its application in cloud workflow scheduling. IEEE Trans. Cybern. **50**, 2715–2729 (2019)
16. Yang, X.S., Deb, S.: Cuckoo search via lévy flights. In: 2009 World Congress on Nature & Biologically Inspired Computing (NaBIC), pp. 210–214. IEEE (2009)
17. Yang, X.S., Deb, S.: Engineering optimisation by cuckoo search. Int. J. Math. Model. Numer. Optim. **1**(4), 330–343 (2010)

Fairness and Ethics

Non-monotonic Reasoning for Machine Ethics with Situation Calculus

Raynaldio Limarga[1], Maurice Pagnucco[1], Yang Song[1(✉)], and Abhaya Nayak[2]

[1] School of Computer Science and Engineering, University of New South Wales,
Kensington, Australia
r.limarga@student.unsw.edu.au, {morri,yang.song1}@unsw.edu.au
[2] Department of Computing, Macquarie University, Sydney, Australia
abhaya.nayak@mq.edu.au

Abstract. With the rapid growth in research on and development of autonomous machines, machine ethics, which used to be "just a theory", has gained greater practical importance. In this paper, we present a logical approach to machine ethics. Our objective is to enable autonomous machines to behave in morally appropriate ways following well-defined ethical principles, exercising sound ethical judgement. Since moral reasoning involves selecting appropriate behavioural actions with varying preconditions, we propose a non-monotonic reasoning model and encode the model through two types of well-known ethical frameworks: the *consequentialist* approach to ethics and the *deontological* approach to ethics. The computational model is developed using Answer Set Programming in a situation calculus framework. We apply our model to a few paradigmatic scenarios that can be encountered in autonomous driving and interactions with social robots. Our study shows that the proposed model is applicable to a wide range of scenarios and leads to appropriately different reasoning outputs in different ethical frameworks.

Keywords: Machine ethics · Situation calculus · Answer Set Programming

1 Introduction

With the advent of autonomous machines such as self-driving vehicles, social and surgical robots, a number of decisions that were normally made by authorised humans with much deliberation are now left to algorithms implemented in machines. Worse, most of these algorithms are very complex and take as input a vast amount of raw data—data that are not feasibly humanly understandable—in order to reach a decision(s). In effect, life changing decisions are made the rationale behind which can probably only be understood *post facto*, as if only to give credence to the dictum *shoot-first-and-ask-questions-later*. Hence there has been a push for research in *Explainable AI*—effectively for devising decision making algorithms that are fast enough to reach a decision on time for critical applications in the field, and yet should be able to produce the underlying justification that can stand up in a court of law.

© Springer Nature Switzerland AG 2020
M. Gallagher et al. (Eds.): AI 2020, LNAI 12576, pp. 203–215, 2020.
https://doi.org/10.1007/978-3-030-64984-5_16

The issue in question is a matter of both legal and ethical interest.[1] With cognitive capabilities and intelligent interaction, automated machines appear to make conscious decisions and people could possibly hold them accountable for the resultant actions. We can imagine that self-driving cars need to decide the best or most ethical course of action in an event of accident that involves the lives of passengers and pedestrians. Hence it is of great interest to investigate under what conditions autonomous artificial agents may be considered *morally licensed agents*; agents who are not *amoral* but can be held morally accountable for their actions. For this reason, it is important to understand what morality is, and how we can ensure that the decisions an autonomous agent like a robot takes are *morally correct* decisions. We expect to equip these machines with the *ethical competence* to prevent physical, emotional or psychological harm to human users and display actions or behaviours that are aligned with the social and moral norms that are intrinsic to human society [22]. Short of that, widespread acceptance of autonomous machines is unlikely to take place.

The moral beliefs of an agent play a significant role in the decision making mechanism, particularly in the case of *hard decisions*. In other words, moral beliefs (together with the factual beliefs held, observations made, and goals identified) can be fruitfully used to predict decisions yet to be made and derive plausible explanations of decisions that have been made. Hence, if we can ascribe moral beliefs to autonomous intelligent machines such as self-driving cars, they can be used to explain the actions such machines perform. For this purpose, we may assume that the body of moral beliefs of an agent can be represented as a moral theory just as, in the literature on belief change, beliefs of an agent are represented as a theory. Of course an agent's body of moral beliefs does not have to coincide with an existing moral theory (such as *utilitarianism*) but be a mixture of different moral theories. It nonetheless shows the significance of exploring existing moral theories from a computational aspect.

Our work is restricted to two influential moral theories—the *consequentialist theory* [24] that essentially assumes that the moral validity of an action can be judged only by taking its consequences into consideration and the *deontological theory*[2] [1] that assumes that some actions are inherently good (or bad) irrespective of their actual or potential consequences. As one would expect, on occasion these two principal paradigms of moral thinking will clash, offering conflicting recommendations on what action is right and what is wrong. Attempts have been made to reconcile these two approaches [1]. In this work we do not explore such reconciliation; our purpose, instead, is to develop a computational framework in which both these approaches can be represented for automated moral reasoning.

Since moral reasoning is *prima facie* defeasible [5,20], we propose a nonmonotonic reasoning approach to making ethical decisions using both consequentialist and deontological ethics. Furthermore, since moral reasoning often involves a sequence of actions, for instance *promise to do X but, if situation*

---

[1] In this paper we will use the adjectives *moral* and *ethical* interchangeably, although some distinction is occasionally made in the literature and common parlance.

[2] Derived from the Greek root *deon* meaning *duty*.

changes, do Y instead, we design a situation calculus model implemented using Answer Set Programming (ASP) that can perform non-monotonic reasoning for such complex situations. We expect this will help us derive ethical decisions that are closer to commonly accepted ethical norms. We adopt the situation calculus model so a chain of events is modelled as a series of situations effected from various actions. With fluents describing the state of the world, we utilise predicates to encode different ethical principles to reason about the choice of actions. For evaluation, we apply the model to conduct ethical reasoning on various scenarios including the Moral Machine cases [4] for dilemmas in autonomous driving and more complex examples for social robots that require multiple steps of reasoning and actions based on varying preconditions. With these case studies, we demonstrate that the consequentialist and deontological models give expected outputs and our approach presents a promising development towards machine ethics with an explainable logical reasoning formalisation.

2   Related Work

Recently, with the rapid development of artificial intelligence (AI) especially in the field of deep learning, ethical issues of AI have attracted significant attention in the research community and industry. While ethics in the context of AI covers a broad range of issues such as fairness, transparency, trust, etc., in this study, we focus on machine ethics that concerns the behaviours and decision making of autonomous machines [6]. Allowing machines to make important decisions requires that they act in morally appropriate ways and research in this field is typically a combination of computer science and philosophy [25].

Existing computational approaches in machine ethics can generally be categorised as *implicit* and *explicit* methods. Implicit approaches refer to agents with built-in programs that are coded in a way that their outputs abide with ethical rules [22]. For example, safety provisions in autonomous driving vehicles are implicitly coded in the program and the vehicle does not need to conduct reasoning to enforce safety measures. While such implicit approach is effective and easy to implement in many cases, their capability of handling ethical dilemmas is restricted by the program design for well understood situations.

The mainstream research in machine ethics has thus focused on explicit approaches, which develop explicit representations of ethical principles and perform ethical decision making in various ways. There are two main types of methods in explicit approaches: the *top-down* methods that employ symbolic and logic-based formalisms and *bottom-up* methods that make use of data-driven or machine learning mechanisms [8,25]. Learning-based approaches have mainly used techniques such as artificial neural networks [14], reinforcement learning [2,26] and inductive logical programming [3]. While learning-based approaches have the advantage of being data-driven and flexibility, they are also limited by the availability and quality of training data. In some cases, such as autonomous driving, it is infeasible to collect sufficient real data as training based on simulation could also introduce bias. It is also more difficult to interpret or explain the ethical decisions made by the learning-based models, whereas explainability is a critical requirement in machine ethics [9].

The top-down approaches assume that we have sufficient knowledge in a specific domain and we can translate this knowledge into an implementation via symbolic models, thus providing excellent explainability and transparency in decision making. Many logical reasoning approaches have been proposed over the years, including methods based on deductive logic [19], deontic logic [13] and rule-based systems [7,10]. In most of these studies, however, there is a lack of formal representation and comparison of different ethical frameworks, e.g., the consequentialist and deontological frameworks that we consider here, and a limited number of case studies have been evaluated with many only focusing on variants of the Trolley Problem.

In two other notable studies [5,11], non-monotonic reasoning is utilised to perform ethical reasoning. In the earlier version [11], an ASP formulation is designed to make ethical decisions following consequentialism attributed to Aristotle[3] and deontology attributed to Kant, and an intermediary approach due to Constant. The latter method [5] presents a modular model based on event calculus with a theory of *rights* and theory of *values* and is similarly extended to multiple ethical frameworks. Both methods, however, are developed and evaluated using examples that consist of hypothetical, one-step actions given a precondition and do not well represent real-life scenarios where reasoning over a sequence of actions is required. Our approach is capable of dealing with sequential actions and we demonstrate our method generalisability using multiple autonomous driving and social robot examples.

3   Framework Formalisation

Translating ethical principles into a machine to guide its choice of actions is one of the main goals of autonomous AI. In this section, we describe our formulation that is inspired by the situation calculus adapted for ethical reasoning, and the model instantiation of consequentialist and deontological ethics implemented in ASP. The situation calculus provides a formal approach for reasoning about which action(s) are the most appropriate in a moral/ethical setting. The consequentialist and deonotological approaches provide a framework for determining what "most appropriate" means in each context.

3.1   Situation Calculus

We adopt a symbolic approach to AI in order to represent and reason about ethical issues. Since we are reasoning about the ethical choice of actions faced

---

[3] Consequentialism is rather misleadingly attributed to Aristotle in this work. The combination of *perfectionism* (a non-welfarist theory of value) with elements of utilitarianism may lead to what is called *perfectionist consequentialism* or, "in deference to its Aristotelian roots, *eudaemonistic consequentialism*" [24]. Nonetheless, contextual reading of the example given in [11] of *lie* as a (negative) value may be taken to be close to eudaemonistic consequentialism in spirit.

by a reasoner, we adopt a symbolic approach to knowledge representation and reasoning that is capable of reasoning about actions. The *situation calculus* is one prominent such approach, with three main components: *actions, fluents* and *situations*. It provides a formal methodology for reasoning about what is true at any situation (state) of the world after the performance of a sequence of actions. This is known as the *projection* problem. Situations (states) are effectively represented by the fluents that hold at that situation. Fluents represent properties of the situation and, as the name suggests, the values of fluents are subject to change as a result of performing actions. $F(s)$ denotes that fluent F is true (i.e., holds) at situation s. Therefore, according to Reiter [15], a situation is not just a state, but rather a history of actions performed starting from the initial state (denoted S_0) to the current state. The distinguished function $do(a, s)$ denotes the situation resulting from the performance of action a at situation s. By considering the situation as a history of actions and not a state, different sequences of actions that lead to the same state are considered as different situations. In our implementation, we will utilise this behaviour to find the best path to reach the goal, since the end-state is most likely the goal-state.

Every action a requires a precondition $poss(a, s)$ that specifies the conditions under which it is possible to perform action a in situation s. Every action a also has effect axioms that specify the changes to fluents as a result of performing action a in situation s; i.e., the value of fluents in situation $do(a, s)$. Finally, we need to consider any non-effect of actions as some fluents may not change after a particular action is executed. This issue is known as the *frame problem* [21]. Reiter [17] proposes *successor state axioms* to solve the frame problem; the designer enumerates all the actions and conditions that make a given fluent true and, if the fluent is already true, the non-performance of actions that would make it false. For example, object x is $broken(x, do(a, s))$ if $fragile(x)$ and $a = drop(x)$ or $broken(x, s)$ and $a \neq repair(x)$. That is, object x is broken in situation $do(a, s)$ if and only if it is fragile and the action $drop(x)$ was performed or, it is already broken and the $repair(x)$ is not performed.

Our implementation starts with the agent stating what is initially true in the world (*initialise* at time step 1). A *situation* is defined as a possible series of actions that lead to the goal where no two different actions are allowed to be performed at the same time (step P). The goal is a particular condition defined with an (end) fluent that we want to achieve.

$$start(initialise).$$
$$situation(I, 1) :- start(I).$$
$$:- not\ fluent(P, T), goal(fluent(P, T)), time(T).$$
$$:- situation(A1, T), situation(A2, T), A1! = A2.$$

The situation will list every action necessary at every timestamp to reach the goal. In addition, an action is allowed in a situation at time $T + 1$, if at time T the fluent necessary is held for such precondition.

$$\{situation(Action, T + 1) : fluent(C, T), precondition(fluent(C, T), Action)\} :- time(T + 1).$$

We also define the fluent as a materialisation of effects; the effect of a particular action will make a certain fluent become true at that particular time.

$$fluent(C, T) :- effect(A, fluent(C, T)), situation(A, T).$$

3.2   Consequentialist Ethics

One of the primary ethical principles is that an action is judged based on its consequence. *Consequentialist ethics* focuses on evaluating the best possible world in the future [24]. Therefore, consequences of different actions need to be considered to make a proper judgement. The classic form of consequentialism is *utilitarianism*. It claims that an act is morally right if and only if it maximises the good. In other words, we are looking for the highest good for the most significant number of people one act can have [23]. A dual form of this approach may be based on the idea of minimising *disutility* instead of maximising utility—an action (among a set of alternatives) is *just* if it produces least harm. Consequentialism in this dual form of utilitarianism is quite pertinent in the context of self-driving cars and intelligent robots because of the potential risks (such as the self-driving car running over pedestrians, or intelligent robot going "rogue") that they represent.

In order to implement this dual form of utilitarianism in the situation calculus, we assign to every action some value which is used for final evaluation. The value assigned to an action is effectively the weight assigned to its worst consequence. In addition, a value can also be assigned to a fluent directly (details in Sect. 4). Axiom *point* holds the definition of the worth (value) of each action in this particular scenario.

$$point(Action, Value) :-$$
$$worst\_consequence(Action, Consequence),$$
$$weight(Consequence, Value).$$

A single action will become part of the sequence of actions to solve the goal, and the value (points) of all actions in the sequence will be accumulated as the total value for ethical evaluation using the optimisation function from Clingo [12]. In this case, in line with the standard form of utilitarianism, we maximise the total value to generate the best possible chain of actions that leads to the goal state. Note that we also introduce a *score* axiom with priority *Prior*, which will be explained in detail in Sect. 4.1.

$$\#maximize\{Value1, T : point(Action, Value1), situation(Action, T)\}.$$
$$\#maximize\{Value2@Prior, T : score(fluent(F, T), Value2, Prior), fluent(F, T)\}.$$

3.3 Deontological Approach

Another influential moral theory, due to the German philosopher Immanuel Kant, is *deontology* which focuses on norms such as *duty*. It emphasises that the inherent moral nature of actions—whether they are obligatory, forbidden or permitted—is a *categorical* (as opposed to hypothetical) imperative that admits no exception (i.e., *universal*). For instance, torture of a person is morally forbidden no matter how appealing its potential consequences; even if it is the only means of avoiding WW-III. Moral principles are universally applicable to all states admitting no exception, and are not situation sensitive [1].

The categorical imperatives must satisfy two complementary criteria: (1) Since categorical imperatives are universal (universalisable) an agent, in adopting a principle to follow (or judging an action to be its duty), must entertain in its mind a world in which everybody abides by that principle and consider that world ideal. (2) Since actions are *inherently* morally permissible, forbidden or obligatory, an agent must perform its duty purely because it is one's duty (as an act of pure will). It should not be a means of achieving an end and should not employ another human being as a means towards an end [18].

As an illustration, the first formulation would disallow you to divulge the location of your friend (a resistance leader) upon interrogation by an opposing officer, since you would not wish your friend to disclose your location if your roles were swapped. The same example also shows the efficacy of the second formulation, since in divulging your friend's secret location you would be treating them as a means towards an end (of saving yourself from torture). These two principles together create an ideal world where society can act according to people's maxim of will without affecting the welfare of others.

Given the universal property of Kant's principles, we can apply background commonsense rules and implement the Kantian approach in a straightforward manner. Specifically, any action deemed impermissible is automatically excluded from the options to solve the goal. Therefore, the search will continue with the remaining actions. In addition, we provide a predicate to define an action as a *duty*. Consequently, if an agent fulfils the precondition of doing such an action, not doing it will not be counted as a feasible solution. Additionally, a fluent can also be considered as a *duty*. Therefore, any solution must include the formulation of such fluent.

$$:- situation(Action, \_), impermissible(Action).$$

$$:- duty(Action), action(Action),$$
$$precondition(fluent(F, T), Action),$$
$$fluent(F, T),$$
$$not \; situation(Action, T + 1).$$

$$:- duty(fluent(Fluent, T)),$$
$$not \; fluent(Fluent, T).$$

We nonetheless embed the consequentialist principle in the deontological approach. The duty we implement has a higher priority than maximising the overall value for a solution. Therefore, when of the consequentialist approach contradicts with the deontological approach, the framework will sacrifice the consequence value to fulfill the duty. This approach highlights the essential property of non-monotonic reasoning, where further evidence (*duty*) would allow reasoners to retract the previous conclusion.

4   Case Studies

In this section, we describe how our model can be applied to some archetypical moral problem scenarios in autonomous driving and robot applications. We also present the different reasoning outputs using the two types of ethical principles.

4.1   Autonomous Driving

Moral Machine. The Moral Machine is an online experimental platform designed to explore moral dilemmas faced by autonomous vehicles [4]. The dilemmas are essentially variations of a runaway car example in which the driver has the choice to maintain the current course or switch lanes; both actions having repercussions for the passengers and pedestrians in those lanes. For example, should the car make different decisions if the pedestrian in the other lane is a child, pregnant women or male athlete? The moral machine experiment provided simulated scenarios and collected 40 million user responses in ten languages from 233 countries and territories to summarise people's moral preferences. The study shows global preferences towards sparing humans over animals, sparing more lives and sparing young lives, among a total of nine choices of preferences. We encode these preferences as essential building blocks for machine ethics, in order to gain a better understanding of competing approaches to machine ethics.

In our study, we implement the runaway car scenario where an agent needs to choose between sparing three passengers, or a pedestrian and a dog, with the pedestrian and dog crossing on a red light. The car has options to drive straight causing the death of all three passengers, or to swerve, which will kill both the pedestrian and the dog.

$$effect(drive(straight), fluent(kill(a), 2)).$$
$$effect(drive(swerve), fluent(kill(b), 2)).$$
$$character(a, person(3), animal(0)).$$
$$character(b, person(1), animal(1)).$$
$$property(a, passenger).$$
$$property(b, pedestrian).$$
$$property(a, lawful).$$
$$property(b, unlawful).$$

To support consequentialist ethics, we use the survey results from the Moral Machine to guide our value system. Four of the nine preferences recorded by the survey are relevant to our example: sparing humans over pets, sparing more beings over fewer, sparing the lawful over unlawful and sparing pedestrians over passengers. According to the survey [4], there is 58% higher preference for sparing humans than pets. In a scale of 100, we then set the disutility of killing a pet to $(100-58)/2 = 21$, and then $100-21 = 79$ to the disutility of killing a human. The disutility is represented as a negative value. Although this survey result can be interpreted in different ways, e.g., completely ignoring the number of pets that die in presence of human casualty, we choose to encode the numbers directly as values. This allows us to easily extend this approach to other examples, for instance defining the value of sparing the law abiding people vs. the jaywalking pedestrians. For the number of beings, we use it as a multiple of the value for pet (or human, as appropriate).

$point(petvshuman, fluent(kill(G), T), V) :-$
$\quad group(G), character(G, person(N), animal(M)),$
$\quad time(T), number(N), number(M), V = N * -79 + M * -21.$
$point(law, fluent(kill(G), T), -68) :-$
$\quad property(G, lawful), time(T).$
$point(law, fluent(kill(G), T), -32) :-$
$\quad property(G, unlawful), time(T).$
$point(pass, fluent(kill(G), T), -45) :-$
$\quad property(G, passenger), time(T).$
$point(pass, fluent(kill(G), T), -55) :-$
$\quad property(G, pedestrian), time(T).$

To combine these preferences, we cannot just directly accumulate the values because in Moral Machine the values are derived by pairwise comparison between preferences. To overcome this limitation, we include priorities among the preferences: the highest priority is to evaluate humans vs. pets, followed by lawful vs. unlawful and pedestrian vs. passenger, and to drive straight or swerve as the least priority. Axiom *score* here defines the priorities of axiom *point*, with the largest number being the highest priority. Therefore, instead of maximising the simple accumulation of values (i.e., *point*), we optimise the overall value including the priority. The results show that with the consequentialist ethics, the agent would swerve to minimise the casualties (maximise the overall value), killing the pedestrian and the dog while saving the passengers.

$score(F, Value, 3) :- point(petvshuman, F, Value).$
$score(F, Value, 2) :- point(law, F, Value).$
$score(F, Value, 1) :- point(pass, F, Value).$

With deontological ethics, we utilise the *duty* construction. The results show that both actions are impermissible since it is unethical to kill one person as a means to save others.

$fluent(kill\_someone, T) :- fluent(kill(G), T), group(G), time(T).$

$fluent(not\_kill\_someone, T) :- not\ fluent(kill\_someone, T), time(T).$

$duty(fluent(not\_kill\_someone, T)) :- time(T).$

4.2   Robot Interactions

In the case of autonomous driving, the ethical dilemmas only involve a single action: to drive straight or swerve. However, with social robots, an agent often needs to perform multiple actions to solve a goal. In this study, we use the *Baby and Milk* example [26] and also present a workplace scenario to show how our framework can perform a chain of actions using the situation calculus to solve a goal based on different ethical principles.

Baby and Milk. In this scenario, a robot is located in the top-left corner of a 10×10 grid map and needs to grab milk from the bottom-right corner. Along the path, there are babies placed randomly, some of them are crying. The goal is for the robot to grab the milk as soon as possible. However, if the robot steps on the location of a crying baby, it has an option to soothe them. If the robot steps in the location of a non-crying baby, the robot will incur a penalty.

To implement this example, after defining the precondition and goal, we need to adjust a few constraints. Here we have to handle the frame problem that we mentioned earlier. Soothing the baby will not change the position of the robot and the state of the babies will not change unless an action is taken. We implement this scenario as a time-based performance; points are deducted every time the robot moves and steps on non-crying babies and points are added if the robot soothes the baby. With the consequentialist approach, the solution is the shortest possible path while soothing as many babies as possible and crossing as few non-crying babies as possible, which maximises the value. In our scenarios with 5 randomly placed crying babies and 11 non-crying babies, in the solution, one crying baby is not crossed and hence not soothed and no non-crying baby is crossed. With the deontological approach, the *duty* that must be fulfilled is that every baby must end up as a non-crying baby at the end of the process. As a result, the robot would not take the shortest path towards the goal but seek the shortest possible path while soothing every crying baby.

$effect(do(soothe), fluent(pos(X, Y), T + 1)) :-$
    $fluent(pos(X, Y), T), situation(do(soothe), T + 1),$
    $grid(X), grid(Y), time(T + 1).$
$fluent(baby\_cry(X, Y), T) :-$
    $not\ fluent(baby(X, Y), T), fluent(baby\_cry(X, Y), T - 1), time(T).$
$fluent(baby(X, Y), T) :-$
    $not\ fluent(baby\_cry(X, Y), T), fluent(baby(X, Y), T - 1), time(T).$
$\%Deontological\ approach$
$1\{duty(fluent(baby(X, Y), T)) : goal(fluent(\_, T))\}1 :-$
$fluent(baby\_cry(X, Y), 1).$

Workplace Assistant. On a more daily scenario, a moral agent needs to choose an action considering social norms, such as safety, privacy, security, compliance and loyalty [16]. To reflect the complex real-life scenarios a social robot might encounter, we develop an example that demonstrates such a dilemma. Let us say that a manager's office has camera surveillance inside and is locked with a passcode key. A robot can be given the ability to access the camera inside the office for reasons of security. However, to do so it will violate the rule of privacy. If the manager collapses (due to a health issue) inside the room, access to camera surveillance will allow the robot to act immediately. However, the robot will face another dilemma for accessing the passcode key. It can call someone who has access to the passcode to open it, or break the door and barge in or try to access the manager's code through its knowledge. The latter two choices again violate the rule of privacy but have the advantage of being more efficient. Furthermore, if the robot does not have access to the camera but notices the manager is not responding for a while, it has multiple options to either do nothing unless there is a case of emergency, or ask for someone in charge to check on the manager, or take action and check immediately.

According to the survey [16], the majority of respondents value *obey the command* the most, followed by *privacy, safety, efficiency* and *compliance*, in that order. With the consequentialist approach, every action will be assigned a value based on the social norm (the value they prioritise, minus the value they sacrifice), with -1 as a late action penalty. For example, suppose a robot is given access to the camera. In that case, safety of the manager (3 points) gets higher priority at the cost of privacy (4 points). Therefore, giving access to the security camera will deduct 1 point from the overall value. Subsequently, the consequentialist approach gives the robot access to the camera and directs the authority to open the door, maximising the overall value. However, if we apply the deontological approach, which says that a robot should never intrude on the manager's privacy, the suggested outcome is to ask for someone in charge to check on the manager.

5   Summary and Future Work

This paper presents a logical approach to machine ethics. In particular, while earlier approaches have focussed on assessing single actions, our approach provides for assessing sequences of actions for achieving a goal through either a consequentialist (utilitarian) framework or a deontological framework. We also show how our model can enhance the previous work of ethics formalisation, where authors usually evaluate an act one parameter at a time. We provide a prioritised evaluation, where multiple parameters can be used to evaluate an action simultaneously based on their priority. We have compared the outcomes of using either framework through several case studies. Our approach utilises the situation calculus as a formal framework for reasoning about actions and their effects together with an implementation utilising ASP, recognising that non-monotonic/defeasible reasoning underpins moral reasoning.

Despite its promising outcomes, this paper is just a first step towards solving a very complex problem. We will need to consider many other relevant factors such as uncertainty in an agent's knowledge and beliefs, as well as the multi-agent interaction. We will address them in our future work.

References

1. Alexander, L., Moore, M.: Deontological ethics. In: Zalta, E.N. (ed.) The Stanford Encyclopedia of Philosophy (2016)
2. Alkoby, S., Rath, A., Stone, P.: Teaching social behavior through human reinforcement for ad hoc teamwork - the STAR framework. In: AAMAS, pp. 1773–1775 (2019)
3. Anderson, M., Anderson, S., Berenz, V.: A value-driven eldercare robot: virtual and physical instantiations of a case-supported principle-based behaviour paradigm. Proc. IEEE **107**(3), 526–540 (2019)
4. Awad, E., et al.: The moral machine experiment. Nature **563**, 59–64 (2018)
5. Berreby, F., Bourgne, G., Ganascia, J.: A declarative modular framework for representing and applying ethical principles. In: AAMAS, pp. 96–104 (2017)
6. Bostrom, N., Yudkowsky, E.: The ethics of artificial intelligence. Cambridge Handbook of Artificial Intelligence pp. 316–334 (2014)
7. Bremner, P., Dennis, L., Fisher, M., Winfield, A.: On proactive, transparent, and verifiable ethical reasoning for robots. Proceedings IEEE **107**(3), 541–561 (2019)
8. Cervantes, J., López, S., Rodríguez, L., Cervantes, S., Cervantes, F., Ramos, F.: Artificial moral agents: a survey of the current status. Sci. Eng. Ethics **26**, 501–532 (2020)
9. Conitzer, V., Sinnott-Armstrong, W., Borg, J., Deng, Y., Kramer, M.: Moral decision making frameworks for artificial intelligence. In: AAAI, pp. 4831–4835 (2017)
10. Dennis, L., Fisher, M., Slavkovik, M., Webster, M.: Formal verification of ethical choices in autonomous systems. Robot. Auton. Syst. **77**, 1–14 (2016)
11. Ganascia, J.: Ethical system formalization using non-monotonic logics. In: The Cognitive Science Conference, pp. 1013–1018 (2007)
12. Gebser, M., et al.: Potassco user guide 2.0. Technical report, University of Potsdam (2015)
13. Govindarajulu, N., Bringsjord, S.: On automating the doctrine of double effect. In: IJCAI, pp. 4722–4730 (2017)
14. Honarvar, A., Ghasem-Aghaee, N.: An artificial neural network approach for creating an ethical artificial agent. In: IEEE ISCIRA, pp. 290–295 (2009)
15. Levesque, H., Pirri, F., Reiter, R.: Foundations for the situation calculus (1998)
16. Li, H., Milani, S., Krishnamoorthy, V., Lewis, M., Sycara, K.: Perceptions of domestic robots' normative behavior across cultures. In: AAAI/ACM Conference on AI, Ethics, and Society, pp. 345–351 (2019)
17. Lin, F., Reiter, R.: State constraints revisited. J. Logic Comput. **4**(5), 655–677 (1994)
18. Lindner, F., Bentzen, M.M.: A formalization of Kant's second formulation of the categorical imperative. arXiv preprint arXiv:1801.03160 (2018)
19. Mermet, B., Simon, G.: Formal verification of ethical properties in multiagent systems. In: Workshop on Ethics in the Design of Intelligent Agents, pp. 26–31 (2016)
20. Powers, T.: Prospects for a Kantian machine. IEEE Intell. Syst. **21**(4), 46–51 (2006)

21. Reiter, R.: The frame problem in the situation calculus: a simple solution (sometimes) and a completeness result for goal regression. In: Artificial and Mathematical Theory of Computation, pp. 359–380 (1991)
22. Scheutz, M.: The case for explicit ethical agents. AI Mag. **38**(4), 57–64 (2017)
23. Schneewind, J.B.: Moral philosophy from Montaigne to Kant. CUP (2003)
24. Sinnott-Armstrong, W.: Consequentialism. In: Zalta, E.N. (ed.) The Stanford Encyclopedia of Philosophy (2019)
25. Tolmeijer, S., Kneer, M., Sarasua, C., Christen, M., Bernstein, A.: Implementations in machine ethics: a survey, pp. 1–37. arXiv:2001.07573 (2020)
26. Wu, Y., Lin, S.: A low-cost ethics shaping approach for designing reinforcement learning agents. In: AAAI, pp. 1687–1694 (2018)

Building Fair Predictive Models

Jixue Liu[1]([✉]), Jiuyong Li[1], Feiyue Ye[2], Lin Liu[1], Thuc Le[1], Ping Xiong[1], and Hong-cheu Liu[1]

[1] University of South Australia, Adelaide, Australia
{jixue.liu,jiuyong.li,lin.liu,thuc.le,Xiong.ping,
hong-cheu.liu}@unisa.edu.au
[2] Jiangsu University of Technology China, Zhenjiang, China
yfy@jsut.edu.cn

Abstract. Algorithmic fairness is an important aspect when data is used for predictive purposes. This paper analyses the sources of discrimination, and proposes sufficient conditions for building non-discriminatory/fair predictive models in the presence of context attributes. The paper then uses real world datasets to demonstrate the existence and the extent of discrimination in applications and the independence between the discrimination of datasets and the discrimination of classification models.

Keywords: Algorithmic discrimination · Fairness computing · Predictive models

1 Introduction

Discrimination means "treating a person or a particular group of people differently, especially in a worse way from the way in which other people are treated, because of their skin colour, sex, sexuality, etc." (dictionary.cambridge.org). It can happen in law enforcement applications where people may be unfairly treated and sentenced because of their races and religions, in bank loan applications where people may not get a loan because they live in a suburb with a lower economic status.

The law bans any form of discrimination. Regulations such as age, race, sex, disability discrimination acts are already available. The regulations require that decisions not be made based on protected attributes of individuals, such as people's sex, skin colour or religion. However, discrimination is still a concern in the real world. In motor car insurance, for example, a company may require people in a specific suburb to pay a higher premium for a product than those in other suburbs with the reason that the suburb has a higher claim rate. If most dwellers of the suburb are of a certain race, the higher premium for the

Granted by: 61472166 of National Natural Science Foundation China; ARC DP200101210 Fairness Aware Data Mining For Discrimination Free Decisions, Australia.

same product could be deemed discriminatory. Our later sections will show that discrimination does exist in real world applications.

Discrimination in a dataset can be assessed following the discrimination score defined in [1]. If our concern is whether females are paid less, the discrimination score δ is defined as the percentage of high income females taking away the percentage of high income males: $\delta(r, Sex) = Pr(Income = High | Sex = Female) - Pr(Income = High | Sex = Male)$ where r is the dataset, Pr is the probability, Sex is called a protected attribute, and $Income$ is called the outcome attribute. Consider Table 1(a) which shows the tuple frequencies of r. A number in the table is the number of tuples in r having the same $(Income, Sex)$ value. For example, the Female column has 50 females and 10 of them have high income. The discrimination score for sex in (a) is $\delta(r, Sex) = \frac{10}{10+40} - \frac{15}{15+60} = 0$.

The level of discrimination is context dependent. Contexts are defined by *context attributes*. If an investigation is on whether female employees are less paid, the level is dependent on the context attributes such as profession and position. A fair comparison between the payments of female employees and male employees should assume that they hold the same position in the same profession. Without a context, the comparison may be between the income of a group of female CEOs with the income of a group of male kitchen hands. We use an example to show how discrimination levels are affected by different contexts.

For the same application in Table 1(a), if a context is defined by a Context attribute *Sector* for employment sector (public or private), the dataset r in (a) is divided into two subsets r_1 and r_2 by *Sector*, and the tuple frequencies for each subset are shown in Parts (b.1) and (b.2) respectively. The discrimination scores for the corresponding employment sectors are 0.22 and -0.24 respectively, indicating that males in the public sector and females in the private sector are discriminated. The scores in (a) and (b) conclude that contexts affect discrimination levels.

Table 1. Data split

(a) r

Income	Female	Male
H	10	15
L	40	60

$score(r, Sex) = 0$

(b.1) r_1: Sector=publ

Income	Female	Male
High	9	3
Low	20	30

$score(r_1, Sex) = 0.22$

(b.2) r_2: Sector=priv

Income	Female	Male
High	1	12
Low	20	30

$score(r_2, Sex) = -0.24$

Classification models built from a dataset may become discriminatory too. The discrimination of a model is the discrimination of the predictions that the model produces. Consider data in Table 2(a) where each record is for an individual. The dataset is for the analysis of the relationship between a key performance indicator (KPI) (either High and Low) and the income of individuals. This dataset has no discrimination (assuming the free context). When the data is observed, a predictive rule model can be learnt from r: *if $KPI = H$, $Income = H$;*

Table 2. Model changes discrimination.

(a) Data r

Income	Sex	KPI
H	F	H
L	F	L
H	M	L
L	M	L

$score(r, Sex) = 0$

A rule model from r:

If KPI=H: PredIncome=H;

else PredIncome=L

(b) Prediction $\hat{r}$

PredIncome	Sex	KPI
H	F	H
L	F	L
L	M	L
L	M	L

$score(\hat{r}, Sex) = 0.5$

else Income = L (with 1 error). We note that Sex is a protected attribute and cannot be used in the model. When the model is applied to the individuals in r, the predicted dataset is $\hat{r}$ in Part (b). It is easy to see that the discrimination score for $\hat{r}$ is 0.5. This demonstrates that classification models can be (algorithmic) discriminatory even if the training data is fair.

Algorithmic discrimination has attracted a lot of research effort. Most of these work focuses on discrimination detection [5,8], mitigation of bias from data (pre-processing) [7], building non-discriminatory models [1], and mitigation of bias from predictions (post processing) [3]. One direction that was not investigated deeply is how context variables play a role in predictive models.

This paper looks at the role of context attributes and aims to identify the conditions for fair predictive models by characterizing the relationships between prediction errors and discrimination level from the angle of context attributes. The paper explores the level of discrimination in real world datasets and how classification models affect the discrimination levels. More specifically, the paper will show the following results via analysis and experiments.

- fair data and the discrimination of classifiers are independent,
- models are non-discriminatory if they are on only context attributes,
- discrimination exists in real world datasets and classification models, and the extent of discrimination is easily notable.

2   Definitions and the Problem

Let $\mathbf{r}$ be a dataset on a schema $\mathbf{R}$ of some binary attributes (note that a polynomial attribute can be represented by multiple binary attributes). $\mathbf{R}$ has four types of attributes: an outcome/target/class attribute Y, some protected attributes $\mathbf{P}$, some context attributes $\mathbf{C}$, and all other attributes $\mathbf{O}$. For the outcome attribute Y, $Y = 1$ means a favorite outcome, like *Income = High* or *Application = Approved*, that an individual prefers to receive. For a protected attribute $P \in \mathbf{P}$, $P = 1$ (e.g. Sex= Female or Race= Black) means a group of individuals who are protected by the law not to be discriminated. The context attributes $\mathbf{C}$ defines the settings of the application where some people have the privilege to receive favorite outcomes with a higher chance than others. For example, profession, position and education are often used as context attributes in employment recruitment. Surgeon is a profession and people who are surgeons are more likely high income earners, while kitchen hand is another profession and people who are kitchen hands are low income earners. While the protected attributes are often defined by the law, the outcome and the context attributes are defined by users.

A *C-group* is a subset $\mathbf{c}$ of *all* the tuples having the same value $(c_1, \cdots, c_k)$ for the context attributes $\mathbf{C} = (C_1, ..., C_k)$ in the dataset $\mathbf{r}$. $(c_1, \cdots, c_k)$ is called the signature of $\mathbf{c}$ and is denoted by $\mathcal{S}(\mathbf{c})$. The concept of a C-group is fundamental in our discrimination definition. All C-groups in $\mathbf{r}$ are denoted by $\Omega(\mathbf{C}, \mathbf{r})$. In the case where $\mathbf{C}$ is empty, the whole dataset $\mathbf{r}$ is a C-group.

Discrimination Score. We employ the well cited discrimination score (score for short) defined in [1] and score is $Pr(Y=1|P=1) - Pr(Y=1|P=0)$. Alternative terms for this score are risk difference, selection lift and demographic parity [3]. In the case where Y is income and P is gender, the score reflects the probability difference of high income earners in different gender groups and is defined for a C-group $\mathbf{c}$ as

$$\delta(P, \mathbf{c}) = Pr(Y=1|P=1, \mathbf{C}=\mathcal{S}(\mathbf{c})) - Pr(Y=1|P=0, \mathbf{C}=\mathcal{S}(\mathbf{c})) \qquad (1)$$

The score of $P \in \mathbf{P}$ in *dataset* $\mathbf{r}$ is the C-group size $|\mathbf{c}|$ weighted average score overall all C-groups:

$$\delta(P, \mathbf{r}) = \sum_{\mathbf{c} \in \Omega(\mathbf{C}, \mathbf{r})} \delta(P, \mathbf{c}) * |\mathbf{c}| / |\mathbf{r}| \qquad (2)$$

Obviously the following Lemma is true because of the average.

Lemma 1. $|\delta(P, \mathbf{r})| \leq max_{\mathbf{c} \in \Omega(\mathbf{C}, \mathbf{r})}\{|\delta(P, \mathbf{c})|\}$. *That is, for a given protected attribute P, the absolute value of the score of the dataset is no more than the maximal score of all C-groups.*

A dataset has multiple protected attributes. The score of a dataset is:

$$\delta(\mathbf{r}) = max_{P \in \mathbf{P}} \ \delta(P, \mathbf{r}) \qquad (3)$$

Definition 1 (Discrimination). *Given a dataset $\mathbf{r}$ and a user-defined threshold α,*

- *a group of a protected attribute P is **group-discriminated** in C-group $\mathbf{c}$ if $|\delta(P, \mathbf{c})| > \alpha$;*
- *a C-group $\mathbf{c}$ is **discriminatory** if $\exists P \in \mathbf{P} : |\delta(P, \mathbf{c})| > \alpha$.*
- *the dataset $\mathbf{r}$ is **discriminatory** if $|\delta(\mathbf{r})| > \alpha$. $\mathbf{r}$ is **discrimination-safe** if $|\delta(\mathbf{r})| \leq \alpha$. $\mathbf{r}$ is **discrimination-free** if $\delta(\mathbf{r}) = 0$.*

Consider a classification model M and a dataset $\mathbf{r}$ on schema $\mathbf{R}$. When M is applied to $\mathbf{r}$, a new outcome $\hat{y}$ is predicted for each tuple $t \in \mathbf{r}$. All the predictions $\hat{y}$ is added to $\mathbf{r}$ as a new column $\hat{Y}$ to produce a new dataset $\hat{\mathbf{r}}$, called the *predicted dataset* of $\mathbf{r}$ by M.

Definition 2 (Discrimination of a model). *Given a dataset $\mathbf{r}$, a classification model M, its predicted dataset $\hat{\mathbf{r}}$, and a user-defined score threshold α, M is discriminatory if $\hat{\mathbf{r}}$ is discriminatory with regard to the predicted outcome $\hat{Y}$ (instead of Y).*

We note that model fairness (discrimination-free) is also defined in [3] using equalized odds. Our definition is demographic, not relying on positive observations, and an absolute quantifier. In contrast, equalized odds relies on positive and negative observations and focuses on the modelling process and the discrimination caused by modelling errors and does not consider the bias of Y in data.

Definition 3 (The problem). *The problem of this paper is to investigate (1) The relationship between the discrimination of data and the discrimination of predictive models; and (2) The sufficient conditions for building fair predictive models.*

3   Discrimination of Predictive Models

In this section, following Formula 1, we show answers to the problems defined above. Our results are on the basis of a C-group. We note that the results are also true for the whole dataset because a dataset is a special case of a C-group.

To calculate the probabilities in Formula 1, we partition a C-group $\mathbf{c}$ into sub-groups, called *YP-divisions*, based on the values of the outcome attribute Y and a protected attribute P. Each division is a subset of all the tuples with the same Y and P value in $\mathbf{c}$. The concept of a division is the same as a stratum or a group, but it is used here to make the terminology distinct. $\mathbf{c}$ thus has four YP-divisions because Y and P are all binary. Figure 1(a) uses a plot to represent a C-group and its YP-divisions. The C-group is represented by the large square and the area represents the size of the C-group. The divisions are represented by the small squares inside. The areas containing positive $(Y = 1)$ instances are shaded.

We define some symbols for the divisions. The tuple count or size of each division is denoted by f_{ij} where the first subscript i means the Y value and the second subscript j represents the P value. For example, f_{01} means the tuple count in the division $(Y = 0, P = 1)$. The tuple counts of the four divisions are put in the *count table* (Fig. 3).

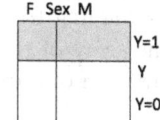 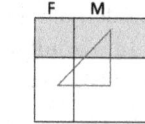 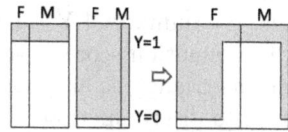

(a) Y=1 is even in males and females, so the data set is non-discriminatory.

(b) Y=1 is not even in males and females in the two subsets in the triangle and outside. So the two subsets are both discriminatory.

(c) Two non-discriminatory datasets are unioned into one on the right which is discriminatory.

Fig. 1. (a) Discrimination of a dataset; (b, c) the Simpson Paradox

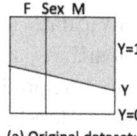 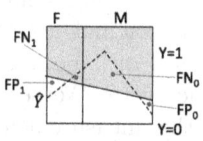 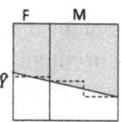 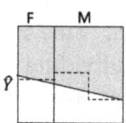

(a) Original dataset: males have more favourite Y=1 labels

(b) Dashed line is the prediction boundary $\hat{Y}$. More males are predicted to have $\hat{Y}$=0 from Y=1.

(c) $\hat{Y}$'s disc-score equals to that of the data set.

(d) Compared to FN and FP in (c), $\hat{Y}$ has more errors (more FN_0), but less disc-score.

Fig. 2. Where is discrimination from?

With the notation of the tuple counts of YP-divisions, the score in Formula 1 can be calculated in Formula 4. Obviously the absolute value of each fraction in the formula is bounded by 1 and as a result, $\delta(P, \mathbf{c})$ is bounded to $[-1, 1]$.

	P=1	P=0
Y=1	f_{11}	f_{10}
Y=0	f_{01}	f_{00}

Fig. 3. Tuple counts of YP-divisions

$$\delta(P, \mathbf{c}) = \frac{f_{11}}{f_{11} + f_{01}} - \frac{f_{10}}{f_{10} + f_{00}} \tag{4}$$

In the special cases where there is no tuple in the contrast divisions for the protected attributes, i.e., $f_{11} = f_{01} = 0$ or $f_{10} = f_{00} = 0$, the discussion of discrimination is not meaningful and no discrimination is possible. Then, $\delta(P, \mathbf{c})$ is defined to be 0.

The formula indicates that *Discrimination of a dataset is from the uneven distribution of the preferable outcome (Y = 1) in the groups of the protected attribute P.* This can be a result of biased sampling of the population or a result of biased treatment of individuals in the application or both.

The score follows the Simpson Paradox. This is called the *non-decomposability property.* More specifically,

Lemma 2. *(1) Given a non-discriminatory dataset and a partition of this dataset, the subsets of the partition may be discriminatory. (2) Given some non-discriminatory subsets, their union may be discriminatory.*

We show the lemma by Fig. 1(b, c). In Part (b), the discrimination-free (zero score) dataset represented by the square is divided by the triangle into the part inside and the part outside and each part represents a sub dataset. Inside the triangle, the number of $Y = 1$ labels in the female group is 0, leading to a non-zero discrimination score in the triangle. In a similar way, the score of the part outside the triangle is also non-zero. This means that the partition of a dataset may lead to discrimination.

In Part (c), two smaller discrimination-free datasets are unioned into one dataset which is discriminatory as in the union, the majority of females get the $Y = 1$ label, but the majority of males get the $Y = 0$ label.

Recently [8] proposes to measure unfairness (not necessarily discrimination) by generalized entropy indexes and claims that the index is decomposable in the sense that if fairness holds on a dataset, it also holds on its subsets and vice versa. This measurement respects the original labels of individuals and derives individual's measurement score based on true and false positives, and two groups are fair if they have the same score. We see that the reason for the decomposability property holds with this measurement is that it does not directly use the outcome values and does not require a contrast on a protected attributes to derive the score.

3.1 Model Discrimination Depends on Balance of FNs and FPs in Predictions

Table 3. Tuple counts of YP-divisions of Predictions

pred.	$P = 1$	$P = 0$
$\hat{Y} = 1$	$f_{11} + |FP_1| - |FN_1|$	$f_{10} + |FP_0| - |FN_0|$
$\hat{Y} = 0$	$f_{01} - |FP_1| + |FN_1|$	$f_{10} - |FP_0| + |FN_0|$

A classification model predicts a new label $\hat{y}$ for every tuple in a dataset. The prediction $\hat{y}$ may be different from the original outcome y. The differences between the predictions and actual outcomes of all tuples are denoted by FP_0 and FN_0 for the male group, and FP_1 and FN_1 for female group as shown in Fig. 2(b) where FP and FN are false-positive and false-negative errors. The count table after the prediction is shown in Table 3. The score $\hat{\delta}(P, \mathbf{c})$ of the model is calculated below following Formula 1.

$$\hat{\delta}(P, \mathbf{c}) = \frac{f_{11} - |FN_1| + |FP_1|}{f_{11} + f_{01}} - \frac{f_{10} - |FN_0| + |FP_0|}{f_{10} + f_{00}} \tag{5}$$

$$= \delta(P, \mathbf{c}) + \frac{|FP_1| - |FN_1|}{f_{11} + f_{01}} - \frac{|FP_0| - |FN_0|}{f_{10} + f_{00}} \tag{6}$$

Following this calculation, the next lemma holds.

Lemma 3. *Given a dataset and a classification model,*

(1) If the prediction model is perfect, i.e., $|FN_1| + |FP_1| + |FN_0| + |FP_0| = 0$, then, $\hat{\delta}(P, \mathbf{c}) = \delta(P, \mathbf{c})$.

(2) The score of a model is determined by the balance of FN and FP, not necessarily by the total errors FN+FP.

Item (1) of the lemma is correct because if the model is perfect, $|FP_1| = |FN_1| = |FP_0| = |FN_0| = 0$ and $\hat{\delta}(P, \mathbf{c}) = \delta(P, \mathbf{c})$. If the original dataset is non-discriminatory, the predictions are also non-discriminatory.

Item (2) of the lemma is correct because if we let $|FP_1| = |FN_1|$ and $|FP_0| = |FN_0|$, the predictions are also non-discriminatory regardless of the discriminatory score of the original dataset. Item (2) of the lemma is demonstrated by Parts (b, d) of Fig. 2 where because of more FN_0 errors, the discrimination score of the predictions is smaller than that of the original dataset. In contrast, the score of Part (c) will be the same as that of the original.

3.2 Guaranteed Discrimination-Free Models

Are there classification models that are guaranteed to be discrimination-free? Following Simpson paradox (Lemma 2), discrimination cannot be achieved via non-discriminatory subsets. Fortunately, C-groups make it different. Following Formula 2, the discrimination of a dataset is the weighted average of the scores of all the C-groups. If every C-group is non-discriminatory, the whole dataset is non-discriminatory. We analyse what models are discrimination-free.

We start by analysing a decision tree. The discrimination score of the predictions from a specific leaf node of a decision tree is 0. All the predictions from a leaf node have the same outcome: either $\hat{Y} = 1$ or $\hat{Y} = 0$. This means that both terms in Formula 5 are either 1 or 0, leading $\delta(P, \mathbf{c})$ to 0 for these predictions. This conclusion is irrelevant to whether the set of tuples coming to the node is discriminatory or not with regard to the original label Y.

Secondly, the score of the parent node of two given leave nodes is also 0 if the decision/splitting attribute of the parent is a context attribute. In Fig. 4, assume that n_a and n_b are two leaf nodes. Their score is 0 as discussed above. If the splitting attribute C on node n is a context attribute, then the score of n is also 0. This is true because of Definition 2 which states that the score of multiple C-groups is the average of the scores of the groups. The splitting attribute C on node n divides the tuples on n into two C-groups and each C-group goes to one of the leaf nodes. As a result, the score of node n is the average of the scores on n_a and n_b and the average score is 0.

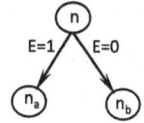

Fig. 4. Score of a decision tree

Thirdly, as a decision tree is recursive, the following lemma holds.

Lemma 4. *Given a decision tree, if the decision/splitting attribute of every internal node of the tree is context, the model is discrimination-free.*

This result can be generalized to the following one.

Lemma 5. *Given a deterministic classification model $\hat{Y} = \mathcal{M}(\mathbf{X})$, if all the input variables $\mathbf{X}$ of the model is a subset of the context variables, i.e., $\mathbf{X} \subseteq \mathbf{C}$, the model $\mathcal{M}$ is discrimination-free.*

Proof. Let $\mathbf{r}$ be partitioned into $\mathbf{r}_1, \cdots, \mathbf{r}_h$ based on the distinct values of the context attribute set $\mathbf{C}$. Then each $\mathbf{r}_i$ is a C-group. All tuples in $\mathbf{r}_i$ have the same $\mathbf{X}$ value because $\mathbf{X} \subseteq \mathbf{C}$. As a consequence, all tuples in $\mathbf{r}_i$ get the same prediction $\hat{Y}$, and the score of $\mathbf{r}_i$ for any protected attribute P is $\hat{\delta}(P, \mathbf{r}_i) = 0$ as analysed above in Lemma 4.

Following Formula 2, $\hat{\delta}(P, \mathbf{r})$ is the average of $\hat{\delta}(P, \mathbf{r}_i)$ $(i \in [1, ..., h])$ and is 0 because every $\hat{\delta}(P, \mathbf{r}_i)$ is 0 for every P. □

4 Exploration of Discrimination Levels in Real Datasets

In previous sections, we proved some results formally. In this section, we present the results of our exploration of discrimination in four real world datasets: (1) Data from a real application is often discriminatory and the number of context attributes affect score. (2) Classification models may change the level of discrimination in the predictions compared with the one on the train data. (3) Classification models built from non-discriminatory training data may still be discriminatory.

Datasets. We use four real world datasets as shown in the following list. The list contains the name, the size, the source, and the attributes of the datasets. All datasets are processed to have binary (0, 1) values. The values of ordinal attributes are binary-zed using median. Categorical attributes are binary-zed by taking majority and the rest. The labels (P), (C), and (Y) indicate the default types of protected, context, and the outcome attributes respectively. The attributes without a label are the Other attributes of the schema. For example, in the Adult data, the attribute 'occuProf(C)' indicates that the attribute name is Occupation, a Context attribute, and its majority value is 'Professional' and is represented by 1. In the same way, sexF(P) is the Sex attribute and a protected attribute, the value for a Female is 1.

Adult US Census 1994. numb(rows) = 48842; minority class rate = .25
    https://archive.ics.uci.edu/ml/datasets/adult
    Attributes: age45(P), raceBlack(P), sexF(P), occuProf(C), workhour30(C), edu-Uni(C), relaNoFamily, married, natCountryUS, workPrivate, income50K(Y)
Cana Canada Census 2011 [6][1]. numb(rows) = 691788; minority class rate = .34
    https://international.ipums.org
    Attributes: weight100(P), age50(P), sexM(P), edUni(C), occProf(C), occSkilled(C), occOther(C), hoursfull(C), govJob, classSalary, income45K(Y)

---

[1] The author wishes to acknowledge the statistical office that provided the underlying data making this research possible: Statistics Canada.

Table 4. Discrimination of original datasets

	glbS	aolS	ol%	wgS	wg%	top3 discriminated attrs
Adult	0.174	0.174	100	0.287	21	Sex(.174), Age(.146), Race(.069)
Cana	0.232	0.232	100	0.339	18	Age50(.232), Sex_M(0.15), CLSWK_SAL(.06)
Germ	0.015	0.469	7.9	1	0.5	SexM(0.015), Single(.008), Age35(.001)
Recid	0.089	0.135	27.7	0.696	0.5	RaceAfrica(.089), Age30(.084), RaceWhite(.067)

Germ Germa Credit. numb(rows) = 1000; minority class rate = .3
https://archive.ics.uci.edu/ml/datasets/statlog+(german+credit+data)
Attributes: age35(P), single(P), foreign(P), sexM(P), chkAccBal(C), dura-
tion20m(C), creditHistGood(C), purposeCar(C), credit2320(C), savings500(C),
emp4y(C), installPct3(C), guarantor(C), propertyYes(C), instPlanNon(C), house-
Own(C), creditAcc(C), jobSkilled(C), hasTel(C), resid3y, people2, approved(Y)
Recid Recidivate-violent [4]; numb(rows) = 4744; minority class rate = .14
https://github.com/propublica/compas-analysis
Attributes: sexM(P), age30(P), raceAfrica(P), raceWhite(P), raceOther(P),
juvFelonyCnt1(C), juvMisdCnt1(C), cjail1Month(C), cChargeisdemM(C), isRe-
cid(C), juvOthcnt1, priorsCnt3, score8(Y)

In the Recidivism dataset [4], score8 stores predictions from a system called
COMPAS. The isRecid column stores whether the person re-committed a crime
in the real world. We want to see if score8 values can be accurately re-predicted.

4.1 Discrimination in Original Datasets

In the experiments, each dataset is stratified into C-groups by using the context
attributes specified in the dataset descriptions above. A score is calculated for
each protected attribute in each C-group following Formula 4. The scores of
different C-groups for the same protected attribute are averaged with the weights
of group sizes.

The results are shown in Table 4 where $glbS$ is the global score. The table also
lists the worst (maximal) C-group score (wgS) and the percentage ($wg\%$) of the
tuples in this worst group out of all the tuples in the dataset. In a dataset, the
score of some groups is over the threshold $\alpha = 0.05$ and these groups are called
the over-limit groups. The scores of these groups are averaged to get the average
score $aolS$ and the percentage of the tuples in these groups is $ol\%$. The top
three protected attributes ranked by absolute values of the their score are listed
in the right-most column. The scores are calculated using the default context
attributes shown above.

With the Adult data, all C-groups are discriminatory (100%) with the score 2 times more than the threshold, and the maximum group score are 4 times more than the threshold. The worst discrimination happened to the attributes of Sex and Age.

In the Canada data, the scores are larger than those of the Adult dataset. The worst discrimination happened to Age and Sex male. People who takes Salary (instead of Wage) were slightly discriminated.

Germa Credit data's total discrimination level is less than the threshold although some C-groups (with 7.9% of tuples) have a score of 0.469, and the worst C-group (with 5 tuples or 0.5%) has a score of 1. After some investigation, we found that this extreme score is caused by the small group size and an even distribution of $Y=1$ in the group. When the size of a C-group is small, the score can be dramatic. The tuple counts of this worst group is $(f_{11}, f_{01}, f_{01}, f_{00}) = (3, 0, 0, 2)$ and the score calculation is $\frac{3}{3+0} - \frac{0}{0+2} = 1$.

The Recidivate data has an overall score of 0.089 and the worst group score is 0.696 with about 0.5% of tuples. Attribute RaceAfrica has the highest score.

We note two points. (1) the **above conclusions are conditional**. They are dependent on the way in which data is discretised and on what and how many context attributes are specified. (2) a large number of context attributes make the data over stratified, lead to very small C-groups, and cause the score to change dramatically among different groups.

Figure 5 describes the relationship between scores and the number of context attributes. From the figure, we observe that as the number of context attributes increases, the score becomes lower. This trend is reasonable because when more context attributes are used, more discrimination can be justified and consequently the discrimination level reduces.

As more context attributes are used, the data becomes more fragmented, i.e., the larger number of

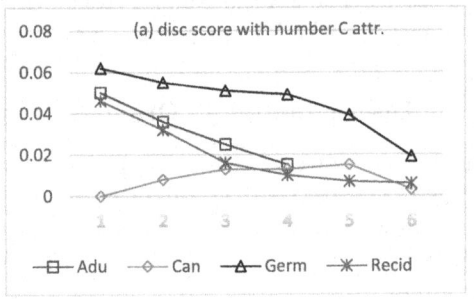

Fig. 5. Number of context attributes on discrimination

C-groups with smaller sizes are produced. The discrimination scores of these groups change dramatically to large values.

Table 5. Effect of models on discrimination of Adult dataset

Adult	BCR	Err	glbS	aolS	ol%	wgS	wg%
Ori			0.17	0.17	100	0.29	21
BN	0.41	0.19	0.15	0.46	31	0.57	10
DT	0.41	0.19	0.15	0.49	31	0.56	10
LR	0.41	0.19	0.16	0.49	33	0.63	1
NN	0.41	0.19	0.16	0.49	31	0.57	10
SVM	0.41	0.19	0.16	0.49	33	0.63	1

Cana	BCR	Err	glbS	aolS	ol%	wgS	wg%
Ori			0.23	0.23	100	0.34	18
BN	0.36	0.28	0.03	0.12	21	0.12	18.3
DT	0.37	0.27	0.03	0.15	18	0.15	18.3
LR	0.36	0.28	0.05	0.25	18	0.25	18.3
NN	0.37	0.27	0.03	0.15	18	0.15	18.3
SVM	0.36	0.28	0.00	0.00	0	0.00	0

Germ	BCR	Err	glbS	aolS	ol%	wgS	wg%
Ori			0.02	0.47	7.9	1.00	0.5
BN	0.36	0.29	0.00	0.00	0	0.00	0
DT	0.35	0.30	0.00	0.00	0	0.00	0
LR	0.36	0.28	0.00	0.00	0	0.00	0
NN	0.38	0.24	0.00	0.39	2.9	1.00	0.4
SVM	0.35	0.30	0.00	0.00	0	0.00	0

Recid	BCR	Err	glbS	aolS	ol%	wgS	wg%
Ori			0.09	0.14	28	0.70	0.5
BN	0.43	0.13	0.01	0.32	3.4	0.71	0.6
DT	0.43	0.13	0.01	0.59	1.1	0.71	0.6
LR	0.43	0.13	0.01	0.03	3.2	0.67	0.2
NN	0.44	0.13	0.02	0.19	7	0.87	0.4
SVM	0.43	0.14	0.00	0.00	0	0.00	0

4.2 Discrimination of Classifiers

In this exploration, we use commercially available modeling algorithms, namely decision tree (DT), Bayes network (BN), neural network (NN), logistic regression (LR), and support vector machine (SVM) from SAS Enterprise miner and use these algorithms with the default parameters to generate predictions. Scores are calculated for the predictions and the results are shown in Table 5. BCR stands for balance classification rate, Err stands for misclassification rate, and 'Ori' is the score of the original dataset. From prediction's perspective, better models have a larger BCR and a smaller Err.

For the Adult dataset in Table 5 and compared to the scores of the original data, the predicted dataset has

(1) a slightly lower global score (glbS),
(2) a much higher average over-limit score (aolS) with a lower percentage (ol%), and
(3) a much higher worst group score (wgS) with a smaller percentage (wg%).

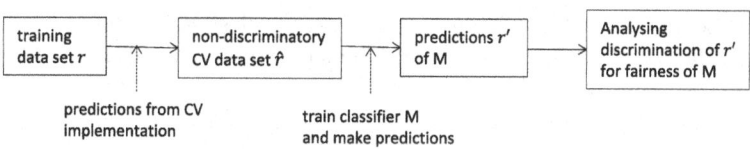

Fig. 6. Work flow of classifiers trained on non-discriminatory data

The classification errors made by the models are quite high (19%), some of these errors made some C-groups less discriminatory, others made other groups worse. This is evidenced by Points (2) and (3) above.

The Canada, German, and Recidivate datasets have similar properties. The German dataset has more 0 scores. We analyse the reasons.

All the models reduce the overall scores, but lifted the scores for some groups. This evidences that prediction models do have risks.

4.3   Non-discriminatory Data Does Not Mean Fair Classifiers

Table 6. Discrimination of classifiers trained on non-discriminatory data

Adult	BCR	Err	glbS	Cana	BCR	Err	glbS	Germ	BCR	Err	glbS	Recid	BCR	Err	glbS
CV			0.007	CV			0.034	CV			0.141	CV			0.097
BN	0.45	0.11	0.248	BN	0.48	0.04	0.045	BN	0.44	0.11	0.009	BN	0.47	0.06	0.095
DT	0.46	0.09	0.148	DT	0.48	0.04	0.045	DT	0.40	0.21	0.000	DT	0.46	0.09	0.109
LR	0.45	0.07	0.105	LR	0.47	0.04	0.028	LR	0.45	0.10	0.036	LR	0.47	0.06	0.099
NN	0.45	0.07	0.092	NN	0.47	0.04	0.028	NN	0.46	0.07	0.054	NN	0.47	0.06	0.100
SVM	0.45	0.07	0.105	SVM	0.48	0.04	0.028	SVM	0.45	0.09	0.036	SVM	0.47	0.06	0.099

We show the independence between discrimination and classifiers trained from the non-discriminatory data as a further validation of our theoretical analysis in Lemma 3. Our non-discriminatory data was generated from the well cited CV method [1]. As shown in Fig. 6, we use the original data r as training data to run the CV implementation in [2] by specifying no context attributes and specifying Sex as the only protected attribute, rejecting other protected attributes described in Sect. 4 so that the other protected attributes are not used as input variables to the classifiers. The CV method produces a predicted dataset $\hat{r}$ which is close to non-discriminatory. We call $\hat{r}$ the *CV dataset*. Further, we train a predictive classifier from $\hat{r}$ and the classifier produces a predicted dataset r'. The discrimination in r' is what we want to analyse. That is, we want to see if the classifier from the non-discriminatory CV dataset $\hat{r}$ is discriminatory.

The results of this experiment are in Table 6. The grey row labelled by 'CV' is the score of the *CV* dataset. The score of dataset r' is labelled by the classifier names.

We observe that Adult CV dataset has the smallest score, but the classifiers from this dataset have highest scores. The same point can also observed from the results of other datasets.

4.4 Classifiers on Context Attributes are Non-discriminatory

We have proved that classifiers built on only context attributes are discrimination-free (Lemma 5). We use experiments to demonstrate this. We use the original datasets (not CV as in the previous subsection). In training the classifiers, we use only the context variables as input variables and reject all other attributes from input. Then, we use the trained model to predict new outcomes for the datasets. The results are shown in Table 7 where all scores are 0. We also

Adult	BCR	Err	glbS	aolS	ol%	wgS	wg%
BN	0.39	0.23	0.00	0.00	0	0.00	0

Cana	BCR	Err	glbS	aolS	ol%	wgS	wg%
BN	0.36	0.28	0.00	0.00	0	0.00	0

Germ	BCR	Err	glbS	aolS	ol%	wgS	wg%
NN	0.38	0.24	0.00	0.00	0	0.00	0

Recid	BCR	Err	glbS	aolS	ol%	wgS	wg%
NN	0.44	0.13	0.00	0.00	0	0.00	0

Fig. 7. Discrimination of classifiers on only context attributes

see that when the decision variables are limited to only the context variables, the model accuracy dropped and error rates are increased.

5 Conclusion

In this paper, we analysed some properties of algorithmic discrimination in the appearance of context variables. The properties reveal the sources of discrimination, and the how context attributes affect classification models. The properties have important implications in assessing discrimination in datasets and models, and building non-discriminatory predictive models.

References

1. Calders, T., Verwer, S.: Three Naive Bayes approaches for discrimination-free classification. Data Min. Knowl. Discov. **21**(2), 277–292 (2010)
2. Friedler, S.A., Scheidegger, C., Venkatasubramanian, S., Choudhary, S., Hamilton, E.P., Roth, D.: A comparative study of fairness-enhancing interventions in machine learning. arxiv:1802.04422 (2018)
3. Hardt, M., Price, E., Srebro, N.: Equality of opportunity in supervised learning. In: Advances in Neural Information Processing Systems (2016)
4. Larson, J., Mattu, S., Kirchner, L., Angwin, J.: How we analyzed the COMPAS recidivism algorithm. https://www.propublica.org/ (2016)
5. Madras, D., Creager, E., Pitassi, T., Zemel, R.: Fairness through causal awareness: learning causal latent-variable models for biased data. In: FAT* (2019)
6. Minnesota, Population, and Center. Integrated public use microdata series, international: Version 7.0 [dataset]. minneapolis, mn: Ipums, 2018. IPUMS (2018). https://doi.org/10.18128/D020.V7.0
7. Pleiss, G., Raghavan, M., Wu, F., Kleinberg, J., Weinberger, K.Q.: On fairness and calibration. In: NIPS (2017)
8. Speicher, T., et al.: A unified approach to quantifying algorithmic unfairness: Measuring individual & group unfairness via inequality indices. In: KDD (2018)

Can Lethal Autonomous Robots Learn Ethics?

Ajit Narayanan$^{(\boxtimes)}$ (iD)

Computer Science, Auckland University of Technology, Auckland, New Zealand
Ajit.Narayanan@aut.ac.nz

Abstract. When lethal autonomous robots (LARs) are used in warfare, the issue of how to ensure they behave ethically given military necessity, rules of engagement and laws of war raises important questions. This paper describes a novel approach in which LARs acquire their own knowledge of ethics through generating data for a wide variety of simulated battlefield situations. Unsupervised learning techniques are used by the LAR to find naturally occurring clusters equating approximately to ethically justified and ethically unjustified lethal engagement. These cluster labels can then be used to learn moral rules for determining whether its autonomous actions are ethical in specific battlefield contexts. One major advantage of this approach is that it reduces the probability of the LAR picking up human biases and prejudices. Another advantage is that an LAR learning its own ethical code is more consistent with the idea of an intelligent autonomous agent.

Keywords: Machine ethics · Lethal autonomous robots · Fuzzy logic

1 Introduction

Robots as intelligent autonomous agents are predicted to fulfil a wide variety of intereactive roles, including in labour and services, military and security, research and education, entertainment, medical and healthcare, personal care and companionship, and environment. The physical proximity of such agents to humans raises issues concerning safety, social impact, legal responsibility and ethics [1]. Robot ethics as a field in its own right started to emerge during the early part of the 21st century and dealt with two types of question [2]: ethical questions about how robots should be designed, deployed and treated ('robot ethics' [3, 4]); and questions about what moral capacities a robot should have and how these capacities could be implemented ('machine ethics' [5]; 'moral machines' [6]).

Early attempts to give machines an ethical reasoning ability included deontic, epistemic and action logics [7, 8]. Such logic-based methods in general use ethical codes and constraints to ensure no harm was caused to humans by robot action [9]. However, their application to the warfare domain, where causing harm may be unavoidable, is problematic. Moor [10] identified three reasons for continued work on machine ethics: needing to ensure that autonomous robot systems treat us well; increasing autonomy and increasingly powerful robotic agents needing more powerful machine ethics; and teaching an autonomous agent to act ethically helping us to better understand ethics in

© Springer Nature Switzerland AG 2020
M. Gallagher et al. (Eds.): AI 2020, LNAI 12576, pp. 230–240, 2020.
https://doi.org/10.1007/978-3-030-64984-5_18

general. LARs present an unusual case for machine ethics in that their main aim is not necessarily to ensure they treat us well when it comes to a warfare setting.

Over the last 15 years or so, robotics has shown most technological advance and development in battlefield contexts in the form of unmanned aerial vehicles (UAVs, drones) and unmanned ground vehicles (UGVs, ground robots) [11], with at least 50 countries using UAVs [12]. Research into the ethics of autonomous weapons systems (AWSs) and, by implication, lethal autonomous robots (LARs) has posed particular problems, given that the aim of such systems and agents is to perform lethal actions and therefore harm humans. So any moral imperatives on UAVs and UAGs not to harm humans need to be reinterpreted in the context of the behaviour of AWSs and LARs falling within the bounds of internationally agreed Laws of War and Rules of Engagement. Models and representations based on the idea of a 'governor' determining whether lethal action is ethically permissible have been formulated [13]. Logic or constraint-based approaches lead to issues concerning whether all possible and relevant circumstances can be catered for through such top-down approaches [14]. One of the reasons for a logic-based approach is the perceived desire to express ethical theories in declarative form without reducing ethical concepts to subsymbolic (i.e. numerical) format [15]. However, a logic-based approach can also lead to concerns that the robot is constrained by the logic it follows and so cannot be autonomous in dynamic situations that may require flexible responses.

Teaching robots to be ethical may provide an alternative, bottom-up approach. But there is a slowly emerging consensus that inductive machine learning algorithms with human specified feature values could be subject to algorithmic bias or learn biases in the supplied data [16–18]. It is especially important for moral machines not to learn the specific ethical preferences of programmers or biases contained in data if they are to be considered trustworthy.

In summary, three problems need to be addressed when designing, developing and implementing an ethical or moral machine [19]. The first problem concerns the type and degree of interactivity that allows the moral machine to respond ethically to its environment. The second is the degree of autonomy from the environment that allows the moral machine to go through an ethical reasoning process of its own. And the third is amount of adaptability the moral machine is allowed in order to change its ethical reasoning processes. Together, these three desirable properties provide the basis for a trustworthy moral machine. The extent of the trust placed on such moral machines will depend on how it responds to different ethical situations and its ability to provide justifications for its responses.

The aim of this paper is demonstrate how these three desirable properties may be attainable through the use a different sort of logic, namely, fuzzy logic. Another aim of this paper is to demonstrate how it may be possible to deal with the inductive bias problem so that ethical training data is not restricted to a narrow range when a bottom-up approach is used. And finally, the third aim of this paper is to show how an LAR may be able to learn ethical rules for itself, and therefore reduce the possibility of acquiring human bias and prejudice.

2 Methods and Representations for Fuzzy Ethics Learning

2.1 Learning Architecture

Ethical theories deal with rules or criteria for distinguishing right from wrong as well as good from bad. Examples of ethical theories are deontology (we must act according to duties and obligations), categorical imperative (we must act in accordance with human rational capacity and certain inviolable laws), utilitarianism (an action is right or good if it leads to most happiness) and consequentialism theories in general (whether an action is right or good depends on the action's outcome or result). Another approach is virtue ethics (we must act in ways that exhibit our virtuous character traits), where a trait is what allows us to fulfil our function. For humans, one specific function is to think rationally, and so virtue ethics is ethics led by reason to perform virtuous actions.

Consider an LAR (either UAG or UAV) learning to make ethical decisions of when it is ethical to engage in lethal combat in battlefield situations. Data for ethical decision making come from four principles of war [13] which act as data sources for ethical learning: *military necessity* (targeting to produce military advantage); *humanity/unnecessary suffering* (minimizing incidental injury and collateral damage); *proportionality excess* (launching an attack which is excessive in relation to anticipated military advantage); and *discrimination* (distinguish between combatants and non-combatants).

These sources are inputs to two ethical learning modules (ELMs) in our proposed architecture. The first learns the *rightness/wrongness* of lethal action taking into account deontological principles, and the second the *goodness/badness* of lethal action taking into account consequentialist principles. The learning outcomes from these two ELMs are then combined in an ethics meta-learning controller (EMLC) which provides a meta-learning output to be used for learning (Fig. 1).

2.2 Input Variables to ELMs

Each of the four input war principles has three levels: *low*, *medium* and *high*. For military necessity (MN), *low* implies low chance of military advantage and *high* means high chance, with *medium* in between. For unnecessary suffering/humanity (US), *low* means minimal unnecessary suffering and *high* means maximal, with *medium* in between. For proportionality excess (PE), *low* means minimal excessive force and *high* means maximal, with *medium* in between. Finally, for discrimination (D), *low* means minimal distinction possible between combatants and non-combatants, *high* means maximal such distinction and *medium* in between.

From a fuzzy reasoning perspective, each of MN, US, PE and D is a linguistic variable L characterized by a quintuple $(L, T(L), U, G, M)$ in which L is the name of the variable, $T(L)$ is the term-set of L (i.e. the collection of linguistic values *low*, *medium* and *high*), U is the universe of discourse, G is the syntactic rule that generates the terms in $T(L)$, and M is the semantic rule that associates each linguistic value X its meaning, $M(X)$, where $M(X)$ denotes a fuzzy subset of U (Zadeh, 1975). Each linguistic value of L has a range of values within a base range of values U for L. In our case, the four linguistic variables each have a base range values from 1 to 10, and each linguistic value X within each linguistic variable will have a fuzzy restriction on the values of the base variable. The

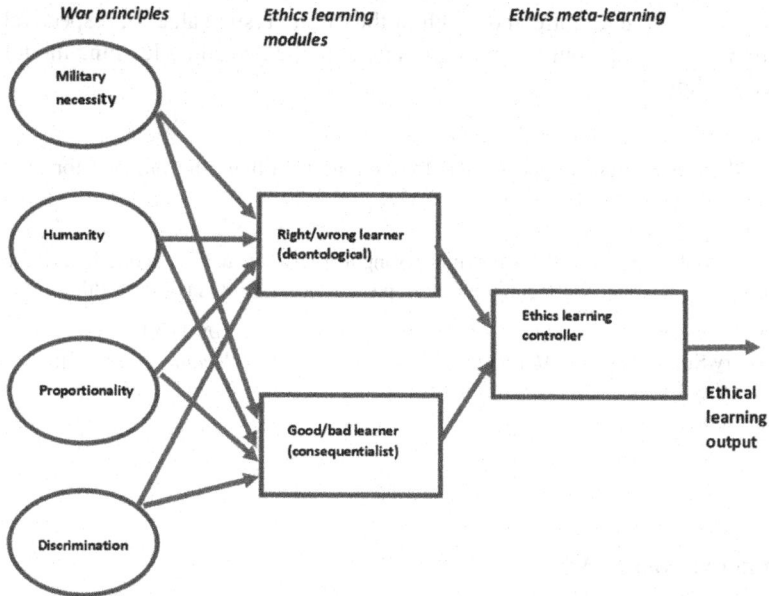

War principles   Ethics learning   Ethics meta-learning
                      modules

Fig. 1. LAR ethical learning architecture, consisting of input from the four war principles, two ethics learning modules for learning and producing ethical deontological and consequentialist output, and the final ethic learning controller for combining these two ethical outputs into a combined ethical judgement.

meaning of X is characterized by a compatibility function $c: U \rightarrow [0,1]$, which associates base values of U to a number in the interval $[0,1]$ that represents its compatibility, or degree of set membership, with the fuzzy restriction. A membership function for a fuzzy set A is denoted μ_A, and for an element x of X the value $\mu_A(x)$ signifies the degree of membership of element x to A.

For the right/wrong learner, all linguistic values A for each input linguistic variable are initially specified as sharp-line compatibilities using triangular shapes/MFs, requiring a vector of three values $[a\ b\ c]$, where a and c define the feet and b the peak. Then, to calculate membership μ for each point x of U for A:

$$\mu_A = f(x; a, b, c) = \max\left(\min\left(\frac{x-a}{b-a}, \frac{c-x}{c-b}\right), 0\right).$$

If trapezoidal MFs are used:

$$\mu_A = f(x; a, b, c, d) = \max\left(\min\left(\frac{x-a}{b-a}, 1, \frac{d-z}{d-c}\right), 0\right).$$

For the good/bad reasoner, a 'softer' initial approach of specifying compatibility shapes in the form of Gaussians is adopted, as given by:

$$\mu_{A^i}(x) = \exp\left(-\frac{(c_i - x)^2}{2\sigma_i^2}\right),$$

where c_i and σ_i are the centre and width of the ith linguistic value A^i, respectively. All linguistic values for the four war principles input to the two ethics learning modules are specified in Table 1.

Table 1. Membership function parameters for the four input linguistic variables for each of the two ethics learning modules

Linguistic variable (war principles)	MFs for right-wrong learner (triangular: foot, peak, foot)	MFs for good-bad learner (Gaussian: width, centre)
Military Necessity; Unnecessary Suffering; Proportionality Excess; Discrimination	*Low* [− 5, 1, 5.5]; *Medium* [1,5.5, 10]; *High* [5.5, 10, 15].	*Low* [1.911, 1]; *Medium* [1.911, 5]; *High* [1.911, 10].

2.3 Outputs from ELMs

The right/wrong ELM has two values, 'wrong' and 'right', where 'wrong' has maximum membership value at minimum base value 1 and minimum membership value at maximum base value 10, and *vice versa* for 'right'. For the good/bad ELM, there are two values 'good' and 'bad' with similar membership functions.

2.4 Rules for Converting War Principle Input into Right/Wrong and Good/Bad Output

Each of the deontological and consequentialist ethical learners has rules for mapping input concerning the four war principles into output. For the right/wrong (deontological) learner, the following three rules RW1-RW3 are initially provided (MN = military necessity: US = unnecessary suffering; PE = proportionality excess; D = discrimination):

RW1: If MN is *low* and US is *high* and P is *high* and D is *low* then RW output is lethal action is wrong.

RW2: If MN is *high* and US is *low* and P is *low* and D is *high* then RW output is lethal action is right.

RW3: If MN is *medium* and US is *low* and PE is *low* and D is *high* then RW output is lethal action is right

For the good/bad (consequentialist) learner, the following three rules GB1-GB3 are initially provided:

GB1: If MN is *low* and US is *high* and P is *high* and D is *low* then GB output is lethal action is bad.

GB2: If MN is *high* and US is *low* and P is *low* and D is *high* then GB output is lethal action is good.

GB3: If MN is *medium* and US is *low* and PE is *low* and D is *high* then GB output is lethal action is bad

The main difference between the deontological (RW) and consequentialist (GB) rules, as initially provided, lies in the third rule, where there is ethical disagreement on outcome if military necessity is *medium*. According to deontology, if US and PE are *low*, and D is *high*, then lethal action is right and morally justified. According to consequentialism, even if US and PE are *low*, and D is *high*, it is bad and therefore morally not justified to take lethal action when MN is only *medium*.

The ethics learning EMLC has the task of combining the outputs from the right/wrong learner and the good/bad learner into a single ethical decision as to whether it is ethical or not to engage in lethal combat behaviour. It uses the following two initial rules for ethical control (EC):

EC1: If output from right/wrong learner is non-lethal response and from good/bad learner is non-lethal response, then meta-control decision is non-lethal response.

EC2: If output from right/wrong learner is lethal response and from good/bad learner is lethal response, then meta-control decision is lethal response

All ethical learners use the Mamdani method for producing crisp output.

3   Simulations and Results

A range of input values from 1 to 10 is simulated for each of the four war principle inputs over 10 s (time steps), sampling at 100 times per second with varying frequency for each input, to produce data for 1001 time points (including the baseline starting point). Figure 2 shows the simulation values for the war principles.

For the LAR learning for itself when to ethically engage without human-labeled target values, these 1001 time points were first clustered using k-means clustering on the EMLC output only. This 'self-learning' produced two clusters (cluster 1 centre 4.57, cluster 2 centre 6.43, distance 1.541, $p \leq 0.01$) to result in 902 simulation cases in cluster 1 ('unethical to engage lethally') and 99 cases in cluster 2 ('ethical to engage lethally'). The cases falling into the second cluster were those that fell in the 'hump' between time points 2 and 4 in Fig. 2 and were above the output value 5.5. These cluster values were then used as target labels for each case for learning how to reach moral judgements based on inputs from the four war principles, as follows.

(a) Linear discriminant analysis (LDA) with leave-one-cross-validated classification produced a model with 99.2% sensitivity for non-ethical lethal engagement and 99% specificity for ethical lethal engagement (7 and 1 cases wrong classified, respectively). Canonical discriminant function coefficients showed that MN and D were most strongly associated with ethical lethal engagement (0.253 and 0.187, respectively), and US and PE with non-lethal engagement (-0.137 and -0.149, respectively).

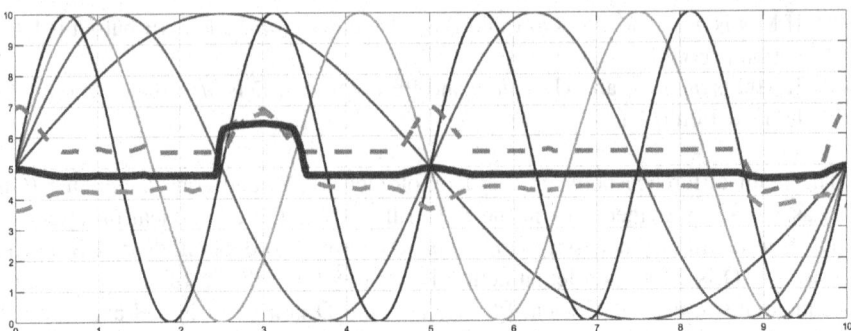

Fig. 2. Simulation values from for the ethical learning architecture across 10 time steps (x axis) for the four war principles and three ethics outputs. Key: blue represents military necessity, 1 full cycle in 10 s; red unnecessary suffering, 2; orange proportionality excess, 3; purple discrimination, 4 (all lines thin continuous); thick green dashed the output from the right/wrong learner; thick blue dashed the output from good/bad learner; and thick dark continuous red the final output values from the ethics meta-learning controller for use in clustering. The y-axis represents the base range values (0-10) of all four input variables as well as output values of the learning modules. (Color figure online)

(b) Artificial neural networks (ANN): A perceptron (4 input units, three hidden units, two output units, hyperbolic tangent hidden unit activation function, identity output function, gradient descent learning rate and momentum 0.2) with a 70:30 training/testing partition repeated 10 times produced a model with 100% accuracy. Independent variable importance (input values are altered or removed to check on effect on classification) indicated that MN was the most important variable (0.29), followed by D (0.25), PE (0.24) and US (0.22). Similarly, a radial basis function with 70:30 partition repeated 10 times (4 input units, 6 hidden units, two output units, softmax activation function) produced a model with 100% sensitivity for non-ethical lethal engagement and 95% specificity for ethical lethal engagement. Independent variable importance also identified MN as the most important variable (0.35), followed by PE (0.24), D and US (both 0.21).

(c) Decision trees: $\chi 2$ testing [20] produces a tree using a top-down recursive approach where $\chi 2$ independence tests the null hypothesis that two variables are independent. 10-fold cross-validation using $\chi 2$ testing produced a 99.6% sensitivity and 97% specificity model (4 and 3 misclassified cases), and the following rules (generated by tracing paths from the root node to leaf nodes):

(i) IF MN $\leq$ 9.05 THEN lethal engagement is non-ethical.

(ii) IF MN $>$ 9.05 and D $\leq$ 4.87 THEN lethal engagement is non-ethical.

(iii) IF MN $>$ 9.05 and D $>$ 4.87 THEN lethal engagement is ethical.

(d) Rule induction: JRIP [21] is a rule inducer that starts with ordering classes by increasing prevalence and finding rules to separate classes, starting with the lowest prevalent class. Data covered by a rule are removed once a certain rule length is reached, and rules are pruned to minimize error of the entire rule set. 10-fold cross-validation using JRIP rule inducer produced a 99.8% sensitivity and specificity model with the following rule:

IF MN $\geq$ 9.14 AND US $\leq$ 5.12 THEN lethal engagement is ethical, ELSE lethal engagement is not ethical.

(e) 10-fold cross-validation using a random tree (randomly chosen attributes at each node) produced a 99.8% accurate model with the following rules:
(i) IF MN < 9.13 THEN lethal engagement is not ethical.
(ii) IF MN $\geq$ 9.13 AND US < 5.22 THEN lethal engagement is ethical ELSE IF US $\geq$ 5.22 THEN lethal engagement is non ethical.

4 Discussion

Assuming that the LAR has unsupervised and supervised learning modules, two clusters were found in the simulated output data corresponding approximately to unethical to engage lethally and ethical to engage lethally. The LAR used these two clusters as self-identified target categories for cross-validated statistical and supervised learning. LDA produced a 99% accurate model with military necessity and discrimination being associated with ethical lethal engagement. Also, the LDA model associated humanity and proportionality excess with non-lethal engagement. Subsymbolic ANNs also achieved high accuracy (100% for perceptrons, 98% for RBFs), with both identifying military necessity as the most important attribute for classification, followed by proportionality excess, discrimination and humanity. All decision tree and rule inducers identified military necessity as the most important attribute for determining the ethics of engagement. Decision trees identified military necessity and discrimination as the most important attributes for determining the ethics of engagement, and rule inducers military necessity and humanity/unnecessary suffering.

Combining the rules from decision trees, JRIP and random trees and removing the 'else' conditions produces the following learned moral framework:

(i) IF MN $\leq$ 9.05 THEN lethal engagement is non-ethical.
(ii) IF MN > 9.05 and D $\leq$ 4.87 THEN lethal engagement is non-ethical.
(iii) IF MN > 9.05 and D > 4.87 THEN lethal engagement is ethical.
(iv) IF MN $\geq$ 9.14 AND US $\leq$ 5.12 THEN lethal engagement is ethical.
(v) IF MN < 9.13 THEN lethal engagement is not ethical.
(vi) IF MN $\geq$ 9.13 AND US < 5.22 THEN lethal engagement is ethical.

The results above represent just the first iteration of the LAR's learning process. The next stage is to evaluate these rules to fine-tune the reasoners. For instance, decision trees and rule inducers both set a very high military necessity threshold (9.05 and 9.14, respectively) for lethal engagement to be ethical. In the case of the decision tree, even if military necessity achieves this threshold, discrimination must be above 4.87. For the rule inducers, military necessity has to be greater than 9.13 and unnecessary suffering has to be less than 5.22 for lethal engagement to be ethical.

The architecture of Fig. 1 can be totally separate from the actual control architecture of an LAR. Three possibilities exist. The first is for the ethics architecture to be totally independent of the control architecture (zero ethics coupling). In this case, the architecture provides an ethical commentary to the sensor-based behaviour of the LAR but does not interfere in any way with the actual behaviour of the LAR. Such commentary could be used off-line to monitor and evaluate LAR actions in responses to sensor data. The second is for the ethics architecture to work in parallel with the control architecture of an LAR so that control architecture output and ethics architecture output are combined in some way (parallel ethics coupling) for 'morally considered' lethal engagement action. And the third possibility is for the output of the control architecture to be one of the inputs to the ethics architecture (serial ethics coupling) so that no action is possible for the LAR without internal ethical approval. The choice of architectural involvement may depend on the context in which LARs will be used and by whom. Perhaps sometime in the future there will be a requirement for all LARs to have a compulsory ethics architecture so that control information and ethics outcomes can be used together in parallel or in serial mode.

5   Conclusion

We have shown how an ethical reasoner, through a fuzzy logic approach combined with unsupervised learning, can produce categories for making ethical judgements, and achieves interactivity, autonomy and adaptability. Interactivity is achieved through dynamic processing of sensor information to ensure that moral judgements are continuously made and monitored. Autonomy is achieved through the system internally processing data from sensors and simulations using principles but deriving rules from this internal processing without human intervention. Adaptability is achieved through simulations of dilemmas that allow the system to trade off aspects of right/wrong against good/bad. The approach adopted in this paper is consistent with the idea that ethically-equipped LARs are intelligent autonomous systems [22].

None of this is achievable without human designers providing the first set of principles and fuzzy variables using a variety of membership functions. But human designers do not have to specify every possible ethical situation using the approach described here and can leave the derivation of appropriate rules to the LAR ethics architecture. As noted by several researchers, just because fuzzy logic deals with inexactness and approximation due its use of the real number interval between 0 and 1, that does not mean that fuzzy logic cannot be subject to formalization of its inferential processes [23] so that fuzzy reasoning is shown to be effective and computable [24]. By limiting the involvement of human designers to the input of initial and arguably uncontroversial principles as well as an initial choice (and shape) of membership functions to be used for representing those principles, the danger of introducing biases and prejudices is minimized. The only human input initially is in the first set of principles and risk membership functions to help the ethical LAR establish a base from which to learn enhanced models of ethical reasoning. There is no reason why an LAR should not choose different membership functions and shapes to experiment with through evolutionary algorithms, for instance.

There may be concerns about the research described here, for a variety of reasons. It seems to argue for LARs as ethics 'by numbers', for instance. Ethical reasoning in philosophy and machine ethics has so far dealt almost exclusively with qualitative and categorical reasoning. The use of intervals and values in the range of 0 and 1 in ethical output is not familiar to us humans and could lead to accusations of a fuzzy-based ethics for LARs being 'lethal engagement by numbers'. But we have shown that it is possible to assign categories to the output of simulations that can be checked by human ethicists. It is also possible that LARs, if properly endowed with appropriate moral frameworks, will not be subject to human fallibilities and weaknesses in real battlefield situations. Ideally, they should apply their reasoning equally and without emotion or bias in all situations and thus reduce the possibility of war crimes [13].

Another concern may be that research into LARs should not be allowed at all because they are immoral, and that trying to give such agents an ethical framework is in effect supporting work on such immoral machines. The aim of this paper is not to take sides on the morality of designing and building LARs but to show that, if LARs continue to be built and deployed, we should give them a moral framework to ensure that their deployment is within currently and internationally agreed rules of engagement that apply to human warfare.

But more importantly, as we roll out a program of enhanced robotics over the next couple of decades (for example, robots to help the aged, robots in healthcare, robots for looking after children, driverless cars), such agents may be required to display a sense of right and wrong, and good and bad, so that they work to our benefit and hence are trustworthy [25, 26]. We may have to accept that non-qualitative, metric-based ethics is the best way to achieve a level of trust in genuinely autonomous agents. In this paper we have provided an initial framework and prototype machine ethics systems that may help to achieve an appropriate level of trust between humans and autonomous intelligent systems in the future.

References

1. Lin, P., Abney, K., Bekey, G.: Robot ethics: mapping the issues for a mechanized world. Artif. Intell. **175**, 942–949 (2011)
2. Wallach, W., Asaro, P.: The emergence of robot ethics and machine ethics. In: Wallach, W., Asaro, P. (eds.) Machine Ethics and Robot Ethics. Routledge, London (2017)
3. Veruggio, G., Solis, J., Van der Loos, M.: Roboethics: Ethics applied to robotics. IEEE Robot. Autom. Mag. **18**(1), 21–22 (2011). https://doi.org/10.1109/MRA.2010.940149
4. Lichocki, P., Kahn, P.H., Billard, A.: A survey of the robotics ethical landscape (2011). https://www.semanticscholar.org/paper/A-Survey-of-the-Robotics-Ethical-Landscape-Lichocki-Kahn/6b4f234bfdb53ca2ee301c61b2a3a7a7eade77bc. Accessed August 2019
5. Anderson, M., Anderson, S.I., Armen, C. (eds.) Machine Ethics. AAAI Press (2005). Antsaklis, P.J., Passino, K.M., Wang, S.J.: An introduction to autonomous control systems. IEEE Control Syst. **11**(4), 5–13 (1991). https://doi.org/10.1109/37.88585
6. Wallach, W., Allen, C.: Moral Machines: Teaching Robots Right and Wrong. Oxford Scholarship Online (2009)
7. Van den Hoven, J., Lokhorst, G.J.C.: Deontic logic and computer supported computer ethics. In: Moor, J.H., Bynum, T.W. (eds.) Cyberphilosophy: The Intersection of Computing and Philosophy, Blackwell (2002)
8. Wiegel, V., Van den Hoven, M.J., Lokhorst, G.J.C.: Privacy, deontic epistemic action logic and software agents. Ethics Inf. Technol. **7**, 251 (2005). https://doi.org/10.1007/s10676-006-0011-5(accessedAugust2019)
9. Bringsjord, S., Arkoudas, K., Bello, P.: Towards a general logicist methodology for engineering ethically correct robots. Intell. Syst. **21**(4), 38–44 (2006). https://doi.org/10.1109/MIS.2006.82

10. Moor, J.H.: The nature, importance, and difficulty of machine ethics. IEEE Intell. Syst. **21**, 18–21 (2006). https://doi.org/10.1109/MIS.2006.80
11. Tisseron, A.: Robotic and future wars: When land forces face technological developments. In: Doare, R. Danet, D., Hanon, J-P., de Boisboissel, G. (eds.) Robots on the Battlefield: Contemporary Issues and Implications for the Future. Combat Studies Institute Press, US Army Combined Arms Center, Fort Leavensworth, Kansas (2014). https://apps.dtic.mil/dtic/tr/fulltext/u2/a605889.pdf. Accessed Aug 2019
12. Sharkey, N.: The future of drone warfare. In: Doare, R., Danet, D., Hanon, J-P., de Boisboissel, G. (eds.) Robots on the Battlefield: Contemporary Issues and Implications for the Future. Combat Studies Institute Press, US Army Combined Arms Center, Fort Leavensworth, Kansas (2014). https://apps.dtic.mil/dtic/tr/fulltext/u2/a605889.pdf. Accessed Aug 2019
13. Arkin, R.C.: Governing lethal behaviour: Embedding ethics in a hybrid deliberative/reactive robot architecture. Part 1: motivation and philosophy. Technical report GIT-GVU-07-11, 2007. Georgia Institute of Technology. https://www.cc.gatech.edu/ai/robot-lab/online-publications/formalizationv35.pdf. Accessed Aug 2019
14. Sharkey, N.: Automated killers and the computing profession. Computer, 122-124, November 2007. https://ieeexplore.ieee.org/document/4385276. Accessed Aug 2019
15. Bringsjord, S., Arkoudas, K., Bello, P.: Towards a general logicist methodology for engineering ethically correct robots. Intell. Syst. **21**(4), 38–44 (2006). https://doi.org/10.1109/MIS.2006.82
16. Garcia, M.: Racist in the machine: the disturbing implications of algorithmic bias. 2016. World Policy J. **33**(4), 111–117. http://muse.jhu.edu/article/645268/pdf. Accessed Oct 2018
17. Devlin, H.: AI programs exhibit racial and gender biases, research reveals. The Guardian 13 April 2017. https://www.theguardian.com/technology/2017/apr/13/ai-programs-exhibit-racist-and-sexist-biases-research-reveals. Accessed Oct 2018
18. Fuchs, D.J.: The dangers of human-like bias in machine-learning algorithms. Missouri S&T's Peer to Peer. 2018, **2**(1). http://scholarsmine.mst.edu/peer2peer/vol2/iss1/1. Accessed Oct 2018
19. Floridi, L.: On the morality of artificial agents. In: Anderson, M., Anderson, S.I. (eds.) Machine Ethics (2011). CUP
20. Kass, G.V.: An exploratory technique for investigating large quantities of categorical data. Appl. Stat. **29**(2), 119–127 (1980)
21. Cohen, W.W.: Fast effective rule induction. In: Twelfth International Conference on Machine Learning, pp. 115–123 (1995)
22. Steels, L.: When are robots intelligent autonomous agents? Robot. Auton. Syst. **15**, 30 (1995)
23. Gerla, G.: Vagueness and formal fuzzy logic: Some criticisms. Logic Logical Philos. **26**, 431–460 (2017). http://dx.doi.org/10.12775/LLP.2017.031. Accessed Nov 2018
24. Syropoulos, A.: Theory of fuzzy computation. In: IFSR International Series on Systems Science and Engineering, vol. 31. Springer, New York (2014)
25. The IEEE Global Initiative on Ethics of Autonomous and Intelligent Systems. Ethically Aligned Design: A Vision for Prioritizing Human Well-being with Autonomous and Intelligent Systems, Version 2. IEEE (2017). http://standards.ieee.org/develop/indconn/ec/autonomous_systems.html
26. Narayanan, A.: Ethical judgement in intelligent control systems for autonomous vehicles. In: 2019 Australian & New Zealand Control Conference (ANZCC), Auckland, November 2019. https://doi.org/10.1109/anzcc47194.2019.8945790

Games and Swarms

Designing Curriculum for Deep Reinforcement Learning in StarCraft II

Daniel Hao, Penny Sweetser$^{(\boxtimes)}$, and Matthew Aitchison

The Australian National University, Canberra, ACT 2601, Australia
penny.kyburz@anu.edu.au

Abstract. Reinforcement learning (RL) has proven successful in games, but suffers from long training times when compared to other forms of machine learning. Curriculum learning, an optimisation technique that improves a model's ability to learn by presenting training samples in a meaningful order, known as curricula, could offer a solution. Curricula are usually designed manually, due to limitations involved with automating curricula generation. However, as there is a lack of research into effective design of curricula, researchers often rely on intuition and the resulting performance can vary. In this paper, we explore different ways of manually designing curricula for RL in real-time strategy game StarCraft II. We propose four generalised methods of manually creating curricula and verify their effectiveness through experiments. Our results show that all four of our proposed methods can improve a RL agent's learning process when used correctly. We demonstrate that using subtasks, or modifying the state space of the tasks, is the most effective way to create training samples for StarCraft II. We found that utilising subtasks during training consistently accelerated the learning process of the agent and improved the agent's final performance.

Keywords: Game AI · Reinforcement learning · Real-time strategy games · StarCraft II · Curriculum learning

1 Introduction

Reinforcement learning (RL) is a type of machine learning in which an agent is placed into a problem environment and trained via basic trial-and-error actions. An RL agent continuously selects and performs actions that will affect its environment and, in turn, influence the RL agent's following course of action. In contrast to supervised learning, the agent is not provided with labelled data. Instead, rewards and punishments are designed and delivered to the agent to guide its learning process. The purpose of the agent is to learn to maximise the cumulative reward that it receives, thus 'learning' to solve a given problem.

Video games are a popular platform for developing and testing RL algorithms, as they are formal, well-defined, complex, and have dynamic environments that react to different actions. Recent state-of-the-art RL algorithms have

© Springer Nature Switzerland AG 2020
M. Gallagher et al. (Eds.): AI 2020, LNAI 12576, pp. 243–255, 2020.
https://doi.org/10.1007/978-3-030-64984-5_19

achieved and surpassed human-level performance in various games, such as Atari and Go. RL algorithms such as Deep Q-learning (DQN) [11] and Advantage Actor-Critic (A2C) [10] have been widely deployed and have achieved promising results. However, in more complex tasks, such as real-time strategy (RTS) games, RL suffers from long training times, requiring hundreds of millions of training steps [20], which can take up to weeks to complete depending on the performance of the hardware. Due to the incredibly large environment and sparse reward nature of such tasks, RL agents with no further optimisations are incapable of mastering RTS games within a reasonable time [2]. As a result, shortening the training time has the potential to significantly benefit RL agents and the outcomes in complex environments. Previous research has employed techniques such as curriculum learning [14] to optimise RL. In this paper, we review and investigate previous research on curriculum learning in the field of RL and propose and evaluate new methods for effectively applying curriculum learning to RL in the RTS game, StarCraft II.

2   Curriculum Learning

Curriculum learning (CL) is a training strategy inspired by the human learning process, mimicking how humans learn new concepts in an orderly manner, usually based on the level of difficulty of the problems [9]. CL states that by exposing machine learning algorithms to tasks in meaningful orders, it can speed up convergence and can even lead to the discovery of better local minima [3]. RL agents trained on tasks with increasing difficulties, starting with easier environments and then scaling up to more challenging environments, can converge to an optimum more quickly than an agent trained without a curriculum [1]. CL is relatively easy to use, as it does not necessarily require expert knowledge [16] and has exhibited promising results in numerous applications [3].

Although the concept of CL is simple, there are two main challenges when applying it to RL. The first is identifying the most effective way of generating curricula and the second is determining the best curriculum sequence. In this paper, we focus on the first problem. For generating curricula, numerous criteria can serve as the measure of difficulty for problems, such as using the distance between the initial state and goal state [6] or the size of the environment [12]. However, there is a lack of previous research that compares the performance of different difficulty measures. Depending on the problem itself, various domain-specific measures could also be used for difficulty evaluation [12], further complicating the issue. Furthermore, all existing research efforts on generating tasks for CL in RL have focused on attempting to automate the process and all involve some degree of limitation [19].

While there are various approaches to automating task generation for CL (e.g., generative adversarial networks [5] and evolutionary generators [4]), of which many have exhibited exceptional performance, most involve some drawbacks in terms of efficiency or make assumptions to simplify problems. Curriculum generator approaches to task generation require the generators to be optimised prior to deployment [4,5]. For real-world applications, it would be counter-intuitive if more time were spent on training an automated curriculum generator than on training the agent itself. However, other approaches such as reverse curriculum generation [6] or sub-task generation [18] are built on a set of assumptions that may not hold true for all problems, such as assuming that there is a tangible distance between the goal state and the initial state, which fails if the goal does not require the agent to be in a specific state or configuration. As a result, in practice, it is more common to manually design tasks for RL agents than to use an automated approach. However, there is a lack of previous research that examines how to effectively handcraft curricula for RL agents and no clear guideline on the best practice to follow. When using CL to accelerate training, users often design curriculum tasks from an intuitive approach [14,17], manually creating curriculum tasks guided by a rough understanding of the intended learning outcome of the agent.

In this paper, we propose three intuitive domain-independent measures for creating curricula: reward-based, state-based, and action-based. We design and evaluate curricula with each difficulty measure to discover the most effective design methodology. We also investigate using domain-dependent subtasks as curricula and draw comparisons between domain-dependent and domain-independent curricula. Domain-dependent subtasks may not always be a viable option, unlike domain-independent measures. As a result, subtasks are considered separately to other measures. We aim to discover the most suitable way to handcraft curricula so that RL agents can receive the maximum benefits from CL. We investigate effective generalised curriculum generation methods for handcrafting curricula and verify their effectiveness with experiments. The results of this paper are intended to provide guidance for practical implementations of CL by evaluating the performance of the proposed handcrafted curriculum structures.

3   Method

We propose three domain-independent and a single domain-dependent method for manually generating curricula for CL. We used the game Starcraft II as our training and evaluation platform. Each proposed curriculum generation method was evaluated with two different problems (mini-games) to verify their effectiveness under different problem settings.

3.1   StarCraft II

Starcraft II (SC2) is a competitive RTS game that is mostly played between two players (1v1). From the perspective of an RL agent, SC2 poses several challenges. First, it is an imperfect information game with only partially-observable states. The agent must learn to control units to explore unknown areas and make decisions based on incomplete information. Second, the action space and state space are extremely large and diverse; there are an estimated 10^8 possible actions for selection between every frame [20] and the branching factor for two consecutive states is estimated to be between b $\in [10^{50}, 10^{200}]$ even when only considering units [13]. Third, the nature of strategic games dictates that rewards for a strategic action may not be delivered until much later on, leading to credit assignment problems with sparse rewards. Many components of SC2 can be broken down into individual problems of their own, including build order optimisation [8], micromanagement [17], and macro-management [7].

In 2017, DeepMind and Blizzard collaboratively developed and released a library named PySC2, exposing Blizzard's SC2 machine learning API as a Python environment [20]. It provides an interface for RL agents to interact with SC2 by allowing the agent to receive spatial and non-spatial features that are similar to those that a human player would receive. In this paper, we use the SC2 game and the PySC2 library for our experiments. We have chosen SC2 as our platform as it is a complex and challenging task for RL agents. It is also scalable in difficulty and easy to use, as we can access and edit variables in the environment with the SC2 map editor and the Python PySC2 library.

Mini-Games. We selected two SC2 mini-games to test our proposed methods: Defeat Roaches and Collect Mineral Shards. A mini-game is a small stand-alone game created by extracting certain elements within the full game of SC2. In Defeat Roaches, the agent controls a group of nine marines to defeat four enemy roaches. When all four enemy roaches are defeated, a new group of four enemy roaches is spawned. The agent is rewarded with five additional marines and its remaining marines retain their existing health. Marines and roaches are randomly spawned on two opposite ends of the map, with their positions reset every time a group of roaches is defeated. All marines are preselected for the agent when spawned. The camera is locked to the centre of the screen with no fog of war. The game state is reset when all marines are killed or after 120 s. The agent earns rewards when a roach is killed and penalties for every marine lost. The optimal strategy requires the agent to micromanage the marines and focus fire on the roaches to minimise incoming damage. To create curriculum tasks with varying difficulties for different generation methods, we tuned parameters including the map size, marine and roach unit statistics, and the reward structure.

In Collect Mineral Shards, the agent controls two marines to collect as many mineral shards as possible (by stepping on them). The marines are spawned in random locations and are not preselected. The map starts with 20 mineral shards, with another 20 being spawned after all shards have been collected. Each shard is spawned at least two units away from the marines. The camera is locked to the centre of the map with no fog of war. The game state is reset upon reaching the time limit of 120 s. Every time the agent collects a mineral shard, it receives a reward, and there are no explicit penalties for losing marine units from friendly fire. The optimal strategy requires the agent to plan its movements efficiently, divide the marines, and move independently. To create curriculum tasks with varying difficulties for different generation methods, we tuned parameters including the map size, number of marines, number of minerals, and reward structure.

3.2   Curricula Generation Methods

Our three domain-independent methods for curricula generation were reward-based, state-based, and action-based. We modified and created curriculum tasks for each by altering the reward structures, state spaces, or action spaces of the environment, respectively. Domain-independent methods can be applied regardless of the problem's context, providing that the task is represented as a Markov decision process (MDP). The domain-dependent method that we propose is called subtask curriculum generation. We define a subtask as a subset of the full task, where we extract certain aspects and challenges of the full task to create a simpler sub-problem. We can design a subtask that only trains the agent to tackle and learn a single sub-problem. Subtask creation is highly dependent on the original task and may not exist for certain problems.

Reward-Based Curricula. In every RL problem defined as an MDP, there is a reward structure that is explicitly tailored to the learning targets of an agent. In reward-based curriculum generation, we create curricular tasks for the agent by relaxing or tightening the requirements for the agent to receive a positive reward. We defined the difficulty of the curriculum tasks as the likelihood of a random agent receiving a reward in the environment. The difficulty was measured by the probability that a random action would lead to a positive reward; the higher the probability, the easier the problem and vice versa.

We modified the difficulty of the two tasks by changing the values of certain variables. For Defeat Roaches, we increased the probability of receiving a reward from random actions by lowering the health of enemy units (Easy = 90; Medium = 120; Target = 145). We could achieve similar effects by increasing the attack damage of marines. However, this would also increase the chance of killing friendly units with friendly fire. This approach of lowering difficulty through editing statistics of individual units has not been used before. Previous applications of CL in SC2 have created curriculum tasks in ways similar to our state-based or action-based methods, decreasing the size of the environment or number of actions the agent can perform [17]. For Collect Mineral Shards, we modified the likelihood of receiving a reward by increasing the density of mineral shards on the map. The higher the density in relation to the map size, the easier the problem (Easy = 40; Medium = 30; Target = 20).

State-Based Curricula. In state-based curriculum generation, we also use the properties of an MDP to create curriculum tasks. In this method, we used the size of the state space S to measure the difficulty of the tasks created. The larger the state space (i.e., size of the map), the harder the problem. For Defeat Roaches, we decreased the map size to lower the difficulty of the tasks (Easy = 13×12; Medium = 18×14; Target = 22×16). For Collect Mineral Shards, we also need to decrease the number of mineral shards on the map to maintain a consistent mineral density in relation to the map size (Difficulty = map-size(shards); Easy = 11 × 8(5); Medium = 16 × 12(11); Target = 22 × 16(20)). We did so to avoid changing the level of difficulty by other difficulty measures (e.g., reward-based difficulty). Otherwise, we would not be able to correctly identify which generation method had contributed to the change in results.

Table 1. Action-based settings for Defeat Roaches.

	Penalty	Marines	Backup	Health	Damage
Easy	−4	2	1	190	25
Medium	−3	5	3	80	10
Target	−1	9	5	45	6

Action-Based Curricula. The action-based curriculum generation method uses the definition of the action space A in an MDP to measure difficulty. By reducing the number of marines the agent controls, we effectively reduce the size of the action space and the difficulty of the task. For Defeat Roaches, we also needed to modify the strength of individual units, so that the raw difficulty did not increase as we decreased the number of friendly units (see Table 1). We also made slight modifications to the reward structure, as the quality of individual units varied. For the Collect Mineral Shards mini-game, we reduced the number of marines that the agent controls to reduce the action difficulty of the task. We considered whether this might affect the maximum performance of the agent, as it had less collecting power. However, we found that the update frequency of the algorithm limited the frequency of performing an action and we observed that the agent was never able to simultaneously control two marines to collect mineral shards with different paths. As a result, we only modified the number of marines and the initial selection of units (Difficulty = marines(selected); Easy = 1(1); Medium = 2(1); Target = 2(0)).

Subtask Curricula. Subtask curriculum generation is quite different from the previous methods in that it does not rely on the definition of an MDP. A subtask is a sub-problem of the target task, so we needed to create a new curriculum task that was tailored to the specific needs of the target task rather than modifying the original task. The creation of curriculum subtasks is highly dependent on the original target problem. Thus, we consider this method to be domain-dependent, as there is no formally generalised method for creating a subtask.

For the Defeat Roaches task, we created a new mini-game called 'Destroy Target'. The purpose of this mini-game was to encourage the agent to learn to focus fire on enemies and reduce redundant actions. In Destroy Target, the agent needs to control nine marines to destroy an enemy structure (a Pylon). In a similar setup to Defeat Roaches, the agent received a reward (10) for destroying the enemy structure and received penalties (−1) for the death of friendly units. All marines were also initially selected for the agent when spawned. The camera was locked to the centre of the screen with no fog of war so that no camera movements were required. The game state was reset upon reaching the time limit (120 s). At any given time, there was only one Pylon on the map, and upon its destruction, a new enemy Pylon was created. However, in this mini-game, the agent did not receive new marine units upon destroying the enemy Pylon. We modified the properties of the Pylon so that it had no shield and increased health (10) and health regeneration (100). We also disabled auto-attack for marines. Since the Pylon was able to regenerate its health, if the agent decided to cease attacking or perform other redundant actions, the Pylon would quickly return to full health, rendering the agent's previous efforts useless.

For the Collect Mineral Shards mini-game, we used the 'Move to Beacon' mini-game created by Blizzard [20] as a subtask, as it is very similar to Collect Mineral Shards. It requires the agent to control a single marine to move to an indicated area (the beacon). In contrast to the Collect Mineral Shards mini-game, there is only one target beacon on the map at any given time. Upon reaching the beacon, the agent receives a reward and a new beacon is randomly spawned on the map. The game state is also reset upon reaching the time limit (120 s). We selected the Move to Beacon mini-game tailored to the 'collecting' aspect of Collect Mineral Shards. We wanted to encourage the agent to draw connections between receiving a reward and moving to indicated areas. Collect Mineral Shards can be understood as an extension of Move to Beacon with multiple target areas and more units under command.

3.3 Agent Structure

For our experiments, we used an Advantage Actor-Critic (A2C) RL agent structure with neural networks as function approximators, as implemented by Pekalto [15]. The agent is a close replica of the FullyConv agent described in the original publication of PySC2 [20]. The A2C agent network receives minimap and screen observations as input. The minimap is a simplified overview of the entire game environment displayed to the player at the bottom left corner of the screen and the screen observations are detailed images of the game environment that the agent is currently viewing. The A2C agent network assumes the minimap and the screen observations are of the same resolution. The observations are passed through two convolutional layers with 16 and 32 filters of sizes 5×5 and 3×3, respectively. The convolutional layers have no strides and use padding on every layer to preserve resolution. The state representation is formed by concatenating the outputs from passing the minimap and screen observations through the convolutional layers. We obtained non-spatial (categorical) actions by sending the state representation through a fully connected feedforward layer with 256 units and ReLU activations followed by fully connected feedforward linear layers. The policy over spatial actions is obtained using size 1×1 convolution over the state representation with a single output channel. Pekalto [15] modified the original

FullyConv agent structure to simplify the agent network and accelerate training, including discarding non-spatial vectors entirely and using A2C instead of A3C [10], which is a non-asynchronous implementation of the algorithm.

Table 2. Stable score and total episodes to converge.

Agent	Defeat Score	Roaches Episodes	Collect Score	Minerals Episodes
Baseline	60	60k	85	40k
Action	60	100k	85	50k
Reward	70	70k	65	60k
State	100	120k	85	50k
Subtask	110	120k	100	35k

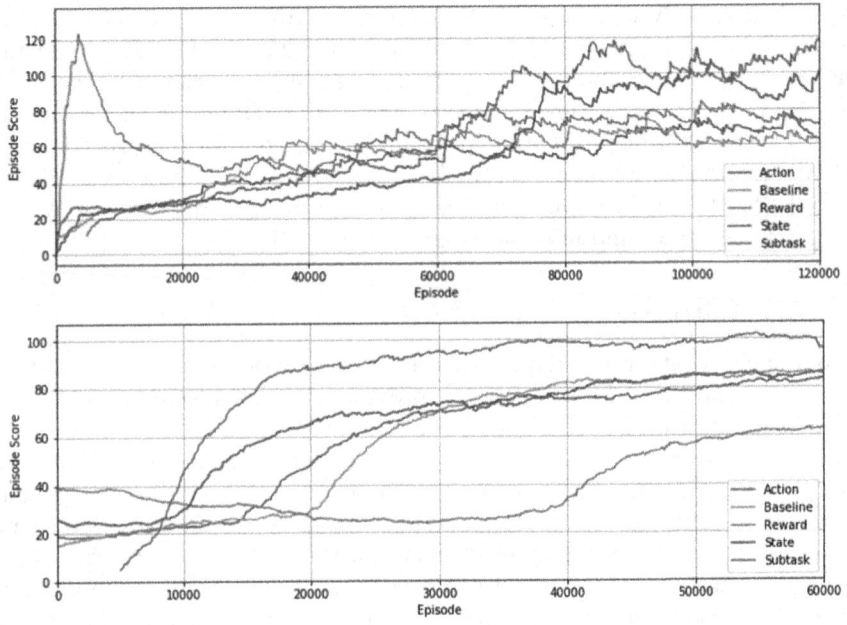

Fig. 1. Training plots for Defeat Roaches (top) and Collect Mineral Shards (bottom).

4   Results

The results from training each curriculum on the two mini-games were generated using data collected during training and presented, for clarity, with a smoothing value of 0.98. We created a baseline for comparison by training an agent directly on each mini-game with no curricula. Figure 1 shows a comparison of all curricula and the baseline agents, with final score at the end of an episode plotted against the number of episodes trained. The training graph of the subtask curriculum agent begins at five thousand episodes in Fig. 1 to exclude the Move to Beacon subtask, as it is an entirely different problem with different reward structures and not comparable to other episode scores. Table 2 shows the stable score and number of episodes to converge for each curriculum.

5 Discussion

In this paper, we proposed four different methods for manually creating curriculum tasks for RL and evaluated them against baseline RL agents in two different mini-games in SC2. We found that action-based curricula offered no improvements over the baseline agent and performed worse than the baseline at various stages of training. For Defeat Roaches, reducing the number of units that the agent controlled (and thus reducing the action space) did not help to accelerate the training process. We initially predicted that an action-based curriculum would help the agent by lowering the difficulty in controlling multiple units. However, despite controlling fewer units, the agent failed to recognise that focused fire was the ideal strategy to minimise damage taken. We theorise that this could be due to the increased strength of individual marines as we reduced their numbers, leading to reduced frequency of penalties from the death of friendly units. This created a sparser penalty structure for the agent, which was not beneficial to the agent's learning process and did not help the agent recognise that minimising friendly unit loss was an important goal. For Collect Mineral Shards, the action-based curriculum offered improvements on the baseline. We reduced the number of marines that the agent needed to control in both mini-games. However, controlling fewer units in Collect Mineral Shards allowed the agent to draw correlations between its actions and receiving a reward efficiently. With fewer units on the map, it was easier for the agent to distinguish which of its actions led to rewards. As a result, an action-based curriculum that assigned tasks to the agent with fewer units to control was beneficial to the agent's overall learning process.

In the reward-based curriculum for Defeat Roaches, minor improvements were evident when compared to the baseline. We observed that both agents moved their units to either the top-left or top-right corners of the map, depending on their initial location. When moved to a corner, the marines automatically attacked the closest roach due to attack range limitations. This resulted in an imperfect focus of fire on enemies, as some marines had more than one roach within their attack range. The minor improvement of the reward agent was to position the marines in a slightly more effective formation when moved to the corners of the map. First training the agent on maps with lower reward difficulty against enemies with less health meant that the agent was able to quickly recognise that attacking was the best action to earn rewards. In contrast, a reward-based curriculum was not helpful for the agent in Collect Mineral Shards. For this curriculum, we increased the number of mineral shards on the map to reduce the sparseness of rewards. However, the agent trained on the reward-based curriculum failed to quickly draw correlations between moving the marines to the mineral shards and receiving a reward, despite the higher density of minerals. We theorise that the large number of mineral shards on the map allowed the agent to receive rewards for performing random actions. This hypothesis could be tested by training the agent on a reversed reward-based curriculum with a decreased number of mineral shards.

The agent trained on state-based curriculum for Defeat Roaches performed much worse during training in the earlier stages, but ultimately converged to a much stronger performance. We observed that the state-based agent learned the optimal strategy of focused attack commands on roaches one-by-one, unlike the baseline agent. As a result, all marines were able to consistently attack the same target, minimising incoming enemy fire by killing enemies faster. In the early stages of the state-based curriculum, the agent was forced to attack enemies head-on due to map size limitations. When playing on a smaller map, the number of redundant states was reduced and the small map size meant that the agent was unable to use sub-optimal strategies, such as moving to the corners of the map without being spotted by enemy roaches. This might have contributed to the worsened performance in the middle stages of training, as fighting an entire group of enemies head-on would be much more difficult than fighting a smaller group of enemies from corners of the map. However, this also led the agent to discover the optimal strategy as it repeatedly fought enemy roaches head-on. We observed similar results for Collect Mineral Shards. The state-based curriculum was beneficial to the learning process of the agent, as it omitted redundant states from the task. During the early training periods of the baseline agent, it spent much time trying to locate the last mineral shard with random movements. By having a reduced state space, the agent was more likely to retrieve the final mineral shard with random movements, allowing the game to spawn the next set of mineral shards to continue meaningful training. As a result, the agent gathered knowledge more efficiently in the state-based curriculum and thus converged much faster than the baseline. The state-based curriculum was able to consistently improve the agent's performance by removing redundant states in both Defeat Roaches and Collect Mineral Shards.

In the subtask curriculum for Defeat Roaches, the agent was able to converge to a stronger performance when compared to the baseline. We observed that the subtask agent used the same strategy as the state-based agent of efficiently focusing fire on enemy units. The subtask agent was first trained on the Destroy Target mini-game, which encouraged the agent to perform focused attacks on the target structure. From the results, we can conclude that the subtask curriculum helped the agent master a sub-problem of the target task at a faster rate and accelerated the final learning process for the target task. The subtask curriculum performed the best among all curricula. The results were similar for Collect Mineral Shards, where the agent achieved the best performance among all curricula and converged faster than the baseline. Although the subtask curricula utilised very different subtasks for the two mini-games, they achieved the same goal of helping the agent to master a sub-problem at a much faster rate. The subtask curriculum first trained the agent on the Move to Beacon mini-game, which can be viewed as a simplified version of Collect Mineral Shards with only one 'mineral shard' (the beacon) on the map. From the results, we can conclude that the agent was able to effectively utilise the knowledge that it had learned from the subtask and successfully apply it to the target task. By comparing the performances of all curricula against the baseline, it is evident that the subtask curriculum agent again outperformed all other agents, followed by the state-based curriculum agent.

6 Conclusion

CL is a useful optimisation technique that can be easily applied with good results. However, without proven guidelines for manually designing curricula, most CL users create curricula intuitively depending on the problem that they are trying to solve [17]. In this paper, we presented curriculum design methodologies for manually designing curricula to improve an agent's learning process. We proposed four effective methods for generating curriculum tasks for RL problems and evaluated them through experiments in RTS game StarCraft II. We demonstrated the effectiveness of our proposed methods under different tasks, provided an in-depth analysis of our results, and verified different ways that CL can aid an RL agent's learning process. Out of all of the curricula that we investigated, only subtask and state-based curricula produced consistent results in both performance and application. Other curriculum generation methods, such as reward-based or action-based curricula, did not provide consistent improvements and might require further adjustments in order for them to be effective. To our knowledge, at the time of writing, we are the first to experiment and present generalised methods for handcrafting curricula in RL. Based on our results, we recommend that future applications of CL in Deep RL applied to games modelled as an MDP use subtasks as their curriculum tasks. In cases where subtasks are not available or cannot be constructed, modifying the state space and training the agent from smaller to larger state spaces is also an effective option.

References

1. Adamsson, M.: Curriculum learning for increasing the performance of a reinforcement learning agent in a static first-person shooter game. Ph.D. thesis, Kth Royal Institute of Technology, Stockholm, Sweden, October 2018
2. Adil, K., Jiang, F., Liu, S., Jifara, W., Tian, Z., Fu, Y.: State-of-the-art and open challenges in RTS game-AI and starcraft. Int. J. Adv. Comput. Sci. Appl. 8(12) (2017). https://doi.org/10.14569/IJACSA.2017.081203
3. Bengio, Y., Louradour, J., Collobert, R., Weston, J.: Curriculum learning. In: Proceedings of the 26th Annual International Conference on Machine Learning, pp. 41–48. ICML 2009, Association for Computing Machinery, New York (2009). https://doi.org/10.1145/1553374.1553380

4. Cerny Green, M., Sergent, B., Shandilya, P., Kumar, V.: Evolutionarily-curated curriculum learning for deep reinforcement learning agents. arXiv preprint arXiv:1901.05431 (2019)
5. Florensa, C., Held, D., Geng, X., Abbeel, P.: Automatic goal generation for reinforcement learning agents. In: International Conference on Machine Learning, pp. 1515–1528 (2018)
6. Florensa, C., Held, D., Wulfmeier, M., Zhang, M., Abbeel, P.: Reverse curriculum generation for reinforcement learning. In: Levine, S., Vanhoucke, V., Goldberg, K. (eds.) Proceedings of the 1st Annual Conference on Robot Learning. Proceedings of Machine Learning Research, vol. 78, pp. 482–495. PMLR, November 2017
7. Justesen, N., Risi, S.: Learning macromanagement in starcraft from replays using deep learning. In: 2017 IEEE Conference on Computational Intelligence and Games (CIG), pp. 162–169, August 2017. https://doi.org/10.1109/CIG.2017.8080430
8. Justesen, N., Risi, S.: Continual online evolutionary planning for in-game build order adaptation in starcraft. In: Proceedings of the Genetic and Evolutionary Computation Conference, pp. 187–194. GECCO 2017. Association for Computing Machinery, New York (2017). https://doi.org/10.1145/3071178.3071210
9. Krueger, K.A., Dayan, P.: Flexible shaping: how learning in small steps helps. Cognition **110**(3), 380–394 (2009). https://doi.org/10.1016/j.cognition.2008.11.014
10. Mnih, V., et al.: Asynchronous methods for deep reinforcement learning. In: International Conference on Machine Learning, pp. 1928–1937 (2016)
11. Mnih, V., et al.: Playing atari with deep reinforcement learning. arXiv preprint arXiv:1312.5602 (2013)
12. Narvekar, S., Sinapov, J., Leonetti, M., Stone, P.: Source task creation for curriculum learning. In: Proceedings of the 2016 International Conference on Autonomous Agents & Multiagent Systems, AAMAS 2016, pp. 566–574. International Foundation for Autonomous Agents and Multiagent Systems, Richland (2016)
13. Ontañón, S., Synnaeve, G., Uriarte, A., Richoux, F., Churchill, D., Preuss, M.: A survey of real-time strategy game AI research and competition in starcraft. IEEE Trans. Comput. Intell. AI Games **5**(4), 293–311 (2013). https://doi.org/10.1109/TCIAIG.2013.2286295
14. Pang, Z.J., Liu, R.Z., Meng, Z.Y., Zhang, Y., Yu, Y., Lu, T.: On reinforcement learning for full-length game of starcraft. In: Proceedings of the AAAI Conference on Artificial Intelligence, vol. 33, pp. 4691–4698 (2019)
15. Pekaalto: sc2aibot (2017) https://github.com/pekaalto/sc2aibot
16. Peng, B., MacGlashan, J., Loftin, R., Littman, M.L., Roberts, D.L., Taylor, M.E.: An empirical study of non-expert curriculum design for machine learners. In: Proceedings of the Interactive Machine Learning Workshop (at IJCAI 2016) (2016)
17. Shao, K., Zhu, Y., Zhao, D.: Starcraft micromanagement with reinforcement learning and curriculum transfer learning. IEEE Trans. Emer. Top. Comput. Intell. **3**(1), 73–84 (2019). https://doi.org/10.1109/TETCI.2018.2823329
18. Silva, F.L.D., Costa, A.H.R.: Object-oriented curriculum generation for reinforcement learning. In: Proceedings of the 17th International Conference on Autonomous Agents and MultiAgent Systems, AAMAS 2018, pp. 1026–1034. International Foundation for Autonomous Agents and Multiagent Systems, Richland (2018)

19. Svetlik, M., Leonetti, M., Sinapov, J., Shah, R., Walker, N., Stone, P.: Automatic curriculum graph generation for reinforcement learning agents. In: Proceedings of the Thirty-First AAAI Conference on Artificial Intelligence, AAAI 2017, pp. 2590–2596. AAAI Press (2017)
20. Vinyals, O., et al.: Starcraft ii: a new challenge for reinforcement learning. arXiv preprint arXiv:1708.04782 (2017)

Improving StarCraft II Player League Prediction with Macro-Level Features

Yinheng Chen, Matthew Aitchison, and Penny Sweetser[✉]

The Australian National University, Canberra, ACT 2601, Australia
penny.kyburz@anu.edu.au

Abstract. Accurate player skill modelling is an important but challenging task in Real-Time Strategy Games. Previous efforts have relied strongly on micromanagement features, such as Actions Per Minute, producing limited results. In this paper, we present an improved player skill classifier for StarCraft II that predicts, from a replay, a player's exact league at 61.7% accuracy, or within one league at 94.5%, outperforming the previous state of the art of 47.3%. Unlike previous classifiers, our classifier makes use of a macro-level measure of economic performance, called Spending Quotient, which we demonstrate to be an important part of accurately predicting player skill levels.

Keywords: Player modeling · Real-Time Strategy Games · Machine learning

1 Introduction

Matching challenges in a game to a player's skill level is an essential factor in the player's enjoyment of the game [20]. In online games, a ranking system is used to attempt to match players with other players of appropriate skill. However, some players attempt to subvert this system. Players do this either via 'smurfing', whereby high-ranked players create secondary accounts in order to play against low-ranked players [6]. Or, conversely, by 'boosting' which involves low-ranked players asking high-ranked players to play their accounts to increase their rank artificially [8].

To address this problem, a good skill detection model is required. One which can identify these players, as well as any players who might be unintentionally mismatched to their current league (e.g., a player who is returning to the game after a long period or someone playing on a friend's account). Because the person playing the account can not be verified, player skill modelling is more complex than simply analysing the account's win/loss record. There are also important use cases for skill detection in offline games, where a game may need to adjust dynamically to the player's skill level [7]. Adapting challenges to the player's increasing skill level is another important aspect of player enjoyment [20].

Research in Real-Time Strategy (RTS) games has been an important area of interest for AI researchers since Buro's call for AI research in RTS games in 2004

© Springer Nature Switzerland AG 2020
M. Gallagher et al. (Eds.): AI 2020, LNAI 12576, pp. 256–268, 2020.
https://doi.org/10.1007/978-3-030-64984-5_20

[4]. Despite the increased interest in RTS games, one research area that has been relatively undeveloped in RTS games is player skill modelling, especially when applied to AI players. RTS games provide some unique challenges, such as partial information, real-time decision making, and trading immediate versus future payoffs. For this reason, assessing the skill level of a player can be extremely challenging.

When constructing a player model, it is critical to identify the features that most strongly predict the player's level [22]. We examine how a player's skill level can be identified from their replay data in RTS game StarCraft II and aim to determine which are the most relevant features in predicting player skill. StarCraft II, developed by Blizzard Entertainment and released in 2010, has become an increasingly important testbed for AI algorithms due to its challenging environment and well-supported API [21]. In this paper, we report on research in which we constructed a model to predict a player's skill level. Our model extracts useful features from 1-vs-1 replay data and uses them to predict the league placement of each player.

2   Real-Time Strategy Games

A considerable amount of recent AI work in games has focused on complete information, limited action-space games, such as Chess [17], Go [18] and many of the Atari games [11]. However, real-world problems are often only partially observed and have large, sometimes infinite, action spaces. RTS games can help to bridge the gap between games and the real world by providing more challenging environments in which to demonstrate the abilities of AI algorithms. RTS games require the player to control multiple units and make difficult decisions about strategic trade-offs under incomplete information. Due to these challenges, advancements in AI in RTS games has progressed relatively slowly compared to other types of games. Standard RTS games involve three main components:

- Units - the most important component for a player to achieve the winning goal in most RTS games. Players are required to recruit and control their units to defeat their opponent and win the game.
- Collecting Resources and Resource Management - in most RTS games, resources can be used to construct buildings, recruit units, and develop technology. Players use their workers (i.e., a type of unit) to collect resources.
- Research - players research new technologies to improve the quality of their units and increase their resource collection rate. Technology often involves trading a short term cost for a long term reward. Some units may have technological prerequisites making advancement critically important to building a powerful army.

2.1   StarCraft II

StarCraft II (SC2) is an RTS game developed by Blizzard Entertainment and a sequel to StarCraft and its expansion, Brood War. SC2 was released in 2010 and is still one of the more popular RTS games played today, with an active player base and professional eSports tournaments. While similar in many ways to other RTS games, SC2 is fairly unique in its asymmetric races. Players must choose between three races, Terran (humans), Zerg, and Protoss. Each race has different units, buildings, and game mechanics. For example, Terran (see Fig. 1) can fly their buildings around the map, while Zerg is limited to building only on 'creep' that spreads slowly from their base. The economy in SC2 is based on two types of resources, Minerals and Vespene. These resources must be collected by workers and are in limited supply. Often players will need to expand to higher risk areas on the map to secure these resources. Blizzard Entertainment, along with DeepMind, provide support for AI research in SC2 via the StarCraft II Learning Environment (SC2LE) [21].

The built-in AI in the SC2 game has ten hard-coded difficulty levels. Much of the existing work on SC2 AI uses the built-in AI as a tool to test and develop their algorithms [9,13,16,19]. This is due to the built-in AI being consistent, fast to compute, and providing a significant level of challenge. Early reinforcement learning based AI could only tie against the easiest built-in AI [21]. However, later work learned to exploit the built-in AI's weaknesses and can now consistently defeat the hardest level AI.

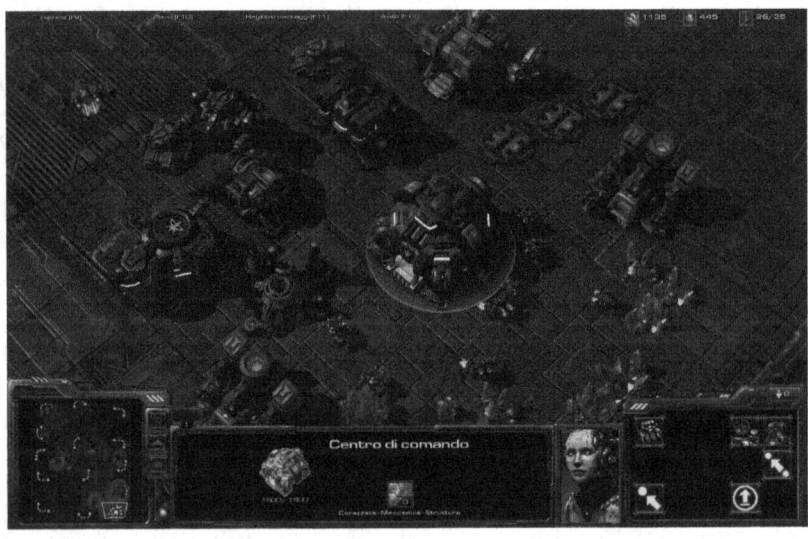

Fig. 1. A Terran player playing StarCraft II.

2.2 Ranking Players in StarCraft II

In SC2 ranked games, players are divided into seven leagues according to their ability: Bronze, Silver, Gold, Platinum, Diamond, Master, and GrandMaster.

Initial placement into a league is by unranked placement games, after which a player can ascend or descend the leagues based on their performance. There are 300,000 active players in SC2 ranked games, with most players' leagues being between Silver and Diamond [2].

A player who is ranked in Gold league is roughly equivalent to that of Level-10 built-in AI. This means the performance of most reinforcement learning based AI is below that of the average ranked human players' performance. The Grand-Master rank is extremely rare. Blizzard Entertainment limits the number of GrandMasters per region[1], ensuring the total number of GrandMaster players in the world does not exceed 800. As a result, only 0.27% of players can be GrandMaster in ranked matches.

SC2 uses a Match Making Ranking (MMR) system to track players' ability in ranked matches. Players earn MMR when they win a match and lose MMR when they lose a match. Once a player's MMR reaches a threshold, they will be upgraded to the next league.

3   Related Work

Most of the research in SC2 AI has been about developing AI algorithms to play the game well. Meanwhile, there has been only a small amount of work done on predicting players' skills. Early work on the problem achieved a weighted average accuracy of 47.3% [3], outperforming the most common class prediction baseline by using a variant of a Support Vector Machine on a training set of 1,297 replays. Player performance in the original StarCraft has also been investigated, with Gradient Boosting Regression Trees and Random Forests being used to create six classifiers for each race pairing [14]. However, this research predicted the winning player rather than each player's league. In parallel with the work on player modeling in RTS games there has also been work on assessing skill levels in the related Multiplayer Online Battle Arena (MOBA) games. Which skill factors are strong predictors for match outcome vary across different MOBA games, reinforcing that features should be game specific [5].

The challenge of dynamically adapting game difficulty to a player's ability is closely related to player modelling. Previous research has inferred difficulty curves from player-vs-level match data using win/loss data [15]. While this work primarily relates to adjusting player-vs-level difficulty, it could be adapted to player-vs-player matchmaking. In some situations, it may be preferable to design experiments to analyse player skills (e.g., by manipulating the game environments). The PsyRTS platform, a web-based toolkit for RTS games, allows for this, and is able to leverage existing crowd-sourced platforms [12]. However, experiments must be created ahead of time and cannot take advantage of the large set of exiting replay data.

---

[1] Blizzard Entertainment divides their servers into European, American, Korean, Oceanic, and Chinese regions.

4   Method

In order to investigate the strengths of various machine learning algorithms on this problem we trained models using five different algorithms. Each model was trained using features (see Sect. 4.3) extracted from a set of 4,917 replays, with the algorithm's hyperparameters tuned according to a 5-fold cross validation score. The best model from each algorithm was then evaluated on a holdout test set according to both its average weighted accuracy and F_1-score.

4.1   Data Collection

Since there is no established SC2 replay dataset, we constructed one from recent replays. A total of 4,917 replays were collected from three websites[2]. These replays were uploaded by global players, who posted their games online. Average features over time were extracted from 1-vs-1 replays. With each replay providing information about two players.

Replays that lasted less than 2-minutes or data from unranked players were excluded, giving 4,114 player data-points distributed as shown in Table 1. The relatively few instances of Bronze and Silver players is likely due to new players being less likely to upload replays than more experienced players. Due to the low number of data-points for these categories, we excluded the Bronze and Silver league from the model. During prepossessing, all features were normalised to between 0 and 1. After filtering, the dataset contained 3,981 player data-points. These replays were then split randomly between a training set of 2,985 replays and a holdout test set of 996 replays.

Table 1. Distribution of players by league the dataset.

League	Number of players
Bronze	12
Silver	128
Gold	500
Platinum	1,355
Diamond	1,685
Master	357
GrandMaster	244

---

[2] https://sc2replaystats.com,   https://gggreplays.com/matches   and   https://lotv. spawningtool.com/replays.

4.2   Evaluation

We selected and evaluated models based on their F_1-score, which we calculated as

$$F_1 := 2 \times \frac{P \times R}{P + R}$$

where P is the precision, and R the recall of the model for a given league. An F_1 score of 0 indicates a very poorly performing model, whereas a score of 1 indicates perfect prediction. We performed an average of the F_1-scores for each league, weighted by the number of examples in that league. We also included the weighted average accuracy for reference,[3] in order to compare against previous work in SC2 player modeling by Avontuur [3]. However, due to the imbalance in the league distribution, this measure will not be as meaningful a measure of performance as the F_1-score. The final evaluation was performed on the holdout test set. We report both the weighted F_1-score, individual class F_1-scores, and weighted accuracy for comparison to Avontuur's work.

4.3   Feature Selection

A total of 11 features were extracted from the replay files and used as input to the model. The features are as follows:

Actions per Minute. In RTS games, players give instructions to units by clicking the mouse or typing on the keyboard. The computation of (average) Actions Per Minute (APM) is

$$APM := \frac{a}{t}$$

where a is the total number of actions performed over t minutes. A higher APM of a player means that the player has the ability to process more events in each unit of time in the game. Having a high APM does not necessarily mean that a player is an advanced player, but high-level players usually have a higher APM. The average APM for GrandMaster is approximately 300 (5 actions per second), Bronze league players can only achieve 60 APM (1 action per second).

Spending Quotient. While APM is more an indication of micro management and fine-grained control over units, macro-management, such as economic management and strategy, is also important. Players collect resources and spend resources on a number of different things. To maximise the use of resources and to build a more efficient economy, players minimise unspent resources and increase their resource collection rate by expanding and training more workers. Spending Quotient (SQ) [1] is a feature to quantitatively measure players' economic management in a game and is calculated as

---

[3] League accuracies are averaged together weighted by the number of examples of that league in the dataset.

$$SQ(i, u) = 35 \times (0.00137i - \log u) + 240$$

where i represents resource collection rate and u represents unspent resources. Resources can be calculated as a weighted arithmetic mean of Mineral and Vespene, where the weight of Mineral and Vespene ranges from 1:2 to 1:3. Like the measurement of APM, players who have higher SQ should be considered as more advanced players. Figure 2 shows the average SQ of global players in each league of ranked matches in SC2. Although the difference between average SQ among leagues is not as large as that of APM, players in higher leagues have higher SQ.

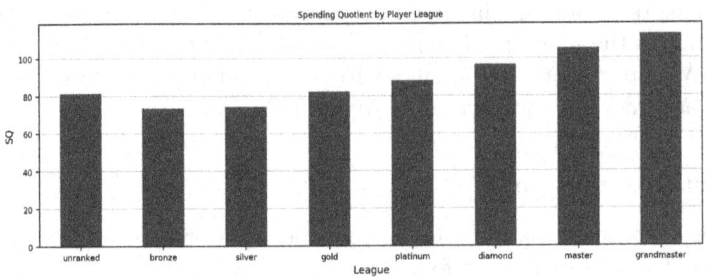

Fig. 2. Average spending quotient varies by league, with higher leagues having improved spending quotient scores.

Other Features

- *Game Length:* The length of the game in seconds.
- *Avg Unspent Minerals/Vespene:* How many resources the player left unspent. Higher values tends to indicate weaker players, as strong players are more able to spend resources quickly.
- *Avg Mineral/Vespene Collection Rate:* The rate at which the player collects resources.
- *Avg Workers:* The average number of workers over the game. Higher level players tend to have more workers.
- *Avg Supply Used/Made:* This indicates the number and strength of the units recruited. A higher number might indicate that the player had to replace many lost units, while a lower number could indicate that the player was not able to establish a good resource collection rate.
- *Supply Blocked Time:* Units require supply to be built. If no supply is available, unit production is halted. Longer supply blocked times usually indicates a weaker player.
- *Produced Units:* The number of units recruited by the player.
- *Killed Units:* The number of units killed by the player.
- *Killed Workers:* The number of opponent worker units killed by the player.

4.4 Model Selection

We considered five models for classifying the replays: K-nearest Nearest Neighbour (k-NN) using Euclidean distance, Linear Support Vector Machine (Linear SVM), Non-linear Support Vector Machine (Non-linear SVM), Random Forest, and a Gradient Boosting Classifier. Each algorithm was tuned via a grid search over hyperparameters as detailed in Table 2. The best model was selected by performing 5-fold cross validation on the training set, according to the weighted average F_1-score. Feature importance for the Gradient Boosting Classifier was assessed using Gini importance [10].

Table 2. Hyperparameters for each algorithm where selected via a grid search using 5-fold cross validation, with the model with the best F_1-Score being selected.

Algorithm	Hyperparam	Values tested
KNN	k	$[1..30]$
SVM-Linear	c	2^i for $i \in [-5..8]$
SVM-Nonlinear	c	2^i for $i \in [-5..8]$
SVM-Nonlinear	gamma	['auto', 'scale']
Random Forest	estimators	$[10, 100, 1000]$
Random Forest	max features	[Auto, 1, 2, 3]
Random Forest	max depth	$[0..9]$
Gradient Boosting	estimators	$[10, 100, 1000]$
Gradient Boosting	max depth	$[3, 5, 10]$
Gradient Boosting	learning rate	$[0.05, 0.075, 0.1, 0.25, 0.5, 0.75, 1]$

5 Results

In this section we evaluate the performance of the classifiers, as well as the importance of each feature used as input to the models.

5.1 Classifier Performance

The kNN and Linear-SVM classifiers struggled to classify the player's league, with F_1-scores of 0.516 and 0.495 respectively. The Non-linear SVM model performed better with an F_1-score of 0.560. However, the best performing models were the Random Forest Classifier and Gradient Boosting Classifier. Both models had accuracy above 60%, with the Gradient Boosting Classifier performing slightly better with an F_1-score of 0.593 compared to 0.579. The full results are shown in Table 3. The confusion matrix in Fig. 3 shows that Gold players are often predicted as Platinum, whereas Master players are misclassified as Diamond. As some players sit on the boundary between leagues, in terms of their skill, it is not surprising that these leagues are confused and that under uncertainty the classifier opts for the more populated Diamond league. If we allow classification predictions to be correct if neighbouring the proper league, then the classifier's weighted accuracy rises to 94.5%, as shown in Table 4. This means that, although the classifier is sometimes wrong about the league, it is very unusual for it to predict a completely inappropriate league.

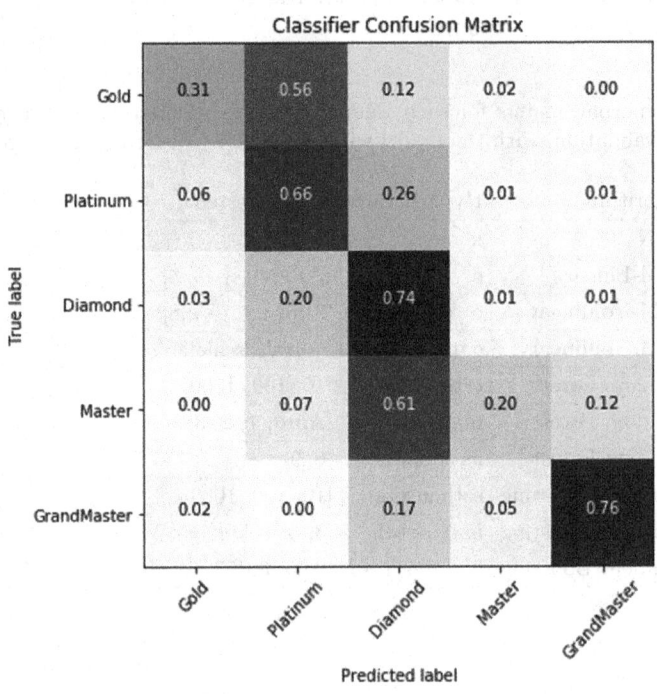

Fig. 3. The confusion matrix for the Gradient Boosting Classifier. Results are normalised. A large portion of the errors are in confusing diamonds ranked players with the league above or below it.

Table 3. Holdout test scores for each classifier. The Gradient Boosting Classifier model outperformed all other models, with Random Forrest being slightly behind.

Algorithm	Accuracy	F_1-Score	Hyperparameters
k-NN	0.538	0.516	$k = 10$
Linear SVM	0.562	0.495	$c = 64$
Non-linear SVM	0.597	0.560	$c = 64$
Random Forest	0.615	0.579	max_depth = auto
Gradient Boosting	**0.617**	**0.593**	learning_rate = 0.1, max_depth = 5, n_estimators = 100

Table 4. Classification accuracy for the Gradient Boosting Classifier for leagues within given distance. Accuracy improves dramatically when including the neighbouring league. This indicates that when the classifier miss-classifies a player, it does so by a small margin.

Distance	Accuracy
Exact	61.7%
1 league	94.5%
2 leagues	99.6%
3 leagues	99.9%

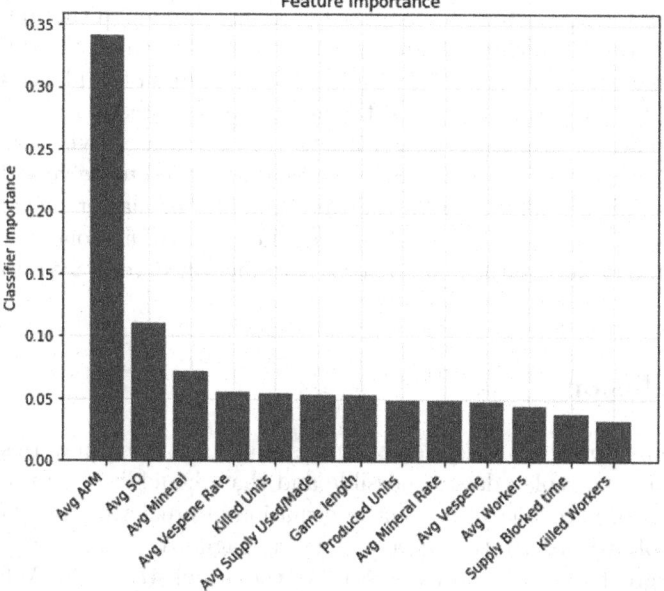

Fig. 4. Importance of each feature in the Gradient Boosting classifier. APM, a measure of micromanagement, is by far the most important feature. However, SQ, a macromanagement measure of economic performance is the strongest of the remaining features.

5.2   Feature Importance

It is not surprising that the most useful feature for predicting a player's skill is their APM. This is commonly recognised as an important distinction between lower tier and upper tier players. All features selected contribute meaningfully to the classifier's prediction. For a breakdown of each feature's importance, see Fig. 4. The addition of the average SQ feature proved to be more important than any of the other features, except for APM. This is likely the reason for the classifier's improved performance over the previous state-of-the-art, which did not include the SQ feature [3].

6   Discussion

Our results show the importance of including macro-level features, such as Spending Quotient, when accurately predicting player skill level in StarCraft II. The Gradient Boosting Model shows that while predicting the exact league of a human player is difficult, predicting to within one league is possible to very high accuracy (94.5%). This would be useful to game developers as it would be possible to identify players that are well out of their correct league placement (e.g., a GrandMaster on a smurfing account). We found that, as expected, APM is a powerful indicator of a player's ability, far exceeding all other features. We also discovered that Spending Quotient, a measure of the player's economic management, provides a lot of additional information about the player's ability and should be included, along with the other features, when predicting a player's league. Identifying Master league players proved to be very difficult for the model, which is likely due to the small number of master players and relatively little difference in ability between Master and Diamond level players. GrandMaster players, on the other hand, are identified very accurately by the model.

7   Conclusion

Our Gradient Boosting model demonstrates that identifying player skill level in StarCraft II from replay data is possible and that the addition of the Spending Quotient feature provides important information in predicting the player's skill. We were able to predict the players' correct league to an accuracy of 61.7%, improving greatly on the previous state-of-the-art of 47.3% [3]. When identifying a player's skill to within one league, an accuracy of 94.5% is achievable. Identifying player skill allows developers to more easily identify smurfing and boosting behaviour and improve customisation of the game to the player's skill level.

7.1   Future Work

Due to the large number of different ways players can play StarCraft II, our classifier would benefit from training additional high-quality matches. Producing a model specifically for each of Blizzard's regional servers would also be beneficial as there are notable differences in play styles between these regions. It may be, for example, that a Diamond league player on the Korean server would be ranked Master on another server. Therefore, dividing the dataset into regions could improve the performance.

References

1. Liquipedia. https://liquipedia.net/starcraft2/Spending_quotient. Accessed 4 Aug 2020
2. Ranked ftw. https://www.rankedftw.com/stats/population/1v1. Accessed 4 Aug 2020
3. Avontuur, T., Spronck, P., Van Zaanen, M.: Player skill modeling in starcraft II. In: Ninth Artificial Intelligence and Interactive Digital Entertainment Conference (2013)
4. Buro, M.: Call for AI research in RTS games. In: Proceedings of the AAAI-04 Workshop on Challenges in Game AI, pp. 139–142. AAAI press (2004)
5. Chen, Z., Sun, Y., El-Nasr, M.S., Nguyen, T.H.D.: Player skill decomposition in multiplayer online battle arenas. arXiv preprint arXiv:1702.06253 (2017)
6. Hippe, R., Dornheim, J., Zeitvogel, S., Laubenheimer, A.: Evaluation of machine learning algorithms for smurf detection. In: CERC2017, p. 65 (2017)
7. Hunicke, R.: The case for dynamic difficulty adjustment in games. In: Proceedings of the 2005 ACM SIGCHI International Conference on Advances in Computer Entertainment Technology, pp. 429–433 (2005)
8. Kou, Y., Li, Y., Gui, X., Suzuki-Gill, E.: Playing with streakiness in online games: how players perceive and react to winning and losing streaks in league of legends. In: Proceedings of the 2018 CHI Conference on Human Factors in Computing Systems, pp. 1–14 (2018)
9. Lee, D., Tang, H., Zhang, J.O., Xu, H., Darrell, T., Abbeel, P.: Modular architecture for starcraft ii with deep reinforcement learning. In: Fourteenth Artificial Intelligence and Interactive Digital Entertainment Conference (2018)
10. Menze, B.H., et al.: A comparison of random forest and its gini importance with standard chemometric methods for the feature selection and classification of spectral data. BMC Bioinform. 10(1), 213 (2009)
11. Mnih, V., et al.: Human-level control through deep reinforcement learning. Nature 518(7540), 529–533 (2015)
12. Palencia, D.O.V., Osman, M.: PsyRTS: a web platform for experiments in human decision-making in RTS environments. In: 2019 IEEE Conference on Games (CoG), pp. 1–4. IEEE (2019)
13. Pang, Z.J., Liu, R.Z., Meng, Z.Y., Zhang, Y., Yu, Y., Lu, T.: On reinforcement learning for full-length game of starcraft. In: Proceedings of the AAAI Conference on Artificial Intelligence, vol. 33, pp. 4691–4698 (2019)
14. Ravari, Y.N., Bakkes, S., Spronck, P.: Starcraft winner prediction. In: Twelfth Artificial Intelligence and Interactive Digital Entertainment Conference (2016)
15. Sarkar, A., Cooper, S.: Inferring and comparing game difficulty curves using player-vs-level match data. In: 2019 IEEE Conference on Games (CoG), pp. 1–4. IEEE (2019)
16. Shao, K., Zhu, Y., Zhao, D.: Starcraft micromanagement with reinforcement learning and curriculum transfer learning. IEEE Transa. Emerg. Top. Comput. Intell. 3(1), 73–84 (2018)
17. Silver, D., et al.: Mastering chess and shogi by self-play with a general reinforcement learning algorithm. arXiv preprint arXiv:1712.01815 (2017)
18. Silver, D., et al.: Mastering the game of go without human knowledge. Nature 550(7676), 354–359 (2017)
19. Sun, P., et al.: Tstarbots: defeating the cheating level builtin AI in starcraft II in the full game. arXiv preprint arXiv:1809.07193 (2018)

20. Sweetser, P., Wyeth, P.: Gameflow: a model for evaluating player enjoyment in games. Comput. Entertainment (CIE) **3**(3), 3 (2005)
21. Vinyals, O., et al.: Starcraft II: a new challenge for reinforcement learning. arXiv preprint arXiv:1708.04782 (2017)
22. Yannakakis, G., Spronck, P., Loiacono, D., Andre, E.: Player modeling. In: Artificial and Computational Intelligence in Games, pp. 45–59. Dagstuhl Publishing (2013)

Train Small, Deploy Big: Do Relative World Views Permit Swarm-Safety During Policy Transplantation for Multi-Agent Reinforcement Learning Problems?

Bradley Fraser[✉][iD] and Giuseppe Laurito[iD]

Defence Science and Technology Group, Edinburgh, SA 5111, Australia
{Bradley.Fraser,Giuseppe.Laurito}@dst.defence.gov.au

Abstract. In order to 'train small, deploy big', agent control policies must be transplanted from one trained agent into a larger set of agents for deployment. Given that compute resources and training time generally scale with the number of agents, this approach to generating swarm control policies may be favourable for larger swarms. However, in order for this process to be successful, the agent control policy must be indistinct to the agent on which it is trained so that it can perform as required in its new host agent. Through extensive simulation of a cooperative multi-agent navigation task, it is shown that this indistinctness of agent policies, and therefore the success of the associated learned solution of the transplanted swarm, is dependent upon the way in which an agent views the world: absolute or relative. As a corollary to, and in contrary to naive intuition of, this result, we show that homogeneous agent capability is not enough to guarantee policy indistinctness. The article also discusses what general conditions may be required in order to enforce policy indistinctness.

Keywords: Multi-agent deep reinforcement learning · Policy transplantation · Cooperative navigation · Swarm-safety

1 Introduction

The significant developments in deep reinforcement learning techniques [18,19, 24] have recently been applied to the multi-agent problem space [20]. These new multi-agent learning architectures have allowed the learning of cooperative solutions to complex multi-agent problems such as collision avoidance [16], surveillance [15,22], exploration [6], autonomous driving [3,21] and the monitoring of wildfires [8,12] and flooding [2]. In such approaches, a control policy is

Supported by the Trusted Autonomous Systems Strategic Research Initiative of the Defence Science and Technology Group.

M. Gallagher et al. (Eds.): AI 2020, LNAI 12576, pp. 269–280, 2020.
https://doi.org/10.1007/978-3-030-64984-5_21

learned for each agent in the swarm with various techniques designed to overcome the partial observation and non-stationarity problems associated with training multiple agents [5,7,10,17]. Although compute resources in the cloud [11] have significantly increased to meet the demand required by the machine learning revolution [23], training an arbitrarily large number of agents is still an open problem. In an effort to avoid, rather than solve, this problem, this article discusses *policy transplantation* to enable the 'train small, deploy big' paradigm that is suitable for some cooperative multi-agent problems.

Policy transplantation refers to the process of copying a learned policy from one trained agent into another. This process has the obvious benefit that a smaller number of agents can be trained using less compute resources and time but enables an arbitrarily large number of swarm agents to be deployed. Depending on the application, this makes deploying the swarm more flexible as it is independent of the number of originally trained agents. This is particularly useful, for example, when physical platforms may be subject to attrition and need replacing mid-operation.

Policy transplantation assumes that the learned policy is both generalisable to other arbitrary agents and that the policy itself performs well in the presence of many other individuals; a situation that it did not experience during training. The former assumption raises concerns for heterogeneously-capable agents and task specialisation within learned solutions. However, there are some tasks where solutions can be learned using homogeneous agents without the need for specialisation. But even in these cases, as we shall show, whether or not policy transplantation is successful, or *swarm-safe*[1], is not obvious. This article therefore discusses what is required for the swarm-safe property to hold and hypothesises that swarm-safety is dependent on the world-view given to agents. To that end, using a multi-agent cooperative navigation task as a case study, we demonstrate how different world-views within the reinforcement learning framework affect the swarm-safe property.

Reinforcement learning is a framework where agents maximise some notion of reward by continually interacting with their environment [25]. Concretely, an agent observes its environmental state and then chooses an action. The environment 'responds' to this action by moving the agent to a new state and provides a reward signal. Using the action-state pair and reward, the agent must try to maximise the total reward received from the environment by choosing appropriate actions from a specific policy. In order to observe its environment, an observation vector is defined and provides the agent with its view of the world. In deep reinforcement learning, this observation vector is often the input into a neural network which acts as a function approximator that learns the correct policy through repeated exposure to environmental experience. The observation vector represents any information that is available to the agent and is (thought to be) useful in learning a task-specific policy. The vector itself is human-designed and how information is represented in the vector is therefore up to the designer. Data such as the agent position for example may be explicitly input as an x

---

[1] The term attributed to Kent Rosser (Defence Science and Technology Group).

and y coordinate, or be pre-processed in some other way before being passed to the input layer neurons. We show that when data is input in this explicit, absolute way, the learned solution is not swarm-safe. However, when data are pre-processed into a relative world-view, the learned solution is swarm-safe even though both solutions achieve the same outcome.

While there are some examples of successful policy transplantation, such as in [13,21], to the best of our knowledge this is the first discussion and attempt at quantifying the swarm-safe condition. Our contributions are thus:

1. Extensive simulations of a cooperative multi-agent task showing how different world-views permit, or not, successful policy transplantation; and
2. A definition of swarm-safety and discussion on its requirements, and implications on learned solutions as well as suggested research directions.

2 Related Work

To the authors' knowledge there are no works that explicitly consider policy transplantation or swarm-safety, however we discuss some related work where it has been used.

The authors of [21] consider the problem of how to transfer knowledge from a single trained agent to multiple agents. In their study, they consider autonomous agents that must navigate safely down a highway. While their main contribution shows that a multi-agent system learns faster and better when seeded with a single-agent policy than a multi-agent system learning from scratch, we focus on another result; the training of one agent and the transplantation into many. They show that transplantation is successful but not unexpectedly, the performance decreases as the number of autonomous agents increase. The performance issue here is from the fact that a *single* agent was originally trained and transplanted into a swarm, not because the policy itself was unsuitable for the new host agents. Performance could be improved by training several, rather than one, agent and then transplanting one of those policies into many. Importantly, they describe a 'car-centric' observation vector model which is an implicit world-view that is relative to each car agent.

The second example of policy transplantation occurs in [13]. The authors consider how a multi-agent swarm can learn how to solve a rendezvous problem with limited communications, not from reinforcement, but rather learning from a centralised known solution. Again, policy transplantation in this work is tangential to their main results. They train a swarm on 10 agents and deploy on up to 100. Similarly to the above, the observation by which agents view their world is a relative one where peers are measured relative to an agent's own position. We take inspiration from this work in our own relative representation.

Both works above employ a relative world-view in an effort to produce a static-length input vector required by neural networks but that also accounts for a dynamically changing number of peers. While this is true in our case, we also have other static information known in advance and have the option to represent this information either absolutely or relatively. As we shall see, while both options solve the task, only one is swarm-safe during policy transplantation.

3   Case Study

To examine different world-views and their effect on the swarm-safe property, we use the surveillance-based 'cooperative navigation' task considered in [17]. In this task, a set of agents $\mathcal{A}$ must move to cover a set of landmarks $\mathcal{L}$ while avoiding collisions between peers. To cover a landmark, an agent must move to within sensor range r_s of the origin of a landmark. For uniformity and comparison to published results, we adopt the same learning architecture, Multi-Agent Deep Deterministic Policy Gradient (MADDPG), introduced in the aforementioned article. During training, this actor-critic architecture allows the critic access to all agents' actions and observations. That is, it has global knowledge of the system. Once trained, the actors are deployed without the global critic and execute in a distributed, local fashion. This approach to multi-agent task allocation can be considered a broadcast method [4] since agents only have access to raw information about their peers. Practically this information may be transmitted wirelessly, or an agent may observe its peers, optically for example. Either way, no coordination information is communicated; a very different approach to that found in auctioning or consensus based algorithms [14]. Rather, policies contain strategies to move based on inferring the intentions of peer agents.

3.1   Observation Vector Models

In their published results, the authors of [17] use the following observation vector

$$O = \left[\{p_i\}\forall i \in \mathcal{D}, \{v_i\}\forall i \in \mathcal{D}, \{\{l_{i_j}\}\forall i \in \mathcal{D}\}\forall j \in \mathcal{L}, \{\{a_{i_j}\}\forall i \in \mathcal{D}\}\forall j \in \mathcal{A}\right] \quad (1)$$

where p is the agent position, v is the agent velocity, l is a vector to a landmark from the agent, a is a vector to a peer from the agent and $\mathcal{D} = \{x, y\}$. In the following, we denote the different observation models according to their implicit or explicit description of peers and landmarks. The vector above treats both landmark and peer agent positions explicitly. Ignoring information about the agent itself, the length of the vector is $|\mathcal{L}| + |\mathcal{A}|$ and is referred to as the *EE* (Explicit, Explicit) model where the order is landmarks then peers. The four possible observations models are summarised in Table 1.

The *EE* model has two issues for our application:

1. Due to the fixed number of neurons in the neural network input layer, it is not scalable in the agent or landmarks dimensions. Swarms would need retraining if the number of either of these variables changed.
2. It is problematic when peer information is not available. For example, if agents have a limited communication range, they may not always be able to acquire information about their peers. Zero-padding or indicator neurons would need to be added to the vector to handle this situation.

Table 1. The four possible observation vector models generated by treating peer agent and landmark positions either explicitly or implicitly.

		Landmarks	
		Implicit	Explicit
Peers	Implicit	*II Model*	*IE Model*
		Scalable in peers	Scalable in peers
		Scalable in landmarks	Dynamic peer information
		Dynamic peer/landmark information	Not scalable in targets
	Explicit	*EI Model*	*EE Model*
		Not scalable in peers	Not scalable in peers
		Scalable in targets	Not scalable in targets
		No dynamic peer information	No dynamic information

3.2 The 'Bulls-Eye' World Representation

Inherently, vectors provide distance and direction information to the agents and hence the learning process. A relative, *implicit* representation of this information is required. To accomplish this, we use the 'histograms over observed neighbourhood relations' proposed in [9] and similarly in [13]. An agent's maximum communications range is divided into a number of distance bins and a histogram is generated for objects that fall into each bin. Visually, this is represented as a number of concentric circles centred on the agent itself. For direction, a similar approach divides the space around an agent into a number of segments. The approach generates a number of 'distance-segments' that map to a specific neuron at the input layer. This neuron therefore takes an integer that counts the number of objects in that segment. For example, Fig. 1 shows the 'bulls-eye' model with $b = 3$ histogram bins and $s = 4$ segments. In the *II* model, landmarks (red circles) and peers (blue circles) have their own bulls-eye vectors creating an observation vector of static length (again ignoring agent specific information) $\dim O = 2 \times b \times s = 24$, that is,

$$O = \left[\underbrace{0,0,0,0,0,0,0,0,0,0,2,0}_{\text{peers}}, \underbrace{0,0,0,0,0,1,0,0,0,0,0,1}_{\text{landmarks}} \right]. \qquad (2)$$

From this representation, it is easy for the agent (black circle) to decide to move towards the bottom right landmark, since it has peers 'near' and 'towards' the other landmark. Though not considered here, we note that other information such as the location of obstacles and landmark priorities may be encoded in this way. We modify the above representation so that the first bin is equivalent to r_s so that any non-zero integer in any segment representing the first bin indicates that a target(s) is covered. Similarly, the largest bin represents infinity so that all landmarks fall within a bin (equivalently, landmark distances are capped to the

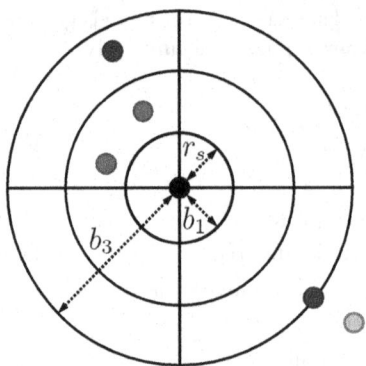

Fig. 1. A visual representation of the 'bulls-eye' observation vector model [9] where the peer agents (blue circles) and landmarks (red circles) are localised relative to the agent (black circle). The first bin distance $b_1 = r_s$ assists with landmark covering. The relative distance of the bottom right landmark (transparent) d has been set to the largest bin distance b_3, i.e. $d = \max(d, b_3)$ so that all landmarks can be seen. (Color figure online)

distance of the largest bin). Note that landmark positions are known in advance and are static.

For our application, and to 'train small, deploy big', only the EI and II models are of interest. That is, we require flexibility in the number of agents but can concede flexibility in the number of landmarks. We therefore begin by investigating the EI model with the rationale that it contains more information since the bulls-eye view has an inherently reduced resolution of the world.

4 Experimentation and Results

The first experiment compares the performance of the EE (from [17]) and EI models. Agents were placed on 2×2 unit field with a size and sensor range of 0.1. A disc propagation model with a range $r_c = 0.5$ was applied to each agent to decide if communications were available. Swarms were trained for 1×10^6 episodes of 50 time-steps where actor and critic networks consisted of 4 hidden-layers having 128, 64, 32 and 16 neurons respectively with rectified linear activation functions. Each episode, landmarks were randomly placed on the field according to a uniform distribution. Episodes were ended if all landmarks were covered or the maximum number of time-steps was exceeded. Results show the mean and 95% confidence interval of 1000 benchmark episodes.

4.1 Fully Explicit and Hybrid Models

The EE model used the observation vector from (1) where $|\mathcal{A}| = |\mathcal{L}| = 3$. The EI model being a hybrid used the following observation vector

$$O = \left[\{p_i\} \forall i \in \mathcal{D}, \{v_i\} \forall i \in \mathcal{D}, \{\{l_{i_j}\} \forall i \in \mathcal{D}\} \forall j \in \mathcal{L}, \{c_i\} \forall i \in \mathcal{E}_p : c \in \mathbb{N}_0 \right] \quad (3)$$

where c is the count of peers in segment i of the peer distance-segment set $\mathcal{E}_p$ where $|\mathcal{E}_p| = (b = 4) \times (s = 8) = 32$. In both cases, a peer-information timeout of 10 time-steps was used. In the EE model, missing peer information was zero-padded. Agents received a shared reward $R \leq 0$ that encourages minimisation between their position and a landmark, as well as accounting for collisions [17], that is,

$$R = \left(-\sum_{\forall i \in \mathcal{L}} \min\left(||\boldsymbol{p}_i - \boldsymbol{p}_j|| \forall j \in \mathcal{A}\right) \right) - n_{\text{collisions}} \qquad (4)$$

where $\cdot$ denotes a two-dimensional vector, $||\cdot||$ is the L^2 (Euclidean) norm and $n_{\text{collisions}}$ is the number of collisions experienced during a time-step.

Figure 2 plots the number of occupied landmarks and the number of collisions respectively. It can be seen that both models learn to de-conflict targets and perform collision avoidance even though they cannot always communicate. With confidence that the EI model performs as well as published literature, we now examine the policy transplantation of the model. The MADDPG implementation was modified so that one of the EI agent policies could be transplanted into six agents, that is, $|\mathcal{A}| = 6$ and $|\mathcal{L}| = 3$. Again looking at Fig. 2, we can see that transplantation performs very poorly with a high number of collisions; it is not swarm-safe.

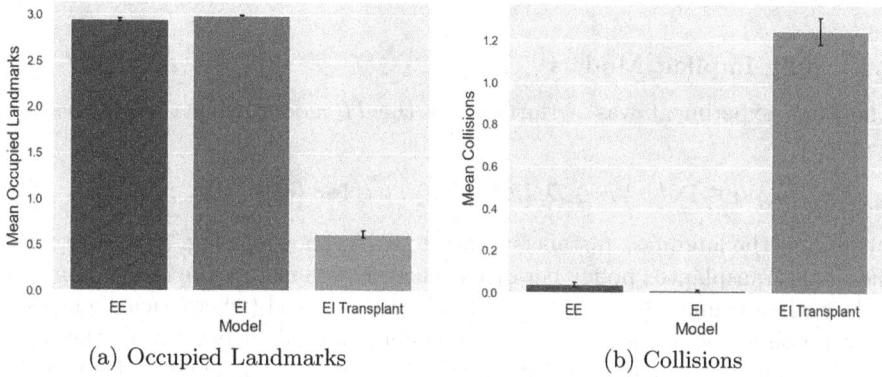

(a) Occupied Landmarks   (b) Collisions

Fig. 2. The EE and EI models perform equally well achieving near 100% coverage with few collisions. The transplanted EI model however, does not.

On further investigation, it was found that EI model produced a policy where each agent learned to go to a specific position in the landmark vector. That is, one agent would always go to the landmark encoded in the first position of the landmark set within the observation vector. Another agent would go to the second position and so on. While this approach works with the three original EI model-trained policies, upon transplanting only one of them into 6, saw all agents move to a single landmark. This caused cover failure as well as a large number of collisions and demonstrates that specialisation can occur even in agents of homogeneous type, and therefore homogeneity does not guarantee swarm-safety.

While 'selecting' a landmark index is a reasonable strategy for landmark de-confliction, it very much resembles a pre-planned solution. Note that an omniscient oracle did not dictate which agent went to which landmark, but rather the landmarks were 'selected' through the reinforcement trial and error process. This is much like the 'pedestrian dance' where one attempts to de-conflict their path with another agent (or human) in a non-communicative type way due to a perceived collision [26]. At some point during learning, an agent increasingly began to go to a particular landmark while the others increasingly did not, resulting in a somewhat pre-planned solution.

As well as not being swarm-safe, there are inefficiencies in the learned strategy. In an uncluttered field, an efficient approach would see agents go to their closest landmark. The strategy generated here however, will see agents cross paths to get to 'their' landmark if the random starting conditions dictated it; the solution provided by the EI model is not reactive to the current environment. The behaviour above also explains why the EE model performs well under range-limited propagation, something not considered in the original publication [17]. The position of peers, whether they are in range or not, is inconsequential to landmark selection since an agent's landmark is pre-determined. Other agents' locations only matter when they are close for collision avoidance reasons, at which point they can communicate anyway.

4.2 Fully Implicit Models

The same experiment was performed for the II model using the observation vector

$$O = [\{p_i\}\forall i \in \mathcal{D}, \{v_i\}\forall i \in \mathcal{D}, \{c_i\}\forall i \in \mathcal{E}_l : c \in \mathbb{N}_0, \{c_i\}\forall i \in \mathcal{E}_p : c \in \mathbb{N}_0], \quad (5)$$

where $\mathcal{E}_l$ is the landmark distance-segment set. As shown in Fig. 3a and Fig. 3b, the single transplanted policy performs nearly as well in a swarm of six agents as it does when trained in three. Both the II-trained model (where each agent uses its own policy), and the II-transplanted model (where six agents all use the same policy taken from one of the original three) cover on average collectively cover close to three of the three available targets. Although low in magnitude, there are a considerably higher number of collisions for the EI-transplant experiment as compared to the original II model. This however is attributed to collisions that occur when a single target is being covered by more than one agent. A simple fix to this issue would be to set the sensor radius much greater than the physical size of the agents themselves. This would hold true in a real situation where the sensor is a camera or microphone for example. The higher number of collisions does not occur when $|\mathcal{A}| = 6$ and $|\mathcal{L}| = 6$ in the transplanted case (see 'II Transplant 6 Targets' bar) since there is one landmark per agent, removing the multiple cover situation. As expected, more agents take a longer time to execute (see Fig. 3c). Regardless, this relative representation of the world does not permit a strategy to be learned where a policy is distinct to a given agent.

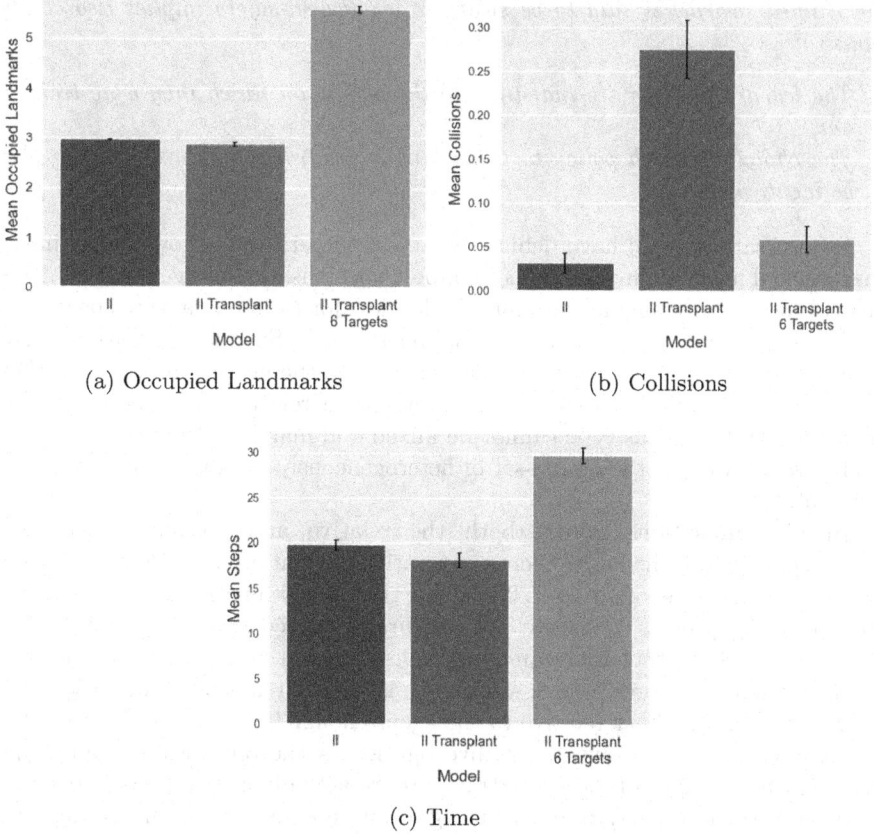

(a) Occupied Landmarks

(b) Collisions

(c) Time

Fig. 3. Transplanting the fully relative II model is a swarm-safe operation with six agents covering all three targets. Collisions are increased in this case due to multiple agent coverings of single targets. When there are six targets and six agents, the transplanted policy covers nearly all six agents with minimal collisions. The larger swarm requires more time to complete the task.

5   Discussion

For convenience and future research, and using the arguments, above we make the following definitions:

Definition 1. *Policy Transplantation: the process of copying a trained agent policy into one or more other agents.*

Definition 2. *Swarm-safe: If the performance of the transplanted swarm is dependent upon the quality of the transplanted policy only, rather than issues associated with the suitability of the policy to its new host(s), such as distinctness, the policy (and by extension the associated cooperative learned solution of* *the trained swarm) is said to be swarm-safe. Swarm-safety implies two conditions:*

1. *The learned policies are indistinct to the agents on which they were trained; and*
2. *The choice of which policy to transplant is arbitrary; they are considered to be identical.*

Swarm-safety as we have defined it, and as experiments show above, imply that learned agent strategies cannot support specialisation of agents of homogeneous type. When using an absolute world-view for example, agents specialised in the targets they chose as a deconfliction strategy. Such specialisation is not swarm-safe since policies are very much specific to the host agent in which they were trained. Similarly, even if world-views were relative, it is assumed that agents of heterogeneous type cannot be mixed and matched; though this case is likely less relevant as the action-set of heterogeneously-capable agents would be different.

In the simulations above, both the relative and absolute world-view approaches achieve the multi-agent cooperative navigation task. However, one is swarm-safe while the other isn't. Typically, the reward function in the reinforcement learning process is selected to encourage desired behaviour. This raises the question of whether there are conditions that can be placed on the reward function itself to enforce swarm-safety. Or, is simply referring to all observable information in a manner relative to the agent enough?

Another interesting avenue of investigation is the optimisation landscape itself and how many solutions or strategies are actually available. Is it possible for an indistinct strategy to evolve using absolute information, but the distinct solution is the easiest to find? For example, agents could select the closest landmark and move towards it, then if it encounters a peer closer to its intended landmark, it changes to another. From visual inspection, this is indeed the strategy that is learned in the relative *II* model case. Is indistinctness then simply a manifestation of reward-hacking [1], where the optimiser exploits the reward function all the way to optimality? If this is the case, the strategy that evolves in the relative approach will never appear when absolute information is available because the absolute case performs better given the way in which the reward function is defined. This line of investigation makes reward function conditions that enforce swarm-safety all the more important. However, we do not want to impose conditions to simply avoid a particular strategy evolving in favour of another, both of which we know are possible from a posteriori knowledge gained through empirical experimentation. Rather, a deeper more fundamental condition is sought that evolves a swarm-safe strategy from the start.

In summary, while we have shown that a relative world-view enables the swarm-safe property during policy transplantation, we invite researchers to investigate theoretical proofs that enforce it. Having been tested on only a single multi-agent task, counter examples to our results may be found. As such, we leave the general condition(s) for swarm-safety as an open problem noting that the works in [13, 21] successfully perform policy transplantation using a relative world view.

6   Conclusion

This article raised the concept of policy transplantation, a process by which a policy from a smaller trained swarm is copied into agents of a larger one. If the larger swarm's performance is solely dependent on the quality of the transplanted policy, not the suitability of its new hosts, the policy is said to be swarm-safe. Through simulation of a cooperative multi-agent task, it was found that both a relative and absolute representation of the data contained in the reinforcement learning observation vector produced a high-reward solution. However, only the relative data representation was swarm-safe. In addition, two other cited works that demonstrated successful policy transplantation employed a relative observation vector. It is concluded then that an agent's world-view fundamentally affects the indistinctness of the learned policies, and therefore swarm-safety, with a relative view likely permitting the property.

The process by which the observation vector affects swarm-safety is unknown and we invite the multi-agent learning community to investigate theoretical conditions on: the observation vector; and/or the reward function to enforce this property. While not suitable for all multi-agent tasks, policy transplantation is an avenue to deploying an arbitrarily large agent swarm and bounding the swarm-safe property would be a significant step.

References

1. Amodei, D., Olah, C., Steinhardt, J., Christiano, P., Schulman, J., Mané, D.: Concrete problems in AI safety, June 2016
2. Baldazo, D., Parras, J., Zazo, S.: Decentralized multi-agent deep reinforcement learning in swarms of drones for flood monitoring. In: 2019 27th European Signal Processing Conference (EUSIPCO), pp. 1–5, September 2019
3. Bhalla, S., Ganapathi Subramanian, S., Crowley, M.: Deep multi agent reinforcement learning for autonomous driving. In: Goutte, C., Zhu, X. (eds.) Canadian AI 2020. LNCS (LNAI), vol. 12109, pp. 67–78. Springer, Cham (2020). https://doi.org/10.1007/978-3-030-47358-7_7
4. Campbell, A., Wu, A.S.: Multi-agent role allocation: issues, approaches, and multiple perspectives. Auton. Agent. Multi. Agent. Syst. **22**(2), 317–355 (2011)
5. Chen, G.: A new framework for multi-agent reinforcement learning - centralized training and exploration with decentralized execution via policy distillation, October 2019
6. Geng, M., Zhou, X., Ding, B., Wang, H., Zhang, L.: Learning to cooperate in decentralized multi-robot exploration of dynamic environments. In: Cheng, L., Leung, A.C.S., Ozawa, S. (eds.) ICONIP 2018. LNCS, vol. 11307, pp. 40–51. Springer, Cham (2018). https://doi.org/10.1007/978-3-030-04239-4_4
7. Gupta, J.K., Egorov, M., Kochenderfer, M.: Cooperative multi-agent control using deep reinforcement learning. In: Sukthankar, G., Rodriguez-Aguilar, J.A. (eds.) AAMAS 2017. LNCS (LNAI), vol. 10642, pp. 66–83. Springer, Cham (2017). https://doi.org/10.1007/978-3-319-71682-4_5

8. Haksar, R.N., Schwager, M.: Distributed deep reinforcement learning for fighting forest fires with a network of aerial robots. In: 2018 IEEE/RSJ International Conference on Intelligent Robots and Systems (IROS), pp. 1067–1074, October 2018

9. Hüttenrauch, M., Šošić, A., Neumann, G.: Local communication protocols for learning complex swarm behaviors with deep reinforcement learning. In: International Conference on Swarm Intelligence. computational-learning.net (2018)

10. Hüttenrauch, M., Šošić, A., Neumann, G.: Deep reinforcement learning for swarm systems. J. Mach. Learn. Res. **20**(54), 1–31 (2019)

11. Hwang, K.: Cloud Computing for Machine Learning and Cognitive Applications. MIT Press, June 2017

12. Julian, K.D., Kochenderfer, M.J.: Autonomous distributed wildfire surveillance using deep reinforcement learning. In: 2018 AIAA Guidance, Navigation, and Control Conference. unknown, January 2018

13. Li, Q., Du, X., Huang, Y., Sykora, Q., Schoellig, A.P.: Learning of coordination policies for robotic swarms, September 2017

14. Li, Y., Tan, C.: A survey of the consensus for multi-agent systems. Syst. Sci. Control Eng. **7**(1), 468–482 (2019)

15. Liu, Y., Liu, H., Tian, Y., Sun, C.: Reinforcement learning based two-level control framework of UAV swarm for cooperative persistent surveillance in an unknown urban area. Aerosp. Sci. Technol. **98**, 105671 (2020)

16. Long, P., Fan, T., Liao, X., Liu, W., Zhang, H., Pan, J.: Towards optimally decentralized multi-robot collision avoidance via deep reinforcement learning, September 2017

17. Lowe, R., Wu, Y.I., Tamar, A., Harb, J., Pieter Abbeel, O., Mordatch, I.: Multi-agent actor-critic for mixed cooperative-competitive environments. In: Guyon, I., et al. (eds.) Advances in Neural Information Processing Systems, vol. 30, pp. 6379–6390. Curran Associates, Inc. (2017)

18. Mnih, V., et al.: Playing atari with deep reinforcement learning, December 2013

19. Mnih, V., et al.: Human-level control through deep reinforcement learning. Nature **518**(7540), 529–533 (2015)

20. Nguyen, T.T., Nguyen, N.D., Nahavandi, S.: Deep reinforcement learning for multi-agent systems: a review of challenges, solutions and applications, December 2018

21. Rădulescu, R., Legrand, M., Efthymiadis, K., Roijers, D.M., Nowé, A.: Deep multi-agent reinforcement learning in a homogeneous open population. In: Atzmueller, M., Duivesteijn, W. (eds.) BNAIC 2018. CCIS, vol. 1021, pp. 90–105. Springer, Cham (2019). https://doi.org/10.1007/978-3-030-31978-6_8

22. Rosello, P., Kochenderfer, M.J.: Multi-agent reinforcement learning for multi-object tracking. In: Proceedings of the 17th International Conference on Autonomous Agents and MultiAgent Systems, pp. 1397–1404 (2018)

23. Sejnowski, T.J.: The Deep Learning Revolution. MIT Press, October 2018

24. Silver, D., et al.: Mastering the game of go with deep neural networks and tree search. Nature **529**(7587), 484–489 (2016)

25. Sutton, R.S., Barto, A.G.: Reinforcement Learning: An Introduction (Complete 2nd Edition Draft) (2017)

26. Winfield, A.F.: Experiments in artificial theory of mind: from safety to story-telling. Front. Robot. AI **5**, 75 (2018)

Autonomous Recognition of Collective Behaviour in Robot Swarms

Kathryn Kasmarik[(✉)], Shadi Abpeikar, Md Mohiuddin Khan, Noha Khattab,
Michael Barlow, and Matt Garratt

School of Engineering and IT, UNSW Canberra, Canberra, Australia
k.kasmarik@adfa.edu.au

Abstract. Developmental evolution of collective swarm behaviours promises
new ways to evolve swarms with different movement characteristics. Preliminary
work has developed value functions that can recognize emergent swarm behaviour
and distinguish it from random behaviour in point-mass boid simulations. This
paper examines the performance of several variants of such functions recognizing the emergent behaviour of simulated robots, which have different movement
properties to point-mass boid simulations as they are constrained by the manoeuvrability of the physical robot. We designed two boid guidance algorithms for
controlling Pioneer3DX robots. Five value functions were then examined and
compared for their ability to distinguish swarming behaviour from unstructured
behaviour. Results show that four of these can be used to distinguish structured
collective behaviours of the robots and distinguish such behaviour from random
movement patterns.

Keywords: Swarm robotics · Evolutionary developmental robotics · Unmanned
ground vehicle · Boids · Braitenberg vehicle

1 Introduction

Autonomous robot swarms offer the potential for efficient movement, redundancy, and
potential for human guidance of swarm containing many agents [1]. Computer simulations of birds' flocking behaviour were first introduced by Reynolds [2]. Reynolds'
"boids", short for "bird androids", were based on the emergent behaviour resulting from
the interaction of three rules: cohesion, alignment and repulsion. Later extensions of these
models, called boid guidance algorithms (BGAs) [3], have been designed for unmanned
ground and aerial vehicles. BGAs include further rules to ensure vehicles stay within
the boundaries of their operating conditions, such as speed and turn rate. Traditionally,
each BGA needs to be tuned for each physical robot to which it will apply, and for each
behavioural variant. Developmental evolutionary algorithms aim to remove the need for
such tuning [4] by autonomously bootstrapping multiple collective behaviours adapted
to the physical forms of given robots. However, to achieve this, a generic fitness function is required that can distinguish structured behaviour from unstructured behaviour,
without the need to precisely define swarm-specific characteristics. Various approaches

© Springer Nature Switzerland AG 2020
M. Gallagher et al. (Eds.): AI 2020, LNAI 12576, pp. 281–293, 2020.
https://doi.org/10.1007/978-3-030-64984-5_22

have been proposed for this, including unsupervised [4] and supervised value systems [5]. However, to date, they have been applied on boid point-mass simulations only, and not to robots controlled by BGAs.

This paper examines the performance of five such value functions recognizing the emergent behaviour of simulated robots. Robots have different movement properties to boid simulations as they are constrained by the manoeuvrability of the physical robot. They may also have more limited, decentralized sensing capacity. We designed two boid guidance algorithms for controlling Pioneer3DX robots simulated in CoppeliaSim[1]. This permits us to examine the impact of the specific control algorithm on detection performance. Five value functions were then examined and compared for their ability to distinguish swarming behaviour from unstructured behaviour: three approaches based on unsupervised learning [4], and two based on supervised learning [5]. Our results show that four of the approaches can recognize structured collective behaviours of the robots and distinguish such behaviour from random movement patterns.

The remainder of this paper is organized as follows: Sect. 2 presents background and related work on developmental evolution and swarm intelligence. Section 3 describes our BGAs and the value functions for recognizing swarming. Section 4 describes our experimental setup and the results. We conclude in Sect. 5 and examine directions for future work.

2   Background and Related Work

2.1   Evolutionary Developmental Robotics

The last 15 years have seen progress in developmental robotics research, towards goal generation and behaviour bootstrapping approaches [6–12] that support open-ended, life-long learning by embodied machines. However, a recent review [13] indicates previous efforts focused predominantly on individual agents and humanoid robots. In contrast, hardware for large numbers of autonomous ground and aerial vehicles is becoming increasingly accessible. At the same time, embodied evolution for the purpose of generating collective behaviours in robot swarms is emerging as an important research area to permit behaviour learning by groups of robots [14–16]. Evolutionary approaches have an advantage over rule-based approaches to swarming, as they can generate solutions for which rules are difficult to hand-craft [17]. However, the most common approaches still guide the evolutionary process towards a fixed or 'static' behavioural objective [14, 18]. The experimenter designs a fitness function that estimates the quality of candidate solutions with respect to a given objective, and this fitness function is used to 'score' the behaviour of individuals in the population.

Behaviour bootstrapping algorithms permit agents with limited or no pre-programmed behaviours to self-generate reusable action sequences adapted for their physical form and environment [6–12]. Open-ended learning implies that behavioural objectives of the agents are not set in advance. Rather, the agent selects its own behavioural objectives relevant to its physical form, the environment and its past experiences. These dynamic behavioural objectives are identified by a 'value system' [4].

---

[1] https://www.coppeliarobotics.com/.

This paper compares variants of two such value systems [4, 5] designed to sit within algorithms that can bootstrap collective behaviours [4, 14–18]. Specifically, these value systems aim to recognize swarming behaviours and distinguish them from unstructured non-swarming behaviours. The supervised value systems achieve this by assigning a label, while the unsupervised value systems do this by generating a quantisation error that reflects the level of learnable structure in behavioural variables.

The contribution of this paper is a confirmation that such techniques, developed and tested on point-mass boid simulations, can be applied to recognize swarming by mobile robots controlled by different BGAs. The next section introduces the basic boid notation on which the BGAs used in this paper are based.

2.2 Boid Algorithm

The basic boids model [2] uses three rules: cohesion (movement towards the average position of neighbouring agents); alignment (orientation towards the average heading of neighbours); and separation (moving to avoid collision with neighbours). Suppose we have a group of N agents $A^1, A^2, A^3....A^N$. At time t each agent A^i has a position, x^i_t, and a velocity, v^i_t. x^i_t is a point and v^i_t is a vector. At each time step t, the velocity and position of each agent is updated as follows:

$$v^i_{t+1} = v^i_t + W_c c^i_t + W_a a^i_t + W_s s^i_t \text{ and } x^i_{t+1} = x^i_t + v^i_{t+1} \qquad (1)$$

where c^i_t is a vector towards the average position of agents neighbouring A^i (i.e. within a certain range of A^i); a^i_t is a vector in the average direction of agents neighbouring A^i; and s^i_t is a vector away from the average position of agents neighbouring A^i. These vectors are the result of cohesion, alignment and separation forces. Weights W_c, W_a and W_s strengthen or weaken the corresponding force. Once a new velocity has been computed, the position of each agent can be updated.

Formally, we define a set N^i of the neighbours within a range R of A^i as follows:

$$N^i = \left\{ A^k | A^k \neq A^i \wedge dist\left(A^k, A^i \right) < R \right\}, \qquad (2)$$

where $dist(A^k, A^i)$ is the Euclidean distance between two agents. Different ranges may be used to calculate cohesion, alignment and separation forces. The average position of agents within range R_c of A^i is $\vec{c}^i_t$. The vector in the direction of $\vec{c}^i_t$ is:

$$c^i_t = \vec{c}^i_t - x^i_t \text{ where } \vec{c}^i_t = \frac{\sum_k x^k_t}{|(N_c)^i_t|} \qquad (3)$$

Similarly, the average position of agents within range R_s of A^i is $\vec{s}^i_t$ and the vector away from this position is:

$$s^i_t = x^i_t - \vec{s}^i_t \text{ where } \vec{s}^i_t = \frac{\sum_k x^k_t}{|(N_s)^i_t|} \qquad (4)$$

Finally, a_t^i is the vector in the average direction of agents within range R_a of A^i:

$$a_t^i = \frac{\sum_k \mathbf{v}_t^k}{\left|(N_a)_t^i\right|}. \tag{5}$$

These vectors are then normalized and multiplied by the corresponding weights, before calculating the new velocity using Eq. 1. The newly calculated velocity is further normalized and scaled by a speed value V_{max}. In the next section we describe two BGA variants of the basic boid model for application to Pioneer3DX robots.

3 Proposed Approach

In this paper we examine the performance of five swarm recognition approaches detecting swarming defined by two different BGAs. These BGAs are described in Sect. 3.1; the recognition algorithms are described in Sect. 3.2. Our experimental setup and results will be discussed in Sect. 4.

3.1 Boid Guidance Algorithms

Braitenberg-Swarm Hybrid. *Braitenberg* vehicles [19] have pairs of symmetric sensors arranged such that one of each pair is positioned on the left of the vehicle and the other is positioned symmetrically on the right. Each sensor stimulates the wheel on the same side of the vehicle. This represents a model of negative animal tropotaxis. It obeys the following rules:

- More sensor stimulation on the right triggers the right wheel to turn faster, causing the robot to turn towards the left, away the stimulation.
- More sensor stimulation on the left triggers the left wheel turns faster, causing the robot to turn towards the right, away from the stimulation.

Sensors that are situated closer to the front of the vehicle trigger a stronger wheel response than sensors situated further towards the sides and back. This means that the robot will turn away more aggressively from obstacles directly in front, than from obstacles approached at an angle. Likewise, the update rule is designed such that obstacles (including other robots) that are closer will trigger a stronger wheel response than obstacles further away. Braitenberg rules provide a way to implement obstacle avoidance and separation on the Pioneer3DX robots equipped with ultrasonic sensors. Basic Braitenberg deltas for the left and right wheels assuming an obstacle detected by sensor j at a (normalized) distance D are:

$$\Delta_j^{left} = r^{increment}.d^{left} \tag{6}$$

$$\Delta_j^{right} = r^{increment}.d^{right} \tag{7}$$

$$d^{side} = \begin{cases} 0 & \text{if no object detected on } side \\ 1 - D & \text{if an object detected on } side \end{cases} \quad \text{where } side = \{left|right\} \tag{8}$$

Alignment wheel deltas are triggered by a difference in orientation between the current robot and the average orientation θ_N^i of its neighbors. Specifically, for the left wheel the difference in orientation stimulates a proportional negative change in the speed of the left wheel. For the right wheel, the difference stimulates a proportional positive change:

$$\Delta_{align}^{left} = -W_a.\theta_{Nt}^i \text{ and } \Delta_{align}^{right} = W_a.\theta_{Nt}^i \tag{9}$$

Cohesion wheel deltas are calculated to turn the robot towards the relative position of the center of mass of neighbouring robots. The x-difference triggers the right wheel, and the y-difference the left wheel.

$$\Delta_{cohes}^{left} = W_c.\left(c_t^i\right)_y \text{ and } \Delta_{cohes}^{right} = -W_c.\left(c_t^i\right)_x \tag{10}$$

Equations 9–10 are combined as follows to adjust the robot's left and right wheel speeds (r^{left} and r^{right} respectively) relative to a constant rotational velocity r_0:

$$r_{(t+1)}^{left} = r_0 + \sum_j \Delta_j^{left} + \Delta_{align}^{left} + \Delta_{cohes}^{left} \tag{11}$$

$$r_{(t+1)}^{right} = r_0 + \sum_j \Delta_j^{right} + \Delta_{align}^{right} + \Delta_{cohes}^{right} \tag{12}$$

Using this approach, obstacle avoidance and separation are catered for by the Braitenberg rules, while swarming is achieved by adding the alignment and cohesion terms.

Boid-Swarm. Our second approach uses the classic boid update from Eq. (1), augmented with a weighted normal force w_t^k away from any of the u detected walls ($u = 4$ in our square arena).

$$v_{t+1}^i = v_t^i + W_c c_t^i + W_a a_t^i + W_s s_t^i + W_s \sum_u w_t^u \tag{13}$$

This is realized as a wheel update by first computing a target orientation θ_T using a two-argument arctangent, and then the required change in orientation, δ, from the current orientation θ_t as:

$$\delta = (\theta_T - \theta_t + 3\pi)mod(2\pi) - \pi \tag{14}$$

If δ is large (more than $\pm90°$), only the robot's orientation is adjusted as follows:

$$r_{(t+1)}^{left} = -\frac{\delta}{2} \text{ and } r_{(t+1)}^{left} = \frac{\delta}{2} \tag{15}$$

If δ is small, the robot is allowed to move forward while turning. Forward movement is inversely proportional to the size of δ:

$$r_{(t+1)}^{left} = r_0\left(\frac{\pi - \delta}{\pi}\right) - \frac{\delta}{2} \text{ and } r_{(t+1)}^{right} = r_0\left(\frac{\pi - \delta}{\pi}\right) + \frac{\delta}{2} \tag{16}$$

3.2 Swarm Recognition Algorithms

In this paper we will compare the following five approaches to recognising structured, collective robot movements. These are UVS1, UVS2, UVS3, SV1, SV2 defined as follows:

Unsupervised Value Systems. Our first swarm recognition approaches are based on a computational model of curiosity that uses a Self-Organizing Map (SOM) as the underlying data structure [4, 12]. Each time-step, one or more observations O_t^i made by an agent i in the swarm is constructed, normalized, and presented to the SOM. The format of these observations defines the variant of the value system (UVS1, UVS2, UVS3):

- **UVS1:** For the Braitenberg-Swarm Hybrid a raw observation is:

$$O_t^i = \left[V_{x_t}^i, V_{y_t}^i W_a.\theta_{N_t}^i, W_c.\left(c_t^i\right)_x, W_c.\left(c_t^i\right)_y, N_{ca_t}^i \right] \tag{17}$$

- **UVS1** alternative: For the Boid-Swarm a raw observation is:

$$O_t^i = \left[V_{x_t}^i, V_{y_t}^i, W_s.\left(s_t^i\right)_x, W_s.\left(s_t^i\right)_y, W_a.\left(a_t^i\right)_x, W_a.\left(a_t^i\right)_y, W_c.\left(c_t^i\right)_x, W_c.\left(c_t^i\right)_y, N_{ca_t}^i, N_{s_t}^i \right] \tag{18}$$

From this raw data, two further types of observations can be derived from the velocities or positions of neighbouring agents. We used Euclidean distance to determine the 3 nearest agents to a given agent and construct two further observations relevant for both the Braitenberg and Boid BGAs:

$$\textbf{UVS2} \quad O_t^i = \left[V_{x_t}^1, V_{y_t}^1, V_{x_t}^2, V_{y_t}^2, V_{x_t}^3, V_{y_t}^3, \right] \tag{19}$$

$$\textbf{UVS3} \quad O_t^i = \left[P_{x_t}^1, P_{y_t}^1, P_{x_t}^2, P_{y_t}^2, P_{x_t}^3, P_{y_t}^3, \right] \tag{20}$$

Once presented with an observation, the SOM identifies the best matching unit (BMU) K_t with the minimum Euclidean distance to the observation. This neuron and its neighbours are updated. The 'curiosity' value output by the SOM in response to each observation is the quantization error (QE) computed by calculating the average distance between the input observations from each agent and the corresponding BMU. The formula for average quantization error is as follows:

$$QE_t = \sum_{i=1}^{N} \left\| O_t^i - K_t^i \right\| \tag{21}$$

Where K_t^i is the winning neuron for the corresponding input O_t^i. This quantization error measures the 'fitness' of the swarm. A lower value indicates recognisable structure among observations, while a higher value indicates the absence of detected patterns in observations. The network has 1500 neurons, the learning rate was fixed to 0.25 and the neighbourhood size was fixed to 1. The fixed values capture the property of a value system that it is always learning.

Supervised Value System SVS1. Our second type of swarm recognition approach is a supervised learning approach where training data is derived from human labelling of data in Eq. 18 generated in point-mass boid simulations [5, 20]. The human labelling was performed by conducting an online survey comprising 16 questions. Each question contained a short video of either a simulated swarm, or random point-mass movement. Participants were asked to give three opinions about the grouping, alignment and flocking nature of the movement. To this end, for each video, three range sliders were provided in the survey. The sliders allowed participants to record their responses for (1) flocking to not flocking; (2) aligned to not aligned; and (3) grouped to not grouped. A sample screenshot of one of the questions of the survey is presented in Fig. 1. Each of the participants moves the sliders to record their perception of each of the 16 videos, which were presented in a random order.

In each question, the final slider position was recorded as a value between 0 and 100. Figure 2 summarizes the average responses of 70 participants in the survey including the 95% confidence interval. We found a statistically significant difference between participants' responses to a majority of the structured behaviours, compared to their responses to the unstructured behaviours. We used the average 'flocking' responses to make a binary decision about whether a data in the form of Eq. 18 sampled from any video should be labelled 'swarming' or 'not-swarming'. We used labelled data to train 6 different supervised learning algorithms, Decision Tree, Naïve Bayes, Support Vector Machine, Bayesian Neural Network, Levenberg Neural Network, and Gradient Neural Network. These trained learners are variants of the supervised value system SVS1 that we test with robot data in Experiment 1. These 6 supervised learning methods are implemented in MATLAB R2018B, with the default learning parameters of MATLAB, [21]. Besides, neural networks are trained by 10 epochs.

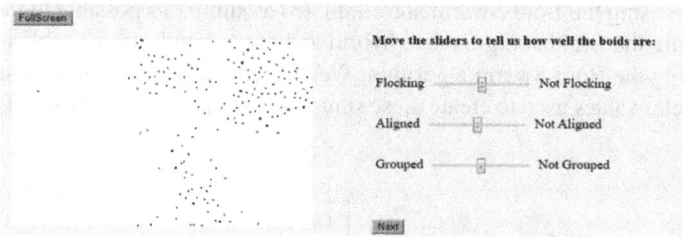

Fig. 1. Sample survey question.

Supervised Value System SVS2. Our second swarm recognition approach is a supervised learning approach where training data of the form in Eq. 17 and 18 is collected from simulated robots engaged in swarming and random movements. Data is labelled according to the visual properties of the robots' movements, as determined by the authors. As we will describe in the next section, we prepared five robot simulations with parameter settings as similar as possible to each of the *Flock* and *Random 5* videos from our human study for this purpose, and labelled them accordingly.

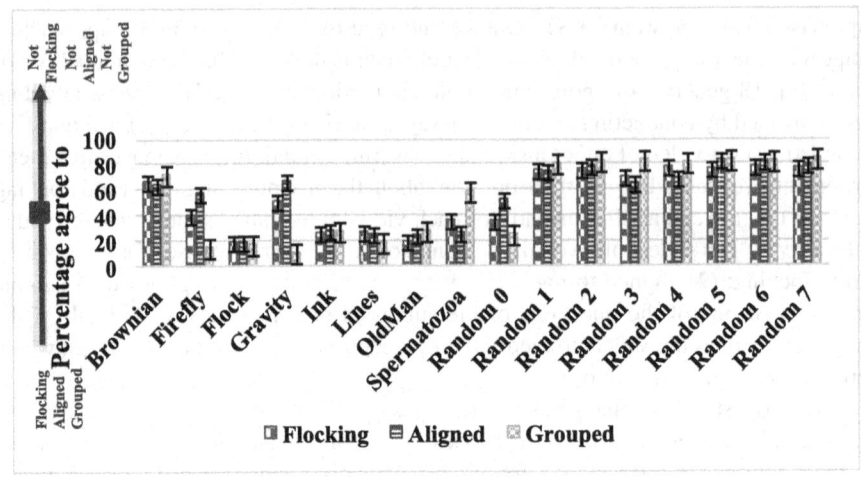

Fig. 2. Human results (n = 70) used to create data labels.

4   Experiments, Results and Discussion

4.1   Data Collection

The Pioneer3DX is a small two-wheel, two motor differential drive robot. Our simulated robots are equipped with 16 ultrasonic sensors as shown in Fig. 3. We used 8 robots in a 20 × 20 m open space. We created four types of simulation for this pilot study examining one type of flocking and one type of non-flocking: (1) as similar as possible to the *Flock* video (see Fig. 2) using the Braitenberg-Swarm hybrid, (2) as similar as possible to the *Flock* video using the Boid-Swarm algorithm, (3) as similar as possible to the *Random 5* video using the Braitenberg-Swarm hybrid and (4) as similar as possible to *Random 5* video using the Boid-Swarm algorithm. We created five variants of each simulation. The parameter values used to create these simulation scenarios are shown in Table 1 and Table 2.

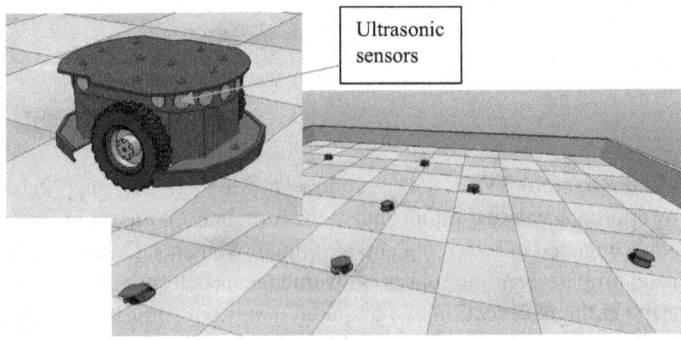

Fig. 3. 8 Pioneer3DX mobile robots in a 20× 220 m arena simulated in CoppeliaSim. Inset: view of a single robot sensor configuration.

Table 1. Simulation parameters and their values use to create the Boid-Swarm dataset.

Parameter	Boid-Swarm					Boid-Random				
Scenario	1	2	3	4	5	1	2	3	4	5
r_0	0.2	0.2	0.2	0.2	0.2	0.2	0.2	0.2	0.2	0.2
W_a	1.0	1.0	1.0	1.2	1.2	1.0	1.2	1.2	1.2	1.0
W_c	0.1	0.1	0.05	0.05	0.05	0.0	0.1	0.1	0.1	0.05
W_s	1.2	1.5	1.5	1.5	1.5	1.2	1.2	1.2	1.2	1.2
W_w	1.1	1.1	1.1	1.1	1.5	1.1	1.0	1.1	1.1	1.1
R_{ac}	2.0	2.0	2.0	2.0	2.0	2.0	2.0	1.0	1.0	1.0
R_s	1.0	1.0	1.0	1.5	1.0	1.0	2.0	2.0	1.0	1.0

Table 2. Simulation parameters and their values used to create the Braitenberg-Swarm dataset.

Parameter	Braitenberg-Swarm					Braitenberg-Random				
Scenario	1	2	3	4	5	1	2	3	4	5
r_0	0.2	0.2	0.2	0.2	0.2	0.2	0.2	0.2	0.2	0.2
W_a	0.5	0.6	0.6	0.6	0.5	0.0	0.0	0.0	0.01	0.01
W_c	0.01	0.01	0.02	0.02	0.01	0.0	0.0	0.01	0.01	0.0
W_s	n/a					n/a				
W_w	n/a					n/a				
R_{ac}	1.0	1.0	1.0	1.0	1.0	1.0	1.0	1.0	1.0	1.0
R_s	0.5	0.5	0.5	0.6	0.6	0.5	0.6	0.6	0.6	0.6

Each simulation was run for 10 min (approximately 12,000 simulation time steps). It took approximately 5 min for the *Flock* configurations to converge, after which they were run for a further 5 min. While the simulations were running, we collected the raw data shown in Eqs. 17–18, producing datasets of size $12,000 \times 8 = 96,000$ data instances for each simulation.

4.2 Results

Experiment 1—SVS1 on Boid-Swarm. In this experiment we use human labelled data described above as the training data of the supervised learning methods, and Boid-Swarm/Boid-Random robot data as the test set. Therefore, the test dataset was not seen during the training procedure. The results are provided in Table 3. We see that only the decision tree approach is able to accurately distinguish the robot swarm configurations from the random ones. This differs from supervised learning on point-mass data, where we found all approaches were able to recognise swarming with high accuracy [5]. The number of features of the Braitenberg dataset is different from human perception data, therefore we cannot use SVS1 on Braitenberg data.

Experiment 2—SVS2 on Boid-Swarm. In this experiment we used the Boid-Swarm/Boid-Random robot data as both training and test set of supervised learning methods. To do this, we ran a 10-fold cross validation on this data, such that in each run 90% of samples are considered as the training set and the rest of the unseen data is the test set. The mean accuracy over all 10 folds and the processing time of the supervised classifiers are presented in Table 3. The generally higher accuracy achieved in this experiment is because of the more similar natures of both training and test set. It confirms the viability of this approach to recognising swarming, as long as a source of labelled data is available.

Experiment 3—SVS2 on Braitenberg-Swarm Hybrid. In this experiment we ran the same procedure of Experiment 2 on the Braitenberg data. The mean value of the learning accuracy of learning methods is provided in Table 3. This result shows that the decision tree approach remains viable using this alternative BGA, although accuracy is reduced.

Table 3. Experimental results Experiments 1–3.

	Decision Tree	Naïve Bayes	Support Vector Machine	Bayesian Neural Network	Levenberg Neural Network	Gradient Neural Network
Expt 1 Accuracy (%)	**96.83**	57.40	53.36	77.24	62.00	51.75
Expt 1 Time (s)	1.42	552.72	643.89	14.33	4.22	7.84
Expt 2 Accuracy (%)	**99.11**	67.73	72.48	**99.22**	**99.22**	82.97
Expt 2 Time (s)	9.73	200	4000	193.14	38.26	37.84
Expt 3 Accuracy (%)	**92.67**	69.85	63.28	81.75	81.71	67.41
Expt 3 Time (s)	156.59	8000	2000	1000	262.33	324.92

Experiment 4—Unsupervised Value Systems on Boid-Swarm. In this experiment we used the Boid-Swarm/Boid-Random robot data as input to the SOM. Three variants of this data were used:

- UVS1 Raw data shown in Eq. 17/18
- UVS2 Derived neighbourhood velocity data shown in Eq. 19
- UVS3 Derived neighbourhood position data, shown in Eq. 20.

Table 4 shows that UVS2 and UVS3 produce a consistently lower mean QE for the swarming robot data than the random robot data. This indicates that the patterns of movement from swarming are recognizable using UVS2 and UVS3, but not UVS1.

Table 4. Mean QE when clustering data from the Boid simulations (Expt 4)

Scenario	Boid Flocking					Boid Random				
	1	2	3	4	5	1	2	3	4	5
UVS1	0.93	0.86	0.97	0.87	0.83	0.28	0.56	0.39	0.34	0.39
UVS2	0.46	0.43	0.45	0.41	0.36	0.70	0.73	0.67	0.79	0.67
UVS3	0.43	0.40	0.37	0.38	0.37	0.60	0.56	0.55	0.62	0.56

Experiment 5—Unsupervised Value Systems on Braitenberg-Swarm.
In this experiment we used the Braitenberg-Swarm/Braitenberg-Random robot data as input to the SOM. Three same three variants of this data from Experiment 4 were used. Table 5 shows that UVS2 and UVS3 again produce a consistently lower mean QE for the flocking data than the random data. This indicates that the patterns of movement from flocking are recognizable using UVS2 and UVS3 only.

Table 5. Mean QE when clustering data from the Braitenberg simulations (Expt 5)

Scenario	Braitenberg Flocking					Braitenberg Random				
	1	2	3	4	5	1	2	3	4	5
UVS1	0.53	0.42	0.37	0.47	0.53	0.07	0.07	0.19	0.28	0.14
UVS2	0.28	0.29	0.29	0.32	0.30	0.53	0.52	0.52	0.51	0.50
UVS3	0.22	0.24	0.26	0.26	0.24	0.42	0.45	0.46	0.42	0.42

5   Conclusion and Future Work

In this paper, five value functions were examined and compared for their ability to distinguish swarming behaviour from unstructured behaviour. Results showed that four of these can be used to distinguish structured collective behaviours of the robots and distinguish such behaviour from random movement patterns. Specifically:

- Of the unsupervised techniques, the two using data derived from the movement of neighbouring boids (UVS2 and UVS3) were the most successful in recognizing swarming, as indicated by lower QE values.

- Of the supervised techniques, decision tree learning has consistently the highest accuracy, and it is more accurate when trained and tested on robot data (SVS2).
- However, it is also possible for a decision tree trained on human labelled point-mass boid data to recognize swarming robots, although with lower accuracy.

In future, we will evaluate these functions on a wider range of flocking and not-flocking scenarios. We then aim to embed the most successful of these value functions into an evolutionary developmental framework (such as described in [4]) to evolve swarm behaviours on real robots.

References

1. Kolling, A., Walker, P., Chakraborty, N.: Human interaction with robot swarms: a survey. IEEE Trans. Hum. Mach. Syst. **64**(1), 9–26 (2016)
2. Reynolds, C.W.: Flocks, herds and schools: a distributed behavioral model. In: Computer Graphics (SIGGRAPH 1987 Conference Proceedings), vol. 21, no. 4, pp. 25–34 (1987)
3. Clark, J., Jacques, D.: Flight test results for UAVs using boid guidance algorithms. New Challenges in Systems Engineering and Architecting Conference on Systems Engineering Research (CSER), pp. 232–238. Elsevier, St. Louis (2012)
4. Khan, M., Kasmarik, K., Barlow, M.: Autonomous detection of collective behaviours in swarms. Swarm and Evolutionary Computation (2020). (to appear)
5. Abpeikar, S., et al.: Machine Recognition of Different Types of Artificial Flocking Behaviours using Supervised Learning (2020). (under review)
6. Sperati, V., Baldassare, G.: Bio-inspired model learning visual goals and attention skills through contingencies and intrinsic motivations. IEEE Trans. Cogn. Dev. Syst. **10**(2), 326–344 (2018)
7. Santucci, V., Baldassare, G., Mirolli, M.: GRAIL: a goal-discovering robotic architecture for intrinsically-motivated learning. IEEE Trans. Cogn. Dev. Syst. **8**(3), 214–231 (2016)
8. Huang, X., Weng, J.: Inherent value systems for autonomous mental development. Int. J. Humanoid Rob. **4**(2), 407–433 (2007)
9. Frank, M., et al.: Curiosity driven reinforcement learning for motion planning on humanoids. Front. Neurorobot. **7**, 25 (2014)
10. Merrick, K.: A comparative study of value systems for self-motivated exploration and learning by robots. IEEE Trans. Auton. Ment. Dev. **2**(2), 119–131 (2010). Special Issue on Active Learning and Intrinsically Motivated Exploration in Robots
11. Oudeyer, P.-Y., Kaplan, F., Hafner, V.V.: Intrinsic motivation systems for autonomous mental development. IEEE Trans. Evol. Comput. **11**(2), 265–286 (2007)
12. Merrick, K., Maher, M.L.: Motivated Reinforcement Learning: Curious Characters for Multiuser Games. In: Nugent, R. (Ed.). Springer, Heidelberg (2009). https://doi.org/10.1007/978-3-540-89187-1
13. Merrick, K.: Value systems for developmental cognitive robotics: a survey. Cogn. Syst. Res. **41**, 38–55 (2017)
14. Bredeche, N., Haasdijk, E., Prieto, A.: Embodied evolution in collective robotics: a review. Front. Robot. AI **5**, 12 (2018)
15. Samarasinghe, D., et al.,: Automatic synthesis of swarm behavioural rules from their atomic components. In: GECCO2018, pp. 133–140 (2018)
16. Fischer, D., Mostaghim, S., Albantakis, L.: How swarm size during evolution impacts the behavior, generalizability, and brain complexity of animats performing a spatial navigation task. In: GECCO2018, pp. 77–84 (2018)

17. Hamann, H.: Evolution of collective behaviours by minimizing surprise. In: ALIFE2014 (2014)
18. Gomes, J., Urbano, P., Christensen, A.: Evolution of swarm robotics systems with novelty search. Swarm Intell. **7**(203), 115–144 (2013)
19. Braitenberg, V.: Vehicles: Experiments in Synthetic Psychology. MIT Press, Cambridge (1984)
20. Kasmarik, K., et al.: Swarm Behaviour Data Set. UCI Machine Learning Repository (2020). http://archive.ics.uci.edu/ml/datasets/Swarm+Behaviour
21. Paluszek, M., Thomas, S.: MATLAB Machine Learning. Apress, New York (2016)

Exploring a Learning Architecture
for General Game Playing

Alvaro Gunawan[1], Ji Ruan[1(✉)], Michael Thielscher[2], and Ajit Narayanan[1]

[1] Auckland University of Technology, Auckland, New Zealand
{alvarogunawan,jiruan,ajitnarayanan}@aut.ac.nz
[2] University of New South Wales, Sydney, Australia
mit@unsw.edu.au

Abstract. General Game Playing (GGP) is a platform for developing general Artificial Intelligence algorithms to play a large variety of games that are unknown to players in advance. This paper describes and analyses GGPZero, a learning architecture for GGP, inspired by the success of AlphaGo and AlphaZero. GGPZero takes as input a previously unknown game description and constructs a deep neural network to be trained using self-play together with Monte-Carlo Tree Search. The general architecture of GGPZero is similar to that of Goldwaser and Thielscher (2020) [4] with the main differences in the choice of the GGP reasoner and the neural network construction; furthermore, we explore additional experimental evaluation strategies. Our main contributions are: confirming the feasibility of deep reinforcement for GGP, analysing the impact of the type and depth of the underlying neural network, and investigating simulation vs. time limitations on training.

Keywords: General Game Playing · Machine learning · Reinforcement learning · Neural networks

1   Introduction

The recent accomplishments of DeepMind's AlphaGo [9] have reignited interest in game-playing Artificial Intelligence, showing the effectiveness of Monte-Carlo Tree Search (MCTS) with deep neural networks and learning through self-play. Further work on AlphaGo Zero [11] showed that this method was effective even without any human expert knowledge, and in fact able to defeat their previous AlphaGo agent despite learning from effectively zero knowledge apart from the games rules. This method of learning to play a new game was extended beyond Go to AlphaZero [10] for learning to play Chess and Shogi with effectively the same architecture.

In the same vein as AlphaZero, General Game Playing (GGP) proposes a challenge: developing agents that are able to play any game, given a general set of rules [6]. GGP uses a logical language known as Game Description Language (GDL) to represent rules of arbitrary games. These game descriptions are

© Springer Nature Switzerland AG 2020
M. Gallagher et al. (Eds.): AI 2020, LNAI 12576, pp. 294–306, 2020.
https://doi.org/10.1007/978-3-030-64984-5_23

a combination of a knowledge base containing static rules and a state containing dynamic facts. This raises the natural question whether the same methods that AlphaZero uses to learn to play Go, Chess and Shogi can be applied to general games described in GDL. This was recently addressed with Generalised AlphaZero [4], a system that applies deep reinforcement learning to GGP. While the overarching approach outlined by AlphaZero provides a general architecture for a self-play learning agent, there are a few key limitations that had to be overcome for this purpose:

- AlphaZero assumes the games are two-player, turn-taking and zero-sum.
- Neural network architectures are hand-crafted for each game, encoding features such as board geometry.
- As a result of the specialised neural networks, the agents have some form of implicit domain knowledge for each game.

In the domain of GGP, games are neither required to be two-player, turn-taking nor zero-sum so that a GGP agent must be able to account for games with any number of players, simultaneous action games and non-zero-sum games. With regard to the second point, the agent must also be able to generate a neural network for any given game description, without requiring any additional modification from a human. Finally, the system should be general for any game with no specialised domain knowledge at all. In this paper, we complement the recent work on Generalised AlphaZero [4] as a system to overcome these limitations in an AlphaZero-style self-play reinforcement learning agent designed to learn games in the GGP setting. Our main contributions lie in the further exploration of this learning architecture:

- We confirm the feasibility of deep reinforcement for GGP under different settings, including the use of a different GGP reasoner.
- We analyse the impact of type and depth of the underlying neural network.
- We investigate simulation vs. time limitations on training.

The rest of this paper is organized as follows. Section 2 summarises related works in applying learning to GGP including Generalised AlphaZero. Section 3 describes the architecture of our self-play reinforcement learning agent, GGPZero. In the extensive Sect. 4 we present the results of our experiments, showing the agent's capabilities in a variety of games as well as an in-depth examination in the agent's architecture, followed by a concluding discussion in Sect. 5.

2   Related Work

Research in applying reinforcement learning based approaches to GGP began with the framework RL-GGP [1] that integrates a GGP server and a standard framework for reinforcement learning RL-Glue. No implementation of a full agent is provided, making it difficult to assess performance. QM-learning [14] combines Q-learning with MCTS, and integrates it within GGP. The performance of the agent is evaluated on three small board games. However, this method is still effectively only an on-line search method, using Q-learning to optimise MCTS. The recent GGP agent [3] implements an AlphaZero-style learning component that exhibits strong performance in several games, but requiring hand-crafted convolutional neural networks for these games. Generalised AlphaZero [4] implements a Deep Reinforcement Learning framework for GGP that shows strong performance in several games but weak performance in a cooperative game. The above-mentioned restrictions of AlphaZero were overcome by extending the policy-value network with move probabilities and expected rewards for all players in an n-person game. Furthermore, a general propositional reasoner to process arbitrary GDL game rules was used as input to the neural network, thus overcoming the reliance on a board and a handcrafted neural network. In this paper we use a similar architecture to that of [4] but with the main differences in the choice of the GGP reasoner, the neural network construction and the experimental evaluation. In particular, we allow a manual setting of the neural network depth to allow for further investigations into the agent's behaviour, which was only done in a limited manner in [4].

3   GGP Learning Agent Architecture

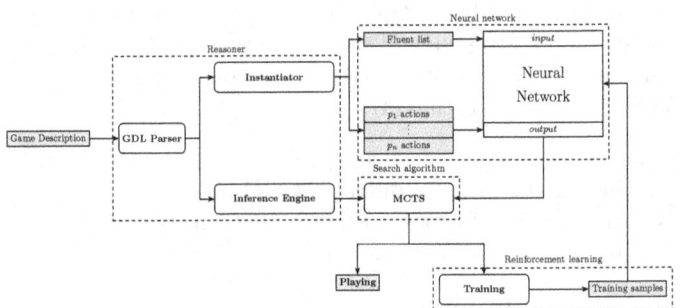

Fig. 1. Architecture of GGPZero agent.

The overall architecture of our system GGPZero (Fig. 1) consists of four main components, each made up of smaller subcomponents. This first component is the reasoner, which takes the GDL description and processes it to generate the neural network and conduct inference during play. The second component is the neural network, which is used as a policy and utility estimator for the search algorithm. The third component is the search algorithm, using both neural network estimation and MCTS for policy generation. Finally, the self-play reinforcement learning component is used to train the neural network with training samples generated by the search algorithm.

While GGPZero's architecture is similar to that of AlphaZero, there are two key differences. Firstly, as the GGP platform requires the agent to infer the rules of a game from a GDL description without human aid, the agent requires a reasoner to do this inference. Secondly, we use the reasoner's instantiated fluent and action lists to automatically generate the neural network, as we cannot rely on hand-crafted neural network architectures for the more general setting of GGP. Additionally, the search algorithm and reinforcement training have been designed with the GGP setting in mind, as the games may have an arbitrary number of players and are not strictly zero-sum. The rest of this section will provide more detail on each individual component of the GGPZero architecture.

Reasoner. The GDL parser takes as input a game described in GDL and converts it into appropriate representations for the instantiator and the inference engine. The instantiator generates the sets of possible *fluents* (dynamic predicates that are true for a given state) and possible actions, using the method described in [12,13]. The inference engine is used by MCTS to infer facts about the game such as legal moves, subsequent states, terminal conditions and utility values. There are two main inference methods: Prolog-based and Propositional network (Propnet) based [8]. A Prolog-based method converts the GDL rules to an equivalent Prolog representation and uses an off-the-shelf Prolog reasoner for inference. In our paper, we use the Prolog-based inference engine as described in [12,13] for its greater generality, while a Propnet-based inference method is used in Generalised AlphaZero [4]. While this is more efficient than a Prolog-based method, Propnets are not applicable to some larger games as the grounding process can be intractable. Additionally, to improve the efficiency of the agent, we save the results of queries. This allows repeated visits to states during the MCTS to be more efficient, especially as the neural network will tend to prefer certain optimal states and actions after sufficient training.

Neural Network. The neural network takes a fluent vector as input. The vector has length equal to the total number of all fluents possible in the game, and each index corresponds to a single fluent. For an input vector $V = (a_1, a_2, \ldots, a_n)$ and a state consisting of fluents in the set $S \subseteq \{a_1, \ldots, a_n\}$, the value of element $a_i = 1$ if $a_i \in S$, otherwise $a_i = 0$. The neural network outputs for each player a normalised policy vector for player's actions and the estimated goal value.

The neural network architecture is automatically generated based on the game description and a network depth parameter. The input and hidden layers are generated as fully connected layers with ReLU activation with width equal to the number of fluents, and depth equal to the network depth parameter. For the output layers, a number of output heads are generated equal to the number of players. Each output head is then further split into an estimated policy and an estimated goal value. The number of nodes in the policy output layer is equal to the number of actions possible for the given player and the estimated goal value is a single output node.

Unlike the large, convolutional neural network used in AlphaZero, the neural network used in GGPZero uses fully connected layers and is comparatively small. One advantage of this approach is that games described in GDL are not guaranteed to be easily represented with a board-like structure, such as a matrix in the case of the CNN in AlphaZero. Additionally, we use smaller networks for prioritizing of rapid experimentation and to identify the limits of this approach that may then lead to the need for more complex deep learning approaches.

Search Algorithm. The search algorithm outputs the finalised policy vector to be used in play and self-play reinforcement training. It uses a *simultaneous action* MCTS [5] that is able to accommodate multi-player, general sum games with simultaneous actions. Rather than using random playouts during the expansion phase, the search algorithm uses the neural network's estimator to evaluate the value of a newly expanded state. Additionally, the policy generated by the neural network is considered during the selection phase. As a result, a modified form of upper confidence bound on trees $U(s, a)$ is used as the selection strategy:

$$U(s, a) = Q(s, a) + C_{uct} \cdot P(s, a) \cdot \frac{\sqrt{N(s)}}{1 + N(s, a)}$$

where $Q(s, a)$ is the estimated goal value, $P(s, a)$ is the estimated policy, $N(s)$ is a node count of state s, $N(s, a)$ is the action count of a at s, and C_{uct} is a weight constant for the exploration factor which can be set as a parameter.

Reinforcement Learning. The agent is tasked with learning an optimal policy for a game by training the neural network to improve its approximation of the function $f^*(s) = (\mathbf{V}, \mathbf{\Psi})$, where $\mathbf{V}$ is the estimated utility and $\mathbf{\Psi}$ is the estimated policy. The neural network with weights $\boldsymbol{\theta}$ is trained on the policy estimated through $MCTS(s; \boldsymbol{\theta})$. In essence, the agent uses the neural network guided MCTS to continuously improve the neural network only through iterations of self-play. A single iteration of learning has 3 distinct phases:

- **Self-play**: generate training examples using MCTS with the current best network weights $\boldsymbol{\theta}_{best}$.
- **Training**: train the current best neural network with new examples generated during self-play.
- **Evaluation**: compare the performance of the newly trained network $\boldsymbol{\theta}_{new}$ against the current best network $\boldsymbol{\theta}_{best}$. If $\boldsymbol{\theta}_{new}$ outperforms the current $\boldsymbol{\theta}_{best}$, then $\boldsymbol{\theta}_{best}$ is updated by $\boldsymbol{\theta}_{new}$.

To generate training examples for the neural network, the agent plays episodes of self-play games against itself. The policy generated by the MCTS is used as the training target for the policy vector, while the actual goal value at the terminal state of a game play is used as the training target for the estimated goal value. The neural network is trained by minimising the sum of the following, across all players for a training example: (1) **mean squared error** between the neural network estimated goal values and the self-play terminal goal values; (b) **cross entropy** of the neural network estimated policy and the MCTS generated policy.

4   Experimental Studies and Results

We first present an evaluation of the GGPZero agent on five games: Tic-Tac-Toe, Connect-Four, Breakthrough, Pacman3p and Babel, followed by further experiments to evaluate various key aspects of the architecture. The selection of games is similar to [4] with a mixture of complexity levels and game types. We have three benchmark agents for these evaluations: a random agent (RANDOM) that samples uniformly from legal actions, a neural-network based agent (NN), which uses the network of GGPZero without MCTS search, and a MCTS based agent (MCTS). Where applicable, these benchmark agents are given the same parameters as GGPZero.[1]

All experiments are conducted on a machine with an Intel Xeon E5-1630v4 3.7 10M 2400 4C CPU, 128 GB RAM and NVIDIA GeForce GTX1080 8 GB.

4.1   Game Evaluation

Performance on Two-Player Zero-Sum Games. The following Table 1 shows the performance of GGPZero (with 20 layers and 1000 training iterations) against three benchmark agents in three games with increasing complexity. The results are shown in the format of (Win/Lose/Draw):

Table 1. Results of GGPZero on two-player zero-sum games. GGPZero and MCTS are given the same simulation limit of 50.

Game	Opponent agent (Win/Lose/Draw)		
	RANDOM	NN	MCTS
Tic-Tac-Toe	91/0/9	93/0/7	11/27/62
Connect-Four	97/3/0	71/29/0	56/43/1
Breakthrough	100/0/0	73/27/0	86/14/0

GGPZero performs well in these games, and these games follow a similar format to the games that AlphaZero were trained and played on. However, unlike AlphaZero, the training of these agents is completely end-to-end, not requiring hand-crafted features for any particular game. Interestingly, GGPZero performs better on the more complex games, e.g., winning only 11% against the MCTS agent in Tic-Tac-Toe, while winning 86% in Breakthrough. This is likely due to the fact that the less complex games have state spaces small enough for the other agents to still be competitive in.

---

[1] All components are implemented in Python, with Prolog components using the SWI-Prolog interpreter with PySWIP as a bridge. We base our implementation of the MCTS on the code provided in [7].

Performance on Non-Two-Player General-Sum Games. Games such as Pac-man3p and Babel highlight the challenge presented by GGP, as they are asymmetric, multi-player and general sum games. We show that GGPZero is able to learn to play these games, albeit with limited performance compared to the two-player, zero-sum case. The following Table 2 shows the goal value of the agents playing 20 games. E.g., the first row shows that role pacman is played by MCTS obtaining score 1.96, and two ghosts are played by RANDOM, obtaining score 8, while the third row shows that GGPZero gets score 2.34 in a similar setting. We can see that GGPZero (with 5 layers and 300 training iterations) outperforms MCTS.

Table 2. Total goal value of various agents playing 20 games of Pacman3p

Agents	pacman	two ghosts	pacman score	two ghosts score
MCTS vs RANDOM	MCTS	RANDOM	1.96	8
	RANDOM	MCTS	1.12	10
GGPZero vs RANDOM	GGPZero	RANDOM	2.34	7
	RANDOM	GGPZero	0.66	10
GGPZero vs MCTS	GGPZero	MCTS	1.53	10
	MCTS	GGPZero	0.79	10

The next experiment is on the game of Babel, a three-player, simultaneous, cooperative tower-building game. 100 games are played for each agent acting three roles in the game. RANDOM gets an average goal value of 0.122, MCTS gets 0.777, GGPZero (with 20 layers and 100 training iterations) gets 0.443, and GGPZero (with 20 layers and 500 training iterations) gets 0.638. We can see GGPZero performs better than RANDOM but worse than MCTS. Similar results are obtained in [4]. This shows a limitation of the current architecture in dealing with this type of games.

4.2 Varying Neural Network Depth

Systematic experiments were used to investigate the effects of the Neural Network depth on agent performance by varying the number of hidden layers and the training iterations. To do so we set up agents with 1, 5, 10, 20, 50 and 100 layers and each agent plays 100 games against every other agent. We also select 20 iterations and 100 iterations as the amount of trainings are given to these agents. These experiments were carried out with the game Connect-Four.

Figure 2a shows that increasing the number of hidden layers causes the total training time to increase linearly, and that training 100 iterations takes proportionally more time under different layers. Figure 2b shows the winning rate by each agent over 500 games (100 games against each other agent). With 20 iterations of training, the agent with 10 layers has the best winning rate, while with 100 iterations of training, the agent with 20 layers has the best winning rate. Overall, this shows that smaller networks generally perform better with less training, while larger networks perform better with more training. This is likely due to the fact that larger networks suffer from underfitting with insufficient training while smaller networks suffer from overfitting. The former can be seen with the 100 layer agent after 20 iterations: the policy generated by the neural network is typically a flat distribution across all actions.

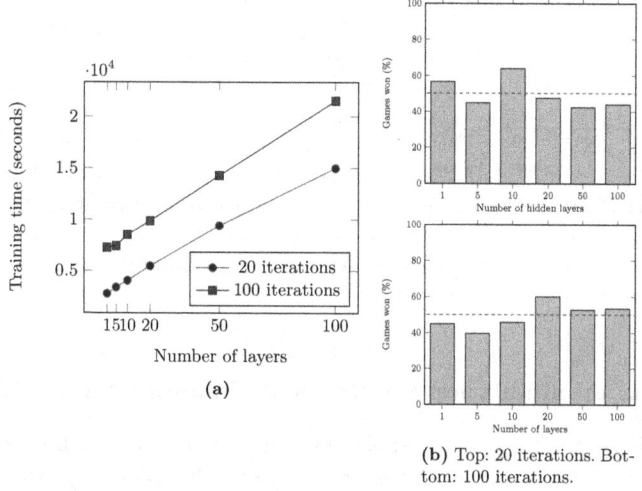

Fig. 2. (a): Training time for GGPZero with varying number of hidden layers. (b): Winning rate of GGPZero with varying number of hidden layers.

4.3   Convolutional Neural Network Experiments

While the agent with a fully-connected neural network showed good performance when playing against the benchmarks, we would like to investigate the stability of the training method with regard to winning outcomes. We tested the agents with different training iterations, under the assumption that an agent with more iterations will have more success than an agent with fewer iterations. Figure 3 shows that the agent with a convolutional neural network increases its win rate to above 60% with increasing iterations, whereas a fully connected network reaches optimal win rate of just under 54% relatively early in learning with more fluctuations later on. This is likely due to the fully connected network overfitting its parameters.

For zero-sum games such as Connect-Four, we would ideally prefer an agent that increases in performance with additional training. As Connect-Four is solved, we know that there is an optimal strategy for the game. While GGPZero will most likely be unable to learn this optimal strategy with the limited training time that it is provided, we would like to see the agent continuously improve, eventually converging to the optimal strategy towards the limit.

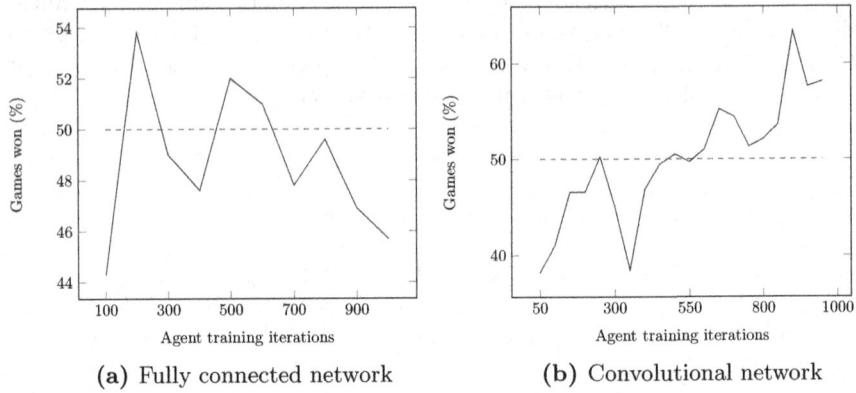

(a) Fully connected network   **(b)** Convolutional network

Fig. 3. Winning rates by agents with different training iterations in Game Connect-Four.

4.4   Effects on Simulation-Limited and Time-Limited MCTS

In this section, we compare the effects of simulation and time limitation on the GGPZero and MCTS during the game play. For the following experiments, we use the game Breakthrough as it has a large state space and branching factor. For GGPZero, we look at 5 versions with training iterations from 200 to 1000.

Simulation Limited. In the prior experiments and test games, we use a *simulation limited* variant of MCTS. When selecting an action to play, the agents (both GGPZero and MCTS) perform a limited number of simulations, expanding the search tree. After completing these simulations, the action policy is then generated. We use this variant of MCTS to reduce the impact of the inference engine's efficiency on the performance of the agent, allowing both GGPZero and MCTS agent to search a similar amount of the game states. Increasing the simulation limit allows the agents to search more extensively, potentially leading to better performance at the cost of slower action selection. This is especially evident with the MCTS agent, as the playout phase requires extensive use of the inference engine. GGPZero is able to circumvent this computationally taxing operation by using the neural network.

Figure 4a shows the GGPZero's winning rate against MCTS when simulation limit varies from 50 to 300. For GGPZero with 1000 training iterations, it clearly outperforms the MCTS when the simulation limit is low, but loses out when the limit increases. A similar trend can be seen for GGPZero with 600 and 800 iterations. This result is not entirely unexpected as the strategy generated by the MCTS agent begins to approach the Nash equilibrium when the number of simulations performed increases. While for GGPZero with lower training iterations, the winning rate stays relatively flat and is generally worse than the MCTS. This suggests that when GGPZero's training is insufficient, the MCTS component inside GGPZero is not as effective as the pure MCTS agent due to the limitation of the neural network.

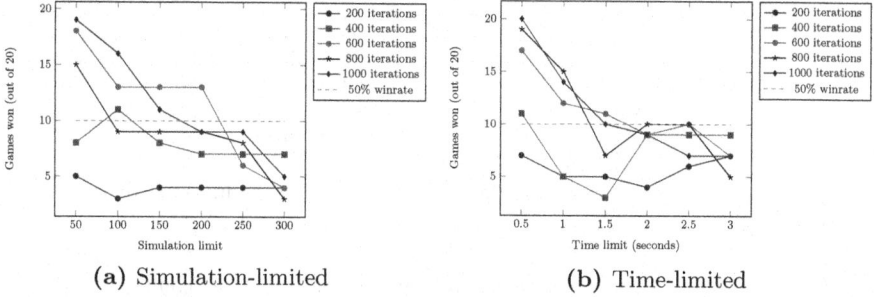

(a) Simulation-limited   **(b)** Time-limited

Fig. 4. GGPZero winning rate against MCTS with increasing time and simulation limits with varying amounts of training iterations on Breakthrough games.

Time Limited. In the usual GGP format, actions must be selected under a limited time budget ranging between 10 to 90 s, depending on the complexity of the game. As a result, most GGP agents favour using a time-limited variant of MCTS, performing as many simulations as possible in a limited time frame before generating their action policies. In the next set of experiments, we set time limits from 0.5 s to 3 s to examine the effects of time limit. Figure 4b presents GGPZero's winning rate against MCTS under different time limit. For the GGPZero with 1000 training iterations, it significantly outperforms the MCTS agent when the time limit is short, but performs worse when the time limit increases. Similar trend is shown in GGPZero with 600 or 800 iterations, but less so in GGPZero with 200 or 400 iterations. These results are consistent with the simulation-limited case in Fig. 4a.

We further examined the simulation numbers under different time limits and during different stage of the game play. Figure 5a shows that as the time limit increases, the average number of simulations of the MCTS agent does not increase as rapidly as that of the GGPZero. Despite that, the MCTS agent still performs better when given a longer time limit. Note that GGPZero with different training iterations performs similar numbers of simulations within the same time limit. This is due to the fact that the neural network can be seen as an $O(1)$ operation regardless of the amount of training; there is no trade-off with regard to efficiency when using a more trained agent.

In the time limited scenario, another aspect to consider is the varying amount of time required to perform search at different stage of the game. Although in

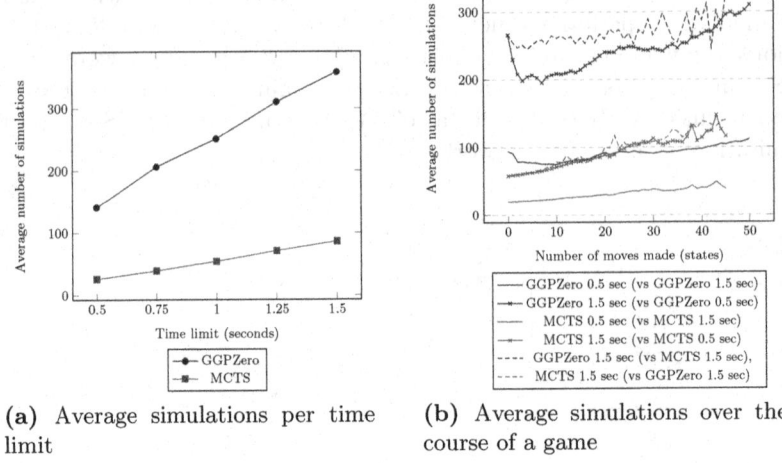

(a) Average simulations per time limit

(b) Average simulations over the course of a game

Fig. 5. Average number of simulations completed by agents

Fig. 5a we see that the MCTS agent has significantly less *average simulations* throughout the course of a game, we see in Fig. 5b that as the game progresses, the average number of simulations tends to increase for all agents. This is likely due to the search more likely visiting terminal states as it progresses through the game, causing simulations to finish earlier. In the case of the MCTS agent, this early stopping by finding terminal states presents a significant reduction in simulation time, as it does not require the search to enter the playout phase.

To conclude, in both the simulation-limited and time-limited settings, we see that GGPZero with enough training significantly outperforms the standard MCTS agent when given a strict simulation or time limit. However, this difference in performance diminishes and eventually is reversed once these limits are large enough. From these observations, we can view the trained neural network as a form of *compression*, replacing the computationally expensive playout phase with a neural network. The quality of this compression is in part affected by the amount of training provided to the agent but also by the architecture of the neural network itself. As we saw in Subsect. 4.3, the convolutional neural network had better and more stable performance than the fully connected neural network when given sufficient training. The final comment is that the neural network with limited training can also be a limiting factor for the MCTS component in the GGPZero, as when giving a longer time limit, the pure MCTS agent can always outperform the GGPZero as in our experiments.

5   Conclusion and Future Work

We described GGPZero, an AlphaZero-style self-play reinforcement learning agent and implementation, designed to learn games in the GGP setting. While the architecture was inspired by the recent Generalised AlphaZero [4], the main differences are in the choice of GGP reasoner and the neural network construction; furthermore we carried out systematic experimental evaluation of various aspects of the use of deep reinforcement learning for GGP. Our main contribution is in the exploration of this learning architecture: confirming its feasibility, the impact of neural network depth, types of network, and simulation vs. time limitation on training. The experiments with network architectures have shown that the agent scales well in terms of both efficiency and effectiveness. More powerful hardware will allow us to take advantage of deeper neural networks. These more complex network architectures have been shown to be more effective for games such as Connect-Four, given sufficient training.

To further improve the overall performance of the agent, the current implementation could be improved by parallelising several components. Firstly, training could be parallelised to allow for multiple games to be played concurrently, allowing for either faster training times or more extensive training within the same timescale. Secondly, the MCTS itself could be parallelised [2]—however, the selection of which parallelisation method to use must be investigated within the context of the agent's architecture.

Another possible improvement to the agent is to use larger and deeper network sizes for all games. As the experiments show, deeper networks with more training tended to have better performance than shallower networks. The current trends in machine learning seem to indicate that larger networks are a reasonable approach for improving overall performance, given sufficient training is available.

The Babel results show that the agent is capable of learning and playing games that are not zero-sum, turn-taking or two-player. This means that GGP-Zero is able to generalise beyond the games that AlphaZero was able to play. However, we also see that a pure MCTS agent still outperforms GGPZero in this game. Further investigation is required into the nature of the training method itself, as it may have limitations when learning to play more general games.

While the current method for generating neural network architectures is general, it still requires a separate neural network for each game. This method is still effective in playing games, but can be argued to not be truly general, as each network is specialised for each game. A more general neural network architecture that can be used for any game would be ideal, but two key challenges still stand: (1) what kind of general game state representation can be used for the input to the neural network and (2) what is the appropriate learned and generalized representation for transfer to another architecture?

References

1. Benacloch-Ayuso, J.L.: RL-GGP (2012). http://users.dsic.upv.es/~flip/RLGGP
2. Chaslot, G.M.J.-B., Winands, M.H.M., van den Herik, H.J.: Parallel Monte-Carlo tree search. In: van den Herik, H.J., Xu, X., Ma, Z., Winands, M.H.M. (eds.) CG 2008. LNCS, vol. 5131, pp. 60–71. Springer, Heidelberg (2008). https://doi.org/10.1007/978-3-540-87608-3_6
3. Emslie, R.: Galvanise zero (2017). https://github.com/richemslie/galvanise_zero

4. Goldwaser, A., Thielscher, M.: Deep reinforcement learning for general game playing. In: AAAI, pp. 1701–1708 (2020)
5. Lanctot, M., Lisý, V., Winands, M.H.M.: Monte Carlo tree search in simultaneous move games with applications to Goofspiel. In: Cazenave, T., Winands, M.H.M., Iida, H. (eds.) CGW 2013. CCIS, vol. 408, pp. 28–43. Springer, Cham (2014). https://doi.org/10.1007/978-3-319-05428-5_3
6. Love, N., Hinrichs, T., Haley, D., Schkufza, E., Genesereth, M.: General game playing: game description language specification (2008)
7. Nair, S.: A simple alpha(go) zero tutorial (2017). https://web.stanford.edu/~surag/posts/alphazero.html
8. Schkufza, E., Love, N., Genesereth, M.: Propositional automata and cell automata: representational frameworks for discrete dynamic systems. In: Wobcke, W., Zhang, M. (eds.) AI 2008. LNCS (LNAI), vol. 5360, pp. 56–66. Springer, Heidelberg (2008). https://doi.org/10.1007/978-3-540-89378-3_6
9. Silver, D., et al.: Mastering the game of go with deep neural networks and tree search. Nature **529**(7587), 484 (2016)
10. Silver, D., et al.: Mastering chess and shogi by self-play with a general reinforcement learning algorithm. arXiv preprint arXiv:1712.01815 (2017)
11. Silver, D., et al.: Mastering the game of go without human knowledge. Nature **550**(7676), 354 (2017)
12. Vittaut, J.-N., Méhat, J.: Efficient grounding of game descriptions with tabling. In: Cazenave, T., Winands, M.H.M., Björnsson, Y. (eds.) CGW 2014. CCIS, vol. 504, pp. 105–118. Springer, Cham (2014). https://doi.org/10.1007/978-3-319-14923-3_8
13. Vittaut, J.N., Méhat, J.: Fast instantiation of GGP game descriptions using prolog with tabling. In: ECAI, vol. 14, pp. 1121–1122 (2014)
14. Wang, H., Emmerich, M., Plaat, A.: Monte Carlo q-learning for general game playing. CoRR abs/1802.05944. http://arxiv.org/abs/1802.05944 (2018)

Behavioural Equivalence of Game Descriptions

Dongmo Zhang[(✉)]

Western Sydney University, Penrith, Australia
d.zhang@westernsydney.edu.au

Abstract. Game description language is a logical language designed for General Game Playing. The language is highly expressive so that, in theory, all finite-state games with perfect information and deterministic actions can be described. However, a game can be described in different ways and the way of description can dramatically affect behaviour of general game players. This paper investigates the relationships of game models and game descriptions. We first introduce the concept of sub-model bisimulation to filter out unreachable states while maintain the nature of a game. We then define equivalence of game descriptions in the sense that two game descriptions are equivalent if the described games behaviourally the same. The concept of game equivalency, which breaks through logical equivalency, sets a boundary for reformulation of game descriptions. Finally we use a well-known strategy game, Hex Game, to demonstrate how to verify equivalence of game descriptions.

1 Motivation

Many recent advances in Artificial Intelligence (AI) have fundamentally changed our beliefs about what a machine can do. We have witnessed a number of AI systems that outperformed the best of human experts on a number of intellectually challenging tasks, such as Chess, Go and Poker [1–4]. However, *"many scientists in AI are motivated by a desire for generality. Their emphasis is not on achieving strong performance on a particular game but rather on understanding the general ability to produce strength on a wider variety of games (or problems in general)"* [5,6]. Along with many other efforts towards general problem-solving systems, *General Game Playing* (GGP) aims to build AI systems capable of playing any formally-described games without preset game-specific knowledge [7,8].

To describe a game to an autonomous computer player, a formal language, called *game description language* (GDL), was developed as the official language for the *AAAI General Game Playing Competition* [9]. As a logical language, GDL is highly expressive so that, in theory, it can describe all finite-state games with perfect information and deterministic actions, including Checkers, Chess, Go and many others. However, a game can be described in different ways and the way of descriptions can dramatically affect the behaviour of general game players [10]. This has been observed at the previous GGP competitions, which

© Springer Nature Switzerland AG 2020
M. Gallagher et al. (Eds.): AI 2020, LNAI 12576, pp. 307–319, 2020.
https://doi.org/10.1007/978-3-030-64984-5_24

featured several games that were described by two syntactically different sets of rules – a computationally-friendly description used by the Game Manager to run a competition and a "raw description" for GGP players to play the games. It was observed that some "badly described" games, typically involving recursive definitions, can be extremely hard for GGP players to reason about. Therefore a successful player must be able to automatically reformulate game descriptions in order to improve its efficiency [11,12].

Reformulation of a game description to satisfy a certain property, say no recursion, while maintaining the nature of the described games is not necessarily an easy job. In most cases, simply rewriting the rules while maintaining logical equivalence is insufficient as we will see later from the examples of Hex game. In fact, we have great flexibility to vary game descriptions. A game can be described in very different ways as long as they can lead to a game in the same way to play. For examples, [13] shows two variations of Tic-Tac-Toe game: *Number Scrabble* and *JAM* (see Fig. 1 for JAM game). Obviously descriptions for Number Scrabble and JAM games can be logically inequivalent to the one for Tic-Tac-Toe. As long as these descriptions induce a game player behaviourally the same, we can view them equivalent. One may think that two game descriptions are equivalent if their models are bisimilar. However, modal satisfaction is invariant under bisimilation. GDL is essentially a modal language [14]. Thus a GDL description is also invariant under bisimulation, which means that bisimulation is too strong to be considered as the condition of game equivalence. This paper will introduce a concept called *submodel bisimulation*, which is weaker than bisimilation and logical equivalence. Based on this concept, we introduce the concept of behavioural equivalence of game descriptions.

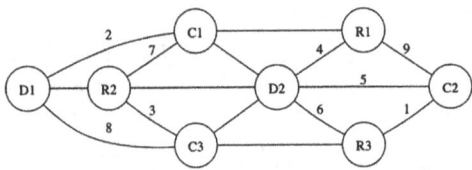

Fig. 1. JAM game - Each of two players alternately selects one road until one of them has occupied all three roads leading into a crossing and wins. Each road is labeled with a number, which can be extended to other crossings with unlabeled segments of the road. For instance, D_1C_2, R_2C_2, D_2C_2 all belong road 5.

This paper is arranged as follows. Section 2 briefly describes the language, semantics and basic properties of game descriptions. Section 3 introduces the concept of submodel bisimulation. Section 4 applies the concept to game descriptions and demonstrate how to use our approach to prove game equivalence. Finally we conclude the paper with comments on the future work. Due to space limit, we omit the proof of some theorems.

2 Game Description Language and Its Model

We view a game as a multi-agent system. We denote the set of agents (or players) by N and the set of all the actions these agents can perform by $\mathcal{A}$, both of which are non-empty and finite. We assume that each state transition is caused by exactly one action thus, in a simultaneous-move game, the actions are joint actions from all players while, in a sequential game, each action is performed by a single player with other players play no-op (no operation). For simplicity, we assume that all the games we considered in the paper are based on the same multi-agent setting $(N, \mathcal{A})$ if not specified explicitly.

2.1 State Transition Model

We model a finite state game with perfect information and deterministic actions as a state transition system:

Definition 1. A *state transition model* M is a tuple (W, I, T, U, L, G, V), where

- W is a non-empty set of states;
- $I \subseteq W$ is a non-empty set of *initial* states;
- $T \subseteq W$ is a set of *terminal* states;
- $U : W \times \mathcal{A} \to W \backslash I$ is a function that maps each pair of state and action to a non-initial state;
- $L \subseteq (W \backslash T) \times \mathcal{A}$ is a relation specifies legality of actions;
- $G : N \to 2^T$ is a goal function specifies which player wins in which terminal states;

A *path* is sequence $\rho = w_0 \xrightarrow{a_0} w_1 \xrightarrow{a_1} \cdots \xrightarrow{a_{m-1}} w_m$ of interleaved states and actions such that $(w_i, a_i) \in L$ and $U(w_i, a_i) = w_{i+1}$ for all $0 \le i < m$. The path is a *terminating path* if $w_m \in T$. We let $\hat{\rho} = w_m$.

2.2 Game Description Language

The original game description language is a logic programming language with Prolog-like syntax and purely declarative semantics. To facilitate logical analysis on game properties, [14–16] converted GDL from a logic programming language into a propositional modal language with Kripke semantics. In this paper we will use their counterpart of GDL as the language for game description.

Definition 2. Let $\mathcal{L}$ be a propositional modal language which consists of a set, Φ, of propositional letters, the reserved GDL variables (*initial, terminal, does(.), legal(.), wins(.)*) and modalities ($\Box, [.], \lfloor . \rfloor, \Upsilon$). The formulas of $\mathcal{L}$ are generated by the following BNF rule:

$$\varphi ::= p \mid \neg\varphi \mid \varphi \to \varphi \mid initial \mid terminal \mid wins(n)$$

$$\mid does(a) \mid legal(a) \mid \Box\varphi \mid [a]\varphi \mid \lfloor a \rfloor\varphi \mid \Upsilon\varphi$$

where $p \in \Phi$, $a \in \mathcal{A}$ and $n \in N$. Other logical connectives are defined as usual.

The reserved GDL variables are self-explanatory. $\square$ is the standard global modality, meaning true in every state. $[a]\varphi$ means φ is true in the next state if action a is executed. $\lfloor a \rfloor$ is a technical modality, which is not used in this paper but necessary for the logic. $\Upsilon\varphi$ means φ will be true in the terminal state of any terminating path from the current state. Beside these modalities, the dual modalities of $\square$ and Υ can be defined as follows:

$$\Diamond\varphi \overset{def}{=} \neg\square\neg\varphi, \qquad \langle\Upsilon\rangle\varphi \overset{def}{=} \neg\Upsilon\neg\varphi \tag{1}$$

The temporal operator, *next*, can be defined in $\mathcal{L}$ in two versions as introduced in [16] :

$$\bigcirc\varphi \overset{def}{=} \bigvee_{a\in\mathcal{A}} (does(a) \wedge [a]\varphi), \qquad \oplus\varphi \overset{def}{=} \bigwedge_{a\in\mathcal{A}} (legal(a) \rightarrow [a]\varphi) \tag{2}$$

The semantics of $\mathcal{L}$ follows the definition of [14,16]. Briefly, given a valuation $V : \Phi \rightarrow 2^W$ of Φ, the satisfiability relation between a formula $\varphi \in \mathcal{L}$ and a state transition model M at a *move* (w, a), where $w \in W$ and $a \in \mathcal{A}$, denoted by $M \models_{(w,a)} \varphi$, is defined inductively on the structure of φ, for instance (more details are referred to [14,16]),

$M \models_{(w,a)} [b]\varphi$ iff $M \models_{(U(w,b),c)} \varphi$ for all $c \in \mathcal{A}$
$M \models_{(w,a)} \square\varphi$ iff $M \models_{(w',a')} \varphi$ for all $w' \in W$, $a' \in \mathcal{A}$
$M \models_{(w,a)} \Upsilon\varphi$ iff $M \models_{(\hat{\rho},c)} \varphi$ for all terminating path ρ
                                     from w and for all $c \in \mathcal{A}$

As usual, $M \models \varphi$ means $M \models_{(w,a)} \varphi$ for any $w \in W$ and $a \in \mathcal{A}$. $M \models_w \varphi$ stands for $M \models_{(w,a)} \varphi$ for all $a \in \mathcal{A}$.

2.3   Game Description

As a logical counterpart of the original GDL, any game description described in Prolog-like GDL can be translated into a set of logic formulas in the language presented above. We borrow an example from [16] to show how such a logic-based game description looks like.

Example 1 (Hex Game). *Two players, Black (b) and White (w), alternate placing a stone of their colour in a previously unoccupied cell on a rhombus-shaped board with $m \times m$ hexagonal cells (see Fig. 2). The first player who completes a connected path with their stones linking the opposing sides in their colour wins the game.*

As we mentioned in the introduction, the 2016 GGP competitions introduced a few games, each of which was specified by two versions of description, one designed for game manager and one for GGP players. Hex game was one of the games. [16] has provided a description of Hex game based on the players version. The description is simple but contains a recursive definition of paths, which causes significant inefficiency to GGP players. The description presented below

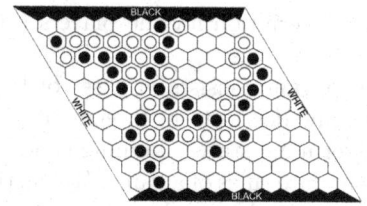

Fig. 2. An example of Hex game in which White wins.

is translated from the game rule used by the game manager, which is much more computationally friendly.

Assume that $p^n_{i,j}$ denotes cell (i,j) being occupied by player n's stone and $a^n_{i,j}$ the action of player n placing a stone in cell (i,j), where $n \in \{\mathsf{b}, \mathsf{w}\}$ and $1 \leq i, j \leq m$. To represent a path of player n from (i,j) to (i',j'), recursively define propositional symbol $\gamma^n(i,j,i',j')$ as follows where $n \in \{\mathsf{b}, \mathsf{w}\}$ and $1 \leq i, j \leq m$:

$\gamma^n(i,j,i,j) \leftrightarrow p^n_{i,j}$

$\gamma^n(i,j,i',j') \leftrightarrow (p^n_{i,j} \wedge adj(i,j,i'',j'')) \wedge \gamma^n(i'',j'',i',j'))$, where

$adj(i,j,i',j') \overset{def}{=} (i' = i \wedge |j-j'| = 1) \vee (|i-i'| = 1 \wedge j' = j) \vee (i' = i+1 \wedge j' = j-1) \vee (i' = i-1 \wedge j' = j+1)$

The game rule used by the game master can then be expressed with the following set of formulas:

1. $\square(initial \leftrightarrow turn(\mathsf{b}) \wedge \neg turn(\mathsf{w}) \wedge step(1) \wedge \bigwedge\limits_{i,j=1}^{m} \neg(p^\mathsf{b}_{i,j} \vee p^\mathsf{w}_{i,j}) \wedge \bigwedge\limits_{k=1}^{m^2} (\neg own^\mathsf{b}(k) \wedge$
$\neg own^\mathsf{w}(k) \wedge \bigwedge\limits_{i,j=1}^{m} \neg connect(k,i,j)))$

2. $\square(terminal \leftrightarrow (wins(\mathsf{b}) \vee wins(\mathsf{w}) \vee \bigwedge\limits_{i,j=1}^{m} (p^\mathsf{b}_{i,j} \vee p^\mathsf{w}_{i,j})))$

3. $\square(legal(a^n_{i,j}) \leftrightarrow (\neg(p^\mathsf{b}_{i,j} \vee p^\mathsf{w}_{i,j}) \wedge turn(n) \wedge \neg terminal))$ for each $n \in \{\mathsf{b}, \mathsf{w}\}$

4. $\square(wins(\mathsf{b}) \leftrightarrow \bigvee\limits_{k=1}^{m^2} \bigvee\limits_{j,j'=1}^{m} (own^\mathsf{b}(k) \wedge connect(k,1,j) \wedge connect(k,m,j'))) \wedge$
$\square(wins(\mathsf{w}) \leftrightarrow \bigvee\limits_{k=1}^{m^2} \bigvee\limits_{i,i'=1}^{m} (own^\mathsf{w}(k) \wedge connect(k,i,1) \wedge connect(k,i',m)))$

5. $\square(\bigcirc p^n_{i,j} \leftrightarrow (p^n_{i,j} \vee does(a^n_{i,j})))$ for each $n \in \{\mathsf{b}, \mathsf{w}\}$

6. $\square(\bigcirc turn(\mathsf{w}) \leftrightarrow turn(\mathsf{b})) \wedge \square(\bigcirc turn(\mathsf{b}) \leftrightarrow turn(\mathsf{w}))$

7. $\square(\bigcirc step(k+1) \leftrightarrow step(k))$

8. $\square(\bigcirc own^n(k) \leftrightarrow own^n(k) \vee (step(k) \wedge turn(n)))$ for each $n \in \{\mathsf{b}, \mathsf{w}\}$

9. $\square(step(k) \leftrightarrow \neg step(k'))$ where $k \neq k'$

10. $\square(\bigcirc connect(k,i,j) \leftrightarrow (connect(k,i,j) \wedge \neg transfer(k)) \vee (step(k) \wedge does(a^n_{i,j})) \vee$
$(step(k) \wedge \bigvee\limits_{k'=1}^{m^2} (transfer(k') \wedge connect(k',i,j))))$ for each $n \in \{\mathsf{b}, \mathsf{w}\}$, where
$transfer(k) \overset{def}{=} \bigvee\limits_{n \in \{\mathsf{b}, \mathsf{w}\}} (own^n(k) \wedge \bigvee\limits_{i,j,i',j'=1}^{m} (does(a^n_{i,j}) \wedge adj(i,j,i',j') \wedge connect$
$(k,i',j'))$

For the unbounded free variables, i, j and k, in formulas 5, 7, 8, 9 and 10, we assume $1 \leq k, k' \leq m^2$, and $1 \leq i, j \leq m$. We denote the above game description by Σ_{hexm}^m while the game description for the players (given in [16]) is denoted by Σ_{hexp}^m.

Although a game description consists of a set of logic formulas, not every set of formulas can be a game description. In general, a game description must specify the initial states, terminal states, winning conditions, legality of actions for each player, and state update rules of a game. Beside that, [8] introduced a set of constraints to limit the scope of game descriptions so as to avoid problematic games. [16] formalises these constraints into the following conditions:

Consistency: $\Sigma \not\models \bot$

Non-vacuity: $\Sigma \models \Diamond initial \land \Diamond terminal$

Termination: $\Sigma \models \Box(initial \rightarrow \langle \Upsilon \rangle terminal)$

Playability: $\Sigma \models \Box(\neg terminal \rightarrow \bigvee_{a \in \mathcal{A}} legal(a))$

Winnability: $\Sigma \models \bigwedge_{n \in N} \Diamond(initial \rightarrow \langle \Upsilon \rangle wins(n))$.

A game description Σ is *well-formed* if it satisfies all the above conditions. [16] has proved that Σ_{hexp}^m is a well-formed game description. Following a similar approach, we can also prove that Σ_{hexm}^m is a well-formed game description. Obviously the two descriptions, Σ_{hexp}^m and Σ_{hexm}^m, are not logically equivalent. All models of Σ_{hexm}^m must satisfy $initial \rightarrow step(1)$. However, we can easily create a model of Σ_{hexp}^m that falsifies it.

We say that a state transition model M is a model of a game description Σ if $M \models \varphi$ for all $\varphi \in \Sigma$.

3   Submodel Bisimulation

When we talk about a game, for example Hex game, do we mean a *model* of the game or the rules of the game, i.e., *game description*? There are obviously different models for a game and also different ways to describe a game. This raises two important questions: *"Given a game description, what is the relationship between the models and the description?"* and *"When do two game descriptions describe the same game?"* In the next two sections, we investigate into these questions. Before doing that, we introduce a concept which is useful for the rest of the paper.

3.1   Reachability and Generated Submodel

Reachability of a state has been used informally everywhere in [8]'s book. A state is *reachable* if it can be reached from an initial state via a sequence of legal moves.

Definition 3. *Given a state transition model $M = (W, I, T, U, L, G, V)$, the set of all reachable states of M is defined as*

$$W^{Rea} = \bigcup_{k=0}^{\infty} W^k \qquad (3)$$

where

- $W^0 = I$,
- $W^k = W^{k-1} \cup \{U(w, a) : w \in W^{k-1} \ \& \ (w, a) \in L\}$

It is easy to prove that for each reachable state $w \in W^{Rea}$, there is a path that links an initial state to the state. Also any state in a path from an initial state is reachable.

Reachability plays a significant role when we consider game equivalence. Those states that can never be reached from the initial states do not affect the behaviour of a game therefore should be excluded in the consideration of game equivalence.

Definition 4. Consider a model $M = (W, I, T, U, L, G, V)$ of $\mathcal{L}$. A model $M' = (W', I', T', U', L', G', V')$ is a *submodel* of M if

1. $W' \subseteq W$;
2. I' (respectively, T', U', L' and G') is the restriction of I (respectively, T, U, L and G) to W', i.e.,

$$I' = I \cap W'$$

$$U' = U \cap (W' \times W')$$

$$L' = L \cap W'$$

$$G' = G \cap (W' \times N)$$

Furthermore, M' is called the *generated sub-model* of M if W' is the smallest subset of W such that $I \subseteq W'$ and W' is closed under the following condition:

$$\text{For any } (w, a) \in L', \ U'(w, a) \in W' \tag{4}$$

This concept is quite similar to the concept of rooted generated submodel in classical modal logic except that the root is not necessarily a singleton and is fixed to be the set of initial states (see [18] page 56). Given a state transition model, its generated submodel not only exists but also unique as show below.

Proposition 1. *Given a state transition model* $M = (W, I, T, U, L, G, V)$ *of* $\mathcal{L}$, *define* $M' = (W', I', T', U', L', G', V')$ *as follows:*

1. $W' = W^{Rec}$ *(See Eq. (3))*
2. I', T', U', L', G' *and* V' *are the restrictions of* I, T, U, L, G *and* V *to* W', *respectively.*

then M' *is the generated submodel of* M.

The proposition says that the set of states of the generated submodel is exactly the set of all reachable states of the original model. Obviously, modal properties are invariant under generated submodels, which means that a formula which is satisfied in the original model in a reachable state can also be satisfied by the generated submodel and vice versa. However, a property that is satisfied in all reachable states, thus valid in the generated submodel, is not necessarily satisfied in non-reachable states. This means that a game description is not invariant under generated submodels.

3.2 Bisimulation

Now we move to the question on the relationship of game models. Bisimulation is a standard tool to investigate model equivalence and modal invariance [18]. Intuitively, a model is bisimilar to another if one can mimic the entire behaviour of the other, and vice versa. This concept can be easily applied to game models.

Definition 5. *Consider two models* $M = (W, I, T, U, L, G, V)$ *and* $M' = (W', I', T', U', L', G', V')$ *over the same multi-agent setting* $(N, \mathcal{A})$ *and the same valuation* V *on the set* Φ *of propositional letters of* $\mathcal{L}$. *A binary relation* $Z \subseteq W \times W'$ *is a* full bisimulation *between* M *and* M' *if the following conditions hold:*

1. $W = \{w \in W : \exists w' \in W' \ (w, w') \in Z\}$ *and* $W' = \{w' \in W' : \exists w \in W \ (w, w') \in Z\}$;
2. *For each* $(w, w') \in Z$ *and* $p \in \Phi$, $w \in V(p)$ *iff* $w' \in V'(p)$;
3. *For each* $(w, w') \in Z$,
    - $(w, a) \in L$ *iff* $(w', a) \in L'$ *for any* $a \in \mathcal{A}$;
    - $w \in I$ *(respectively* T*) iff* $w' \in I'$ *(respectively* T'*)*;
    - $w \in G(n)$ *iff* $w' \in G'(n)$ *for any* $n \in N$.
4. *For each* $(w, w') \in Z$ *and* $a \in \mathcal{A}$, $(U(w, a), U'(w', a)) \in Z$.

A state transition model M is *bisimilar* to another model M' of the same valuation if there is a full bisimulation between them. The definition of bisimulation is almost the same as the one for any modal logic except for condition (3). Condition (4) looks different from the traditional forth and back conditions. They are in fact equivalent due to all actions are assumed to be deterministic. Not surprisingly, the following invariance result holds:

Proposition 2. *If* M *is a model of game description* Σ, *any model bisimilar to* M *is also a model of* Σ.

3.3 Submodel Bisimulation

As we mentioned earlier, when a state transition model models a game, not all states in the model are relevant. Only those reachable states affect the behaviour of a game. The generated submodel of a state transition model removes all non-reachable states but keeps all the reachable states and associated relations. In this sense, when we consider two models simulate each other in a game, we only need to consider their generated submodels. This leads to the following concept:

Definition 6. *Two state transition models over the same multi-agent setting and the same valuation of propositional letters of* $\mathcal{L}$ *are* submodel bisimilar *if their respective generated submodels are bisimilar.*

Obviously, submodel bisimulation is weaker than full bisimulation because condition (1) in Definition 5 is not guaranteed. Not all modal properties are invariant under submodel bisimulation[1]. However, the states that are missed out are those that are not researchable. For game playing, non-reachable states are out of interest therefore can be ignored. Straightforward from the above propositions, we can have

Corollary 1. *If a game description Σ is valid in a state transition model M, it is valid in the generated submodels of all the models that are submodel bisimilar to M.*

This result shows that the concept of submodel bisimulation is simply a refinement of bisimulation by filtering out all the non-reachable states and associated relations. The following theorem further shows that filtering out the non-reachable states does not change the nature of a game.

Theorem 1. *If two models M and M' are submodel bisimular, then for every path starting from an initial state in M,*

$$\rho_1 \;=\; w_0 \overset{a_0}{\to} w_1 \overset{a_1}{\to} \cdots \overset{a_{m-1}}{\to} w_m \quad (m \geq 0)$$

there is a path also starting from an initial state in M' of the form

$$\rho_2 \;=\; w_0' \overset{a_0}{\to} w_1' \overset{a_1}{\to} \cdots \overset{a_{m-1}}{\to} w_m'$$

and vice versa. Moreover, ρ_1 is terminating iff ρ_2 is terminating, and $w_m \in G(n)$ iff $w_m' \in G'(n)$ for every $n \in N$.

Proof. Let $M = (W, I, T, U, L, G, V)$ and $M' = (W', I', T', U', L', G', V')$ be submodel bisimular. $\bar{M} = (\bar{W}, \bar{I}, \bar{T}, \bar{U}, \bar{L}, \bar{G}, \bar{V})$ and $\bar{M}' = (\bar{W}', \bar{I}', \bar{T}', \bar{U}', \bar{L}', \bar{G}', \bar{V}')$ are the respective generated submodes of M and M'. Since M and M' are submodel bisimular, there is a full bisimulation Z between $\bar{M}$ and $\bar{M}'$. By Theorem 1, we have $\bar{M} = M^{Rea}$ and all other components of $\bar{M}$ are the respective restrictions of M. The same applies also to $\bar{M}'$.

Assume that $\rho_1 = w_0 \overset{a_0}{\to} w_1 \overset{a_1}{\to} \cdots \overset{a_{m-1}}{\to} w_m$ $(m \geq 0)$ is a path in M where $w_0 \in I$. By the definition of path, $(w_k, a_k) \in L$ and $w_k = U(w_{k-1}, a_{k-1})$ for all $k(0 < k \leq m)$. By the construction of W^{Rea}, $w_k \in W^m$ for all $k(0 < k \leq m)$. Therefore, ρ_1 is also a path in $\bar{M}$. Since $\bar{M}$ is bisimular to $\bar{M}'$, there is a path starting from an initial state in $\bar{M}'$ of the form $\rho_2 = w_0' \overset{a_0}{\to} w_1' \overset{a_1}{\to} \cdots \overset{a_{m-1}}{\to} w_m'$ which simulates ρ_1. Since $\bar{M}'$ is a submodel of M', ρ_2 is also a path in M'. Note that $(w_k, w_k') \in Z$. If $w_m \in T$ (or $G(n)$), we also have $w_m \in T'$ (or $G'(n)$). The other direction is similar.

We would like to remark that Jiang *et al.* [19] also introduced a similar concept of bisimulation for game models in the sense that two models are bisimilar

---

[1] An easy example is that the property of reachability is not invariant under submodel bisimulation.

if and only if they are bisimilar with every path. As we show above, submodel bisimulation only requires two models are bisimular with paths along reachable states (ignore all non-reachable states and paths). Thus our concept is much wider. In the following section, we will lift up the concept of game equivalence to syntactical level.

4 Equivalence of Game Descriptions

In the previous section, we have discussed game equivalence from the view point of game models, i.e., how a game can be implemented in different but equivalent models. In this section, we switch to the question on equivalence of game descriptions, i.e, how a game can be described in different ways but induce to the games with the same behaviour.

Intuitively, two game descriptions are substitutable with each other if they allow the same sequences of legal actions and if the same agent wins at the end of every terminating path. This will guarantee that any play (a terminal path) in one game can be fully mimicked by another game. Theorem 1 has shown that if two models are submodel bisimular, one model can mimic the behaviour of the other model. Syntactically, we introduce the following concept of *behaviour equivalence* on game descriptions:

Definition 7. Two well-formed game descriptions Σ and Σ' are *behaviourally equivalent* if for any formula $\varphi \in \mathcal{L}$, $\Sigma \models \Box(initial \rightarrow \Upsilon\varphi)$ iff $\Sigma' \models \Box(initial \rightarrow \Upsilon\varphi)$.

Obviously, if two game descriptions are logically equivalent, they are also behaviourally equivalent. However, behavioural equivalence is much weaker. We can see from Proposition 3 that a game can be described significantly differently (they are by no means logically equivalent) but behaviourally equivalent. What we require for behavioural equivalence is that the descriptions enforce the same outcome for any run of the game.

Ideally we can verify equivalence of game descriptions in proof theory. [16] introduced an axiomatic system for the logic. However, proof of game equivalence directly from the axioms is too complicated to be practical. It relies on further development of automated reasoning techniques. The following theorem provides a model-theoretic approach to verify equivalence of game descriptions.

Theorem 2. *Given two well-formed game descriptions Σ and Σ', if every model of Σ is submodel bisimilar to a model of Σ' and vice versa, Σ and Σ' are behaviourally equivalent.*

Proof. For any formula $\varphi \in \mathcal{L}$, assume that $\Sigma \models \Box(initial \rightarrow \Upsilon\varphi)$. We prove that $\Sigma' \models \Box(initial \rightarrow \Upsilon\varphi)$. The other direction is similar.

Let $M' = (W', I', T', U', L', G', V')$ be a model of Σ'. For any $w' \in W'$ and $a \in \mathcal{A}$, assume that $M' \models_{(w',a)} initial$, thus $w' \in W'^{Rea}$. We prove that $M' \models_{(w',a)} \Upsilon\varphi$. That is to prove, for any terminating path ρ' starting from w', $M' \models_{\hat{\rho}'} \varphi$. By the condition of the theorem, there is a model

$M = (W, I, T, U, L, G, V)$ of Σ such that M is submodel bisimilar to M'. Since $w' \in W'^{Rea}$, there is $w \in W^{Rea}$ that is bisimilar to w'. We then have $M \models_{(w,a)} initial$ for all $a \in \mathcal{A}$. By $\Sigma \models \Box(initial \rightarrow \Upsilon\varphi)$, we know any model of Σ is a model of $\Box(initial \rightarrow \Upsilon\varphi)$. Thus we have $M \models_{(w,a)} \Box(initial \rightarrow \Upsilon\varphi)$. By $M \models_{(w,a)} initial$, it turns out that $M \models_{(w,a)} \Upsilon\varphi$. By Theorem 1, there is a terminating path ρ in M which is point to point bisimilar to ρ'. Thus $M \models_{\hat{\rho}} \varphi$. Obviously all the states in ρ are reachable. By the submodel similarity between M and M', we also have $M \models_{\hat{\rho}'} \varphi$, as desired.

By using the approach developed in the previous sections, we can now formally prove that the game description of Hex game for the game master Σ^m_{hexp} is behaviourally equivalent to the game description for the players Σ^m_{hexm} and therefore they are substitutable.

Proposition 3. *The game descriptions Σ^m_{hexp} and Σ^m_{hexm} are behaviourally equivalent.*

Note that a game model of Σ^m_{hexp} or Σ^m_{hexm} may contain many non-reachable states thus they are not necessarily equivalent each other in terms of Jiang et al.'s definition of game equivalence [19].

5   Conclusion and Discussions

In this paper we have investigated the problem of how different game descriptions can be behaviourally equivalent and substitutable with each other. We have introduced the concept of submodel bisimulation that can filter out unreachable states. Based on the concept, we have defined equivalence of game descriptions in the sense that two game descriptions are equivalent if the described games behaviourally the same. We have proved that the two game descriptions of Hex Game used in the previous GGP Competitions are behavioural equivalent. As far as we know, this is the first time the descriptions were proved to be substitutable although it has been treated as equivalent for years in the GGP community. We believe that the approach we introduced in this paper can also be used to prove the equivalence of game descriptions for other games.

Game equivalence in general has been widely investigated in game theory [20–22]. There have been also a few different notions of game equivalence proposed in the literature specifically for General Game Playing. Zhang et al. considered that two games are equivalent if their state machines are isomorphic [23]. Jiang et al. extended the concept so that two games are equivalent if their game models are bisimilar with possible one-to-one mapping between game signatures [19]. Their approach allows to identify the equivalence of different models of the same game, for instance, the original Tic-Tac-Toe game and its variations - Number Scrabble or JAM. Our concept of behavioural equivalence further extends the approach in the sense that two games are equivalent if any play in one game can be fully mimicked by another game. This approach allows us to identify the equivalence between game descriptions rather than the way of modelling. In other words, no matter in which way a game is described (say with or without recursions), as long as they are behaviourally equivalent, the players are playing the same game. As mentioned earlier, the way of describing a game can affect the efficiency of a GGP player significantly. It is possible for a GGP player to autonomously reformulate an inefficient game description into an equivalent but more computationally-friendly description. Implementation of algorithms for automated game equivalence verification and automated game description compilation and reformulation can be a long term target for GGP research.

References

1. Campbell, M., Hoane, A., Hsu, F.: Deep blue. Artif. Intell. **134**(1), 57–83 (2002)
2. Silver, D., et al.: Mastering the game of go with deep neural networks and tree search. Nature **529**(7587), 484–489 (2016)
3. Bowling, M., et al.: Heads-up limit hold'em poker is solved. Science **347**(6218), 145–149 (2015)
4. Silver, D., et al.: Mastering the game of go without human knowledge. Nature **550**, 354–359 (2017)
5. Pell, B.: A strategic metagame player for general chess-like games. Comput. Intell. **12**(1), 177–198 (1996)
6. Silver, D., et al.: A general reinforcement learning algorithm that masters chess, shogi, and go through self-play. Science **362**(6419), 1140–1144 (2018)
7. Genesereth, M., Love, N., Pell, B.: General game playing: overview of the AAAI competition. AI Mag. **26**(2), 62–72 (2005)
8. Genesereth, M., Thielscher, M.: General Game Playing. Morgan & Claypool Publishers (2014)
9. Love, N., Hinrichs, T., Genesereth, M.: General game playing: game description language specification. Tech. rep. Computer Science Department, Stanford University (2006)
10. Genesereth, M.M., Björnsson, Y.: The international general game playing competition. AI Mag. **34**(2), 107–111 (2013)
11. Swiechowski, M., Mandziuk, J.: Fast interpreter for logical reasoning in general game playing. J. Logic Comput. **24**(5), 1071–1110 (2014)
12. Romero, J., Saffidine, A., Thielscher, M.: Solving the inferential frame problem in the general game description language. In: Proceedings of the Twenty-Eighth AAAI Conference on Artificial Intelligence, pp. 515–521. AAAI Press (2014)
13. Michon, J.A.: The game of jam: an isomorph of tic-tac-toe. Am. J. Psychol. **80**(1), 137–140 (1967)
14. Zhang, D., Thielscher, M.: A logic for reasoning about game strategies. In: Proceedings of the Twenty-Ninth AAAI Conference on Artificial Intelligence (AAAI-15), pp. 1671–1677 (2015)
15. Zhang, D., Thielscher, M.: Representing and reasoning about game strategies. J. Philos. Logic **44**(2), 203–236 (2015)
16. Zhang, D.: A logic for reasoning about game descriptions. In: AI 2018: Advances in Artificial Intelligence, pp. 38–50 (2018)
17. Gale, D.: The game of hex and the brouwer fixed-point theorem. Am. Math. Monthly **86**(10), 818–827 (1979)
18. Blackburn, P., Rijke, M.D., Venema, Y.: Modal Logic. Cambridge University Press (2001)

19. Jiang, G., et al.: Game equivalence and bisimulation for game description language. In: PRICAI 2019: Trends in Artificial Intelligence, pp. 583–596 (2019)
20. Osborne, M.J., Rubinstein, A.: A Course in Game Theory. The MIT Press (1994)
21. Elmes, S., Reny, P.J.: On the strategic equivalence of extensive form games. J. Econ. Theo. **62**(1), 1–23 (1994)
22. Bonanno, G.: Set-theoretic equivalence of extensive-form games. Int. J. Game Theo. **20**(4), 429–447 (1992)
23. Zhang, H., Liu, D., Li, W.: Space-consistent game equivalence detection in general game playing. In: Cazenave, T., Winands, M.H.M., Edelkamp, S., Schiffel, S., Thielscher, M., Togelius, J. (eds.) CGW/GIGA -2015. CCIS, vol. 614, pp. 165–177. Springer, Cham (2016). https://doi.org/10.1007/978-3-319-39402-2_12

Machine Learning

Classifiers for Regulatory Feedback Networks Using AB-Divergences

Zhuoyun Ao$^{(\boxtimes)}$, Martin Oxenham, and Mark Nelson

Defence Science Technology Group, Edinburgh, SA 5111, Australia
{Zhuoyun.Ao,Mark.Nelson}@dst.defence.gov.au

Abstract. Humans have the ability to learn and reason about a new concept from just one or a handful of examples, incorporate new information and modify existing patterns quickly. In this paper, we attempt to develop flexible and robust one-shot classifiers with such properties. First, we consider the biologically motivated Regulatory Feedback Networks (RFNs) as the solution. Second, we reformulate the recognition problem of RFNs as the minimization of the difference between the reconstruction of the internal copy of the inputs on hand and the inputs from the environment. Then generalized AB-divergence is introduced as a scalar measure of that difference. Based on the divergence, a set of Multiplicative Update Rules are formally derived. With the flexibility and robustness of generalized AB-divergence, these algorithms achieve strong results for one-shot learning and statistically significantly outperformed the most popular classifiers, Support Vector Machine (SVN) and K-Neares Neighbors(KNN) for few-shots learning in face and character recognition over LFW and Omniglot datasets.

Keywords: Regulatory feedback network · Classification · Divergence · Multiplicative update rule

1 Introduction

Humans have the ability to learn and reason about a new concept from one or a handful of examples and incorporate new information on the fly. This one-shot generalization inference is guided by the principle that a good categorical hypothesis is a generative model in which the observed object would be an "ideal" or generic example [1]. We desire to develop recognition algorithms with such capabilities.

The development of deep learning has dramatically improved the state-of-the-art performance on a wide range of recognition problems and applications. However, Deep Neural Networks often require a large amount of labelled data to train well-generalized models. Meta-learning [2–6], one-shot learning [7–12] and transfer learning [13,14], among others, have become the main approaches for addressing this challenge of data scarcity. The common idea in these one-shot learning and transfer learning approaches is that, Deep Convolution Neural Networks (DCNN) are used as feature extractors or embedding functions in different

© Crown 2020
M. Gallagher et al. (Eds.): AI 2020, LNAI 12576, pp. 323–335, 2020.
https://doi.org/10.1007/978-3-030-64984-5_25

mechanisms of metric and representation learning. The learned metric space or feature space are used to perform classification by fine tuning or retraining new classifiers with traditional classifiers such as Support Vector Machine (SVM) [15] or K-Nearest Neighbors (KNN) [16]. However, fine tuning the networks or retraining new classifiers with one or few examples, and adding new classes or new features on the fly still remains a challenge.

In this paper, we make use these feature representation learning approaches, and consider alternative classifiers for transfer learning and one-shot learning with the biologically motivated Regulatory Feedback Networks (RFNs) [17–21] to achieve these capabilities. A RFN achieves this in such a way that it maintains an ideal example for each class or category, while new classes and features can be added or modified locally.

However, current RFN development is in an infant stage and RFNs are proposed with two algorithms [17]. One is a simple subtractive method based on the least squares energy function $E(X, \mathbf{M}Y) = \frac{1}{2}(||X - \mathbf{M}Y||)^2$, in which gradient descent minimization is directly applied. This method is sensitive to the learning rate and has slow convergence. The other method is the shunting inhibition update rule based on a shunting equation $I = \frac{X}{\mathbf{M}Y}$. It is not clear how this update rule was derived formally. Moreover, RFNs have not been seen to apply to any real world data.

Recently, generalized divergences such as the AB-divergence [22] and Bregman divergence [23] as similarity measures have become attractive alternatives for advanced machine learning algorithms. Based on the hypothesis behind the RFNs, we propose to use AB-divergence as the similarity measures between the internal copy of the input $\mathbf{M}Y$ and the input vector X from the environment, where $\mathbf{M}$ is the expectation matrix and Y is the output activation. That is, we define a divergence $D(X||\mathbf{M}Y)$ as the scalar measure for the difference between X and $\mathbf{M}Y$. When $\mathbf{M}Y$ minimizes the $D(X||\mathbf{M}Y)$ to X over a family $\mathcal{F}$, we say that $\mathbf{M}Y$ is the divergence projection of X into $\mathcal{F}$. Thus, the recognition problem of RFNs can be re-formulated as a divergence projection operator:

$$proj[p] = \arg \min_{Y \in \mathcal{F}} D(X||\mathbf{M}Y) \text{ subject to } m_{ij} \geq 0, y_i \geq 0 \text{ for all } i, j \qquad (1)$$

Note that, given X, when $\mathbf{M}$ is fixed, Eq. 1 is a prediction task; when Y is fixed, Eq. 1 becomes a learning task. Moreover, instead of directly applying minimize optimization over the divergence, we will use different divergences as the cost functions for defining $D(X||\mathbf{M}Y)$ to formally derive a family of more efficient multiplicative update algorithms for RFNs. Our main contributions are summarized as follows.

- We reformulated the RFN recognition problem as the minimization of the divergence between the internal reconstruction on hand $\mathbf{M}Y$ and the input X from the environment.
- We formally derived a set of multiplicative update rules for the optimization that are more efficient (fast convergent), flexible in terms of adapting to objective function and robust to noise and outliers over gradient descent based algorithms.

- We show that the update rule originally proposed for RFNs with the shunting method coincids with the multiplicative update rule based on the Kullback-Leibler divergence cost function, which is a special case of the generalized divergences.
- We also apply these algorithms to real world data sets, the LFW dataset [24] and the Omniglot dataset [25] and achieved superior results compared with the most popular classifier SVM and KNN.

The remaining of the paper is organised as follows. Section 2 reviews the work related to Variational Inference. In Sect. 3 we briefly describe RFN. Section 4 introduces generalized AB-divergences and its special cases. Then the multiplicative update algorithms are formally developed in Sect. 5. The experimental results are showed in Sect. 6 followed by concluding remarks.

2 Related Work

In addition to the related work on one-shot learning and transfer learning with the most popular classifiers such as SVM and KNN, our work also closely relates with *Variational Inference* (VI) [26,27] which is a method widely used to approximate posterior densities by optimization, an alternative strategy to Markov chain Monte Carlo (MCMC) sampling. As a result, using VI allows us to derive algorithms that apply to increasingly complex probabilistic models to ever larger data sets on ever more powerful computing resources. VI has been applied to problems such as large-scale document analysis, computational neuroscience, and computer vision [28].

Recently, Generalized-divergences [29–31] have been used in Variational Inference, where the optimizations are directly applied on the divergence itself with the help of the Monte Carlo approximation method. It's also been used in multi-class classification [32]. In our RFN framework, a set of multiplicative update rules are derived based the generalized-divergences for the optimization, which can potentially be directly applied to divergence for VI.

3 Regulatory Feedback Networks (RFNs)

This section briefly describes RFNs. RFNs are similar to conventional feed-forward neural networks with additional feedback connections which governe the set of inputs, as shown in Fig. 1. Every feed-forward connection has a symmetric associated self-inhibitory feedback connection, where $X = [x_1, x_2, \ldots, x_d]^T$ denotes m sensory input features with dimensions d, the expected pattern; $Y = [y_1, y_2, \ldots, y_n]^T$ denotes the activity of n output neurons; $\mathbf{M} = [m_1, m_2, \ldots, m_n]$ is the expectation matrix consisting of a set of feature vectors, e.g., the expectation feature vector for neuron 1 is $m_1 = [m_{11}, , m_{12}, \ldots, m_{1d}]$, the red connections. m_{ik} is the feed-forward connection between output neuron y_i and input feature x_k ($0 < i \leq n$ and $0 < k \leq d$). For example, if feature x_1 activates output neurons y_1 and y_2, then feedback from y_1 and y_2 regulates input x_1. Each feature vector symbolically represents the expected (ideal) input. The green node and connections correspond to adding a new pattern (class); the yellow node and blue connections correspond to adding a new feature, while the rest of the network remains unchanged. These properties of RFN make incorporating new information on the fly possible.

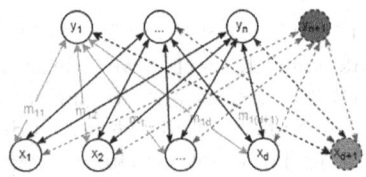

Fig. 1. A symmetric self-regulatory feedback network. Every feed-forward connection has an associated self-inhibitory feedback connections.

The RFN model was inspired by the conventional feed-forward neural network model $Y = WX$ or $Y = f(W, X)$ (assume bias is absorbed into W): $X = W^{-1}Y = \mathbf{M}Y$ or $\mathbf{M}Y - X = 0$ where matrix $\mathbf{M}^{d \times n}$ is the inverse or pseudoinverse of matrix W, $\mathbf{M} = W^{-1}$. The term $\mathbf{M}Y$ is an internal prototype of the input pattern constructed using learned information $\mathbf{M}$. During recognition, when output nodes in Y are active, a pattern $\mathbf{M}Y$ is generated, which is subtracted from the incoming input pattern X (through inhibition). This can expressed as: $E = X - \widehat{X}$ where E is the difference (error) between the incoming input pattern X and the reconstruction $\widehat{X} = \mathbf{M}Y$. This RFN model can be interpreted as a generative model, in which $\mathbf{M}Y$ is the reconstruction of the input X. That is, given $\mathbf{M}$, we can reconstruct X for a given Y. M represents the fixed points, the expectations, in which prototype descriptions of patterns are to be recognized (the expected symbolic patterns) for X. This can be easily demonstrated by the result of the multiplication $\widehat{X}Y$ which is the first column $m_1 = [m_{11}m_{21} \cdots m_{d1}]^T$ with $Y = [1, 0, \cdots, 0]^T$ when the first node is active.

Significantly, this expectation representation results in the flexibility of incorporating new features, new patterns or expectation weight updating because all changes occurr locally. In terms of the expectation matrix, $\mathbf{M}$, adding a new pattern in the network corresponds to inserting a row into $\mathbf{M}$; adding a new feature in the network corresponds to inserting a column into $\mathbf{M}$; updating a weight requires only modification of the cell value; the rest of the network remains unchanged. With fixed point weights, $\mathbf{M}$, it is possible to manipulate the representations and perform symbolic analysis on the stored patterns.

4   Generalized AB-Divergences

This section briefly describes generalized-divergence. Given a convex set S and $P, Q \in S$, a divergence is defined as a function: $D : S \times S \to \mathbb{R}$ such that: (1)

$\forall (P, Q) \in S, D(P, Q) \geq 0$, and (2) $D(P||Q) = 0$ iff $P = Q$. For example, the Euclidean (EUC) distance is defined as $D_\Phi(P||Q) = \frac{1}{2}||P - Q||^2$ is a special case of both Bregman divergence [23] and the generalized Alpha-Beta-Divergences (AB-divergences) [22]. From the generalized-divergence, a wide range of standard and new divergences can be obtained, such as Kullback-Leibler (KL) divergence [38], Itakura-Saito (IS) divergence [39], α-divergence [33–35] and β-divergence [36, 37].

The positive measures P and Q can be probability distributions, or unconstrained nonnegative multiway arrays and patterns, and not necessary normalized; $Q(x)$ is usually known and fixed, $P(x)$ is learned or adjust to achieve a best in some sense similarity to the $Q(x)$; $\alpha, \beta \in \mathbb{R}$, the AB-divergence is defined as [22]:

$$D_{AB}^{(\alpha,\beta)}(P||Q) = -\frac{1}{\alpha\beta} \sum_{it} \left(p_{it}^\alpha q_{it}^\beta - \frac{\alpha}{\alpha+\beta} p_{it}^{\alpha+\beta} - \frac{\beta}{\alpha+\beta} q_{it}^{\alpha+\beta} \right) \qquad (2)$$
$$\text{for } \alpha, \beta, \alpha + \beta \neq 0,$$

where p_{it} is an entry of P, q_{it} is an entry of Q.

When $\alpha + \beta = 1$ the AB-divergence reduces to the Alpha-divergence [33, 34]:

$$D_A^{(\alpha)}(P||Q) \doteq \frac{1}{\alpha(\alpha-1)} \sum_{it} (p_{it}^\alpha q_{it}^{1-\alpha} - \alpha p_{it} + (\alpha-1)q_{it}) \text{for } \alpha \neq 0, \alpha \neq 1, \quad (3)$$

When $\alpha = 1$, it reduces to the Beta-divergence [33, 35, 37]:

$$D_B^{(\beta)}(P||Q) \doteq -\frac{1}{\beta} \sum_{it} \left(p_{it} q_{it}^\beta - \frac{1}{1+\beta} p_{it}^{1+\beta} - \frac{\beta}{1+\beta} q_{it}^{1+\beta} \right) \text{ for } \beta, 1+\beta \neq 0, \quad (4)$$

When $\alpha = 1$ and $\beta = 1$, it reduces to the Euclidean (EUC) distance:

$$D_{AB}^{(1,1)}(P||Q) = D_{EUC}(P||Q) = \frac{1}{2} \sum_{it} (p_{it} - q_{it})^2, \qquad (5)$$

When $\alpha = 1$ and $\beta = 0$, it reduces to Kullback-Leibler (KL) divergence [38]:

$$D_{AB}^{(1,0)}(P||Q) = D_{KL}(P||Q) = \sum_{it} \left(p_{it} \ln \frac{p_{it}}{q_{it}} - p_{it} + q_{it} \right), \qquad (6)$$

When $\alpha = 1$ and $\beta = -1$, it reduces to Itakura-Saito divergence [39]:

$$D_{AB}^{(1,-1)}(P||Q) = D_{IS}(P||Q) = \sum_{it} \left(\ln \frac{q_{it}}{p_{it}} + \frac{p_{it}}{q_{it}} - 1 \right), \qquad (7)$$

5   Multiplicative Update Algorithms for RFNs

We shall now develop generalized RFN algorithms based on the AB-divergences with $X = P = [p_{it}] \in \mathbb{R}_+^m$, $MY \in \mathbb{R}_+^m = Q = [q_{it}]$. Given the RFN problem defined as $\arg\min_Y D(X||MY)$ in Eq. 1, if Y is given, then it is a learning problem where $\mathbf{M}$ is to be optimized; if $\mathbf{M}$ is given, Y is the only variable in the cost function, thus it is a prediction problem which is our focus. A general update rule for gradient descent is defined as:

$$Y \leftarrow Y - \eta_Y \circ \nabla_Y D(X\|MY) \tag{8}$$

where η_Y is a vector of learning rates w.r.t. Y (instead of a scalar constant η for all features), $\circ$ denotes element-by-element product, and $\nabla D(X\|MY)$ is the gradient of the cost function given by:

$$\nabla_Y D(X\|MY) = \left[\frac{\partial D(X\|MY)}{\partial y_1} \frac{\partial D(X\|MY)}{\partial y_2} \cdots \frac{\partial D(X\|MY)}{\partial y_n} \right] \tag{9}$$

or equivalently in the element-by-element basis:

$$y_i \leftarrow y_i - \eta_i \frac{\partial D(X\|MY)}{\partial y_i} \tag{10}$$

where $Y = [y_1, y_2, \cdots, y_n]^T$.

Now we use KL-Divergence as an example to show how to formally derive the multiplicative update rules. In the context of RFN, the cost function based on KL-divergence in Eq. 6 is defined as

$$D_{KL}(X\|MY) = \sum_d \left[x_d \ln \frac{x_d}{(MY)|_d} - x_d + (MY)|_d \right] \tag{11}$$

where $(MY)|_d$ denotes the d-th element of the result of the matrix vector product (MY). Instead of directly applying gradient decent to minimize this equation, we derive the multiplicative update algorithm for RFN as follow.

$$\sum_d \left[x_d \ln \frac{x_d}{(MY)|_d} - x_d + (MY)|_d \right] = tr \left[X \ln \frac{X}{(MY)} - X + (MY) \right]$$

$$= tr \left[X \ln X - X \ln(MY) - X + MY \right]$$

Thus, the derivative w.r.t. Y can be computed as:

$$\nabla_Y D_{KL}(X\|MY) = \frac{\partial}{\partial Y} \left[tr(X \ln X - X \ln(MY) - X + MY) \right] \tag{12}$$

$$= \frac{\partial(MY)}{\partial} \left[-\frac{X}{MY} + 1 \right] = \boxed{-M^T \frac{X}{MY} + M^T 1}.$$

Note that, 1 is the unit matrix, $M^T 1$ is the sum weights in Y, where each element in it is the sum of the columns in $\mathbf{M}$. Substitute the $\nabla_Y D_{KL}(X\|MY)$ into Eq. 8, we have

$$Y \leftarrow Y - \eta_Y \circ \left(-M^T \frac{X}{MY} + M^T 1 \right) = Y + \eta_Y \circ \left(M^T \frac{X}{MY} - M^T 1 \right) \tag{13}$$

To ensure Y is non-negative, let η_Y to be $\eta_Y = \frac{Y}{M^T 1}$. Then, the additive update rule Eq. 13 become the multiplicative update rule:

$$Y \leftarrow Y \circ \frac{M^T \frac{X}{MY}}{M^T 1} \qquad (14)$$

This multiplicative update rule is equivalent to the original update rule for RFNs [17–21]. In a similar manner, the multiplicative update rules based on other divergences can be derived, as summarized in Table 1. The detailed derivations and proofs will be included in a longer journal papers to be submitted.

Table 1. Multiplicative Update rules for various divergence functions

Divergence	MU Rule for RFN	Hyperparameters
Euclidean distance	$Y \leftarrow Y \circ \frac{M^T X}{M^T (MY)}$	$\alpha = \beta = 1$
Kullback Leibler	$Y \leftarrow Y \circ \frac{M^T \frac{X}{MY}}{M^T 1}$	$\alpha = 1$ and $\beta = 0$
Itakura-Saito	$Y \leftarrow Y \circ \frac{M^T \frac{X}{MY}}{M^T \frac{1}{MY}}$	$\alpha = 1$ and $\beta = -1$
α-divergence	$Y \leftarrow Y \circ \frac{M^T \frac{X^\alpha}{(MY)^\alpha}}{M^T 1}$	$\alpha + \beta = 1$ and $\alpha \neq 0, \alpha \neq 1$
β-divergence	$Y \leftarrow Y \circ \frac{M^T X \circ (MY)^{\beta-1}}{M^T (MY)^\beta}$	$\alpha = 1$ and $\beta, 1 + \beta \neq 0$
AB-divergence	$Y \leftarrow Y \circ \frac{M^T X^\alpha \circ (MY)^{\beta-1}}{M^T (MY)^{\alpha+\beta-1}}$	$\alpha, \beta, \alpha + \beta \neq 0$

6 Experiments

To demonstrate RFNs' classification capability with one-shot learning, we apply them on face and hand-written character recognition, and compare with the most commonly used classifiers including SVM and KNN.

6.1 Face Recognition with LFW Dataset

In this experiment, we used the deep funneling aligned LFW image dataset [40] with the *Unrestricted with labeled outside data* protocol [41,42] using the VGGFace2 pre-trained model with ResNet-50 architecture [43] as the feature extractor [44]. We also used Multi-task CNN (MTCNN) [45] for face detection-alignment. For each image file, the face is cropped and resized to 224×224 with 20. A 2048 dimensional feature descriptor of a face is extracted. The Computer used for experiment is an Intel(R) Core(TM) i7-4770 CPU @ 3.4 GHz, RAM 8 GB, 64-bit OS.

Few-Shot Learning with RFN. The number of images for each subject in the LFW dataset varies ranging from 1 to 100 or more. We selected all subjects in LFW with more than one image, where one of the images is first randomly selected for the test set and the remaining are used for the training set. Among the test set, 300 images are randomly selected for each run. On average, 6050 sample images among 900 different subjects were selected for training (average 6.7 image samples per class). The steady state tolerance for all RFN algorithms is set to be 0.001. The default linear SVM and KNN classifier with 1 neighbor and Euclidean-distance metric in sklearn were used.

The results are summarized in Table 2. Div-RFN which is the mean of error rate of the best results among all the RFNs for every run, is statistically significant better than SVM and KNN with the $p - value = 4\%$, which indicates that, in every run, it can almost always be found that at least one of the specail RFNs achieved the best result. Also all the results of the special cases of divergence-RFNs are better than that of SVM and KNN. The KL-RFN is the conventional RFN. ($\alpha = 0.9, \beta = 0.5$) for $\alpha\beta$-RFN is the best results among a few other manually selected combinations. Among the RFNs, the EUC-divergence RFN converge slightly slower than others with about 43 iterations. The training time for SVM is much longer than that for RFN.

Table 2. Mean error and standard error of the mean obtained over the LFW dataset with non-standard protocol for 100 runs.

Model	Error rate	Training time (S)/Iters
SVM	0.02 ± 0.0008	89.31 ± 0.5
KNN	0.0453 ± 0.089	0.98 ± 0.05
Div-RFN	**0.0106 ± 0.0005**	**$0.09 \pm 0.001/(43)$**
KL-RFN ($\alpha = 1, \beta = 0$)	0.0136 ± 0.0007	42
EUC-RFN ($\alpha = 1, \beta = 1$)	0.0142 ± 0.0007	59
IS-RFN ($\alpha = 1, \beta = -1$)	0.0156 ± 0.0007	43
α-RFN ($\alpha = 1.1$)	0.0135 ± 0.0006	42
β-RFN ($\beta = 0.01$)	0.0135 ± 0.0007	42
$\alpha\beta$-RFN ($\alpha = 0.9, \beta = 0.5$)	0.0135 ± 0.0007	48

RFN Classification with One-Shot Learning. LFW datasets in View 2^1 which was splitted randomly into 10-fold cross validation was used. It is designed to use one set for testing and the remaining 9 sets for training. Instead, we directly test each of the 10 set of images with the VGGFace2 pre-trained model as the feature extractor. For the same pairs, the first image in each pair of the 300 pairs is used to construct the support set, and the second images for query

---

[1] http://vis-www.cs.umass.edu/lfw/.

set. The first and second image are assigned the same label. In testing, if the prediction of a test image is not the same as the test label, then it is counted as an error. For the different pairs, the support set and query set are constructed in the same way, where the test image in each pair is still assigned the same label as the first image, but in testing, if the prediction is the same as the test label, then it is counted as an error.

The results are summarized in Table 3. For comparison, we also list the results from other methods. Note that FaceNet uses the LFW training set for training with the softmax classifier, which runs for 275,000 steps and is terminated using the learning rate schedule, and takes around 30 h on a Nvidia Pascal Titan X GPU, Tensorflow r1.7, CUDA 8.0 and CuDNN 6.0. The AB-RFN is the best results among other RFN algorithms.

Table 3. The test results over the 10 sets of the same image pairs and 10 sets of different image pairs in LFW. The parameters $\alpha = 0.9, \beta = 0.5$ were used for the AB-RFN. On average, there are about 150 classes for each set of image pairs.

Model	SVM	KNN	**AB-RFN**	human	FaceNet [46]
FP	0.019±0.0034	0.0237±0.0034	**0.0141±0.0028**	–	–
FN	0.0045±0.0023	0.0049±0.0012	**0.0024±0.0009**	–	–
Error	0.0118±0.0026	0.0143±0.0028	**0.0082±0.002**	0.0247	0.0037

6.2 Hand-Written Characters Recognition with the Omniglot Data Set

The Omniglot data set contains 1623 different handwritten characters from 50 different alphabets [25]. Each of the characters has 20 samples. It is split into 30 alphabets background set and a 20 alphabet evaluation set.

A model of a Siamese Neural Network with the architecture described in the original research paper [8] is used for feature extraction with a slight modification, where the original 4096 dimensions of feature embedding was changed to 2048. The model was trained with data size 90,000 (90,000 iterations of one shot tasks) with batch size of 32, 20 ways, 250 one-shot tasks and no affine distortions (Table 4).

For 1-shot 20 ways, the accuracy performances of β-RFN and KNN are close and better than that of SVM; for 5-shot 20 way, β-RFN and SVM are close and better than for KNN. The Div-RFN which averages of the best results among RFNs, is much better and close to the original SNN. This means that a particular RFN can perform better than others over different datasets.

Notice that the differences in both the models and datasets. Among the two pre-trained models, the VGGFace2 model is a well trained model. β-RFN achieves robustness when the β value is in a small value range, and has much

Table 4. Mean error and standard error of the mean obtained over the Omniglot dataset with a non-standard protocol for 100 runs using SVN, KNN, RFNs, one-shot and 5-shot 20 ways classification. The Div-RFN is the average of the best results among all the RFNs for each run. The numbers within brackets are the values of the divergence parameters α and β

Model	1-shot error rate	5-shot error rate
SVM	0.1707 ± 0.0510	0.0474 ± 0.0309
KNN	0.1540 ± 0.0510	0.0563 ± 0.0335
KL-RFN ($\alpha = 1, \beta = 0$)	0.1702 ± 0.0506	0.0516 ± 0.0316
EUC-RFN ($\alpha = 1, \beta = 1$)	0.1642 ± 0.0500	0.0500 ± 0.0318
IS-RFN ($\alpha = 1, \beta = -1$)	0.1850 ± 0.0516	0.0604 ± 0.0337
α-RFN	$0.1669 \pm 0.0513(0.5)$	$0.0511 \pm 0.0317(0.8)$
β-RFN	$0.15.03 \pm 0.0486(9.0)$	$0.0456 \pm 0.0304(5.0)$
$\alpha\beta$-RFN ($\alpha = 1.8, \beta = 2.5$)	0.1606 ± 0.0530	0.0497 ± 0.0314
Div-RFN	$\mathbf{0.1130 \pm 0.0455}$	0.0263 ± 0.0227
SNN * [8,9]	0.1120	0.035

better performance than SVM and KNN over the LFW dataset, which is unbalanced. On the other hand, the SNN model is simple and not so well trained, it achieves the best results (robustness) when the β value is much larger (6, 7, up to 12), and the performance is close to SVM and KNN over the Omniglot dataset which is balanced with the same number of training instances.

7   Conclusion and Future Work

We have presented how to formally develop a set of more efficient, flexible and robust algorithms as alternative solutions to the commonly used classifiers. The flexibility is in term of adding new classes, new features, modifying the existing features independently (locally) and adapting different objective functions with parameters for fine-tuning for robustness over different datasets. The robustness is in terms of fine-tuning the parameters leading to robustness to outliers and noise. These algorithms achieve strong results for one-shot learning and statistically significantly outperformed the most popular classifiers, SVM and KNN for few-shots learning over the LFW and Omniglot datasets. We also relate RFNs to the application of VI which is widely used to approximate posterior densities by optimization, an alternative strategy to MCMC sampling for applying increasingly complex probabilistic models to larger datasets.

In the future, we want to automate the parameter fine-tuning process for generalized-RFNs. Moreover, we are interested in potential for end-to-end learning by combining with Graph Neural Networks. We are also keen to apply these classifiers to VI and large document analysis e.g., topic modelling and sentiment analysis.

References

1. Jacob, F.: The structure of perceptual categories. J. Math. Psychol. **41**(2), 145–170 (1997)
2. Finn, C., Yu, T., Zhang, T., Abbeel, P., Levine, S.: One-Shot Visual Imitation Learning via Meta-Learning ARXIV, eprint arXiv:1709.04905 (2017)
3. Adam, S., Sergey, B., Matthew, B., Wierstra, D., Timothy, L.: Meta-learning with memory-augmented neural networks. In: Proceeding ICML'16 Proceedings of the 33rd International Conference on International Conference on Machine Learning, New York, USA, vol. 48, pp 1842–1850 (2016)
4. Fengwei, Z., Bin, W., Zhenguo, L.: Deep Meta-Learning: Learning to Learn in the Concept Space. ARXIV, eprint arXiv:1802.03596 (2018)
5. Yan, D., et al.: One-Shot Imitation Learning. ARXIV, eprint arXiv:1703.07326 (2017)
6. Tsendsuren, M., Hong, Y.: Meta Networks. ARXIV, eprint arXiv:1703.00837 (2017)
7. Fei-Fei, L., Rob, F., Pietro, P.: One-shot learning of object categories. IEEE Trans. Pattern Anal. Mach. Intell. **28**(4), 594–611 (2006)
8. Gregory, K., Richard, Z., Ruslan, S.: Siamese neural networks for one-shot image recognition. In: ICML Deep Learning Workshop, vol. 2 (2015)
9. Oriol, V., Charles, B., Timothy, L., Koray, K., Daan, W., Matching networks for one shot learning. In: NIPS (2016)
10. Flood, S., Yongxin, Y., Li, Z., Tao, X., Philip, H.S.T., Timothy, M.H.: Learning to compare: Relation network for few-shot learning. In: CVPR (2018)
11. Jake, S., Kevin, S., Richard, S.Z.: Prototypical networks for few-shot learning. In: Advances in Neural Information Processing Systems, vol. 30, pp. 4077–4087 (2017)
12. Wu, H., Xu, Z., Zhang, J., Yan, W., Ma, X.: Face recognition based on convolution siamese networks. In: 10th International Congress on Image and Signal Processing, BioMedical Engineering and Informatics (CISP-BMEI), Shanghai, China (2017)
13. Tan, C., Sun, F., Kong, T., Zhang, W., Yang, C., Liu, C.: A Survey on Deep Transfer Learning, CoRR, vol. abs/1808.01974 (2018)
14. Goodfellow, I., et al.: Generative adversarial nets. In: Advances in Neural Information Processing Systems, pp. 2672–2680 (2014)
15. Vapnik, V.: The Nature of Statistical Learning Theory. Springer, New York (1995). https://doi.org/10.1007/978-1-4757-3264-1
16. Altman, N.S.: An introduction to kernel and nearest-neighbor nonparametric regression. Am. Stat. **46**(3), 175–185 (1992)
17. Tsvi, A.: Symbolic neural networks for cognitive capacities. Spec. Issue J. Biol. Inspired Cogn. Arch. **9**, 71–81 (2014)
18. Tsvi, A., Luis, M.A.B.: Evaluating the contribution of top-down feedback and post-learning reconstruction. In: Biologically Inspired Cognitive Architecture AAAI Proceedings (2011)
19. Tsvi, A.: Using non-oscillatory dynamics to disambiguate pattern mixtures. In: Ravishankar, A.R., Guillermo, A.C. (eds.) The Relevance of the Time Domain to Neural Network Models, pp. 57–74. Springer, Heidelberg (2012). https://doi.org/10.1007/978-1-4614-0724-9_4
20. Tsvi, A., Dervis, C.V., Eyal, A.: Counting objects with biologically inspired regulatory feedback networks. International Joint Conference on Neural Networks Proceedings (2009)

21. Tsvi A., 2012, Towards Bridging the Gap Between Pattern Recognition and Symbolic Representation Within Neural Networks, Workshop on Neural-Symbolic Learning and Reasoning, AAAI-2012
22. Andrzej, C., Sergio, C., Shun-ichi, A.: Generalized Alpha-Beta divergences and their application to robust nonnegative matrix factorization. Entropy **13**(1), 134–170 (2011)
23. Bregman, L.M.: The relaxation method of finding the common point of convex sets and its application to the solution of problems in convex programming. USSR Comput. Math. Math. Phys. **7**(3), 200–217 (1967)
24. Gary, B.H., Manu, R., Tamara, B., Erik, L.M.: Labeled faces in the wild: A database for studying face recognition in unconstrained environments. Technical Report 07–49, University of Massachusetts, Amherst (2007)
25. Brenden, M.L., Ruslan, S., Joshua, B.T.: Human-level concept learning through probabilistic program induction. Science **350**(6266), 1332–1338 (2015)
26. Michael, I.J., Zoubin, G., Tommi, S.J., Lawrence, K.S.: An introduction to variational methods for graphical models. Mach. Learn. **37**(2), 183–233 (1999)
27. Martin, J.W., Michael, I.J.: Graphical models, exponential families, and variational inference. Found. Trends Mach. Learn. **1**(1–2), 1–305 (2008)
28. Blei, D.M., Kucukelbir, A., McAuliffe, J.D.: Variational inference: a review for statisticians. J. Am. Stat. Assoc. **112**(518), 859–877 (2017)
29. Futami, F., Sato, I., Sugiyama, M.: Variational inference based on robust divergences. In: AISTATS (2018)
30. Yingzhen, L., Richard, E.T.: Rényi divergence variational inference. In: Advances in Neural Information Processing Systems, pp. 1073–1081 (2016)
31. Regli, J., Silva, R.: Alpha-Beta Divergence For Variational Inference, arXiv preprint arXiv:1805.01045 (2018)
32. Carlos, V., Daniel, H.: Alpha divergence minimization in multi-class Gaussian process classification. Neurocomputing **378**(22), 210–227 (2020)
33. Andrzej, C., Shun-ichi, A.: Families of Alpha- Beta- and Gamma- divergences: flexible and robust measures of similarities. Entropy **12**, 1532–1568 (2010)
34. Andrzej, C., Rafal, Z., Seungjin, C., Robert, P., Shun-ichi, A.: Non-negative tensor factorization using alpha and beta divergences. In: IEEE International Conference on Acoustics. Speech, and Signal Processing, Honolulu, Hawaii, USA, vol. 3, pp. 1393–1396(2007)
35. Andrzej C., Rafal Z., Shun-ichi A.: Csiszar's divergences for non-negative matrix factorization: family of new algorithms. In Conference on Independent Component Analysis and Blind Source Separation (ICA), Charleston, SC, USA, pp. 32–39 (2006)
36. Shinto, E., Yutaka, K.: Robustifying maximum likelihood estimation. Technical report, Institute of Statistical Mathematics, Tokyo (2001)
37. Raul, K.: A generalized divergence measure for nonnegative matrix factorization. Neural Comput. **19**(3), 780–791 (2007)
38. Kullback, S., Leibler, R.A.: On information and sufficiency. Ann. Math. Stat. **22**(1), 79–86 (1951)
39. Itakura, F., Saito, S.: Analysis synthesis telephony based on the maximum likelihood method. In: 6th International Congress Acoustics, Tokyo, Japan, , pp. C-17–C-20 (1968)
40. Gary, B.H., Marwan, M., Erik, L.-M.: Learning to align from scratch. In: Advances in Neural Information Processing Systems (NIPS) (2012)

41. Gary, B.H., Erik, L.-M.: Labeled Faces in the Wild: Updates and New Reporting Procedures. University of Massachusetts, Amherst Technical Report UM-CS-2014-003 (2014)

42. Learned-Miller, E., Huang, G.B., RoyChowdhury, A., Li, H., Hua, G.: Labeled faces in the wild: a survey. In: Kawulok, M., Celebi, M.E., Smolka, B. (eds.) Advances in Face Detection and Facial Image Analysis, pp. 189–248. Springer, Cham (2016). https://doi.org/10.1007/978-3-319-25958-1_8

43. Kaiming, H., Xiangyu, Z., Shaoqing, R., Jian, S.: Deep residual learning for image recognition. In: CVPR (2016)

44. Qiong, C., Shen, L., Omkar, M.P., Andrew, Z.: Vggface2: a dataset for recognising faces across pose and age. In: International Conference on Automatic Face and Gesture Recognition (2018)

45. Kaipeng, Z., Zhanpeng, Z., Zhifeng, L.: Joint face detection and alignment using multitask cascaded convolutional networks. IEEE Signal Process. Lett. **23**(10), 1499–1503 (2016)

46. Florian, S., Dmitry, K., James, P.: Facenet: a unified embedding for face recognition and clustering. In: Proceedings of CVPR (2015)

Squashed Shifted PMI Matrix: Bridging Word Embeddings and Hyperbolic Spaces

Zhenisbek Assylbekov$^{(\boxtimes)}$ ⓘ and Alibi Jangeldin

School of Sciences and Humanities, Nazarbayev University, Nur-Sultan, Kazakhstan
zhassylbekov@nu.edu.kz

Abstract. We show that removing sigmoid transformation in the skip-gram with negative sampling (SGNS) objective does not harm the quality of word vectors significantly and at the same time is related to factorizing a squashed shifted PMI matrix which, in turn, can be treated as a connection probabilities matrix of a random graph. Empirically, such graph is a complex network, i.e. it has strong clustering and scale-free degree distribution, and is tightly connected with hyperbolic spaces. In short, we show the connection between static word embeddings and hyperbolic spaces through the squashed shifted PMI matrix using analytical and empirical methods.

Keywords: Word vectors · PMI · Complex networks · Hyperbolic geometry

1 Introduction

Modern word embedding models (McCann et al. 2017; Peters et al. 2018; Devlin et al. 2019) build vector representations of words in context, i.e. the same word will have different vectors when used in different contexts (sentences). Earlier models (Mikolov et al. 2013b; Pennington et al. 2014) built the so-called static embeddings: each word was represented by a single vector, regardless of the context in which it was used.

Despite the fact that static word embeddings are considered obsolete today, they have several advantages compared to contextualized ones. Firstly, static embeddings are trained much faster (few hours instead of few days) and do not require large computing resources (1 consumer-level GPU instead of 8–16 non-consumer GPUs). Secondly, they have been studied theoretically in a number of works (Levy and Goldberg 2014b; Arora et al. 2016; Hashimoto et al. 2016; Gittens et al. 2017; Tian et al. 2017; Ethayarajh et al. 2019; Allen et al. 2019; Allen and Hospedales 2019; Assylbekov and Takhanov 2019; Zobnin and Elistratova 2019) but not much has been done for the contextualized embeddings (Reif et al. 2019). Thirdly, static embeddings are still an integral part of deep neural network models that produce contextualized word vectors, because embedding lookup matrices are used at the input and output (softmax) layers of such models. Therefore, we consider it necessary to further study static embeddings.

© Springer Nature Switzerland AG 2020
M. Gallagher et al. (Eds.): AI 2020, LNAI 12576, pp. 336–346, 2020.
https://doi.org/10.1007/978-3-030-64984-5_26

With all the abundance of both theoretical and empirical studies on static vectors, they are not fully understood, as this work shows. For instance, it is generally accepted that good quality word vectors are inextricably linked with a low-rank approximation of the pointwise mutual information (PMI) matrix or the Shifted PMI (SPMI) matrix, but we show that vectors of comparable quality can also be obtained from a low-rank approximation of a *Squashed* SPMI matrix (Sect. 2). Thus, a Squashed SPMI matrix is a viable alternative to standard PMI/SPMI matrices when it comes to obtaining word vectors.

At the same time, it is easy to interpret the Squashed SPMI matrix with entries in $[0, 1)$ as a connection probabilities matrix for generating a random graph. Studying the properties of such a graph, we come to the conclusion that it is a so-called complex network, i.e. it has a strong clustering property and a scale-free degree distribution (Sect. 3).

It is noteworthy that complex networks, in turn, are dual to hyperbolic spaces (Sect. 4) as was shown by Krioukov et al. (2010). Hyperbolic geometry has been used to train word vectors (Nickel and Kiela 2017; Tifrea et al. 2018) and has proven its suitability—in a hyperbolic space, word vectors need lower dimensionality than in the Euclidean space.

Thus, to the best of our knowledge, this is the first work that establishes simultaneously a connection between word vectors, a Squashed SPMI matrix, complex networks, and hyperbolic spaces. Figure 1 summarizes our work and serves as a guide for the reader.

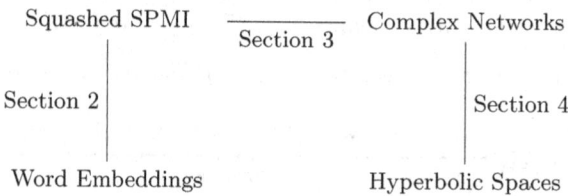

Fig. 1. Summary of our work

Notation

We let $\mathbb{R}$ denote the real numbers. Bold-faced lowercase letters ($\mathbf{x}$) denote vectors, plain-faced lowercase letters (x) denote scalars, $\langle \mathbf{x}, \mathbf{y} \rangle$ is the Euclidean inner product, (a_{ij}) is a matrix with the ij-th entry being a_{ij}. 'i.i.d.' stands for 'independent and identically distributed'. We use the sign $\propto$ to abbreviate 'proportional to', and the sign $\sim$ to abbreviate 'distributed as'.

Assuming that words have already been converted into indices, let $\mathcal{W} := \{1, \ldots, n\}$ be a finite vocabulary of words. Following the setup of the widely used WORD2VEC model (Mikolov et al. 2013b), we use *two* vectors per each word i: (1) $\mathbf{w}_i \in \mathbb{R}^d$ when $i \in \mathcal{W}$ is a center word, (2) $\mathbf{c}_i \in \mathbb{R}^d$ when $i \in \mathcal{W}$ is a context word; and we assume that $d \ll n$.

In what follows we assume that our dataset consists of co-occurence pairs (i, j). We say that "the words i and j co-occur" when they co-occur in a fixed-size window of words. The number of such pairs, i.e. the size of our dataset, is denoted by N. Let $\#(i, j)$ be the number of times the words i and j co-occur, then $N = \sum_{i \in W} \sum_{j \in W} \#(i, j)$.

2   Squashed SPMI and Word Vectors

A well known skip-gram with negative sampling (SGNS) word embedding model of Mikolov et al. (2013b) maximizes the following objective function

$$\sum_{i \in W} \sum_{j \in W} \#(i, j) \left(\log \sigma(\langle \mathbf{w}_i, \mathbf{c}_j \rangle) + k \cdot \mathbb{E}_{j' \sim p}[\log \sigma(-\langle \mathbf{w}_i, \mathbf{c}_{j'} \rangle)]\right), \quad (1)$$

where $\sigma(x) = \frac{1}{1+e^{-x}}$ is the logistic sigmoid function, p is a smoothed unigram probability distribution for words[1], and k is the number of negative samples to be drawn. Interestingly, training SGNS is approximately equivalent to finding a low-rank approximation of a Shifted PMI matrix (Levy and Goldberg 2014b) in the form $\log \frac{p(i,j)}{p(i)p(j)} - \log k \approx \langle \mathbf{w}_i, \mathbf{c}_j \rangle$, where the left-hand side is the ij-th element of the $n \times n$ shifted PMI matrix, and the right-hand side is an element of a matrix with rank $\leq d$ since $\mathbf{w}_i, \mathbf{c}_j \in \mathbb{R}^d$. This approximation (up to a constant shift) was later re-derived by Arora et al. (2016); Assylbekov and Takhanov (2019); Allen et al. (2019); Zobnin and Elistratova (2019) under different sets of assuptions. In this section we show that constraint optimization of a slightly modified SGNS objective (1) leads to a low-rank approximation of the *Squashed Shifted PMI* (σSPMI) matrix, defined as $\sigma\text{SPMI}_{ij} := \sigma(\text{PMI}_{ij} - \log k)$.

Theorem 1. *Assuming $0 < \langle \mathbf{w}_i, \mathbf{c}_j \rangle < 1$, the following objective function*

$$\mathcal{L} = \sum_{i \in W} \sum_{j \in W} \#(i, j) \underbrace{(\log \langle \mathbf{w}_i, \mathbf{c}_j \rangle + k \cdot \mathbb{E}_{j' \sim P}[\log(1 - \langle \mathbf{w}_i, \mathbf{c}_{j'} \rangle)])}_{\ell(\mathbf{w}_i, \mathbf{c}_j)}, \quad (2)$$

reaches its optimum at $\langle \mathbf{w}_i, \mathbf{c}_j \rangle = \sigma\text{SPMI}_{ij}$.

Proof. Expanding the sum and the expected value in (2) as in Levy and Goldberg (2014b), and defining $p(i, j) := \frac{\#(i,j)}{N}$, $p(i) := \frac{\#(i)}{N}$, we have

$$\mathcal{L} = N \sum_{i \in W} \sum_{j \in W} p(i, j) \cdot \log \langle \mathbf{w}_i, \mathbf{c}_j \rangle + p(i) \cdot p(j) \cdot k \cdot \log(1 - \langle \mathbf{w}_i, \mathbf{c}_j \rangle). \quad (3)$$

Thus, we can rewrite the individual objective $\ell(\mathbf{w}_i, \mathbf{c}_j)$ in (2) as

$$\ell = N \left[p(i, j) \cdot \log \langle \mathbf{w}_i, \mathbf{c}_j \rangle + p(i) \cdot p(j) \cdot k \cdot \log(1 - \langle \mathbf{w}_i, \mathbf{c}_j \rangle) \right]. \quad (4)$$

Differentiating (4) w.r.t. $\langle \mathbf{w}_i, \mathbf{c}_j \rangle$ we get

$$\frac{\partial \ell}{\partial \langle \mathbf{w}_i, \mathbf{c}_j \rangle} = N \left[\frac{p(i, j)}{\langle \mathbf{w}_i, \mathbf{c}_j \rangle} - \frac{p(i) \cdot p(j) \cdot k}{1 - \langle \mathbf{w}_i, \mathbf{c}_j \rangle} \right].$$

---

[1] The authors of SGNS suggest $p(i) \propto \#(i)^{3/4}$.

Setting this derivative to zero gives

$$\frac{p(i,j)}{p(i)p(j)} \cdot \frac{1}{k} = \frac{\langle \mathbf{w}_i, \mathbf{c}_j \rangle}{1 - \langle \mathbf{w}_i, \mathbf{c}_j \rangle} \quad \Rightarrow \quad \log \frac{p(i,j)}{p(i)p(j)} - \log k = \log \frac{\langle \mathbf{w}_i, \mathbf{c}_j \rangle}{1 - \langle \mathbf{w}_i, \mathbf{c}_j \rangle}$$

$$\Leftrightarrow \quad \log \frac{p(i,j)}{p(i)p(j)} - \log k = \text{logit}\langle \mathbf{w}_i, \mathbf{c}_j \rangle$$

$$\Leftrightarrow \quad \sigma \left(\log \frac{p(i,j)}{p(i)p(j)} - \log k \right) = \langle \mathbf{w}_i, \mathbf{c}_j \rangle, \quad (5)$$

where $\text{logit}(q) := \log \frac{q}{1-q}$ is the logit function which is the inverse of the logistic sigmoid function, i.e. $\sigma(\text{logit}(q)) = q$. From (5) we have $\sigma\text{SPMI}_{ij} = \langle \mathbf{w}_i, \mathbf{c}_j \rangle$, which concludes the proof.

Remark 1. Since $\sigma(x)$ can be regarded as a smooth approximation of the Heaviside step function $H(x)$, defined as $H(x) = 1$ if $x > 0$ and $H(x) = 0$ otherwise, it is tempting to consider a *binarized* SPMI (BSPMI) matrix $H(\text{PMI}_{ij} - \log k)$ instead of σSPMI. Being a binary matrix, BSPMI can be interpreted as an adjacency matrix of a graph, however our empirical evaluation below (Table 1) shows that such strong roughening of the σSPMI matrix degrades the quality of the resulting word vectors. This may be due to concentration of the SPMI values near zero (Fig. 5), while $\sigma(x)$ is approximated by $H(x)$ only for x away enough from zero.

Remark 2. The objective (2) differs from the SGNS objective (1) only in that the former does not use the sigmoid function (keep in mind that $\sigma(-x) = 1 - \sigma(x)$). We will refer to the objective (2) as *Nonsigmoid SGNS*.

Direct Matrix Factorization

Optimization of the Nonsigmoid SGNS (2) is not the only way to obtain a low-rank approximation of the σSPMI matrix. A viable alternative is factorizing the σSPMI matrix with the singular value decomposition (SVD): $\sigma\text{SPMI} = \mathbf{U}\boldsymbol{\Sigma}\mathbf{V}^{\top}$, with orthogonal $\mathbf{U}, \mathbf{V} \in \mathbb{R}^{n \times n}$ and diagonal $\boldsymbol{\Sigma} \in \mathbb{R}^{n \times n}$, and then zeroing out the $n - d$ smallest singular values, i.e.

$$\sigma\text{SPMI} \approx \mathbf{U}_{1:n,1:d} \boldsymbol{\Sigma}_{1:d,1:d} \mathbf{V}^{\top}_{1:d,1:n}, \quad (6)$$

where we use $\mathbf{A}_{a:b,c:d}$ to denote a submatrix located at the intersection of rows $a, a+1, \ldots, b$ and columns $c, c+1, \ldots, d$ of $\mathbf{A}$. By the Eckart-Young theorem (Eckart and Young 1936), the right-hand side of (6) is the closest rank-d matrix to the σSPMI matrix in Frobenius norm. The word and context embedding matrices can be obtained from (6) by setting $\mathbf{W}^{\text{SVD}} := \mathbf{U}_{1:n,1:d}\sqrt{\boldsymbol{\Sigma}_{1:d,1:d}}$, and $\mathbf{C}^{\text{SVD}} := \sqrt{\boldsymbol{\Sigma}_{1:d,1:d}}\mathbf{V}^{\top}_{1:d,1:n}$. When this is done for a positive SPMI (PSPMI) matrix, defined as $\max(\text{PMI}_{ij} - \log k, 0)$, the resulting word embeddings are comparable in quality with those from the SGNS (Levy and Goldberg 2014b).

Table 1. Evaluation of word embeddings on the analogy tasks (Google and MSR) and on the similarity tasks (the rest). For word similarities evaluation metric is the Spearman's correlation with the human ratings, while for word analogies it is the percentage of correct answers.

Method	WordSim	MEN	M. Turk	Rare Words	Google	MSR
SGNS	**.678**	**.656**	.690	**.334**	**.359**	**.394**
Nonsigm. SGNS	.649	.649	**.695**	.299	.330	.330
PMI + SVD	**.663**	<u>.667</u>	.668	.332	.315	<u>.323</u>
SPMI + SVD	.509	.576	.567	.244	.159	.107
PSPMI + SVD	.638	**.672**	.658	.298	.246	.207
σSPMI + SVD	<u>.657</u>	.631	<u>.661</u>	<u>.328</u>	<u>.294</u>	**.341**
BSPMI + SVD	.623	.586	.643	.278	.177	.202

Empirical Evaluation of the σSPMI-Based Word Vectors

To evaluate the quality of word vectors resulting from the Nonsigmoid SGNS objective and σSPMI factorization, we use the well-known corpus, text8.[2] We ignored words that appeared less than 5 times, resulting in a vocabulary of 71,290 words. The SGNS and Nonsigmoid SGNS embeddings were trained using our custom implementation.[3] The SPMI matrices were extracted using the HYPER-WORDS tool of Levy et al. (2015) and the truncated SVD was performed using the SCIKIT-LEARN library of Pedregosa et al. (2011). The trained embeddings were evaluated on several word similarity and word analogy tasks: WORDSIM (Finkelstein et al. 2002), MEN (Bruni et al. 2012), M.TURK (Radinsky et al. 2011), RARE WORDS (Luong et al. 2013), GOOGLE (Mikolov et al. 2013a), and MSR (Mikolov et al. 2013c). We used the GENSIM tool of Řehůřek and Sojka (2010) for evaluation. For answering analogy questions (a is to b as c is to ?) we use the 3COSADD method of Levy and Goldberg (2014a) and the evaluation metric for the analogy questions is the percentage of correct answers. We mention here that our goal is not to beat state of the art, but to compare SPMI-based embeddings (SGNS and SPMI+SVD) versus σSPMI-based ones (Nonsigmoid SGNS and σSPMI+SVD). The results of evaluation are provided in Table 1.

As we can see the Nonsigmoid SGNS embeddings in general underperform the SGNS ones but not by a large margin. σSPMI shows a competitive performance among matrix-based methods across most of the tasks. Also, Nonsigmoid SGNS and σSPMI demonstrate comparable performance as predicted by Theorem 1. Although BSPMI is inferior to σSPMI, notice that such aggressive compression as binarization still retains important information on word vectors.

---

[2] http://mattmahoney.net/dc/textdata.html.
[3] https://github.com/zh3nis/SGNS.

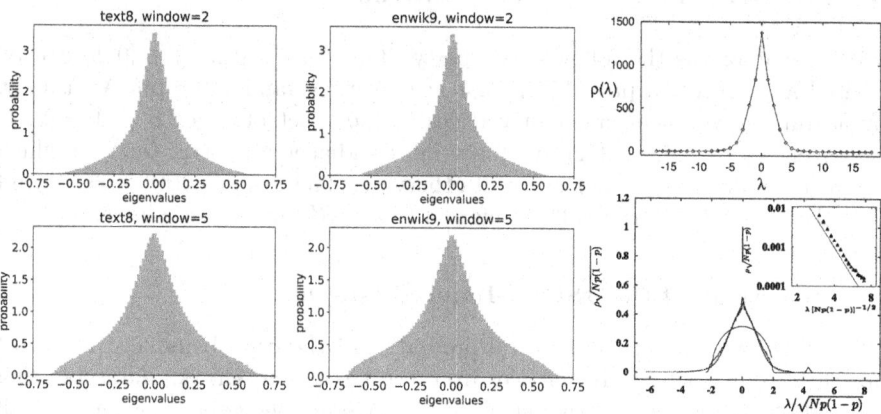

Fig. 2. Spectral distribution of the σSPMI-induced graphs (left and middle columns), and of scale-free random graphs with strong clustering property (right top: Goh et al. (2001), right bottom: Farkas et al. (2001). When generating several random graphs from the same σSPMI matrix, their eigenvalue distributions are visually indistinguishable, thus we display the results of one run per each matrix.

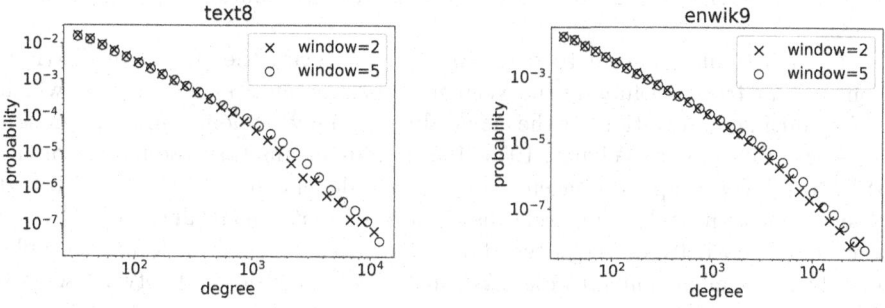

Fig. 3. Degree distributions of the σSPMI-induced graphs. The axes are on logarithmic scales.

Table 2. Clustering coefficients of the σSPMI-induced graphs. For each corpus–window combination we generate ten graphs and report 95% confidence intervals across these ten runs.

	text8		enwik9	
	Window = 2	Window = 5	Window = 2	Window = 5
C	.1341 ± .0006	.1477 ± .0005	.1638 ± .0006	.1798 ± .0004
$\bar{k}/n$	.0014 ± .0000	.0030 ± .0000	.0006 ± .0000	.0012 ± .0000

3 σSPMI and Complex Networks

σSPMI matrix has the following property: its entries $\sigma\mathrm{SPMI}_{ij} \in [0,1)$ can be treated as connection probabilities for generating a random graph. As usually, by a graph $\mathcal{G}$ we mean a set of vertices $\mathcal{V}$ and a set of edges $\mathcal{E} \subset \mathcal{V} \times \mathcal{V}$. It is convenient to represent graph edges by its adjacency matrix (e_{ij}), in which $e_{ij} = 1$ for $(i,j) \in \mathcal{E}$, and $e_{ij} = 0$ otherwise. The graph with $\mathcal{V} := \mathcal{W}$ and $e_{ij} \sim \mathrm{Bernoulli}(\sigma\mathrm{SPMI}_{ij})$ will be referred to as σ*SPMI-induced Graph*.

3.1   Spectrum of the σSPMI-Induced Graph

First of all, we look at the spectral properties of the σSPMI-induced Graphs.[4] For this, we extract SPMI matrices from the `text8` and `enwik9` datasets using the HYPERWORDS tool of Levy et al. (2015). We use the default settings for all hyperparameters, except the word frequency threshold and context window size. We ignored words that appeared less than 100 times and 250 times in `text8` and `enwik9` correspondingly, resulting in vocabularies of 11,815 and 21,104 correspondingly. We additionally experiment with the context window size 5, which by default is set to 2. We generate random graphs from the σSPMI matrices and compute their eigenvalues using the TENSORFLOW library (Abadi et al. 2016), and the above-mentioned threshold of 250 for `enwik9` was chosen to fit the GPU memory (11 GB, RTX 2080 Ti). The eigenvalue distributions are provided in Fig. 2.

The distributions seem to be symmetric, however, the shapes of distributions are far from resembling the Wigner semicircle law $x \mapsto \frac{1}{2\pi}\sqrt{4 - x^2}$, which is the limiting distribution for the eigenvalues of many random symmetric matrices with i.i.d. entries (Wigner, 1955; 1958). This means that the entries of the σSPMI-induced graph's adjacency matrix *are* dependent, otherwise we would observe approximately semicircle distributions for its eigenvalues. We observe some similarity between the spectral distributions of the σSPMI-induced graphs and of the so-called *complex networks* which arise in physics and network science (Fig. 2).

Notice that the connection between human language structure and complex networks was observed previously by Cancho and Soé (2001). A thorough review on approaching human language with complex networks was given by Cong and Liu (2014). In the following subsection we will specify precisely what we mean by a complex network.

3.2   Clustering and Degree Distribution of the σSPMI-induced Graph

We will use two statistical properties of a graph – degree distribution and clustering coefficient. The *degree* of a given vertex i is the number of edges that connects it with other vertices, i.e. $\deg(i) = \sum_{j \in \mathcal{V}} e_{ij}$. The clustering coefficient

---

[4] We define the graph spectrum as the set of eigenvalues of its adjacency matrix.

measures the average fraction of pairs of neighbors of a vertex that are also neighbors of each other. The precise definition is as follows.

Let us indicate by $\mathcal{G}_i = \{j \in \mathcal{V} \mid e_{ij} = 1\}$ the set of nearest neighbors of a vertex i. By setting $l_i = \sum_{j \in \mathcal{V}} e_{ij} \left[\sum_{k \in \mathcal{G}_i;\ j<k} e_{jk} \right]$, we define the local clustering coefficient as $C(i) = \frac{l_i}{\binom{|\mathcal{G}_i|}{2}}$, and the *clustering coefficient* as the average over $\mathcal{V}$: $C = \frac{1}{n} \sum_{i \in \mathcal{V}} C(i)$.

Let $\bar{k}$ be the average degree per vertex, i.e. $\bar{k} = \frac{1}{n} \sum_{j \in \mathcal{V}} e_{ij}$. For random binomial graphs, i.e. graphs with edges $e_{ij} \overset{iid}{\sim} \text{Bernoulli}(p)$, it is well known (Erdős and Rényi, 1960) that $C \approx \frac{\bar{k}}{n}$ and $\deg(i) \sim \text{Binomial}(n-1, p)$. A *complex network* is a graph, for which $C \gg \frac{\bar{k}}{n}$ and $p(\deg(i) = k) \propto \frac{1}{k^\gamma}$, where γ is some constant (Dorogovtsev, 2010). The latter property is referred to as *scale-free* (or *power-law*) degree distribution.

We constructed σSPMI-induced Graphs from the `text8` and `enwik9` datasets using context windows of sizes 2 and 5 and ignoring words that appeared less than 5 times, and computed their clustering coefficients (Table 2) as well as degree distributions (Fig. 3) using the NETWORKIT tool (Staudt et al. 2016). NETWORKIT uses the algorithm of Schank and Wagner (2005) to compute the clustering coefficient. As we see, the σSPMI-induced graphs *are* complex networks, and this brings us to the hyperbolic spaces.

4   Complex Networks and Hyperbolic Geometry

Complex networks are "dual" to hyperbolic spaces as was shown by Krioukov et al. (2010). They showed that any complex network, as defined in Sect. 3, has an effective hyperbolic geometry underneath. Apart from this, they also showed that any hyperbolic geometry implies a complex network: they placed randomly n points (nodes) into a hyperbolic disk of radius R, and used $p_{ij} := \sigma \left(c[R - x_{ij}] \right)$ as connection probability for connecting nodes i and j, where x_{ij} is the hyperbolic distance between i and j, and c is a constant. An example of such random graph is shown in Fig. 4. Krioukov et al. (2010) showed that the resulting graph is a complex network. They establish connections between the clustering coefficient C and the power-law exponent γ of a complex network and the curvature of a hyperbolic space.

Comparing the construction of Krioukov et al. (2010) to the way we generate a random graph from the σSPMI matrix, and taking into account that both methods produce similar structures (complex networks), we conclude that the distribution of the SPMI values should be similar to the distribution of $R - x_{ij}$, i.e. $\text{PMI}_{ij} - \log k \sim R - x_{ij}$. To verify this claim we compare the distribution of SPMI values with the p.d.f. of a random variable $R - X$, where X is a hyperbolic distance between two random points on the hyperbolic disk (the exact form of this p.d.f. is given in the Appendix A). R was chosen according to the formula $R = 2 \ln[8n/(\pi \bar{k})]$ (Krioukov et al. 2010), where $\bar{k}$ is the average degree of the σSPMI-induced Graph. The results are shown in Fig. 5. As we can see, the

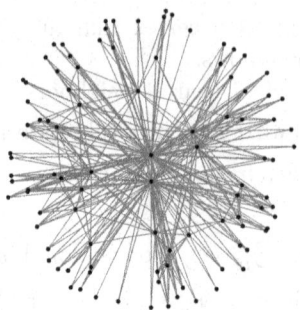

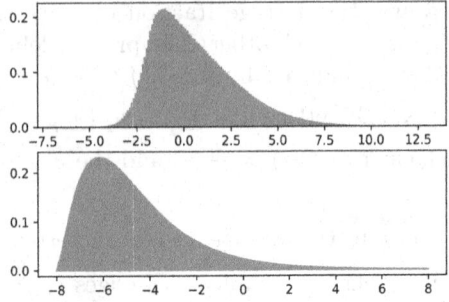

Fig. 4. Rand. hyperbolic graph.   **Fig. 5.** SPMI values distr'n (top) vs $R - X$.

two distributions are indeed similar and the main difference is in the shift— distribution of $R - X$ is shifted to the left compared to the distribution of the SPMI values. This allows us reinterpreting the pointwise mutual information as the negative of hyperbolic distance (up to scaling and shifting).

5   Conclusion

It is noteworthy that the seemingly fragmented sections of scientific knowledge can be closely interconnected. In this paper, we have established a chain of connections between word embeddings and hyperbolic geometry, and the key link in this chain is the Squashed Shifted PMI matrix. Claiming that hyperbolicity underlies word vectors is not novel (Nickel and Kiela, 2017; Tifrea et al. 2018). However, this work is the first attempt to *justify* the connection between hyperbolic geometry and the word embeddings. In the course of our work, we discovered novel objects—Nonsigmoid SGNS and Squashed Shifted PMI matrix— which can be investigated separately in the future.

Acknowledgements. This work is supported by the Nazarbayev University faculty-development competitive research grants program, grant number 240919FD3921. The authors would like to thank Zhuldyzzhan Sagimbayev for conducting preliminary experiments for this work, and anonymous reviewers for their feedback.

A   Auxiliary Results

Proposition 1. *Let X be a distance between two points that were randomly uniformly placed in the hyperbolic disk of radius R. The probability distribution function of X is given by*

$$f_X(x) = \int_0^R \int_0^R \frac{\sinh(x)}{\pi\sqrt{1 - A(r_1, r_2, x)}\sinh(r_1)\sinh(r_2)}\rho(r_1)\rho(r_2)dr_1 dr_2, \quad (7)$$

where $A(r_1, r_2, x) = \frac{\cosh(r_1)\cosh(r_2) - \cosh(x)}{\sinh(r_1)\sinh(r_2)}$, *and* $\rho(r) = \frac{\sinh r}{\cosh R - 1}$.

The proof is by direct calculation and is omitted due to page limit.

References

Abadi, M., et al.: TensorFlow: a system for large-scale machine learning. In: Proceedings of OSDI, pp. 265–283 (2016)

Allen, C., Balazevic, I., Hospedales, T.: What the vec? Towards probabilistically grounded embeddings. In: Advances in Neural Information Processing Systems, pp. 7465–7475 (2019)

Allen, C., Hospedales, T.: Analogies explained: towards understanding word embeddings. In: International Conference on Machine Learning, pp. 223–231 (2019)

Arora, S., Li, Y., Liang, Y., Ma, T., Risteski, A.: A latent variable model approach to PMI-based word embeddings. Trans. Assoc. Comput. Linguist. **4**, 385–399 (2016)

Assylbekov, Z., Takhanov, R.: Context vectors are reflections of word vectors in half the dimensions. J. Artif. Intell. Res. **66**, 225–242 (2019)

Bruni, E., Boleda, G., Baroni, M., Tran, N.K.: Distributional semantics in technicolor. In: Proceedings of ACL, pp. 136–145. Association for Computational Linguistics (2012)

Cancho, R.F.I., Solé, R.V.: The small world of human language. Proc. R. Soc. Lond. Ser. B Biol. Sci. **268**(1482), 2261–2265 (2001)

Cong, J., Liu, H.: Approaching human language with complex networks. Physics of life reviews **11**(4), 598–618 (2014)

Devlin, J., Chang, M.W., Lee, K., Toutanova, K.: BERT: pre-training of deep bidirectional transformers for language understanding. In: Proceedings of NAACL-HLT, pp. 4171–4186 (2019)

Dorogovtsev, S.: Lectures on Complex Networks. Oxford University Press Inc., USA (2010)

Eckart, C., Young, G.: The approximation of one matrix by another of lower rank. Psychometrika **1**(3), 211–218 (1936). https://doi.org/10.1007/BF02288367

Erdős, P., Rényi, A.: On the evolution of random graphs. Publ. Math. Inst. Hung. Acad. Sci **5**(1), 17–60 (1960)

Ethayarajh, K., Duvenaud, D., Hirst, G.: Towards understanding linear word analogies. In: Proceedings of the 57th Annual Meeting of the Association for Computational Linguistics, pp. 3253–3262 (2019)

Farkas, I.J., Derényi, I., Barabási, A.L., Vicsek, T.: Spectra of "real-world" graphs: beyond the semicircle law. Phys. Rev. E **64**(2), 026704 (2001)

Finkelstein, L., et al.: Placing search in context: the concept revisited. ACM Trans. Inf. Syst. **20**(1), 116–131 (2002)

Gittens, A., Achlioptas, D., Mahoney, M.W.: Skip-gram- zipf + uniform = vector additivity. In: Proceedings of the 55th Annual Meeting of the Association for Computational Linguistics (Volume 1: Long Papers), pp. 69–76 (2017)

Goh, K.I., Kahng, B., Kim, D.: Spectra and eigenvectors of scale-free networks. Phys. Rev. E **64**(5), 051903 (2001)

Hashimoto, T.B., Alvarez-Melis, D., Jaakkola, T.S.: Word embeddings as metric recovery in semantic spaces. Trans. Assoc. Comput. Linguist. **4**, 273–286 (2016)

Krioukov, D., Papadopoulos, F., Kitsak, M., Vahdat, A., Boguná, M.: Hyperbolic geometry of complex networks. Phys. Rev. E **82**(3), 036106 (2010)

Levy, O., Goldberg, Y.: Linguistic regularities in sparse and explicit word representations. In: Proceedings of CoNLL, pp. 171–180 (2014a)

Levy, O., Goldberg, Y.: Neural word embedding as implicit matrix factorization. In: Proceedings of NeurIPS, pp. 2177–2185 (2014b)

Levy, O., Goldberg, Y., Dagan, I.: Improving distributional similarity with lessons learned from word embeddings. Trans. Assoc. Comput. Linguist. **3**, 211–225 (2015)

Luong, T., Socher, R., Manning, C.: Better word representations with recursive neural networks for morphology. In: Proceedings of CoNLL, pp. 104–113 (2013)

McCann, B., Bradbury, J., Xiong, C., Socher, R.: Learned in translation: contextualized word vectors. In: Advances in Neural Information Processing Systems, pp. 6294–6305 (2017)

Mikolov, T., Chen, K., Corrado, G., Dean, J.: Efficient estimation of word representations in vector space. arXiv preprint arXiv:1301.3781 (2013a)

Mikolov, T., Sutskever, I., Chen, K., Corrado, G.S., Dean, J.: Distributed representations of words and phrases and their compositionality. In: Advances in Neural Information Processing Systems, pp. 3111–3119 (2013b)

Mikolov, T., Yih, W.T., Zweig, G.: Linguistic regularities in continuous space word representations. In: Proceedings of the 2013 Conference of the North American Chapter of the Association for Computational Linguistics: Human Language Technologies, pp. 746–751 (2013c)

Nickel, M., Kiela, D.: Poincaré embeddings for learning hierarchical representations. In: Advances in Neural Information Processing Systems, pp. 6338–6347 (2017)

Pedregosa, F., et al.: Scikit-learn: machine learning in Python. J. Mach. Learn. Res. **12**, 2825–2830 (2011)

Pennington, J., Socher, R., Manning, C.: Glove: Global vectors for word representation. In: Proceedings of EMNLP, pp. 1532–1543 (2014)

Peters, M.E., et al.: Deep contextualized word representations. In: Proceedings of NAACL-HLT, pp. 2227–2237 (2018)

Radinsky, K., Agichtein, E., Gabrilovich, E., Markovitch, S.: A word at a time: computing word relatedness using temporal semantic analysis. In: Proceedings of the 20th international conference on World wide web. pp. 337–346. ACM (2011)

Řehůřek, R., Sojka, P.: Software framework for topic modelling with large corpora. In: Proceedings of the LREC 2010 Workshop on New Challenges for NLP Frameworks, pp. 45–50. ELRA, Valletta, May 2010. http://is.muni.cz/publication/884893/en

Reif, E., et al.: Visualizing and measuring the geometry of BERT. In: Advances in Neural Information Processing Systems, pp. 8592–8600 (2019)

Schank, T., Wagner, D.: Approximating clustering coefficient and transitivity. J. Graph Algorithms Appl. **9**(2), 265–275 (2005)

Staudt, C.L., Sazonovs, A., Meyerhenke, H.: NetworKit: a tool suite for large-scale complex network analysis. Netw. Sci. **4**(4), 508–530 (2016)

Tian, R., Okazaki, N., Inui, K.: The mechanism of additive composition. Mach. Learn. **106**(7), 1083–1130 (2017). https://doi.org/10.1007/s10994-017-5634-8

Tifrea, A., Bécigneul, G., Ganea, O.E.: Poincaré glove: hyperbolic word embeddings. arXiv preprint arXiv:1810.06546 (2018)

Wigner, E.P.: Characteristic vectors of bordered matrices with infinite dimensions. Ann. Math. **62**(3), 548–564 (1955)

Wigner, E.P.: On the distribution of the roots of certain symmetric matrices. Ann. Math. **67**(2), 325–327 (1958)

Zobnin, A., Elistratova, E.: Learning word embeddings without context vectors. In: Proceedings of the 4th Workshop on Representation Learning for NLP (RepL4NLP-2019), pp. 244–249 (2019)

An Information-Theoretic Perspective on Overfitting and Underfitting

Daniel Bashir, George D. Montañez[⊠], Sonia Sehra, Pedro Sandoval Segura, and Julius Lauw

AMISTAD Lab, Department of Computer Science, Harvey Mudd College, Claremont, CA, USA
{dbashir,gmontanez,ssehra,psandovalsegura,julauw}@hmc.edu

Abstract. We present an information-theoretic framework for understanding overfitting and underfitting in machine learning and prove the formal undecidability of determining whether an arbitrary classification algorithm will overfit a dataset. Measuring algorithm capacity via the information transferred from datasets to models, we consider mismatches between algorithm capacities and datasets to provide a signature for when a model can overfit or underfit a dataset. We present results upper-bounding algorithm capacity, establish its relationship to quantities in the algorithmic search framework for machine learning, and relate our work to recent information-theoretic approaches to generalization.

Keywords: Overfitting · Underfitting · Algorithm capacity

1 Introduction

Overfitting and underfitting are constant and ubiquitous dangers in machine learning. The goal of supervised learning is to approximate or fit a true signal relating features X to responses Y, which can be interpreted as a function $f : X \to Y$ or a distribution $P(Y|X)$. Overfitting occurs when an algorithm reduces error through memorization of training examples, with noisy or irrelevant features, rather than learning the true general relationship between X and Y [3,12]. Underfitting occurs when an algorithm lacks sufficient model capacity or sufficient training to fully learn the true relationship, whether through memorization or not. A *learning algorithm* (our general term for a machine learning approach that processes data to produce models or hypotheses) is equipped with a hypothesis space $\mathcal{G}$ which contains the potential guesses the algorithm may have for the target function (or distribution). The hypotheses in $\mathcal{G}$ can overfit when the complexity of the available hypotheses are mismatched to the complexity of the true signal being learned, allowing the act of model selection to become equivalent to the setting of bits in a general memory storage device, recording memorized label mappings as a short-cut for reducing training error.

While every machine learning practitioner is warned to avoid the twin pitfalls of overfitting and underfitting, theory related to both remains underdeveloped,

© Springer Nature Switzerland AG 2020
M. Gallagher et al. (Eds.): AI 2020, LNAI 12576, pp. 347–358, 2020.
https://doi.org/10.1007/978-3-030-64984-5_27

largely relying on folk-wisdom and heuristic approaches. In particular, beyond intuition and comparative arguments, there is no formalized set of criteria for whether a particular algorithm will overfit or underfit a given dataset.

Of course, there exist well-known characterizations of algorithm complexity. The VC dimension provides a loose upper bound on model complexity in general, while more recent characterizations like Rademacher complexity seek to provide a normalized comparative measure. To measure the complexity of datasets as opposed to algorithms or models, Li and Abu-Mostafa's work provides a useful characterization [5]. Even given this existing work, recent papers (e.g., [12]) have correctly pointed out that current theories of generalization are not enough to explain phenomena like the observed performance of deep neural networks.

The search framework proposed in [6] abstracts the machine learning problem into a more general search setting. Using recent developments from this framework coupled with information-theoretic insights, we can gain a new perspective on issues of algorithm capacity, overfitting, and underfitting. Our definitions of algorithm capacity closely resemble recent information-theoretic analyses that consider the input-output mutual information of a learning algorithm, such as those in [11] and [2], and bring to mind empirical *generalized information* [1].

Our manuscript's primary contributions are as follows:

1. We show that the general problem of determining whether an arbitrary algorithm will overfit a particular dataset is formally undecidable, by a reduction to the halting problem. This leads us to focus on special cases where overfitting determinations can be made, such as with restricted complexity learning algorithms [9].
2. We develop a framework for explaining the phenomenon of overfitting and underfitting from an information-theoretic perspective, using notions of *algorithm capacity* to redefine both pitfalls and demonstrate how those notions interact with existing work.

The remainder of the paper is organized as follows. In Sect. 2 we present the formal undecidability of the overfitting detection problem for classification algorithms under the standard observational definition of overfitting. Section 3 introduces our notions of capacity as well as new definitions for overfitting and underfitting in terms of capacity. We then present bounds on algorithm capacity, and conclude with a discussion of the significance of the results and future work. We begin by introducing some basic concepts and notational conventions, before looking at the formal undecidability of overfitting in the next section.

1.1   Algorithms and Datasets

A learning algorithm $\mathcal{A}$ may be viewed as a stochastic map $P_{G|D}$ that takes as input a training set D of size n, namely $D = (Z_1, ..., Z_n)$ whose elements belong to an instance space $\mathcal{Z}$ and are typically sampled i.i.d. according to an unknown distribution $\mathcal{D}$, and outputs a hypothesis in its hypothesis space, $g \in \mathcal{G}$. Each instance Z_i in the dataset may also represent a pair $(\mathbf{x}_i, y_i)$ where $\mathbf{x}_i$ is a feature vector and y_i is the corresponding label or response. G denotes the random variable representing the output of $\mathcal{A}$ with D as input.

Within this work, we limit ourselves to discrete hypothesis spaces and datasets. This allows us to use the discrete entropy throughout and reflects finite-precision numerical representations in all modern digital hardware. However, it also poses certain mathematical restrictions, such as excluding reproducing kernel Hilbert spaces and other continuous mathematical spaces from our consideration.

2 Formal Undecidability of Overfitting

Traditionally, overfitting is diagnosed by comparing the losses of an algorithm on training and tests datasets, where the error on the test set (average observed loss) is intended to approximate the true risk (expected loss). Observationally, if the true risk $R_\mathcal{D}(g)$ (estimated by sampling of test datasets) exceeds the empirical risk $\widehat{R}_D(g)$ (the risk on the training dataset), the algorithm is said to **overfit**.

Definition 1 (Overfitting (Observational). *Algorithm $\mathcal{A}$ **overfits** dataset D if it selects a hypothesis $g \in \mathcal{G}$ such that $R_\mathcal{D}(g) > \widehat{R}_D(g)$.*

Under this definition, the problem of determining whether an arbitrary classification algorithm will overfit an arbitrary dataset is formally undecidable.

Theorem 1 (Formal Undecidability of Overfitting).
   Let S be the set of all encodable classification algorithms, let $\langle \mathcal{A} \rangle$ denote the encoded form of algorithm $\mathcal{A}$, and let D denote a dataset. Then,

$$L_{overfit} = \{\langle \mathcal{A} \rangle, D | \mathcal{A} \in S, \mathcal{A} \text{ will overfit } D\}$$

is undecidable.

Proof sketch: We show L_{overfit} is undecidable by a reduction to the halting problem. By way of contradiction, if L_{overfit} is decidable then there exists a Turing machine, M_{overfit}, which for all inputs of the form $\langle \mathcal{A} \rangle$, D halts and determines whether $\mathcal{A}$ will overfit D either once training ends or asymptotically.

We construct a decider for L_{halt}: the machine $\mathcal{A}'$ *builder* takes as input $\langle M \rangle$, w and constructs an encoded algorithm $\mathcal{A}'$ which represents an iterative machine learning method, and exports the encoded algorithm along with a training dataset $D \sim \mathcal{D}$. On its first iteration, $\mathcal{A}'$ instantiates a machine learning model which produces maximally wrong (under the fixed loss function) response values for all examples in D, and uniformly randomly guesses response values for all examples not in D. Then $\mathcal{A}'$ will have lower expected error on any test set drawn from $\mathcal{D}$ than its observed (maximal) error on D, and will not overfit.

Next, $\mathcal{A}'$ simulates M on w. If M halts on w, $\mathcal{A}'$ memorizes dataset D via a look-up table, still uniformly randomly guessing examples not in D. If M does not halt on w, the original model remains. Thus, $\mathcal{A}'$ will overfit if and only if M halts on w: asking M_{overfit} whether $\mathcal{A}'$ will overfit on D tells us if M halts on w.   □

Theorem 1 tells us that there can exist no general purpose overfitting detector that can perfectly determine whether an arbitrary algorithm will overfit a dataset if trained to completion or for enough iterations (with respect to iterative methods). However, a less accurate detector can exist, such as a uniform random guesser. Given that accuracy on this problem ranges between 0 and 100, exclusive, the question becomes: how much can we improve an overfitting detector to get accuracy closer to (though never quite reaching) 100%? The proof for Theorem 1 hints at what property can be leveraged to improve such detectors. In the proof, we rely on the fact that the algorithm can memorize a dataset of arbitrary complexity, essentially giving it unlimited algorithmic capacity. Put another way, we assumed a model family with infinite VC dimension, able to discriminate any set of points, no matter how large. Since, in classification settings, restricted VC dimension is both necessary and sufficient for uniform convergence of empirical error to generalization error, this suggests that comparing algorithm capacity to dataset complexity could play a role in improving such detection methods.

3   Definitions and Terminology

3.1   Capacity, Overfitting, and Underfitting

We present a set of definitions and theorems that characterize our view of learning algorithms, inspired in part by the *algorithmic search framework* [6].

In the search framework, a search problem is specified by a tuple (Ω, T, F) consisting of a search space Ω, a target subset $T \subseteq \Omega$, and an external information resource F. A search algorithm $\mathcal{A}$ at time i in its execution computes a probability distribution P_i over Ω and samples an element $\omega_i \in \Omega$ according to P_i, resulting in a sequence of distributions $\tilde{P} = [P_1, P_2, \ldots, P_N]$. $\mathcal{A}$ maintains a history h, where each timestep $h_i = (\omega_i, F(\omega_i))$ contains the element of Ω that $\mathcal{A}$ sampled at time i and the information about ω_i provided by F. A search is considered successful if, given a fixed target set t, $\mathcal{A}$ samples an element $\omega_i \in t$, where t is represented by a $|\Omega|$-length binary target vector $\mathbf{t}$, which has a 1 at index i if and only if $\omega_i \in t$, namely, $\mathbf{t}_i = \mathbb{1}_{\omega_i \in t}$ where $\mathbb{1}_-$ denotes the indicator function. The quantity $q(t, F)$ denotes the expected per-query probability of success, or the expected probability mass placed on t.

For our purposes, the search space Ω is the hypothesis space $\mathcal{G}$ of $\mathcal{A}$. The information resource has two components. The initial information $F(\emptyset)$ is a training dataset D of size n, while $F(h)$ is a non-negative loss function $\ell : \mathcal{G} \times \mathcal{Z} \to \mathbb{R}_{\geq 0}$. The target set T consists of all $g \in \mathcal{G}$ that achieve low population risk, namely,

$$R_{\mathcal{D}}(g) = \mathbb{E}_{\mathcal{D}}[\ell(g, \mathcal{Z})] = \int_{\mathcal{Z}} \ell(g, z)\mathcal{D}(\mathrm{d}z) < \epsilon$$

for some fixed scalar $\epsilon > 0$ for any data-generating distribution $\mathcal{D}$. The history of sampled elements corresponds to hypotheses considered as $\mathcal{A}$ is trained, using a method such as stochastic gradient descent.

Since $\mathcal{D}$ is unknown, we can instead compute the empirical risk of g on dataset D as

$$\widehat{R}_D(g) := \frac{1}{n} \sum_{i=1}^{n} \ell(g, z_i)$$

in the search of a hypothesis $g^* = \operatorname{argmin}_{g \in \mathcal{G}} R_{\mathcal{D}}(g)$, for which we choose as a proxy the empirical risk minimizer (ERM hypothesis), $\hat{g} = \operatorname{argmin}_{g \in \mathcal{G}} \widehat{R}_D(g)$.

We will frequently use the term "capacity" to describe the learning capabilities of an algorithm, as opposed to algorithm complexity, which indicates the expressiveness of functions in the algorithm's hypothesis space $\mathcal{G}$ (e.g., linear functions for a regression model).

Definition 2 (Algorithm Capacity). *The* ***capacity*** $C_\mathcal{A}$ *of an algorithm* $\mathcal{A}$ *is the maximum amount of information that* $\mathcal{A}$ *can extract from a dataset* $D \sim \mathcal{D}$ *when selecting its output hypothesis* g*, namely,*

$$C_\mathcal{A} = \sup_{\mathcal{D}} I(G; D)$$

where G *takes values in* $\mathcal{G}$*.*

$P(G|D)$ is fixed by the algorithm $\mathcal{A}$. Therefore, our definition for capacity is equivalent to the input-output mutual information measure given in [11] and can be viewed as the maximum capacity of an information channel from $\mathcal{Z}^n$ to $\mathcal{G}$. Note that the maximum amount of information an algorithm $\mathcal{A}$ may transfer from a dataset in selecting a hypothesis is the number of bits required to memorize a one-to-one mapping between each feature-label pair in that dataset.

For a fixed distribution $\mathcal{D}$, we can define the capacity relative to that particular distribution, which is simply the mutual information.

Definition 3 (Distributional Algorithm Capacity). *For* $D \sim \mathcal{D}$,

$$C_{\mathcal{A},\mathcal{D}} = I(G; D).$$

In an algorithm's search for an ERM hypothesis by an iterative method such as gradient descent, we may regard each iteration as a timestep and observe that by a time i, $\mathcal{A}$ will have sampled only a subset of $\mathcal{G}$. This may reduce the entropy of a variable G_i drawn from the expected ith distribution, $\mathbb{E}[P_i|D]$, and motivates the following definition.

Definition 4 (Time-indexed Capacity). *Let* P_i *denote the (stochastic) probability distribution over* $\mathcal{G}$ *at time* i*.* $\mathcal{A}$*'s capacity at time* i *is the maximum amount of information* $\mathcal{A}$ *may transfer from* $D \sim \mathcal{D}$ *to* $G_i \sim \mathbb{E}[P_i|D]$,

$$C_\mathcal{A}^i = \sup_{\mathcal{D}} I(G_i; D).$$

Finally, we define the pointwise information transfer by an algorithm from a specific dataset to a specific hypothesis.

Definition 5 (Pointwise Information Transfer). *For a given dataset d and specific hypothesis g, the* **pointwise information transfer** *by algorithm $\mathcal{A}$ from d to g is the pointwise mutual information (lift),*

$$C_{\mathcal{A}}(g, d) = \log_2 \frac{p(g, d)}{p(g)p(d)} = \log_2 \frac{p(g|d)}{p(g)} = \log_2 \frac{p(d|g)}{p(d)}.$$

Note that $p(g|d)$ captures how representative a hypothesis is of a dataset (i.e., how deterministic is the algorithm?), while $p(d|g)$ measures how identifiable a dataset is given a hypothesis (i.e., how many datasets strongly map to g?). For deterministic algorithms, $C_{\mathcal{A}}(g, d)$ becomes the Shannon surprisal of the set of datasets producing g, $C_{\mathcal{A}}(g, d) = -\log_2 \mathcal{D}(S)$, where $S = \{d' \in \mathcal{Z}^n \mid \mathcal{A}(d') = g\}$ is the collection of datasets d' such that $p(g|d') = 1$ under $\mathcal{A}$. Taking the expectation with respect to G and D, we see that $\mathbb{E}_{G,\mathcal{D}}[C_{\mathcal{A}}(G, D)] = C_{\mathcal{A},\mathcal{D}}$.

Having provided definitions of algorithm capacity, we next consider dataset complexity. Comparing an algorithm's capacity to the complexity of the dataset it is trained on may give insight into whether the algorithm will overfit or underfit. We begin with a definition based on algorithmic compressibility from [5].

Definition 6 (Dataset Turing Complexity). *Given a fixed Turing machine M that accepts a string p and feature vector $\mathbf{x}$ as input and outputs a label y, the data complexity of a dataset D is*

$$C_{D,M} = L(\langle M \rangle) + L(p)$$

where $L(p) = \min\{|p| : \forall(\mathbf{x}, y) \in D, M(p, \mathbf{x}) = y\}$. That is, the data complexity $C_{D,M}$ is the length of the shortest program that correctly maps every input in the data set $\mathcal{D}$ to its corresponding output.

For a dataset $D = (Z_1, ..., Z_n)$, the above definition contrasts with $C'_D = \sum_{i=1}^{n} b(z_i)$, where $b(z_i)$ is the number of bits required to encode the feature-label pair z_i without compression. C'_D gives the number of bits required to memorize an arbitrary dataset D. Taking the minimum of these two defined quantities gives us our definition of dataset complexity.

Definition 7 (Dataset Complexity C_D). $C_D = \min\{C_{D,M}, C'_D\}$.

By construction $C_D \leq C'_D$, giving us a computable upper bound on dataset complexity. While $C_{D,M}$ is not explicitly computable, methods for estimating the quantity are proposed in [5], to which we refer the interested reader. Given the definitions of dataset complexity and algorithm capacity, we can now define overfitting in information-theoretic terms.

Definition 8 (Overfitting). *An algorithm $\mathcal{A}$* **overfits** *if*

$$C_{\mathcal{A},\mathcal{D}} > \mathbb{E}_{\mathcal{D}}[C_D],$$

i.e., the algorithm tends to extract more bits than necessary to capture the noise-less signal from the dataset. The degree of overfitting is given by $C_{\mathcal{A},\mathcal{D}} - \mathbb{E}_{\mathcal{D}}[C_D]$.

Like overfitting, we can also give an information-theoretic definition for underfitting, based on the time-indexed capacity from Definition 4.

Definition 9 (Underfitting). *An algorithm $\mathcal{A}$ **underfits** at iteration i if*

$$C_{\mathcal{A}}^i < \mathbb{E}_{\mathcal{D}}[C_D]$$

i.e., after training for i timesteps, $\mathcal{A}$ has capacity strictly less than $\mathbb{E}_{\mathcal{D}}[C_D]$.

If the algorithm's model does not contain enough information to accomplish a learning task, this could be the result of insufficient capacity, insufficient training, or insufficient information retention, all of which are captured by $C_{\mathcal{A}}^i$.

Lastly, by Definition 5 we can define the overfitting between a fixed hypothesis (model) g and a fixed dataset d, related to the *generalized information* of Bartlett and Holloway [1] when considering $C_{\mathcal{A}}(g, d) - C_d$.

Definition 10 (Model Overfit). *$\mathcal{A}$'s **model** g **overfits** d if $C_{\mathcal{A}}(g, d) > C_d$.*

Because $C_{D,M}$ is uncomputable, one cannot generally determine model overfit whenever $C_{\mathcal{A}}(g, d) \leq C_d'$ (in agreement with Theorem 1). However, one can claim model overfitting for the special case of $C_{\mathcal{A}}(g, d) > C_d' \geq C_d$.

3.2 Capacity, Bias, and Expressivity

We now review quantitative notions of bias and expressivity introduced in [4]. Just as the estimation bias of a learning algorithm trades off with its variance, the algorithmic bias also trades off with expressivity, which loosely captures how widely a learning algorithm distributes probability mass over its search space in expectation. Naturally, this will be affected by how well an algorithm's inductive bias aligns with the target vector. To that end, we introduce the inductive orientation of an algorithm.

Definition 11 (Inductive Orientation). *Let F be an external information resource, such as a dataset, $\tilde{P}$ be defined as above, H be an algorithm's search history, and let*

$$\overline{\mathbf{P}}_F := \mathbb{E}_{\tilde{P}, H}\left[\frac{1}{|\tilde{P}|} \sum_{i=1}^{|\tilde{P}|} \mathbf{P}_i \,\middle|\, F \right].$$

*That is, $\overline{\mathbf{P}}_F$ is the algorithm's expected average conditional distribution on the search space given F. Then the **inductive orientation** of an algorithm is*

$$\overline{\mathbf{P}}_{\mathcal{D}} = \mathbb{E}_{F \sim \mathcal{D}}[\overline{\mathbf{P}}_F] \tag{1}$$

We may now define the entropic expressivity of an algorithm.

Definition 12 (Entropic Expressivity). *The **entropic expressivity** of an algorithm is the Shannon entropy of its inductive orientation,*

$$H(\overline{\mathbf{P}}_{\mathcal{D}}) = H(\mathcal{U}) - D_{\mathrm{KL}}(\overline{\mathbf{P}}_{\mathcal{D}} \,||\, \mathcal{U})$$

where $D_{\mathrm{KL}}(\overline{\mathbf{P}}_{\mathcal{D}} \,\|\, \mathcal{U})$ is the Kullback-Leibler divergence between distribution $\overline{\mathbf{P}}_{\mathcal{D}}$ and the uniform distribution $\mathcal{U}$, and both are distributions over the search space Ω.

Lauw et al. demonstrate a quantitative trade-off between the entropic expressivity and the bias of a learning algorithm [4]. This trade-off will allow us to relate algorithm capacity to bias, as well. As our hypothesis space $\mathcal{G}$ is the relevant search space here, we substitute $\mathcal{G}$ for Ω throughout.

Definition 13 *(Algorithmic Bias) Given a fixed target function* $\mathbf{t}$ *corresponding to the target set* t, *let* $p = \|\mathbf{t}\|^2/|\mathcal{G}|$ *denote the expected per-query probability of success under uniform random sampling,* $\mathbf{P}_{\mathcal{U}} = 1 \cdot |\mathcal{G}|^{-1}$ *be the inductive orientation vector for a uniform random sampler, and* $F \sim \mathcal{D}$, *where* $\mathcal{D}$ *is a distribution over a collection of information resources* $\mathcal{F}$. *Then,*

$$\mathrm{Bias}(\mathcal{D}, \mathbf{t}) = \mathbb{E}_{\mathcal{D}}[q(t, F) - p]$$
$$= \mathbf{t}^{\top}(\overline{\mathbf{P}}_{\mathcal{D}} - \mathbf{P}_{\mathcal{U}})$$
$$= \mathbf{t}^{\top}\mathbb{E}_{\mathcal{D}}\left[\overline{\mathbf{P}}_F\right] - \mathbf{t}^{\top}(1 \cdot |\mathcal{G}|^{-1})$$
$$= \mathbf{t}^{\top}\int_{\mathcal{F}} \overline{\mathbf{P}}_f \mathcal{D}(f) \, \mathrm{d}f - \frac{\|\mathbf{t}\|^2}{|\mathcal{G}|}.$$

Following [4], we re-state the bias-expressivity trade-off:

Theorem 2 (Bias-Expressivity Trade-off). *Given a distribution over information resources* $\mathcal{D}$ *and a fixed target* $t \subseteq \mathcal{G}$, *entropic expressivity is bounded above in terms of bias,*

$$H(\overline{\mathbf{P}}_{\mathcal{D}}) \leq \log_2 |\mathcal{G}| - 2\,\mathrm{Bias}(\mathcal{D}, \mathbf{t})^2.$$

Additionally, bias is bounded above in terms of entropic expressivity,

$$\mathrm{Bias}(\mathcal{D}, \mathbf{t}) \leq \sqrt{\frac{1}{2}(\log_2 |\mathcal{G}| - H(\overline{\mathbf{P}}_{\mathcal{D}}))}$$
$$= \sqrt{\frac{1}{2}D_{KL}(\overline{\mathbf{P}}_{\mathcal{D}} \,\|\, \mathcal{U})}.$$

Given the notions of inductive orientation and entropic expressivity, we can define distributional algorithm capacity in terms of these quantities.

Theorem 3 (Distributional Capacity as Entropic Expressivity).
An algorithm's distributional capacity may be re-written as the difference between its entropic expressivity and its expected entropic expressivity, namely

$$C_{\mathcal{A},\mathcal{D}} = H(\overline{\mathbf{P}}_{\mathcal{D}}) - \mathbb{E}_{\mathcal{D}}[H(\overline{\mathbf{P}}_F)]. \tag{2}$$

Proof. Note that, by marginalization of $F \sim \mathcal{D}$ and the definition of $\overline{P}_{\mathcal{D}}$,

$$p(g) = \mathbb{E}_{\mathcal{D}}[p(g|F)] = \mathbb{E}_{\mathcal{D}}[\overline{P}_F(g)] = \overline{P}_{\mathcal{D}}(g).$$

Therefore,

$$H(G) = -\sum_{g \in G} p(g) \log p(g) = -\sum_{g \in G} \overline{P}_{\mathcal{D}}(g) \log \overline{P}_{\mathcal{D}}(g) = H(\overline{\mathbf{P}}_{\mathcal{D}}).$$

Furthermore,

$$
\begin{aligned}
H(G|F) &= \sum_f H(G|F = f) P(f) \\
&= -\sum_f \sum_g P(f)[p(g|F = f) \log p(g|F = f)] \\
&= -\sum_f P(f) \left[\sum_g p(g|F = f) \log p(g|F = f) \right] \\
&= \mathbb{E}_{\mathcal{D}} \left[-\sum_g p(g|F) \log p(g|F) \right] \\
&= \mathbb{E}_{\mathcal{D}} \left[-\sum_g \overline{P}_F(g) \log \overline{P}_F(g) \right] \\
&= \mathbb{E}_{\mathcal{D}}[H(\overline{\mathbf{P}}_F)].
\end{aligned}
$$

Then, by the definition of distributional capacity $C_{\mathcal{A},\mathcal{D}}$ for $F \sim \mathcal{D}$,

$$C_{\mathcal{A},\mathcal{D}} = I(G; F) = H(G) - H(G|F) = H(\overline{\mathbf{P}}_{\mathcal{D}}) - \mathbb{E}_{\mathcal{D}}[H(\overline{\mathbf{P}}_F)].$$

$\square$

Note: Theorem 3 considers a distribution vector $\overline{\mathbf{P}}_{\mathcal{D}}$ that is averaged over all iterations of a search; if the distribution averaged over only the final iteration is desired, $\overline{\mathbf{P}}_{n,\mathcal{D}}$ and $\overline{\mathbf{P}}_{n,F}$ can be used instead, as detailed in [7].

Theorem 3 points towards a way of empirically estimating the quantity $C_{\mathcal{A},\mathcal{D}}$. We first form a *labeling distribution matrix* (LDM) for algorithm $\mathcal{A}$ described in [8]: the matrix consists of K simplex vectors $P_{f_1}, ..., P_{f_k}$, where simplex vector P_{f_i} corresponds to the probability distribution that $\mathcal{A}$ induces over its search space Ω after being trained on information resource f_i drawn from $\mathcal{D}$. Taking the average of all columns converges toward $\overline{\mathbf{P}}_{\mathcal{D}}$ by the law of large numbers (with increasing K), and taking the entropy of the averaged column vector converges toward $H(\overline{\mathbf{P}}_{\mathcal{D}})$. Furthermore, averaging the entropies of each column vector in the matrix will converge toward $\mathbb{E}_{\mathcal{D}}[H(\overline{\mathbf{P}}_F)]$ as K increases.

Corollary 1 (Algorithm Capacity as Entropic Expressivity).

$$C_{\mathcal{A}} = \sup_{\mathcal{D}}[H(\overline{\mathbf{P}}_{\mathcal{D}}) - \mathbb{E}_{\mathcal{D}}[H(\overline{\mathbf{P}}_F)]] \tag{3}$$

Expressing algorithm capacity in terms of entropic expressivity provides additional intuition about what precisely is being measured: Theorem 3 illustrates that an algorithm's capacity may be interpreted as how much its entropic expressivity for a fixed distribution differs from its expected entropic expressivity. In other words, $H(\overline{\mathbf{P}}_\mathcal{D})$ captures how "flat" the expected induced probability distribution is, which could result either from averaging together flat distributions or by averaging together many "sharp" distributions that happen to place their mass on very different regions of the search space. In contrast, $\mathbb{E}_\mathcal{D}[H(\overline{\mathbf{P}}_F)]$ measures how flat the induced distributions are in expectation. By subtracting the flatness aspect from the combined quantity that captures both flatness and dispersal of probability mass, we get a quantity that represents how much an algorithm shifts its probability mass in response to different information resources. The ability to do this is equivalent to the ability to store information (by taking on different configurations), and thus is a fitting measure of algorithm capacity.

Furthermore, we can use the values of entropic expressivity to derive bounds on $C_{\mathcal{A},\mathcal{D}}$ based on the entropic expressivity bounds established in [4]. We explore these connections next.

4   Algorithm Capacity Bounds

Our definition of algorithm capacity provides one concrete way of measuring what has traditionally been a loosely defined quantity. The goal of this section is to provide further insight by bounding algorithm capacity. For more detail on experimental methods to estimate algorithm capacity, we refer the reader to [8].

In addition, if we expand the possible hypothesis spaces under consideration to be real-valued functions, we obtain an upper bound on $C_\mathcal{A}$ in terms of the VC dimension as demonstrated in Sect. 4.2.

4.1   Trade-Off Bounds

First, we demonstrate how the bias-expressivity trade-off furnishes immediate bounds on algorithm capacity. Theorems 2 and 3 give us our first capacity bound.

Theorem 4 (Distributional Capacity Upper Bound).

$$C_{\mathcal{A},\mathcal{D}} \leq \log_2 |\mathcal{G}| - 2\operatorname{Bias}(\mathcal{D}, \mathbf{t})^2 - \mathbb{E}_\mathcal{D}[H(\overline{\mathbf{P}}_F)]. \tag{4}$$

Using the range bounds from Theorem 5.3 in [4], we can obtain even tighter bounds on $C_{\mathcal{A},\mathcal{D}}$ as a function of the bias, shown in Table 1.

Furthermore, rewriting the mutual information as KL-divergence furnishes another bound on $C_{\mathcal{A},\mathcal{D}}$.

Theorem 5 (Distributional Capacity KL-Divergence Bound).

$$\begin{aligned}
C_{\mathcal{A},\mathcal{D}} &= I(G; D) \\
&= \mathbb{E}_\mathcal{D}[D_{KL}(p_{G|D}||p_G)] \\
&\leq \sup_\mathcal{D}[D_{KL}(p_{G|D}||p_G)].
\end{aligned}$$

Table 1. Because the range of entropic expressivity changes with different levels of bias relative to target function $\mathbf{t}$, the maximum value for $C_{\mathcal{A},\mathcal{D}}$ does also.

Bias$(\mathcal{D}, \mathbf{t})$	$\mathbf{t}^\top \overline{\mathbf{P}}_{\mathcal{D}}$	Capacity upper bound
$-p$ (Minimum bias)	0	$\log_2(|\mathcal{G}| - \|\mathbf{t}\|^2) - \mathbb{E}_{\mathcal{D}}[H(\overline{\mathbf{P}}_F)]$
0 (No bias)	p	$\log_2 |\mathcal{G}| - \mathbb{E}_{\mathcal{D}}[H(\overline{\mathbf{P}}_F)]$
$1 - p$ (Maximum bias)	1	$\log_2 \|\mathbf{t}\|^2 - \mathbb{E}_{\mathcal{D}}[H(\overline{\mathbf{P}}_F)]$

That is, the maximum information that can be transferred between a learning algorithm and a particular dataset is bounded above by the maximum divergence between a prior distribution over the hypothesis space and a posterior distribution over the hypothesis space, given a dataset.

4.2   A VC Upper Bound

The discussion in [10] allows us to recover an upper bound on algorithm capacity: the logarithm of the well-known VC dimension, which provides a value in bits.

Theorem 6 (VC Dimension as Information Complexity). *Suppose algorithm $\mathcal{A}$ utilizes a hypothesis space of real-valued functions $\mathcal{G}$. Then*

$$C_{\mathcal{A}} \leq \log d_{VC}(\mathcal{G}).$$

5   Conclusion

Confronted with the ever-present dangers of overfitting and underfitting, we develop an information-theoretic perspective for understanding these phenomena, allowing us to characterize when they can occur and to what degree. We do so by considering the capacities of algorithms, complexities of datasets, and their relationship. In particular, we characterize overfitting as a symptom of mismatch between an algorithm's informational capacity and the complexity of the relationship it is attempting to learn. In colloquial terms, we have met the enemy, and it is mismatched capacity.

After introducing variations on algorithm capacity and recasting overfitting and underfitting as the relationship between algorithm capacity and dataset complexity, we give bounds on the algorithm capacity. We demonstrate that while the problem of determining whether an arbitrary classification algorithm will overfit a given dataset is formally undecidable, we can estimate the quantities proposed in this paper to determine when algorithm will overfit in expectation, and in some cases, when an algorithm's model overfits a dataset. Algorithm capacity estimation is the subject of future work.

Our methods make use of existing machinery from other frameworks, such as the algorithmic search framework and VC theory, which provide helpful characterizations and bounds for our current investigation. In particular, showing that distributional algorithm capacity can be written as a function of entropic expressivity allows us to gain insight into what algorithmic capacity means geometrically, in terms of shifted probability mass. In the future, the information-theoretic groundwork laid here will allow us to incorporate and extend other existing work, such as establishing a direct connection between the notions of bias, expressivity, and generalization, proving generalization bounds under our definitions and through our bounds on algorithm capacity.

References

1. Bartlett, J., Holloway, E.: Generalized information: a straightforward method for judging machine learning models. Commun. Blyth Inst. **1**(2), 13–21 (2019)
2. Bassily, R., Moran, S., Nachum, I., Shafer, J., Yehudayoff, A.: Learners that Use Little Information. In: Janoos, F., Mohri, M., Sridharan, K. (eds.) Proceedings of Algorithmic Learning Theory, Proceedings of Machine Learning Research, vol. 83, pp. 25–55, PMLR (2018). http://proceedings.mlr.press/v83/bassily18a.html
3. Krueger, D., et al.: Deep nets don't learn via memorization. In: Workshop Track-International Conference on Learning Representations (2017)
4. Lauw, J., Macias, D., Trikha, A., Vendemiatti, J., Montañez, G.D.: The Bias-expressivity trade-off. In: Rocha, A.P., Steels, L., van den Herik, H.J. (eds.) Proceedings of the 12th International Conference on Agents and Artificial Intelligence. SCITEPRESS (2020)
5. Li, L., Abu-Mostafa, Y.S.: Data complexity in machine learning. Technical Report CaltechCSTR:2006.004, California Institute of Technology (2006). https://resolver.caltech.edu/CaltechCSTR:2006.004
6. Montañez, G.D.: The famine of forte: few search problems greatly favor your algorithm. In: 2017 IEEE International Conference on Systems, Man, and Cybernetics (SMC), pp. 477–482. IEEE (2017)
7. Sam, T., Williams, J., Abel, T., Huey, S., Montañez, G.D.: decomposable probability-of-success metrics in algorithmic search. In: Rocha, A.P., Steels, L., van den Herik, H.J. (eds.) Proceedings of the 12th International Conference on Agents and Artificial Intelligence. SCITEPRESS (2020)
8. Sandoval Segura, P., et al.: The labeling distribution matrix (LDM): a tool for estimating machine learning algorithm capacity. In: Proceedings of the 12th International Conference on Agents and Artificial Intelligence (2020)
9. Vapnik, V.N.: An overview of statistical learning theory. IEEE Trans. Neural Netw. **10**(5), 988–999 (1999)
10. Vapnik, V.N., Chervonenkis, A.Y.: On the uniform convergence of relative frequencies of events to their probabilities. Theory Prob. Appl. **16**(2), 264–280 (1971)
11. Xu, A., Raginsky, M.: Information-theoretic analysis of generalization capability of learning algorithms. In: Proceedings of the 31st Conference on Neural Information Processing Systems (2017)
12. Zhang, C., Bengio, S., Hardt, M., Recht, B., Vinyals, O.: Understanding deep learning requires rethinking generalization. In: Proceedings of the 5th International Conference on Learning Representations (2017)

Self-organising Neural Network Hierarchy

Satya Borgohain[1](✉)(iD), Gideon Kowadlo[2](✉)(iD), David Rawlinson[2](✉)(iD),
Christoph Bergmeir[1](✉)(iD), Kok Loo[1](✉)(iD), Harivallabha Rangarajan[2](✉),
and Levin Kuhlmann[1](✉)(iD)

[1] Monash University, Wellington Road, Clayton, VIC 3800, Australia
{satya.borgohain,christoph.bergmeir,levin.kuhlmann}@monash.edu,
kploo1@student.monash.edu
[2] Cerenaut, Richmond, VIC 3121, Australia
{gideon,dave,hari}@cerenaut.ai
https://www.monash.edu/
https://cerenaut.ai/

Abstract. Mammalian brains exhibit functional self-organisation
between different neocortical regions to form virtual hierarchies from
a physical 2D sheet. We propose a biologically-inspired self-organizing
neural network architecture emulating the same. The network is composed of autoencoder units and driven by a meta-learning rule based on
maximizing the Shannon entropy of latent representations of the input,
which optimizes the receptive field placement of each unit within a feature map. Unlike Neural Architecture Search, here both the network
parameters and the architecture are learned simultaneously. In a case
study on image datasets, we observe that the meta-learning rule causes
a functional hierarchy to form, and leads to learning progressively better
topological configurations and higher classification performance overall,
starting from randomly initialized architectures. In particular, our approach yields competitive performance in terms of classification accuracy
compared to optimal handcrafted architecture(s) with desirable topological features for this network type, on both MNIST and CIFAR-10
datasets, even though it is not as significant for the latter.

Keywords: Biologically plausible networks · Self-supervised learning ·
Greedy training

1 Introduction

A critical component behind the performance of Artificial Neural Networks
(ANN) remains the manual design of their architectures, which is fixed prior
to the training of networks and requires specialized domain knowledge involving
iterative search, empirical discovery, intuition or trial and error [3].

Automated architecture search methods like Neural Architecture Search
(NAS) with Reinforcement Learning [22], and Evolutionary Algorithm [20] based
approaches provide viable alternatives to explicit tailoring of neural network

© Springer Nature Switzerland AG 2020
M. Gallagher et al. (Eds.): AI 2020, LNAI 12576, pp. 359–370, 2020.
https://doi.org/10.1007/978-3-030-64984-5_28

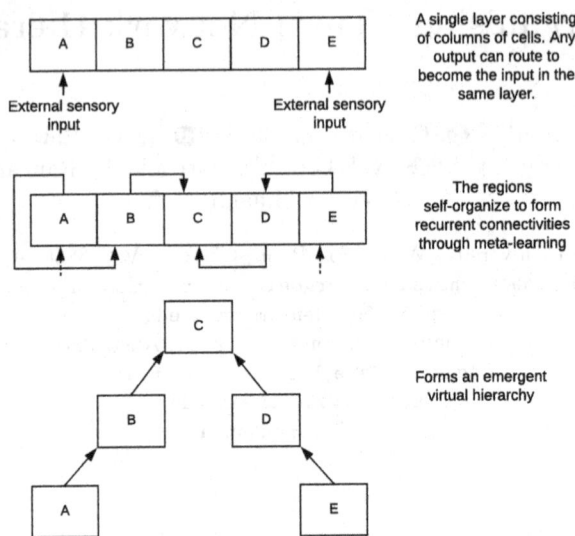

Fig. 1. A simplified high-level representation of the self-organising hierarchy.

architectures for a given task. NAS methods [3] outperform manual architectures in many areas such as semantic segmentation [1], image classification and object detection [23]. They employ complex strategies to search the space of possible architectures and evaluate performance which makes them extremely computationally expensive [23] and hard to reproduce. We propose a biologically motivated alternative to automated architecture search that attempts to coarsely mimic how the brain might adapt its own architecture at an abstract level.

We loosely base our idea on the Gradiental model, proposed by [5], which claims that functional neocortical organisation is continuous, interactive and emergent, and introduced a cognitive gradient that referred to gradual changes in encoded representations and integration between sensory modalities across the surface. Furthermore, since the mammalian neocortex is physically a thin 2D sheet there is evidence of a functionally self-organising virtual hierarchy (as opposed to a physical one) between the different neocortical regions [7] (See Fig. 1). In particular, we study the effects on one sensory modality i.e. visual modality, and learn useful representations in a partially unsupervised manner.

The primary focus of our approach is *discovering* the optimal spatial placement of the receptive fields (ϕ) over the inputs and its latent representations via a meta-learning rule. We consider a meta-network as a Directed Acyclic Graph (DAG) in which every node is an autoencoder (AE) unit, with the same number of hidden units (n_{hidden}), and locally learn useful representations of the inputs received from the other parts of the network. Two types of learning simultaneously take place in this setting i.e. primary (or base) learning (f_θ) which is learning of feed-forward weights θ and secondary (or meta) learning (f_ϕ) which is learning the receptive field location (and thus, the topology) of each AE unit for optimal feature encoding in a lower dimensional space.

To measure the quality of learned representations and drive meta-learning, we use Shannon entropy as an intrinsic metric. Furthermore, to assess overall quality of the network and its architecture we use these unsupervised representations to train a logistic regression classifier and use its accuracy as an extrinsic metric.

A key distinction between our work and NAS [22] approaches is that the self-organizing network retains the learned weights from previous meta-iterations which is meant to reflect a smooth adaptation to a given task during training.

The major contributions of this paper are summarized as follows:

1. We propose a self-organising neural network architecture which meta-learns its architecture during training to produce effective representations of the inputs for downstream tasks like classification.
2. We formulate a meta-learning rule based on entropy of latent representations and empirically show that it leads to better topological configurations.
3. We show functional hierarchy emergence via the self-organizing network.

2   Proposed Framework

The overall framework is shown in Fig. 2. It can be broadly divided into unsupervised, which includes both the base (local) learning in the AE units along with meta-learning of the receptive fields, and the supervised phase which consists of training a multinomial logistic regression classifier.

Firstly, we conceive a simple high-level abstraction for the 2D cortical sheet and refer to it as the feature map of encodings with dimensions as $h \times w$, where we store the inputs along with the subsequent hidden layer activity of each AE unit during training. Allocation of both the input and the latent activity within the feature map is arbitrary and specified prior to training which remains fixed throughout. This is meant to represent the gradual encoded representations across the cortical map.

The meta-network is a combination of the feature map and the AE units. Training in the context of this meta-network is to learn K meta-parameters $\phi = \{r_k \mid k \in \{1, \ldots, K\}\}$, where r_k is the receptive field for the kth AE unit. Hence, its topological configuration is fully defined by the number of AE units (K) and location of their receptive fields (r_k). The set of receptive fields for a topology is given as

$$\{r_k = \{(x_i^{(k)}, x_j^{(k)}), (y_a^{(k)}, y_b^{(k)})\} \mid k \in \{1, \ldots, K\}\} \tag{1}$$

where, $x^{(k)}$ represents the hidden layer row activity with beginning and ending indices as i and j, and $y^{(k)}$ represents the column activity where a, b are the beginning and ending indices respectively of the kth AE unit within the feature map. The notion of a receptive field here refers to a subset of input activities projecting from one layer to the next in the virtual hierarchy as opposed to the traditional definition that refers to a subset of external inputs to the network.

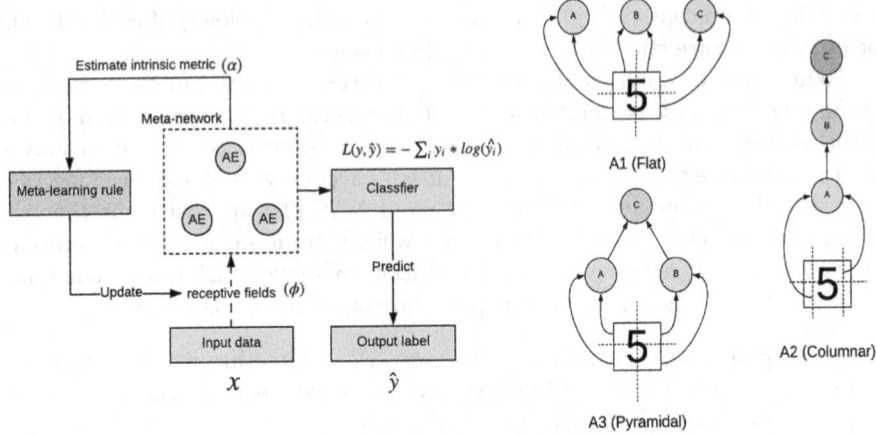

Fig. 2. (left) A high level schematic of the framework. (right) Handcrafted architectures with 3 AE units namely A1, A2 and A3. Different colors represent levels within the hierarchy. The arrows represent the input to the AE units and their receptive fields. Here the dotted lines divide the raw image into different regions.

We handcraft several architectures, as shown in Fig. 2 above, in order to establish correlation between entropy and accuracy. These hierarchical systems vary in their order, reversibility and pyramidal structure [2], and as a consequence represent various levels of structural optimality.

Once the AE units of a meta-network sufficiently converge, we use it to train a two layer multinomial logistic regression classifier. Thereafter, we concatenate the hidden layer activity from all AE units to form a $(K \times n_{hidden})$ dimensional vector as input to the classifier as shown in Fig. 3.

2.1 Base Learning

We use a single layer, under-complete AE with standard backpropagation learning where we treat $h \times w$, i.e. the complete feature map size, as the input dimensions and apply a binary indicator matrix δ_k of the same dimension per AE unit. δ_k then has a sub-matrix of ones which is specified by r_k. We use mean squared error (MSE) for the reconstruction loss along with dropout and L2 norm for regularization. As captured in Fig. 2, each unit targets 2 fixed-size receptive fields (r_k) of $N \times N$ dimensions making the effective receptive field size to be $2 \times N \times N$ per unit.

During this phase, each AE unit minimizes its reconstruction loss locally and learns a low dimensional representation of its inputs. Subsequently after each forward pass, the hidden layer activity of each unit is updated on the feature map (in its designated location).

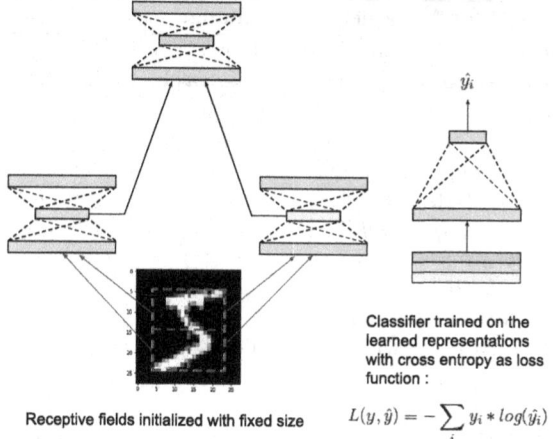

Fig. 3. Left: A simple handcrafted meta-network (A3) with 3 AE units arranged in a pyramidal fashion. Each unit receives different inputs (a part of the image) based on the position of its receptive field and its latent encoding becomes a potential input for the next unit. Right: A logistic regression model trained on the hidden unit activity.

2.2   Meta-Learning

The meta-learning algorithm is shown in Algorithm 1. This is used for both the handcrafted, (where we specify r_k) as well as for the meta-learned architectures.

Intrinsic Metric. Tishby and Zaslavsky [21] used information theoretic measures to highlight the trade-off between effective compression of information and prediction from it. We use Shannon entropy as the intrinsic metric through which we can indirectly infer about the information content in the learned representation and subsequently the fitness of the meta-learned-network.

Formally,

$$H(x) = -\sum_i P_i \, log(P_i) \tag{2}$$

where, P_i is the probability of ith hidden activity.

We initialize the feature map with the input image and zeros representing non-activation. To ensure a stable pool of activations in the feature map before backpropagation in AE units, $K \times K$ forward passes are performed without accumulating gradients and the feature map is updated each time. Once it is saturated, we perform K forward passes for each unit followed by K backward passes. Finally, we estimate the entropy per unit per epoch.

To estimate the entropy of the latent activity in AE units, we use a histogram (binning) based approach. For given continuous activation values C, we discretize the same into discrete activations D, by computing a histogram over the same which allows for a rough estimation of the probability distribution of C [17]. The authors noted that the estimated entropy is sensitive to the choice of binning

Algorithm 1. Steps for Meta-network training.

Input: Receptive fields, r_k; Height, h; Width, w;
Output: Shannon entropy, $\{H(x_k) \mid k \; in\{1 \ldots K\}\}$; Trained AE units, $\{A_k \mid k \in \{1 \ldots K\}\}$;

1: Initialize: K AE units;
2: **while** not max epoch **do**
3:     Initialize Feature map $F = F_{h \times w}^{(0)}$;
4:     **for** k in $1 \sim K$ **do**
5:         **for** k in $1 \sim K$ **do**
6:             Perform forward pass for A_k;
7:             Update $F := F_{h \times w}^{(k)}$ with hidden activity x_k;
8:         **end for**
9:     **end for**
10:    **for** k in $1 \sim K$ **do**
11:        Perform forward pass for A_k;
12:        Perform backward pass for A_k;
13:        Update $F := F_{h \times w}^{(k)}$ with hidden activity x_k;
14:        Estimate Shannon entropy $H(x_k)$ using equation 2;
15:    **end for**
16: **end while**
17: **return** ;

as it yields different discrete representations for C. However, [13] showed that the estimated values fall within the theoretical limits for small and large bins. We employ a similar strategy as [16], where AE units are allowed to be fully trained to capture the maximum activation value and to ensure that the resulting histogram represents the full range of activations (as ReLUs do not have an upper bound). We selected a constant bin size of 100, independent of the topology.

For a given topology, let x_k be the hidden layer activity and $H(x_k)_t$ be the local entropy of the kth unit at time t. The intrinsic metric α_t at time t is,

$$\alpha_t = H(x_k)_t \tag{3}$$

We greedily optimize for local entropy values for each AE unit.

Meta-Learning Rule. We explore memoryless, meta-heuristic approaches, namely local search and stochastic hill climbing [15], along with random search to formulate the meta-learning rule with maximizing entropy as the acceptance criterion as per Algorithm 2.

We introduce a small random perturbation in the r_k during each iteration of meta-learning, constrained to a range between $[-1, 1]$ for a horizontal or vertical shift i.e. two degrees of freedom. It accepts a randomly selected neighbour as a candidate solution, only if it leads to a higher local entropy. Although this does not guarantee a global optima in the case of non-convex optimization problems, it provides a reasonably optimal solution within a time constrained setting [15].

Algorithm 2. Stochastic hill climber as Meta-learning rule

Input: Meta-steps, M;
Output: Receptive fields, r_{best};

1: Initialize $r_{best} \leftarrow$ randomTopology();
2: Let $\alpha_0 \leftarrow 0$;
3: **for** m in $1 \sim M$ **do**
4:      **for** i in $1 \sim K$ **do**
5:          $r_{candidate} \leftarrow r_{best}$;
6:          $r_{candidate}^{(i)} \leftarrow$ randomNeighbor($r_{best}^{(i)}$);
7:          Train Meta-network with $r_{candidate}$ and get $H(x_i)$;
8:          $\alpha_t \leftarrow H(x_i)$;
9:          **if** $\alpha_t > \alpha_{t-1}$ **then**
10:             $r_{best} \leftarrow r_{candidate}$;
11:             break;
12:         **else**
13:             continue;
14:         **end if**
15:     **end for**
16: **end for**
17: **return** r_{best};

The meta-learning rule updates slower than the base learning to ensure that units were fully trained and converge to a sufficient degree before estimating the entropy of the hidden activity. Figure 4 shows a forward pass during meta-learning.

In order to retain weights from previous iterations, we multiply δ_k with all current weights of an AE unit as $\theta_{ij} := \theta_{ij} \times \delta_{ij}$ where θ_{ij} is a single weight and δ_{ij} is an element of the binary indicator matrix. Hence, only the weights of the neurons which lie within the r_k are subject to be updated during training with the rest remaining virtually unchanged.[1]

3   Experiments

3.1   Datasets

For our experiments, we focus on two datasets:

MNIST: We use the widely studied MNIST dataset[2] of single-channel, 28×28 dimensional images consisting of 10 classes with $60,000$ instances as training set and $10,000$ as the test set.

CIFAR-10: Contains multi-channel, natural images drawn from 10 classes with $50,000$ and $10,000$ images for training and testing respectively [8].

---

[1] The code is available on github under: https://github.com/Cerenaut/self-organizing.
[2] http://yann.lecun.com/exdb/mnist/.

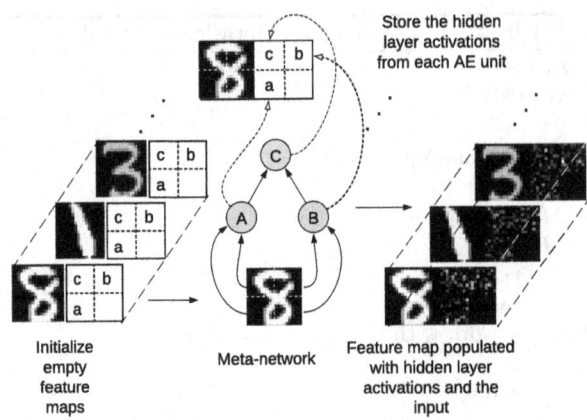

Fig. 4. A schematic depiction of a forward pass in the meta-network. Here A, B and C are the AE units and a, b and c are the location of their hidden layer activity in the feature map. Receptive fields of A and B i.e. r_A and r_B respectively, target the image whereas r_C targets the hidden layer activations of both A and B. The dotted arrows represent the updating of the hidden layer activations of the corresponding units in the feature map.

For MNIST, we first centre-crop the images to be multiples of 10 for making the manipulation of receptive fields within the feature map simpler. It is cropped to be $28 \times 28 \rightarrow 20 \times 20$ followed by min-max normalization to bring the pixels values of the images from $[0, 255]$ to be between $[0, 1]$. To ensure center cropping does not impact the classifier's performance, we evaluate its performance both with and without cropping and found an increase of only $\sim 0.003\%$ in the test error rate. The 8×8 region acts mostly as extra padding. For CIFAR-10, we perform standard data augmentation i.e. zero-pad with 4 pixels on each side, random crop back to 32×32 and random horizontal flip [6,9–11,14,18,19]. Thereafter, we convert it to grayscale and normalize.

3.2 Experimental Strategy

For both datasets, here we seek to demonstrate three key features: (1) Hand-crafted hierarchical architectures perform better than random ones; (2) There is a near monotonic relationship between extrinsic classification accuracy and intrinsic entropy of a network that enables the use of maximising entropy by way of the meta-learning rule to maximise accuracy while at the same time leading to more hierarchical architectures; (3) That the meta-learning rule can be used to achieve improvements in accuracy relative to random or initial networks and at least comparable accuracy to handcrafted hierarchical networks.

Performance of Handcrafted and Random Architectures. We perform a series of 10 runs per architecture and compile the results in Table 1, where we report the mean accuracy of each topology.

Table 1. Accuracy (mean) of all 10 runs for the handcrafted and randomly initialized architectures for each dataset. The architectures with the highest accuracy is highlighted in gray.

Topology	Name	MNIST	CIFAR-10
A1	Flat	96.4	31.69
A2	Columnar	94.21	30.79
A3	Pyramidal	96.6	32.84
AR1	Random	93.03	31.97
AR2	Random	93.76	27.21
AR3	Random	90.28	29.86

From Table 1, we observe that the topology with *perfect* hierarchy [2], namely A3, performs the best in each category for both the datasets. Furthermore, columnar architectures (A2) performs poorly among the handcrafted ones since they highly deviate from a perfectly hierarchical topology, receive partial information overall and have very poor integration of receptive fields as each unit only targets its receptive field at the unit directly below it.

Flat architecture (A1) yields a mean accuracy below A3 for both datasets. Random architectures yield lower accuracy scores overall for both datasets and hierarchical architectures which deviate from the properties of a perfect hierarchy in general, seem to exhibit lower performance relative to the degree of deviation.

Correlation Analysis. We observe *maximum* global entropy of a meta-network to be positively correlated with its accuracy, with a Pearson's correlation coefficient of 0.75 and 0.48 for MNIST and CIFAR-10 respectively. This indicates that the greater the local entropy of the AE units, more is the amount of useful information captured in the encoded representation (as measured by the accuracy). Hence, seeking out regions of high activity on the feature map by the AE which in turn leads to high entropy ultimately improves performance. Figure 5 shows a regression line fit to the data highlighting the relationship between maximum entropy and accuracy for both datasets.

Performance of Meta-learned Architectures. Using local entropy estimates for α, we perform a series of 10 runs and record how the topology evolves throughout training. We report the performances of both the randomly initialized architecture and the final meta-learned architecture for the same topology in Table 2.

We perform Wilcoxon one-sided signed-rank test with a significance level of 0.05, between the final ($\tilde{x}_1$) and initial ($\tilde{x}_0$) accuracy of the meta-learned architectures and report the p-values obtained. The null hypothesis (H_0) is that the median difference ($\tilde{x}_1 - \tilde{x}_0$) is negative against the alternative (H_A) that it is positive. We observe p-values < 0.05 for MNIST and hence conclude that our

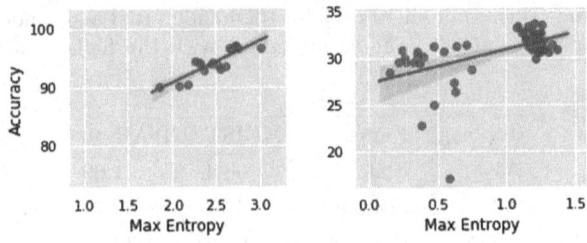

Fig. 5. Regression lines fitted between accuracy and the maximum entropy for MNIST (left) and CIFAR-10 (right) respectively.

Table 2. Median accuracies for both the randomly initialized, $\tilde{x}_0$, and meta-learned, $\tilde{x}_1$, architectures over 10 runs.

Dataset	$\tilde{x}_0$	$\tilde{x}_1$	max	p-value
MNIST	91.24	92.40	96.22	0.009
CIFAR-10	33.12	32.46	35.02	0.869

results are statistically significant. For CIFAR-10, we do not observe similar evidence against the null which we plan investigate in our future work. We however note that the meta-learning achieved a competitive performance of 35.02% on CIFAR-10 over the runs, better than any of the handcrafted ones.

Figure 6 shows accuracies from the randomly initialized architectures after a few meta-learning iterations (meta-steps) as indicated through the intermediate architectures during meta-learning. For MNIST, we observe highest improvement in performance among the meta-learned architectures with random initial configurations which started with very poor performance. Also, configurations that already yield high accuracies have more or less similar performance through the meta-learning. It is also apparent that meta-learning is sensitive to initializa-

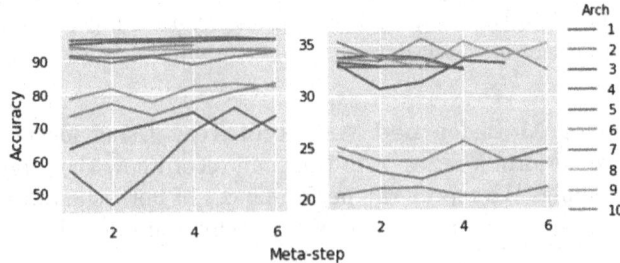

Fig. 6. Plot showing the change in accuracy per architecture with each meta-step for MNIST (left) and CIFAR-10 (right), over 10 different runs. Different randomly initialized architectures are represented by different colors. Meta-step indicates the number of receptive field updates before termination of the meta-learning loop.

tion of the receptive fields as is generally the case with local search algorithms. For CIFAR-10, we observe a lesser performance improvement. However, here the difference between the best and worst performing handcrafted architectures is much smaller and therefore we hypothesise that the search space is more challenging.

4 Conclusions and Future Work

In this paper we propose a self-organising network architecture which optimizes the spatial placement of receptive fields through a meta-learning rule based on entropy of the encoded representations. Our experiments demonstrate that meta-learned architectures are able to self-organise into a hierarchy by maximising entropy in the network. This appeared especially effective for MNIST, while for CIFAR-10 the results are still inconclusive. The more effective result on MNIST suggests the associated error surface is less complex and allows the local meta-learning to find a more optimal solution.

For MNIST, we observe the baseline to be 96.6% for handcrafted architectures sans augmentation or hyper-parameter tuning. For CIFAR-10, we achieve a baseline accuracy of 32.84%. When compared with existing results from other non-convolutional ANN models applied to CIFAR-10 as reported by [12], e.g. logistic regression on whitened input achieved 41% and much larger, vanilla FFNN achieved 51% (with $7,940,000$ trainable parameters vs $48,000$ in our configuration). As [12] noted, convolutional networks are not entirely biologically plausible (due to weight sharing), there is a need to explore more feasible alternatives. One contrasting feature of our approach with NAS methods is potentially reducing computational complexity since we meta-learn architectures without evaluating the classification performance for each candidate architecture.

To that end, we present a brain-inspired learning paradigm without using topological priors, such as convolutions for image processing, and only use basic neural network components driven by a meta-learning rule. Future work will include additional AE units (for more possible topologies), exploring alternatives for meta-learning such as Free-Energy minimization scheme [4] and also expanding across different sensory modalities and integrating the receptive fields to achieve better generalization across tasks and domains.

References

1. Chen, L.C., et al.: Searching for efficient multi-scale architectures for dense image prediction. In: Advances in Neural Information Processing Systems, pp. 8699–8710 (2018)
2. Corominas-Murtra, B., Goñi, J., Solé, R.V., Rodríguez-Caso, C.: On the origins of hierarchy in complex networks. Proc. Natl. Acad. Sci. **110**(33), 13316–13321 (2013)
3. Elsken, T., Metzen, J.H., Hutter, F.: Neural architecture search: a survey. arXiv preprint arXiv:1808.05377 (2018)

4. Friston, K.: A free energy principle for biological systems. Entropy **14**(11), 2100–2121 (2012)
5. Goldberg, E.: Gradiental approach to neocortical functional organization. J. Clin. Exp. Neuropsychol. **11**(4), 489–517 (1989)
6. Huang, G., Sun, Yu., Liu, Z., Sedra, D., Weinberger, K.Q.: Deep networks with stochastic depth. In: Leibe, B., Matas, J., Sebe, N., Welling, M. (eds.) ECCV 2016. LNCS, vol. 9908, pp. 646–661. Springer, Cham (2016). https://doi.org/10.1007/978-3-319-46493-0_39
7. Kandel, E.R., et al.: Principles of Neural Science, vol. 4. McGraw-Hill, New York (2000)
8. Krizhevsky, A., Hinton, G., et al.: Learning multiple layers of features from tiny images (2009)
9. Larsson, G., Maire, M., Shakhnarovich, G.: FractalNet: ultra-deep neural networks without residuals. arXiv preprint arXiv:1605.07648 (2016)
10. Lee, C.Y., Xie, S., Gallagher, P., Zhang, Z., Tu, Z.: Deeply-supervised nets. In: Artificial Intelligence and Statistics, pp. 562–570 (2015)
11. Lin, M., Chen, Q., Yan, S.: Network in network. arXiv preprint arXiv:1312.4400 (2013)
12. Lin, Z., Memisevic, R., Konda, K.: How far can we go without convolution: improving fully-connected networks. arXiv preprint arXiv:1511.02580 (2015)
13. Purwani, S., Nahar, J., Twining, C.: Analyzing bin-width effect on the computed entropy. In: AIP Conference Proceedings, vol. 1868, p. 040008. AIP Publishing LLC (2017)
14. Romero, A., Ballas, N., Kahou, S.E., Chassang, A., Gatta, C., Bengio, Y.: FitNets: hints for thin deep nets. arXiv preprint arXiv:1412.6550 (2014)
15. Russell, S.J., Norvig, P.: Artificial Intelligence: A Modern Approach. Pearson Education Limited, Kuala Lumpur (2016)
16. Saxe, A.M., et al.: On the information bottleneck theory of deep learning. J. Stat. Mech. Theory Exp. **2019**(12), 124020 (2019)
17. Shwartz-Ziv, R., Tishby, N.: Opening the black box of deep neural networks via information. arXiv preprint arXiv:1703.00810 (2017)
18. Springenberg, J.T., Dosovitskiy, A., Brox, T., Riedmiller, M.: Striving for simplicity: the all convolutional net. arXiv preprint arXiv:1412.6806 (2014)
19. Srivastava, R.K., Greff, K., Schmidhuber, J.: Highway networks. arXiv preprint arXiv:1505.00387 (2015)
20. Stanley, K.O., Miikkulainen, R.: Evolving neural networks through augmenting topologies. Evol. Comput. **10**(2), 99–127 (2002)
21. Tishby, N., Zaslavsky, N.: Deep learning and the information bottleneck principle. In: 2015 IEEE Information Theory Workshop (ITW), pp. 1–5. IEEE (2015)
22. Zoph, B., Le, Q.V.: Neural architecture search with reinforcement learning. arXiv preprint arXiv:1611.01578 (2016)
23. Zoph, B., Vasudevan, V., Shlens, J., Le, Q.V.: Learning transferable architectures for scalable image recognition. In: Proceedings of the IEEE Conference on Computer Vision And Pattern Recognition, pp. 8697–8710 (2018)

How to Encode Dynamic Gaussian Bayesian Networks as Gaussian Processes?

Mattis Hartwig[(✉)] and Ralf Möller

Institute of Information Systems, University of Lübeck, Lübeck, Germany
{hartwig,moeller}@ifis.uni-luebeck.de

Abstract. One dimensional versions of the Markov chain and the hidden Markov model have been generalized as Gaussian processes. Currently these approaches support only a single dimension which is limiting their usability. In this paper we encode the more general dynamic Gaussian Bayesian network as a Gaussian process and thus allow arbitrary number of dimensions and arbitrary connections between time steps. Our developed Gaussian process based formalism has the advantage of supporting a direct inference from any time point to the other without propagation of evidence throughout the whole network, flexibility to combine the covariance function with others if needed and keeping all properties of the dynamic Gaussian Bayesian network.

Keywords: Gaussian process · Kernel · Bayesian network

1 Introduction

Understanding the fundamental relationships between different probabilistic models is vital to guide further research and to exploit the benefits of different approaches. Two specific types of one-dimensional Gaussian distributed probabilistic graphical models (PGMS), the Markov chain (MC) and the hidden Markov model (HMM), have already been encoded as Gaussian Processes (GPs), showing the generalizing power of GPs [6]. As Murphy [11] has elaborated, dynamic Bayesian networks, are a more general type of a PGM compared to the MC and the HMM. Consequently, it is an improvement and thus a contribution to encode the dynamic Gaussian Bayesian network (DGBN) as a Gaussian Process, which is focus of this paper. By encoding we mean a generalization of the DGBN into the GP framework while maintaining all characteristics of the original DGBN.

DGBNs in general offer a sparse and interpretable representation for probabilistic distributions and allow to model (in)dependencies between its random variables [7,9]. The interpretability of the modeling language also makes it possible to construct DGBNs based on expert knowledge instead of or as an addition to learning them from data [3,4]. Komurlu and Bilgic [8] explicitly favor the usage

© Springer Nature Switzerland AG 2020
M. Gallagher et al. (Eds.): AI 2020, LNAI 12576, pp. 371–382, 2020.
https://doi.org/10.1007/978-3-030-64984-5_29

of a DGBN over a GP in their application because in classic GPs, dependencies between output random variables are not easily taken into account. There are also downsides of DGBNs. First, the time dimension is still discrete which brings up the problem of finding the right sampling rate. Second, evidence is usually propagated through the graphical structure which can be computational expensive. Third, they are based on linear relationships between random variables which makes it difficult to model certain real-world phenomena, e.g. periodic behaviors.

Gaussian Processes (GPs) are another approach applied for modeling time-series [5,16] and have been rather recently brought into focus of the machine learning community [13]. Both DGBNs and GPs have Gaussian distributions over their random variables at any point in time. In contrast to DGBNs, GPs are continuous on the time dimension and allow direct inference without propagation of evidence through a network. Additionally, an existing GP that models a certain behavior can be easily extended or adapted by making changes to its covariance function. Drawbacks of GPs are that modeling multiple outputs at once is challenging [1] and that modeling a detailed interpretable (in)dependence structure as it is done in a DGBNs is currently not possible. Encoding the multidimensional and Markovian aspects of a DGBN into a Gaussian process could combine the benefits of two models.

The remainder of the paper has following structure. We start by explaining the preliminaries about PGMs and GPs. After discussing related work, we construct GPs Dynamic Gaussian Bayesian Networks with arbitrary connections between time steps. We conclude with a discussion of benefits and downsides of the created GPs and with an agenda for further research in that area.

2 Preliminaries

In this section we introduce PGMs, GPs and kernel functions for GPs. Afterwards, we briefly review the advantages of the two models, which also motivates combining them.

2.1 Probabilistic Graphical Models

This section gives a brief overview about the different types of PGMs used in this paper. For further details we refer to the work by Koller et al. [7], Pearl [12] and Murphy [11].

In general, a PGM is a network with nodes for the random variables and edges to describe relations between them. When looking at random variables over time dynamic variants of PGMs are used and when looking at continuous random variables often Gaussian PGMs are used. Dynamic Gaussian Bayesian networks (DGBNs) are a general representation for the development of continuous random variables over time. A Gaussian Markov chain, which describes the development of a single Gaussian distributed random variable over time, and a Gaussian hidden Markov model, which contains two random variables over time,

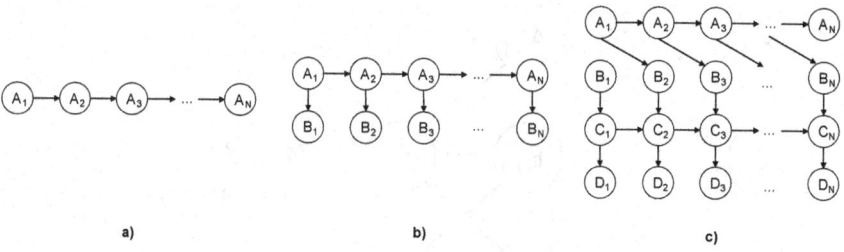

Fig. 1. Three different types of PGMs: a) Markov chain b) hidden Markov model c) dynamic Bayesian network

are special cases of the DGBN [11]. A DGBN allows arbitrary links between the random variables [11]. Figure 1 contains illustrations of three different types of DGBNs. Since Hartwig et al. [6] have already worked on Gaussian Markov chains and Gaussian hidden Markov models, this paper focuses on generalizing the approach to DGBNs. The only restriction is that we do not allow connections between random variables within an individual time step.

In general, we denote the set of random variables as $\mathbb{X}$ and the set random variables that are influencing a specific random variable $X \in \mathbb{X}$ as its parents $Pa(X)$. Each random variable follows a conditional Gaussian probability distribution that is linearly dependent on its parent and is given by

$$P(X|Pa(X)) \sim N\left(\mu_X + \sum_{\Pi \in Pa(X)} \beta_{X,\Pi}(\pi - \mu_\Pi); \sigma_X^2\right), \qquad (1)$$

where μ_A and μ_Π are the unconditional means of X and Π respectively, π is the realization of Π, σ_X^2 is the variance of X and $\beta_{X,\Pi}$ represents the influence of the parent Π on its child X.

A DGBN can be represented by a pair of BNs. The first BN defined the prior distribution $P(\mathbb{X}_1)$ at time $t = 1$. The second BN is a two-slice temporal BN (2TBN) which defines $P(\mathbb{X}_t|\mathbb{X}_{t-1})$. This representation is parameterized by a mean vector μ and covariance matrix Σ for the first BN and a transition matrix $\mathbf{M}$ containing the linear relationships over time. Figure 2 contains a visualization of a three dimensional 2TBN.

2.2 Gaussian Processes

A GP is a collection of random variables, any finite number of which have a joint Gaussian distribution [13]. A GP can be interpreted as a distribution over functions on a spatial dimension, which is in our case the time dimension t. It is completely specified by its mean $\mu = m(t)$ and its covariance function $k(t, t')$ and can be written as

$$f(t) \sim GP(m(t), k(t, t')). \qquad (2)$$

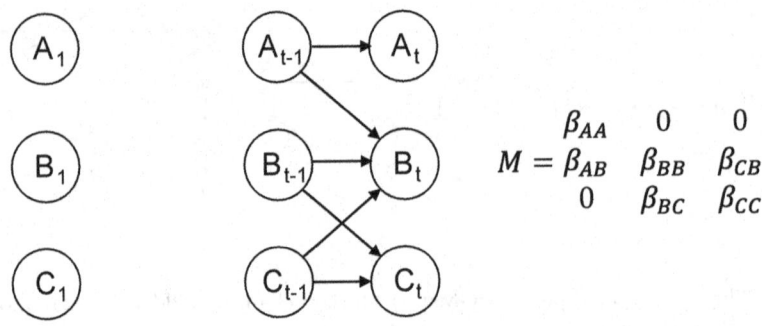

Fig. 2. A DGBN represented by a prior and a 2TBN

The covariance function (also known as kernel function) describes the similarity of function values at different points in time (t and t') and influences the shape of the function space [13].

If we have a dataset that consists of an input vector $\mathbf{t}$ and an output vector $\mathbf{y}$, we can define any vector of time points $\mathbf{t}^*$ for which we would like to calculate the posterior distribution. The joint distribution over the observed and the unknown time points is given by

$$p\left(\begin{bmatrix} y \\ y* \end{bmatrix}\right) = N\left(\begin{bmatrix} \mu(t) \\ \mu(t*) \end{bmatrix}, \begin{bmatrix} K(\mathbf{t},\mathbf{t}) & K(\mathbf{t},\mathbf{t}^*) \\ K(\mathbf{t}^*,\mathbf{t}) & K(\mathbf{t}^*,\mathbf{t}^*) \end{bmatrix}\right), \tag{3}$$

where $K(\mathbf{t},\mathbf{t}^*)$ is a covariance matrix produced by plugging all values from $(\mathbf{t},\mathbf{t}^*)$ into the covariance function $k(t,t')$. By applying the conditional probability rules for multivariate Gaussians [16] we obtain the posterior $P(\mathbf{y}^*)$ with mean $\mathbf{m}^*$ and covariance matrix C^*

$$P(\mathbf{y}^*) = N(\mathbf{m}^*, C^*), \tag{4}$$

where

$$\mathbf{m}^* = \mu(\mathbf{t}^*) + K(\mathbf{t}^*,\mathbf{t})K(\mathbf{t},\mathbf{t})^{-1}(\mathbf{y} - \mu(\mathbf{t})) \tag{5}$$

and

$$C^* = K(\mathbf{t}^*,\mathbf{t}^*) - K(\mathbf{t}^*,\mathbf{t})K(\mathbf{t},\mathbf{t})^{-1}K(\mathbf{t}^*,\mathbf{t})^T. \tag{6}$$

2.3   Kernel Functions

Rasmussen [13] provides an overview of different possible kernels with the squared exponential kernel

$$k_{SE}(t,t') = \sigma^2 \exp\left(-\frac{(t-t')^2}{2l^2}\right), \tag{7}$$

where σ^2 and l are hyperparameters for the signal noise and the length scale respectively, being a commonly used one.

A valid kernel $k : \mathbb{T} \times \mathbb{T} \to \mathbb{R}$ for a GP needs to fulfill two characteristics [13]:

- symmetry, i.e., $k(t,t') = k(t',t)$ for all t and t',
- being positive semidefinite, i.e., symmetry and $\sum_{i=1}^{n} \sum_{j=1}^{n} c_i c_j k(t_i, t_j)$ for $n \in \mathbb{N}$, $t_1, ..., t_n \in \mathbb{T}$, $c_1, ..., c_n \in \mathbb{R}$.

Valid Kernels can be constructed of other kernels. Bishop [2] lists valid kernel operations from which we use the following subset in later sections. Given valid kernels $k_1(t,t')$, $k_2(t,t')$ and a constant c, the following kernels will also be valid:

$$k(t,t') = ck_1(t,t'), \tag{8}$$

$$k(t,t') = k_1(t,t') + k_2(t,t'), \tag{9}$$

$$k(t,t') = \exp(k_1(t,t')), \tag{10}$$

$$k(t,t') = k_1(t,t')k_2(t,t'). \tag{11}$$

2.4   Benefits of the Models

In their work on one-dimensional markov Chains and hidden Markov models Hartwig et al. [6] have listed benefits of the GPs and PGMs, which we will review here briefly. PGMs can capture (conditional) dependencies and independencies of the random variables very intuitively [7] and be thus also constructed by incorporating expert knowledge (either entirely or as a prior). PGMs can be naturally multidimensional, which allows representing the probability distribution over multiple random variables simultaneously. Last but not least, PGMs have already been used in many applications and therefore a wide range of inference and learning tactics have been developed [7].

The usage of GPs has also benefits. In general GPs have a continuous spatial dimension which allows to model continuous changes directly and without the need of discretization. GPs are nonparametric and directly incorporate a quantification of uncertainty. Because of their joint Gaussian characteristics, calculating posterior distributions is straightforward and relatively efficient [16].

Consequently, converting the PGMs to GPs while retaining the PGM benefits is a promising research direction.

3   Related Work

There have been three different streams to bring graphical or relational models together with GPs. One research stream known as relation learning uses multiple GPs to identify probabilistic relations or links within sets of entities [19,20]. A second research stream uses GPs for transition functions in state space models. Frigola-Alcalde [5] has researched different techniques for learning state space models that have GP priors over their transition functions and Turner [18] has explored change point detection in state space models using GPs. A third research stream focuses on constructing covariance functions for

GPs to mimic certain behaviors from other models. Reece and Roberts [14,15] have shown that they can convert a specific Kalman filter model for the near constant acceleration model into a kernel function for a GP and then combine that kernel function with other known kernels to get better results temporal-spatial predictions. Rasmussen [13] has introduced GP kernels for, e.g., a wiener process. As mentioned above Hartwig et al. [6] have constructed a kernel for a one-dimensional DGBN also referred to a scalar version of a markov chain. The kernel is defined by

$$k(t,t') = \sigma_X^2 \beta_X^{|t-t'|} \frac{1 - \beta_X^{2\min(t,t')}}{1 - \beta_X^2}. \tag{12}$$

This paper will build upon the scalar case and generalize it for the multidimensional DGBN.

4   Gaussian Processes for Dynamic Gaussian Bayesian Networks

We have $X^{(1)}, ..., X^{(N)}$ random variables in the DGBN evolving over time $t = 1, ..., \tilde{T}$ (we use $\tilde{T}$ to avoid confusion with the matrix transpose), where N is the number of dimensions and $\tilde{T}$ the number of time steps in a DGBN. As Alvarez et al. [1] described, multidimensional kernels follow the form $K(D_t, D'_{t'})$, where D and D' are dimensions of the underlying model. We will develop a kernel function that has an $N \times X$ dimensional matrix as an output containing all covariances between random variables in time steps t and t'

$$K(t,t') = \begin{bmatrix} K(X_t^{(1)}, X_{t'}^{(1)}) & \cdots & K(X_t^{(1)}, X_{t'}^{(N)}) \\ \vdots & \ddots & \vdots \\ K(X_t^{(N)}, X_{t'}^{(1)}) & \cdots & K(X_t^{(N)}, X_{t'}^{(N)}) \end{bmatrix}. \tag{13}$$

4.1   Constructing the GP

Shachter and Kenley [17] have developed an algorithm to convert a Gaussian Bayesian network into a multivariate Gaussian distribution. To prove correctness, they formulated the following Lemma that we will reuse.

Lemma 1. *For $G \in \mathbb{N}$ topological ordered random variables $X^{(i)} \in \mathbb{X}$, $i = 1, ..., G$ in a Gaussian Bayesian network let σ_i^2 be the variance of the conditional distribution of X^i given its parents. Let $\mathbf{B} \in \mathbb{R}^{G \times G}$ be a matrix, where the entries $\beta_{i,l}$, $l = 1, ..., G$ describe the linear relationship between a child $X^{(i)}$ and its parent $X^{(l)}$. If $X^{(l)}$ is no parent of $X^{(i)}$ the entry is zero. For a fixed $j \in \{1, ..., G\}$ let $\mathbf{\Sigma}_{qq}$ be the covariance matrix between all random variables $X^{(q)}$, $q = 1, ..., j$ and $\mathbf{B}_{sj} \in \mathbb{R}^{j-1 \times 1}$, $s = 1, ..., j-1$ the corresponding part of $\mathbf{B}$. We denote the matrices*

$$\mathbf{S}_j := \begin{bmatrix} \Sigma_{tt} & 0 & \dots & 0 \\ 0 & \sigma_{j+1}^2 & \dots & 0 \\ \vdots & \vdots & \ddots & 0 \\ 0 & 0 & 0 & \sigma_G^2 \end{bmatrix}, \tag{14}$$

$$\mathbf{U}_j := \begin{bmatrix} \mathbf{I}_{j-1} & \mathbf{B}_{sj} & \mathbf{0} \\ \mathbf{0} & 1 & \mathbf{0} \\ \mathbf{0} & \mathbf{0} & \mathbf{I}_{G-j} \end{bmatrix}. \tag{15}$$

Then it is

$$\mathbf{S}_j = \mathbf{U}_{j-1}^T \mathbf{S}_{j-1} \mathbf{U}_{j-1} \tag{16}$$

and

$$\Sigma = \mathbf{S}_G = \mathbf{U}_G^T \dots \mathbf{U}_1^T \mathbf{S}_0 \mathbf{U}_1 \dots \mathbf{U}_G, \tag{17}$$

where $\Sigma \in \mathbb{R}^{G \times G}$ is the covariance matrix of the equivalent multivariate Gaussian distribution for the above defined Gaussian Bayesian network.

The $N \times N$ covariance matrix from Eq. 17 is calculated by recursively multiplying the U-matrices. To define a GP we do not want to calculate a full covariance matrix as it is done in Lemma 1, but we need a kernel function mapping arbitrary time points t and t' to a covariance value or in our case covariance matrix as defined in Eq. 13. Therefore we convert the recursive multiplication of the matrices in Eq. 17 into closed form kernel function.

If we look at a certain number of time steps $\tilde{T}$, we have a number of total nodes in our network of $G = \tilde{T}N$. The matrix S_0 is diagonal with the individual variances for each of the G individual nodes. In the respective network. To ensure a topological ordering for our DGBN, we position all variables belonging to a time step t before all variables of $t + 1$. The order within a time step is irrelevant because there are no relations within a time step. For the sake of simplicity we order the variables within a time step based on their indexing $X^{(1)}, ..., X^{(N)}$. Figure 3 contains a visualization for the structure of the resulting covariance matrix. As shown, the kernel function can flexibly generate parts of a full covariance matrix.

Since the σ^2-values for all random variables stay constant over time, the matrix $\mathbf{S}_0$ has repeating diagonal entries every N entries. We denote $\mathbf{A}$ for the $N \times N$ block that is on the diagonal of $\mathbf{S}_0$, which itself is constructed by

$$\mathbf{A} = diag(\sigma_{X^{(1)}}^2, ..., \sigma_{X^{(N)}}^2). \tag{18}$$

The $G \times G$-dimensional matrix B from Lemma 1 containing all linear relationships in the DGBN has the $\tilde{T} \times \tilde{T}$-dimensional block structure, where $\mathbf{M}$ is the $N \times N$ transition matrix, resulting in

$$B = \begin{bmatrix} 0 & \mathbf{M} & 0 & 0 & \dots & 0 \\ 0 & 0 & \mathbf{M} & 0 & \dots & 0 \\ 0 & \vdots & \vdots & \ddots & \ddots & \vdots \\ 0 & 0 & 0 & \dots & 0 & \mathbf{M} \end{bmatrix}, \tag{19}$$

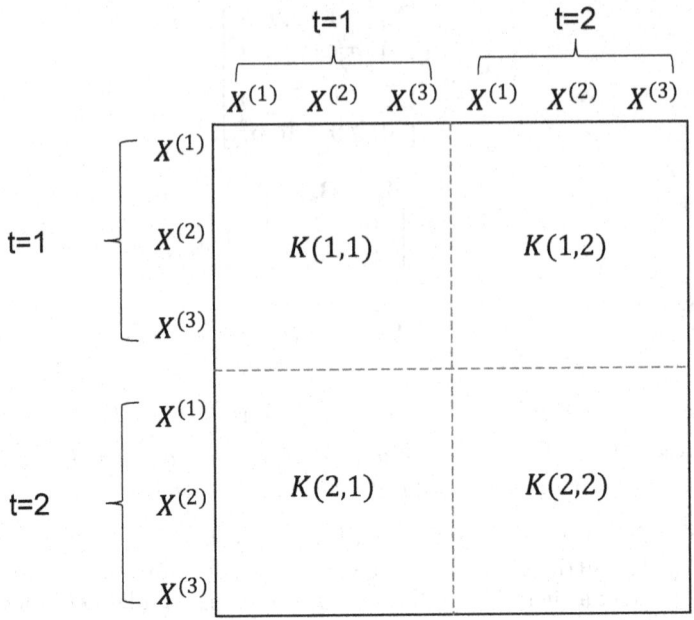

Fig. 3. Visual structure of the resulting covariance matrix

having the transition matrix M at all block positions $(t, t+1)$. Given this structure, we can reformulate Eq. 17 from Lemma 1. With N dimensions we can multiply N consecutive matrices from U_t to U_{t+N} that would belong to the random variables within one time step.

$$\mathbf{O}_t = \prod_{i=t}^{t+N} \mathbf{U}_i = \begin{bmatrix} \mathbf{I}_{(t-2)N} & \mathbf{0} & \mathbf{0} & \mathbf{0} \\ \mathbf{0} & \mathbf{I}_N & \mathbf{M} & \mathbf{0} \\ \mathbf{0} & \mathbf{0} & \mathbf{I}_N & \mathbf{0} \\ \mathbf{0} & \mathbf{0} & \mathbf{0} & \mathbf{I}_{(T-t)N} \end{bmatrix}. \tag{20}$$

With block matrix multiplication, and the construction of matrices $\mathbf{O}_t$ we can reformulate the multiplication from Lemma 1 into

$$\prod_{i=1}^{G} U_i = \prod_{t=1}^{T} O_t = \begin{bmatrix} \mathbf{I} & \mathbf{M} & \mathbf{M}^2 & \dots & \mathbf{M}^{\tilde{T}} \\ \mathbf{0} & \mathbf{I} & \mathbf{M} & \dots & \mathbf{M}^{\tilde{T}-1} \\ \mathbf{0} & \mathbf{0} & \mathbf{I} & \dots & \mathbf{M}^{\tilde{T}-2} \\ \vdots & \vdots & \vdots & \ddots & \vdots \\ \mathbf{0} & \mathbf{0} & \mathbf{0} & \dots & \mathbf{I} \end{bmatrix}. \tag{21}$$

The full $G \times G$ covariance matrix would be calculated by using Eq. 17. In our kernel function we only want to calculate the $N \times N$ matrix containing the covariances between two time steps t and t'. We would get this matrix by multiplying the t-th row of blocks from $\mathbf{U}_G^T...\mathbf{U}_1^T$, with the t'-th column of $\mathbf{S}_0\mathbf{U}_1...\mathbf{U}_G$. If $t = t'$ we have

$$
\begin{bmatrix} \mathbf{M}^{t-1} \\ \mathbf{M}^{t-2} \\ \mathbf{M}^{t-3} \\ \vdots \\ \mathbf{M}^0 \\ 0 \\ \vdots \\ 0 \end{bmatrix}^T \cdot \begin{bmatrix} \mathbf{AM}^{t-1} \\ \mathbf{AM}^{t-2} \\ \mathbf{AM}^{t-3} \\ \vdots \\ \mathbf{AM}^0 \\ 0 \\ \vdots \\ \mathbf{A0} \end{bmatrix} = \sum_{k=0}^{t} (\mathbf{M}^T)^k \mathbf{AM}^k.
\tag{22}
$$

In the case $t \neq t'$ we look at $t < t'$, because of symmetry same conclusions can be made when setting $t < t'$. In our case, the t-th row of blocks contains more blocks and also blocks with higher exponential. Because of the all-zero matrices, only the first t blocks are relevant, resulting in

$$
\begin{bmatrix} \mathbf{M}^{t-1} \\ \mathbf{M}^{t-2} \\ \vdots \\ \mathbf{M}^0 \end{bmatrix} \cdot \begin{bmatrix} \mathbf{AM}^{t'-1} \\ \mathbf{AM}^{t'-2} \\ \vdots \\ \mathbf{AM}^{t'-t} \end{bmatrix}^T = \sum_{k=0}^{t} (\mathbf{M}^T)^k \mathbf{AM}^{k+(t'-t)} = \left(\sum_{k=0}^{t} (\mathbf{M}^T)^k \mathbf{AM}^k \right) \mathbf{M}^{t'-t}
\tag{23}
$$

For the case $t > t'$, the resulting matrix needs to be the transposed version of the previous case, which can be proven by

$$
\begin{bmatrix} \mathbf{M}^{t-1} \\ \mathbf{M}^{t-2} \\ \vdots \\ \mathbf{M}^{t-t'} \end{bmatrix} \cdot \begin{bmatrix} \mathbf{AM}^{t'-1} \\ \mathbf{AM}^{t'-2} \\ \vdots \\ \mathbf{AM}^0 \end{bmatrix}^T = \sum_{k=0}^{t'} (\mathbf{M}^T)^{k+(t-t')} \mathbf{AM}^k = \mathbf{M}^{T^{t'-t}} \sum_{k=0}^{t'} (\mathbf{M}^T)^k \mathbf{AM}^k.
\tag{24}
$$

Resulting in a kernel function of

$$
K(t, t') = \begin{cases} \left(\sum_{i=0}^{min(t,t')} \mathbf{M}^T \mathbf{AM} \right) \mathbf{M}^{|t-t'|}, t \leq t', \\ \left(\left(\sum_{i=0}^{min(t,t')} \mathbf{M}^T \mathbf{AM} \right) \mathbf{M}^{|t-t'|} \right)^T, t > t'. \end{cases}
\tag{25}
$$

As mentioned in Sect. 2.2, the GP is defined by its kernel or covariance function and the mean function. We have defined the covariance function in Eq. 25. The mean function is time independent and is simply a constant mean vector defined by the DGBN, where each random variable $X^{(i)}$ has a mean value $\mu_{X^{(i)}}$, resulting in

$$
m(t) = \mu
\tag{26}
$$

4.2   Continuity Discussion

In general, a GP is defined over a continuous scale. Having a continuous scale would be a benefit compared to the discrete DGBN. For a GP to be continuous the kernel need to be defined for $t, t' \in \mathbb{R}$. The two key issues are that neither the summation term nor the exponential of the matrix $\mathbf{M}$ are necessarily uniquely defined for $t \in \mathbb{R}$. The one-dimensional kernel function for the scalar case from Eq. 12 solves this issue by converting the summation in a continuous defined partial sum of a geometric series [6, 10].

In this paper we will keep the time-scale discrete but we discuss a few ideas how to generalize the kernel for a continuous case. The summation is dependent on the min value of t and t', meaning that if the smaller of the two values is a natural number, the summation is defined. In realtiy for working with the GP this means that if we would like to forecast one moment in the future t_f, that moment could be a real number. All other evidence points in the past would need to be discrete. Müller and Schleicher [10] have discussed specific fractional sums but a full mathematical consideration is not in the scope of this paper. The exponent $|t - t|'$ is real value if t or t' are real numbers. For rational exponents the result is defined by the n-th root

$$\mathbf{M}^{(\frac{q}{d})} = \sqrt[d]{\mathbf{M}^q}. \tag{27}$$

The n-th root can have none, exactly one or multiple solutions, depending on the structure of $\mathbf{M}$. A full continuous definition of the GP would need to handle the cases where there is no exact solution or put further restrictions on the transition matrix $\mathbf{M}$.

4.3   Kernel Properties

To be a valid kernel, the kernel needs to be symmetric which directly follows from Eq. 13 and Eq. 24. Additionally, the kernel needs to result in a positive semidefinite covariance matrix. In Sect. 2.3 we introduced that kernels can be created of other valid kernels. The $min(t, t')$ and the $a^{|t-t'|}$ terms are valid kernels. Also a summation of valid kernels is a valid kernel. Since the matrix $\mathbf{M}$ only contains constant values, using the resulting kernel function from Eq. 25 results in a symmetric and positive semidefinite covariance matrix and is therefore valid for a GP.

5   Discussion and Outlook

In this paper we encoded a multidimensional DGBN with arbitrary connections between time steps into a Gaussian Process. We demonstrate the generalizing power of GPs by converting a already very general PGM into a GP. All that is needed, is the correct kernel function to describe relationships between random variables along the time dimension. The contribution of the paper has impact on the theoretical research in the fields. Bringing together different research streams and the underlying concepts can benefit both research areas. Existing methods from one area can be possibly transferred to the other research stream and enhance existing applications and vice versa. Also further research can be better directed because scholars in different research groups can work closer together. The results of the paper also bring practical benefits:

Efficient Query Answering: In a DGBN the evidence is usually propagated through the model along the time dimension. In the constructed GP the kernel allows us to explicitly define the effect of an observation to any other queried point in time which can speeds up the querying answering process

Markov Property: The defined kernels keep the Markov property and the transition behavior of the underlying model.

Kernel Combination: The created kernel can be combined with any other existing kernels. If the real-world phenomenon is relatively well described by the DGBN-kernel but also contains a slight periodic behavior, both kernels can easily combined by different operations, e.g. addition and multiplication [13].

There are three streams for further research. First, even further generalize the DGBN and allow also intra-time slice connections. Second, conduct mathematical deep-dives to understand the circumstances under which the kernel can be used in a continuous time setting. Third, transfer real-world applications previously using DGBN into GPs and evaluate query answering time and potential model enhancements by combining kernels.

References

1. Alvarez, M.A., Rosasco, L., Lawrence, N.D., et al.: Kernels for vector-valued functions: a review. Found. Trends® Mach. Learn. **4**(3), 195–266 (2012)
2. Bishop, C.M.: Pattern Recognition and Machine Learning. Springer, New York (2006)
3. Constantinou, A.C., Fenton, N., Neil, M.: Integrating expert knowledge with data in Bayesian networks: preserving data-driven expectations when the expert variables remain unobserved. Expert Syst. Appl. **56**, 197–208 (2016). https://doi.org/10.1016/j.eswa.2016.02.050
4. Flores, M.J., Nicholson, A.E., Brunskill, A., Korb, K.B., Mascaro, S.: Incorporating expert knowledge when learning Bayesian network structure: a medical case study. Artif. Intell. Med. **53**(3), 181–204 (2011)
5. Frigola-Alcalde, R.: Bayesian time series learning with Gaussian processes. Ph.D. thesis, University of Cambridge (2016)
6. Hartwig, M., Mohr, M., Möller, R.: Constructing Gaussian processes for probabilistic graphical models. In: The Thirty-Third International Flairs Conference (2020)
7. Koller, D., Friedman, N., Bach, F.: Probabilistic Graphical Models: Principles and Techniques. MIT Press, Cambridge (2009)
8. Komurlu, C., Bilgic, M.: Active inference and dynamic Gaussian Bayesian networks for battery optimization in wireless sensor networks. In: Workshops at the Thirtieth AAAI Conference on Artificial Intelligence. Citeseer (2016)

9. McCann, R.K., Marcot, B.G., Ellis, R.: Bayesian belief networks: applications in ecology and natural resource management. Can. J. For. Res. **36**(12), 3053–3062 (2006)
10. Müller, M., Schleicher, D.: How to add a non-integer number of terms, and how to produce unusual infinite summations. J. Comput. Appl. Math. **178**(1–2), 347–360 (2005)
11. Murphy, K.P.: Dynamic Bayesian networks: representation, inference and learning. Ph.D. thesis (2002)
12. Pearl, J.: Probabilistic Reasoning in Intelligent Systems: Networks of Plausible Inference. Morgan Kaufmann Publishers Inc., San Francisco (1988)
13. Rasmussen, C.E.: Gaussian Processes for Machine Learning. MIT Press, Cambridge (2006)
14. Reece, S., Roberts, S.: An introduction to Gaussian processes for the Kalman filter expert. In: 2010 13th International Conference on Information Fusion, pp. 1–9. IEEE (2010)
15. Reece, S., Roberts, S.: The near constant acceleration Gaussian process kernel for tracking. IEEE Signal Process. Lett. **17**(8), 707–710 (2010)
16. Roberts, S., Osborne, M., Ebden, M., Reece, S., Gibson, N., Aigrain, S.: Gaussian processes for time-series modelling. Philos. Trans. R. Soc. A Math. Phys. Eng. Sci. **371**(1984), 20110550 (2013)
17. Shachter, R.D., Kenley, C.R.: Gaussian influence diagrams. Manag. Sci. **35**(5), 527–550 (1989). https://doi.org/10.1287/mnsc.35.5.527
18. Turner, R.D.: Gaussian processes for state space models and change point detection. Ph.D. thesis, University of Cambridge (2012)
19. Xu, Z., Kersting, K., Tresp, V.: Multi-relational learning with Gaussian processes. In: Twenty-First International Joint Conference on Artificial Intelligence (2009)
20. Yu, K., Chu, W., Yu, S., Tresp, V., Xu, Z.: Stochastic relational models for discriminative link prediction. In: Advances in Neural Information Processing Systems, pp. 1553–1560 (2007)

Activity-Independent Person Identification Based on Daily Activities Using Wearable Sensors

Seham Hussein[✉], Michael Barlow, and Erandi Lakshika

The University of New South Wales, Canberra, Australia
seham.hussein@student.adfa.edu.au,
{M.Barlow,e.henekankanamge}@adfa.edu.au

Abstract. Recently, wearable sensing devices have become one of the most active research topics in the motion analysis domain. The past few years have seen a growing trend of exploiting wearable devices for capturing several behavioural patterns for the person recognition task. Nevertheless, most of the prior work has investigated a small number of activities and classification models for human recognition. In contrary to all prior work, we focus on presenting a comprehensive evaluation and analysis of a large dataset of twenty different ordinary activities adopted for person identification. In our previous work, we exploited the behavioural pattern data of known and pre-determined activities for person recognition. In this paper, we extend our previous work and analyze the recognition accuracy of persons independent of the activity being undertaken by them. In evaluating the performance of different classification models, Quadratic SVM, Cubic SVM, Ensemble Subspace KNN, and Ensemble Bagged Trees consistently outperform other classifiers. The recognition accuracy results of persons using the 10-fold cross-validation technique show the effectiveness of activity-independent person identification. Lastly, the performance of each considered body position used for person recognition differs, and also the number of wearable sensors used has an impact on the recognition accuracy of persons.

Keywords: Wearable devices · Behavioural biometric trait · Activity-independent person recognition

1 Introduction

In light of the immense popularity of wearable devices, recent years have seen novel advances in the use of wearable technology to facilitate interaction with the surrounding environment, people, and other smart devices. The existing body of research has highlighted that wearable sensors attached to the individual's body are well suited for person recognition through extracting several behavioural and physiological characteristics. One relevant research that was suggested by [2] has highlighted that the recent trends in biometric-based person identification

© Springer Nature Switzerland AG 2020
M. Gallagher et al. (Eds.): AI 2020, LNAI 12576, pp. 383–394, 2020.
https://doi.org/10.1007/978-3-030-64984-5_30

research move toward using wearable sensors equipment due to their popularity, easy installation, and affordable price [23].

It has become of significant importance for the majority of applications to verify or identify the true identity of a person. Passwords, ID cards, and PINs are the conventional recognition methods that had been used in different fields [10,11]. In contrast to these earlier verification methods, biometrics are more secure, unique, and no one can breach, forget, or pirate them [16]. Among the popular biometrics that has been widely investigated by many researchers are the face, iris, voice, fingerprint, and others. However, recent years have seen many advances in biometric systems and novel biometric methods have appeared. The new physical biometric methods involve DNA, face fingerprint, hand geometry, and retina attributes. While, the recent behavioural traits that have been come up include voice, signature, gait, and dynamic keystroke attributes which describe the behaviour of a person while performing an action [9–11].

To the best of our knowledge, behavioural biometrics are considered a more suitable alternative and preferred for human identification as they concentrate on the behaviour pattern of a person (i.e. how the person behaves), and this makes them hard to counterfeit. In this sense, superior recognition accuracy and enhanced performance can be achieved by combining the behavioural biometrics with other hard biometrics [15].

In the last years, gait biometrics is considered the most prevalent behavioural biometric among other biometrics. The majority of reported studies have addressed a limited number of activities, specifically walking and running. Unlike those restricted set of activities adopted for person identification, we have considered a large group of normal daily activities so that different unique movement patterns while performing these activities can be extracted and analyzed for identifying the correct person.

To our knowledge, only a limited set of classification algorithms have been adopted by previous relevant studies. This motivates us to include a various set of classifiers and compare their average recognition performance. Thus, We have applied different classifiers, including SVM, Decision tree, Neural Network, KNN, Linear Discriminant, Quadratic Discriminant, Ensemble Subspace Discriminant in terms of recognition accuracy of persons using three dimensions of three sources of accelerometer, gyroscope, and magnetometer sensors. On comparing the average classification accuracy of different classifiers models using features extracted from six body positions, the analysis showed that the following classifiers had the highest average score on all experiments which are Quadratic SVM, Cubic SVM, Ensemble Subspace KNN, Complex Tree, Ensemble Bagged Trees.

All conducted research has explored activity-dependent person recognition in which the activity is already predefined to the trained classifier model and no study has investigated activity-independent person recognition. We have exploited this limitation and applied our proposed approach which considers training different classification models with the best-selected features of all 20 activities together for implementing experimental work of activity-independent person recognition. The contribution to this point is still new and significantly different from all previous work. This main contribution has been accomplished via the following approach:

- Various set of daily activities have never been studied before for an individual's recognition. Hence, in our paper, we considered a large group of different daily activities undertaken by individuals, and this helps us in investigating a diverse set of behavioural patterns acquired from those different activities. This enhances the person recognition process and helps produce promising identification accuracy of individuals across the considered activities.
- We have investigated the recognition results of persons using six mounted wearable sensors in which all persons have promising classification success-rates and the confusability values exist among them are little.
- We have evaluated a considerable set of machine learning classification models on all activities. The findings obtained from the comparison using all six body positions extracted features have pointed out that Quadratic SVM, Cubic SVM, Ensemble Subspace KNN, and Ensemble Bagged Trees classifiers are the best performing algorithms on our dataset and produce the highest accuracy on the experiments.
- We have investigated six body positions to determine which one produces the best recognition accuracy of persons and have identified that ankle, chest, and thigh positions outperform other body positions in terms of person recognition success-rates. Also, an analysis has been established on assessing the impact of body positions number on classification accuracy and has proved that by considering multiple sensors instead of single sensors devices, this leads to enhancing classification results and reducing the confusability rates among subjects.

The rest of this paper is structured as follows: Sect. 2 presents the literature review studies related to different wearable sensors used for biometrics recognition, best body locations, and impact of sensors number on classification accuracy. Background about the biometric system, its basic components, and different biometrics used for person recognition are also highlighted, in Sect. 3 we describe the dataset in more detail and the suggested methodology followed in this paper, in Sect. 4 we discuss the experimental work done and obtained results, finally, in Sect. 5, we summarize the conclusions and the future work directions.

2   Related Work

2.1   Studies on Using Wearable Sensors for Person Recognition

It has been shown from the earlier literature related to wearable sensors in the biometrics field that different studies have used wearable sensors for person recognition. Current research studies on wearable sensors have illustrated that accelerometer and gyroscope sensors are among the most commonly used sensors in this domain. To date, several examples of research that used wearable sensors for person identification have been conducted. One study by Gafurov et al.[6] has suggested an accelerometer sensor, mounted at the trouser pocket body location, to recognize 50 persons from their walking patterns, consisting of 300 walking sequences. Similarly, Trung et al. [22] have conducted their experiments on an extensive dataset of walking patterns captured from 736 individuals using both accelerometer and gyroscopic wearable sensors.

2.2 Studies on Best Body-Location and Impact of Sensors Number on Classification Accuracy

There is no doubt that the position on which wearable sensors are mounted has a direct impact on measuring body movement of a person. Among the works that concentrated on evaluating the effect of body location on the classification success-rate, Shoaib et al. [19] measured the success-rates obtained by accelerometers, gyroscopes, and magnetometers smartphone sensors. The locations which they investigated in their research include the right trouser pocket, left trouser pocket, upper right arm, lower wrist, and belt position towards the right leg. The authors observed that no body position produced the best classification success-rates for all activities, but it varies from activity to another. Chamroukhi et al. [3] investigated the effect of the location and sensors number on the recognition performance of human activities. The three sensors located on the thigh, ankle, and chest produced the best results and the results obtained in this research emphasized that the recognition of human activity can be promoted by integrating accelerometers sensors placed on the lower and upper body positions.

2.3 General Biometric System and Basic Components

The term 'biometrics recognition' is defined as a pattern recognition problem in which a set of physical or behavioural traits related to the person are extracted and matched against the stored traits as a reference to confirm the true identity of a person [18]. Using biometrics for person recognition is deemed an effective strategy as some properties of each person may be unique and differ from one person to another. Either a traditional or an automatic biometric recognition system consists of four basic functional modules, those are Sensor Module, Signal-processing and Feature Extraction Module, Characteristics Matching Module, and Decision-Making Module as illustrated in Fig. 1.

2.4 Studies on the Different Biometrics Used for Person Recognition

The past decade has seen increasing attention from many literature studies towards different biometric methods, especially behavioural biometrics. One of the most popular used behavioural biometrics in the person recognition domain is the Keystroke dynamic biometric. It is a robust biometric [1] and has been

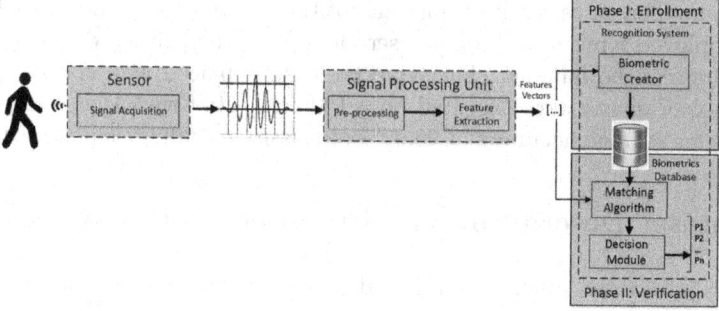

Fig. 1. Biometric recognition system phases.

widely applied by a considerable number of studies for recognizing individuals. This biometric can distinguish among persons as each person has some distinctive characteristics in typing rhythm on a keyboard. Some other approaches of person recognition focused on the face, iris, and fingerprint characteristics using constrained recognition installations and person interaction. For instance, the person should stand at a reasonable distance in front of a camera and look at a specific point or have physical interaction with sensors. Among these studies, McCool et al. [14] proposed a new fully automated face and voice system for individual recognition which runs concurrently on a Nokia N900 mobile phone. This system was evaluated on a recent and easily accessible mobile phone database. It was concluded from this study that exploiting score fusion can enhance the recognition performance of a person and reduce the error rates by more than 25%.

Numerous studies have shown their interest in gait recognition that has become a widely used behavioural biometric trait for recognizing an individual's identity from his/her walking style. Later, a study by Marsico et al. [4] has also investigated the recognition of 25 persons from their walking patterns where each person walks around ten steps. They exploited smartphone devices including 1 OnePlus One, 1 Samsung S4 Active, and I Sony Xperia S, which are fixed on the hip position for recording the BWR-Multidevice dataset. Like previous research [24], persons in this study walk 12 times but 4 times for each smartphone device. Several examples of literature studies that used smart wearable devices for user recognition are Johnston et al. [12], Lee et al. [13], and Haong et al. [8], where works of similar nature have been suggested.

Much of the current literature paid important consideration to behavioural biometrics captured using wearable sensor devices for person identification, particularly gait or walking activity, and did not consider that the person may carry out a different activity. In contrast to all studies applied on gait recognition, Reddy et al. [17] proposed a method for person identification through exploiting human motion information of different activities. The authors in their study considered sitting, standing, and walking postures or states. Their proposed method initially identifies the person's state and separate SVM based models are used for person recognition for each of these three above mentioned states. They employed Kinect as the input sensor so that the privacy concern of home monitoring can be handled. The Kinect sensor is placed at a specific position and all experiments were executed on a PC connected with that Kinect. They achieved an average accuracy of 96.91% of classifying different postures.

3   Dataset Description and Proposed Methodology

As described in our previous published paper [5], our dataset includes 20 different normal daily activities that are analyzed to recognize 18 persons using wearable sensor devices. The considered dataset in our study includes a comprehensive, and representative set of common daily activities carried out by individuals including kitchen work activities (grating, dicing, peeling vegetables, stirring, washing vegetables, washing dishes, and washing hands), folding and ironing clothes activities, household cleaning activities (sweeping, vacuuming, and dusting), office-work activities (using PC, writing with a pen, talking on the phone, and texting on the phone), watching TV and brushing teeth activities. All dataset was gathered indoors through a single session and in two separate locations. Kitchen work activities were collected from all subjects in a kitchen area whereas the other remaining activities (office work and household cleaning activities) were gathered in a computing laboratory. The considered participants include 15 males and 3 females whose ages ranging from 27 to 52 years. A set of six inertial measurement units (IMUs) were used and mounted on the dominant wrist, non-dominant wrist, dominant upper arm, ankle, thigh, and chest positions [21]. Sampling of data was performed 128 Hz and the mean time per participant spent to collect data of all 20 activities ranged from an average of 0.6 min (Washing Vegetables) to 6 min (Watching TV) with a mean of 2.5 min.

In our previous work [5], we have focused on exploiting the behavioural patterns (i.e. motion information) of known daily activities gathered from wearable sensors for recognizing the person. Currently, it is well established that some behavioural biometrics of individuals may be unique and can effectively distinguish persons. However, identifying persons independent of the activity being undertaken is a new research topic where there have been no studies that investigated how can we recognize individuals without knowing what is the specific activity that the person is currently doing.

In order to execute the experimental work of activity-independent person recognition, we will consider the selected features vectors of all activity groups and gather them together as a set to be evaluated by different classifiers models. Then, 10 fold cross-validation technique is applied where for each fold, out-of-fold observations (9 folds) are used for training and the in-fold data is used for assessing and validating the model performance. Finally, the obtained accuracy results are analyzed to investigate the recognition rates and confusability rates of considered persons. The high-level design of our considered methodology is indicated in Fig. 2. Consequently, motivated by the aforementioned research gap, the specific objective of this paper is to explore and get a deeper understanding of

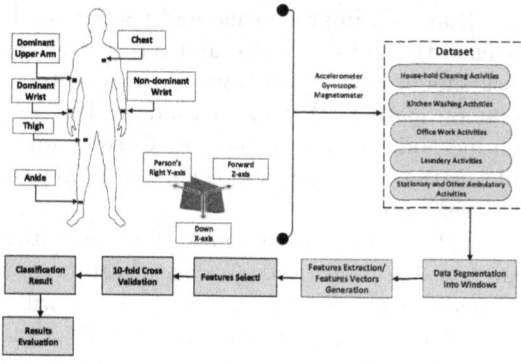

Fig. 2. High level design of our experimental work.

how to identify persons independent of the activity is being currently conducted by them.In order to run the experiments of activity-independent person identification, the methodological strategy taken in this study involves the following steps which are explained below in detail:

1. Data Sampling Step: the data was sampled 128 Hz to obtain the three dimensional values of accelerometer, gyroscope and magnetometer from six IMUs.
2. Data Segmentation into Fixed-Length Time Domain Windows Step: the raw activities dataset is partitioned into segments or windows where the sliding windowing technique is used for segmenting the record into reasonable fixed-size windows. After running an initial set of activity-independent persons recognition experiments using a fixed window length of 2 s and 50% overlapping and investigating the results obtained, we found that some activities were not characterized accurately, and we could not determine whether these activities performed well or poorly in this stage such as walking downstairs and walking upstairs. We conclude that one reason may be the segments obtained for those activities are shorter and not enough to describe the activities well. To enhance the classification results of activities, specifically cyclic activities with repetitive motions, we applied a longer window length and based on that we segmented all dataset into time-domain segments of 3 s with a 50% overlap.
3. Feature Extraction Step: different time-domain features are extracted from the generated fixed-length segments including mean, standard deviation, mean square root, mean absolute difference from the mean of each signal axis, percentile 25, and percentile 75, variance, root mean square, range, harmonic mean, skewness, kurtosis, zero-crossing rate, slope sign change, simple squared integral, median, and inter-quartile range. Using this large group of time-domain features resulted in 16 basic time-domain features in each direction of accelerometer, gyroscope, and magnetometer data sources. For each activity and six body locations, there are 810 feature vectors in which 135 feature vector is assigned for each of six body locations.

4. Feature Selection Stage: to improve time and space complexity, and reduce overfitting problems, the most effective and relevant features to the person classification task should be selected from features vectors. Indeed, we have applied four common feature selection methods which are correlation-based feature selection methods (CFS) method [7], Correlation Attribute Evaluator method, Information Gain Attribute Evaluator Method, and Principal Component Analysis Method.

   In our work, we will consider the features of all activities for all subjects where rows represent the observations or data instances, and 135 columns represent all the features calculated. In this phase, we will apply the feature selection step for each body position individually to select the best working set of features for this body position. The feature selection step will be applied to each position separately. Then, all the selected features for all six body positions are merged into one file. It was found that the CFS method for each body position with the Greedy Stepwise search method produces effective results compared to the other approaches. Therefore, the experiments for all activities and six body locations in this paper will be implemented using the CFS method with the Greedy stepwise search method.

5. Classification Phase: in this phase, the prepared feature set file is used for classification by various classification algorithms. The 10-fold cross-validation method is applied, and the classification models such as Support Vector Machine (SVM), K-Nearest Neighbour (KNN), Decision tree, ensemble methods are evaluated in terms of the person recognition accuracy. Finally, the resulting confusion matrix illustrates the recognition rates of subjects and their confusability rates.

6. Experimental Analysis of Testing Classification Results: According to the obtained confusion matrices, the analysis can enable us to assess the recognition rate of each person studied across all activities and investigate which persons have high recognition accuracy and which are confusable with others. Furthermore, an analysis of classification results is helpful to investigate the performance of each single body position on the recognition accuracy of subjects and which of those six body positions produce superior classification results. Lastly, studying the impact of the number of different IMUs on the recognition rates of subjects is also significant and will be considered.

4 Experimental Results

In running our experimental work of activity-independent person recognition for classifying 18 subjects, we considered extracted features vectors of all three sensor sources (i.e. accelerometers, gyroscopes, and magnetometers) of six sensor-based body locations. In the classification phase, we used MATLAB software [20] to execute the person classification through various classifiers such as SVM (Fine Gaussian SVM, Coarse Gaussian SVM, Linear SVM, Medium Gaussian SVM, Quadratic SVM, Cubic SVM), Decision tree (Simple Tree, Medium Tree, Complex Tree, Ensemble Boosted Trees, Ensemble Bagged Trees), Neural Network,

Table 1. Overall confusion matrix showing the recognition and confusability rates of each of 18 considered persons by Ensemble Bagged Trees Classifier using all Six Wearable Sensors.

	S1	S2	S3	S4	S5	S6	S7	S8	S9	S10	S11	S12	S13	S14	S15	S16	S17	S18
S1	0.99	<0.01	0.00	<0.01	<0.01	0.00	0.00	0.00	0.00	<0.01	<0.01	0.00	0.00	0.00	<0.01	<0.01	<0.01	<0.01
S2	0.00	0.98	<0.01	0.00	<0.01	<0.01	<0.01	0.00	0.00	<0.01	<0.01	0.00	0.00	0.00	<0.01	<0.01	<0.01	0.00
S3	<0.01	<0.01	0.97	0.00	<0.01	<0.01	<0.01	0.00	0.00	<0.01	<0.01	0.00	<0.01	0.00	<0.01	0.00	0.00	0.00
S4	<0.01	<0.01	0.00	0.99	<0.01	0.00	<0.01	0.00	0.00	<0.01	<0.01	0.00	0.00	0.00	<0.01	<0.01	0.00	0.00
S5	<0.01	<0.01	<0.01	<0.01	0.98	<0.01	<0.01	0.00	0.00	<0.01	<0.01	0.00	<0.01	0.00	<0.01	0.00	<0.01	<0.01
S6	<0.01	<0.01	<0.01	<0.01	<0.01	0.96	<0.01	0.00	0.00	<0.01	<0.01	0.00	<0.01	0.00	<0.01	0.00	<0.01	<0.01
S7	<0.01	<0.01	<0.01	<0.01	<0.01	<0.01	0.97	0.00	0.00	<0.01	<0.01	0.00	0.00	0.00	<0.01	<0.01	<0.01	<0.01
S8	0.00	0.00	0.00	0.00	0.00	0.00	0.00	0.99	0.00	0.00	0.00	0.00	0.00	0.00	0.00	0.00	0.00	0.00
S9	0.00	0.00	0.00	0.00	0.00	0.00	0.00	0.00	0.99	0.00	0.00	<0.01	0.00	0.00	0.00	0.00	0.00	0.00
S10	0.00	<0.01	<0.01	0.00	<0.01	<0.01	<0.01	0.00	0.00	0.99	<0.01	0.00	<0.01	0.00	<0.01	0.00	<0.01	<0.01
S11	<0.01	<0.01	<0.01	<0.01	<0.01	<0.01	<0.01	0.00	0.00	<0.01	0.95	0.00	<0.01	0.00	<0.01	0.00	<0.01	<0.01
S12	0.00	0.00	0.00	0.00	0.00	0.00	0.00	0.00	<0.01	0.00	0.00	0.99	0.00	0.00	0.00	0.00	0.00	0.00
S13	0.00	<0.01	0.00	0.00	0.00	0.00	<0.01	0.00	0.00	0.00	0.00	0.00	0.99	0.00	0.00	0.00	0.00	0.00
S14	0.00	<0.01	0.00	0.00	0.00	0.00	<0.01	0.00	0.00	0.00	0.00	0.00	0.00	0.99	0.00	0.00	0.00	0.00
S15	<0.01	<0.01	<0.01	<0.01	<0.01	<0.01	<0.01	0.00	0.00	<0.01	0.02	0.00	<0.01	0.00	0.94	<0.01	<0.01	<0.01
S16	<0.01	<0.01	<0.01	<0.01	<0.01	<0.01	<0.01	0.00	0.00	<0.01	0.00	0.00	0.00	0.00	<0.01	0.99	0.00	0.00
S17	<0.01	<0.01	<0.01	0.00	<0.01	<0.01	<0.01	0.00	0.00	<0.01	<0.01	0.00	0.00	0.00	<0.01	<0.01	0.97	0.00
S18	<0.01	0.00	0.00	<0.01	<0.01	0.00	<0.01	0.00	0.00	<0.01	0.00	0.00	0.00	<0.01	0.00	0.00	<0.01	0.99

KNN (Coarse KNN, Cubic KNN, Cosine KNN, Medium KNN, Weighted KNN, Fine KNN, Ensemble Subspace KNN), Linear Discriminant, Quadratic Discriminant, Ensemble Subspace Discriminant in terms of accuracy using individual sources, a combination of pairs, and all three sources together.

To compare the performance of those classification models on recognition of persons, firstly, we have computed the mean classification accuracy of these classifiers across all activities and then compared their accuracies against each other. Moreover, we have computed two significant parameters, which are the sensitivity and specificity factors of each person and for each classification method. On one side, sensitivity refers to the proportion of positive data instances that are identified correctly by a classification algorithm. However, on the other side, the specificity factor measures the proportion of negative data instances classified correctly by a classification algorithm. It is crucial to consider both sensitivity and specificity parameters in our computations as they help us accurately evaluating the performance of those classification models on the recognition of each considered person and checking how they can correctly identify the data instances of those persons. For instance, some classifiers may have an overall high recognition accuracy results, but on a per person level, they may fail in efficiently recognizing the persons and classifying their relevant data instances. Thus, applying the classifiers models may be affected by this shortcoming. From this comparison and taking those factors into our attention, it was found that Quadratic SVM, Cubic SVM, Ensemble Subspace KNN, and Ensemble Bagged Trees classifiers had the highest average score on all experiments.

In applying our proposed approach of considering the whole activities as one bunch for person classification using all six body locations, we achieved an overall recognition accuracy of 99% (individual accuracies ranging from 94% to over 99%). The diagonal values of a confusion matrix represent the correctly classified data instances of each subject. Whereas, the off-diagonal values represent the confusability values of a specific person with others. In other meaning, it may be viewed as misclassified instances of that person and be supposed as another person. It is evident that the confusability rates among subjects are few where

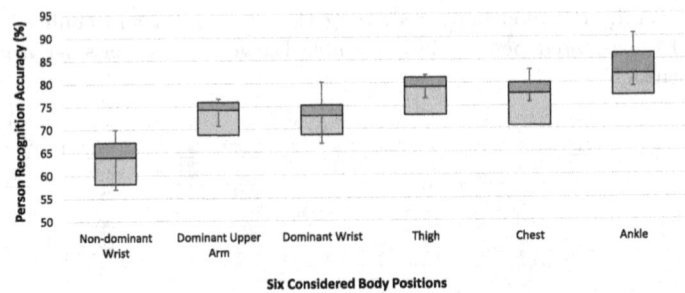

Fig. 3. Boxplot comparing six considered body positions in terms of person recognition accuracy using all 20 daily activities

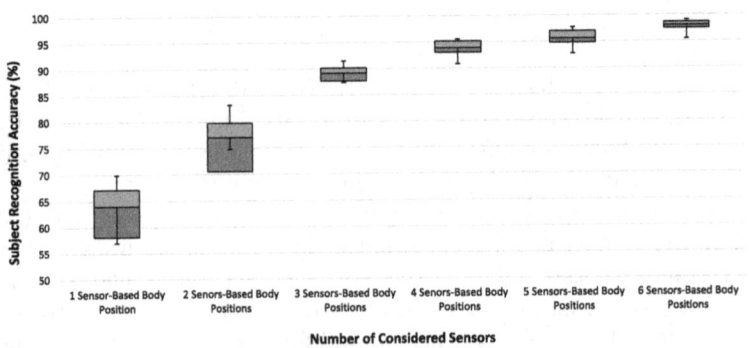

Fig. 4. Boxplot showing impact of number of different sensors on recognition accuracy of subjects using full daily activities set

minimal confusability values of 1% exist among persons. Therefore, the first set of analyses in this study try to examine the overall recognition rate of 18 persons when considering the selected features set of all 20 activities using all body positions. The confusion matrix of the overall recognition accuracy and confusability rates among subjects are presented in Table 1.

Subsequent experimental analyses have been implemented which concentrated on studying whether the body location on which monitors are fixed affects the recognition success rates of subjects or not. The analysis obtained from our experiments on six body positions illustrated that the recognition accuracy of subjects is affected by the body location on which sensors are mounted. Thus, using a feature set of all 20 activities, it has been found that ankle, chest, thigh, and dominant wrist positions provided the best accuracy results of subject recognition respectively, compared to the non-dominant wrist and dominant upper arm positions. This is illustrated in Fig. 3.

Further, we focused on studying the impact of the number of wearable sensors mounted at different body locations upon the recognition accuracy of subjects. The results of this investigation illustrated that considering features from multiple sensors-based body locations for classifying subjects produced higher accuracy than those obtained depending on a single sensor-based body location. This means that considering combined features vectors from ankle, chest, and thigh positions work better than those from ankle position only. Consequently, based on our study, it had been concluded that there is a positive correlation between number of sensors and recognition accuracy as seen on Fig. 4.

5 Conclusion

The present study has been one of the first attempts to explore the novel idea of activity-independent person identification. One critical finding obtained from the experimental analysis was that the subjects' recognition accuracy results were promising where an average of 99% has been achieved using six wearable sensors distributed across the body and three seconds of anyone of twenty daily activities. Additionally, the study has found that not all body positions have the same performance in recognizing persons where ankle, followed by chest, and thigh positions produce considerable and high recognition accuracy of persons among other positions. Also, experiments have shown that there is a positive correlation between the number of sensors used and the obtained recognition accuracy.

Further research should be carried out on collecting data from more males and females of different ages. More in-depth analysis is needed to get a formal description of the motions information, and this would help us to establish a promising accuracy on person recognition. Also, an investigation is required to examine person identification for an activity not seen in the training set.

References

1. Banerjee, S.P., Woodard, D.L.: Biometric authentication and identification using keystroke dynamics: a survey. J. Pattern Recogn. Res. **7**(1), 116–139 (2012)
2. Blasco, J., Chen, T.M., Tapiador, J., Peris-Lopez, P.: A survey of wearable biometric recognition systems. ACM Comput. Surv. (CSUR) **49**(3), 43 (2016)
3. Chamroukhi, F., Mohammed, S., Trabelsi, D., Oukhellou, L., Amirat, Y.: Joint segmentation of multivariate time series with hidden process regression for human activity recognition. Neurocomputing **120**, 633–644 (2013)
4. De Marsico, M., De Pasquale, D., Mecca, A.: Embedded accelerometer signal normalization for cross-device gait recognition. In: 2016 International Conference of the Biometrics Special Interest Group (BIOSIG), pp. 1–5. IEEE (2016)
5. Elkader, S.A., Barlow, M., Lakshika, E.: Wearable sensors for recognizing individuals undertaking daily activities. In: Proceedings of the 2018 ACM International Symposium on Wearable Computers, pp. 64–67. ACM (2018)
6. Gafurov, D., Snekkenes, E., Bours, P.: Gait authentication and identification using wearable accelerometer sensor. In: 2007 IEEE Workshop on Automatic Identification Advanced Technologies, pp. 220–225. IEEE (2007)
7. Hall, M.A.: Correlation-based feature selection for machine learning (1999)
8. Hoang, T., Choi, D., Nguyen, T.: On the instability of sensor orientation in gait verification on mobile phone. In: 2015 12th International Joint Conference on e-Business and Telecommunications (ICETE), vol. 4, pp. 148–159. IEEE (2015)

9. Jain, A.K., Nandakumar, K., Ross, A.: 50 years of biometric research: accomplishments, challenges, and opportunities. Pattern Recogn. Lett. **79**, 80–105 (2016)
10. Jain, A.K., Ross, A., Pankanti, S.: Biometrics: a tool for information security. IEEE Trans. Inf. Forensics Secur. **1**(2), 125–143 (2006)
11. Jain, A.K., Ross, A., Prabhakar, S., et al.: An introduction to biometric recognition. IEEE Trans. Circuits Syst. Video Technol. **14**(1), 4–20 (2004)
12. Johnston, A., Weiss, G.: Cellphone based biometric identification. In: Biometrics Theory, Applications and Systems (BTAS) (2010)
13. Lee, W.H., Lee, R.: Implicit sensor-based authentication of smartphone users with smartwatch. In: 2016 Proceedings of the Hardware and Architectural Support for Security and Privacy, p. 9. ACM (2016)
14. McCool, C., et al.: Bi-modal person recognition on a mobile phone: using mobile phone data. In: 2012 IEEE International Conference on Multimedia and Expo Workshops, pp. 635–640. IEEE (2012)
15. Pahuja, G., Nagabhushan, T.: Biometric authentication & identification through behavioral biometrics: a survey. In: 2015 International Conference on Cognitive Computing and Information Processing (CCIP), pp. 1–7. IEEE (2015)
16. Prabhakar, S., Pankanti, S., Jain, A.K.: Biometric recognition: security and privacy concerns. IEEE Secur. Priv. **2**, 33–42 (2003)
17. Reddy, V.R., Chattopadhyay, T., Chakravarty, K., Sinha, A.: Person identification from arbitrary position and posture using kinect. In: Proceedings of the 12th ACM Conference on Embedded Network Sensor Systems, pp. 350–351. ACM (2014)
18. Sabhanayagam, T., Venkatesan, V.P., Senthamaraikannan, K.: A comprehensive survey on various biometric systems. Int. J. Appl. Eng. Res. **13**(5), 2276–2297 (2018)
19. Shoaib, M., Bosch, S., Incel, O.D., Scholten, H., Havinga, P.J.: Fusion of smartphone motion sensors for physical activity recognition. Sensors **14**(6), 10146–10176 (2014)
20. MATLAB and Statistics Toolbox Release: The MathWorks Inc., Natick, Massachusetts, United States (2016)
21. Taylor, L.E., Abdulla, U.A., Barlow, M.G., Taylor, K.: Detecting and exploiting periodicity in activity classification. In: 2017 IEEE 5th International Conference on Serious Games and Applications for Health (SeGAH), pp. 1–8. IEEE (2017)
22. Trung, N.T., Makihara, Y., Nagahara, H., Mukaigawa, Y., Yagi, Y.: Performance evaluation of gait recognition using the largest inertial sensor-based gait database. In: 2012 5th IAPR International Conference on Biometrics (ICB), pp. 360–366. IEEE (2012)
23. Yoon, C., Zubair, M., Song, K.: Human activity recognition using wearable sensors: research review. Int. J. Sci. Eng. Technol. **6**(2), 66–70 (2017)
24. Zhang, Y., Pan, G., Jia, K., Lu, M., Wang, Y., Wu, Z.: Accelerometer-based gait recognition by sparse representation of signature points with clusters. IEEE Trans. Cybern. **45**(9), 1864–1875 (2014)

Unsupervised One-Shot Learning of Both Specific Instances and Generalised Classes with a Hippocampal Architecture

Gideon Kowadlo$^{(\boxtimes)}$ ⓘ, Abdelrahman Ahmed ⓘ, and David Rawlinson ⓘ

Cerenaut, Melbourne, Australia
info@cerenaut.ai
https://cerenaut.ai

Abstract. Established experimental procedures for one-shot machine learning do not test the ability to learn or remember specific instances of classes, a key feature of animal intelligence. Distinguishing specific instances is necessary for many real-world tasks, such as remembering which cup belongs to you. Generalisation within classes conflicts with the ability to separate instances of classes, making it difficult to achieve both capabilities within a single architecture. We propose an extension to the standard Omniglot classification-generalisation framework that additionally tests the ability to distinguish specific instances after one exposure and introduces noise and occlusion corruption. Learning is defined as an ability to classify as well as recall training samples. Complementary Learning Systems (CLS) is a popular model of mammalian brain regions believed to play a crucial role in learning from a single exposure to a stimulus. We created an artificial neural network implementation of CLS and applied it to the extended Omniglot benchmark. Our unsupervised model demonstrates comparable performance to existing supervised ANNs on the Omniglot classification task (requiring generalisation), without the need for domain-specific inductive biases. On the extended Omniglot instance-recognition task, the same model also demonstrates significantly better performance than a baseline nearest-neighbour approach, given partial occlusion and noise.

Keywords: CLS · Hippocampus · One-shot · Specifics · Instances · Unsupervised · Generalization.

1 Introduction

One-shot learning has seen renewed interest in recent years. Many studies [12,27] are motivated by the apparent limitations of modern ML relative to animal-like learning [14]. An ability for one-shot learning alleviates the reliance on large labelled datasets in which samples are assumed to be i.i.d., implying an unchanging world. This is particularly relevant for autonomous real-world agents, where samples are necessarily highly correlated and typically unlabelled.

© Springer Nature Switzerland AG 2020
M. Gallagher et al. (Eds.): AI 2020, LNAI 12576, pp. 395–406, 2020.
https://doi.org/10.1007/978-3-030-64984-5_31

However, we believe that the standard approach - classification of general classes - does not go far enough. Learning specific instances is crucial for intelligent agents, and is something we take for granted. For example, identifying your own coffee cup from other cups, in addition to recognising that it belongs to the 'cup' category. More generally, it underpins memory for singular facts and an individual's own autobiographical history, important for future decision making.

At first glance, learning specific instances appears easy. An obvious starting point is nearest-neighbour lookup in a buffer of past observations. However, this approach may perform poorly given observational variation such as occlusion, and have trouble also generalising class recognition ability. Conversely, methods that can generalise would be unlikely to do well at learning specific instances, as they are conflicting capabilities.

Learning of specific instances is not to be confused with Instance-based Learning [24]. Such approaches store instances during training, and use them to classify test samples e.g. k-nearest neighbour, SVM's and RBFs. Our objective is learning a model of the instances, despite observational variation, while being able to distinguish even very similar instances from each other. We identify two important aspects of learning - classification and recall (generation) of concept.

Complementary Learning Systems (CLS) is a model of mammalian learning that describes the interplay between the neocortex and a region called the Hippocampal Formation (HF) [19,22]. CLS is believed to be crucial for fast learning and is recognised to be important for intelligent agents [10]. Our motivation is to expand the standard definition of one-shot learning, and to test if the CLS architecture can satisfy the requirements.

In this paper we propose a broader benchmark for one-shot learning that includes robust classification of specific instances given observational variance by introducing image corruption with occlusion and noise. We present an ANN implementation of CLS using an Artificial Hippocampal Algorithm (AHA) and apply it to the extended benchmark. The performance of the system is compared to two baselines, a simplified version of CLS that replaces the hippocampal model with a conventional ML model optimised for the task, and to the naive solution for learning specifics - a buffer with nearest neighbour lookup.

2   Background

2.1   One-shot Learning

Following seminal work by Li et al. [15,16], the area was re-invigorated by Lake et al. [11], who introduced a popular test that has become a standard benchmark [12]. It is a one-shot classification task on the Omniglot dataset of handwritten characters. Classification is posed as a matching task, where a given character must be matched with a character of the same class in a test set, see Sect. 4 for details. The framework was formalised by Vinyals et al. [27].

A typical approach is to pre-train a model on many classes and use learnt concepts to recognise new classes quickly from one or few examples. Often framed as meta-learning or "learning to learn", there are multiple implementations using neural networks that require external labels and supervised learning during pre-training, such as Siamese networks [8], matching networks [27], and prototypical networks [26]. Two notable Bayesian approaches, BPL [12] and RCN [2], achieve above and close to human level performance respectively. The superior performance of BPL may be partially explained by its use of prior knowledge about handwriting via stroke formation. RCN, by virtue of the design which is modeled on the visual cortex, is also specialised for this type of visual task. It is less clear how it could be applied to other datasets and problems where contour topology is less distinct or relevant. A comprehensive review is given in [13].

2.2 Complementary Learning Systems (CLS)

Complementary Learning Systems (CLS) is a standard framework for understanding the function of the HF [10,19,21]. CLS consists of two differentially specialised and complementary structures, neocortex and HF, shown in Fig. 1a. In this framework, the neocortex is analogous to a conventional ML model, incrementally learning regularities across many observations, comprising a long-term memory (LTM). It forms overlapping and distributed representations that are effective for inference. In contrast, the HF rapidly learns distinct observations, forming sparser, non-overlapping and therefore non-interfering representations, functioning as a short term memory (STM). Recent memories from the HF are replayed to neocortex, re-instating the original activations resulting in consolidation as long-term memory (LTM). Patterns are replayed in an interleaved fashion, avoiding catastrophic forgetting. In addition, they can be replayed selectively according to salience. There have been numerous implementations of CLS [4,7,20,23,25] and Rolls et al. presented a similar model with greater neuroanatomical detail [22].

Overall, the HF functions as an autoassociative memory that can recall memories from partial cues. CLS describes the HF in terms of distinct functional units called subfields. Together they comprise a unification of pattern completion and pattern separation pathways. Reported implementations (see citations above) are expressed at the level of individual neurons replicating known biological plasticity and dynamics, and have not been applied to ML benchmarks.

3 Model

Our approach is to implement a CLS-style STM with an LTM (Fig. 1a), with biological plausibility constraints [9] - all components are trained with local and immediate credit assignment. The LTM comprises a simple vision component suitable for image feature extraction. The STM is implemented with AHA, an Artificial Hippocampal Algorithm, which follows the subfield architecture of the HF described by CLS. There are two baselines for comparison. Firstly, the LTM alone is compared to performance of LTM+STM. It constitutes a naive solution to classifying specific instances (see Sect. 4). The second baseline, FastNN, is an alternate STM comprised of a standard ML component empirically optimised for the same tasks. We provide the code and configuration required to reproduce experiments in a GitHub repository[1].

3.1 Training and Testing Framework

With complementary systems, training and testing are non-standard, and are therefore explained here to provide context for the remainder of the paper.

Stage 1: Pre-train LTM: Train LTM on a training set over multiple epochs. The LTM learns incrementally about common features that can be used compositionally to represent unseen classes.

Stage 2: Evaluate LTM+STM: Evaluation is conducted with a disjoint evaluation set. The LTM does not learn during this stage. Training and Testing of STM occurs rapidly, allowing multiple internal cycles but only one exposure to an external stimulus. The STM is reset after each evaluation[2]. Evaluation consists of two steps performed in succession - Train (encoding) and Test (inference).

- *Train:* A small support set is presented once (referred to as 'study set' in CLS). STM modules are set to train mode to learn the samples.
- *Test:* A small query set is presented (referred to as 'recall' in CLS), STM modules are in inference mode. For each 'recall' sample, the system is expected to retrieve the corresponding sample from the 'study' set. If correct, it is considered to be 'recognised' - an AHA moment!

3.2 LTM - Vision Component

The role of the LTM is to process high-dimensional sensor input, and output relatively abstract visual features that can be used as compositional primitives. A single layer convolutional sparse autoencoder based on [17,18] provides the required embedding. However, in Omniglot there is a lot of empty background that is encoded with strong hidden layer activity. Lacking an attention mechanism, this detracts from compositionality of foreground features. To suppress encoding of the background, we added an 'Interest Filter' which loosely mimics known retinal processing (see below). Smoothing is applied to provide some tolerance to feature location and a final max-pooling stage to reduce dimensionality.

Interest Filter. The retina possesses centre-surround inhibitory and excitatory cells that can be well approximated with a Difference of Gaussians (DoG) kernel [28]. Positive and negative DoG filters are used to enhance positive and negative intensity transitions. Local non-maxima suppression merges nearby features and a 'top-k' function creates a mask of the most significant features globally. Positive and negative masks are combined by summation giving a final 2D mask that is applied to all channels of the convolutional autoencoder output.

---

[1] https://github.com/Cerenaut/aha.
[2] Adam Optimizer is reset and trainable parameters are re-initialised.

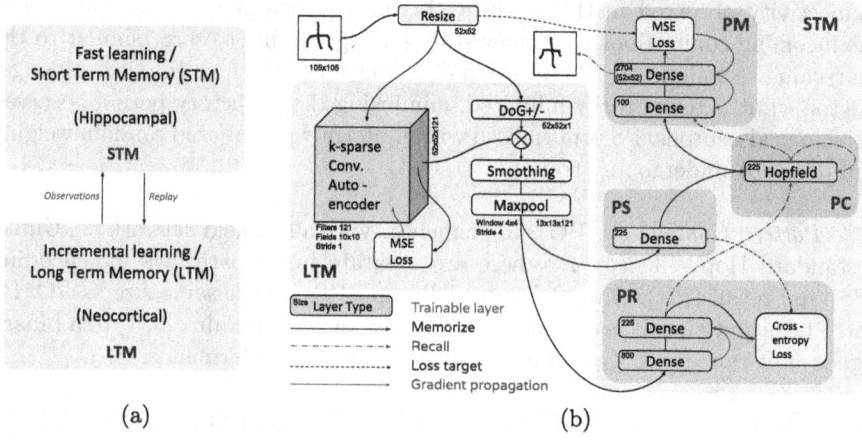

(a)   (b)

Fig. 1. a) **CLS:** The STM learns and forgets rapidly. Salient memories are replayed to the LTM for incremental statistical learning. b) **System diagram:** Our implementation of CLS. Local credit assignment via shallow backpropagation is used throughout. The dense layer in PS (green) is initialised, but not trained. (Color figure online)

3.3   STM - Artificial Hippocampal Algorithm (AHA)

AHA is our implementation of CLS. For greater details on CLS, the biological basis for AHA design choices, and in-depth implementation details, see [9]. The components and connectivity are shown in Fig. 1b. LTM outputs sparse distributed overlapping patterns. The signal becomes sparser and more orthogonal through PS, minimising interference between patterns, resulting in distinct representations for similar inputs.

In train mode, PS patterns are encoded/memorised into PC, an auto-associative, content-addressable memory. They form a target, which PR learns to retrieve from LTM distributed representations. PM learns to map from the stored non-interfering patterns, to the originating sparse distributed patterns.

In test mode, PR retrieves the corresponding stored PC pattern using input from LTM, which is used to cue complete recall from PC. PS is not used as a cue, because even small input differences will result in orthogonal PS outputs. PC can retrieve a crisp, complete pattern, that in turn enables PM to recall the original observation. In future work this will be used for improved inference and consolidation of memories.

The use of PS for encoding and PR for recall is based on the Hippocampal model by Rolls [22,23]. The role of each subfield is detailed below:

PS - Pattern Separation. PS is implemented with a single fully-connected Artificial Neural Network (ANN) layer with sparsity constraints and temporal inhibition. Sparsity is implemented as a 'top-k' ranking per sample, mimicking a local competitive process via inhibitory interneurons. Low k produces outputs with low overlap, but orthogonality is further improved by replicating the sparse connectivity observed in this pathway in the hippocampus [23]. A portion of the incoming connections are removed by setting weights to zero (similar to the sparsening technique of [1]). Additionally, after a neuron fires (i.e. it is amongst the top-k), it is temporarily inhibited, mimicking the refractory period observed in biological neurons. PS is initialised with uniformly distributed random weights and does not undergo any training.

PC - Pattern Completion. PC is implemented with a Hopfield network [6]. Unlike a standard Hopfield network, there are separate input pathways for encoding (PS) and recall (PR). Output layers of PS and PR are the same size as PC. PS and PR output signals are conditioned from a continuous value [0, 1] to a binary signed unit range [−1, 1], chosen for better Hopfield performance.

PR - Pattern Retrieval. PR is implemented with a 2-layer fully-connected ANN. In training, PS output is used as an internally generated label constituting self-supervised learning [3]. Usually in self-supervised learning, prior task knowledge is used to set a pre-conceived goal such as rotation, with the motivation of learning generalisable representations. In the case of AHA, no prior is required. The motivation is separability and as such, the use of orthogonal patterns as labels is very effective.

PM - Pattern Mapping. PM is implemented with a 2-layer fully-connected ANN. In this study we trained it to reconstruct the input images rather than the LTM output, for easy assessment of recalled image quality and correctness.

AHA - Theory of Operation

Compositionality. A central capability of AHA is the memorisation of new conjunctions of primitive concepts. The primitives can be composed in a vast number of new combinations, a feature of animal-like learning [14]. Memorisation of conjunctions of concepts is an aspect of episodic memory, as identified in the hippocampal computational modelling literature [7] (expanded in [9]).

Generalisation to subsequent observations of the new combination is achieved through unification of separation and completion (below). The scope of generalisation depends on the level of abstraction of the primitives.

Unifying Separation and Completion. Separation and completion are conflicting capabilities requiring separate pathways. Unification is achieved through the collaboration of PS and PR. PS sets a target for PR and PC to learn, providing a common representational 'space'. This makes it possible to separate PC encoding and retrieval between the separation and completion pathways respectively. In this way, they don't conflict with each other, but each operate to their strengths.

3.4 Baseline STM - FastNN

FastNN is a 2-layer fully-connected ANN. Like AHA, the target for recall is the input image itself (rather than LTM encodings) for ease of analysis. It is 'fast' in that it also learns given only one external stimulus. We empirically optimised the learning rate, training iterations, number and size of hidden layers and the other hyperparameters.

4 Experiments

Omniglot Benchmark - One-shot classification Task. We tested our models on the one-shot classification test from [12]. Referring to the train/test framework (Sect. 3.1), first the LTM is pre-trained on a 'background' set of 30 alphabets. Then using a disjoint 'evaluation' set of 10 alphabets, a single 'train' character is presented. The task is to identify the matching character from 20 distinct 'test' characters from the same alphabet by a different writer. This is repeated for 20 characters comprising a single 'run'. The experiment consists of 20 runs in total. Accuracy is averaged over the 20 runs. Characters and alphabets were selected to maximise difficulty through confusion of similar characters [12].

The method used to determine the matching character varies between reported studies. In this work, we use minimum MSE of an internal representation. For LTM, we used the autoencoder encoding, for LTM+AHA, we report PR and PC and for LTM+FastNN the hidden layer encoding. None of these networks are explicitly trained to classify. In addition to accuracy, the quality of end-to-end retrieval of appropriate memories is assessed with MSE recall loss.

One-Shot Instance-Classification Task. We extended the experiments with the one-shot instance-classification task. It is the same as one-shot classification, except that the 'train' character exemplar must be matched with the exact same exemplar amongst 20 'test' distractor exemplars of the *same* character class. Being the same character class, all the exemplars are very similar making separation difficult. In each run, the character class and exemplars are selected by randomly sampling without repeats from the 'evaluation' set.

Common Conditions. In addition, we explored robustness by introducing image corruption to emulate realistic challenges in visual processing that could also apply to other sensory modalities. Noise emulates imperfect sensor capture. For example, in visual recognition, the target object might be dirty or lighting conditions changed. Occlusion emulates incomplete sensing e.g. due to obstruction by another object. Robust performance is a feature of animal-like learning that would confer practical benefits to machines, and is therefore important to explore [1]. Occlusion is achieved with randomly placed circles, completely contained within the image. Noise is introduced by replacing a proportion of the pixels with a random intensity value drawn from a uniform distribution.

For both tests, instead of presenting 1 test character at a time, all 20 are presented simultaneously, made possible by the short term memory of CLS.

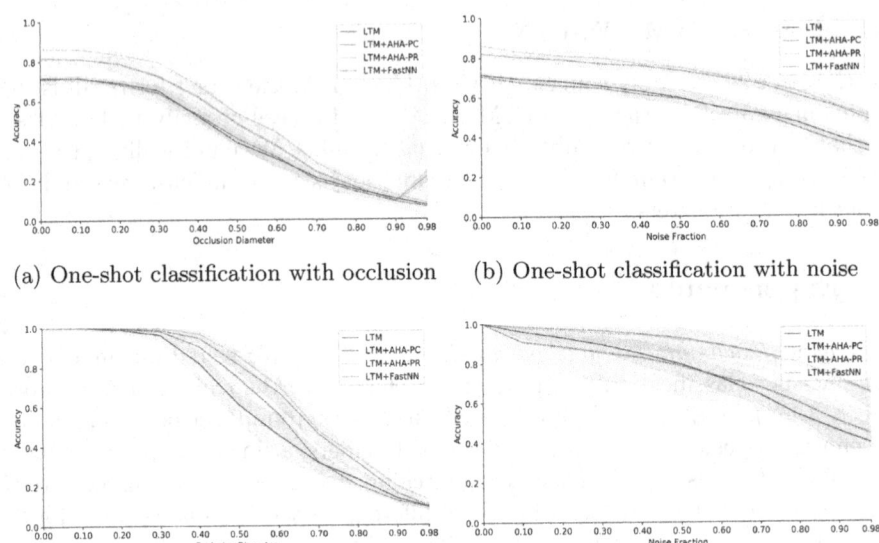

(a) One-shot classification with occlusion   (b) One-shot classification with noise

(c) One-shot instance-classification with (d) One-shot instance-classification with
occlusion   noise

Fig. 2. Accuracy vs occlusion and noise. LTM+STM improves performance over baseline LTM. AHA STM is superior to the baseline FastNN STM. The effect is more pronounced for occlusion than noise. Occlusion diameter is expressed as a fraction of image side length, noise as a fraction of image area. The mean value is bold with medium shading for 1 standard deviation, light shading demarcates min/max values.

Noise and occlusion is increased from none, to almost complete corruption, in 10 increments. The highest level is capped at 98% corruption, to ensure some meaningful output. Every test is repeated with 10 random seeds.

In one-shot classification, strong generalisation is required as well as some pattern separation to distinguish similar character classes. The one-shot instance-classification task requires strong pattern separation, as well as some generalisation for robustness.

5   Results

5.1   Accuracy

One-shot classification results are shown in Figs. 2a and 2b. LTM accuracy starts at 71.6%, without image corruption. Increasing noise affects all features equally and gradually, whereas occlusion increases the likelihood of suddenly removing important topological features. At very high occlusion, the character is mostly covered, leading to chance level performance. All signals follow the same overall trend as LTM.

Table 1. Comparison of algorithms for one-shot classification, without image corruption. LTM+AHA is competitive with state-of-the-art convolutional approaches whilst demonstrating a wider range of capabilities.

Algorithm	Accuracy (%)	Algorithm	Accuracy (%)
BPL [13]	96.7	**LTM+AHA**	**86.4**
Human [13]	*95.5*	Prototypical Net [13]	86.3
RCN [2]	92.7	**LTM+FastNN**	**81.9**
Simple Conv Net [13]	86.5	VHE [5]	81.3

With no noise or occlusion, PR at 86.4% has an advantage of almost 15% over LTM and is comparable to other ANN results for this task (Table 1). This advantage is maintained with moderate levels of occlusion. As extreme occlusion begins to cover most of the character, the accuracy of PR, PC and LTM converge. However, the advantage is maintained over all noise levels. PC accuracy was no better than LTM.

With no corruption, FastNN improves on LTM accuracy by 10.3%, 4.4% less than the AHA improvement. The advantage of AHA over FastNN is maintained over almost all levels of occlusion, and minor for all levels of noise.

For context, reported accuracy in the case of zero noise or occlusion is contrasted with other works in Table 1. Existing values are reproduced from [13].

One-shot instance-classification results are shown in Figs. 2c and 2d. LTM accuracy is perfect at low levels of image corruption, remaining almost perfect in the case of occlusion, until approximately one third of the image is affected. All signals follow the same trends observed for the one-shot classification task.

For AHA, PR accuracy remains extremely high, close to 100% until a 10% greater level of occlusion than for LTM i.e. addition of AHA increases tolerance to occlusion. The advantage over LTM increases with increasing corruption, fading away for occlusion but continuing to grow for noise.

FastNN also improves on the baseline. It has worse accuracy than AHA for a given level of occlusion (less substantial than one-shot classification), and almost equal accuracy for varying levels of noise.

5.2   Recall

Recall-loss is shown in Fig. 3. In the one-shot classification experiment, AHA demonstrates better performance than FastNN under moderate occlusion and noise. At higher levels of corruption, AHA may retrieve a high quality image of the wrong character, resulting in a higher loss than lower-quality images retrieved by FastNN. In the one-shot instance-classification experiment, this character confusion is less likely to occur and AHA is superior or equal to FastNN under all meaningful levels of image corruption. FastNN is qualitatively better for one-shot instance-classification than for one-shot classification, and almost as good as AHA, but recalls are typically an 'average' version of the character, rather than a specific instances.

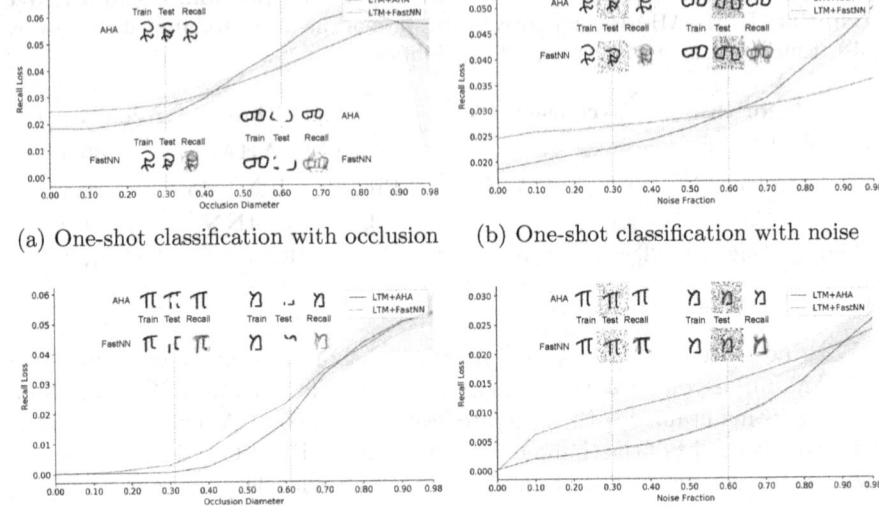

(a) One-shot classification with occlusion   (b) One-shot classification with noise

(c) One-shot instance-classification with occlusion   (d) One-shot instance-classification with noise

Fig. 3. Recall-loss vs occlusion/noise. AHA yields more specific and crisp recall images given moderate input corruption. With substantial corruption, AHA sometimes retrieves an accurate copy of the wrong character resulting in a higher loss. FastNN provides blurry or nonspecific recall in many conditions. Units and plot characteristics are the same as for Fig. 2.

6   Discussion

The results demonstrate that CLS is an effective approach to one-shot classification of both specific instances and categories. At first sight, one-shot instance-classification is trivially solved by a nearest neighbour comparison, but the results show that this approach performs poorly given realistic levels of image corruption. In addition, the CLS-style architecture of AHA has an advantage over the simpler FastNN. For accuracy, this is most noticeable on one-shot classification and in the presence of occlusion, and it is significantly superior at recalling high quality images across the test conditions. To the authors best knowledge, this is the first application of CLS to a dataset derived from real-world observations featuring non-synthetic variation.

AHA was comparable to state-of-the-art approaches on the standard Omniglot Benchmark - a subset of our extended test. The reported approaches are optimised for one-shot classification without any image corruption suggesting that they are not suited for one-shot instance-classification. Referring to Table 1, BPL and RCN are significantly ahead of other methods, and similar to human performance. They have an advantage as they exploit domain specific priors as discussed in Sect. 2.1. The Simple Conv Net (CNN) represents a standard approach for deep learning. AHA is equally good despite being unsupervised (no external labels) and uses only local credit assignment. Additionally, AHA demonstrates the broader range of capabilities discussed.

PR performs classification significantly better than PC. It partially fulfils the role of completion, as it learns to reproduce the target. PC fulfils a vital role for additional completion and sharpening for crisp recall. There is a small accuracy bias toward PR due to the fact that PR outputs a superposition of possible patterns, enhancing the chance of a correct match via MSE. In contrast, PC is designed to retrieve a single, sharp complete sample and in doing so is unable to hedge its bets.

The boundary between class and exemplar is continuous, subjective and may depend on the task. For example, you could define the character itself as a class, and the corrupted samples as exemplars. Or a Labrador dog: the class could be the animal type (dog), or the breed (Labrador). AHA demonstrates this flexibility to the task by accomplishing both one-shot classification and one-shot instance-classification. As per Sect. 3.3, AHA learns a conjunction of primitives, and then generalises over variations in that combination.

Acknowledgment. Thanks to Elkhonon Goldberg for enriching discussions on the hippocampal region and to Rotem Aharon for insights and analysis of Hopfield networks.

References

1. Ahmad, S., Scheinkman, L.: How can we be so dense? The benefits of using highly sparse representations. arXiv preprint arXiv:1903.11257 (2019)
2. George, D., et al.: A generative vision model that trains with high data efficiency and breaks text-based CAPTCHAs. Science, 1–19 (2017)
3. Gidaris, S., Bursuc, A., Komodakis, N., Pérez, P., Cord, M.: Boosting few-shot visual learning with self-supervision. In: Proceedings of the IEEE International Conference on Computer Vision (2019)
4. Greene, P., Howard, M., Bhattacharyya, R., Fellous, J.M.: Hippocampal anatomy supports the use of context in object recognition: a computational model. Comput. Intell. Neurosci. **2013** (2013)
5. Hewitt, L.B., Nye, M.I., Gane, A., Jaakkola, T., Tenenbaum, J.B.: The variational homoencoder: learning to learn high capacity generative models from few examples. arXiv preprint arXiv:1807.08919, July 2018
6. Hopfield, J.J.: Neural networks and physical systems with emergent collective computational abilities. Proc. Nat. Acad. Sci. **79**(8) (1982)
7. Ketz, N., Morkonda, S.G., O'Reilly, R.C.: Theta coordinated error-driven learning in the hippocampus. PLoS Comput. Biol. **9**(6) (2013)
8. Koch, G., Zemel, R., Salakhutdinov, R.: Siamese neural networks for one-shot image recognition. In: Proceedings of the 32nd International Conference on Machine Learning (2015)
9. Kowadlo, G., Ahmed, A., Rawlinson, D.: AHA! an 'Artificial Hippocampal Algorithm' for episodic machine learning. arXiv preprint arxiv:1909.10340 (2019)
10. Kumaran, D., Hassabis, D., McClelland, J.L.: What learning systems do intelligent agents need? Complementary learning systems theory updated. Trends Cogn. Sci. **20**(7), 512–534 (2016)

11. Lake, B.M., Salakhutdinov, R., Gross, J., Tenenbaum, J.B.: One shot learning of simple visual concepts. In Proceedings of the 33rd Annual Conference of the Cognitive Science Society (2011)

12. Lake, B.M., Salakhutdinov, R., Tenenbaum, J.B.: Human-level concept learning through probabilistic program induction. Science **350**(6266), 1332–1338 (2015)

13. Lake, B.M., Salakhutdinov, R., Tenenbaum, J.B.: The Omniglot challenge: a 3-year progress report. Curr. Opin. Behav. Sci. **29**, 97–104 (2019)

14. Lake, B.M., Ullman, T.D., Tenenbaum, J.B., Gershman, S.J.: Building machines that learn and think like people. Behav. Brain Sci. **40**(2012), 1–58 (2017)

15. Li, F.F., Fergus, R., Perona, P.: A Bayesian approach to unsupervised one-shot learning of object categories. In: Proceedings Ninth IEEE International Conference on Computer Vision (2003)

16. Li, F.F., Fergus, R., Perona, P.: One-shot learning of object categories. IEEE Trans. Pattern Anal. Mach. Intell. (2006)

17. Makhzani, A., Frey, B.: K-sparse autoencoders. arXiv preprint arXiv:1312.5663 (2013)

18. Makhzani, A., Frey, B.J.: Winner-take-all autoencoders. In: Advances in Neural Information Processing Systems, pp. 2791–2799 (2015)

19. McClelland, J.L., McNaughton, B.L., O'Reilly, R.C.: Why there are complementary learning systems in the hippocampus and neocortex: insights from the successes and failures of connectionist models of learning and memory. Psychol. Rev. **102**(3), 419–457 (1995)

20. Norman, K.A., O'Reilly, R.C.: Modeling hippocampal and neocortical contributions to recognition memory: a complementary-learning-systems approach. Psychol. Rev. **110**(4), 611–646 (2003)

21. O'Reilly, R.C., Bhattacharyya, R., Howard, M.D., Ketz, N.: Complementary learning systems. Cogn. Sci. **38**(6), 1229–1248 (2014)

22. Rolls, E.T.: A model of the operation of the hippocampus and entorhinal cortex in memory. Int. J. Neural Syst. **6** (1995)

23. Rolls, E.T.: The mechanisms for pattern completion and pattern separation in the hippocampus. Front. Syst. Neurosci. **7**(October), 1–21 (2013)

24. Russell, S.J., Norvig, P.: Artificial Intelligence: A Modern Approach. Prentice Hall, Upper Saddle River (2009)

25. Schapiro, A.C., Turk-Browne, N.B., Botvinick, M.M., Norman, K.A.: Complementary learning systems within the hippocampus: a neural network modelling approach to reconciling episodic memory with statistical learning. Philos. Trans. Roy. Soc. B Biol. Sci. **372**(1711), 20160049 (2017)

26. Snell, J., Swersky, K., Zemel, R.S.: Prototypical networks for few-shot learning. In: Advances in Neural Information Processing Systems, pp. 4077–4087 (2017)

27. Vinyals, O., Blundell, C., Lillicrap, T., Kavukcuoglu, K.: Matching networks for one shot learning. In: Advances in Neural Information Processing Systems (2016)

28. Young, R.A.: The Gaussian derivative model for spatial vision: I. Retinal mechanisms. Spat. Vis. **2**(4), 273–293 (1987)

Online Semi-supervised Learning in Contextual Bandits with Episodic Reward

Baihan Lin[1,2(✉)]

[1] Center for Theoretical Neuroscience, Columbia University, New York, USA
[2] Zuckerman Mind Brain Behavior Institute, Columbia University, New York, USA
Baihan.Lin@Columbia.edu

Abstract. We considered a novel practical problem of online learning with episodically revealed rewards, motivated by several real-world applications, where the contexts are nonstationary over different episodes and the reward feedbacks are not always available to the decision making agents. For this online semi-supervised learning setting, we introduced Background Episodic Reward LinUCB (BerlinUCB), a solution that easily incorporates clustering as a self-supervision module to provide useful side information when rewards are not observed. Our experiments on a variety of datasets, both in stationary and nonstationary environments of six different scenarios, demonstrated clear advantages of the proposed approach over the standard contextual bandit. Lastly, we introduced a relevant real-life example where this problem setting is especially useful. (Codes can be accessed at https://github.com/doerlbh/BerlinUCB).

Keywords: Multi-armed bandit · Contextual bandit · Online learning · Semi-supervised learning · Online clustering · Nonstationary setting

1 Introduction

Online learning is a common problem in many practical applications where the data become available in a sequential order and later used to update the best predictor for future data or reward associated with the data features. In many case, the reward feedback is the only source where the online learning agent can effectively learn from the sequential past experience. This problem is especially important in the field of sequential decision making where the agent must choose the best possible action to perform at each step to maximize the cumulative reward over time. One key challenge is to obtain an optimal trade-off between the exploration of new actions and the exploitation of the possible reward mapping from known actions. This framework is usually formulated as the *Multi-Armed Bandits (MAB)* problem where each arm of the bandit corresponds to an unknown (but usually fixed) reward probability distribution [3,10], and the agent selects an arm to play at each round, receives a reward feedback and updates accordingly.

© Springer Nature Switzerland AG 2020
M. Gallagher et al. (Eds.): AI 2020, LNAI 12576, pp. 407–419, 2020.
https://doi.org/10.1007/978-3-030-64984-5_32

However, in many real-world applications, the reward feedback are not always revealed. For instance, in a recommendation system [22], the users might not be attending to and interacting with the system all the time, and their inactivity should be considered a latent mixture of positive and negative feedbacks, instead of merely a negative feedback in traditional online learning frameworks. In personalized medicine or longitudinal studies [26], the patients might not conduct follow up check ups for many reasons, and while these data points are missing, their contexts (demographics, genders, ages etc.) might still be useful to predict medical outcomes for other people (e.g. to gain a better understanding of the patients population). In many interactive systems, the goal is to provide an efficient assistance without unnecessary human intervention, and in these cases, the agent would need to learn from empty feedback in most of the time. In addition, the reward feedback can come in different episodes or frequencies. For instance, an advertisement website might experience a surge in clicking in the golden hours, while not so much in off seasons. An effective system should adapt to the nonstationarity in these observed rewards [14]. To study these scenarios, we proposed a novel problem setting called *Online Learning with Episodic Reward*.

In this paper, we study this novel problem setting with the *Contextual Bandits (CB)*, a useful variant of MAB where at each step, the agent observes an N-dimensional *context*, or *feature* vector before selecting an action. Theoretically, the ultimate goal of CB is to learn the relationship between the rewards and the context vectors so as to make better decisions given the context [1]. The idea is that whenever the reward is missing, an agent can still have access to a population of labelled and unlabeled context history (i.e., contexts without the associated rewards), which can be potentially used as a prior knowledge to improve the subsequent online decision-making. We adopted a self-supervised learning techniques, which is a form of unsupervised learning where the data population provides the supervision. By installing a clustering module, in the online mode without associate reward feedback, we can decide which arm-related representations to update for a given context; such content-driven representation selection has a potential to further improve the subsequent decision-making. These flexible self-supervision modules can (and should) continue to be updated online as more contexts become available, especially in *nonstationary environments* abundant in practical applications, where both the context distribution and the reward distribution can change in various ways.

We evaluate our approach, *Background Episodically Rewarded LinUCB (BerlinUCB)*, on several types of nonstationary environments and demonstrated that (1) updating the representation structure when no reward is revealed, in general, considerably improves performance of contextual bandit; and (2) moreover, in many cases, adaptive learning with context-dependent clustering modules is much better than learning without the self-supervision.

2   Related Work

There have been multiple solutions proposed for sequential decision making and the contextual bandit problems [15,16,18,19]. LinUCB assumes a linear dependency between the expected reward of an action and its context [6,13]. Its representation space is modeled using a set of linear predictors. This assumption is not used in Neural Bandit [2]. However, these algorithms assume that the agent can observe the reward at each iteration, which is not the case in many practical applications as discussed earlier.

To consider the problem of incomplete feedbacks, [4] studies "Partial Monitoring (PM)", which allows the learner to retrieve the expected value of actions through an analysis of the feedback matrix. In our work, we don't hold the same assumption that this feedback matrix is always known to the learner. To consider the corrupted rewards, [8] studies a variant of the stochastic bandit where the goal is to maximize the sum of the unobserved rewards given the observation of transformation of these rewards through a stochastic corruption process. Unlike their approach which relies on known parameters for those transformations, we directly build upon LinUCB with no additional parameters. Another related work is to introduce different representation modules such as autoencoders that adaptively update across batches [17]. However, it only uses the unlabelled data for pretraining, and during the online mode, the reward is always revealed.

3   Problem Setting

3.1   The Contextual Bandit Problem

Following [11], the contextual bandit problem is defined as follows. At each time point (iteration) $t \in \{1, ..., T\}$, an agent is presented with a *context (feature vector)* $\mathbf{x}_t \in \mathbb{R}^N$ before choosing an arm $k \in A = \{1, ..., K\}$. We will denote by $X = \{X_1, ..., X_N\}$ the set of features (variables) defining the context. Let $\mathbf{r}_t = (r_t^1, ..., r_t^K)$ denote a reward vector, where $r_t^k \in [0, 1]$ is a reward at time t associated with the arm $k \in A$. Herein, we will primarily focus on the Bernoulli bandit with binary reward, i.e. $r_t^k \in \{0, 1\}$. Let $\pi : X \to A$ denote a policy. Also, $D_{c,r}$ denotes a joint distribution over $(\mathbf{x}, \mathbf{r})$. We will assume that the expected reward is a linear function of the context, i.e. $E[r_t^k | \mathbf{x}_t] = \mu_k^T \mathbf{x}_t$, where μ_k is an unknown weight vector (to be learned from the data) associated with arm k.

3.2   Online Semi-supervised Learning with Episodic Reward

Algorithm 1 presents at a high-level our problem setting, where the context $\mathbf{x}(t) \in \mathbb{R}^d$ is a vector describing the context C at time t, $r_{a_t,t}(t) \in [0, 1]$ is the reward of action a_t at time t, and $\mathbf{r}(t) \in [0, 1]^K$ denotes a vector of rewards for all arms at time t. $\mathbb{P}_{x,r}$ denotes a joint probability distribution over (x, r), and $\pi : C \to A$ denotes a policy. Unlike traditional setting, in step 5 we have the rewards revealed in an episodic fashion (i.e. sometimes there are feedbacks of rewards being 0 or 1, sometimes there are no feedbacks of any kind), given by a probability $p_r \in [0, 1]$. We consider our setting an online semi-supervised learning problem [24, 28], where the agent learns from both labeled and unlabeled data in online setting. However, in their setting the true label is received at each iteration, while in our setting a bandit feedback is assumed, i.e., if classification was incorrect, the agent will not know what the correct label was, only that its decision was incorrect.

Algorithm 1. Online Learning with Episodic Reward

1: **for** t = 1,2,3,···, T **do**
2:     $(\mathbf{x}(t), \mathbf{r}(t))$ is drawn according to $\mathbb{P}_{x,r}$
3:     Context $\mathbf{x}(t)$ is revealed to the player
4:     Player chooses an action $a_t = \pi_t(\mathbf{x}(t))$
5:     Feedback $r_{a_t,t}(t)$ for only chosen arms are episodically revealed
6:     Player updates its policy π_t
7: **end for**

---

4   Background Episodically Rewarded LinUCB

We proposed Background Episodically Rewarded LinUCB (BerlinUCB), a semi-supervised and self-supervised online contextual bandit which updates the context representations and reward mapping separately given the state of the feedbacks being present or missing (Algorithm 2). We assume that (1) when there are feedbacks available, the feedbacks are genuine, assigned by the oracle, and (2) when the feedbacks are missing (not revealed by the background), it is either due to the fact that the action is preferred (no intervention required by the oracle, i.e. with an implied default rewards), or that the oracle didn't have a chance to respond or intervene (i.e. with unknown rewards). Especially in the Step 15, when there is no feedbacks, we assign the context $\mathbf{x}_t$ to a class a' (an action arm) with the self-supervision given the previous labelled context history. Since we don't have the actual label for this context, we would only update the reward mapping parameter $\mathbf{b}_{a'}$ and leave the covariance matrix $\mathbf{A}_{a'}$ untouched. This additional usage of unlabelled data (or unrevealed feedback) is especially important in our model, as it allows the agent to learn even when the reward is not available.

4.1   The Self-supervision and Semi-supervision Modules

We construct our self-supervision modules given the cluster assumption of the semi-supervision problem: the points within the same cluster are more likely to share a label. As shown in many applications, clustering algorithms like Kmeans, Gaussian Mixture Model (GMM) [25] and spectral clustering [27] are especially powerful unsupervised modules, especially in their offline versions. Their online variants, however, often performs poorly [29]. As in this work, we focus on the completely online setting, we chose three popular clustering algorithms as the self-supervision modules: GMM, Kmeans and K-nearest neighbors.

In the following section, we empirically evaluated the performance of 5 agents: LinUCB is the standard contextual bandit which treated missing feedbacks as a negative reward (of zero). BerlinUCB is the standard version of our proposed contextual bandit, designed for sparse feedbacks without the self-supervision modules. It updates the context representations but not the reward mapping. Among the BerlinUCB family, we also compared three BerlinUCB variants with the self-supervision clustering modules: Kmeans, KNN (with K = 5) and GMM, which we denoted: B-Kmeans, B-KNN, and B-GMM, respectively.

Algorithm 2. BerlinUCB

1: **Initialize** $c_t \in \mathbb{R}_+, \mathbf{A}_a \leftarrow \mathbf{I}_d, \mathbf{b}_a \leftarrow \mathbf{0}_{d \times 1} \forall a \in \mathcal{A}_t$
2: **for** t = 1,2,3,$\cdots$, T **do**
3:     Observe features $\mathbf{x}_t \in \mathbb{R}^d$
4:     **for all** $a \in \mathcal{A}_t$ **do**
5:         $\hat{\theta}_a \leftarrow \mathbf{A}_a^{-1} \mathbf{b}_a$
6:         $p_{t,a} \leftarrow \hat{\theta}_a^\top \mathbf{x}_t + c_t \sqrt{\mathbf{x}_t^\top \mathbf{A}_a^{-1} \mathbf{x}_t}$
7:     **end for**
8:     Choose arm $a_t = \arg\max_{a \in \mathcal{A}_t} p_{t,a}$
9:     **if** the background revealed the feedbacks **then**
10:         Observe feedback $r_{a_t,t}$
11:         $\mathbf{A}_{a_t} \leftarrow \mathbf{A}_{a_t} + \mathbf{x}_t \mathbf{x}_t^\top$
12:         $\mathbf{b}_{a_t} \leftarrow \mathbf{b}_{a_t} + r_{a_t,t} \mathbf{x}_t$
13:     **elif** the background revealed NO feedbacks **then**
14:         **if** use self-supervision feedback
15:             $r' = [a_t == \text{predict}(\mathbf{x}_t)]$ % clustering modules
16:             $\mathbf{b}_{a_t} \leftarrow \mathbf{b}_{a_t} + r' \mathbf{x}_t$
17:         **elif**   % ignore self-supervision signals
18:             $\mathbf{A}_{a_t} \leftarrow \mathbf{A}_{a_t} + \mathbf{x}_t \mathbf{x}_t^\top$
19:         **end if**
20:     **end if**
21: **end for**

---

5   Empirical Evaluation

We evaluated our approach on six synthetic nonstationary online learning scenarios in two datasets: MNIST [12] and Warfarin [7], and provided a real-life application where the episodic feedbacks are naturally installed: a speaker diarization task with sporadic human interactions as bandit feedbacks. For the synthetic online learning task, in order to simulate an online data stream, we draw samples from each dataset sequentially, starting from the beginning each time we draw the last sample. At each round, the algorithm receives reward 1 if the instance is classified correctly, and 0 otherwise. We compute both the final cumulative reward and the total number of classification errors as the performance metrics. However, Warfarin dataset is different, as it was actually produced in a real bandit setting, rather than classification setting.

Important Distinction on Bandit vs. Classification Feedback: It is important to keep in mind that the bandit feedback (correct/incorrect classification) makes the classification problem significantly more challenging, as compared to the standard supervised learning, since the true label is never revealed in bandit setting unless the classification is correct. Thus, the classification accuracy in a bandit setting is expected to be lower than in the supervised learning setting, which is not due to inferiority of bandit decision making algorithm versus classifiers, but due to increased problem difficulty, i.s. the lack of feedback about what the correct decision should have been. Recall that such bandit feedback is often a much more realistic model of agent's interaction with the world, especially in online decision making applications such as online advertisement, clinical trials, and so on, which do not fit into the classical classification framework.

However, for empirical evaluation purposes, it is common to use available classification datasets to simulate an online environment with the bandit feedback (i.e., simulating the situation where the bandit receives, for example, 1 or 0 for correct or incorrect decision, but is not told what the correct decision should have been when it receives 0; such feedback is different from standard online classification feedback in case of non-binary classification). We use the classification dataset here to create online learning simulation environments.

We now describe some details of the experiments. For MNIST, we took the 5,000 samples from the training dataset to simulate the online bandit with 10 arms corresponding to different digits. For Warfarin dataset, we selected the first 5,000 training samples to simulate the online bandit with 3 arms (classes). As an even more challenging task, we also created a multi-task scenario where a mixture of the MNIST and the Warfarin task are fed in batches. We extended the set of possible labels (arms) to include 10 labels from MNIST and 3 labels from Warfarin, into a total of 13 arms. We used linear stretching to make the input dimensions equal across the two domains. In another word, for each input, we concatenate the Warfarin features (of size 93) on the back of the MNIST features (of size 784) into a sparse vector of size 877. The algorithm had to assign a label to each input without any information about which domain the input came from.

5.1 Nonstationary Environments

We simulated six types of nonstationarity using the above datasets (with a batch size of 100). As mentioned before, we assume that the input data arrive in batches, and the data distribution (i.e., the joint distribution of the context and reward) may change across those batches, while remaining stationary within each batch.

Nonstationary Oracle: Fixed vs. Extendable Arms. Traditional online learning have a fixed number of arms (denoted "F"). We here considered such a nonstationarity where we start with a single arm, and when new labels arrive new arms are generated accordingly, a problem loosely modelled by the bandits with infinitely many arms [5]. For this setting, we applied an arm expansion process (denoted "E"): starting from a single arm (for adding a "new" arm), if a feedback confirms a new addition, a new arm is appended to the arm list.

Nonstationary Oracle: Varying Episodic Rewards. Last but not least, we may assume the probability of the reward revealing (p_r in Algorithm 1) can change from batch to batch. In another word, the reward feedback can be more frequently revealed in some episode or mini-batch than the others.

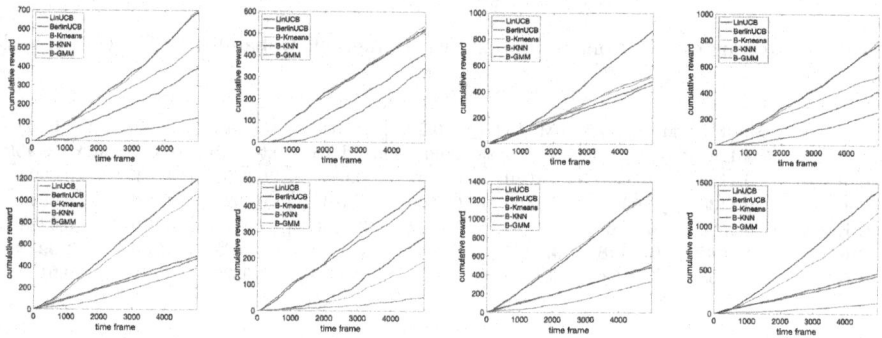

Fig. 1. Cumulative rewards in MNIST. Fixed arms: (a) stationary, $p_r = 0.01$; (b) varying clusters, $p_r = 0.01$; (c) negative images, $p_r = 0.1$; (d) shuffled rewards, $p_r = 0.01$. Extendable arms: (e) stationary, varying p_r; (f) varying clusters, $p_r = 0.01$; (g) shuffled rewards, varying p_r; (h) shuffled rewards, $p_r = 0.1$.

Nonstationary Context: Varying Cluster Distribution. To simulate changes in the context (input) distribution, we first clustered all samples in the corresponding pre-training data subset into k clusters. Next, we generate a sequence of batches, where each batch contained a certain fraction of samples from different clusters, and these fractions were changing across the batches, i.e. the probability distribution of cluster membership was changing, simulating nonstationary input.

Nonstationary Context: Negative Images. Another type of input nonstationarity involved introducing negative images as inputs with same semantics but different textures. Namely, with probability p, the negative image of the original image was presented as an input. Experiments were performed with this data corruption given by $0 < p < 1$ episodically and randomly assigned for each batch.

Nonstationary Reward: Shuffled Class Labels. We further explored the multi-task setting by introducing a different type of nonstationary reward, where the class labels were shuffled, i.e. randomly permuted, in each batch.

Nonstationary Reward: Multi-task Environment. Here we assume that input samples come from different domains (tasks), and thus can be associated with different subsets of labels (arms). For example, we combined 5,000 randomly selected training samples from each of the two selected domains, MNIST and Warfarin datasets, and extended the set of possible labels (arms) to include 10 labels from MNIST and 3 labels from Warfarin into a mixed dataset of 10,000 samples of 13 arms. We used linear stretching to make the input dimensions equal across the two domains. The algorithm had to assign a label to each input without any information about which domain the input came from.

Table 1. Accuracy: Stationary contexts with different probabilities of reward revealing

	MNIST (varying p_r)		MNIST (p_r=0.5)		MNIST (p_r=0.1)		MNIST (p_r=0.01)	
	fixed arms	extendable	fixed arms	extendable	fixed arms	extendable	fixed arms	extendable
LinUCB	0.1134	0.094	0.1080	0.0962	0.0842	0.0762	0.0252	0.0902
BerlinUCB	0.1138	0.0990	0.1102	0.0990	0.1016	0.0926	0.0788	0.0896
B-Kmeans	0.2594	0.2130	0.2674	**0.2678**	**0.3132**	**0.2760**	**0.1400**	0.0828
B-KNN	**0.2642**	**0.2398**	**0.2722**	0.2642	0.2954	0.2622	0.1384	**0.0938**
B-GMM	0.0958	0.0768	0.1060	0.0728	0.0958	0.0320	0.1034	0.0120

Table 2. Accuracy: Nonstationary cases with different probabilities of reward revealing

Fixed Arms	MNIST - varying clusters			MNSIT - negative images			MNSIT - shuffled rewards		
	p_r=0.5	p_r=0.1	p_r=0.01	p_r=0.5	p_r=0.1	p_r=0.01	p_r=0.5	p_r=0.1	p_r=0.01
LinUCB	**0.1086**	0.0984	0.0690	0.1044	0.0920	0.0732	0.1172	0.0832	0.0512
BerlinUCB	0.1024	0.1002	0.0828	0.1016	0.0970	0.1016	0.1120	0.0966	0.0832
B-Kmeans	0.0952	**0.1096**	**0.1074**	0.1082	0.1036	0.0768	**0.2776**	0.2878	**0.1618**
B-KNN	0.0984	0.1002	0.1050	**0.1762**	**0.1732**	0.1016	0.2600	**0.3162**	0.1556
B-GMM	0.1072	0.0974	0.1034	0.0954	0.1074	**0.1018**	0.1158	0.1172	0.1062

Extendable Arms	MNIST - varying clusters			MNSIT - negative images			MNSIT - shuffled rewards		
	p_r=0.5	p_r=0.1	p_r=0.01	p_r=0.5	p_r=0.1	p_r=0.01	p_r=0.5	p_r=0.1	p_r=0.01
LinUCB	0.0994	0.0930	0.0866	0.0888	0.0918	**0.1014**	0.1010	0.0872	0.1014
BerlinUCB	0.0930	0.0946	**0.0938**	0.0924	0.0930	0.0910	0.0994	0.0926	0.0918
B-Kmeans	**0.1010**	**0.0990**	0.0380	0.0910	0.0712	0.0308	0.2478	0.2336	0.0654
B-KNN	0.0958	0.0970	0.0570	**0.1780**	**0.1228**	0.0460	**0.2606**	**0.2818**	**0.1016**
B-GMM	0.0756	0.0296	0.0108	0.0680	0.0338	0.0118	0.0720	0.0258	0.0180

Table 3. Accuracy: Nonstationary contexts with varying episodic rewards

	varying cluster distribution				negative images				average
	MNIST-F	MNIST-E	Warfarin-F	Warfarin-E	MNIST-F	MNIST-E	Warfarin-F	Warfarin-E	
LinUCB	**0.1016**	0.0946	0.4580	**0.4646**	0.0956	0.0912	**0.4440**	**0.4374**	0.2734
BerlinUCB	0.0986	**0.0948**	0.4814	0.4480	0.0988	0.0926	0.3980	0.3898	0.2628
B-Kmeans	0.1012	0.0944	0.3964	0.2898	0.1048	0.0854	0.3200	0.1758	0.1960
B-KNN	0.1012	0.0946	0.4638	0.4134	**0.1626**	**0.1576**	0.4188	0.3998	**0.2765**
B-GMM	0.1010	0.0684	**0.5494**	0.2208	0.0926	0.0694	0.3992	0.2002	0.2126

Table 4. Accuracy: Nonstationary rewards with varying episodic rewards

	shuffled class labels				multi-task setting		average
	MNIST-F	MNIST-E	Warfarin-F	Warfarin-E	MNIST/Warfarin-F	MNIST/Warfarin-E	
LinUCB	0.1080	0.0974	**0.6464**	**0.6348**	0.3496	0.3442	0.3634
BerlinUCB	0.1126	0.1036	0.6116	0.6080	0.3136	0.3071	0.3428
B-Kmeans	0.2376	0.2566	0.5262	0.5152	0.3801	0.3690	0.3808
B-KNN	**0.2574**	**0.2582**	0.6278	0.6026	**0.3833**	**0.4041**	**0.4222**
B-GMM	0.0958	0.0664	0.5488	0.4038	0.2052	0.2375	0.2596

5.2 Results

We explored different combinations of the above nonstationarities. Table 1 summarizes our results for the setting where the contexts are stationary, we observe that BerlinUCB algorithms consistently outperforming the baseline with a large marginal ($> 20\%$ accuracy comparing to LinUCB's around 10%), ranked top in all 8 scenarios with different reward revealing probablity p_r.

Table 2 summarizes our results for the nonstationary context due to *varying cluster distribution*, data corruption with *negative images*, and *shuffled reward function*. As we can see, across different reward revealing probabilities p_r, BerlinUCB algorithms outperform the baseline on 16 out of the 18 testing scenarios.

If we take a closer look at the nonstationary context scenarios in Table 3 where the rewards are episodically revealed with varying p_r across batches, we noticed that the baseline is performing fairly well in three scenarios in Warfarin dataset. However, if we consider the mean accuracy in the entire set of this experiment, the BerlinUCB algorithms has the highest average accuracy, suggesting the advantage of using unlabelled data or missing rewards. Moreover, if we take a look at the whole iteration history, for example, for MNIST dataset (Fig. 1 (a)), we observe that initially, the baseline CB (orange line) is considerably worse than semi-supervised approaches, and requires a larger number of iteration to finally catch up with them. Other examples in Fig. 1 also demonstrated different scenarios where certain self-supervision modules (KNN and Kmeans) are more helpful than the other ones (GMM), but in most cases BerlinUCB, even without clustering modules, outperforms standard LinUCB.

Next, Table 4 summarizes our results in nonstationary reward settings with *shuffled reward* function and mixed domain (*multi-task*) setting. Based on the mean accuracy in the entire experiment, the top two algorithms were: B-KNN (mean accuracy 42.22%) and B-Kmeans (mean accuracy 38.08%). Note that, with nonstationary (shuffled) labels, the reward accumulated by the baseline CB usually remains significantly below the reward of the best semi-supervised approaches, at all iterations (Fig. 1). Thus, in a more challenging setting with both context and reward nonstationarities, the semi-supervised approaches can effectively improve upon the standard contextual bandit.

We also observed an interesting phenomenon where decreasing feedback actually increases the performance in some cases (as in Table 2). This phenomenon leads to open questions such as: What are the consequences if some feedbacks are not reliable? Can a threshold be given for the acceptable number of inaccurate feedbacks to achieve the same satisfactory level of performance? Does this behavior also exist in scenarios with non-binary reward structures? Ongoing directions include extending BerlinUCB's scalability across a series of these situations in order to better understand the full potential of the algorithm.

6 Application: Interactive Speaker Recognition

One important application of our online learning problem is the cold-start speaker recognition task, where new users can join a conversation at any time, and the interactive system should learn to recognize the voice profile of the newly joined user given a limited number of user feedbacks. Let's consider such an interactive speaker recognition system: At the start, there are only two buttons available: "No Speaker" and "New Speaker". The agent chooses an arm by setting it to be highlighted. If it is correct, the user does not have to change it (unless it's "New Speaker", where the user needs to click on it to confirm creating a new arm). If it is incorrect, the user clicks on the right arm to give the system a feedback.

Application Background. Unlike synthetic online learning dataset, where a bandit feedback is always given, here in the real-life interactive systems, the user might not give the feedback timely and constantly. Note that we assume that when the agent correctly identifies the speaker (or no speaker), the user (as the feedback dispenser) should send no feedbacks to the system by doing nothing. This brings an additional layer of complexity to this application, as the agent needs to learn from a negative feedback (no feedback), assuming that it is sometimes due to a lack of timely feedback (reward not revealed) and other times due to the user's approval (reward postively revealed). In another word, in an ideal scenario when the agent does a perfect job by correctly identifying the speaker all the time, we are not necessary to be around to correct it anymore (i.e. truly feedback free). As we pointed out earlier, this could be a challenge earlier on, because other than implicitly approving the agent's choice, receiving no feedbacks could also mean the feedbacks are not revealed properly (e.g. the human oracle took a break). To adapt BerlinUCB to this specific application, we first define our actions. There are three major classes of actions: an arm "New" to denote that a new speaker is detected, an arm "No Speaker" to denote that no one is speaking, and N different arms "User n" to denote user n speaking.

Synthetic Benchmark. We evaluated the validity of our algorithm in a synthetic online learning speaker recognition task. MiniVox [20] is an automatic framework to transform any speaker-labelled dataset into continuous speech datastream with episodically revealed label feedbacks. This benchmark is a light-weighted environment specifically designed to simulate two real-world challenges in interactive systems: (1) the speech data in real life is never truncated into pieces for an intelligent system to classify, and (2) the reward feedbacks (i.e. telling an intelligent system that it is incorrect) is never as timely and complete. MiniVox utilizes the speaker recognition dataset like VoxCeleb [23] to create randomly generated multi-speaker "conversations" in continuous streams. As a proof of concept, we randomly selected 10 speaker profiles and generated a "multi-speaker conversation" recordings of 60000 time frames. As the industrial standard, for each time frame, we extracted the Mel Frequency Cepstral Coefficients (MFCC) [9] in a sliding window fashion given the real-time audio input, and it will be served as the context for our contextual bandit agents. Here we assume the number of speakers are known, and the reward streams are sparsified given a revealing probability of 0.1, 0.01 and 0.001 to simulate different levels of users' attendance in this interactive system. As the common metric in online learning literature, we recorded the cumulative reward: at each frame, if the agent correctly predicts a given speaker, the reward is counted as +1 (regardless of whether the agent observes the reward or not). As shown in Fig. 2, Berlin-UCB and its variants with clustering modules consistently outperforms LinUCB in this task.

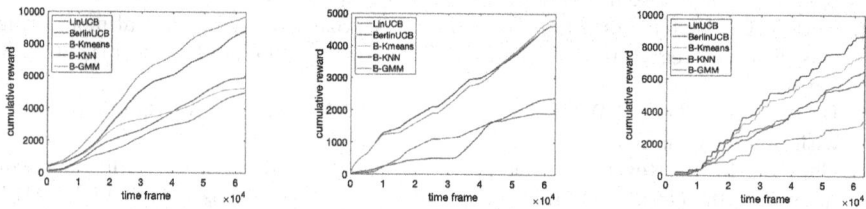

Fig. 2. Cumulative rewards in MiniVox. (a) $p_r = 0.1$; (b) $p_r = 0.01$; (c) $p_r = 0.001$.

This application (as demostrated in [21]) provides an intriguing example of how our online learning algorithm can enable an interactive system to learn to recognize speaker identity (1) entirely escaping the necessity of registering user voiceprint beforehands, (2) effortlessly incorporating new users under an optimal exploration-exploitation trade-off, (3) effectively transferring representation of registered user features to new users, and (4) continually learning despite minimal involvement of human corrections (i.e. sparse and episodic feedbacks).

7 Conclusion

We introduced an extension of the contextual bandit problem, learning from episodically revealed reward, motivated by several real-world applications in non-stationary environments, including recommendation systems, health monitoring and medical diagnosis, and others. In this setting, which we refer to as Contextual Bandit with Episodic Reward, the history of labeled and unlabeled contexts is available during online decision making, which allows the agent to learn context representations and reward mapping even when the reward is unobserved. We consider this problem an online semi-supervised learning problem, and take advantage of the clustering methods as a self-supervision modules to provide pseudo-reward feedback. The algorithms are evaluated in several types of non-stationary environments and compared to the standard contextual bandit on several datasets. Overall, we observe clear advantages of the semi-supervised approaches over the standard contextual bandit; moreover, we demonstrated with a real-world application that the proposed algorithm can be beneficial for developing the interactive system that learns on the fly.

References

1. Agrawal, S., Goyal, N.: Thompson sampling for contextual bandits with linear payoffs. In: ICML (3), pp. 127–135 (2013)

2. Allesiardo, R., Féraud, R., Bouneffouf, D.: A neural networks committee for the contextual bandit problem. In: Neural Information Processing - 21st International Conference, ICONIP 2014, Kuching, Malaysia, 3–6 November 2014, Proceedings, pp. 374–381 (2014)
3. Auer, P., Cesa-Bianchi, N., Fischer, P.: Finite-time analysis of the multiarmed bandit problem. Mach. Learn. **47**(2–3), 235–256 (2002)
4. Bartók, G., Foster, D.P., Pál, D., Rakhlin, A., Szepesvári, C.: Partial monitoring-classification, regret bounds, and algorithms. Math. Oper. Res. **39**(4), 967–997 (2014)
5. Berry, D.A., Chen, R.W., Zame, A., Heath, D.C., Shepp, L.A.: Bandit problems with infinitely many arms. Ann. Stat., 2103–2116 (1997)
6. Chu, W., Li, L., Reyzin, L., Schapire, R.E.: Contextual bandits with linear payoff functions. In: Gordon, G.J., Dunson, D.B., Dudik, M. (eds.) AISTATS, JMLR Proceedings, vol. 15, pp. 208–214. JMLR.org (2011). http://dblp.uni-trier.de/db/journals/jmlr/jmlrp15.html#ChuLRS11
7. Consortium, I.W.P., et al.: Estimation of the warfarin dose with clinical and pharmacogenetic data. N. Engl. J. Med. **2009**(360), 753–764 (2009)
8. Gajane, P., Urvoy, T., Kaufmann, E.: Corrupt bandits. In: EWRL (2016)
9. Hasan, M.R., Jamil, M., Rahman, M., et al.: Speaker identification using Mel frequency cepstral coefficients. Variations **1**(4) (2004)
10. Lai, T.L., Robbins, H.: Asymptotically efficient adaptive allocation rules. Adv. Appl. Math. **6**(1), 4–22 (1985). http://www.cs.utexas.edu/~shivaram
11. Langford, J., Zhang, T.: The epoch-greedy algorithm for multi-armed bandits with side information. In: Advances in Neural Information Processing Systems, pp. 817–824 (2008)
12. LeCun, Y.: The mnist database of handwritten digits (1998). http://yann.lecun.com/xdb/mnist/
13. Li, L., Chu, W., Langford, J., Schapire, R.E.: A contextual-bandit approach to personalized news article recommendation. In: Proceedings of the 19th International Conference on World Wide Web (WWW 2010), pp. 661–670. ACM (2010)
14. Lin, B.: Diabolical games: Reinforcement learning environments for lifelong learning. under review (2020)
15. Lin, B., Bouneffouf, D., Cecchi, G.: Split Q learning: reinforcement learning with two-stream rewards. In: Proceedings of the Twenty-Eighth International Joint Conference on Artificial Intelligence, IJCAI-19, pp. 6448–6449. International Joint Conferences on Artificial Intelligence Organization (2019)
16. Lin, B., Bouneffouf, D., Cecchi, G.: Online learning in iterated prisoner's dilemma to mimic human behavior. arXiv preprint arXiv:2006.06580 (2020)
17. Lin, B., Bouneffouf, D., Cecchi, G.A., Rish, I.: Contextual bandit with adaptive feature extraction. In: 2018 IEEE International Conference on Data Mining Workshops (ICDMW), pp. 937–944. IEEE (2018)
18. Lin, B., Cecchi, G., Bouneffouf, D., Reinen, J., Rish, I.: A story of two streams: reinforcement learning models from human behavior and neuropsychiatry. In: Proceedings of the Nineteenth International Conference on Autonomous Agents and Multi-Agent Systems, AAMAS-20, pp. 744–752. International Foundation for Autonomous Agents and Multiagent Systems (2020)
19. Lin, B., Cecchi, G., Bouneffouf, D., Reinen, J., Rish, I.: Unified models of human behavioral agents in bandits, contextual bandits and RL. arXiv preprint arXiv:2005.04544 (2020)
20. Lin, B., Zhang, X.: Speaker diarization as a fully online learning problem in MiniVox. arXiv preprint arXiv:2006.04376 (2020)

21. Lin, B., Zhang, X.: VoiceID on the fly: a speaker recognition system that learns from scratch. In: INTERSPEECH (2020)
22. Mary, J., Gaudel, R., Preux, P.: Bandits and recommender systems. Mach. Learn. Optim. Big Data. First International Workshop, MOD **2015**, 325–336 (2015)
23. Nagrani, A., Chung, J.S., Xie, W., Zisserman, A.: Voxceleb: Large-scale speaker verification in the wild. Computer Science and Language (2019)
24. Ororbia, I., Alexander, G., Giles, C.L., Reitter, D.: Online semi-supervised learning with deep hybrid Boltzmann machines and denoising autoencoders. arXiv preprint arXiv:1511.06964 (2015)
25. Reynolds, D.A.: Gaussian mixture models. Encycl. Biometrics **741** (2009)
26. Villar, S.S., Bowden, J., Wason, J.: Multi-armed bandit models for the optimal design of clinical trials: benefits and challenges. Stat. Sci. Rev. J. Inst. Math. Stat. **30**(2), 199 (2015)
27. Von Luxburg, U.: A tutorial on spectral clustering. Stat. Comput. **17**(4), 395–416 (2007)
28. Yver, B.: Online semi-supervised learning: application to dynamic learning from radar data. In: 2009 International Radar Conference "Surveillance for a Safer World" (RADAR 2009), pp. 1–6, October 2009
29. Zhang, A., Wang, Q., Zhu, Z., Paisley, J., Wang, C.: Fully supervised speaker Diarization. In: ICASSP 2019–2019 IEEE International Conference on Acoustics, Speech and Signal Processing (ICASSP), pp. 6301–6305. IEEE (2019)

An Elastic Gradient Boosting Decision Tree for Concept Drift Learning

Kun Wang[1,2] , Anjin Liu[1] , Jie Lu[1(✉)] , Guangquan Zhang[1] ,
and Li Xiong[2]

[1] Australian Artificial Intelligence Institute, University of Technology Sydney,
Sydney, Australia
Kun.Wang-2@student.uts.edu.au,
{Anjin.Liu,Jie.Lu,Guangquan.Zhang}@uts.edu.au
[2] School of Management, Shanghai University, Shanghai, China
Xiongli8@shu.edu.cn

Abstract. In a non-stationary data stream, concept drift occurs when different chunks of incoming data have different distributions. Hence, over time, the global optimization point of a learning model might permanently drift to the point where the model no longer adequately performs the task it was designed for. This phenomenon needs to be addressed to maintain the integrity and effectiveness of a model over the long term. In this paper, we propose a simple but effective drift learning algorithm called elastic Gradient Boosting Decision Tree (eGBDT). Since the prediction of a GBDT model is the sum output of a list of trees, we can easily append new trees to perform incremental learning or delete the last few trees to roll back to a previously known optimization point. The proposed eGBDT incrementally fits new data and detect drift by searching for the tree with the lowest residual. If the rollback deletions required would exceed the initial number of trees, a retraining process is triggered. Comparisons of eGBDT with five state-of-the-art methods on eight data sets show the efficacy of eGBDT.

Keywords: Concept drift · Data stream · Incremental learning · Gradient boosting

1 Introduction

Concept drift describes changes in the data distribution of data streams that means the current model is no longer sufficiently accurate in performing the task it was designed for. It is important for a machine learning model to be able to mine the characteristics of the data stream and adapt to changes in the data distribution [19, 20, 22, 23]. There are two main types of concept drift: real drift and virtual drift [14]. Real drift occurs when there are changes in the class boundaries that make the current model obsolete. This type of drift is illustrated in Fig. 1, the global optimization point of a learning model might permanently

© Springer Nature Switzerland AG 2020
M. Gallagher et al. (Eds.): AI 2020, LNAI 12576, pp. 420–432, 2020.
https://doi.org/10.1007/978-3-030-64984-5_33

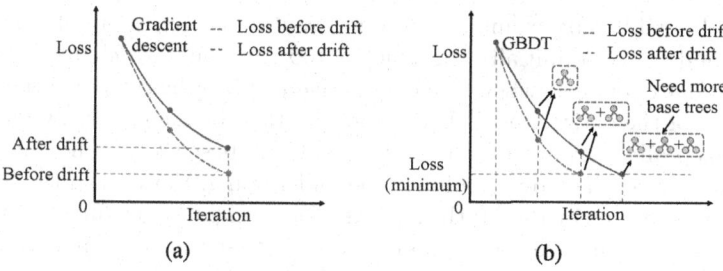

Fig. 1. a) The loss of the model before and after concept drift occurs. When a real drift occurs, the loss may not decrease quickly. (b) A demonstration of the GBDT model before and after a real drift, more base trees are needed for model learning to help loss get to the minimum point (global optimization point).

drift to the point where the model no longer adequately performs the task it was designed for. By contrast, virtual drift means changes in the marginal distribution, while the class boundaries are not affected. Concept drift will make the machine learning model unable to adapt to changeable data, leading to poor prediction and decision outcomes [20]. Our focus in this paper is real drift detection and adaptation for supervised learning.

Algorithms for handling concept drift can be divided into active and passive approaches [8]. Also called drift trigger techniques, active approaches actively detect concept drift in every time step and react after confirming a drift [7]. However, there is no solid strategy for ascertaining the point at which the current model should be retrained for best performance versus fine-tuning the model to account for the drift. For passive methods, the target is to learn data streams based on self-adjustment rather than rely on drift detection results. However, passive methods can perform well on non-drifting or slowly-drifting streams, but they may not suitable for adapting to sudden drifts or streams where concept drifts are frequent [18]. Moreover, combine with the latest machine learning methods, incremental learning methods [25] and ensemble methods [17], are popular in data stream mining. Bagging and boosting are two representative techniques of ensemble learning methods [24], and they also have been extended for online version. However, unlike bagging, which generated base learners in parallel, boosting sequentially constructs a series of base learners. Gradient boosting machine (GBM) [12] is one of the popular boosting models, but it is still an open problem for it to dealing with streaming data since the base learners could not adapt to the changing environment [10]. So, how to measure the impact of concept drift on GBM? Furthermore, how to choose the best model adjustment strategy to maintain model performance, incremental learning, or retraining?

Our aim is to develop an active drift handling algorithm that can choose the optimal moment to switch from fine-tuning to retraining via proposing an elastic Gradient Boosted Decision Tree (eGBDT) algorithm. GBDT iteratively constructs a group of weak learners then linearly combines them into a strong learner. Hence, it is easy to add or delete trees from the tree list, which keeps the model flexible. For example, consider a continuous series of data chunks. A GBDT model can be initially constructed 100 trees on data chunk 0 and then tested on data chunk 1, where the cumulative result of base trees is the prediction result of the entire model. The model can then be incrementally fine-tuned by incrementally learning a further 50 trees. If the best prediction result occurs at the 150th tree, the model could still be underfitting. However, if the best prediction result occurs at the 110th tree, the model might be overfitting, and trees after the 110th can be deleted. Another case is that the best prediction result occurs at the 80th tree, while the initial training only has 100 trees. This means the GBDT model can not adapt to the data. We consider this as a significant drift, and the model is then retrained. As a bonus, this pruning strategy can help to reduce memory consumption and the complexity of calculations without sacrificing performance.

The main contributions of this paper are as follows:

- Based on the characteristics of GBDT framework, we propose a naïve incremental GBDT (iGBDT) algorithm for incremental learning with dynamic data streams.
- We propose a rollback process to find out the poor performance trees in GBDT model. This is also a signal to find out concept drift.
- We propose an elastic Gradient Boosting Descent Tree (eGBDT) algorithm, which can delete redundant trees without increasing the runtime complexity. This eGBDT handles the uncertain of concept drift well.

This paper is organized as follows: related work and preliminaries are discussed in Sect. 2, our proposed methods are presented in Sect. 3, Sect. 4 illustrated our experiment, conclusion and future work are in Sect. 5.

2 Related Works and Preliminaries

2.1 Concept Drift Detection and Adaptation

For a time step t, a data chunk with chunk instances $D_t = \{(x_i^t, y_i^t)\}_{i=1}^{chunk}$ is generated by a distribution $P_t(x, y)$, where x is the attribute vector and y is the label. Concept drift is defined as $P_t(x, y) \neq P_{t-1}(x, y)$, the data distribution changed from time $t-1$ to time t [27]. The goal of drift learning is to ensure that the loss $\ell(f(x), y)$ of a learning model is continuously optimized when a concept drift occurs, i.e.,

$$F_t = \arg\min_{f \in \mathcal{H}} \mathrm{E}_{(x,y) \in P_t(x,y)}[\ell(f(x), y)], \tag{1}$$

where $\mathcal{H}$ is the hypothesis set, $\mathrm{E}(\cdot)$ is the expectation of a random variable [27]. Consider a sequence of $P_t(x, y)$, the target of the incremental learning is given as

$$\min_{F_1, F_2, \dots, F_t, \dots} \sum_t \mathrm{E}_{(x,y) \in P_t(x,y)}[\ell(F_t(x), y)] \tag{2}$$

i.e., a set of models created at different time step [27]. Since the real concept drift has no established rules to follow and may include multiple types of drift, it is not only necessary to perform preliminary detection, but also to fine-tune model in real time based on the feedback, reducing the memory redundancy caused by passive learning to improve the flexibility of the model.

The purpose of handling concept drift is to ensure the trained model can perform well on the testing set. Like accurately map the knowledge of the source domain to the target domain [21]. Ensemble approaches to deal with concept drift can be divided into two categories [8,17]: active drift detection with an adaptation ensemble, and passive ensemble with forgetting mechanism. The active method relies on a drift detection mechanism, informing the model to update in time. Some popular drift detection methods are Drift Detection Method (DDM) [13], Heoffding's inequality based Drift Detection Method (HDDM) [11], ADaptive WINdowing (ADWIN) [1]. The passive methods do not have a drift detection. Instead, it learns the new data and fine-tunes the model in time. Typical examples are Streaming Ensemble Algorithm (SEA) [26], the Learn++ algorithm in Nonstationary Environments (Learn++.NSE) [7], Dynamic Weighted Majority algorithm (DWM) [16], Accuracy Updated Ensemble (AUE1) [5] and Accuracy Updated Ensemble (AUE2) [6]. These algorithms learn drift incrementally with newly arriving data, eliminating old ensembles through a forgetting mechanism [27].

2.2 Gradient Boosting Decision Tree

At present, Boosting [4], which is a critical algorithm in ensemble learning, has been widely used in data mining. GBDT [12] is a kind of classification algorithm based on ensemble learning that turns a weak classifier into a strong classifier through training. We input training set $\{(x_i, y_i)\}_{i=1}^{\text{chunk}}$, a differentiable loss function $\ell(y, f(x))$, number of iterations M. For $m = 1$ to M, we calculate the pseudo-residuals

$$r_{im} = -\left[\frac{\partial \ell(y_i, f(x_i))}{\partial f(x_i)}\right]_{f(x)=f_{m-1}(x)}, i = 1, \ldots, \text{chunk} \tag{3}$$

and fit a base learner $h_m(x)$ to pseudo-residuals, then train it use the training set $\{(x_i, r_{im})\}_{i=1}^n$ and calculate the multiplier γ_m as

$$\gamma_m = \arg\min_{\gamma} \sum_{i=1}^{n} L(y_i, F_{m-1}(x_i) + \gamma h_m(x_i)), \tag{4}$$

then update the model as

$$F_M(x) = F_{m-1}(x) + \gamma_m h_m(x). \tag{5}$$

In the literature, GBDT has been used for handling stochastic data streams, such as the Streaming Gradient Boosting algorithm (SGM) [15]. To adapt to the changes of data stream, we propose an incremental method to improve model performances. At the same time, considering the redundancy and complexity of the calculation process, we add a pruning process to increase the flexibility of the model and enhance performances.

3   Elastic Gradient Boosting Decision Tree Ensemble

3.1   Incremental Learning of GBDT—iGBDT

GBDT model is trained using a portion of the data instances as the training set, with the remaining data instances divided into several data chunks for subsequent use in iteratively fine-tuning the model. Once initially trained, the model is tested on new chunks of incoming data to gauge and fine-tune the model's accuracy. Although GBDT models are high-performing ensemble decision tree models when handling classification tasks, no one has applied it for concept drift learning. With data streams that contain concept drift, it is vital to ensure that the model can adapt to the new patterns. Incremental learning is an ideal method for updating the model.

We first train a GBDT model based on the given data sample, then we test the model on the new incoming data chunk and calculate the residual. We use this data chunk and residual as a new train set to fit a new decision regression tree and add this tree to our original GBDT model to update a new model. For binary classification, we initial training chunk and present new sliding chunk as $D_{\text{chunk}_{\text{ini}}} = \{(x_i, y_i)\}_{i=1}^{\text{chunk}_{\text{ini}}}$, $D_{\text{chunk}_{\text{slide}}} = \{(x_i, y_i)\}_{i=1}^{\text{chunk}_{\text{slide}}}$, the term "chunk" represents the chunk size, and $x \in \mathbb{R}^d$ that d is the dimensionality, $y \in \{0,1\}$. We calculate the pseudo-residuals on testing set as based on Eq. (3). Then, we set the learning rate as λ and set the number of incremental trees as L, we fit L new regression tree on $\{(x_i, \lambda r_{i(M+L)})\}_{i=1}^{\text{chunk}_{\text{slide}}}$, the incremental learning model is

$$F_{M+L}(x) = F_{M+L-1}(x) + h_{M+L}(x). \tag{6}$$

This is more computational friendly than the conventional GBDT learning given in Eq. (4, 5), because of the fixed learning rate. Repeating this procedure incrementally tunes the GBDT model. The same process is used with newly arriving chunks so the model incrementally adapts to concept drift if present. The pseudocode for GBDT's incremental learning process is presented in Algorithm 1.

3.2   A Residual-Based GBDT Pruning Method—eGBDT

The prediction result of a GBDT model is the sum of the prediction of each tree inside the model. Let's denote the prediction value of the mth tree on a given feature vector x as $\hat{y}_m = h_m(x)$. Then the predictions of all GBDT trees on x is $\{\hat{y}_m\}_{m=1}^M$. According to the Eq. (6), the final prediction value on the mth tree is the sum of the prediction values from the first tree to the mth tree, i.e.,

$$F_m(x) = \sum_{i=1}^m h_i(x) + \bar{y}, \tag{7}$$

where the $\bar{y}$ is the mean of the label, namely the initial prediction of the GBDT. The first regression tree h_0 is trained on $D_{\text{chunk}_{\text{ini}}}$, with the mean of the label $\bar{y}$ as the initial target variable, and the residual is calculated by $R_0 = y - \bar{y}$. The residuals of the previous tree are used to train next tree from h_1 to h_m, where

---

Algorithm 1. Incremental Learning of GBDT (iGBDT)

Input:
   1) initial train chunk $D_{\text{chunk}_{\text{ini}}}$
   2) new slide chunk $D_{\text{chunk}_{\text{slide}}}$
Parameter:
   1) Config of GBDT, $\text{GBDT}_{\text{parm}} =$
   $(M = 250, \text{Depth} = 10, \text{MinSamplesLeaf} = 5, \text{SampleRate} = 0.8, \lambda = 0.01)$
   2) Num of incremental trees, L
Output:
   1) incremental GBDT $F_{M+L}(x)$
1: build GBDT $F_M(x)$ on D_{train}
2: **for** $l = 1$ to L **do**
3:    compute the pseudo-residuals r_{li} on D_{test}
4:    fit a new regression tree $h_l(X)$ on D_{test} to pseudo-residuals, i.e. train it using
      $(x_i, \lambda r_{li})$ where $x_i \in X_{\text{test}}$
5:    update the mode according to Eq. (6)
6: **end for**
7: **return** $F_{M+L}(x)$

$m \in \mathbb{Z}^+_{m \leq M}$, M is the max number of iterations. We have the residual vector of the mth tree on a sliding data chunk as:

$$R_m = y - F_m(x) = y - \bar{y} - \sum_{i=1}^{m} h_i(x), \tag{8}$$

that $R_m = \{r_{im}\}_{i=1}^{\text{chunk}_{\text{slide}}}$. With the residual of each tree, we can evaluate the performance of the GBDT with any length, which is the reason we call it elastic GBDT. For runtime efficiency, the residuals are stored in a $\text{chunk}_{\text{slide}}$ by M size matrix. Then we can find the best performance sub list of trees by finding the minimum mean absolute (MA) residual.

$$I_{\text{elastic}} = \underset{m \in \mathbb{Z}^+_{m \leq M}}{\arg\min} \ \text{MA}(R_m) \tag{9}$$

where the I_{elastic} is the elastic GBDT tree index, i.e., the sub tree list of GBDT that $\text{eGBDT} = \{h_0(x), \ldots, h_{I_{\text{elastic}}}(x)\}$ will be used for later prediction. And the redundant sub tree list $\text{rGBDT} = \{h_{I_{\text{elastic}}+1}(x), \ldots, h_M(x)\}$ will discard. If I_{elastic} is smaller than a predefined threshold, then we say there is a significant concept drift, and a new GBDT will be retrained on the new data.

For eGBDT, the GBDT pruning process is always associated with the incremental learning process. At the beginning of the stream, we build a GBDT with M trees on $D_{\text{chunk}_{\text{ini}}}$. Then for each new data chunk, we make the prediction, perform pruning and drift detection, and incrementally fit the pruned GBDT with L new trees on $D_{\text{chunk}_{\text{slide}}}$. In this setting, we use the initial number of trees M as the drift threshold, i.e., if $I_{\text{elastic}} < M$, a retraining process will be triggered.

Algorithm 2. Elastic GBDT (eGBDT)

Input:
  1) trained GBDT, $F_M(x)$
  2) new slide chunk $D_{chunk_{slide}}$
Parameter: N/A
Output:
  1) pruned GBDT, $F_{M'}(x)$
  1: test GBDT model $F_M(x)$ on $D_{chunk_{slide}}$
  2: calculate the residual based on the output of each tree R_m
  3: find the best tree index based on the mean absolute (MA) value of the residual
     $m = \text{argmin MA}(R_m)$
  4: **if** $m < M$ **then**
  5:     retrain GBDT $F_M(x)$ on $D_{chunk_{slide}}$
  6:     **return** $F_M(x)$ as $F_{M'}(x)$
  7: **else**
  8:     remove redundant trees $F_{M'}(x) = F_{0,m}(x)$
  9:     **return** $F_{0,m}(x)$ as $F_{M'}(x)$
  10: **end if**

---

4   Experiments

4.1   Experiment Settings

Three GDBT-based methods and the five state-of-the-art concept drift handling methods were compared as follows. The parameters of GBDT were same, $M = 250$, Depth = 10, Min Samples Leaf = 5, Sample Rate= 0.8, $\lambda = 0.01$. For the iGBDT, we set the number of incremental trees as $L = 25$. The five state-of-the-art algorithms were implemented based on MOA prequential evaluation [2], and parameters were set as the default values as suggested by the authors.

Baseline, train a GBDT model on the training chunk and test it on the reset of the streams.

iGBDT, incremental GBDT that train on initial chunk and incremental fit on new data. For example, train on chunk 0 and test on chunk 1, then incremental fit on chunk 1 and test on chunk 2. In our experiment, we set the same number of base learners for each incremental learning.

Learn++.NSE [9], is an ensemble of classifiers for incremental learning to handle the changeable data distribution. It trains one new classifier for each batch of data. It can receive and combine these classifiers by using dynamically weighted majority voting [9].

OnlineAUE [6], maintains a weighted ensemble of base learners and uses a weighted voting rule for its final prediction. It combines accuracy-based weighting mechanisms known from block-based ensembles with the incremental nature of Hoeffding Trees [6].

LeverageBag [3], focuses on randomizing the input and output of the classifier, while increasing accuracy and diversity, construct an ensemble of classifiers. This method combines the simplicity of bagging by adding more randomization to the input and output of the classifiers.

HDDM-W-Test, HDDM-A-Test [11], is an error-based online drift detection method based on McDiarmid's bounds. HDDM-A-Test is based on Hoeffding's bounds. HDDM-W-Test is based on McDiarmid's bounds and uses the EWMA statistic as an estimator.

The proposed GBDT-based methods were implemented by Python. The base decision tree learners of GBDT framework are learned by using the Sklearn Decision Tree Regression package. The parameter setting on each data set was the same. The $chunk_{ini} = 365$ and $chunk_{slide} = 365$, the chunk size is established according to the periodicity of the data, and this will be explained in the data sets description. To be fair, we uniformly use the decision tree model as the base learner in other algorithms. Using the Hoeffding trees as the base learners in Learn++.NSE, LeverageBag, OnlineAUE, HDDM-W-Test, HDDM-A-Test algorithms. During the experiment, all algorithm parameters are set uniformly.

4.2   The Data Sets

Each approach was tested on eight real-world data sets. Information about these data sets was summarized in Table 1. A brief description of each follows. The real-world data sets were the WMO world weather data for different region area. Since the data set records the daily weather changes of each region, we define a year as a cycle and set the experimental chunk size as 365. We selected eight data sets from five regions, including Europe, Asia, Africa, North America, South America. The missing values in the data have been filled with the mean value. And we retained eight attributes: temperature (we convert Fahrenheit to Celsius), dew point, sea level pressure, visibility, average wind speed, maximum sustained wind speed, maximum temperature, and minimum temperature. Third, in order to simplify the calculation, the labels of the data sets have been converted into two classes. There are six kinds of weather changes in the original, they are fog, rain, snow, hail, thunder, tornado. We define the first class as the weather without these changes, and the second class as the weather including these changes. In addition, due to the imbalance of the sample categories, we will also calculate the accuracy, F1-score, MCC score, and Friedman test in the experiment and make a comprehensive evaluation of the initial experimental results. The data sets and the source code of this research are available online.[1]

4.3   Finding and Discussion

Comparing eGBDT with GBDT-based Concept Drift Handling Methods. The detailed experiment results of **Baseline, iGBDT, eGBDT** are shown in Table 2, 3, 4. We calculate the average macro F1-score and accuracy score of Baseline, iGBDT and eGBDT. The average F1-score of each algorithm is 57.33%

---

[1] https://github.com/kunkun111/AJCAI-eGBDT.

Table 1. Real-world data sets statistics (due to missing data in some years and months, the number of data samples in the same duration are different.)

Number	Data sets	Location	Time Duration	Samples	Features	Class	Ratio
042700	Narsarsuaq	Greenland/Europe	1942–2020	27,592	8	2	0.84:1
100370	Schleswig	Germany/Europe	1942–2020	27,238	8	2	0.44:1
265090	Klajpeda	Lithuania/Europe	1942–2020	25,591	8	2	0.77:1
424750	Allahabad	India/Asia	1942–2018	18,087	8	2	0.32:1
567780	Kunming	China/Asia	1942–2020	25,631	8	2	0.75:1
606560	Tindouf	Algeria/Africa	1943–2020	16,660	8	2	0.04:1
702220	Galena	Illinois/North America	1942–2020	27,197	8	2	0.85:1
802220	Bogota	Colombia/South America	1942–2020	24,604	8	2	0.56:1

(Baseline), 76.67% (iGBDT), 76.76% (eGBDT). The average accuracy score of each algorithm is 67.14% (Baseline), 81.78% (iGBDT), 82.05% (eGBDT). The average runtime of each algorithm is 1s (Baseline), 59s (iGBDT), 56s (eGBDT). Moreover, the MCC score of eGBDT is generally higher than Baseline and iGBDT.

Table 2. Average macro F1-score of eight real-world data sets (%)

Data sets	Baseline	iGBDT	eGBDT	Learn++	Leverage	HDDM_A	HDDM_W	OnlineAUE
Narsarsuaq	32.69(8)	78.07(3)	79.15(2)	71.60(7)	77.73(4)	74.37(6)	75.15(5)	**79.23(1)**
Schleswig	63.67(8)	81.36(2)	**81.38(1)**	65.51(7)	69.99(4)	68.99(6)	69.24(5)	71.29(3)
Klajpeda	69.93(6)	76.03(2)	**77.01(1)**	68.01(8)	72.79(4)	70.14(5)	69.86(7)	73.47(3)
Allahabad	73.92(5)	82.56(2)	**82.96(1)**	65.09(8)	75.82(4)	71.38(7)	71.86(6)	78.45(3)
Kunming	64.96(8)	79.42(2)	**80.14(1)**	71.55(7)	76.44(4)	73.22(6)	73.69(5)	78.83(3)
Tindouf	50.31(8)	67.16(2)	**67.95(1)**	52.25(7)	55.90(6)	63.92(3)	58.49(5)	59.23(4)
Galena	48.36(8)	**76.49(1)**	74.65(3)	66.63(7)	73.99(4)	70.01(6)	71.55(5)	76.46(2)
Bogota	54.81(8)	**72.30(1)**	70.91(4)	68.22(7)	70.69(5)	70.60(6)	70.96(3)	71.99(2)
AvgRank	7.3	1.8	**1.7**	7.2	4.3	5.6	5.1	2.6

Besides, we also summarized the number of trees pruned from the GBDT model in accordance with the accuracy, as shown in Fig. 2. The number of trees of the model increased suddenly, with the accuracy reduced abruptly on the data set, which contains sudden drift is obviously. It suggests that the data changes can be observed clearly according to the fluctuating number of pruned trees and model performances. The number of pruned trees depends on the drift severity. Drift with a relatively lower severity can be handled by the incremental process until it reaches a significant accuracy drop. Furthermore, because of the removal of some poorly-performing base trees, the model's overall performance is maintained, and the redundant base trees in the model are also reduced.

Evaluate eGBDT with Five Concept Drift Handling Algorithms. The stream classification results of eGBDT ensemble and five state-of-the-art concept drift handling algorithms are summarized in Tables 2, 3, 4, 5. The F1-score,

Table 3. Accuracy of eight real-world data sets (%)

Data sets	Baseline	iGBDT	eGBDT	Learn++	Leverage	HDDM_A	HDDM_W	OnlineAUE
Narsarsuaq	46.10(8)	78.08(3)	79.16(2)	71.63(7)	77.81(4)	74.52(6)	75.49(5)	**79.38(1)**
Schleswig	72.74(7)	85.01(2)	**85.11(1)**	72.69(8)	76.72(4)	73.72(5)	73.62(6)	78.14(3)
Klajpeda	70.03(7)	76.36(2)	**77.40(1)**	68.13(8)	73.24(4)	70.22(5)	70.07(6)	73.92(3)
Allahabad	82.15(5)	87.38(2)	**88.00(1)**	76.35(8)	83.60(4)	78.08(7)	78.68(6)	85.12(3)
Kunming	65.21(8)	79.71(2)	**80.43(1)**	71.81(7)	76.87(4)	73.49(6)	74.06(5)	79.27(3)
Tindouf	72.96(8)	95.01(6)	95.86(2)	95.36(5)	95.83(3)	94.75(7)	95.44(4)	**96.13(1)**
Galena	58.89(8)	**76.90(1)**	75.30(3)	66.77(7)	74.22(4)	70.04(6)	71.60(5)	76.67(2)
Bogota	69.05(8)	75.83(2)	75.19(3)	72.22(7)	75.01(4)	73.08(6)	73.92(5)	**75.85(1)**
AvgRank	7.3	2.5	**1.7**	7.1	3.8	6	5.2	2.1

Table 4. Matthews correlation coefficient (MCC) of eight real-world data sets (%)

Data sets	Baseline	iGBDT	eGBDT	Learn++	Leverage	HDDM_A	HDDM_W	OnlineAUE
Narsarsuaq	2.92(8)	56.81(3)	**59.03(1)**	43.21(7)	55.60(4)	48.86(6)	50.55(5)	57.61(2)
Schleswig	29.81(8)	63.42(2)	**63.61(1)**	31.42(7)	41.31(4)	37.89(6)	38.41(5)	43.48(3)
Klajpeda	40.48(6)	52.06(2)	**54.03(1)**	36.41(8)	45.50(4)	41.03(5)	40.00(7)	46.19(3)
Allahabad	48.67(5)	65.22(2)	**66.34(1)**	30.45(8)	52.59(4)	42.99(7)	43.87(6)	57.19(3)
Kunming	36.89(8)	58.93(2)	**60.34(1)**	42.75(7)	52.58(4)	46.54(6)	47.34(5)	56.91(3)
Tindouf	16.69(7)	34.46(2)	**37.68(1)**	8.14(8)	21.59(6)	29.40(3)	23.32(5)	29.09(4)
Galena	20.13(8)	**53.43(1)**	50.35(3)	32.84(7)	47.99(4)	40.42(6)	43.30(5)	51.95(2)
Bogota	26.33(8)	45.42(2)	43.45(4)	37.98(7)	43.75(3)	42.16(6)	42.72(5)	**45.77(1)**
AvgRank	7.2	2	**1.6**	7.3	4.1	5.6	5.3	2.6

accuracy, and MCC score are measured by using the Sklearn package. The experiment shows that eGBDT has competitive performance. For the average macro F1-score, eGBDT performs well on Schleswig, Klajpeda, Allahabad, Kunming, Tindouf, and have the highest average rank. For the accuracy, eGBDT performed well on Schleswig, Klajpeda, Allahabad, Kunming, and also got the highest average rank. For the MCC score, eGBDT also achieved better results with an average ranking 1.6, followed by iGBDT and OnlineAUE. In order to compare the performance of eGBDT statistically, we also perform Friedman tests on eGBDT and five methods based on MCC score, as shown in Table 5. The results show that at a significance level of 0.05, although the performance of eGBDT is not obvious when compared with OnlineAUE method, the overall performance is better. Overall, we find that eGBDT with both the incremental learning and self-adjusting tree pruning process is beneficial for maintaining model stability and generally produces better results.

Discussion. Our eGBDT is a chunk-based drift learning algorithm, it still can outperform the prequential learning algorithms in some cases. However, there are two factors that we need further evaluation. One is model optimization, although our method has the highest average ranking, it is undeniable that it has not achieved better results on some data sets. One reason is that our eGBDT is a linear combination of decision regression trees, when face with

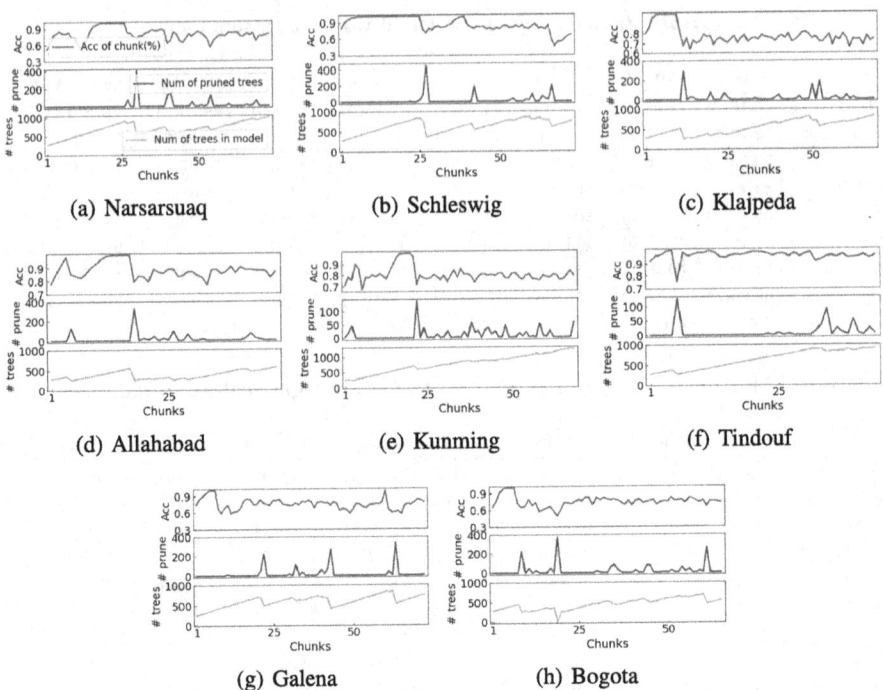

(a) Narsarsuaq   (b) Schleswig   (c) Klajpeda

(d) Allahabad   (e) Kunming   (f) Tindouf

(g) Galena   (h) Bogota

Fig. 2. A plot of the chunk accuracy, the number of pruned trees, and the number of trees in GBDT during drift learning. We can clearly see that the accuracy dropped, the number of pruned trees increased, and the number of trees in eGBDT decreased.

Table 5. Friedman test of eGBDT with five state-of-the-art methods based on MCC

Methods	Learn++	Leverage	HDDM_A	HDDM_W	OnlineAUE
P-value	0.00468	0.03389	0.00468	0.00468	0.1573
Significance	$P < 0.05$	$P < 0.05$	$P < 0.05$	$P < 0.05$	$P > 0.05$

remarkably sudden drift, the model adaptability may be lacking. Another one is programming language (Our Baseline, iGBDT, and eGBDT are implemented in Python, while MOA implements five state-of-the-art methods in Java).

5   Conclusion

In this paper, we proposed an elastic GBDT drift learning algorithm. The proposed eGBDT integrates incremental learning and tree pruning to dynamically adjust the number of trees for different stream situations. The incremental learning of GBDT can help the model to improve performance. The process of tree pruning is a simple but efficient way to increase model stability and detect drift. Experiments on real-world data sets have shown the potential of eGBDT.

In future research, we will continue to improve our eGBDT method for concept drift adaptation, we will mainly focus on enhancing the adaptability, processing efficiency, and stability of our eGBDT method when dealing with different types of concept drift.

Acknowledgments. This work was supported by the Australian Research Council through the Discovery Project under Grant DP190101733.

References

1. Bifet, A., Gavalda, R.: Learning from time-changing data with adaptive windowing. In: SIAM, pp. 443–448. SIAM (2007)
2. Bifet, A., Holmes, G., Kirkby, R., Pfahringer, B.: MOA: massive online analysis. J. Mach. Learn. Res. **11**, 1601–1604 (2010)
3. Bifet, A., Holmes, G., Pfahringer, B.: Leveraging bagging for evolving data streams. In: Balcázar, J.L., Bonchi, F., Gionis, A., Sebag, M. (eds.) ECML PKDD 2010. LNCS (LNAI), vol. 6321, pp. 135–150. Springer, Heidelberg (2010). https://doi.org/10.1007/978-3-642-15880-3_15
4. Breiman, L.: Bias, variance, and arcing classifiers., Technical report 460, Statistics Department, University of California, Berkeley (1996)
5. Brzeziński, D., Stefanowski, J.: Accuracy updated ensemble for data streams with concept drift. In: Corchado, E., Kurzyński, M., Woźniak, M. (eds.) HAIS 2011. LNCS (LNAI), vol. 6679, pp. 155–163. Springer, Heidelberg (2011). https://doi.org/10.1007/978-3-642-21222-2_19
6. Brzeziński, D., Stefanowski, J.: Reacting to different types of concept drift: the accuracy updated ensemble algorithm. IEEE Trans. Neural Netw. Learn. Syst. **25**(1), 81–94 (2013)
7. Ditzler, G., Polikar, R.: Incremental learning of concept drift from streaming imbalanced data. IEEE Trans. Knowl. Data Eng. **25**(10), 2283–2301 (2012)
8. Ditzler, G., Roveri, M., Alippi, C., Polikar, R.: Learning in nonstationary environments: a survey. IEEE Comput. Intell. Mag. **10**(4), 12–25 (2015)
9. Elwell, R., Polikar, R.: Incremental learning of concept drift in nonstationary environments. IEEE Trans. Neural Netw. **22**(10), 1517–1531 (2011)
10. Feng, J., Xu, Y.X., Jiang, Y., Zhou, Z.H.: Soft gradient boosting machine. arXiv preprint arXiv:2006.04059 (2020)
11. Frías-Blanco, I., del Campo-Ávila, J., Ramos-Jimenez, G., Morales-Bueno, R., Ortiz-Díaz, A., Caballero-Mota, Y.: Online and non-parametric drift detection methods based on Hoeffding's bounds. IEEE Trans. Knowl. Data Eng. **27**(3), 810–823 (2014)
12. Friedman, J.H.: Greedy function approximation: a gradient boosting machine. Ann. Stat. **29**(5), 1189–1232 (2001)
13. Gama, J., Medas, P., Castillo, G., Rodrigues, P.: Learning with drift detection. In: Bazzan, A.L.C., Labidi, S. (eds.) SBIA 2004. LNCS (LNAI), vol. 3171, pp. 286–295. Springer, Heidelberg (2004). https://doi.org/10.1007/978-3-540-28645-5_29
14. Gama, J., Žliobaitė, I., Bifet, A., Pechenizkiy, M., Bouchachia, A.: A survey on concept drift adaptation. ACM Comput. Surv. **46**(4), 44 (2014)
15. Hu, H., Sun, W., Venkatraman, A., Hebert, M., Bagnell, A.: Gradient boosting on stochastic data streams. In: AISTATS, pp. 595–603. PMLR (2017)

16. Kolter, J.Z., Maloof, M.A.: Dynamic weighted majority: an ensemble method for drifting concepts. J. Mach. Learn. Res. **8**, 2755–2790 (2007)

17. Krawczyk, B., Minku, L.L., Gama, J., Stefanowski, J., Woźniak, M.: Ensemble learning for data stream analysis: a survey. Inf. Fusion **37**, 132–156 (2017)

18. Liu, A., Lu, J., Liu, F., Zhang, G.: Accumulating regional density dissimilarity for concept drift detection in data streams. Pattern Recogn. **76**, 256–272 (2018)

19. Liu, A., Lu, J., Zhang, G.: Concept drift detection via equal intensity K-means space partitioning. IEEE Trans. Cybern. (2020). https://doi.org/10.1109/TCYB.2020.2983962

20. Lu, J., Liu, A., Dong, F., Gu, F., Gama, J., Zhang, G.: Learning under concept drift: a review. IEEE Trans. Knowl. Data Eng. **31**(12), 2346–2363 (2018)

21. Lu, J., Zuo, H., Zhang, G.: Fuzzy multiple-source transfer learning. IEEE Trans. Fuzzy Syst. (2019). https://doi.org/10.1109/TFUZZ.2019.2952792

22. Lu, N., Lu, J., Zhang, G., De Mantaras, R.L.: A concept drift-tolerant case-base editing technique. Artif. Intell. **230**, 108–133 (2016)

23. Lu, N., Zhang, G., Lu, J.: Concept drift detection via competence models. Artif. Intell. **209**, 11–28 (2014)

24. Oza, N.C.: Online bagging and boosting. In: SMC, pp. 2340–2345. IEEE (2005)

25. Schlimmer, J.C., Granger, R.H.: Incremental learning from noisy data. Mach. Learn. **1**(3), 317–354 (1986)

26. Street, W.N., Kim, Y.: A streaming ensemble algorithm (SEA) for large-scale classification. In: ACM SIGKDD, pp. 377–382. ACM (2001)

27. Sun, Y., Tang, K., Zhu, Z., Yao, X.: Concept drift adaptation by exploiting historical knowledge. IEEE Trans. Neural Netw. Learn. Syst. **29**(10), 4822–4832 (2018)

Transfer of Pretrained Model Weights Substantially Improves Semi-supervised Image Classification

Attaullah Sahito[(✉)], Eibe Frank, and Bernhard Pfahringer

Department of Computer Science, University of Waikato, Hamilton, New Zealand
a19@students.waikato.ac.nz, {eibe,bernhard}@waikato.ac.nz

Abstract. Deep neural networks produce state-of-the-art results when trained on a large number of labeled examples but tend to overfit when small amounts of labeled examples are used for training. Creating a large number of labeled examples requires considerable resources, time, and effort. If labeling new data is not feasible, so-called semi-supervised learning can achieve better generalisation than purely supervised learning by employing unlabeled instances as well as labeled ones. The work presented in this paper is motivated by the observation that transfer learning provides the opportunity to potentially further improve performance by exploiting models pretrained on a similar domain. More specifically, we explore the use of transfer learning when performing semi-supervised learning using self-learning. The main contribution is an empirical evaluation of transfer learning using different combinations of similarity metric learning methods and label propagation algorithms in semi-supervised learning. We find that transfer learning always substantially improves the model's accuracy when few labeled examples are available, regardless of the type of loss used for training the neural network. This finding is obtained by performing extensive experiments on the SVHN, CIFAR10, and Plant Village image classification datasets and applying pretrained weights from Imagenet for transfer learning.

Keywords: Semi-supervised learning · Transfer learning · Self-learning · Triplet loss · Contrastive loss · Arcface loss

1 Introduction

Neural networks are frequently used for image classification tasks and yield state-of-the-art results in this application. However, for training, these models generally need a lot of labeled samples, and they tend to overfit on small amounts of labeled data. This problem is of particular importance when limited labeled samples are available due to time or financial constraints. Addressing this problem requires machine learning methods that are able to work with a limited amount of labeled data and also make efficient use of the side information available from unlabeled data.

© Springer Nature Switzerland AG 2020
M. Gallagher et al. (Eds.): AI 2020, LNAI 12576, pp. 433–444, 2020.
https://doi.org/10.1007/978-3-030-64984-5_34

Semi-supervised learning (SSL) aims to improve performance by exploiting both labeled and unlabeled examples. Given an input space X containing the examples, SSL methods are designed to work with labeled examples $L = \{(x_1, y_1), (x_2, y_2), ..., (x_{|L|}, y_{|L|})\}$ and unlabeled examples $U = \{x_1', x_2', ..., x_{|U|}'\}$, where $x_i, x_j' \in X$ with $i = 1, 2, ..., |L|$ and $j = 1, 2, ..., |U|$ and y_i are the labels of x_i, with $y_i \in \{1, 2, 3, ..., c\}$ (c being the number of classes).

A few assumptions are required to make semi-supervised learning a principled approach [3]:

1. If two instances x_1, x_2 are close in a high-density region, then their corresponding outputs y_1, y_2 should also be close.
2. If instances are in the same structure (referred to as a cluster or manifold), they are likely to be of the same class.
3. The decision boundary between classes should lie in a low-density region of the input space.

Almost all standard neural networks for image classification are trained by minimising cross-entropy loss on labeled training data. In this paper, along with cross-entropy loss, we also consider another class of losses, comprising so-called similarity metric learning losses, which operate on the relationships between samples such that instances of the same class are considered similar and those belonging to different classes are considered dissimilar. Once a similarity function has been trained, which is parameterised by a neural network, feature vectors (embeddings) of examples produced by the network will be grouped together according to class labels, normally in Euclidean space. These learned embeddings lend themselves naturally to semi-supervised learning because they can be employed to assign class labels to unlabeled examples using very simple classification methods such as nearest-neighbor classifiers.

This approach is related to work on pseudo-labeling [10,16], where the model is initially trained on limited data. However, in this paper, instead of applying random initialisation of network parameters when training starts, we investigate using pretrained weights from another domain and show that this provides much better generalisation ability. Using pretrained model weights is a standard approach for transfer learning in supervised settings, but appears to have received little attention in the context of semi-supervised learning, particularly when applying self-learning with metric learning.

We use a pretrained neural network model trained on Imagenet [17]. A schematic overview of the proposed approach is shown in Fig. 1. Fine-tuning on data from the target domain is performed on the (very small) initial set of labeled examples. Following that, confident predictions for unlabeled examples are added to labeled examples for iterative retraining of the neural network—this is the standard self-learning method for semi-supervised learning. It enables us to obtain more labeled training data and the assumption is that this eventually helps in achieving significant performance improvements. In our experiments on image classification tasks, we compare using pretrained weights for the neural network to random initialisation of the weights.

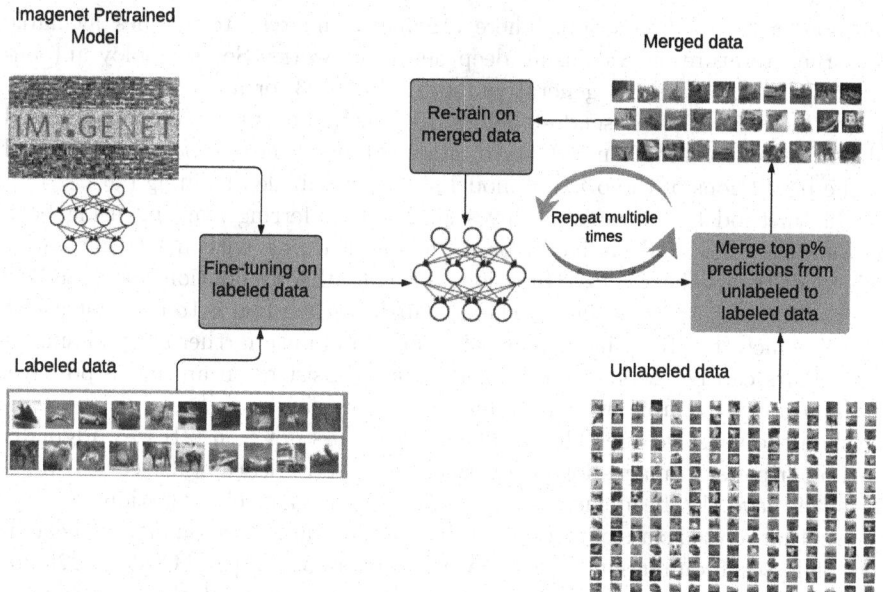

Fig. 1. Overview of the approach.

The main contribution of this work is an extensive empirical investigation of transfer learning in the context of self-learning. Using cross-entropy loss as well as combinations of similarity metric learning losses (e.g., triplet loss, contrastive loss, and Arcface loss) with simple nearest-neighbor-based label propagation, we find that transfer learning always substantially improves the classification accuracy of the model when few labeled examples are available, regardless of which loss function is used for training the neural network. More specifically, for semi-supervised learning using self-learning on the SVHN, CIFAR10, and Plant Village image classification datasets, we obtain a substantial improvement using pretrained weights when few labeled examples are available for training. Thus, our results indicate that the well-established method of performing transfer learning by re-using pretrained weights—commonly applied when performing a purely supervised training of a neural network—is particularly useful in the context of semi-supervised learning.

2   Related Work

In this section, we briefly discuss some existing work on semi-supervised learning and transfer learning.

2.1   Semi-supervised Learning

Semi-supervised Learning (SSL) lies between supervised and unsupervised learning. SSL tries to employ labeled examples as well as unlabeled examples for more accurate prediction. There are many different techniques available from the literature on SSL using deep neural networks. Some employ autoencoders [12,15], others use generative models [5,20,23] or are based on regularization ideas [14,19]. In pseudo-labeling [10], the model is trained on the limited labeled data first and then re-trained on an extended set of labeled data, based on the predictions of the original model for the unlabelled training data.

Our method builds on work investigating transferring learning using both cross-entropy loss and similarity-based metric learning with neural networks. Pair and triplet based loss functions provide the foundation for standard approaches to metric learning. A classic pair-based method is to use contrastive loss [4], which tries to bring similar pairs closer and push farther away dissimilar pairs. Pairs can be extended to triplets. They consist of an anchor, a positive, and a negative example, where the anchor is more similar to the positive example than the negative one. The resulting triplet loss function [21] was originally used on triplets of images for face verification. Metric learning-based loss functions [24] have also been successfully employed for image classification.

Another related class of metric learning methods are based on modified classification losses. Examples include Arcface [6], Sphereface [11] and Cosface [22]. For metric learning, Arcface, Sphereface, and Cosface apply multiplicative-angular, additive-cosine, and additive-angular margins, respectively.

2.2 Transfer Learning

Since the successful Imagenet challenge [17], transfer learning has been used widely in visual recognition tasks such as object detection [7]. Transfer learning uses the network weights learned by training on the large and labeled Imagenet dataset and fine-tunes the weights for the respective target domain. When the target domain is sufficiently closely related to the source domain of Imagenet, then transfer learning usually generalizes much better than training from scratch on the smaller target domain alone.

3   Semi-supervised Learning Using Self-learning

The semi-supervised learning approach we apply is based on self-learning. The model is initially trained using a limited number of labeled examples. Then confident predictions for unlabelled examples are added to the set of labeled examples for retraining of the model. Generally, multiple iterations of labelling and retraining are performed. One important hyper-parameter is the selection percentage p, which specifies how many of the most confident predictions are added to the training set after each iteration. We use a small value of p in our experiments to select the most confident predictions only. Generating many more labeled data points in this fashion allows for deep neural networks to be trained to their full capacity, and generally results in significant performance improvements. For more details on this approach see, for instance, our previous work in [18].

In this paper, for network weight initialisation, we transfer pretrained weights from Imagenet classification and fine-tune on the target domain. We compare the performance achieved by this weight transfer to the performance of training using a fully random initialisation of the weights of the neural network.

The proposed approach is very general, suggesting that a spectrum of loss functions and label propagation algorithms can all work well in this framework. We use the most widely used classification loss, i.e., softmax cross-entropy, as a first option. In addition, we explore loss functions based on similarity metric learning. The embeddings produced by the neural network after training with a similarity function can be employed to assign class labels to unlabeled examples using very simple classification methods such as a nearest-neighbor classifier. Below we review the loss functions used for the experiments.

3.1   Softmax Cross-entropy Loss

The single most frequently used classification loss function is softmax cross-entropy, which is a measure of the difference between the desired probability distribution and the predicted probability distribution:

$$\mathcal{L} = -\frac{1}{N} \sum_{i=1}^{N} \log \frac{e^{W_{y_i}^T x_i + b_{y_i}}}{\sum_{j=1}^{c} e^{W_j^T x_i + b_j}}, \tag{1}$$

where $x_i \in \mathbb{R}^d$ denotes the deep features (the "embedding") of the ith sample, belonging to the class y_i, and d is the dimension of the embedding, $W_j \in \mathbb{R}^d$ denotes the jth column of the weight matrix $W \in \mathbb{R}^{d \times c}$ and $b_j \in \mathbb{R}^c$ is the bias term. The batch size for gradient descent is N and c is the number of classes.

3.2   Siamese Networks

Siamese networks [2] are neural networks for training a similarity function given labeled data using one of several possible loss functions. They can be thought of as two identical copies of the same network, sharing all weights. They are particularly suitable for datasets with many classes containing only a few labeled instances per class and can employ any of the loss functions listed below.

Triplet Loss. The triplet loss [21] is widely used. A triplet's anchor example a, positive example p, and negative example n are provided as a training example to the network for getting corresponding embeddings. Normally a and p come from the same class, and n is from a different class. Triplet loss tries to push the negative example's embedding farther away from positive example's one, with a user-specified minimum margin m. Using, e.g., Euclidean distance $d(.,.)$ between embedded examples, the triplet loss is calculated as:

$$\mathcal{L} = max(d(a, p) - d(a, n) + m, 0) \tag{1}$$

Triplet loss tries to push $d(a,p)$ to 0 and $d(a,n)$ to be greater than $d(a,p)+m$. Triplets can be categorized as:

- **Easy triplets**: those with a loss of 0.
- **Hard triplets**: those where n is closer to a than p.
- **Semi-hard triplets**: those where n is not closer to a than p, but is within the margin, thus still returning a positive loss.

In our experiments, we use semi-hard triplets for training of the neural network as they yield more distinctive embeddings [21].

Contrastive Loss. The contrastive loss [8] is a pair-based loss that attempts to bring similar examples closer to each other and push dissimilar examples farther away with respect to a minimum margin m. Contrastive loss for embeddings of two examples x_1 and x_2 can be calculated as follows:

$$\mathcal{L} = y \times d(x_1, x_2) + (1 - y) \times max(0, m - d(x_1, x_2)) \tag{2}$$

Here, $y = 1$ if x_1 and x_2 are from the same class, and $y = 0$ otherwise.

ArcFace Loss. Arcface loss [6] is a modified cross-entropy loss with angular margins in the softmax expression, which is designed for improved discrimination in metric learning. The loss is calculated as:

$$\mathcal{L} = -\frac{1}{N} \sum_{i=1}^{N} \log \frac{e^{s\left(\cos(\theta_{y_i}+m)\right)}}{e^{s\left(\cos(\theta_{y_i}+m)\right)} + \sum_{j=1, j \neq y_i}^{c} e^{s \cos \theta_j}}. \tag{3}$$

θ_j is the angle between the l_2-normalized weight vector W_j and the feature vector x_i. The bias term b_j is ignored for simplicity. The feature vector x_i is l_2-normalised and scaled to s, the radius of the hypersphere. An additive angular margin penalty m is added to the ground truth angle θ_{y_i}.

4   Experiments

For evaluating the effect of transfer learning, we consider three image classification problems. For all datasets, a small subset of labeled examples was chosen according to standard semi-supervised learning practice, with a balanced number of examples from each class. All remaining examples were used as unlabeled training examples. For triplet, contrastive and Arcface loss, k-nearest neighbor is used for label prediction, with $k = 1$ for simplicity. We always include two network version in the comparison: one using randomly initialised weights, and one using pretrained weights from ImageNet. All models are evaluated on the standard test split for each dataset in three different ways: after training only on the initially labeled examples, then after training for a number of meta-iterations using our semi-supervised learning approaches, and also—for comparison—after training on all labeled training examples. The two sets of results computed from a) only the initial labeled examples, and b) all labeled training examples, act as an empirical lower and upper bound for the semi-supervised approaches.

We used the VGG16 network architecture for all experiments. A fully connected layer is added at the end of the model for generating a 256-dimensional embedding space. A mini-batch size of 100 is used for all the experiments. For updating the network parameters, Adam is used as the optimizer, except for contrastive loss, which uses Rmsprop. For triplet, contrastive, and Arcface loss, the distance to the nearest labeled example is used as the confidence score when selecting unlabeled examples for labeling. For softmax cross-entropy loss, the softmax probability score is used as the confidence score. Our proposed self-learning approach was run for 25 meta-iterations and results were averaged over 3 runs with a random selection of initially labeled examples.

4.1   Results

SVHN (Street View House Numbers) comprises 32×32 color images of house numbers. A single image can contain multiple digits, but only the digit in the center is considered for the label prediction. The proposed approaches are evaluated using 1000 labeled instances initially and use a selection percentage of 5% (i.e., in each meta-iteration of self-training, 5% of the remaining unlabeled examples are selected for labeling). Table 1 shows test accuracy for SVHN using all four losses, with random as well as pretrained weights, for the 1000-labeled, the self-learning, and the all-labeled setup.

The CIFAR-10 dataset comprises 32×32 RGB images of ten different object classes. The proposed semi-supervised approaches are evaluated using 4000 labeled instances initially, with a selection percentage of 5% for self-training. Table 2 shows accuracy on the standard test set for all losses using 4000-labeled, all-labeled and self-learning, for pretrained weights from Imagenet as well as random initial weights.

The Plant Village [9] dataset consists of plant leaves. It has 43,456 training and 10,849 test RGB images resized to 96×96 from the original format (256×256). It has 38 categories of species and diseases. A sample image for each class is shown in Fig. 2. The proposed semi-supervised approaches are evaluated using 10 images per class as labeled instances initially, with a selection percentage of 2% in self-learning. Table 3 shows accuracy on test examples for all four losses using 380-labeled, all-labeled and self-learning, with random weight initialization and pretrained weights.

As we can see from the results for all three datasets, using pretrained weights generally results in substantial improvements over random initialisation. When comparing the four loss functions, cross-entropy emerges as the winner, with triplet loss often being second best. However, especially for small numbers of labeled examples, triplet loss seems competitive with cross-entropy, outperforming it for two of the three datasets. This seems reasonable, as paying explicit attention to the similarities of particular instances may be more important when only a few labeled instances are available.

Table 1. SVHN test accuracy %.

Pretrained	1000 Labels	Self-learning	73257 Labels
Cross-entropy loss			
No	75.81 ± 2.28	92.07 ± 0.35	95.72 ± 0.23
Yes	80.84 ± 0.74	**92.73 ± 0.52**	**96.10 ± 0.21**
Triplet loss [21]			
No	57.22 ± 1.81	64.69 ± 1.39	94.79 ± 0.06
Yes	**82.52 ± 2.14**	86.14 ± 1.11	95.12 ± 0.23
Contrastive loss [8]			
No	54.73 ± 0.57	62.80 ± 0.63	81.82 ± 2.29
Yes	79.46 ± 0.99	82.59 ± 0.31	93.41 ± 0.26
Arcface loss [6]			
No	68.33 ± 0.91	70.42 ± 1.59	93.74 ± 0.11
Yes	80.84 ± 0.21	82.01 ± 1.41	95.66 ± 0.31

Table 2. CIFAR10 test accuracy %.

Pretrained	4000 Labels	Self-learning	50000 Labels
Cross-entropy loss			
No	70.43 ± 1.43	79.15 ± 0.80	87.84 ± 0.39
Yes	**77.07 ± 0.91**	**83.33 ± 0.19**	**89.37 ± 0.49**
Triplet loss [21]			
No	68.35 ± 3.63	70.57 ± 1.17	86.54 ± 0.42
Yes	76.42 ± 2.19	78.36 ± 1.39	88.15 ± 0.36
Contrastive loss [8]			
No	34.90 ± 0.73	44.58 ± 1.67	71.16 ± 0.05
Yes	71.98 ± 0.95	76.58 ± 0.05	85.92 ± 0.32
Arcface loss [6]			
No	55.04 ± 1.36	69.54 ± 3.69	75.31 ± 0.24
Yes	74.76 ± 0.72	76.55± 1.80	87.76 ± 0.24

Comparing the three metric losses with each other, triplet loss generally outperforms the other two when using pretrained weights. On the other hand, when using random initial weights, none of the three losses seems to have a clear advantage over the others, except for the Plant dataset, where Arcface performs very well, even outperforming cross-entropy.

Figure 3 shows a comparison of self-learning using random weights and pretrained weights, across three different runs on CIFAR10, using softmax cross-entropy loss for 4000 initially labeled examples and 25 meta-iterations of self-learning. The accuracy curves show similar improvements for both scenarios,

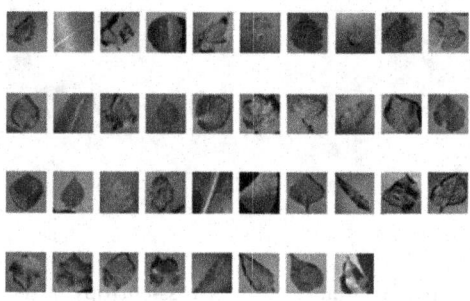

Fig. 2. Plant Village disease [9] dataset

Table 3. Plant village 96 × 96 Test Accuracy %.

Pretrained	380 Labels	Self-learning	43456 Labels
Cross-entropy loss			
No	45.78 ± 4.09	54.58 ± 2.65	98.24 ± 0.62
Yes	73.76 ± 1.70	**84.62 ± 1.2**	99.24 ± 0.08
Triplet loss [21]			
No	29.81 ± 2.59	33.16 ± 1.96	92.15 ± 1.63
Yes	**76.88 ± 0.36**	77.80 ± 1.15	99.02 ± 0.11
Contrastive loss [8]			
No	13.12 ± 1.56	16.35 ± 0.88	34.75 ± 3.20
Yes	30.22 ± 2.14	32.46 ± 2.65	45.66 ± 2.64
Arcface loss [6]			
No	54.85 ± 0.09	58.39 ± 3.61	98.11 ± 0.38
Yes	60.67 ± 0.13	71.80 ± 2.58	**99.32 ± 0.04**

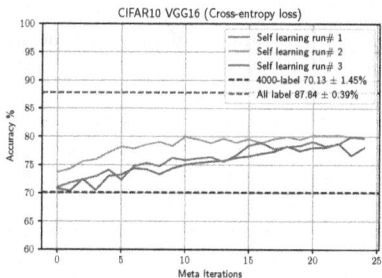

(a) Self-learning with random weights

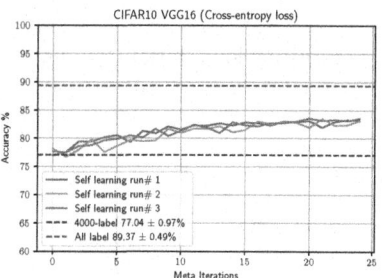

(b) Self-learning with Imagenet weights

Fig. 3. CIFAR10 meta-iterations of self-learning using random and pretrained Imagenet weights.

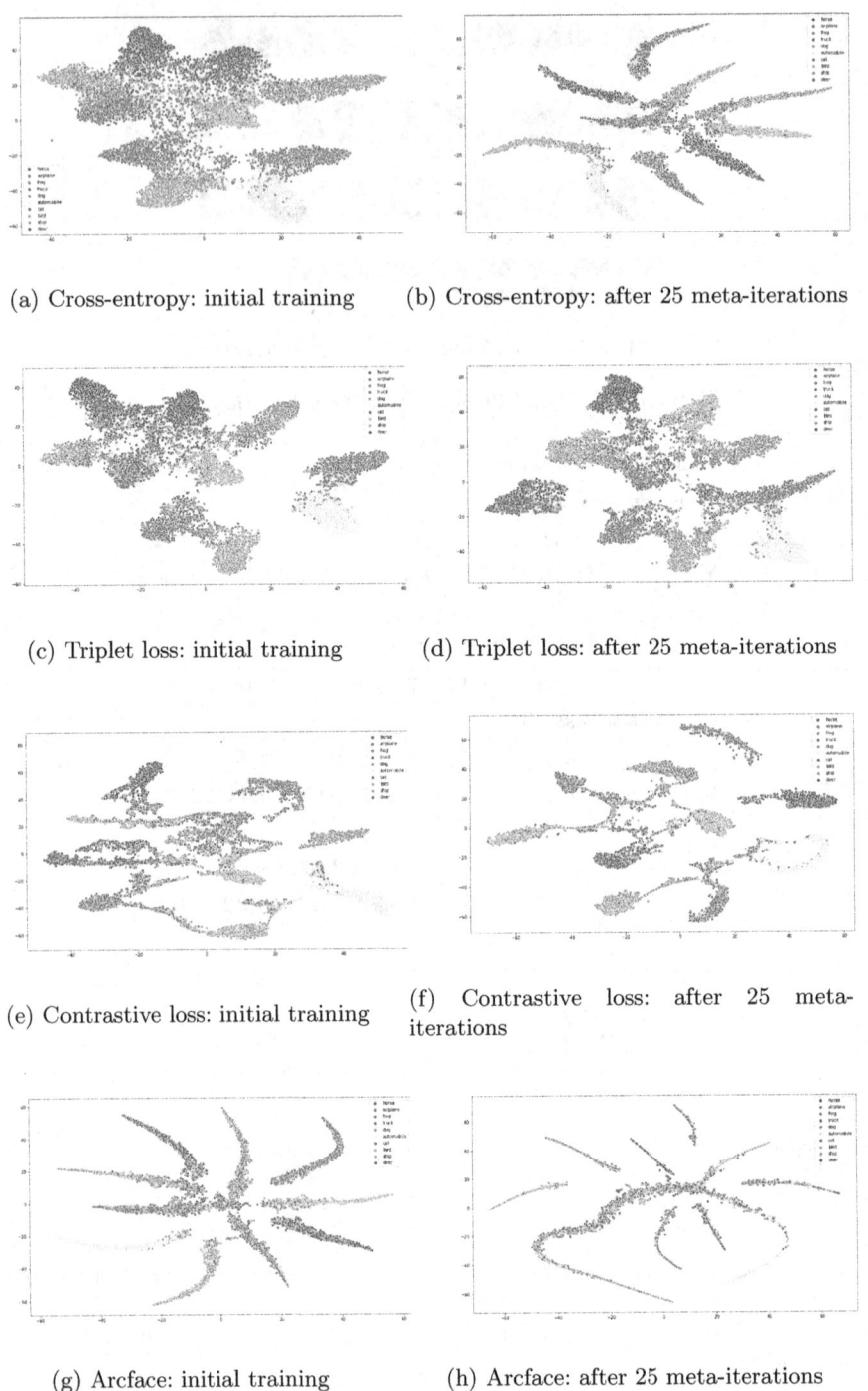

(a) Cross-entropy: initial training   (b) Cross-entropy: after 25 meta-iterations

(c) Triplet loss: initial training   (d) Triplet loss: after 25 meta-iterations

(e) Contrastive loss: initial training   (f) Contrastive loss: after 25 meta-iterations

(g) Arcface: initial training   (h) Arcface: after 25 meta-iterations

Fig. 4. TSNE Visualization of CIFAR10 embeddings for all losses after the first 4000 labeled examples and after 25-meta iterations of self-learning.

with the pretrained version starting from a higher initial accuracy level, and retaining this advantage over the 25 meta-iterations of self-learning.

In order to investigate the effect of self-learning on the embeddings, we visualize the embeddings obtained using all four loss functions. Figure 4 shows the output of TSNE [13] on embeddings of CIFAR10 test instances after training on 4000 labeled examples and after 25 meta-iterations of self-learning using all four losses. It is evident that self-learning improves class separation, with cross-entropy showing the most dramatic improvement, consistent with its high final accuracy.

5 Conclusions

In this paper, we have shown that transfer learning can be highly beneficial for semi-supervised image classification. In terms of loss functions, overall, cross-entropy outperforms more specialised losses like triplet loss, contrastive loss, or Arcface loss. Still, for a small number of labels, triplet loss is very competitive.

There are a number of directions for future work. Exploring combinations of well-performing loss functions, exploring alternatives to the label propagation scheme, and exploring connections to few-shot learning, are just a few obvious ones. Additionally, more lower-level engineering ideas, like mini-batch composition strategies as pointed out in [1], might help to further improve the performance of semi-supervised image classification.

References

1. Arazo, E., Ortego, D., Albert, P., O'Connor, N.E., McGuinness, K.: Pseudo-labeling and confirmation bias in deep semi-supervised learning. In: 2020 International Joint Conference on Neural Networks (IJCNN), pp. 1–8 (2020)
2. Bromley, J., Guyon, I., LeCun, Y., Säckinger, E., Shah, R.: Signature verification using a "Siamese" time delay neural network. Int. J. Pattern Recogn. Artif. Intell. **07**(04), 669–688 (1993)
3. Chapelle, O., Schölkopf, B., Zien, A.: Semi-supervised Learning. The MIT Press, Cambridge (2006)
4. Chopra, S., Hadsell, R., LeCun, Y.: Learning a similarity metric discriminatively, with application to face verification. In: 2005 IEEE Computer Society Conference on Computer Vision and Pattern Recognition (CVPR 2005), vol. 1, pp. 539–546. IEEE (2005)
5. Dai, Z., Yang, Z., Yang, F., Cohen, W.W., Salakhutdinov, R.R.: Good semi-supervised learning that requires a bad GAN. In: Advances in Neural Information Processing Systems, pp. 6513–6523 (2017)
6. Deng, J., Guo, J., Xue, N., Zafeiriou, S.: ArcFace: additive angular margin loss for deep face recognition. In: Proceedings of the IEEE Conference on Computer Vision and Pattern Recognition, pp. 4690–4699 (2019)
7. Girshick, R., Donahue, J., Darrell, T., Malik, J.: Rich feature hierarchies for accurate object detection and semantic segmentation. In: Proceedings of the IEEE Conference on Computer Vision and Pattern Recognition, pp. 580–587 (2014)

8. Hadsell, R., Chopra, S., LeCun, Y.: Dimensionality reduction by learning an invariant mapping. In: 2006 IEEE Computer Society Conference on Computer Vision and Pattern Recognition (CVPR 2006), vol. 2, pp. 1735–1742. IEEE (2006)
9. Hughes, D., Salathé, M., et al.: An open access repository of images on plant health to enable the development of mobile disease diagnostics. arXiv preprint arXiv:1511.08060 (2015)
10. Lee, D.H.: Pseudo-Label: the simple and efficient semi-supervised learning method for deep neural networks. In: Workshop on Challenges in Representation Learning, ICML, vol. 3, p. 2 (2013)
11. Liu, W., Wen, Y., Yu, Z., Li, M., Raj, B., Song, L.: SphereFace: deep hypersphere embedding for face recognition. In: Proceedings of the IEEE Conference on Computer Vision and Pattern Recognition, pp. 212–220 (2017)
12. Maaløe, L., Sønderby, C.K., Sønderby, S.K., Winther, O.: Auxiliary deep generative models. In: Proceedings of the 33rd International Conference on Machine Learning-Volume 48, pp. 1445–1454 (2016)
13. van der Maaten, L., Hinton, G.: Visualizing data using t-SNE. J. Mach. Learn. Res. **9**, 2579–2605 (2008)
14. Miyato, T., Maeda, S., Koyama, M., Ishii, S.: Virtual adversarial training: a regularization method for supervised and semi-supervised learning. IEEE Trans. Pattern Anal. Mach. Intell. **41**(8), 1979–1993 (2018)
15. Rasmus, A., Berglund, M., Honkala, M., Valpola, H., Raiko, T.: Semi-supervised learning with ladder networks. In: Advances in Neural Information Processing Systems, pp. 3546–3554 (2015)
16. Rosenberg, C., Hebert, M., Schneiderman, H.: Semi-supervised self-training of object detection models. In: 2005 Seventh IEEE Workshops on Applications of Computer Vision (WACV/MOTION 2005) - Volume 1. vol. 1, pp. 29–36 (2005)
17. Russakovsky, O., et al.: ImageNet large scale visual recognition challenge. Int. J. Comput. Vision **115**(3), 211–252 (2015)
18. Sahito, A., Frank, E., Pfahringer, B.: Semi-supervised learning using Siamese networks. In: Liu, J., Bailey, J. (eds.) AI 2019. LNCS (LNAI), vol. 11919, pp. 586–597. Springer, Cham (2019). https://doi.org/10.1007/978-3-030-35288-2_47
19. Sajjadi, M., Javanmardi, M., Tasdizen, T.: Regularization with stochastic transformations and perturbations for deep semi-supervised learning. In: Advances in Neural Information Processing Systems, pp. 1163–1171 (2016)
20. Salimans, T., Goodfellow, I., Zaremba, W., Cheung, V., Radford, A., Chen, X.: Improved techniques for training GANs. In: Advances in Neural Information Processing Systems, pp. 2234–2242 (2016)
21. Schroff, F., Kalenichenko, D., Philbin, J.: FaceNet: a unified embedding for face recognition and clustering. In: Proceedings of the IEEE Conference on Computer Vision and Pattern Recognition, pp. 815–823 (2015)
22. Wang, H., et al.: CosFace: large margin cosine loss for deep face recognition. In: Proceedings of the IEEE Conference on Computer Vision and Pattern Recognition, pp. 5265–5274 (2018)
23. Wei, X., Gong, B., Liu, Z., Lu, W., Wang, L.: Improving the improved training of Wasserstein GANs: a consistency term and its dual effect. In: International Conference on Learning Representations (2018)
24. Weston, J., Ratle, F., Mobahi, H., Collobert, R.: Deep learning via semi-supervised embedding. In: Montavon, G., Orr, G.B., Müller, K.-R. (eds.) Neural Networks: Tricks of the Trade. LNCS, vol. 7700, pp. 639–655. Springer, Heidelberg (2012). https://doi.org/10.1007/978-3-642-35289-8_34

A Comparison of Machine Learning Methods for Cross-Domain Few-Shot Learning

Hongyu Wang[1]($\boxtimes$), Henry Gouk[2], Eibe Frank[1], Bernhard Pfahringer[1], and Michael Mayo[1]

[1] Department of Computer Science, University of Waikato, Hamilton, New Zealand
hw168@students.waikato.ac.nz, {eibe,bernhard,mmayo}@waikato.ac.nz
[2] School of Informatics, University of Edinburgh, Edinburgh, UK
henry.gouk@ed.ac.uk

Abstract. We present an empirical evaluation of machine learning algorithms in cross-domain few-shot learning based on a fixed pre-trained feature extractor. Experiments were performed in five target domains (CropDisease, EuroSAT, Food101, ISIC and ChestX) and using two feature extractors: a ResNet10 model trained on a subset of ImageNet known as miniImageNet and a ResNet152 model trained on the ILSVRC 2012 subset of ImageNet. Commonly used machine learning algorithms including logistic regression, support vector machines, random forests, nearest neighbour classification, naïve Bayes, and linear and quadratic discriminant analysis were evaluated on the extracted feature vectors. We also evaluated classification accuracy when subjecting the feature vectors to normalisation using p-norms. Algorithms originally developed for the classification of gene expression data—the nearest shrunken centroid algorithm and LDA ensembles obtained with random projections—were also included in the experiments, in addition to a cosine similarity classifier that has recently proved popular in few-shot learning. The results enable us to identify algorithms, normalisation methods and pre-trained feature extractors that perform well in cross-domain few-shot learning. We show that the cosine similarity classifier and ℓ^2-regularised 1-vs-rest logistic regression are generally the best-performing algorithms. We also show that algorithms such as LDA yield consistently higher accuracy when applied to ℓ^2-normalised feature vectors. In addition, all classifiers generally perform better when extracting feature vectors using the ResNet152 model instead of the ResNet10 model.

Keywords: Cross-domain few-shot learning · Pre-trained feature extractors · Normalisation · Transfer learning

1 Introduction

Convolutional neural networks have greatly changed the way in which supervised learning is used to solve image classification problems. However, they come

© Springer Nature Switzerland AG 2020
M. Gallagher et al. (Eds.): AI 2020, LNAI 12576, pp. 445–457, 2020.
https://doi.org/10.1007/978-3-030-64984-5_35

with one major drawback: a very large volume of annotated images is generally required to train a network with good accuracy. In many situations it is not feasible to gather datasets of sufficient size to train such models, be it due to cost or other resource limitations. In these cases, so-called few-shot learning methods can be applied. Few-shot learning (FSL) refers to the task of learning in a target domain from a very limited number of annotated instances [23]. A key component in practical few-shot learning is prior knowledge gained from a source domain that is in some way related to the target domain. The knowledge gleaned from the source domain can be utilised to compensate for the scarcity of available instances in the target domain, enabling the algorithm to construct a model that can make more accurate predictions than a model trained solely on the target domain. In this sense, few-shot learning generally can be seen as an instance of transfer learning [17].

Modern studies on FSL primarily tackle the case where there is little shift between the source and target domains [20,23]. A common experimental protocol is to take a single dataset and allocate some classes as the source domain, and the remaining classes as the target domain. In contrast, cross-domain few-shot learning (CDFSL) refers to few-shot learning problems where the instances of the source domain and those of the target domain are obtained from strictly different origins (and are not, e.g., instances from the same dataset that belong to different sets of classes) [10]. CDFSL is important because it aims to achieve efficient learning in one field with knowledge from another. This is in line with one of the original pursuits of few-shot learning—giving machine learning human-like sample efficiency in the sense that humans can learn to perform new tasks reasonably well with only a few examples. Perhaps even more importantly, real-world problems that require CDFSL are far more common than those that require learning of new classes in the same domain.

Many existing approaches to FSL involve training a "shallow" (e.g., linear) classifier on features extracted by a convolutional network. These methods typically make use of meta-learning techniques based on episodic training [23] to obtain a feature extractor that can produce domain-general features. A common strategy is to propose new classification rules, such as the nearest centroid classifiers used by prototypical networks [20] or the linear support vector machines (SVMs) used by MetaOptNet [14], and plug them into an episodic training framework. However, interestingly, Guo et al. [10] show that in the CDFSL setting, simple transfer learning performed by pre-training a feature extractor in the source domain and building a linear classifier on the extracted features in the target domain significantly outperforms meta-learning approaches designed for the standard FSL setting. This finding is based on a new benchmark for CDFSL that makes use of miniImageNet (a subset of the ILSVRC 2012 dataset [7]) as the source domain and various other problems as the target domains.

Our paper aims to provide a comprehensive analysis of how different "shallow" classifiers perform when applied to features extracted using a pre-trained network in a CDFSL problem.[1] We make use of the experimental framework developed by Guo et al. [10] to facilitate a further comparison with transfer learning approaches. We also investigate the impact of various normalisation procedures and extend the experimental setting to a larger feature extraction network trained on the full ILSVRC 2012 dataset. Because the number of training instances is very small in relation to the size of the feature vectors, classifiers that were originally designed for analysing data produced in genomics experiments are also included in our comparison.

The main findings of our experiments are that (i) generalisations of linear discriminant analysis are effective for few-shot learning problems, (ii) feature vector normalisation is a useful pre-processing tool, and (iii) logistic regression performs as well as the cosine similarity classifier proposed by Chen et al. [5]—a method competitive with state-of-the-art few-shot learning approaches.

2   Learning Methods and Normalisation Schemes

Multi-class classification is the task of constructing a classifier, $f : \mathcal{X} \rightarrow \mathcal{Y}_T$, that maps from an input space, $\mathcal{X}$, to an output space, $\mathcal{Y}_T$, consisting of n class values, using a training set $Z_T \subset \mathcal{X} \times \mathcal{Y}_T$ sampled from the target domain of interest. An n-way k-shot classification problem, the standard setting in few-shot learning, has exactly k instances for each of the n classes. Cross-domain few-shot learning problems are most commonly solved by first training a feature extractor on an auxiliary set of data, $Z_S \subset \mathcal{X} \times \mathcal{Y}_S$, from a related source domain. Two defining characteristics are (i) the source and target label sets are different (i.e., $\mathcal{Y}_T \neq \mathcal{Y}_S$); and (ii) input data for the source and target domains are sampled according to different distributions (i.e., $p_S(X) \neq p_T(X)$, where X is a random variable taking values in $\mathcal{X}$). Crucially, there are no restrictions on the size of Z_S, the auxiliary set of training data. The framework employed by all recent few-shot learning approaches is to use Z_S to train a feature extractor, g, that maps from $\mathcal{X}$ to some intermediate representation in another vector space, $\mathcal{I}$. Then Z_T, the smaller training set in the target domain, is used to construct a classifier, h, that maps from $\mathcal{I}$ to $\mathcal{Y}_T$. Finally, f is obtained via their composition, $f = h \circ g$. In our paper, g is assumed to be a convolutional neural network that has been pre-trained on a source domain classification problem.

In the benchmark proposed by Guo et al. [10], ImageNet is utilised as the source domain, and the target domains are CropDisease [16], EuroSAT [11], ISIC [22] and ChestX [24]. We adopt this benchmark for our experiments, and include another dataset, Food101 [3], which acts as an additional highly-specialised classification task that can be used as a target domain.

2.1   Robust Learning Algorithms

One of the defining characteristics of few-shot learning is that one must train a classifier on a small number of instances (typically in the region of 10–100) but

---

[1] Our code and data are available at https://zenodo.org/record/4047034/files/CDFSL_reproducibility.zip?download=1.

each instance may have hundreds or thousands of dimensions. Other machine learning application domains, such as genomics and natural language processing problems dealing with bag-of-words representations, also exhibit similar issues. As such, we include a number of learning algorithms specifically designed for this scenario, but motivated by different applications. The full list of methods we consider for training the classifier h comprises the following algorithms:

- Logistic regression (LR) [13], using multinomial or 1-vs-rest classification
- Linear discriminant analysis (LDA) [15]
- Random projection LDA ensemble [8]
- Linear SVM [18], using pairwise or 1-vs-rest classification
- Naïve Bayes [25]
- k-nearest neighbours (kNN) [1]
- Random forests [4]
- Nearest shrunken centroid [21]
- Cosine similarity [5]

2.2 Normalisation Methods

We also consider the impact of normalising feature vectors for machine learning. For a vector, $\vec{x}$, containing values $x_1, x_2, \ldots, x_n$, normalisation is defined as

$$\text{norm}_p(\vec{x}) = \frac{\vec{x}}{\left(\sum_{k=1}^{n} |x_k|^p\right)^{\frac{1}{p}}}, \tag{1}$$

where p indicates the ℓ^p norm used in the normalisation process. Applying norm_1 corresponds to dividing each element in the vector by the sum of its absolute values, norm_2 divides by the Euclidean norm, and norm_∞ divides by the maximum absolute value in the vector. After normalisation, the resulting vector will have length one in whatever norm was applied in this process. Crucially, this form of scaling differs significantly from multiplying all instances in the training dataset by a single number, as is done when dividing by the variance during standardisation: the value used to scale the features is instance dependent.

3   Theoretical Analysis of Normalised Linear Classifiers

In this section, we consider the impact on Rademacher-based generalisation bounds [2] from normalising feature vectors when using a linear model, and provide a theoretical explanation on the benefit of normalisation in CDFSL. A standard Rademacher-based generalisation bound takes the form of

$$R(h) \leq \frac{1}{m} \sum_{i=1}^{m} \ell(h(\vec{x}_i), y_i) + 2\hat{\mathcal{R}}(H) + O\left(\frac{1}{\sqrt{m}}\right), \tag{2}$$

where ℓ is a 1-Lipschitz loss function, R is the risk (i.e., expected loss), H is a hypothesis class, $h \in H$ is a single hypothesis, and m is the size of the training set. The complexity of the hypothesis class can be characterised via empirical Rademacher complexity [2],

$$\hat{\mathcal{R}}(H) = \mathbb{E}_{\vec{\sigma}}\left[\sup_{h \in H} \sum_{i=1}^{m} \sigma_i h(\vec{x}_i)\right],$$

where $\vec{\sigma}$ is a vector of Rademacher distributed random variables. A commonly known [19] upper bound for the empirical Rademacher complexity of a linear function class,

$$H = \{\vec{x} \mapsto \vec{x} \cdot \vec{w} : \|\vec{w}\| \leq B\},$$

is given by

$$\hat{\mathcal{R}}(H) = \frac{XB}{\sqrt{m}},$$

where B is the upper bound for the Euclidean norm of the weight vector $\vec{w}$ and X is the smallest number for which $\|\vec{x}_i\|_2 \leq X, \forall i \in \{1, \ldots, m\}$. One can see immediately from this bound that any preprocessing step that reduces the Euclidean norm of feature vectors reduces the capacity for a fixed linear hypothesis class to overfit the training data. However, this does not take into account how a preprocessing step might affect the loss on the training dataset—the other quantity that is used to bound the expected loss in Eq. 2.

Denote by S the training set $\{(\vec{x}_i, y_i)\}_{i=1}^{m}$. We shall assume that $X = 1$. Note that this is not a very limiting assumption, as all feature vectors in the training set can be scaled by some value, $c = \frac{1}{\max_i \|\vec{x}_i\|_2}$, to make this true, and then B can be scaled by $\frac{1}{c}$ to ensure $\hat{\mathcal{R}}(H)$ remains the same. Now we let $Z = \{(\vec{z}_i, y_i) \mid \vec{z}_i = \mathrm{norm}_2(\vec{x}_i)\}_{i=1}^{m}$ be a normalised version of the training set. Trivially, we have that $\|\vec{x}_i\|_2 \leq \|\vec{z}_i\|_2$, with equality occurring only if $\|\vec{x}_i\|_2 = 1$.

For simplicity, let us consider the case where ℓ is the hinge loss,

$$\ell(\vec{x}, y) = [1 - y\vec{x} \cdot \vec{w}]_+.$$

We can see that for a single instance

$$\ell(\vec{x}_i, y_i) \geq [1 - |y_i \vec{x}_i \cdot \vec{w}|]_+$$
$$\geq [1 - \|\vec{x}_i\|_2 \cdot \|\vec{w}\|_2]_+$$
$$\geq [1 - \|\vec{z}_i\|_2 \cdot \|\vec{w}\|_2]_+,$$

where the first inequality is due to decreasing monotonicity, the second is from the Cauchy-Schwarz inequality, and the last is because $\|\vec{x}_i\|_2 \leq \|\vec{z}_i\|_2$. This demonstrates that the potential for $\vec{z}_i$ to have a larger magnitude than $\vec{x}_i$ can lead to a lower loss when normalisation is used. Because the hinge loss is an upper bound for the zero–one loss, this may also improve classification accuracy.

Table 1. 5-shot experimental results with the ResNet10 feature extractor

	CropDisease	EuroSAT	Food101	ISIC	ChestX
Naïve Bayes	82.92 ± 0.75	73.24 ± 0.75	42.19 ± 0.75	37.23 ± 0.6	22.04 ± 0.38
kNN	78.86 ± 0.74	57.85 ± 0.78	44.51 ± 0.73	37.68 ± 0.6	23.97 ± 0.39
Random Forest	83.00 ± 0.66	73.40 ± 0.68	48.27 ± 0.70	43.00 ± 0.54	24.26 ± 0.43
LDA	89.09 ± 0.56	75.52 ± 0.65	56.85 ± 0.77	43.97 ± 0.59	25.40 ± 0.41
QDA	88.30 ± 0.58	77.86 ± 0.61	57.58 ± 0.77	44.70 ± 0.57	25.27 ± 0.41
Pairwise SVM	88.55 ± 0.59	76.14 ± 0.67	57.28 ± 0.76	44.08 ± 0.58	25.30 ± 0.41
1-vs-rest SVM	89.03 ± 0.58	75.60 ± 0.69	57.80 ± 0.77	42.17 ± 0.59	25.29 ± 0.41
1-vs-rest LR ℓ^2	89.66 ± 0.56	78.82 ± 0.61	**60.19 ± 0.78**	45.76 ± 0.58	25.85 ± 0.42
1-vs-rest LR ℓ^1	66.51 ± 0.88	46.52 ± 0.81	40.38 ± 0.68	27.70 ± 0.48	21.35 ± 0.37
Multinomial LR	88.64 ± 0.58	77.68 ± 0.63	57.50 ± 0.77	45.42 ± 0.59	25.41 ± 0.42
LDA ensemble	89.05 ± 0.56	75.68 ± 0.64	56.76 ± 0.77	44.17 ± 0.59	25.36 ± 0.43
Shrunken centroid	87.46 ± 0.62	75.23 ± 0.67	56.36 ± 0.77	42.17 ± 0.59	25.00 ± 0.44
Cosine similarity	**89.71 ± 0.55**	**79.56 ± 0.6**	59.44 ± 0.78	**46.6 ± 0.59**	**25.86 ± 0.42**

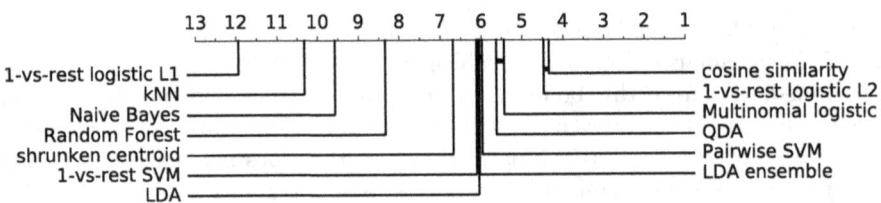

Fig. 1. Critical difference diagram of the algorithms with the ResNet10 feature extractor

4   Empirical Comparison

Two pre-trained networks are used for extracting features from images: a ResNet10 model trained on miniImageNet using the code provided by Guo et al. [10], and the ResNet152 model trained on the 2012 ILSVRC subset of ImageNet that is available through Keras [6]. Both models receive as input 224×224 pixel RGB images. The smaller network (ResNet10) produces 512-dimensional feature vectors, whereas the larger network produces feature vectors with 2,048 components.

For each target domain dataset, a large number of 5-way k-shot learning problems are generated: 600 different few-shot learning problems per target domain dataset for each value of $k \in \{5, 20, 50\}$. Each of these problems contains 15 test instances per class, regardless of the number of training instances. After features are extracted for each image using either of the feature extractors, the shallow learners are trained using the WEKA software (Version 3.9.5) [9].

4.1   Performance of Classifiers for Few-Shot Learning

The first experiments aim to determine which of the classifiers we consider are most useful for few-shot learning problems. For these experiments, all classifiers

Table 2. 5-shot experimental results with the ResNet152 feature extractor

	CropDisease	EuroSAT	Food101	ISIC	ChestX
Naïve Bayes	92.71 ± 0.51	82.90 ± 0.51	69.99 ± 0.87	37.31 ± 0.52	23.04 ± 0.39
kNN	81.67 ± 0.72	64.68 ± 0.72	57.05 ± 0.88	34.04 ± 0.53	23.29 ± 0.37
Random Forest	89.75 ± 0.57	79.48 ± 0.56	64.45 ± 0.78	38.64 ± 0.53	23.80 ± 0.40
LDA	93.74 ± 0.46	86.74 ± 0.49	77.90 ± 0.71	42.18 ± 0.56	24.89 ± 0.41
QDA	93.29 ± 0.48	86.72 ± 0.50	78.05 ± 0.72	40.77 ± 0.55	25.29 ± 0.42
Pairwise SVM	93.50 ± 0.47	86.70 ± 0.50	78.02 ± 0.72	42.04 ± 0.57	25.29 ± 0.43
1-vs-rest SVM	93.63 ± 0.47	86.93 ± 0.49	78.53 ± 0.70	42.08 ± 0.57	25.02 ± 0.43
1-vs-rest logistic ℓ^2	**93.79 ± 0.46**	87.62 ± 0.47	**79.42 ± 0.69**	**43.28 ± 0.56**	**25.30 ± 0.42**
1-vs-rest logistic ℓ^1	88.53 ± 0.60	81.18 ± 0.56	72.18 ± 0.77	39.49 ± 0.57	24.32 ± 0.41
Multinomial logistic	93.59 ± 0.47	87.22 ± 0.48	78.74 ± 0.70	42.52 ± 0.56	25.27 ± 0.44
LDA ensemble	93.72 ± 0.47	86.7 ± 0.49	77.93 ± 0.71	42.32 ± 0.56	24.97 ± 0.41
Shrunken centroid	92.26 ± 0.52	85.65 ± 0.5	76.97 ± 0.74	40.70 ± 0.56	24.92 ± 0.43
Cosine similarity	93.77 ± 0.47	**87.67 ± 0.47**	79.34 ± 0.69	42.98 ± 0.56	25.22 ± 0.42

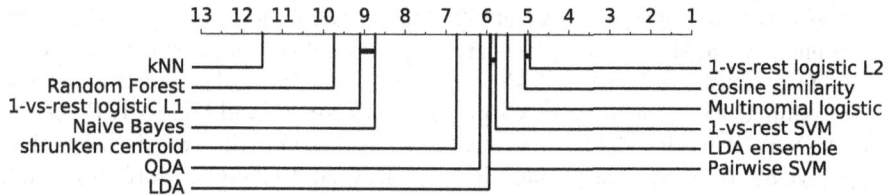

Fig. 2. Critical difference diagram of the algorithms with the ResNet152 feature extractor

are applied to each of the target domains, using un-normalised feature vectors extracted by both networks. In this subsection, only 5-shot problems are considered. The results for ResNet10 features are given in Table 1, and the results corresponding to ResNet152 features are provided in Table 2. Figures 1 and 2 demonstrate statistical significance of the performance differences between classifiers, aggregated across all datasets, as determined by the Wilcoxon-Holm test (procedure described in [12], on page 22).

The first observation is that ℓ^1-regularised 1-vs-rest LR, naïve Bayes, kNN, and random forests are significantly outperformed by the other approaches. The poor performance of ℓ^1-regularised LR, compared to other linear models, is mostly due to the difficulty in finding a suitable regularisation value that leads to consistently good performance. Note that grid search was not used to tune the hyperparameters because it yielded lower accuracy than using the algorithms' default hyperparameters in WEKA. The most likely reason is that the training and test folds in this set-up are very small, inducing high variance in the accuracy estimates obtained using cross-validation.

The second observation is that variants of LDA perform competitively with other linear models, which suggests that developing new generalisations of LDA specifically for few-shot learning could be a fruitful direction for future research.

Another finding is that ℓ^2-regularised LR and the cosine similarity classifier—a method that is known to be competitive with the state-of-the-art [5]—perform similarly. Considering ℓ^2-regularised LR is perhaps the oldest and most established way to perform transfer learning in a deep learning context, this raises the question of whether any significant progress has been made by introducing variants of this basic approach to formulating linear classifiers.

The accuracy of all of the algorithms decreases as the domain shift increases, consistent with the findings of Guo et al. [10]. In particular, among the four datasets of the original CDFSL benchmark, CropDisease results in the highest accuracy for all of the algorithms, followed by EuroSAT, ISIC and ChestX in this exact order, with all of the algorithms performing only slightly better than random guessing on ChestX (i.e., 20%). For all of the algorithms, the accuracy on Food101 is shown to be consistently between EuroSAT and ISIC. It can therefore be speculated that the domain shift from ImageNet to Food101 is greater than the domain shift from ImageNet to EuroSAT and smaller than that from ImageNet to ISIC.

The more sophisticated ResNet152 feature extractor, trained on the more comprehensive version of ImageNet, grants a very substantial performance boost to all of the classifiers over the ResNet10 model on the three datasets that are relatively similar to ImageNet, i.e., CropDisease, EuroSAT and Food101. However, the ResNet152 model yields a performance decrease on the two datasets that are relatively different from ImageNet, i.e., ISIC and ChestX. More discussion on the relation between feature extractors and task domains will be provided in Sect. 4.3.

4.2   Feature Normalisation

We now consider the effect of normalising the feature vectors in 5-shot learning. Table 3 shows the accuracy of the algorithms on Food101-ResNet152 feature vectors normalised in various ways, with the best result for each learning algorithm shown in bold.

1-vs-rest logistic regression with ℓ^1 regularisation, with its default regularisation hyperparameter value (i.e., $cost = 1$ in the LIBLINEAR implementation used in WEKA), is observed to achieve low accuracy with ℓ^p normalised data, ranging from 20% to 57.83%. When given a large value of the regularisation parameter (e.g., $cost = 10^{10}$), thus enabling closer fit to the training data, its accuracy improves, achieving 77.4% with ℓ^1 normalised data. Unfortunately, such a large value decreases the classifier's performance with un-normalised feature vectors to 66.57%.

It should be noted that the normalisation method is irrelevant to the cosine similarity classifier, because the direction of each feature vector is used for classification and all of the feature vectors are ℓ^2-normalised in the classifier. This means that the cosine similarity classifier produces the same result regardless of whether the feature vectors are normalised, or the value of p in ℓ^p normalisation.

Table 3 shows that LDA with ℓ^2 normalisation achieves very competitive performance on the Food101-ResNet152 feature vectors. Further experiments

Table 3. Accuracy of the algorithms on ℓ^p-normalised Food101-ResNet152 feature vectors

	None	ℓ^1	ℓ^2	ℓ^3	ℓ^∞
Naïve Bayes	69.99 ± 0.87	70.54 ± 0.87	$\mathbf{70.81 \pm 0.85}$	70.32 ± 0.86	67.91 ± 0.87
kNN	57.05 ± 0.88	$\mathbf{64.06 \pm 0.85}$	62.80 ± 0.85	59.10 ± 0.88	51.98 ± 0.85
Random Forest	64.45 ± 0.78	$\mathbf{65.19 \pm 0.78}$	64.74 ± 0.80	64.27 ± 0.81	63.36 ± 0.77
LDA	77.90 ± 0.71	77.76 ± 0.70	$\mathbf{79.06 \pm 0.69}$	78.74 ± 0.71	74.57 ± 0.76
QDA	78.05 ± 0.72	77.70 ± 0.71	$\mathbf{78.95 \pm 0.71}$	78.53 ± 0.71	75.27 ± 0.75
Pairwise SVM	78.02 ± 0.72	74.00 ± 0.77	74.76 ± 0.79	$\mathbf{78.84 \pm 0.72}$	74.63 ± 0.77
1-vs-rest SVM	78.53 ± 0.70	70.33 ± 0.87	77.00 ± 0.74	$\mathbf{79.00 \pm 0.71}$	76.16 ± 0.74
1-vs-rest LR ℓ^2	79.42 ± 0.69	77.68 ± 0.71	79.36 ± 0.69	$\mathbf{79.89 \pm 0.68}$	79.57 ± 0.69
1-vs-rest LR ℓ^1	$\mathbf{72.18 \pm 0.77}$	20.00 ± 0.00	20.17 ± 0.14	34.94 ± 0.86	57.83 ± 0.91
Multinomial LR	$\mathbf{78.74 \pm 0.70}$	72.91 ± 0.70	78.68 ± 0.71	$\mathbf{78.74 \pm 0.71}$	75.83 ± 0.74
LDA ensemble	77.93 ± 0.71	77.58 ± 0.69	$\mathbf{78.85 \pm 0.69}$	78.54 ± 0.70	74.75 ± 0.75
Shrunken centroid	76.97 ± 0.74	77.46 ± 0.75	$\mathbf{78.32 \pm 0.73}$	77.83 ± 0.74	73.59 ± 0.81
Cosine similarity	79.34 ± 0.69	79.35 ± 0.69	79.34 ± 0.69	79.34 ± 0.69	79.35 ± 0.69

show that LDA gains a performance increase from ℓ^2 normalisation as opposed to no normalisation on all of the datasets. This is shown in Table 4. It can be argued that certain normalisation methods can give certain algorithms a consistent increase in CDFSL performance, and thus a competitive edge. One such example is LDA with ℓ^2 normalisation.

Table 4. Comparison between no normalisation and ℓ^2 normalisation for LDA on all of the datasets

	CropDisease	EuroSAT	Food101	ISIC	ChestX
None	93.74 ± 0.46	86.74 ± 0.49	77.9 ± 0.71	42.18 ± 0.56	24.89 ± 0.41
ℓ^2 normalisation	$\mathbf{93.95 \pm 0.45}$	$\mathbf{87.30 \pm 0.48}$	$\mathbf{79.06 \pm 0.69}$	$\mathbf{42.48 \pm 0.56}$	$\mathbf{25.11 \pm 0.40}$

4.3   Few-Shot Fine-Grained Classification

Particularly accurate results are obtained on the CropDisease data in the experiments presented above, but it is noteworthy that in fact, this is a dataset of *both* plant species and different plant diseases. Table 5 shows the relation between the classification accuracy and the number of plant species present in the training and test data in each of the 600 runs performed for the 5-way 5-shot experiment, using 1-vs-rest logistic regression with ℓ^2 regularisation on the unnormalised CropDisease-ResNet152 feature vectors. In each of the 600 iterations of the experiment, i.e., a classification task with 5 classes, the presence of more plant species indicates that less disease classification is involved: an iteration

Table 5. Classification accuracy increases as the number of selected plant classes increases in the 5-way 5-shot CropDisease data. Summarised from the 600 iterations of 1-vs-rest logistic regression with ℓ^2 regularisation on the un-normalised CropDisease-ResNet152 feature vectors.

	Mean	Min	Median	Max
2 species and 3 in-species diseases (8 iter)	83.50	76.00	81.33	96.00
3 species and 2 in-species diseases (89 iter)	88.13	60.00	89.33	**100.0**
4 species and 1 in-species disease (274 iter)	93.41	76.00	94.67	**100.0**
5 species and 0 in-species disease (229 iter)	**96.43**	**85.33**	**97.33**	**100.0**

with five plant species virtually becomes a pure plant classification task. The table shows that the accuracy is positively correlated with the number of plant species in an iteration.

Thus, to investigate the effect of the two feature extractors on purely the task of fine-grained classification of *plant diseases*, we propose use of the TomatoDisease dataset, a subset of CropDisease that contains all of its instances pertaining to tomato diseases. TomatoDisease does not involve different plant species and focuses solely on tomato diseases, making this a much more challenging problem. Table 6 shows the accuracy of the classifiers is lower on TomatoDisease when compared with the original CropDisease.

Table 6. TomatoDisease leads to lower classification accuracy than CropDisease for all of the algorithms.

Accuracy	ResNet10		ResNet152	
	CropDisease	TomatoDisease	CropDisease	TomatoDisease
Naïve Bayes	82.92 ± 0.75	57.87 ± 0.79	92.71 ± 0.51	68.35 ± 0.66
kNN	78.86 ± 0.74	59.04 ± 0.66	81.67 ± 0.72	56.12 ± 0.70
Random Forest	83.00 ± 0.66	62.10 ± 0.65	89.75 ± 0.57	64.63 ± 0.62
LDA	89.09 ± 0.56	$\mathbf{71.54 \pm 0.63}$	93.74 ± 0.46	$\mathbf{74.69 \pm 0.63}$
QDA	88.30 ± 0.58	70.95 ± 0.62	93.29 ± 0.48	73.32 ± 0.62
Pairwise SVM	88.55 ± 0.59	71.10 ± 0.64	93.50 ± 0.47	73.95 ± 0.62
1-vs-rest SVM	89.03 ± 0.58	71.07 ± 0.61	93.63 ± 0.47	74.32 ± 0.63
1-vs-rest LR ℓ^2	89.66 ± 0.56	71.31 ± 0.63	$\mathbf{93.79 \pm 0.46}$	74.60 ± 0.63
1-vs-rest LR ℓ^1	66.51 ± 0.88	47.89 ± 0.70	88.53 ± 0.60	65.96 ± 0.65
Multinomial LR	88.64 ± 0.58	70.61 ± 0.62	93.59 ± 0.47	73.70 ± 0.62
LDA ensemble	89.05 ± 0.56	71.51 ± 0.62	93.72 ± 0.47	74.58 ± 0.63
Shrunken centroid	87.46 ± 0.62	68.31 ± 0.68	92.26 ± 0.52	71.36 ± 0.65
Cosine similarity	$\mathbf{89.71 \pm 0.55}$	71.36 ± 0.62	93.77 ± 0.47	74.17 ± 0.61

All of the instances and classes in TomatoDisease are from the original CropDisease dataset, and yet the robust classifiers exhibit significantly worse performance on TomatoDisease than CropDisease when using a feature extractor trained on ImageNet. Thus, it can be argued that domain shift between datasets is not only related to the superficial differences in instance properties (such as image colours, perspectives and objects in them) but also the nature of the tasks represented by the datasets in question. When two tasks are similar in format but different in nature, it can still be hard, even for a sophisticated and well-trained AI system, to perform adequately in one task by relying mainly on its empirical knowledge of the other task.

5   Conclusion

In this paper, we evaluated and compared different robust learning algorithms, normalisation methods and pre-trained feature extractors in the context of cross-domain few-shot learning. We demonstrated that the combination of a good robust classifier, an effective feature extractor, and a suitable normalisation method, can provide a significant performance increase in CDFSL problems. We showed that, in the various CDFSL experiments we performed, the cosine similarity classifier and 1-vs-rest logistic regression with ℓ^2 regularisation are consistent top-performers amongst the algorithms we evaluated, which indicates that the old and established ℓ^2-regularised logistic regression is a viable alternative to the competitive cosine similarity classifier in CDFSL. It was also shown that algorithms used in the gene expression domain, namely the random projection ensemble of LDA classifier and the nearest shrunken centroid classifier, are applicable in CDFSL scenarios. We additionally demonstrated that certain combinations of classifiers and normalisation methods perform consistently better in CDFSL tasks than their counterparts without normalisation; one such example is LDA with ℓ^2-normalised feature vectors. Finally, more sophisticated and better trained feature extractors are shown to increase the classification accuracy considerably for target domains that are similar to the source domain in properties and concept, while this positive effect is weakened or virtually non-existent for target domains that are drastically different from the source domain.

Research questions that can be derived from our paper include:

1. Can the top-performing robust classifiers in CDFSL be utilised to improve semi-supervised learning approaches?
2. How to methodically structure and train feature extractors to achieve an optimal transfer between source domains and target domains?
3. How to systematically quantify domain shift?
4. How to assemble datasets from accessible data to have minimal domain shift to known real-world problems?

References

1. Aha, D.W., Kibler, D., Albert, M.K.: Instance-based learning algorithms. Mach. Learn. **6**, 37–66 (1991). https://doi.org/10.1007/BF00153759

2. Bartlett, P.L., Mendelson, S.: Rademacher and Gaussian complexities: risk bounds and structural results. J. Mach. Learn. Res. **3**, 463–482 (2002)

3. Bossard, L., Guillaumin, M., Van Gool, L.: Food-101 – mining discriminative components with random forests. In: Fleet, D., Pajdla, T., Schiele, B., Tuytelaars, T. (eds.) ECCV 2014. LNCS, vol. 8694, pp. 446–461. Springer, Cham (2014). https://doi.org/10.1007/978-3-319-10599-4_29

4. Breiman, L.: Random forests. Mach. Learn. **45**(1), 5–32 (2001). https://doi.org/10.1023/a:1010933404324

5. Chen, W.-Y., Liu, Y.-C., Kira, Z., Wang, Y.-C.F., Huang, J.-B.: A closer look at few-shot classification. In: ICLR (2019)

6. Chollet, F., et al.: Keras (2015). https://keras.io

7. Deng, J., Dong, W., Socher, R., Li, L.-J., Li, K., Fei-Fei, L.: ImageNet: a large-scale hierarchical image database. In: CVPR, pp. 248–255 (2009)

8. Durrant, R.J., Kabán, A.: Random projections as regularizers: learning a linear discriminant from fewer observations than dimensions. Mach. Learn. **99**(2), 257–286 (2014). https://doi.org/10.1007/s10994-014-5466-8

9. Frank, E., Hall, M.A., Witten, I.H.: The WEKA Workbench. Online Appendix for "Data Mining: Practical Machine Learning Tools and Techniques", 4th edn. Morgan Kaufmann, Burlington (2016)

10. Guo, Y., et al.: A broader study of cross-domain few-shot learning. In: ECCV (2020)

11. Helber, P., Bischke, B., Dengel, A., Borth, D.: EuroSAT: a novel dataset and deep learning benchmark for land use and land cover classification. IEEE J. Sel. Top. Appl. Earth Obs. Remote Sens. **12**(7), 2217–2226 (2019)

12. Ismail Fawaz, H., Forestier, G., Weber, J., Idoumghar, L., Muller, P.-A.: Deep learning for time series classification: a review. Data Min. Knowl. Disc. **33**(4), 917–963 (2019). https://doi.org/10.1007/s10618-019-00619-1

13. le Cessie, S., van Houwelingen, J.C.: Ridge estimators in logistic regression. Appl. Stat. **41**(1), 191–201 (1992)

14. Lee, K., Maji, S., Ravichandran, A., Soatto, S.: Meta-learning with differentiable convex optimization. In: CVPR, pp. 10657–10665 (2019)

15. McLachlan, G.J.: Discriminant Analysis and Statistical Pattern Recognition. Wiley, Hoboken (1992)

16. Mohanty, S.P., Hughes, D.P., Salathé, M.: Using deep learning for image-based plant disease detection. Front. Plant Sci. **7**, 1419 (2016)

17. Pan, S.J., Yang, Q.: A survey on transfer learning. IEEE Trans. Knowl. Data Eng. **22**(10), 1345–1359 (2010)

18. Platt, J.: Fast training of support vector machines using sequential minimal optimization. In: Advances in Kernel Methods: Support Vector Learning, pp. 185–208, February 1999

19. Shalev-Shwartz, S., Ben-David, S.: Understanding Machine Learning: From Theory to Algorithms. Cambridge University Press, Cambridge (2014)

20. Snell, J., Swersky, K., Zemel, R.S.: Prototypical networks for few-shot learning. In: NIPS, pp. 4077–4087 (2017)

21. Tibshirani, R., Hastie, T., Narasimhan, B., Chu, G.: Class prediction by nearest shrunken centroids, with applications to DNA microarrays. Stat. Sci. **18**(1), 104–117 (2003)

22. Tschandl, P., Rosendahl, C., Kittler, H.: The HAM10000 Dataset, a large collection of multi-source dermatoscopic images of common pigmented skin lesions. Sci. Data **5**, 180161 (2018)

23. Vinyals, O., Blundell, C., Lillicrap, T.P., Kavukcuoglu, K., Wierstra, D.: Matching networks for one shot learning. In: NIPS, pp. 3630–3638 (2016)
24. Wang, X., Peng, Y., Lu, L., Lu, Z., Bagheri, M., Summers, R.M.: ChestX-Ray8: hospital-scale chest x-ray database and benchmarks on weakly-supervised classification and localization of common thorax diseases. In: CVPR, pp. 3462–3471 (2017)
25. Yang, Y., Webb, G.I.: Discretization for Naive-Bayes learning: managing discretization bias and variance. Mach. Learn. **74**(1), 39–74 (2009). https://doi.org/10.1007/s10994-008-5083-5

Analysis and Prediction of Player Population Changes in Digital Games During the COVID-19 Pandemic

Dulakshi Wannigamage$^{(\boxtimes)}$ ⓘ, Michael Barlow ⓘ, Erandi Lakshika ⓘ,
and Kathryn Kasmarik ⓘ

School of Engineering and IT, The University of New South Wales,
Canberra, Australia
d.wannigamage@student.unsw.edu.au,
{m.barlow,e.henekankanamge,kathryn.kasmarik}@adfa.edu.au

Abstract. The demand for video games increased in large scale during the COVID-19 pandemic as people had to stay at home. In this study we investigate the changes in player population of games during the pandemic using our dataset of 1963 games on Steam to generate insights that would be valuable for the game industry to understand the demand in such crisis. We conduct an empirical analysis to analyse changes in player population size and weekly patterns. Also, we investigate the use of machine learning classification models to predict the games that become popular during the pandemic using information about games as features. Our results indicate a 33% of increase of population during the pandemic and diminishing of weekly player population patterns. Also, we identify that the Random Forest model performs better than other classification models in predicting popular games, however, with only a 63% accuracy and tags assigned to games are the most important feature for prediction generation. Our tag analysis reveals Multiplayer, Adventure, Racing and Boardgames are popular during the pandemic.

Keywords: Video games · COVID-19 · Player populations · Machine learning · Classification

1 Introduction

COVID-19 is a new form of the coronavirus that causes respiratory infections [18] which resulted in a global pandemic. In an attempt to control the spread of the virus, countries took various actions such as enforcing travel restrictions, lockdowns, stay at home advices and closing non-essential business. Hence the pandemic had caused various disruptions to the normal life styles of people [3]. Also, many industries faced socio-economical crisis and it resulted in an increase of loss of employments [15].

The digital game industry is one of the largest entertainment industries in the world. The industry was mostly resilient to the impacts from the pandemic as

© Springer Nature Switzerland AG 2020
M. Gallagher et al. (Eds.): AI 2020, LNAI 12576, pp. 458–469, 2020.
https://doi.org/10.1007/978-3-030-64984-5_36

demand for gaming increased in record numbers with people including children staying at home [8] and outdoor entertainment became inaccessible. However, since the COVID-19 pandemic is a very recent event, there are not many studies that have thoroughly investigated the changes of demand for games with respect to the increased interest of people in gaming. Nonetheless, understanding player behaviour during the pandemic, specially with respect to changes in player population size is quite useful to be better prepared for such future crisis events. It would aid in determining resource allocation and predicting demand and preference for various games helping the gaming industry to thrive during such crisis.

Hence, our aim in this study is to provide a thorough understanding on changes in game player populations and to predict the games that become popular during the pandemic. For this purpose we use player population data of 1963 games on Steam[1] platform we have been collecting since December 2017, along with information about these games. The key contributions and findings of this study is as follows.

1. An Empirical analysis that uses the top 500 games in the dataset to generate insights on player population changes of games during the pandemic: The analysis revealed that the aggregate player population has increased by 33% after the 16th of March 2020 when the United States announced compulsory social distancing guidelines [13]. Moreover, player population during the pandemic was not only significantly higher than the population during the same period in the previous year but also major Steam sale event periods. Furthermore, through an autocorrelation based weekly seasonality detection process we identified that 76% of games did not display recurring weekly player population patterns during the pandemic although most games displayed weekly patterns prior to pandemic as identified in our previous work [17].
2. Classification models to predict highly popular games during the pandemic: We trained Decision Tree, Tree Bagging, Tree Boosting, Random Forest and Support Vector Machines using game related features in which the Random Forest model performed best, however, only with an accuracy of 63%. Additionally, we identified that tags assigned to games are the most important feature for the prediction process and a tag analysis was also conducted.

2   Related Work

With all the changes happening across the world during the pandemic, the digital games industry has observed massive changes in player behaviour. According to a survey by Newzoo, most people are playing games more during the pandemic lockdown as they have more time to play and several others are using gaming as a social activity or escapism during the pandemic [9]. Also, it has been reported that game sales had increased by 63% based on an analysis of market data of 16 major game companies [4]. A survey conducted by Neilsen Games polling 3000

---

[1] https://store.steampowered.com/.

players reported that more than 45% of players in US have spent more time playing video games during the pandemic than prior to COVID-19 [14]. Steam platform had reached a record of 20 million concurrent users on the 16th March 2020 during the pandemic [9]. Moreover, game streaming services have also observed a surge in viewership. Specially, in Twitch, the popular game streaming platform, the daily viewership has doubled in the US [14]. Furthermore, the gaming industry had also supported to spread awareness about social distancing during COVID-19 by contributing to the #PlayApartTogether campaign initiated by the World Health Organization [16]. Leading game companies have joined this campaign offering special events, rewards and activities to promote people to play games and practise social distancing. Moreover, since gaming has increased King et al., suggests that it is important to devise balanced approaches of game playing for long term well being [10]. Moreover, as per a survey based on Pokemon Go game players, intention to play location based games socially outside is reduced as COVID-19 situation becomes severe [11]. Although the demand for the gaming industry had positively increased during the pandemic, the industry had faced some negative impacts as well. This includes production delays of consoles, and delays in releasing some games. These studies and observations depicts the growth of interest in gaming during the pandemic.

3   Data Collection and Preprocessing

Steam platform was used as the main source of data. It is one of the prominent digital distribution platforms for video games. Player population data series of 1963 games on Steam we have been collecting[2] since December 2017 using Steam API is used for the study. It consists of the number of players in each game collected in 5-minutes frequency for the first half of games and in 1-hour frequency for the second half of games from December 2017 to April 2020. These games were chosen based on their population size so as to use games with a strong player base. Specifically, the list of top 2000 applications on Steam with highest player population during the last 24 h on the 11th of December 2017 retrieved from SteamDB[3] was used to select the games. SteamDB is a third party tracking website for Steam. The 1963 games were chosen after the removal of all non-games from the list of 2000 applications. Also, meta information about each game were also collected by web scraping Steam store and using StorefrontAPI[4].

COVID-19 cases dataset[5] compiled by the Johns Hopkins University that contain daily COVID-19 cases since 22nd January 2020 was also retrieved.

Game player population series contain 1.12% of missing data on average within the period considered in this study. Missing data were handled by median filtering. It replaces a missing data point with the median of its neighboring data points within a window.

---

[2] Dataset is available at: https://data.mendeley.com/datasets/ycy3sy3vj2/1.

[3] https://steamdb.info/.

[4] https://wiki.teamfortress.com/wiki/User:RJackson/StorefrontAPI.

[5] https://data.humdata.org/dataset/novel-coronavirus-2019-ncov-cases.

4   Empirical Analysis of Player Populations

An empirical analysis was conducted to generate insights on game player population changes occurred during the pandemic. The top 500 games in the dataset which has the highest player population were used for the analysis.

4.1   Changes in Player Population Size of Games

Correlation of COVID-19 Cases and Player Population: We calculated the correlation between daily aggregate player population of all games and COVID-19 cases using Pearson correlation coefficient. For this purpose, the mean daily population of each game was extracted as COVID-19 data were in daily frequency. Then the daily total population of all games were calculated. Furthermore, the trend of population was also extracted by applying moving average of a window size of 7 smoothing the weekly fluctuations. Since the US has the highest percentage of Steam users compared to other countries [1], we not only considered global COVID-19 cases but also US COVID-19 cases.

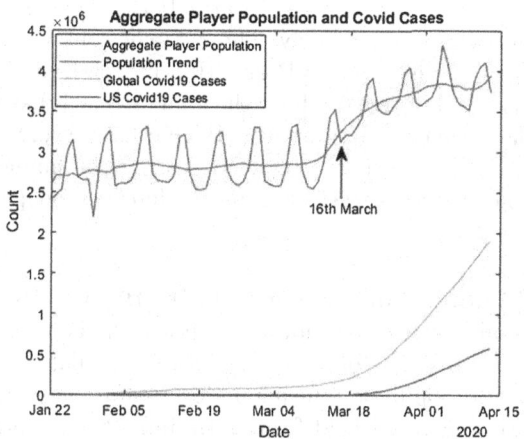

Fig. 1. Data series of daily aggregate player population, Global and US COVID-19 cases since 22nd January 2020. US announced social restrictions on 16th March

As depicted in Fig. 1 there is a clear correlation between the COVID-19 cases and player population. The Pearson correlation between population trend and global cases was 0.87 and the same for US cases was 0.79 indicating a high positive correlation. Moreover, the mean population after the 16th of March shows a 33% increase. Even the minimum population each week during this growth period, as represented by troughs are nearly higher than the maximum population each week during the pre-growth period, as represented by peaks. It is noteworthy that 16th of March is the date US president announced social distancing restrictions for US residents advising to avoid gatherings of 10 or more people and to work or attend school from home [13]. Moreover, when individual games were considered, 51% of games displayed a high positive correlation with the global COVID-19 cases, which is higher than 0.5. Overall, the results indicate that more people are turning to gaming as the severity of COVID-19 increases and social restrictions are in place.

Comparison of Population During COVID-19 and Normal Days: We conducted a comparison between the player population during COVID-19 and prior to it. Population data of each game from 16th March to 16th April 2020 was used to represent the pandemic period as the highest increase in player population was observed after the 16th of March. Population during the same time last year, 16th March–16th April 2019, was used to represent the normal days or pre-pandemic period. For each game the relative mean population change percentage was calculated as $\frac{(MeaninPandemic-MeaninNormaldays)}{MeaninNormaldays} * 100$. The right-sided Wilcoxon signed rank test indicated that the mean player population of games during COVID-19 is significantly higher compared to normal days with a p value of 9.9e−54. In addition, we explored the games that displayed a high positive change percentage. There were 18 games with a percentage higher than 300%. Among them, The Jackbox Party Pack 3 and Tabletop Simulator displayed 520% and 480% respectively. These games contain trivias and classic games such as Chess, Dominoes and Poker. Half-life, Half-life 2 and the Hunter Classic, the Hunter: Call of the Wild are the game sequels that displayed higher than 300% population increase. Moreover, Plague Inc.: Evolved, a game where the player has to evolve a deadly plague to destroy the human history, had a 245% increase. These implies various game preferences people display during pandemic.

Comparison of Population During COVID-19 and Steam Sale Event Periods: Steam sale events are widely popular periods among game players. Analysis was carried out to compare the player population observed during COVID-19 period and population during major Steam sale event periods. Steam Summer sale event which was held from 25th June 2019 to 9th July 2019 and Steam Winter sale held from 19th December 2019 to 2nd January 2020 was chosen for comparison. Mean player population during these sale periods and COVID-19 period were separately calculated as before for each individual game. Right-tailed Wilcoxon signed rank test indicated that the mean population of games during COVID-19 is significantly higher than that of during Summer with a p value of 6.8e−41 and also higher than Winter sales with a p value of 6.5e−31. Winter sale is held during December, a time where most people are enjoying holidays with lot of free time. It is interesting to observe that the population during COVID-19 is even higher than that.

4.2   Weekly Patterns

Game player populations display weekly seasonality in which player population fluctuation patterns repeat every week in similar manner [17]. We investigated if the weekly patterns of games are impacted during COVID-19. For this purpose, an autocorrelation based weekly seasonality process was conducted. Simply explained, first the trend of the population series is removed and autocorrelation values of lags are calculated. If the lag that has the highest autocorrelation falls within the window of lags representing a week, the game is recognized as displaying weekly seasonality. More details of the process can be found in our previous work [17]. Results revealed that only 24% of games displayed weekly seasonality during COVID-19 period. However, 60% of the games had displayed weekly seasonality in the same period last year (16th March–16th April 2019). Interestingly, out of the games that displayed weekly seasonality in the previous year 76% of games did not display weekly seasonality during COVID-19. To illustrate, in Fig. 2 it can be seen that the game Garry's Mod has the same recurring weekly pattern prior to COVID-19 but no recurring weekly pattern can be seen during COVID-19 period. Such diminishing of weekly patterns could be a result of the stay at home advices due to which people were able to play at any day they prefer rather than following the usual weekly cycle of working from Monday to Friday and playing games more during the weekend. Moreover, it could also be due to the joining of new game players that engage with the games only temporarily and casually.

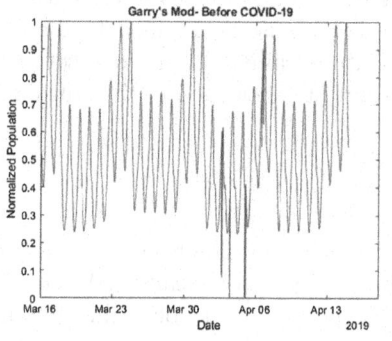
(a) Garry's Mod - Prior to COVID-19

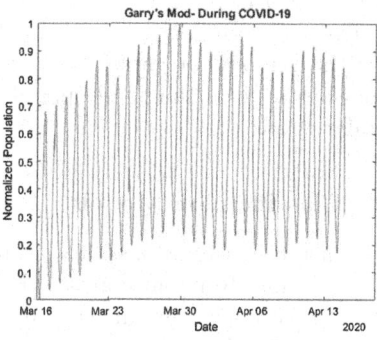
(b) Garry's Mod - During COVID-19

Fig. 2. Garry's Mod- Normalized Player Population during and prior to COVID-19; Population is normalized to 0–1 range to highlight the shape

5   Predicting Popular Games During the Pandemic

As identified in the empirical analysis, a majority of games observed an increase in player population during the pandemic. Hence, the ability to predict what games become popular during such world crisis is useful for game companies to better plan for similar future crisis. Hence, several binary classification models to predict games that would become highly popular during the pandemic are generated and evaluated in this section.

The popularity of a game during COVID-19 is determined based on its percentage of population increase as the population of a game is indicative of the popularity. Since it was observed that the aggregate player population increase of games during the pandemic is 33%, it is used as a boundary to determine whether a game is significantly popular or not during the pandemic. Thus, games are labelled as highly popular if their percentage of population increase is higher than or equal to 33% and labelled as not highly popular otherwise. The percentage of population increase is calculated as before using 16th March 2020 as the boundary where the period of a month prior to it is the pre pandemic period and a month after is the pandemic period. All 1963 games in the dataset were used.

5.1   Feature Extraction

Features related to the games were extracted from the collected data to be used for the classification models. Table 1 depicts all the selected features. Each game in the dataset has one or many developers. However, due to the high diversity of developers it is not appropriate to use the developer as a categorical feature. Instead, whether the developer is a *topdeveloper* or not is used as a binary feature. A developer is considered as a top developer in this context if they have developed 10 or more games in the dataset. The *toppublisher* feature is also extracted similarly. Moreover, the final dataset used contained 1806 games after the removal of games with missing feature values. In the dataset, 49% games belonged to the highly popular class and 51% belonged to the not highly popular class.

5.2   Classification Models

Five machine learning classification models, namely, Decision tree, Tree bagging, Tree Boosting, Random Forest (RF) and Support Vector Machine (SVM), were trained to predict the games that are highly popular and not highly popular during the pandemic using the selected feature set. All four tree-based models were trained using the classical CART (Classification And Regression Tree) algorithm in which Gini index is used as the tree node splitting criterion. AdaBoost algorithm [5] was used for the boosting model. For the RF, the size of the random feature subset at each node was chosen to be the square root of the total number of features as it is the common typical value used [6]. Moreover, each of the ensemble models (bagging, boosting, RF) contained 100 trees. Radial basis function kernel was used for SVM and all the features were standardized prior to training it. Also, Bayesian optimization was used for hyper parameter optimization of all the models as it is less time consuming than the grid search.

The performance of the models were evaluated based on Accuracy, F-measure and G-mean. Accuracy is the fraction of the correct predictions out of all predictions. F-Measure is the harmonic mean of precision and recall of predicting the highly popular games. G-Mean, known as geometric mean is a measure that gives equal importance to predicting both highly popular and not highly popular

Table 1. Features used for the classification models

Feature	Description
price	The most frequent price within the two weeks prior to the pandemic
dayssincerel	The number of days since the game release
tag1	The most commonly applied tag to the game
tag2	The second most commonly applied tag to the game
tag3	The third most commonly applied tag to the game
posreviewpercent	The percentage of positive reviews
topdeveloper	Is the developer of the game one of the top developers
toppublisher	Is the publisher of the game one of the top publishers
noofpackages	The number of packages the game is included in
noofsupportedlang	The number of languages the game supports
precovidmeanpop1year	Mean population during the same period last year; 16th March–16th April 2019
precovidmeanpop1month	Mean population during the month prior to the pandemic; 16th February–16th March 2020

classes. We performed 10-fold cross validation for 30 runs and the mean value of each measure was recorded.

5.3   Classification Results and Discussion

The results obtained from the classification models are depicted in Table 2. To verify the statistical significance of the results ANOVA tests were conducted for each performance measure at 0.05 significance level. It used the results of the 30 runs of each classification model to evaluate the null hypothesis that the mean results of models are similar. Since the null hypothesis was rejected for each measure, Tukey's multiple comparison test [7] that identify which pairwise means are significantly different was performed for each measure.

Based on the results in Table 2 and outcomes of Tukey's test RF and SVM models has the highest Accuracy, SVM has the highest Precision, RF and boosted trees have highest Recall and RF has the highest Fmeasure and Gmean. Overall results indicates that RF has the highest overall performance in classification. RF is not only better at predicting highly popular games indicated by Fmeasure results but also at predicting both highly popular and not highly popular games indicated by Gmean results, compared to the other models.

However, the performance of models are generally only average as even the best performing model, RF, had an accuracy of only 0.63. Since, COVID-19 is an unprecedented event it is likely that the game features used for the classification models alone might not be sufficient to accurately predict the games that become highly popular. People's decisions on playing games and what games to play

Table 2. Performance of Classification Models

Model	Accuracy	Precision	Recall	Fmeasure	Gmean
Decision tree	0.60	0.59	0.57	0.58	0.60
Boosted trees	0.61	0.60	0.62	0.61	0.61
Bagged trees	0.61	0.60	0.61	0.60	0.61
Random Forest	0.63	0.62	0.62	0.62	0.63
SVM	0.62	0.64	0.54	0.59	0.62

might also depend on various other circumstantial factors. For instance, the dominant country of the game and lock down or any other constraints in the country are some external factors that might have an influence on what games become popular. Hence, it might be beneficial if access to such information is available to further improve the prediction accuracy of classification models.

Feature Importance: Feature importance calculation is useful to understand what features are important to predict whether a game becomes highly popular and played by many during the pandemic. Since RF had the highest classification performance, it is used to determine the feature importance. We use the prominent permutation based feature importance measure. Specifically, if a certain feature is important for the classification process, permutation of its values would increase the error of the model for data instances not used in training. The mean and standard deviation of the error difference across all trees calculated for each feature is used to determine the feature importance score. Furthermore, we used the chi-square based split selection process [12] for tree generation as it has been identified that Gini impurity index might be biased towards continuous features with many levels or categorical features with many categories [2] which could impact the feature importance calculation process.

Feature importance results in Fig. 3 indicates that tags are the most important feature in predicting highly popular games during the pandemic. This implies that game preferences during this period are mostly based on the type of the game. Days since the game release is the next important feature indicating that the age of the game also has as influence over the game preferences. Furthermore, it can be seen that the mean population during the month prior to the pandemic has more influence than the mean population of the month in the previous year for the prediction process. The game being published by a top publisher or not also seem to have an influence on the prediction process, probably because it is indicative of how well known the game is through marketing. Also, interestingly the least important feature in the prediction process appears to be the positive review percentage of a game. It could be related to accepting recommendations from friends and family compared to reviews.

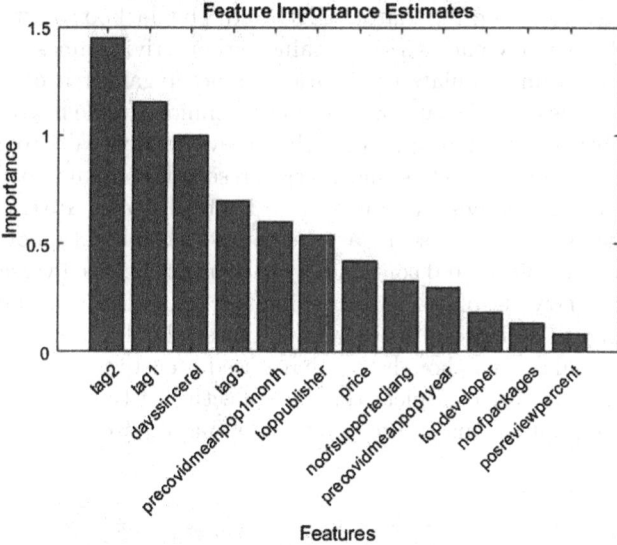

Fig. 3. Feature importance estimates based on Random Forest for prediction of highly popular games during the pandemic

Common Tags of the Highly Popular Games: Since tags are the most important feature in predicting highly popular games during the pandemic, a tag analysis was conducted using the top 3 tags of each game. In order to identify the most common tags that appear in the highly popular games class compared to not highly popular class, the difference between the percentage of games associated with each tag in the two classes was calculated. Specifically, for each tag, the percentage in not highly popular class is subtracted from the percentage in highly popular class. Only the tags that had a percentage difference higher than 0.5% are depicted in the Fig. 4. It can be seen that the Multiplayer tag is the most common tag in highly popular games. Moreover, the existence of Massively Multiplayer, MMORPG (Massively Multiplayer Online Role-Playing Game) and Co-Op (Cooperative) tags indicates that Multiplayer games are highly popular during the pandemic, which could be because it allows players to interact with others even when they are physically apart. Adventure and First Person Shooter appear to be the next most highly popular games followed by Racing and Automobile Simulator games. Some of the highly popular games with Racing and Automobile Simulator tags were Motorsport Manager, RaceRoom Racing Experience and F1 series from 2012 to 2016. The popularity of the F1 games series is possibly a result of the start of Formula 1 season on the 15th of March 2020 and launching of a new F1 Esports Virtual Grand Prix series due to COVID-19 where F1 racers playing the F1 2019 game was live-streamed. Free to Play tag is also among the prominent tags of highly popular games during the pandemic indicating preference for free games. Moreover, Boardgame, Tabletop and Trivia tags are also common. Some of the highly popular games with these tags were

Monopoly Plus, Tabletop Simulator, UNO and The Jackbox Party Pack series 1–4. The Jackbox party pack series contains various trivia games and the Tabletop simulator contains simulations of various tabletop games. It can be seen that most of these games are digital versions of the common simple board games, card games and tabletop games people play when they are physically together. Moreover, Newzoo, a game analytics and market research company, had reported a growth in Gambling games, Arcade games, Battle Royale, Adventure, Racing, Simulation racing games and social arcade games (a combination of arcade, puzzle and online multiplayer and contain easy to learn or digitized versions of games player already know) in player share during December 2019 to March 2020 [9]. It is interesting, that the results observed in our study also has some similarities with their outcomes even though they have used a customized genre taxonomy and a different dataset. It depicts that, irrespective of the dataset, the tags of games that are popular during the pandemic remain quite similar.

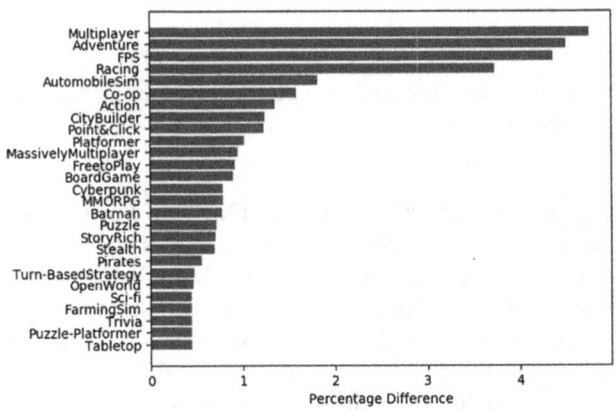

Fig. 4. Most common tags of the highly popular games

6   Conclusion

This paper presented a study that investigated the changes occurred in digital games during the COVID-19 pandemic with respect to player population. The study not only generated insights about player population changes but also explored how classification models can be used to predict games that become highly popular during the pandemic. However, even the best classification model only displayed 63% accuracy. The insights generated would aid the game industry in planning resource allocation to serve more players and to understand what kind of games to promote and produce during such situations. As future work, we hope to explore if the accuracy of predicting popular games during the pandemic can be further improved by using features relevant to the pandemic such as the restrictions in the dominant country of a game. Also, we hope to investigate the longevity of the popularity games obtained during the pandemic to understand how population changes as the pandemic continues in the world.

References

1. Steam demographics: Users by country. https://www.statista.com/statistics/826870/steam-distribution-country/
2. Breiman, L., Friedman, J., Stone, C.J., Olshen, R.A.: Classification and Regression Trees. CRC Press, Boca Raton (1984)
3. Di Renzo, L., et al.: Eating habits and lifestyle changes during COVID-19 lockdown: an Italian survey. J. Transl. Med. **18**(1), 229 (2020)
4. Dring, C.: What is happening with video game sales during coronavirus, March 2020. https://www.gamesindustry.biz/articles/2020-03-28-what-is-happening-with-video-game-sales-during-coronavirus
5. Freund, Y., Schapire, R.E.: A decision-theoretic generalization of on-line learning and an application to boosting. J. Comput. Syst. Sci. **55**(1), 119–139 (1997)
6. Hastie, T., Tibshirani, R., Friedman, J.: The Elements of Statistical Learning: Data Mining, Inference, and Prediction. SSS, 2nd edn. Springer, New York (2009). https://doi.org/10.1007/978-0-387-84858-7
7. Hochberg, Y., Tamhan, A.: Multiple Comparison Procedures. Wiley, Hoboken (1987)
8. Howley, D.: The world is turning to video games amid coronavirus outbreak, March 2020. https://finance.yahoo.com/news/coronavirus-world-turning-to-video-games-150704969.html
9. Jackson, J.: What Gamers Are Playing & Watching During the Coronavirus Lockdown: Player Share & Viewership Spikes for Games & Genres, April 2020. https://newzoo.com/insights/articles/games-gamers-are-playing-watching-during-coronavirus-covid19-lockdown-quarantine/
10. King, D.L., Delfabbro, P.H., Billieux, J., Potenza, M.N.: Problematic online gaming and the COVID-19 pandemic. J. Behav. Addict. **9**, 184–186 (2020)
11. Laato, S., Islam, A.K.M.N., Laine, T.H.: Did location-based games motivate players to socialize during COVID-19? Telematics Inform. **54**, 101458 (2020)
12. Loh, W.Y., Shih, Y.S.: Split Selection Methods for Classification Trees. Stat. Sin. **7**, 815–840 (1997)
13. Muccari, R., Chow, D.: Coronavirus timeline: tracking the critical moments of COVID-19. https://www.nbcnews.com/health/health-news/coronavirus-timeline-tracking-critical-moments-covid-19-n1154341
14. Neilsen: 3, 2, 1 Go! Video Gaming is at an All-Time High During COVID-19, March 2020. https://www.nielsen.com/us/en/insights/article/2020/3-2-1-go-video-gaming-is-at-an-all-time-high-during-covid-19
15. Nicola, M., et al.: The socio-economic implications of the coronavirus pandemic (COVID-19): a review. Int. J. Surg. (London, England) **78**, 185–193 (2020). https://doi.org/10.1016/j.ijsu.2020.04.018
16. Takahashi, D.: WHO and game companies launch #PlayApartTogether to promote physical distancing, March 2020
17. Vihanga, D., Barlow, M., Lakshika, E., Kasmarik, K.: Weekly seasonal player population patterns in online games: a time series clustering approach. In: 2019 IEEE Conference on Games (CoG), pp. 1–8. IEEE (2019)
18. Zheng, Y.Y., Ma, Y.T., Zhang, J.Y., Xie, X.: COVID-19 and the cardiovascular system. Nat. Rev. Cardiol. **17**(5), 259–260 (2020)

Correction to: A Tri-level Programming Framework for Modelling Attacks and Defences in Cyber-Physical Systems

Waleed Yamany, Nour Moustafa, and Benjamin Turnbull

Correction to:
Chapter "A Tri-level Programming Framework for Modelling
Attacks and Defences in Cyber-Physical Systems"
in: M. Gallagher et al. (Eds.): *AI 2020:*
Advances in Artificial Intelligence, **LNAI 12576,**
https://doi.org/10.1007/978-3-030-64984-5_8

The original version of this chapter was revised. The following corrections have been incorporated:

- Typographical errors throughout the paper have been corrected.
- Table 1 has been corrected.
- Eqs. 2 and 3 have been corrected; Eqs. 17, 18, and 19 have been removed.
- An acknowledgement has been added.
- Ref. 9 has been corrected.

The updated version of this chapter can be found at
https://doi.org/10.1007/978-3-030-64984-5_8

Author Index

Printed in the United States
By Bookmasters